Beginning Java Objects

Jacquie Barker

apress™

Beginning Java Objects

ISBN (pbk): 1-59059-146-1

Printed and bound in the United States of America 345678910

Trademarked names may appear in this book. Rather than use a trademark symbol with every occurrence of a trademarked name, we use the names only in an editorial fashion and to the benefit of the trademark owner, with no intention of infringement of the trademark.

Technical Reviewers: Gregory Beekman, Allan Jones, Robert F E Shaw

Editorial Directors: Dan Appleman, Gary Cornell, Martin Streicher, Jim Sumser, Karen Watterson, John Zukowski

Project Manager: Chandima Nethisinghe

Development Editor: Tim Briggs

Proofreader: Helena Sharman

Indexer: Alessandro Ansa

Distributed to the book trade in the United States by Springer-Verlag New York, Inc., 175 Fifth Avenue, New York, NY, 10010 and outside the United States by Springer-Verlag GmbH & Co. KG, Tiergartenstr. 17, 69112 Heidelberg, Germany.

In the United States: phone 1-800-SPRINGER, email orders@springer-ny.com, or visit http://www.springer-ny.com. Outside the United States: fax +49 6221 345229, email orders@springer.de, or visit http://www.springer.de.

For information on translations, please contact Apress directly at 2560 Ninth Street, Suite 219, Berkeley, CA 94710. Phone 510-549-5930, fax 510-549-5939, email info@apress.com, or visit http://www.apress.com.

The information in this book is distributed on an "as is" basis, without warranty. Although every precaution has been taken in the preparation of this work, neither the author(s) nor Apress shall have any liability to any person or entity with respect to any loss or damage caused or alleged to be caused directly or indirectly by the information contained in this work.

The source code for this book is available to readers at http://www.apress.com in the Downloads section.

About the Author

Jacquie Barker

Jacquie Barker is a professional software engineer and adjunct faculty member at The George Washington University. With over 25 years of experience as a software developer and project manager, she has been focusing on object technology since 1991, and has become proficient as a 'hands-on' object modeler and as a Sun Microsystems certified Java programmer. Jacquie is currently employed as a principal member of the technical staff at SRA International, Inc. in Fairfax, Virginia, where she consults for both public and private sector clients, and is also the founder of ObjectStart LLC, an object technology mentorship and training firm.

Acknowledgements

Writing this book was perhaps the biggest professional challenge that I've faced in my career to date, as well as being one of the most gratifying. I'd like to offer my sincere, heartfelt thanks to everyone who helped me to achieve this goal:

❑ To Timothy Briggs, for sharing in my vision and for taking a chance with a new author; to Gregory Beekman, for helping me across the 'finish line' and for his many words of inspiration along the way; and to *both* Tim and Greg, for patiently responding to my seemingly *millions* of email messages! Thanks to Allan Jones and Robert Shaw, as well, for their wonderful editorial support.

❑ To John DiCarlo, for his instrumental role in getting me "jump started" with Java many years ago, and for serving as my Java mentor ever since.

❑ To Mary Helms, a touchstone in my life, for inspiring me to always seek new adventures and to be true to my dreams.

❑ To John Kopsky, John Walton, Sandy Tucker, and Barb Power, for their willingness to review and help me shape early drafts of my book. And, to *all* of my Wrox reviewers, whose thoughtful comments kept me honest!

❑ To John Carson, for our many Starbucks sessions and shared 'war stories' – good and bad – about what it takes to survive writing a book, and for giving me permission to use our jointly developed Java lecture materials as the basis for some of the examples in Chapter 16.

❑ To Dave Pappas, without whose encouragement (and vision for what I could achieve) I might never have begun teaching in the first place. And, to my entire management team at SRA International, for providing me with a rewarding workplace that fosters professional development.

❑ To all my dear friends: 'Linder', Ron and Renee; Mimi and Bill; Sandy, Ed and Charlie; Susan, Dave, Emily, and Amanda; Lisa, Mike, Ryan, Kelly, and Brianna; Donna, Chuck, and Michael; Bonnie, Tom, Katarina, and Larissa; Curt, Kathy, Harrison, and Chelsea; Dan, Katrina, Magda, and John; Dave, Debbie, Daniel, and Elaina; Richard and Bob; Dave, Martha, Michelle and Julie; Denise; Dianne; Rich, Cathy, Scott, and Ryan; Jeanne, Dan, and Gregory; Linda; Chris, Karen, Steven, and Kyle; Mary; Ari; Anne; Sue; and 'Grandma' Jennie; for allowing me to drop off the face of the earth (well, almost!) for the better part of a year.

❑ To my wonderfully supportive family: Cheryl, Mike, and Michaela; Doug and Sam; Ginny, Dick, Colleen, Katie, and Barb; and Louann and Rod; for believing in me and for cheering me on, and for forgiving me for not making it to the many fun family events that took place during my book writing adventure.

❑ And most of all, to my husband, Steve, for being such a loving, supportive partner through my many 3 AM writing frenzies and the 'roller coaster ride' known as getting published – I love you whole bunches, 'Mellie'!

To the two most important men in my life:

My husband, Steve, for being my soul mate, best friend, and the best partner in life anyone could ever wish for.

In loving memory of my Dad, Bill Jost.

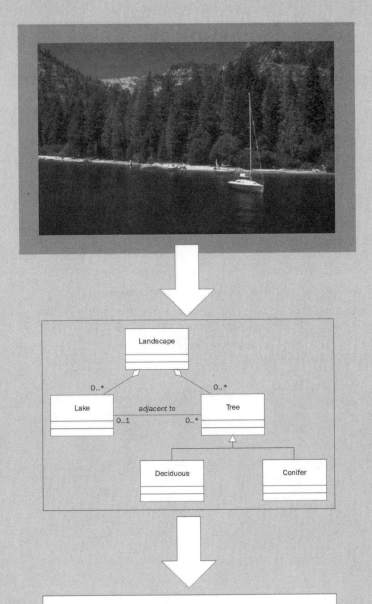

```
public class Tree {
    protected Landscape landscape;
    protected Lake nextTo;

    public void setNextTo(Lake l) {
        nextTo = l;
    }
    public Lake getNextTo() {
        return nextTo;
    }

    public abstract Color getLeafColor();
}
```

Table of Contents

Table of Contents

Table of Contents

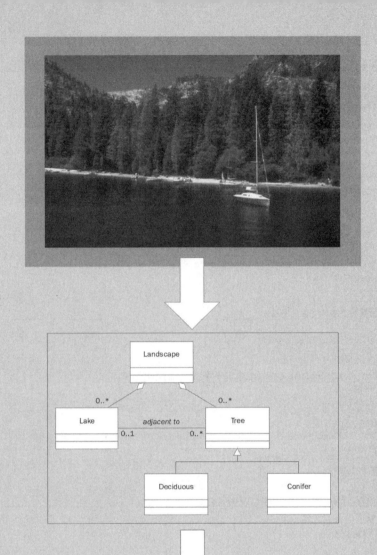

```
public class Tree {
    protected Landscape landscape;
    protected.Lake nextTo;

    public void setNextTo(Lake l) {
        nextTo = l;
    }
    public Lake getNextTo() {
        return nextTo;
    }

    public abstract Color getLeafColor();
}
```

Introduction

Goals for this Book

This is a book, first and foremost, about software objects: what they are, why they are so 'magical' and yet so straightforward, and how one goes about structuring a software application to use objects appropriately.

This is also a book about Java: not a hard core, 'everything there is to know about Java' book, but rather a gentle yet comprehensive introduction to the language, with special emphasis on how to transition from an object model to a fully functional Java application, something that few, if any, other books provide.

My goals in writing this book (and, hopefully, yours for buying it) are to:

- **Make you comfortable with fundamental object-oriented (OO) terminology and concepts.**

- **Give you hands-on, practical experience with object modeling:** that is, with developing a 'blueprint' that can be used as the basis for subsequently building an object-oriented software system.

- **Illustrate the basics of how such an object model is translated into a working software application – a Java application, to be specific,** although the techniques that you'll learn for object modeling apply equally well to any OO language.

If you are already experienced with the Java language (but not with object fundamentals), it is critical to your successful use of the language that you learn about its object-oriented roots. On the other hand, if you are a newcomer to Java, then this book will get you properly 'jump-started'. **Either way, this book is a 'must-read' for anyone who wishes to become proficient with an OO programming language like Java.**

Just as importantly, this book is **not** meant to:

❑ **Turn you into an overnight 'pro' in object modeling.** Like all advanced skills, becoming totally comfortable with object modeling takes two things: a good educational foundation and a lot of practice! We give you the foundation in this book, along with suggestions for projects and exercises that will enable you to apply and practice your new-found knowledge. But the only way you will really get to be proficient with object modeling is by participating in OO modeling and development projects over time. This book will give you the skills and, hopefully, the confidence to begin to apply object techniques in a professional setting, which is where the real learning will take place, particularly if you have an OO-experienced mentor to guide you through your first 'industrial strength' project.

❑ **Make you an expert in any particular OO methodology.** There are dozens of different formal methods for OO software development, new variations continue to emerge, and no one methodology is necessarily better than another. For example, UML (which stands for 'Unified Modeling Language') notation is the newest, OMT (which stands for 'Object Modeling Technique') notation one of the oldest, yet the two are remarkably similar because UML is based to a great extent on OMT. By making sure that you understand the generic **process** of object modeling along with the specifics of UML, you will be armed with the knowledge you need to read about, evaluate, and select a specific methodology (or to craft your own – who knows, maybe someday you will even write a book yourself on the methodology that you invent!).

❑ **Teach you everything you'll ever need to know about Java.** Java is a very rich language, consisting of dozens of class libraries, hundreds of built-in classes, and literally thousands of operations that can be performed with and by these classes. If Java provides a dozen alternative ways to do something in particular, we'll explain the one or two ways that we feel best suit the problem at hand, to give you an appreciation for how things are done. Nonetheless, you'll definitely see enough of the Java language in this book to be able to build a complete application.

Armed with the foundation you gain from this book, you will be poised and ready to appreciate a more thorough treatment of Java such as that offered by one of the many other Java references that are presently on the market, or an in-depth UML reference.

Why Is Understanding Objects So Critical To Being a Successful OO Programmer?

Time and again, I meet software developers – at my place of employment; at clients' offices; at professional conferences; on college campuses – who have attempted to master an OO programming language like Java by taking a course in Java, reading a book about Java, or installing and using a Java integrated development environment (IDE) such as Forte, Visual Café, JBuilder, Power J, or Kawa. However, there is something fundamentally missing: a basic understanding of what objects are all about, and more importantly, knowledge of how to structure a software application from the ground up to make the most of objects.

Imagine that you have been asked to build a house, and that you know the basics of home construction. In fact, you are a world-renowned home builder whose services are in high demand! Your client tells you that all of the materials you will need for building this home are going to be delivered to you. On the day construction is to begin, a truck pulls up at the building site and unloads a large pile of strange, blue, star shaped blocks with holes in the middle. You are totally baffled! You have built countless homes using materials like lumber, brick, and stone, and know how to approach a building project using these familiar materials; but you haven't got a clue about how to assemble a house using blue stars.

Scratching your head, you pull out a hammer and some nails and try to nail the blue stars together as if you were working with lumber, but the stars don't fit together very well. You then try to fill in the gaps with the same mortar that you would use to adhere bricks to one another, but the mortar doesn't stick to these blue stars very well. Because you are working under tight cost and schedule constraints for building this home for your client, however (and because you are too embarrassed to admit that you, as an 'expert' builder, don't know how to work with these modern materials), you press on. Eventually, you wind up with something that looks (on the outside, at least) like a house.

Your client comes to inspect the work, and is terribly disappointed. One of reasons he had selected blue stars as a construction material was that they are extremely energy efficient; but, because you have used nails and mortar to assemble the stars, they have lost a great deal of their inherent ability to insulate the home. To compensate, your client asks you to replace all of the windows in the home with thermal glass windows so that they will allow less heat to escape. You are panicking at this point! Swapping out the windows will take as long, if not longer, than it has taken to build the house in the first place, not to mention the cost of replacing stars that will be damaged in the renovation process. When you tell your customer this, he goes ballistic! Another reason that he selected blue stars as the construction material was because of their recognized flexibility and ease of accommodating design changes; but, because of the ineffective way in which you assembled these stars, you are going to have to literally rip them apart and replace a great many of them.

This is, sad to say, the way many programmers wind up building an OO application when they don't have appropriate training in how to approach the project from the perspective of objects. Worse yet, the vast majority of would-be OO programmers are blissfully ignorant of the need to understand objects in order to program in an OO language. So, they take off programming with a language like Java and wind up with a far from ideal result: a program which lacks flexibility when an inevitable 'mid-course correction' occurs in terms of a change in the requirements specification, as when new functionality needs to be introduced after an application has been deployed.

Who Is This Book Written For?

Anyone who wants to get the most out of an object-oriented programming language like Java! It has been written for:

- ❑ Anyone who has yet to tackle Java, but wants to get off on the right foot with the language.

- ❑ Anyone who has ever purchased a book on Java, and who has read it faithfully; who understands the 'bits and bytes' of the language, but doesn't quite know how to structure an application to best take advantage of the OO features of the language.

- Anyone who has purchased a Java integrated development environment (IDE) software tool, but really only knows how to drag and drop graphical user interface (GUI) components and to add a little bit of logic behind buttons, menus, etc. without any real sense of how to properly structure the core of the application around objects.

- Anyone who has built a Java application, but was disappointed with how difficult it was to maintain or modify it when new requirements were presented later in the application's lifecycle.

- Anyone who has previously learned something about object modeling, but is 'fuzzy' on how to transition from an object model to real, live code (Java or otherwise).

The bottom line is that anyone who really wants to master an OO language like Java **must** become an expert in objects **first**!

In order to gain the most value from this book, you should have some programming experience under your belt; virtually any language will do. You should understand simple programming concepts such as:

- Simple data types (integer, floating point, etc.)

- Variables and their scope (including the notion of global data)

- Control flow (if-then-else statements, for/do/while loops, etc.)

- What arrays are, and how to use them

- The notion of a function/subroutine/subprogram: how to pass data in and get results back out

but, you needn't have had any prior exposure to Java (we'll give you a taste of the language at the beginning of Part 1, and will go into the language in depth in Part 3). And, you needn't have ever been exposed to objects, either – in the software sense, at least! As you'll learn in Chapter 2, human beings naturally view the entire world from the perspective of objects.

Even if you have already developed a full-fledged Java applet or application, it is certainly not too late to read this book if you still feel 'fuzzy' when it comes to the object aspects of structuring an application. I teach two university level courses – Object Methods for Software Development and Beginning Java Programming. Although it is ideal for students to take the two courses in that order, I often have students that, for one reason or another, arrive at my object modeling course having already taken a stab at learning Java. Even for such folks, who will see some familiar landmarks (in the form of Java code examples) in this book, many new insights are gained as they learn the rationale for why we do many of the things that we do when programming in Java (or any other OO programming language for that matter). It ultimately makes someone a better Java programmer to know the whys of object orientation rather than merely the mechanics of the language. If you have had prior experience with Java, you may find that you can quickly skim those chapters that provide an introduction to the language – namely, Chapter 1 in Part 1 and Chapter 13 in Part 3.

Because this book has its roots in the courses that I teach, it is ideally suited for use as a textbook for a semester-long graduate or upper-division undergraduate course in either object modeling or Java programming. We've included some suggestions for how to use the book in that fashion in Appendix A.

What if You are Interested in Object Modeling, But Not Necessarily in Java Programming?

Will this book still be of value to you? Definitely! Even if you don't plan on making a career of programming (as is true of many of my Object Methods students), I have found that being exposed to a smattering of code examples written in an OO language like Java really helps to cement object concepts. So, you are encouraged to read Part 3 – at least through Chapter 14 – even if you never intend to set your hands to the keyboard for purposes of Java programming.

How This Book is Organized

The book is structured around three major topics, as follows:

Part 1

The ABC's of Objects: Before we dive into the how-to's of object modeling and the details of OO programming in Java, it is important that we all speak the same language with respect to objects. This section starts out slowly, by defining basic concepts that underlie all software development approaches, OO or otherwise. But, the chapters quickly ramp up to a discussion of advanced object concepts so that, by the end of Part 1, you should be 'object savvy'.

Part 2

Object Modeling: In this section, we focus on the underlying principles of how and, more importantly, why we do the things that we do when we develop an object model of an application – principles that are common to all object modeling techniques. It is important to be conversant in UML notation, as this is the emerging industry standard and is most likely what the majority of your colleagues/clients will be using, and so we teach you the basics of UML and use UML for all of our concrete modeling examples. Using the modeling techniques presented in these chapters, we'll develop an object model 'blueprint' for a Student Registration System (SRS), the requirements specification for which is presented at the end of this introduction.

Part 3

Translating an Object 'Blueprint' Into Java Code: Here, we illustrate how to render the SRS object model that we've developed in Part 2 into a fully-functioning Java application, complete with a graphical user interface and a way to persist data from one user logon to the next. All of the code examples that we present in this section are available for download from the Apress web site – http://www.press.com – and we strongly encourage you to download and experiment with this code. In fact, we provide exercises at the end of each chapter that encourage such experimentation. The requirements specification for the SRS is written in the narrative style with which software system requirements are often expressed. You may feel confident that you could build an application today to solve this problem, but by the end of this book you should feel much more confident in your ability to build it as an *object-oriented* application. Two additional case studies – for a Conference Room Reservation System and an Airline Ticketing System, respectively – are presented in Appendix B; these serve as the basis for many of the exercises presented at the end of each chapter.

To round out the book, we have included a final section entitled 'Next Steps' which provides suggestions for how you might wish to continue your object-oriented discovery process after finishing this book. We furnish you with a list of recommended books that will take you to the next level of proficiency, depending on what your intention is for applying what you've learned in this book.

Conventions

To help you get the most from the text and keep track of what's happening, we've used a number of conventions throughout the book.

For instance:

> **These boxes hold important, not-to-be forgotten information which is directly relevant to the surrounding text.**

While the background style is used for asides to the current discussion.

As for styles in the text:

When we introduce important words, we **highlight** them.

We show keyboard strokes like this: *Ctrl-A*.

We show filenames and code within the text like so: writeObject()

Text on user interfaces and URLs are shown as: Menu.

Example code is shown:

```
In our code examples, the code foreground style shows new, important, pertinent code
while code background shows code that's less important in the present context, or
has been seen before.
```

Which Version of Java is this Book Based On?

It seems like every time I blink my eyes, a new version of the Java language is being released by Sun Microsystems! The good news is that, because we focus only on core Java language syntax in this book – language features that have become quite stable since Java's inception – this book is not version specific. The way that graphical user interfaces and event handling are approached changed significantly from Java version 1.0 to 1.1; but, as long as you are using Java version 1.1 or later, the lessons provided by this book should serve you equally well.

A Final Thought Before We Get Started

A lot of the material in this book – particularly at the beginning of Part 1 – may seem overly simplistic to experienced programmers. This is because much of object technology is founded on basic software engineering principles that have been in practice for many years, and, in many cases, just repackaged slightly differently! There are indeed a few new tricks that make OO languages extremely powerful and which were virtually impossible to achieve with non-OO languages – **inheritance** and **polymorphism**, for example, which you'll learn more about in Chapters 5 and 7, respectively. (Such techniques can be simulated by hand in a non-OO language, just as programmers could program their own database management system (DBMS) from scratch instead of using a commercial product like Access, Oracle, or Sybase – but who'd want to?)

The biggest challenge for experienced programmers in becoming proficient with objects is in reorienting the manner in which they think about the problem they will be automating.

❑ Software engineers/programmers who have developed applications using non-object-oriented methods often have to 'unlearn' certain approaches used in the traditional methods of software analysis and design.

❑ Paradoxically, people just starting out as programmers (or as OO modelers) sometimes have an easier time when learning the OO approach to software development as their only approach.

Fortunately, the way we need to think about objects when developing software turns out to be the natural way that people think about the world in general. So, learning to 'think' objects – and to program them in Java – is as easy as 1, 2, 3!

Tell Us What You Think

We've worked hard to make this book as useful to you as possible, so we'd like to know what you think. We're always keen to know what it is you want and need to know.

We appreciate feedback on our efforts and take both criticism and praise to heart in our future editorial efforts. If you've anything to say, let us know at:

info@apress.com

or:

http://www.apress.com

or contact the author at:

http://objectstart.com

Student Registration System Case Study

Student Registration System (SRS) Requirements Specification

We have been asked to develop an automated Student Registration System (SRS). This system will enable students to register on-line for courses each semester, as well as tracking a student's progress toward completion of their degree.

When a student first enrolls at the university, he/she uses the SRS to set forth a plan of study as to which courses he/she plans on taking to satisfy a particular degree program, and chooses a faculty advisor. The SRS will verify whether or not the proposed plan of study satisfies the requirements of the degree that the student is seeking.

Once a plan of study has been established, then, during the registration period preceding each semester, students are able to view the schedule of classes on line, and choose whichever classes he/she wishes to attend, indicating the preferred section (day of the week and time of day) if the class is offered by more than one professor. The SRS will verify whether or not the student has satisfied the necessary prerequisites for each requested course by referring to the student's on-line transcript of courses completed and grades received (the student may review his/her transcript on-line at any time).

Assuming that (a) the prerequisites for the requested course(s) are satisfied, (b) the course(s) meet(s) one of the student's plan of study requirements, and (c) there is room available in each of the class(es), the student is enrolled in the class(es).

If (a) and (b) are satisfied, but (c) is not, the student is placed on a first-come, first-served waiting list. If a class/section that he/she was previously wait-listed for becomes available (either because some other student has dropped the class or because the seating capacity for the class has been increased), the student is automatically enrolled in the wait-listed class, and an e-mail message to that effect is sent to the student. It is his/her responsibility to drop the class if it is no longer desired; otherwise, he/she will be billed for the course.

Students may drop a class up to the end of the first week of the semester in which the class is being taught.

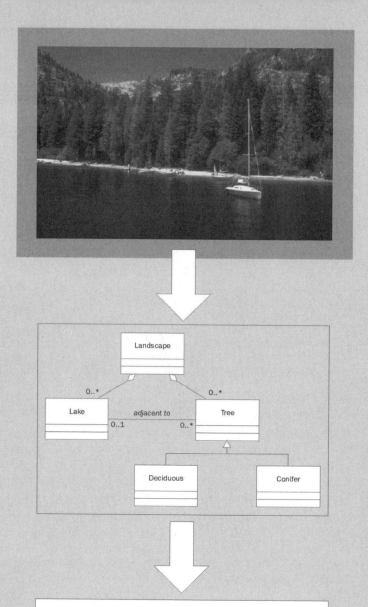

```
public class Tree {
    protected Landscape landscape;
    protected Lake nextTo;

    public void setNextTo(Lake l) {
        nextTo = l;
    }
    public Lake getNextTo() {
        return nextTo;
    }

    public abstract Color getLeafColor();
}
```

Part 1

The ABC's of Objects

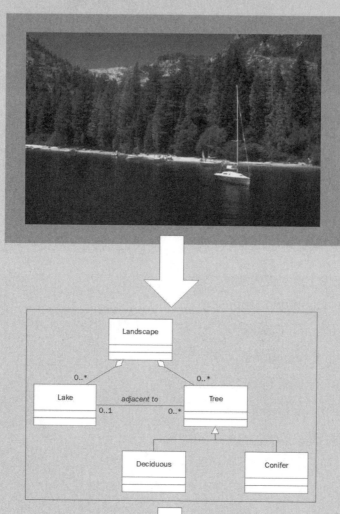

Landscape

0..*   0..*

Lake   Tree
        adjacent to
      0..1   0..*

Deciduous   Conifer

```java
public class Tree {
    protected Landscape landscape;
    protected Lake nextTo;

    public void setNextTo(Lake l) {
        nextTo = l;
    }
    public Lake getNextTo() {
        return nextTo;
    }

    public abstract Color getLeafColor();
}
```

A Little Taste of Java

If the first part of this book is supposed to be about general object concepts, then why are we starting out with a chapter on Java? Because we've found that seeing a sprinkling of code examples definitely helps to cement object concepts. But, objects are 'language neutral': what you'll learn conceptually about objects in Part 1 of this book, and about object modeling in Part 2, could apply equally well to Java, or C++, or Ada, or Smalltalk, or an as-yet-to-be-invented object oriented (OO) language. So, we *could* have used language neutral **pseudocode** – a natural language way of expressing computer logic without worrying about the syntax of a specific language like Java – for all of our code 'snippets' in Parts 1 and 2. This brings us back full circle to our initial question, why are we introducing Java syntax so soon?

The reason is that we'd like you to become comfortable with Java syntax from the start, because our goal for this book is not only to teach you about objects and object modeling, but also to ultimately show you how objects translate into Java code. So, although we do indeed use a bit of pseudocode to hide some of the more complex logic of our code examples throughout Parts 1 and 2 – things that simply aren't relevant to learning object concepts – we focus for the most part on real Java syntax. Just remember that the object concepts you'll learn in Parts 1 and 2 are equally applicable to other OO languages, unless otherwise noted.

In this chapter, you will learn about:

- ❏ The many strengths of the Java programming language (along with a few of its weaknesses).
- ❏ The anatomy of a simple Java program.
- ❏ Built-in Java data types, operators on those types, and expressions formed with those types.
- ❏ Java's block structured nature.
- ❏ Printing messages to the screen, primarily for use in testing our code as it evolves.
- ❏ Controlling a program's execution flow with 'if', 'for', and 'while' statements.

If you are a proficient C or C++ programmer, you will find much of Java syntax – at least as it relates to the non-OO aspects of the language – to be very familiar, and should be able to breeze through this chapter fairly quickly.

If you have already been exposed to Java language basics, please feel free to skip to Chapter 2.

Why Java?

After learning what makes objects 'tick' in Part 1 of the book, and how to model an application to take advantage of objects in Part 2, we'll be ready for the grand finale: rendering our object model in code in order to produce a working Student Registration System (SRS) application in Part 3. We *could* build the SRS using any OO programming language: C++, or Ada, or Smalltalk, or Eiffel, or Java, or any of the OO flavors of conventional programming languages such as COBOL, Fortran, or Visual Basic. So, why have we chosen Java? Read on, and you'll quickly see why!

Java is Architecture Neutral

In order to execute a program written in a compilable language like C or C++, the source code must first be compiled into an executable form known as binary code or machine code. Binary code, in essence, is a pattern of 1's and 0's understandable by the underlying **hardware architecture** of the computer on which the program is intended to run.

Even if the original source code is written to be platform-independent – that is, the program does not take advantage of any platform-specific language extensions such as a specific type of file access or graphical user interface (GUI) manipulation – the resultant executable version will nonetheless still be tied to a particular platform's architecture, and can therefore only be run on that architecture. That is, a version of the program compiled for a Sun workstation will not run on a PC, a version compiled for a PC will not run on a Mac, and so forth.

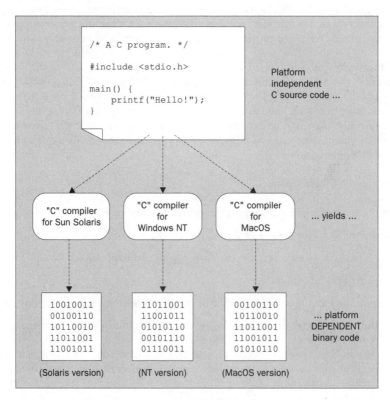

In contrast, Java source code is not compiled for a particular platform, but rather into a special format known as **byte code**, which happens to be platform independent, a.k.a. **architecture neutral**. That is, no matter whether a Java program is compiled under Sun Solaris, or Windows NT, or MacOS, or any other operating system for which a Java compiler is available, the resultant byte code turns out to be the same, and hence can be run on any computer that supports a **Java Virtual Machine (JVM)**.

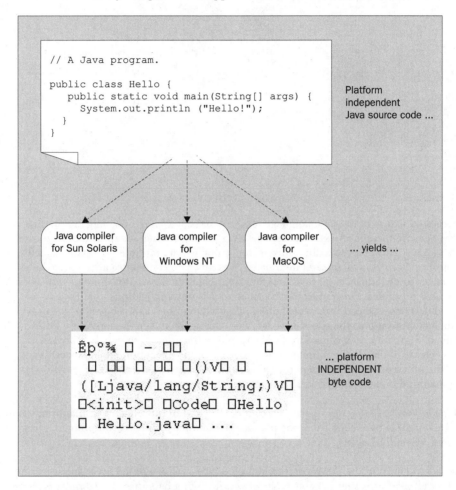

The JVM is a special piece of software that knows how to **interpret** and execute Java byte code. That is, instead of a Java program running directly under control of the operating system the way traditionally compiled programs do, the JVM itself runs under direct control of the operating system, and the Java program in turn runs under control of the JVM, as illustrated in the following diagram. The JVM in essence serves as a 'translator', turning the byte code 'language' into the machine code 'language' that a particular computer can understand.

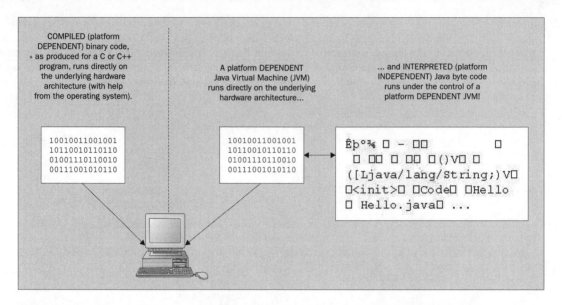

The interpreted nature of the Java language tends to make it a bit slower, in general, than compiled languages because there is an extra processing layer involved when an application executes, as illustrated above. However, this difference is noticeable when real-time processing speeds are required, such as in shop floor control or satellite tracking systems, you sometimes also notice the lag when the browser needs to download large Java programs and compile them, also there may be some lag in some complex GUI programs. For traditional information systems applications, that involve a human in the loop, the difference in speed is imperceptible; other factors, such as the speed of the network in the case of distributed applications, the speed of a database management system server if a DBMS is used, and even human 'think time' can cause any JVM's response time delays to pale by comparison. In addition, each new release of the JVM continues to improve upon the execution efficiency of its predecessors. Finally, when it comes to large-scale enterprise applications, Java's scalability actually makes it more efficient than traditionally compiled languages in many respects.

So, as long as you have the appropriate version of the JVM to run on a given platform, you can **migrate** (transfer) executable byte code from one platform to another without recompiling the original source code, and it will still be able to run!

Because new versions of the JVM, corresponding to new versions of the Java language, don't always get released for all platforms simultaneously, however, it is not a bad idea to recompile programs before transferring them from one platform to another, if you have that luxury.

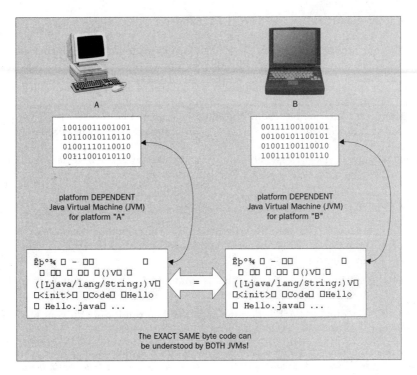

For this reason, Sun Microsystems (the company that invented the Java language) describes Java as the 'write once, run anywhere' language.

As we'll learn in Chapter 16, this slogan would be better phrased 'write once, TEST EVERYWHERE, run anywhere', especially for programs with graphical user interface front-ends.

Java and the World Wide Web

Java's platform independent nature makes it an ideal language for deploying software over the World Wide Web, and **applets** are designed for this exact purpose. An applet is a 'mini' Java program, typically with a graphical user interface front-end, that can be embedded in a HyperText Markup Language (HTML) page. An applet is written in Java and compiled just like any other Java program. Then, a reference to the applet is embedded in an HTML page using an **applet tag**, as illustrated in the trivially simple HTML example that follows:

```
<HTML>
  <HEAD>
    <TITLE>My Home Page</TITLE>
  </HEAD>
  <BODY>
    <APPLET CODE=MyApplet WIDTH=80 HEIGHT=100></APPLET>
  </BODY>
</HTML>
```

When you get to such an HTML page, here's what happens:

- ❑ Step 1: Your browser downloads the HTML for that page from the appropriate Web server to your local machine, and interprets the HTML; in this case, it detects an applet tag.

- ❑ Step 2: An applet can only execute under the control of either a **Java-enabled browser**, such as Sun Microsystem's HotJava browser, or more recent versions of Netscape Communicator and Microsoft's Internet Explorer. Assuming your particular browser is 'applet aware', your browser next downloads the byte code version of the applet to your computer.

  *Applets may also be run via a special tool called an **appletviewer**, which is included in the standard Java Software Developer's Kit that we'll talk about later in the chapter.*

- ❑ Step 3: The byte code is verified to ensure that:

  - ❑ The version of Java used to write the applet matches the version of Java that your browser understands (browsers sometimes lag behind in terms of which version of Java they support).

  - ❑ That the applet can be trusted: that is, that no malicious instructions are present which could do damage to your computer.

- ❑ Step 4: If all is found to be in order, the applet is then run locally on your machine, under control of the JVM embedded in the browser.

  *In the interest of security, the browser restricts what all the applet can do in terms of accessing your local machine's hard drive, talking with servers other than the Web server from which it was downloaded, and so forth; this is often referred to as keeping the applet within a 'sandbox'. Of course, with any security measures, there are 'hackers' in the world who strive to break them, and applet security is no different. For up to date discussions on applet security, please refer to Sun's website (*www.java.sun.com*).*

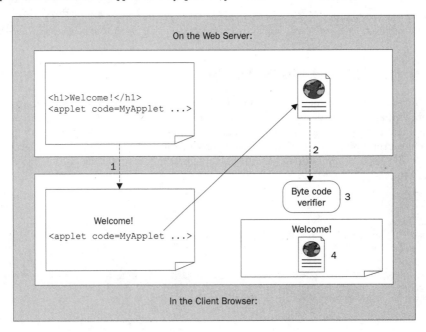

Because users can be surfing the Web with virtually any type of computer, it is particularly important that the byte code which gets downloaded be platform independent.

This approach to dynamically distributing application code also proves to be useful for organizations interested in deploying applications via their respective intranets.

Of course, Java is not used just to create applets. Java is an elegant and powerful programming language that can be used to develop full-blown, stand-alone applications of the sort you might have alternatively written using C, C++, or Visual Basic. And, in addition to the two client side types of Java program – applets and stand-alone applications – Java is also used to develop platform-independent server-side programs/components such as **servlets, Java Server Pages (JSPs),** and **Enterprise Java Beans (EJBs)**. The Enterprise Edition of Java – known as J2EE for short – encompasses all of these server-side technologies, but is beyond the scope of this book to address.

We'll focus on Java applications (versus either applets or J2EE server-side components) for the remainder of this book; the techniques that you will learn for application development are *directly* applicable to all of these other technologies, however. If after completing this book you are interested in learning more about any of these other Java technologies, please see the other Java titles available at the Apress web site (www.apress.com).

Java Provides 'One Stop Shopping'

With most conventional programming languages, the core language does not automatically provide everything that you'll need in order to build an industrial strength application, with a graphical user interface and access to a database management system. For these capabilities, you must typically integrate platform-specific (and in some cases, even *vendor*-specific) libraries into your application, as illustrated below.

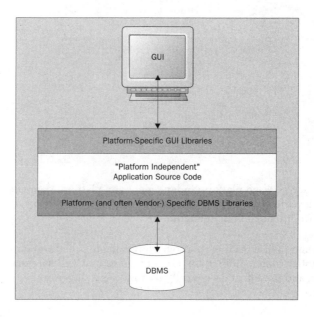

The inclusion of such platform- and vendor-specific components hinders application migration from one platform to another. To migrate a GUI-oriented C++ application originally written to run under Windows NT using the Microsoft Foundation Classes as GUI components so that it instead runs under Sun Solaris using Motif GUI components, for example, we have several choices, *none* of which are very appealing:

1. We can replace the entire NT-specific GUI library calls with their Solaris-specific equivalent calls. There are two problems with this approach:

❏ Not all library calls for a given platform 'X' necessarily *have* an equivalent for a target platform 'Y'.

❏ The preceding figure implies a rosier situation than actually exists, because the boundary between the platform independent and platform/vendor dependent code is not really so clean. Calls to these libraries are often scattered throughout an application as illustrated below, making the chore of migrating an application from one platform to another troublesome at best, and prohibitive in the worst cases.

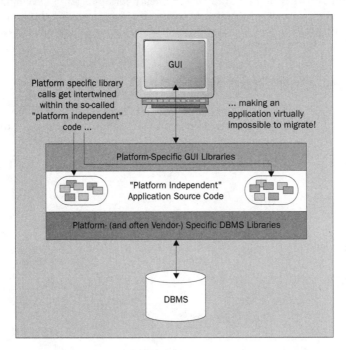

2. If the boundary between platform independent and platform dependent components of an application is particularly messy, it is sometimes the lesser of two evils to rewrite the entire application from scratch than to migrate it!

3. There are some special third party programs available called **emulators** that will simulate one operating system under another, but not all applications will necessarily run properly under an emulator, and those that do typically perform very sluggishly.

Once again, Java comes to our rescue! The Java language provides an extensive set of **application programming interfaces (APIs)** that provide a consistent, *platform-independent* means of accessing all underlying operating system functions, including GUI rendering and DBMS access. We'll learn about the following Java APIs later, in Part 3 of the book:

❏ java.io – used for file system access (Chapter 15).

❏ java.sql – the Java Database Connectivity (JDBC) API, used for communicating with relational databases in a vendor independent fashion (Chapter 15).

❏ java.awt – the Abstract Windowing Toolkit, used for GUI development (Chapter 16).

❏ javax.swing – Swing components, also used for GUI development (Chapter 16).

and there are *many* more! If these built-in Java libraries are used in developing applications, the resultant Java code is truly portable. So, to migrate a Java application from Windows NT to Solaris, for example, there is no need to rip out code (or your hair!) – simply transfer the byte code for the application to the new platform, and as long as:

❏ The new platform has a platform-appropriate JVM installed,

❏ The new target database management system is 'Java aware' (virtually all of the leading DBMS vendors are), and

❏ No vendor-specific extensions to the SQL (Structured Query Language) were assumed in writing the Java code, then you are good to go!

As mentioned earlier, many Java practitioners recommend recompiling an application specifically for a new target platform, to avoid possible discrepancies in the versions of the JVM that the respective platforms are running.

Practice Makes Perfect

As one of the latest OO languages to emerge, the Java language designers at Sun Microsystems had the advantage of seeing what had previously worked well in earlier OO languages, and conversely which language features had proven to be the most troublesome. Therefore, Java is actually a hybrid of the best features from leading OO languages such as Eiffel, Smalltalk, and C++, with some extra 'sizzle' thrown in by way of new features. This is not to say that Java is a 'perfect' language – no language is! – but simply that it has made some significant improvements over languages that have preceded it.

The improvements that Java makes over C++ are particularly noteworthy; we talk about these in some depth in Appendix E.

Java is Heavily Object Oriented

One of the most widely used OO languages, C++, is actually an object-oriented descendant of the non-OO C language. As such, C++ provides a lot of 'back doors' that make it very easy to write decidedly 'un-OO' code. (We discuss a number of these 'back doors' in Appendix E, but it would be best to defer reading that appendix until you've made it through all of the chapters on object concepts in Part 1.)

In contrast, Java is object-oriented to its very core. As we will learn in more detail in the chapters that follow, just about *everything* in Java is an object:

❑   All of your data, with the exception of a few simple data types, are objects.

❑   All of the GUI building blocks – windows, buttons, text input fields, scroll bars, lists, menus, and so on – are objects.

❑   All functions are attached to objects, and are known as **methods** – there can be no 'free floating' functions as there were in C or C++.

❑   Even the main program (now called a **main method**) no longer stands alone, but is instead bundled within a **class**, the reasons for which we'll explore in depth in chapters to come.

Because of this, Java lends itself particularly well to writing applications that uphold the object-oriented paradigm. Yet, as we pointed out in the Introduction to this book, merely using such an object-oriented language does not *guarantee* that the applications you produce will be *true* to this paradigm! You must be knowledgeable both in how to design an application from the ground up to make the best use of objects, and in how to apply the language correctly, which are the primary intents of this book.

As it turns out, the Smalltalk and Eiffel programming languages are also more purely object oriented than C++, and predate Java by several years. So, why didn't either of these two languages gain as widespread an acceptance as Java – the 'new kid on the block' – seems to have gained within the OO community? The answer is simple: with so many things in life, timing is everything! Although object technology had certainly gotten a lot of attention when these more mature languages emerged on the scene, it hadn't quite gained the groundswell level of interest that it had by the time Java was developed. More significantly, however, was the fact that Java's release coincided with the explosion of World Wide Web 'fever' – and as we've already discussed, its platform independent nature made it 'Internet-friendly' from the start.

> *The fact that Java remedies many of the ills of C++ hasn't hurt, either, as many former C++ programmers (myself included!) jumped on the Java bandwagon. C++ programmers found Java to be a language with familiar syntax that also eliminated many of the headaches associated with C++, e.g., pointers, memory leaks, platform dependence, and so forth, as we discuss at length in Appendix E.*

Java is an Open Standard

What does this mean to you? For one thing, all of the source code behind all of the built-in Java libraries is available for you to study and to use as a basis for your own software design. Also, the IT industry as a whole – as defined in large part by the vendor community – has been quick to embrace Java because nobody has been 'shut out' as is often the case with a proprietary, closed technology. Quite the contrary: Sun Microsystems is encouraging other vendors to adopt the Java standard, and to incorporate Java capability in their products, by actually allowing vendors to participate in the development of Java technology specifications through Sun's Java Community Process program.

And, if all the preceding reasons aren't enough to convince you of the merits of Java:

Java is Free!

Sun Microsystems has ensured that Java enjoys widespread adoption, in part, by making the language, and all of the basic tools necessary to develop Java applications, free! Appendix C provides information on what you'll need to do to download the Java **Software Development Kit (SDK)** from Sun's website (http://java.sun.com) in order to get started with Java development.

Of course, you can certainly use a Java integrated development environment (IDE) tool if you wish to, but please wait until after you've read Chapter 13, where you'll hear my biases against using such a tool when first learning Java.

Java Language Basics

Because we realize that some of you may have never seen Java code before, we'd like to introduce Java syntax now. This section presents only those basics of the Java language that you'll need to understand in order to appreciate the code examples in Parts 1 and 2 of this book. We'll revisit Java in a great deal more depth in Part 3 (Chapters 13 – 17), where we'll delve deeply into the OO aspects of the language in preparation for building a fully functional Student Registration System (SRS) application.

> *If you haven't taken the time to read the Introduction to this book, now is a good time to do so! The SRS application requirements are introduced as a case study at the end of the Introduction.*

A Note Regarding Pseudocode versus Real Java Code

As we mentioned in the beginning of this chapter, we occasionally use little bits of pseudocode in our code examples throughout Parts 1 and 2 of the book to hide irrelevant logic details. To make it clear as to when we are using pseudocode vs. real code, we've used *italic* versus regular Courier font:

```
for (int i = 0; i <= 10; i++) {          ← This is real Java syntax.
    compute the grade for the iᵗʰ Student ← This is pseudocode!
}
```

We'll remind you of this fact a few more times later in the book, so that you don't forget and accidentally try to type in and compile pseudocode somewhere along the line!

Anatomy of a Simple Java Program

One of the simplest of all Java applications is shown below.

```
// Simple.java
//
// A trivially simple example for illustrating the anatomy
// of a (non-OO) Java program.
//
// Written by Jacquie Barker.

public class Simple {
    public static void main(String[] args) {
        System.out.print ln("Wheee!!!!") ;
    }
}
```

introductory comment

class "wrapper"

main method

It consists of:

❑ An introductory comment. Java supports several different comment styles; we'll review two of them here:

❑ The C language style of block comments, which begin with a forward slash followed by an asterisk (/*) and end with an asterisk followed by a forward slash (*/). Everything enclosed between these delimiters is treated as a comment and is therefore ignored by the compiler, no matter how many lines the comment spans.

```
/* This is a single line C-style comment. */

/* This is a handy way to temporarily comment out entire sections
   of code. From the time that the compiler encounters the first
   'slash asterisk' above, it doesn't matter what we type here;
   even legitimate lines of code, as shown below, are treated as
   comment lines until the first 'asterisk slash' combination
   is encountered.
x = y + z;
a = b / c;
j = s + c + f;
*/
```

❑ The C++ single line form of comment, using a double slash (//) to comment just to the end of a line:

```
x = y + z;    // text of comment starts here through the end of the line
a = b / c;
```

```
// Here is a block of C++ style comments.
// This serves as an alternative to using the C style
// of block comments (/* ... */).
m = n * p;
```

❑ A main function, called a **main method** in Java, is where the program starts; this contains the logic to be executed on startup by the program. (With trivial applications such as this 'Simple' example, all logic can be contained within this single function; for more complex applications, on the other hand, the main method cannot possibly contain all of the logic for the entire system, and so we'll learn how to construct an application that transcends the boundaries of the main method.)

The first line of the method:

```
public static void main(String[] args) {
```

known as the main method's **signature**, must appear exactly as shown (with one minor exception that we'll explain later in the book, after we learn enough about objects to appreciate all of what this signature is doing).
Our main method body consists of a single statement:

```
System.out.println("Wheee!!!!!!");
```

which prints the message
  Wheee!!!!!!

to the screen; we'll talk more about this statement's syntax in a bit.

❑ A class 'wrapper' of the form:

```
public class name { ... }
```

where curly braces surround the main method, as well as enclosing other building blocks of a class that we'll learn about in Chapter 2. The words 'public' and 'class' are two of Java's reserved words. Reserved words are words that have special meaning in a language, and which therefore may not be used by programmers as the names of variables, functions, or any of the other Java building blocks that we'll be learning about.
In later chapters, we'll learn all about classes, how to name them, and in particular why we even need a class wrapper in the first place.

Built-In Java Data Types

Java defines four types of integer numeric data:

❑ byte: 8 bits

❑ short: 16 bits

❑ int: 32 bits

❑ long: 64 bits

and two floating point numeric types:

- ❏   `float`: 32 bit floating point
- ❏   `double`: 64 bit floating point

Other built-in data types defined by Java include:

- ❏   `char`: a single character, stored using 16 bit Unicode encoding versus 8 bit ASCII encoding, thus enabling Java to handle a wide range of international character sets. Note that we use single quotes, not double quotes, to surround a character literal when assigning it to a `char` variable:

```
char c = 'A';
```

- ❏   `boolean`: a variable that may only assume one of two values – `true or false` (both of these are reserved words). Booleans are often used as flags to signal whether or not some code should be conditionally performed:

```
boolean error = false;  // Initialize the flag.
// Later in the program:
if (some situation arises)
  error = true;
// ...

// Still later in the program:
if (error) take some corrective action
```

Assuming that variable 'done' is declared to be a `boolean`, and is set to a value of `true` or `false` somewhere along the line in a program, the following two tests are considered equivalent for testing for a value of `true`:

```
if (done) do something ...
if (done == true) do something ...   // note the use of == to test
                                     // for equality
```

and the following two tests are considered equivalent for testing for a value of `false`:

```
if (!done) do something ...          // note the use of ! meaning 'not'
if (done == false) do something ...
```

(We'll talk specifically about the syntax of the 'if' statement, one of several different kinds of Java flow-control statements, a bit later.)

- ❏   `String`: Java has 'real' character strings, as opposed to the use of `char`(acter) arrays to simulate strings in C and early versions of C++.

The reserved word `String` *starts with a capital 'S', whereas the names of all of the other built-in data types that we've seen so far start with a lower case letter; this is intentional, and we'll explain its significance in due time.*

```
String aString = "I am a string!";
```

Note that we use double quotes, not single quotes, to surround a `String` literal when assigning it to a `String` variable, even if it consists of only a single character:

```
String shortString = "A";  // Use double quotes when assigning a
                           // value to a String ...

String longString = "supercalifragilisticexpialadocious";  // (ditto)

char c = 'A';              // ... and single quotes when assigning
                           // a value to a char.
```

The plus sign (+) operator is used to concatenate `Strings`:

```
String x = "foo";
String y = "bar";
String z = x + y + "!";  // z now equals "foobar!"
```

There are many other operations that can be performed with/on Strings, which we'll learn about in Chapter 13.

When variables of any of these data types are declared, their values are not automatically initialized; trying to access such variables without explicitly initializing them, will result in a compilation error. For example, this next bit of code:

```
public static void main(String[] args) {
  int i;  // not automatically initialized
  int j;  // ditto
  j = i;  // compilation error!
}
```

would produce the compilation error on the second to the last line:

Variable i may not have been initialized.

because we are trying to copy the value of `i` – which is undefined – into variable `j`. We can resolve this problem by explicitly initializing `i`:

```
public static void main(String[] args) {
  int i = 0; // Explicit initialization.
  int j;     // No need to initialize - j is on the 'receiving' end.
  j = i;     // This line compiles fine now!
}
```

And, although it isn't necessary to do so for this example, it is a good practice to explicitly initialize all variables, primarily as a communication tool:

```
public static void main(String[] args) {
  int i = 0;   // manual initialization
  int j = 0;   // document our intent for j to start out with the value 0.
  j = i;       // compiles fine now!
}
```

Common practice is to initialize booleans to false, numerics to either 0 or 0.0, chars to ' ' (a blank space), and Strings to the value **null**, another reserved word in Java:

```
String name = null;
```

In Chapter 13, we'll learn that the rules of automatic initialization are somewhat different when dealing with the 'inner workings' of objects.

Autoincrement/Autodecrement Operators

Java provides **autoincrement** (++) and **autodecrement** (--) operators; when applied to a variable declared to be of any of the following built-in data types, these operators increase or decrease the value of that variable by the amount indicated:

❑   1, for bytes, shorts, ints, and longs;

❑   1.0, for floats and doubles;

❑   One alphabetic character, for chars (for example, 'A' becomes 'B').

The location of the autoincrement/decrement operator – i.e. whether it is in front of the variable, known as **prefix notation,** or after the variable, known as **postfix notation** – affects whether the increment/decrement operation takes place before or after the variable's value is used in a statement. Here is a simple example:

```
int i, j, k;

i = 1;

j = i++;    // j receives the value 1, because i is incremented from
            // 1 to 2 AFTER its value is used in the assignment statement.

k = ++i;    // k receives the value 3, because i is incremented from
            // 2 to 3 BEFORE its value is used in the assignment statement.
```

Java Expressions

A **simple expression** in Java is either:

- ❑ A constant: 7, `false`

- ❑ A String literal: `"foo"`

- ❑ A variable declared to be of one of the built-in types that we've seen so far: aString, x

- ❑ Any two of the above that are combined with one of the Java **binary operators** (+, -, *, /, etc.): x + 2

- ❑ Any one of the above that is modified by one of the Java **unary operators** (++, --, !, etc.): i++

- ❑ Any of the above simple expressions enclose in parentheses: (x + 2)

plus a few more expression types having to do with objects that we'll learn about in Chapter 13.

Expressions of arbitrary complexity can then be built up around these different simple expression types by nesting parentheses – for example, `((((4/2) + z) * 7) + y)`. We evaluate such expressions from innermost to outermost parentheses, left to right.

Given two (simple or complex) expressions *exp1* and *exp2*, we may then apply any one of the following `Boolean` operators, which cause the entire resultant expression to evaluate to a value of either `true` or `false`:

- ❑ *exp1 == exp2*   true if *exp1* equals *exp2*

- ❑ *exp1 > exp2*   true if *exp1* is greater than *exp2*

- ❑ *exp1 >= exp2*   true if *exp1* is greater or equal to *exp2*

- ❑ *exp1 < exp2*   true if *exp1* is less than *exp2*

- ❑ *exp1 <= exp2*   true if *exp1* is less than or equal to *exp2*

- ❑ *exp1 != exp2*   true if *exp1* is not equal *exp2* (! is read as 'not')

- ❑ *! exp1*   true if *exp1* is `false`, and `false` if *exp1* is true

When we wish to make up a complex 'if' clause that involves two or more `boolean` expressions, we can use the **logical operators** '&&' (and) and '||' (or) operators to combine these, as illustrated by the next few examples:

```
// If x is a positive number AND y is a positive number ...
if ((x > 0) && (y > 0)) ...

// If x is a negative number OR y is a negative number ...
if ((x < 0) || (y < 0)) ...

// If both x AND y are negative, OR z is positive ...
if (((x < 0) && (y < 0)) || (z > 0)) ...
```

Automatic Type Conversions and Explicit Casting

Java supports **automatic type conversions**. This means that if you try to transfer the value of some variable y to another variable x:

```
x = y;
```

and the two variables were originally declared to be of different types, then Java will attempt to make the transfer, automatically converting the type if it makes sense to do so. Unlike languages like C and C++, however, where automatic type conversion occurs even if precision is lost in the conversion, automatic type conversions will only occur if no precision is going to be lost in doing so. This is best understood by looking at an example:

```
int x;
double y;
y = 2.7;
x = y;   // This line will compile in C and C++, but not in Java.
```

In the preceding code snippet, we are attempting to copy the double value of y, 2.7, into x, which is declared to be an int. If this transfer were to take place, this would cause the fractional part of y to be truncated, and x would wind up with the value of 2. This represents a loss in precision, and so the Java compiler will generate an error on the last line:

Incompatible type for =. Explicit cast needed to convert double to int.

In order to signal to the Java compiler that we are willing to accept the loss of precision, we must perform an **explicit cast**, which involves preceding the expression whose value is to be transferred with the desired target data type enclosed in parentheses. In other words, we'd have to rewrite the last line of the example above as follows in order for the Java compiler to accept it:

```
int x;
double y;
y = 2.7;
x = (int) y;    // This will compile in Java now! The compiler 'relaxes',
                // because we have explicitly told it that we WANT the
                // conversion to occur.
```

Note that there is an idiosyncrasy with regard to assigning constant values to floats in Java; the statement

```
float y = 3.5;   // won't compile!
```

will generate a compiler error, because a floating point constant value like 3.5 is automatically treated by Java as a more precise double value, and so the compiler will once again refuse to make a transfer that causes precision to be lost. To make such an assignment, you must explicitly cast the floating point constant into a float:

```
float y = (float) 3.5;   // OK; we're using a cast here.
```

or, alternatively, force the constant on the right hand side of the assignment statement to be treated as a float by using the suffix 'F', as shown below:

```
float y = 3.5F;   // OK, because we're indicating that the constant is to be
                  // treated as a float, not as a double.
```

We'll typically use `doubles` instead of `floats` whenever we need to declare floating point variables in our SRS application, just to avoid these hassles of type conversion.

We'll see other applications of casting, involving objects, later in the book.

Block Structured Languages and the Scope of a Variable

Java (like C and C++) is a **block structured language.** A 'block' of code is a series of zero or more lines of code enclosed within curly braces { ... }.

❑ A method, like the `main` method of our 'Simple' program, defines a block.

❑ A class definition, like the 'Simple' class as a whole, is also a block.

❑ As we will see a bit later, many **control flow statements** also involve defining blocks of code.

Blocks may be nested inside one another to any arbitrary depth:

```
public class Simple {
    // We're inside of the 'class' block (one level deep).
    public static void main(String[] args) {
        // We're inside of the 'main' block (two levels deep).
        int x = 3;
        int y = 4;
        int z = 5;

        if (x > 2) {
            // We're now one level deeper (level 3), in a nested block.
            if (y > 3) {
                // We're one level deeper still (level 4), in yet another
                // nested block.
                // (We could go on and on!)
            } // We've just ended the level 4 block.
            // (We could have additional code here, at level 3.)
        } // Level 3 is done!
        // (We could have additional code here, at level 2.)
    } // That's it for level 2!
    // (We could have additional code here, at level 1.)
} // Adios, amigos! Level 1 has just ended.
```

The **scope** of a variable is defined as that portion of code for which a variable name remains defined to the compiler: namely, from the point where it is first declared down to the closing (right) curly brace for the block of code that it was declared in. In the pseudocode example that follows, we've highlighted the scope of variable x:

```
{ // Start of an outer block; x has not yet been declared.
  int y = 3;

  // Declare x to be of type int.
  int x;
  // x is now considered to be 'in scope'! Whenever the compiler sees a
  // reference to x, it will know it to be a reference to THIS PARTICULAR
  // integer variable.

  {
     // Start of a nested inner block ... this doesn't affect x –
     // it's still in scope, and we can refer to the variable as necessary:
     x = x + 2;
     // etc.
  } // end of the inner nested block

  // We can still manipulate x, because it is still in scope here (we're still
  // within the block in which x was first declared.
  x = x + 17;
} // end of the outer block in which x was first declared;
// x has just gone out of scope, which means essentially
// that the compiler forgets that we ever declared it;
// any subsequent references to x in our program will result
// in compilation errors (unless we declare a DIFFERENT
// variable with the name 'x' later on).
```

Printing to the Screen

Most applications communicate information to users by displaying messages via the application's GUI. However, it is also useful at times to be able to display simple text messages to the command line window from which you are running a program as a 'quick and dirty' way of verifying that a program is working properly (we'll learn how to run Java programs later in the book). And, until you have learned how to craft a Java GUI in Chapter 16 – a non-trivial matter! – then this will be your program's primary way of communicating with the 'outside world' as you learn the language.

To print text messages to the screen, we use the following Java statement:

```
System.out.println(the String expression to be printed);
```

For now, don't worry about the 'strange' syntax of this statement – there's a lot that we need to cover about objects before we can do justice to explaining it in detail. By the time we get to Chapter 13, we'll be able to do so.

The System.out.println() method can accept very complex expressions, and does its best to ultimately turn these into a single String value, which then gets displayed on the screen. Here are a few examples:

```
System.out.println("Hi!");      // Printing a String literal/constant.

String s = "Hi!";
System.out.println(s);          // Printing a String variable.

String s = "foo";
String t = "bar";
System.out.println(s + t);      // Using the String concatenation operator (+) to
                                // print "foobar".

int x = 3;
int y = 4;

System.out.println(x);          // Converts x's int value into a String and
                                // prints the value "3" to the screen.

System.out.println(x + y);      // Automatically computes the sum of x and y, then
                                // prints the value "7" to the screen.
```

Note in the last line of code above that the plus sign (+) is interpreted as the *integer* addition operator, not as the String concatenation operator, because it separates two variables that are both declared to be of type int. So, the sum of 3 + 4 is computed to be 7, which is what is printed. In the next example, however, we get different behavior:

```
System.out.println("The sum of x plus y is:   " + x + y);
```

The preceding line of code causes the following to be printed:

> The sum of x plus y is: 34

Why is this?

❑ We evaluate expressions from left to right, and so since the first of the two plus signs separates a String literal and an int, it is interpreted as a String concatenation operator, and the value of x is thus converted into a String, producing the intermediate String value 'The sum of x plus y is: 3'.

❑ The second plus sign separates this intermediate String value from an int as well (y), so it, too, is interpreted as a String concatenation operator, and the value of y is thus converted into a String, producing the final String value 'The sum of x plus y is: 34', which is what finally gets printed.

To print the correct sum of x and y, we must force the second plus sign to be interpreted as an integer addition operator by enclosing the addition expression in nested parentheses:

```
System.out.println("The sum of x plus y is: " + (x + y));
```

The nested parentheses cause the innermost expression to be evaluated first; the second plus sign is now seen as separating two int values, and will thus serve as the integer addition operator, ultimately causing this print statement to display the correct message on the screen:

> The sum of x plus y is: 7

Any time you write code that involves a complex expression, it is a good idea to use parentheses liberally to make your intentions clear to the compiler.

print vs. println

When we use `System.out.println(...)`, whatever `String` expression is enclosed inside the parentheses will be printed, followed by a 'hard return' character. The following code snippet:

```
System.out.println("First line.");
System.out.println("Second line.");
System.out.println("Third line.");
```

produces as output:

```
First line.
Second line.
Third line.
```

By contrast, the statement:

```
System.out.print(the String expression to be printed);
```

causes whatever expression is enclosed in parentheses to be printed *without* a hard return. Using `print` in combination with `println` allows us to build up a single line of output with a series of `print` statements, as shown by the following example:

```
System.out.print("J");      // Using print here.
System.out.print("AV");     // Using print here.
System.out.println("A");    // Note use of println on the last statement.
```

This code snippet produces the single line of output:

```
JAVA
```

Using the String Concatenation Operator in a Print Statement

When a single print statement gets too long to fit on a single line:

```
statement;
another statement;
System.out.println("Here is an example of a single print statement that is
very long ... SO long that it wraps around and makes the program listing difficult
to read.");
yet another statement;
```

you can make your program listing more readable by breaking up the contents of your print statement into multiple concatenated `String`s, and then breaking the statement along plus-sign boundaries:

```
statement;
another statement;
System.out.println("Here is an example of how " +
                   "to break up a long print statement " +
                   "along plus sign boundaries.");
yet another statement;
```

Even though the preceding print statement is broken across three lines of code, it will be printed as a single line:

Here is an example of how to break up a long print statement along plus sign boundaries.

Escape Sequences

We use **escape sequences** to insert special characters in a String expression to be printed. An escape sequence consists of a backslash (\) followed by one of several predefined characters:

❑ To insert a tab character in a String literal, use \t:

```
System.out.println("DOG\tCAT\tBIRD\tRAT\tFISH");
```

This produces as output:

DOG   CAT   BIRD   RAT   FISH

where each word is separated from the next by a tab character.

❑ To insert a hard return in the middle of a String literal, use \n:

```
System.out.println("One sentence.\nAnother sentence.");
```

This produces as output:

One sentence.
Another sentence.

on two separate lines.

❑ To insert a double quote in the middle of a String literal, use \":

```
System.out.println("I want to print a \"quoted\" string.");
```

The preceding line of code produces the output:

I want to print a "quoted" string.

❑ To insert a backslash in the middle of a String literal, use \\:

```
System.out.println("I want to print a backslash here:  \\");
```

The preceding line of code produces the output:

I want to print a backslash here: \

Controlling a Program's Execution Flow

The Java language provides several means of altering the sequential flow of a program; if you have programmed in C or C++ (or virtually any higher level language), these should all be familiar to you.

If

The 'if' statement is a traditional conditional execution control structure; its syntax is as follows:

```
if (boolean expression ) statement
```

where *statement* can be a **simple statement** – a single line of Java code terminating in a semicolon (;) – or a **compound statement** – that is, a block of statements enclosed in curly braces ({ ... }). Here are a few simple examples:

```
int total;
int limit;
boolean done;

// Assume that variables total, limit, and done are set to appropriate
// values in the execution of the program; details omitted.

// A simple statement is associated with this 'if'.
if (total > limit) j = 2;

// A compound statement is associated with this 'if'.
if (!done) {
  x = 3;
  y = 4;
  System.out.println("foo!");
}
```

In the C/C++ languages, which do not define a data type of `boolean`, 'if' tests are performed on integer expressions, where a value of zero implies `false` and any non-zero value implies `true`. In Java, there are no automatic conversions between the `int` and `boolean` data types, so the following code, while valid in C/C++, would fail to compile in Java:

```
// This works for C and C++, but not for Java:
int ok = 0;
// ...
if (!ok) { do something }
// The preceding line generates a compilation error in Java; an 'if'
// statement in Java expects a boolean expression.
```

An 'if' statement may optionally be paired with an 'else' statement:

```
if (boolean expression) statement to be performed if true
else statement to be performed if false
```

where again either *statement to be performed* in this example may be simple or compound:

```
if (!done) x = 3;   // simple statement
else {              // compound statement
  y = 4;
  System.out.println("foo!");
  // etc.
}
```

The Java compiler is pretty smart about matching up 'else' clauses with the proper 'if' clause when these are nested, but it is best to use curly braces to explicitly state what you mean. For example, the following pseudocode snippet:

```
if (A ) aaa;
else if (B ) bbb;
else if (C ) ccc;
else ddd;
```

is understood by the compiler to mean:

```
if (A ) aaa;
else {
  if (B ) bbb;
  else {
    if (C ) ccc;
    else ddd;
  }
}
```

and, in fact, the first of these two examples would be the preferred coding style for complex 'if – else' statements.

How about the following poorly constructed code?

```
if (x <= 0)
if (x < 0) System.out.println(x + " is negative");
else System.out.println(x + " equals zero");
else System.out.println(x + " is positive");
```

Believe it or not, this code will compile and run – here's how the compiler assumes we meant it to be interpreted:

```
if (x <= 0) {
  if (x < 0) System.out.println(x + " is negative");
  else System.out.println(x + " equals zero");
}
else System.out.println(x + " is positive");
```

The compiler will automatically associate the first 'else' that it finds with the most recent 'if' that it saw, the *next* 'else' with the *next to last* 'if', and so forth. This example illustrates how useful proper indentation and the liberal use of curly braces can be in making code easier to understand and, therefore, easier to debug and maintain. When in doubt, use curly braces profusely! We'll talk more about proper indentation style shortly.

For

The 'for' statement is another type of flow control statement, typically used for iteration (for example, stepping through all of the elements in an array, more information on arrays will occur later in the chapter). There are three parts to the 'for' clause syntax, separated by semicolons (;):

```
for (initialization expression;
    boolean test for completion;
    increment or decrement expression)
        statement to be performed
```

with all parts of the 'for' clause usually appearing on the same line.

Again, the *statement to be performed* can be either a simple or compound statement:

```
// Print out the integer values from 1 to 4.
// Simple statement (all in one line).
for (int i = 1; i <= 4; i++) System.out.println(i);
```

versus:

```
int sum = 0;

// Print out the integer values from 1 to 4, and compute a running total.
for (int i = 1; i <= 4; i++) {
    // Compound statement to be executed.
    System.out.println(i);
    sum = sum + i;
}
```

Note that you can either declare the **iterator variable** (i, in the above examples) *inside* of the 'for' clause or *outside* and *before* the 'for' clause, depending on whether or not you want the scope of that variable to persist after the loop:

```
// Declare j before the loop begins.
int j;

for (j = 1; j <= 4; j++) {
    do something with j!   // pseudocode
}

// The loop has ended, and j still exists as far as the compiler is concerned!
System.out.println(j);   // j has the value of 5 here
```

versus:

```
// Declare k inside of the 'for' clause;
// The 'scope' of k is simply inside of the loop.
for (int k = 1; k <= 4; k++) {
    do something with k!   // pseudocode
}

System.out.println(k);   // Compiler error; k is no longer in scope!
```

While

The 'while' statement is another commonly used form of loop:

```
while (boolean expression ) statement to be executed
```

where again the statement to be executed may be either simple or compound. Here's an example:

```
int i = 1;
int sum = 0;

// Print all integers between 1 and 4, and compute their total.
while (i < 5) {
  System.out.println(i);
  sum = sum + i;
  // Remember to increment i!
  i++;
}
```

Unlike a 'for' loop, which is programmed to terminate after a fixed number of iterations, a 'while' loop is dependent on the state of the program and/or its environment for its stopping criteria. For example, in the preceding code snippet, if we hadn't remembered to autoincrement the value of i each time we went through the loop (a common oversight), the loop would run forever.

This next example illustrates the use of a boolean variable to signal when a 'while' loop should terminate:

```
boolean finished = false;
int maximum = 2000;
int x = 0;
int y = 0;

// As long as the 'finished' flag is set to false, this 'while' loop will
// continue to execute.
while (!finished) {
  do some processing which affects the value of x in some fashion
  do some other processing which affects the value of y in some fashion

  // Test for stopping condition, and set the 'finished' flag accordingly.
  if (x > maximum || y > maximum) finished = true;   // an "or" test

  perhaps some additional processing occurs
}
```

There are two ways to prematurely get out from within the middle of a 'for' or 'while' loop.

❑   The **break** statement is used when we want to abruptly terminate a loop:

```
// We go into this loop intending to execute it 4 times (j = 0, 1, 2, 3).
for (int j = 0; j < 4; j++) {
    // But, as soon as j equals 2 the following 'if' test passes and
    // we break out of the loop
    if (j == 2) break

    // if on the other hand, the 'if' test fails, and we skip over the
    // 'break' statement, we print the value of j, and continue looping.
    System.out.println(j);
}

// We continue our execution at the line of code immediately after the loop
System.out.println("Loop finished");
```

The printed output produced by the preceding code snippet would be as follows:

```
0
1
Loop finished!
```

❑   The **continue** statement, on the other hand, is used when we want to advance to the next iteration of a loop without finishing the current iteration:

```
// We go into this loop intending to execute it 4 times.
for (int j = 0; j< 4; j++) {
    // But, as soon as j= 2, this next 'if' test passes, and we 'jump'
    // back to the beginning of the loop, with j being incremated to 3 ...
    if (j == 2) continue;

    // ... so the following line doesn't get executed for j = 2.
    System.out.println(j);
}

System.out.println("Loop finished!");
```

The printed output produced by this code would be as follows:

```
0
1
3
Loop finished!
```

Indentation Style

When we employ nested blocks of code, the symbols { and } are not always easy to see – we rely on proper indentation to make them more visible. There are two styles commonly used for the positioning of opening and closing curly braces when indenting blocks of code with Java; both are illustrated below. Use whichever one you prefer, but try to be consistent so that people reading your code can become accustomed to your style.

```
// Style 1: this example shows the opening brace tacked onto the
// end of the line that begins the block.
while (a < b) {
  a = in.get( );
  i += in.total( );
} // Note that the closing brace aligns with the leftmost edge of
  // the statement that begins the block.

// Style 2: this example shows the opening brace on its own line, left
// aligned with the 'while' line.
while (a < b)
{
  a = in.get( );
  i += in.total( );
} // Note that closing brace aligns with the opening brace.
```

Sometimes, you have so many levels of nested indentation, and/or individual statements are so long, that lines 'wrap' when viewed in an editor or printed as hardcopy:

```
while (a < b) {
  while (c > d) {
    for (int j = 0; j < 29; j++) {
      x = y + z + a + b - (c * (d / e) + f) - g + h + j - 1 - m - n + o + p * q /
r + s;
    }
  }
}
```

To avoid this, it is best to break the line in question along white space or punctuation boundaries:

```
while (a < b) {
  while (c > d) {
    for (int j = 0; j < 29; j++) {
      // This is cosmetically preferred.
      x = y + z + a + b - (c * (d / e) + f) - g +
          h + j - 1 - m - n + o + p * q / r + s;
    }
  }
}
```

This enables us to visually align the opening and closing curly braces:

```
while (a < b) {
  while (c > d) {
    for (int j = 0; j < 29; j++) {
      // This is cosmetically preferred.
      x = y + z + a + b - (c * (d / e) + f) - g +
          h + j - l - m - n + o + p * q / r + s;
    }
  }
}
```

Failure to properly indent makes programs unreadable and hence harder to debug – if you get a compilation error due to imbalanced curly braces, for example, the error message often occurs much later in the program than where the problem exists. For example, the following program is missing an opening curly brace on line 9, but the compiler doesn't report an error until line 23!

```
public class Indent2 {
  public static void main(String[] args) {
    int x = 2;
    int y = 3;
    int z = 1;

    if (x >= 0) {
      if (y > x) {
        if (y > 2) // missing opening brace here, but ...
          System.out.println("A");
          z = x + y;
        }
        else {
          System.out.println("B");
          z = x - y;
        }
      }
      else {
        System.out.println("C");
        z = y - x;
      }
    }
    else System.out.println("D");  // compiler first complains here!  (line 23)
  }
}
```

The error message that the compiler generates in such a situation is rather 'cryptic'; it points to line 23 as the problem:

```
Indent.java:23: Type expected.
```

and doesn't really help us much in locating the real problem on line 9. However, at least we've properly indented, so it might be easier to hunt down the missing brace than it would be if our indentation were sloppy.

Getting 'Hands On' With Java

You are most likely eager to get started with writing and compiling Java programs. But, we're purposely not going to get into the details of downloading and installing Java, or the mechanics of compiling programs, or any of that just yet.

❑ Part 1 of the book focuses on object concepts – in other words, the 'what' of objects; we don't want you to be distracted from learning these basic concepts by the bits and bytes of getting your Java environment up and running.

❑ Part 2 of the book focuses on object modeling – that is, the 'how' of designing an application to make the best use of objects. We don't want you to be trying to program without an appropriate OO 'blueprint' to work from.

❑ Part 3 takes the 'how' another step further, by showing you how to program an object-oriented application.

If you can remain patient, and resist the temptation to dive into Java coding until we get to Part 3, we promise that you will have ample opportunity to get your hands dirty with Java code at the appropriate stage in your learning process.

Summary

We haven't sung all of Java's praises in this chapter; there are other advanced Java language features, beyond the scope of this book to address, which give Java added 'punch'. But, the advantages that we have discussed – namely:

- ❑ Java's platform independence.

- ❑ Its 'one stop shopping' approach to providing comprehensive APIs.

- ❑ Its strong object orientation.

- ❑ The openness of the Java language standard, and the extensive vendor support that has ensued.

- ❑ The low cost to get started.

are all very compelling.

In addition, we've been introduced to some basic Java syntax:

- ❑ The anatomy of a simple Java program, consisting of a class 'wrapper' around a main method.

- ❑ Several forms that Java comments can take.

- ❑ Some of the data types built into the Java language – `byte`, `short`, `int`, `long`, `float`, `double`, `char`, `boolean`, and `String`.

- ❑ The nature of Java expressions, and how these are evaluated.

- ❑ Automatic type conversion and explicit casting.

- ❑ The block structured nature of the Java language, and how variables are scoped in such a language.

- ❑ How to print messages to the command-line window, a useful technique for testing an application.

- ❑ Various statements for controlling the execution flow of a Java program: `if` – `then` – `else`, `for`, and `while` statements; and, the use of `break` and `continue` statements to alter their behavior.

We'll expand your knowledge of the object-oriented aspects of Java in Chapter 13 – things you'll need to know in building the SRS – but we need to explain a number of object concepts first. So, on to Chapter 2!

Exercises

1. Research Java on Sun's website, http://www.java.sun.com, and cite any of the advantages of Java not mentioned in this chapter.

2. Do some 'web surfing' to see how various vendors have embraced the Java language, for example: IBM; Oracle; Sybase.

3. Research the differences between an applet and an application.

4. Compare what you've learned about Java so far to another programming language with which you are already familiar. What is similar about the two languages? What is different?

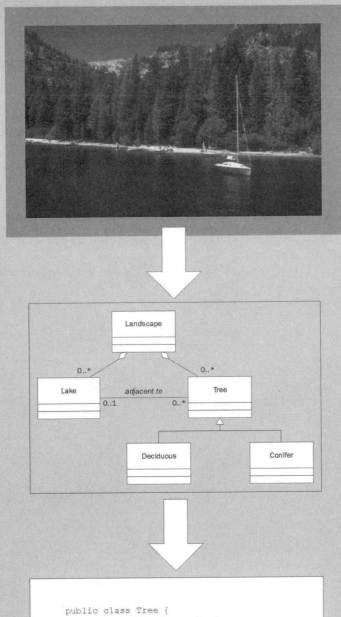

```
public class Tree {
    protected Landscape landscape;
    protected Lake nextTo;

    public void setNextTo(Lake l) {
        nextTo = l;
    }
    public Lake getNextTo() {
        return nextTo;
    }

    public abstract Color getLeafColor();
}
```

Abstraction and Modeling

As human beings, we are flooded with information every day of our lives. Even if we could temporarily turn off all of the sources of 'e-information' that are constantly bombarding us – emails, voicemails, news broadcasts, and the like – our five senses alone collect millions of bits of information per day just from our surroundings. Yet, we manage to make sense out of all of this information, typically without getting overwhelmed. Our brains naturally simplify the details of all that we observe so that these details are manageable through a process known as **abstraction**.

In this chapter, you will learn:

❑   How abstraction serves to simplify our view of the world.

❑   How we organize our knowledge hierarchically to minimize the amount of information that we have to mentally 'juggle' at any given time.

❑   The relevance of abstraction to software development.

❑   The inherent challenges that we face as software developers when attempting to model a real-word situation in software.

Simplification Through Abstraction

Take a moment to look around the room in which you are reading this book. At first, you may think that there really aren't that many things to observe: some furniture, light fixtures, perhaps some plants, artwork, even some other people, and/or pets. Maybe there is a window to gaze out of, which opens up the outside world to observation. Now, look again: for each thing that you see, there are a myriad of details to observe: its size, its color; its intended purpose; the components from which it is assembled (the legs on a table; the lightbulbs in a lamp), etc. In addition, each one of these components in turn has details associated with it: the type of material used to make the legs of the table (wood or metal); the wattage of the lightbulbs; etc. Now, factor in your other senses: the sound of someone snoring (hopefully not while reading this book!), the smell of popcorn coming from the microwave oven down the hall, and so forth. Finally, think about all of the unseen details of these objects – who they were manufactured by, or what their chemical, molecular, or genetic composition is. It is clear that the amount of information to be processed by our brains is truly overwhelming! For the vast majority of people, this does not pose a problem, however, because we are innately skilled at **abstraction**: a process that involves recognizing and focusing on the important characteristics of a situation or object, and filtering out or ignoring all of the unessential details.

One familiar example of an abstraction is a road map. As an abstraction, a road map represents those features of a given geographic area relevant to someone trying to navigate with the map, perhaps by car: major roads and places of interest, obstacles such as major bodies of water, etc. Of necessity, a road map cannot include every building, tree, street sign, billboard, traffic light, fast food restaurant, etc. that physically exists in the real word. If it did, then it would be so cluttered as to be virtually unusable; none of the important features would stand out.

Compare a road map with a topographical map, a climatological map, and a population density map of the same region: each abstracts out different features of the real world – namely, those relevant to the intended user of the map in question.

As another example, consider a landscape. An artist may look at the landscape from the perspective of colors, textures, and shapes as a prospective subject for a painting. A homebuilder may look at the same landscape from the perspective of where the best building site may be on the property, assessing how many trees will need to be cleared to make way for a construction project. An ecologist may closely study the individual species of trees and other plant/animal life for their biodiversity, with an eye toward preserving and protecting them, a child may simply be looking at all of the trees in search of the best site for a treehouse! Some elements are common to all of these four observers' abstractions of the landscape – the types, sizes, and locations of trees, for example – while others are not relevant to all of the abstractions.

Generalization Through Abstraction

If we eliminate enough detail from an abstraction, it becomes generic enough to apply to a wide range of specific situations or instances. Such generic abstractions can often be quite useful. For example, a diagram of a generic cell in the human body might include only a few features of the structures that are found in an actual cell:

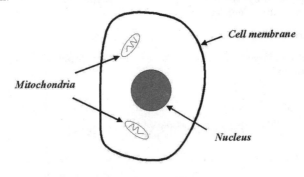

A "Generic" Cell

This overly simplified diagram doesn't look like a real nerve cell, or a real muscle cell, or a real blood cell; and yet, it can still be used in an educational setting to describe certain aspects of the structure and function of all of these cell types – namely, those features that the various cell types have in common.

The simpler an abstraction – that is, the fewer features it presents – the more general it is, and the more versatile it is in describing a variety of real-world situations. The more complex an abstraction, the more restrictive it is, and thus the fewer situations it is useful in describing.

Organizing Abstractions Into Classification Hierarchies

Even though our brains are adept at abstracting concepts such as road maps and landscapes, that still leaves us with hundreds of thousands, if not millions, of separate abstractions to deal with over our lifetimes. To cope with this aspect of complexity, human beings systematically arrange information into categories according to established criteria; this process is known as **classification**.

For example, science categorizes all natural objects as belonging to either the animal, plant, or mineral kingdom. In order for a natural object to be classified as an animal, it must satisfy the following rules:

❑ It must be a living being.

❑ It must be capable of spontaneous movement.

❑ It must be capable of rapid motor response to stimulation.

The rules for what constitute a plant, on the other hand, are different:

❑ It must be a living being (same as for an animal).

❑ It must lack an obvious nervous system.

❑ It must possess cellulose cell walls.

Given clear-cut rules such as these, placing an object into the appropriate category, or **class**, is rather straightforward. We can then 'drill down', specifying additional rules which differentiate various types of animal, for example, until we've built up a hierarchy of increasingly more complex abstractions from top to bottom. A simple example of an **abstraction hierarchy** is shown below.

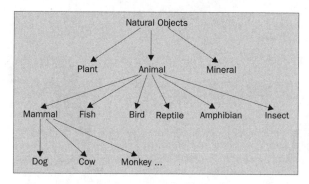

When thinking about an abstraction hierarchy such as the one shown above, we mentally step up and down the hierarchy, automatically zeroing in on only the single layer or subset of the hierarchy (known as a **subtree**) that is important to us at a given point in time. For example, we may only be concerned with mammals, and so can focus on the mammalian subtree:

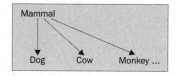

temporarily ignoring the rest of the hierarchy. By doing so, we automatically reduce the number of concepts that we mentally need to 'juggle' at any one time to a manageable subset of the overall abstraction hierarchy; in the simplistic example above, we are now dealing with only four concepts rather than the original 13. No matter how complex an abstraction hierarchy grows to be, it needn't overwhelm us if it is properly organized.

Coming up with precisely which rules are necessary to properly classify an object within an abstraction hierarchy is not always easy. Take, for example, the rules we might define for what constitutes a bird: namely, something which:

- ❑ Has feathers

- ❑ Has wings

- ❑ Lays eggs

- ❑ Is capable of flying

Given these rules, neither an ostrich nor a penguin could be classified as a bird, because neither can fly.

If we attempt to make the rule set less restrictive by eliminating the 'flight' rule, we are left with:

- ❑ Has feathers

- ❑ Has wings

- ❑ Lays eggs

According to this rule set, we now may properly classify both the ostrich and the penguin as birds.

This rule set is still unnecessarily complicated, because as it turns out, the 'lays eggs' rule is redundant: whether we keep it or eliminate it, it doesn't change our decision of what constitutes a bird versus a non-bird. Therefore, we simplify the rule set once again:

- ❑   Has feathers
- ❑   Has wings

Feeling particularly daring (!), we try to take our simplification process one step further, by eliminating yet another rule, defining a bird as something which:

- ❑   Has wings

We've gone too far this time: the abstraction of a bird is now so general that we'd include airplanes, insects, and all sorts of other non-birds in the mix!

The process of rule definition for purposes of categorization involves 'dialing in' just the right set of rules – not too general, not too restrictive, and containing no redundancies – to define the correct membership in a particular class.

Abstraction as the Basis for Software Development

When pinning down the requirements for an information systems development project, we typically start by gathering details about the real world situation on which the system is to be based. These details are usually a combination of:

❑ Those that are explicitly offered to us as we interview the intended users of the system.

❑ Those that we otherwise observe.

We must make a judgment call as to which of these details are relevant to the system's ultimate purpose. This is essential, as we cannot automate them all! To include too much detail is to overly complicate the resultant system, making it that much more difficult to design, program, test, debug, document, maintain, and extend in the future.

As with all abstractions, all of our decisions of inclusion versus elimination when building a software system must be made within the context of the overall purpose and **domain**, or subject matter focus, of the future system. When representing a person in a software system, for example, is their eye color important? How about their genetic profile? Salary? Hobbies? The answer is, any of these features of a person may be relevant or irrelevant, depending on whether the system to be developed is a:

❑ Payroll system

❑ Marketing demographics system

❑ Optometrist's patient database

❑ FBI 'most wanted criminals' tracking system

❑ Public library

Once we've determined the essential aspects of a situation – something that we'll learn how to do in Part 2 of this book – we can prepare a **model** of that situation. **Modeling** is the process by which we develop a pattern for something to be made. A blueprint for a custom home, a schematic diagram of a printed circuit, and a cookie cutter are all examples of such patterns. As we will learn in Parts 2 and 3, an **object model** of a software system is such a pattern. Modeling and abstraction go hand in hand, because a model is essentially a physical or graphical portrayal of an abstraction; before we can model something effectively, we must have determined the essential details of the subject to be modeled.

Reuse of Abstractions

When learning about something new, we automatically search our 'mental archive' for other abstractions/models that we've previously built and mastered, to look for similarities that we can build upon. When learning to ride a two-wheeled bicycle for the first time, for example, you may have drawn upon lessons that you learned about riding a tricycle as a child. Both have handlebars that are used to steer; both have pedals that are used to propel the bike forward. Although the abstractions didn't match perfectly – a two-wheeled bicycle introduced the new challenge of having to balance oneself – there was enough of a similarity to allow you to draw upon the steering and pedaling expertise you already had mastered, and to focus on learning the new skill of how to balance on two wheels.

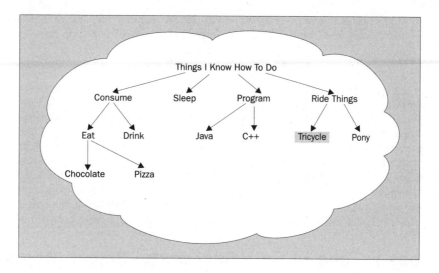

This technique of comparing features to find an abstraction that is similar enough to be reused successfully is known as **pattern matching and reuse**. As we will learn in Chapter 12, pattern reuse is an important technique for object oriented software development, as well, because it spares us from having to reinvent the wheel with each new project. If we can reuse an abstraction or model from a previous project, we can focus on those aspects of the new project that differ from the old, gaining a tremendous amount of productivity in the process.

Inherent Challenges

Despite the fact that abstraction is such a natural process for human beings, developing an appropriate model for a software system is perhaps the most difficult aspect of software engineering, because:

❑   There are an unlimited number of possibilities. Abstraction is to a certain extent in the eye of the beholder: several different observers working independently are almost guaranteed to arrive at different models. Whose is the best? Passionate arguments have ensued!

❑   To further complicate matters, there is virtually never only one 'best' or 'correct' model, only better or worse models relative to the problem to be solved. The same situation can be modeled in a variety of different, equally valid ways. As you'll see when we get into actually doing some modeling in Part 2 of this book, we'll look at a number of valid alternative abstractions for our Student Registration System (SRS) case study that was presented at the end of the Introduction.

❑   Note, however, that there IS such a thing as an incorrect model: namely, one that misrepresents the real-world situation (for example, modeling a person as having two different blood types).

❑   There is no 'acid test' to determine if a model has adequately captured all of a user's requirements. The ultimate evidence of whether or not an abstraction was appropriate is in how successful the resultant software system turns out to be. We don't want to wait until the end of a project before finding out that we've gone astray. Because of this, it is critical that we learn ways of communicating our model concisely and unambiguously to:

❑ The intended future users of our application, so that they may sanity check our understanding of the problem to be solved before we embark upon software development,

❑ Our fellow software engineers, so that team members share a common 'vision' for what we are to build collaboratively.

Despite all of these challenges, it is critical to get the up-front abstraction 'right' before beginning to build a system. Fixing mistakes in the abstraction once a system is modeled, designed, coded, and documented, and undergoing acceptance testing is much more costly (by orders of magnitude) than correcting the abstraction when it is still a gleam in the project team's eye. This is not to imply that an abstraction should be rigid: quite the contrary! The art and science of object modeling, when properly applied, yields a model that is flexible enough to withstand a wide variety of functional changes. In addition, the special properties of objects further lend themselves to flexible software solutions, as we'll learn throughout the rest of the book. However, all things being equal, we'd like to harness this flexibility to expand a system's capabilities over time, rather than repairing mistakes.

What Does It Take to Be a Successful Object Modeler?

Coming up with an appropriate abstraction as the basis for a software system model requires:

❑ **Insight into the problem domain**: ideally, you'll be able to draw upon your own real-world experience, such as your former or current experience as a student, which will come in handy when determining the requirements for the SRS.

❑ **Creativity**: to enable us to think 'outside the box', in case the future users that we are interviewing have been immersed in the problem area for so long, that they fail to see innovations that might be made.

❑ **Good listening skills**: as future users of the system describe how they do their jobs currently, or how they envision doing their jobs in the future, with the aid of the system that we're about to develop.

❑ **Good observational skills**: actions often speak louder than words; just by observing users going about their daily business, we may pick up an essential detail that they have neglected to mention because they do it so routinely that it has become a habit.

But all this is not enough, we also need:

❑ An organized **process** for determining what the abstraction should be. If we follow a proven checklist of steps for producing a model, then we greatly reduce the probability that we'll omit some important feature or neglect a critical requirement.

❑ A way to **communicate** the resultant model concisely and unambiguously to our fellow software developers, and to the intended users of our application. While it is certainly possible to describe an abstraction in narrative text, a picture is worth 1000 words, and so the language with which we communicate a model is often a **graphical notation**. Throughout this book, we'll focus on the Unified Modeling Language (UML – see following figure) notation as our model communication language (you'll learn the basics of UML in Chapters 10 and 11). Think of a graphical model as a 'blueprint' of the software application to be built.

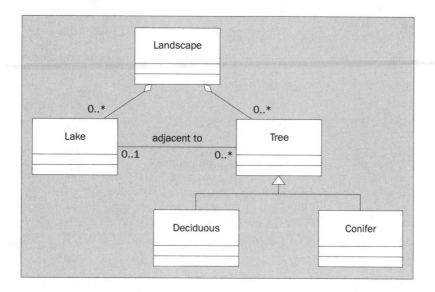

- ❏ Ideally, we'll also have a **software tool** to help us automate the process of producing such a 'blueprint'.

Part 2 of this book covers these three aspects of modeling – process, notation, and tool – in detail; for starters, however, let's make sure that we understand the basics of objects, which is the focus of the remainder of Part 1.

Summary

In this chapter, we've learned that:

- ❏ Abstraction is a fundamental technique that people use to perceive the world, and is a necessary first step of all software development.

- ❏ We naturally organize information into classification hierarchies based upon rules that we carefully structure, so that they are neither too general nor too restrictive.

- ❏ We often reuse abstractions when attempting to model a new concept.

- ❏ Producing an abstraction of a system to be built, known as a model, is in some senses second nature to us, and yet paradoxically is one of the hardest things that software developers have to do in the lifecycle of an information systems project. Yet, it is also one of the most important.

Exercises

1. Sketch a class hierarchy that relates all of the following classes in a reasonable manner:

> Apple
> Banana
> Beef
> Beverage
> Cheese
> Consumable
> Dairy Product
> Food
> Fruit
> Green Bean
> Meat
> Milk
> Pork
> Spinach
> Vegetable

Note any challenges you faced in doing so.

2. What aspects of a television set would be important to abstract from the perspective of:

- ❏ A consumer wishing to buy one?

- ❏ An engineer responsible for designing one?

- ❏ A retailer who sells them?

- ❏ The manufacturer?

3. Select a problem area that you would like to model from an object-oriented perspective. Ideally, this will be a problem that you are actually going to be working on at your place of employment, or that you have a keen interest in. Assume that you are going to write a program to automate some aspect of this problem area; write a one page overview of the requirements for this program, patterned after the Student Registration System case study.

Make certain that your first paragraph summarizes the intent of the system, as the first paragraph in the SRS case study does. Also, emphasize the **functional requirements** – that is, those which a non technical end user might state as to how the system should behave – and avoid stating **technical requirements** – for example, "This system must run on a Windows NT platform, and must use the TCP/IP protocol to ...".

4. Read the case study for a Conference Room Reservation System (CRRS) in Appendix B. In your opinion, how effective is this case study as an abstraction: are there details that you think could have been omitted, and/or missing details that you think would have been important to include? If you had an opportunity to interview the intended users of the CRRS, what additional questions might you ask them to better refine this abstraction?

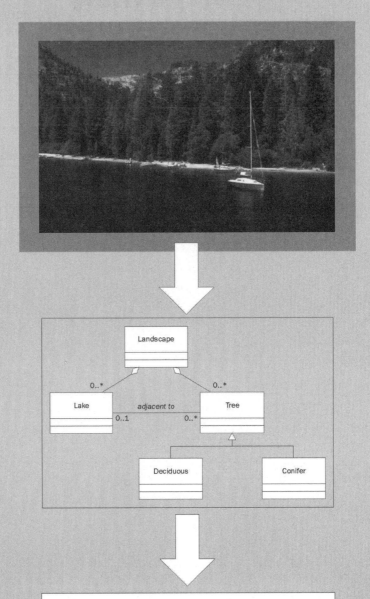

```
public class Tree {
    protected Landscape landscape;
    protected Lake nextTo;

    public void setNextTo(Lake l) {
        nextTo = l;
    }
    public Lake getNextTo() {
        return nextTo;
    }

    public abstract Color getLeafColor();
}
```

Objects and Classes

Objects are the fundamental building blocks of an object-oriented (OO) system. Just as abstraction involves producing a model of the real world as we discussed in Chapter 2, objects are 'mini abstractions' of various real-world components.

In this chapter, you will learn:

- ❑ What makes up a software object.
- ❑ How we use classes to specify an object's data and behavior.
- ❑ How we create objects based on a class definition.
- ❑ How objects keep track of one another.

What Is an Object?

Before we talk about software objects, let's talk about real-world objects in general. According to Merriam-Webster's dictionary, an object is:

> *"(1) Something material that may be perceived by the senses; (2) something mental or physical toward which thought, feeling, or action is directed."*

The first part of this definition refers to objects as we typically think of them: as physical 'things' that we can see and touch, and which occupy space. Because we intend to use the Student Registration System (SRS) case study as the basis for learning about objects throughout this book, let's think of some examples of **physical objects** that make sense in the general context of an academic setting, namely:

- ❑ The **students** who attend classes
- ❑ The **professors** who teach them
- ❑ The **classrooms** in which class meetings take place
- ❑ The **furniture** in these classrooms
- ❑ The **buildings** in which the classrooms are located
- ❑ The **textbooks** students use

and on and on. Of course, while all of these objects are commonly found on a typical college campus, not all of them are relevant to registering students for courses, nor are they all necessarily called out by the SRS case study; but, we won't worry about that for the time being. In Part 2 of this book, we'll learn a technique for using a requirements specification as the basis for identifying which objects are relevant to a particular abstraction.

Now, let's focus on the second half of the definition, particularly on the phrase *'something mental ...toward which thought, feeling, or action is directed'*. There are a great many **conceptual objects** that play important roles in an academic setting; some of these are:

❑   The **courses** that students attend

❑   The **departments** that faculty works for

❑   The **degrees** that students receive

and, of course, many others. Even though we can't see, hear, touch, taste, or smell them, conceptual objects are every bit as important as physical objects are in describing an abstraction.

Let's now get a bit more formal, and define a **software object**:

> *"A (software)* **object** *is a software construct that bundles together* **data** *(***state***) and* **functions** *(***behavior***) which, taken together, represent an abstraction of a 'real-world' (physical or conceptual) object."*

Let's explore the two sides of objects – their **state** and **behavior** – separately, in more depth.

Data/State/Attributes

If we wish to record information about a student, what data might we require? Some examples might be:

❑   The student's name

❑   His or her student ID and/or social security number

❑   The student's birthdate

❑   His or her address

❑   The student's designated major field of study, if the student has declared one yet

❑   His or her cumulative grade point average (GPA)

❑   Who the student's faculty advisor is

❑   A list of the courses that the student is currently enrolled in this semester (a.k.a. the student's current course load)

❑   A history of all of the courses that the student has taken to date, the semester/year in which each was taken, and the grade that was earned for each: in other words, the student's transcript and so on. Now, how about for a course? Perhaps we'd wish to record:

- ❑ The course number (for example, 'ART 101')

- ❑ The course name (for example, 'Introductory Basketweaving')

- ❑ A list of all of the courses which must have been successfully completed by a student prior to allowing that student to register for *this* course (i.e. the course's prerequisites)

- ❑ The number of credit hours that the course is worth

- ❑ A list of the professors who have been approved to teach this course

In object nomenclature, the data elements used to describe an object are referred to as the object's **attributes**.

An object's attribute values, when taken collectively, are said to define the **state**, or condition, of the object. For example, if we wanted to determine whether or not a student is 'eligible to graduate' (a state), we might look at a combination of:

- ❑ The student's transcript (an attribute), and

- ❑ The list of courses they are currently enrolled in (a second attribute)

to see if the student indeed is expected to have satisfied the course requirements for their chosen major field of study (a third attribute) by the end of the current academic year.

A given attribute may be simple – for example, 'GPA', which can be represented as a simple floating point number, – or complex – for example, 'transcript', which represents a rather extensive collection of information with no simple representation.

Behavior/Operations/Methods

Now, let's revisit the same two types of object – a student and a course – and talk about these objects' respective behaviors. A student's behaviors (relevant to academic matters, that is!) might include:

- ❑ Enrolling in a course

- ❑ Dropping a course

- ❑ Choosing a major field of study

- ❑ Selecting a faculty advisor

- ❑ Telling you his or her GPA when asked

- ❑ Telling you whether or not he or she has taken a particular course, and if so, when the course was taken, which professor taught it, and what grade the student received

It is a bit harder to think of an inanimate, conceptual object like a course as having behaviors, but if we were to imagine a course to be a living thing, then we can imagine that a course's behaviors might include:

- ❑ Permitting a student to register

- ❑ Determining whether or not a given student is already registered

- ❑ Telling you how many students have registered so far, or conversely, how many seats remain before the course is full

- ❑ Telling you what its prerequisite courses are

- ❑ Telling you how many credit hours it is worth

- ❑ Telling you which professor is assigned to teach the course this semester

and so on.

When we talk about software objects specifically, we define an object's behaviors, also known as its **operations,** as both the things that an object does to **access** its data (attributes), and the things that an object does to **modify/maintain** its data (attributes).

If we take a moment to reflect back on the behaviors we expect of a student as listed above, we see that each operation involves one or more of the student's attributes. For example:

- ❑ Telling you his or her GPA involves accessing the value of the student's 'GPA' attribute

- ❑ Choosing a major field of study updates the value of the student's 'major' attribute

- ❑ Enrolling in a course updates the value of the student's 'course load' attribute

Since we recently learned that the collective set of attribute values for an object defines its state, we now can see that operations are capable of **changing an object's state**.

Let's say that we define the state of a student who has not yet selected a major field of study as an 'undeclared' student. Asking a student object representing an 'undeclared' student to perform its 'choosing a major field of study' method, will cause that object to update the value of its 'major field of study' attribute to reflect the newly selected major field. This then changes the student's state from 'undeclared' to 'declared'.

Yet another way to think of an object's operations are as **services** that can be requested of the object. For example, one service that we might call upon a course object to perform, is to provide us with a list of all of the students who are currently registered for the course (a.k.a. a student roster).

When we actually get around to programming an object in a language like Java, we refer to the programming language representation of an operation as a **method**, whereas, strictly speaking, the term 'operation' is typically used to refer to a behavior conceptually. However, these two terms are often used interchangeably, and we'll do so throughout the rest of this book.

Classes

A **class** is an abstraction describing the common features of all members in a group of similar objects. For example, a class called 'Student' could be used to describe all student objects recognized by the Student Registration System.

A class defines:

- ❏ The data structure (names and types of attributes) needed to define an object belonging to that class.

- ❏ The operations (methods) to be performed by such objects: specifically, what these operations are, how an object belonging to that class is formally called upon to perform them, and what 'behind the scenes' things an object has to do to actually carry them out.

For example, the Student class might be defined to have the following nine attributes:

Attribute Name	(Java) Data Type
name	String
studentId	String
birthdate	Date
address	String
major	String
gpa	Float
advisor	???
courseLoad	???
transcript	???

which means that each and every Student object must have these same nine attributes. Note that many of the attributes can be represented by data types built into a programming language (e.g. String, Float, and Date) but that a few – advisor, courseLoad, and transcript – are too complex for a built-in data type to handle; we'll learn how to tackle such attributes a bit later on.

In terms of operations, the Student class might define five methods as follows:

- ❏ registerForCourse
- ❏ dropCourse
- ❏ chooseMajor
- ❏ changeAdvisor
- ❏ printTranscript

Note that an object can only do those things for which methods have been defined by the object's class. In that respect, an object is like an appliance: it can do whatever it was designed to do (a VCR provides buttons to play, pause, stop, rewind, and record movies), and nothing more (you cannot ask a VCR to toast a bagel – at least not with much chance of success!). So, an important aspect of successfully designing an object is making sure to anticipate all of the behaviors it will need in order to carry out its 'mission' within the system. We'll learn how to determine what an object's mission, data structure, and behaviors should be, based on the requirements for a system, in Part 2 of the book.

The term **feature** is used to refer interchangeably to either an attribute or a method of a class. Features are the building blocks of a class: virtually everything found within a class definition is either an attribute or a method of the class.

In the Java language, several other types of things wind up getting included within the boundaries of a class definition, but we won't worry about these until we get to Part 3 of the book. Conceptually, it is perfectly appropriate to think of an object as consisting only of attributes and methods at this point in time.

A Note Regarding Naming Conventions

It is recommended practice to name classes starting with an upper case letter, but to use mixed case for the name overall: `Student`, `Course`, `Professor`, and so on. When the name of a class would ideally be stated as a multi-word phrase, such as 'course catalog', start each word with a capital letter, and concatenate the words without using spaces, dashes, or underscores to separate them: for example, `CourseCatalog`.

Method and attribute names use the same mixed-case concatenation convention, except that they start with a lower case letter. Example method names could be `getName` and `registerForCourse`, with `name`, `studentId`, or `courseLoad` as attribute names.

Instantiation

A class definition may be thought of as a template for creating software objects – a 'cookie cutter' used to:

❑ Stamp out a prescribed data structure in memory to house the attributes of a new object.

❑ Associate a certain set of behaviors with that object.

The term **instantiation** is used to refer to the process by which an object is created/constructed based upon a class definition. From a single class definition – for example, `Student` – we create many objects/instances of the class, in the same way that we use a single cookie cutter to make many cookies. Another way to refer to an object, then, is as an **instance** of a particular class. We'll talk about the physical process of **instantiating** objects as it occurs in Java in a bit more detail later in this chapter.

Classes may be differentiated from objects, then, as follows:

❑ A **class** defines the attributes – names and data types – that all objects belonging to the class must possess, and the methods that all objects belonging to the class must be able to perform, and can be thought of as an empty template.

❑ An **object**, on the other hand, is a *filled-in* template to which attribute *values* have been provided.

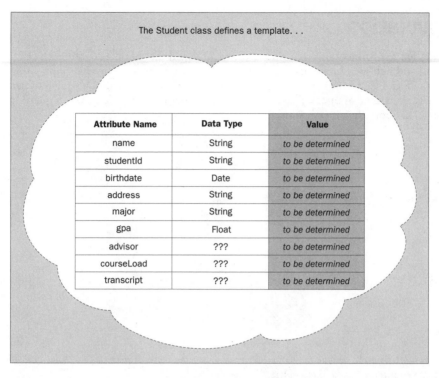

The Student class defines a template. . .

Attribute Name	Data Type	Value
name	String	*to be determined*
studentId	String	*to be determined*
birthdate	Date	*to be determined*
address	String	*to be determined*
major	String	*to be determined*
gpa	Float	*to be determined*
advisor	???	*to be determined*
courseLoad	???	*to be determined*
transcript	???	*to be determined*

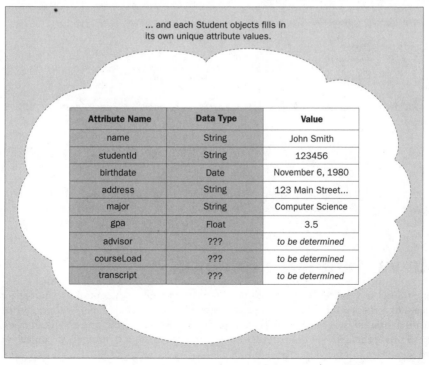

... and each Student objects fills in
its own unique attribute values.

Attribute Name	Data Type	Value
name	String	John Smith
studentId	String	123456
birthdate	Date	November 6, 1980
address	String	123 Main Street...
major	String	Computer Science
gpa	Float	3.5
advisor	???	*to be determined*
courseLoad	???	*to be determined*
transcript	???	*to be determined*

Encapsulation

Encapsulation is a formal term referring to the mechanism that bundles together the state information (attributes) and behavior (methods) of an object into a single logical unit. Everything that we need to know about a given student is, in theory, contained within the 'walls' of the student object, either directly as an attribute of that object or indirectly as a method that can answer a question or make a determination about the object's state.

Encapsulation is not unique to OO languages, but in some senses is perfected by them. For those of you familiar with C, you know that:

A C struct(ure) encapsulates data:

```
struct employee {
    char name[30];
    int age;
}
```

and a C function encapsulates logic – data is passed in, operated on, and an answer is optionally returned:

```
float average(float x, float y) {
    return (x + y)/2.0;
}
```

But only with OO programming languages is the notion of encapsulating data and behavior in a single construct called a class, to represent an abstraction of a real-world entity, truly embraced.

Objects vs. Database Records

As we mentioned in Chapter 2, when people are learning a new concept, they automatically try to map that concept to a mental model with which they are already familiar. Folks who are knowledgeable about relational databases (Sybase, Oracle, SQL Server, Access, DB2, and the like), therefore, have a tendency to relate the concept of an object to that of a record in a database. (If you are not familiar with relational databases, please skip this section.)

The object-record analogy holds up to a point:

- ❑ Each class of object is analogous to a table in a relational database
- ❑ Each record, or row, in the table is analogous to a different object instance
- ❑ Each column in a table corresponds to a different attribute of the associated class

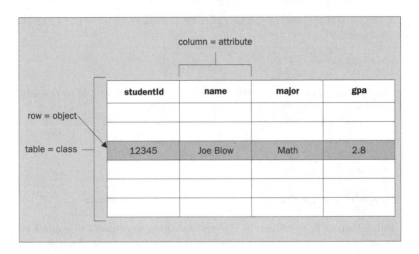

This correlation between objects and records has several flaws, however:

- ❑ Objects exhibit behavior, whereas records typically do not.

    One can argue that the behavior of an object can be modeled by relational database triggers or stored procedures, but this is really the database management system operating on the data versus an individual record taking action on its own behalf.

- ❑ Objects have unique identities, which is the characteristic that distinguishes one object from all others, *even if all of their attribute values are the same*. For example, if we happened to have two professors with the *same* name, and the *same* address, and the *same* birthdate, and so on, then the two objects representing these two professors could still exist as separate instances of the Professor class. In a relational database, on the other hand, identical records cannot, strictly speaking, coexist in the same table, so we'd be forced to add an attribute/column known as a **primary key** to the table – perhaps inventing a unique professor ID number – so that we could differentiate the two professors. In an object-oriented system, objects need not have a unique key - objects *inherently* have identity.

Classes as Abstract Data Types

In a non-OO programming language such as C, the statement

```
int x;
```

is a **declaration** that variable 'x' is an integer, one of several simple, **built-in data types** defined to be part of the C (C++, Java) language.

What does this really mean? It means that:

❑ 'x' is a symbolic name that represents an integer value.

❑ The 'thing' that we have named 'x' understands how to respond to a number of different operations such as addition (+), subtraction (-), multiplication (*), division (/), logical comparisons (>, <, =), and so on that have been defined for the int data type.

❑ Whenever we want to operate on this particular integer value in our program, we refer to 'x' instead:

```
if (x > 17) x = x + 5;
```

In an object-oriented language like Java, we can define a class such as Student, and then declare a variable as follows:

```
Student y;
```

What does this mean? It means that:

❑ 'y' is a symbolic name that refers to a Student object/instance.

❑ The 'thing' that we have named 'y' understands how to respond to a number of different service requests – how to register for a course, drop a course, and so on – that have been defined by the Student class.

❑ Whenever we want to operate on this particular object, we refer to 'y' instead:

```
if (y hasn't chosen an advisor yet ) System.out.println("Oh oh ...");
```

Note the parallels between x as an int in the previous example and y as a Student above. Just as int is referred to as a simple, or built-in, data type in a language like C or Java, we can refer to a user-defined class such as Student as an **abstract data type (ADT)**: that is, a **user-defined data type** that specifies structure as well as behavior. It is called 'abstract' because a class is an abstraction of a real-word object that reflects only its relevant details. And, because 'y' in the above example is a variable that **refers to** an instance (object) of the class Student, 'y' may be alternatively referred to as either a **reference variable** or sometimes just as a **reference** – a reference to a Student object, to be precise.

Names for reference variables follow the same convention as method and attribute names: they start with a lower case letter and use mixed case to separate 'words' within the name. Some sample reference variable declarations are as follows:

```
Student x;
Student aStudent;
Course prerequisiteOfThisCourse;
Professor myAdvisor;
```

Instantiating Objects: A Closer Look

Different OO languages differ in terms of when an object is actually conceived. In Java, when we declare a variable to be of a user-defined type, like:

```
Student y;
```

we haven't actually created an object in memory yet. Reference variable 'y' merely has the **potential** to be a reference to a Student object, but, until we initialize y by assigning it a specific object to refer to, y is said to have the value null, which as we learned in Chapter 1 is a reserved word in the Java language. We have to take the distinct step of using a special Java operator, the new operator, to actually carve out a brand new object in memory, as follows:

```
y = new Student();
```

(Don't worry about the parentheses at the end of this statement; we'll talk about their significance in Chapter 4.)

Think of the newly created object as a helium balloon, and a reference variable as the string that allows us to hold onto and access (reference) the object whenever we'd like.

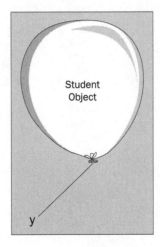

Because a reference variable is said to 'hold onto' an object, we often use the informal term **handle** as a synonym to the term 'reference'.

We could also create a new object without immediately assigning it to a reference variable, as in the following line of code:

```
new Student();
```

but such an object would be like a helium balloon whose string had been let go: it would indeed exist, but we'd never be able to access this object in our program. It would in essence, 'float away' from us in memory.

Note that we can combine the two steps – declaring a reference variable and actually instantiating an object for that variable to refer to – into a single line of code:

```
Student y = new Student();
```

Another way to initialize a reference variable is to hand it a **preexisting** object: that is, an object ('helium balloon') whose handle ('string') is already being held by some **other** reference variable. Let's look at an example:

```
// We instantiate our first Student object.
Student x = new Student();

// We declare a second reference, but do not instantiate a second object.
Student y;

// We pass y a 'handle' on the same object that x is holding
// (x continues to hold onto it, too).  We now, in essence,
// have two 'strings' tied to the same 'balloon'.
y = x;
```

The conceptual outcome of the preceding code is illustrated below: two 'strings' tied to the same 'balloon' – that is, two reference variables referencing the same object.

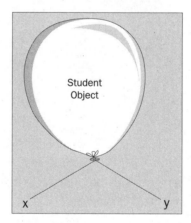

We therefore see that the same object can have many reference variables holding onto it; but, as it turns out, any one reference variable can only hold onto *one* object at a time. To grab onto a new object handle means that a reference variable must let go of the old object handle that it was previously holding onto, if any.

If there comes a time when *all* references holding onto a particular object have let go of the object's handle, then as we discussed earlier the object is no longer accessible to the program, like a helium balloon that has been let loose. Continuing with our previous example:

```
// We instantiate our first Student object.
Student x = new Student();

// We declare a second reference, but do not instantiate a second object.
Student y;

// We pass y a 'handle' on the same object that x is holding
// (x continues to hold onto it, too).  We now, in essence,
// have TWO 'strings' tied to the same 'balloon'.
y = x;
```

```
// We now declare a third reference and instantiate a second Student object.
Student z = new Student();
```

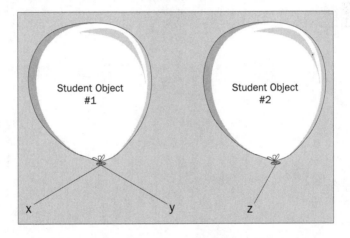

```
// y now lets go of the first Student object and grabs onto the second.
  y = z;
```

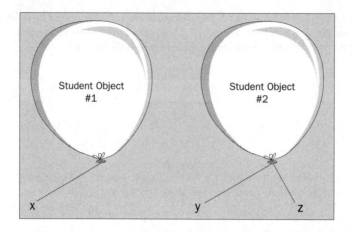

```
// Finally, x lets go of the first Student object, and grabs onto
// the second, as well; the first Student object is now lost to
// the program because we no longer have any reference variables
// maintaining a 'handle' on it!
x = z;
```

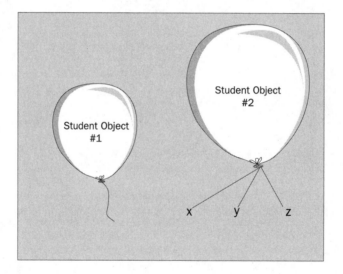

As it turns out, if all of an object's handles are lost, it might seem as though the memory that the object occupies is permanently 'wasted'. In a language like C++, this is indeed the case, and programmers have to take care to 'recycle' the memory of an object that is no longer needed before all of its handles are dropped. In Java, on the other hand, there is a utility called the garbage collector built into the JVM which automatically recycles 'lost' objects' memory for us. We'll revisit this topic in Chapter 13.

Objects as Attributes

When we first discussed the attributes and methods associated with the Student class, we stated that some of the attributes could be represented by built-in data types provided by the Java language, whereas the types of a few others (advisor, courseLoad, and transcript) were left undefined. Let's now put what we learned about abstract data types to good use. Rather than declaring the Student class's advisor attribute as simply a String representing the advisor's name, we'll declare it to be of an abstract data type – namely, type Professor, another user-defined class/type:

Attribute Name	Data Type
name	String
studentID	String
birthdate	Date
address	String
major	String
gpa	float
advisor	**Professor**
courseLoad	???
transcript	???

(We'll still leave the courseLoad and transcript attributes' data types undefined for the time being; we'll see how to handle these attributes a bit later.) By having declared the advisor attribute to be of type Professor, we've just enabled a Student object to maintain a handle on its actual Professor advisor object.

The Professor class, in turn, might be defined to have attributes as follows:

Attribute Name	Data Type
name	String
employeeID	String
birthdate	Date
address	String
worksFor	String (or Department)
studentAdvisee	**Student**
teachingAssignments	???

(We will leave the type of teachingAssignments open for the time being.) Again, by having declared the studentAdvisee attribute to be of type Student, we've just given a Professor object a way to hold onto its actual Student advisee object.

The methods of the `Professor` class might be as follows:

- ❏ `transferToDepartment`
- ❏ `adviseStudent`
- ❏ `agreeToTeachCourse`
- ❏ `assignGrades`

A few noteworthy points about the `Professor` class:

- ❏ It is likely that a professor will be advising several students simultaneously, so having an attribute like `studentAdvisee` that can only track a single `Student` object is not terribly useful. We'll discuss techniques for handling this in Chapter 6, when we talk about **collections**, which we'll also see as being useful for defining the `teachingAssignments` attribute of `Professor` and the `courseLoad` and `transcript` attributes of `Student`.

- ❏ The `worksFor` attribute represents the department to which a professor is assigned. We can choose to represent this as either a simple `String` representing the department name – for example, `'MATH'` – or as a reference to a `Department` object – specifically, the `Department` object representing the 'real-world' Math Department. As we'll see in Part 2 of this book, the decision of whether or not we need to invent an abstract data type to represent a particular real-world concept is not always clear-cut.

Composite Classes

Whenever we have a class, such as `Student` or `Professor`, in which one or more of the attributes are themselves references to other objects, we refer to the class as a **composite class**. The number of levels to which objects can be conceptually bundled inside one another is endless, and so composite classes enable us to model very sophisticated real world concepts. As it turns out, most 'interesting' classes are composite classes.

With composite class instances, it appears as though we are nesting objects one inside the other:

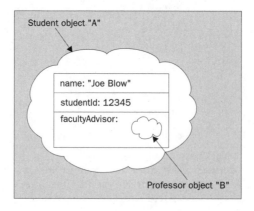

Object nesting does indeed sometimes make sense: namely, if an object 'A' doesn't have a life of its own, and only exists for the purpose of serving enclosing object 'B'.

❑ Think of your brain, for example, as an object that exists only within the context of your body (another object).

❑ As an example of object nesting relevant to the SRS, let's consider a grade book used to track student performance in a particular course. If we were to define a `GradeBook` class, and then create `GradeBook` objects as attributes – one per `Course` object – then it might be reasonable for each `GradeBook` object to exist wholly within its associated `Course` object. No other objects would need to communicate with the `GradeBook` directly; if a `Student` object wished to ask a `Course` object what grade the `Student` has earned, the `Course` object might internally consult its embedded `GradeBook` object, and simply hand a letter grade back to the `Student`.

However, as we saw in the sample `Student` and `Professor` classes above, we often encounter a situation where an object 'A' needs to refer to an object 'B', object 'B' needs to refer back to 'A', and both objects need to be able to respond to requests independently of each other. In such a case, we cannot physically embed one object wholly inside the other; this would lead to infinitely recursive nesting.

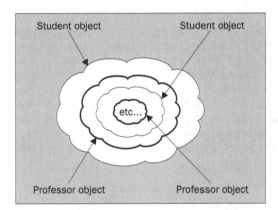

Handles come to the rescue! In reality, we are typically not storing whole objects as attributes inside of other objects, but rather **references** to objects. When an attribute of an object 'A' is defined in terms of an object reference 'B', the two objects exist separately in memory, and simply have a convenient way of finding one another whenever it is necessary for them to interact. Think of yourself as an object, and your cellular phone number as your handle. Other people – 'objects' – can reach you to speak with you whenever they need to, even though they don't know where you are physically located, using your phone number.

Memory allocation using handles might look something like this conceptually:

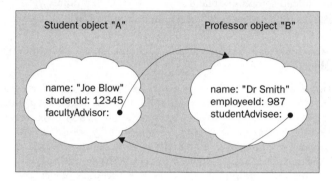

With this approach, each object is allocated in memory only once; the Student object knows how to find and communicate with its advisor (Professor) object whenever it needs to through its handle, and vice versa.

What do we gain by defining the Student's advisor attribute as a reference to a Professor object, instead of merely storing the name of the advisor as a String attribute of the Student object?

❑ For one thing, we can ask the Professor object its name whenever we need it by invoking its getName method. Why is this important? **To avoid data redundancy and the potential for loss of data integrity.** If the Professor object's name changes for some reason, the name will only be stored in one place: encapsulated as an attribute within the Professor object that 'owns' the name, which is precisely where it belongs. If we instead were to store the Professor's name both as a String attribute of the Professor object and as a String attribute of the Student object, we'd have to remember to update the name in two places any time the name changed (or three, or four, or however many places this Professor's name is referenced as an advisor of countless Students). If we were to forget to do so, then the name of the Professor would be 'out of synch' from one instance to another.

❑ Just as importantly, by maintaining a handle on the Professor object via the advisor attribute of Student, the Student object can also request other services of this Professor object via whatever methods are defined for the Professor class. A Student object may, for example, ask its advisor (Professor) object where the Professor's office is located, or what classes the Professor is teaching so that the Student can sign up for one of them.

❑ Another advantage of using object handles from an implementation standpoint is that they also reduce memory overhead. Storing a handle to an object only requires 32 or 64 bits of memory, depending on the programming language, instead of however many bytes of storage the referenced object as a whole occupies in memory. If we were to have to make a copy of an entire object every place we needed to refer to it in our application, we'd quickly exhaust available memory.

Three Distinguishing Features of an Object-Oriented Programming Language

In order to be considered truly object oriented, a programming language must provide support for three key mechanisms:

- ❏ **(Programmer creation of) Abstract Data Types (ADTs)**
- ❏ Inheritance
- ❏ Polymorphism

We've just learned about the first of these – ADTs – and will discuss the other two in chapters to follow.

Summary

In this chapter, we've learned that:

- ❏ An object is a software abstraction of a physical or conceptual real-world object.
- ❏ A class serves as a template for defining objects: specifically, a class defines:
  - ❏ What data the object will house, known as an object's attributes.
  - ❏ What behaviors or services an object will be able to perform, known as an object's operations or methods.
- ❏ An object may then be thought of as a filled-in template, where attribute values have been provided.
- ❏ Just as we can declare variables to be of simple built-in data types such as int, float, and char, we can also declare variables to be of an abstract data type, based on the classes that we define. Such variables are known as reference variables, or simply references.
- ❏ When we create a new object (a process known as instantiation), we store a handle on that object in a reference variable. We can then use that handle to communicate with the object.
- ❏ We can define attributes of a class 'A' to be references to objects belonging to another class 'B'. In doing so, we allow each object to encapsulate the information that rightfully belongs to that object, but enable objects to share information by contacting one another whenever necessary.

Exercises

1. From the perspective of an academic setting (and not necessarily the SRS case study), think about what the appropriate attributes and methods of the following classes might be:

❑   Classroom

❑   Department

❑   Degree

Which of the attributes of each of these classes might be declared as built-in Java data types, and which might be declared as abstract data types? Explain your rationale.

2. For the problem area whose requirements you defined for exercise no. 3 in Chapter 2, list the abstract data types/classes that you might need to model.

3. List the abstract data types/classes that you might need to model for the Conference Room Reservation System discussed in Appendix B.

4. Would 'Color' make a good abstract data type? Why or why not?

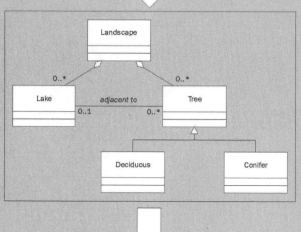

```java
public class Tree {
    protected Landscape landscape;
    protected Lake nextTo;

    public void setNextTo(Lake l) {
        nextTo = l;
    }
    public Lake getNextTo() {
        return nextTo;
    }

    public abstract Color getLeafColor();
}
```

Object Interactions

As we learned in Chapter 3, objects are the building blocks of an object oriented software system. In such a system, objects collaborate with one another to accomplish common system goals, similar to the ants in an anthill, or the employees of a corporation, or the cells in your body. Each object has a specific structure and 'mission'; these respective missions complement one another in accomplishing the mission of the system as a whole.

In this chapter, you will learn:

❑   How external events set the objects within an OO application in motion.

❑   How objects publicize their methods as services to one another.

❑   How they communicate to request one another's services.

❑   How objects maintain their data, and how they 'guard' their data to ensure its integrity.

Events Drive Object Collaboration

At its simplest, the process of object-oriented software development involves:

❑   Properly establishing the functional requirements for, and overall mission of, an application.

❑   Designing the appropriate classes necessary to fulfill these requirements and mission.

❑   Instantiating the classes to create objects.

❑   Setting the objects in motion through external triggering events.

Think of an anthill: at first glance, you may see no apparent activity taking place. But if you drop an ice cream cone nearby, a flurry of activity suddenly begins as ants rush around to gather up the 'goodies', as well as to repair any damage that may have been caused if you dropped the ice cream cone *too close* to the anthill! Within an OO application (the 'anthill'), the objects ('ants') may be set in motion by an external event such as:

- ❏ The click of a button on the Student Registration System (SRS) graphical user interface (GUI), indicating a student's desire to register for a particular course.

- ❏ The receipt of information from some other automated system, such as when the SRS receives a list of all students who have paid their tuition from the university's Billing System.

As soon as such a triggering event has been noted by an OO system, the appropriate objects react, performing services themselves and/or requesting services of other objects in chain-reaction fashion, until some overall system goal has been accomplished. For example, the request to register for a course made by a student user via the SRS application's GUI may involve the collaboration of many different objects:

- ❏ A Student object (an abstraction of the *real* student)

- ❏ A DegreeProgram object, to ensure that the requested course is truly required for the student to graduate

- ❏ The appropriate Course object, to make sure that there is a seat available in the course for the student

- ❏ A Classroom object, representing the room in which the course will be meeting, to verify its seating capacity

- ❏ A Transcript object – specifically, the Transcript of the Student of interest – to ensure that the student has met all prerequisites for the course

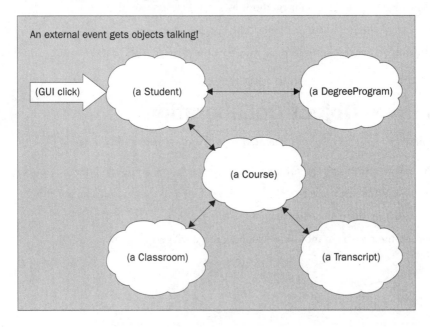

Meanwhile, the user of the SRS is blissfully ignorant of all the objects that are 'scurrying around' behind the scenes to accomplish their goal; the student merely fills in a few fields and clicks a button on the SRS GUI and a few moments later sees a message which either confirms or rejects their registration request.

Once the ultimate goal of an event chain has been achieved (for example, registering a student for a course), an application's objects may become effectively idle, and may remain so until the next such triggering event occurs. An object-oriented application is in some ways similar to a game of pool: hit the cue ball with your cue, and it (hopefully!) hits another ball, which might collide with three other balls, and so on. Eventually, however, all balls will come to a standstill until the cue ball is hit again.

Method Signatures

Let's talk in a bit more detail about how we specify an object's behaviors. Recall from Chapter 3 that an object's methods may be thought of as services that the object can perform. In order for an object A to request some service of an object B, A needs to know the specific language with which to communicate with B. That is:

❑ **Object A needs to be clear as to exactly which of B's methods/services A wants B to perform.** Think of yourself as object A, and a pet dog as object B. Do you want your dog to sit? Stay? Heel? Fetch?

❑ **Depending on the service request, object A may need to give B some additional information so that B knows exactly how to proceed.** If you tell your dog to fetch, the dog needs to know *what* to fetch: A ball? A stick? The neighbor's cat?

❑ **Object B in turn needs to know whether object A expects B to report back the outcome of what it has been asked to do.** In the case of a command to fetch something, your dog will hopefully bring the requested item to you as an outcome. However, if your dog is in another room and you call out the command 'sit', you won't see the result of your command; you have to trust that the dog has done what you have asked it to do.

We take care of communicating these three aspects of each method by defining a method signature, which is a formal specification (from a programming standpoint) of how that method is to be invoked. A method signature consists of:

❑ A method's **name**.

❑ An optional list of comma-separated **arguments** (names and types of variables) to be passed to the method enclosed in parentheses.

❑ A method's **return type** – that is, the data type of the information that is going to be passed back by object B to object A, if any, when the method is finished executing.

As an example, here is a typical method signature that we might define for the Student class:

```
boolean registerForCourse (String courseID, String secNo);
return type   method name        list of argument types (and names) enclosed in parentheses.
```

When casually referring to a method such as isHonorsStudent in narrative text, we often append an empty set of parentheses () to the end of the method name, for example isHonorsStudent(). This does not necessarily imply that the formal signature has no arguments, however.

For those of you who are familiar with C or C++ syntax, a method is a function, and a method signature is exactly the same thing as a function prototype or function signature. The purpose of such a signature is to instruct the compiler on the details of how a function/method is to be called. The conceptual difference between a (C) function and a (C++ or Java) method is, that a method happens to be encapsulated within a particular class, whereas a function can be 'floating freely' within an application.

Passing Arguments

The purpose of passing arguments into a method is either to provide the object receiving the request with the 'fuel' necessary to do its job and/or to guide its behavior in some fashion. In the `registerForCourse` method signature above, for example, it is necessary to tell the receiving `Student` object which course we want it to register for by passing in the course ID (for example, 'MATH 101') and the section number (for example 10, which happens to meet Monday nights from 8 – 10 PM). Had we instead defined this method signature as:

```
boolean registerForCourse();
```

with an **empty argument list**, the request would be ambiguous: the receiving `Student` object would have no idea as to which course it was expected to register for.

Not all methods require such 'fuel', however; some methods are able to produce results solely based on the information stored internally within an object, in which case no additional guidance is needed in the form of arguments. For example, the method signature:

```
int getAge();
```

requires no arguments because a `Student` object can presumably tell you its age (based on its `birthdate` attribute, perhaps) without having to be given any qualifying information. Let's say, however, that we wanted a `Student` object to be able to report its age expressed either in years (rounded to the nearest year), or in months; in such a case, we might wish to define the `getAge` method as follows:

```
int getAge(int ageType);
```

We would pass in an `int`(eger) argument to serve as a control flag for informing the `Student` object of how we want the answer to be returned; that is, we might program the `getAge` method so that:

❑ If we pass in a value of 1, it means that we want the answer to be returned in terms of years (for example, 30).

❑ If we pass in a value of 2, we want the answer to be returned in terms of months (for example, 30 x 12 = 360).

However, the preferred OO way of handling this requirement to retrieve the age of a `Student` object in two different formats, would be to define two separate methods, such as perhaps:

```
int getAgeInYears();
int getAgeInMonths();
```

One more bit of terminology: the term **argument signature** refers to the order, types, and number of arguments comprising a method signature, but not their specific names. Some examples of method signatures and their corresponding argument signatures are shown in the table below; we'll find argument signatures to be important when we discuss the concept of **overloading** in Chapter 5.

Method Signature	Corresponding Argument Signature
`int getAge(int ageType);`	`(int)`
`void switchMajor(String newDepartment,` `                  Professor newAdvisor);`	`(String, Professor)`
`int getName();`	`()`

Return Types

The `registerForCourse` method signature as previously defined is shown to have a return type of `boolean`, which implies that this method will return one of two values:

❑ A value of `true`, to signal 'mission accomplished' – namely, that the `Student` object has successfully registered for the course that it was instructed to register for.

❑ A value of `false`, to signal that the mission has failed for some reason: perhaps the desired section was full, the student didn't meet the prerequisites of the course, or the requested course/section has been cancelled, etc.

> *In Part 3 of the book, we'll learn techniques for determining precisely why the mission has failed.*

Note that a method need not return anything – it may go about its business silently, without reporting the outcome of its efforts. If so, its return type is said to be `void` (another Java reserved word).

Here are additional examples of method signatures that we might define for the `Student` class:

❑ `void setName(String newName);`

This method requires one argument – a `String` representing the new name that we want this `Student` to assume – and performs 'silently' by setting the `Student`'s internal name attribute to whatever value is being passed into the method, returning no answer in response.

❑ `void switchMajor(String newDepartment, Professor newAdvisor);`

This method represents a request for a `Student` to change their major field of study, which involves designating both a new academic department (for example, `'BIOLOGY'`) as well as a reference to the `Professor` object that is to serve as the student's advisor in this new department.

The preceding example demonstrates that we can define arguments in terms of either abstract or built-in data types; the same is true for the return type of a method:

❑ `Professor getAdvisor();`

This method is used to ask a `Student` object who its advisor is. Rather than returning the name of the advisor, the `Student` object returns a reference to the `Professor` object (as stored in `Student` attribute `facultyAdvisor`) in its entirety! We'll see a need for returning 'handles' to objects in this fashion shortly, when we explore how objects interact.

Note that a method can only return one result or answer – a simple data type or a single object reference – which may seem limiting. What if, for example, we want to ask a `Student` object for a list of all of the courses that the student has ever taken: must we ask for these one-by-one through multiple method calls? Fortunately not: the result handed back by a method can actually be an object of arbitrary complexity, including a special type of object called a **collection** that can contain multiple other objects. We'll talk about collections in more depth in Chapter 6.

Method Bodies

When we design and program a class in an OO language, we must not only provide formal signatures for all of its methods, but also must program the internal details of how each method should behave when it is invoked. These internal programming details, known as the **method body**, are enclosed within curly braces ({ ... }) immediately following the method signature, as follows:

```
class Student {
  // Attributes.
  float gpa;
  // others omitted ...

    // Here is a full-blown method, complete with a body of code to be executed
    // when the method is invoked.
    boolean isHonorsStudent() {
      // The programming details of what this method (function) is to do
      // go between the curly braces ... this is the method body.

      // 'gpa' is an attribute of the Student class.
      if (gpa >= 3.5) return true;
        else return false;
      } // end of the method body
    // etc.
}
```

Naming Suggestions

Inventing descriptive names for both methods and arguments helps to make method signatures self-documenting. For example, the method signature:

```
void switchMajor(String newDepartment, Professor newAdvisor);
```

is much more self-explanatory than this alternative version:

```
void switch(String dept, Professor p);
```

yet, to the compiler, they are equally acceptable.

Message Passing and Dot Notation

Now that we understand how methods are formally specified, how do we represent in code that a method is being invoked on an object? We create what is known as a **message**. A message is an expression, formed by taking the name of the reference variable representing the object that is to receive the message, followed by a 'dot' (period), followed by a 'filled in' method signature; for example,

```
// Instantiate a Student object.
Student x = new Student();

// Send a message to Student object 'x' asking it to register for course
// MATH 101, section 10.
x.registerForCourse("MATH 101", 10);  // This is a message!
```

Again, for people familiar with C/C++, this is nothing more that a function call.

Because we are using a 'dot' to 'glue' the reference variable to the method signature, this is informally known as using 'dot notation'.

Let's now look at a simple message-passing example involving two objects. Assume that we have two classes defined – Student and Course – and that the following methods are defined for each:

Student Method:	
`boolean successfully Completed(Course c);`	Given a reference 'c' to a particular Course object, we are asking the Student object receiving this message to confirm that they have indeed taken the course in question and received a passing grade.
Course Method:	
`boolean register (Student s);`	Given a reference 's' to a particular Student object, we are asking the Course object receiving this message to do whatever is necessary to register the student. In this case, we expect the Course to ultimately respond true or false to indicate success or failure of the registration request.

The following diagram reflects one possible message interchange between a Course object c and a Student object s; note that this is not necessarily the 'best' interchange between objects for accomplishing this goal, but is simply an example that we've chosen for purposes of illustration. (In Chapter 11, we'll learn how to design appropriate object interactions for the SRS.) The numbered steps involved in this message exchange are described below.

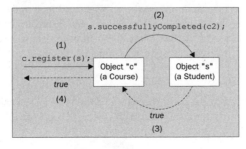

1. A `Course` object c receives the message:

> `c.register(s);`

where s represents a particular `Student` object. (For now, we won't worry about the origin of this message; it was most likely triggered by a user's interaction with the SRS GUI.)

2. In order for `Course` object c to officially determine whether or not s should be permitted to register, c sends the message:

> `s.successfullyCompleted(c2);`

to `Student` s, where c2 represents a reference to a *different* `Course` object that happens to be a prerequisite of `Course` c. (Don't worry about how `Course` c knows that c2 is one of its prerequisites; this involves interacting with c's internal `prerequisites` attribute, which we haven't talked about. Also, `Course` c2 is not depicted in the diagram above because, strictly speaking, c2 is not engaged in this 'discussion' between objects c and s; c2 is being talked about, but not doing any talking itself!)

3. `Student` object s replies with the value `true` to c, indicating that s has successfully completed the prerequisite course. (We will for the time being ignore the details as to how s determines this; it involves interacting with s's internal `transcript` attribute, of which we haven't fully explained the structure just yet.)

4. Convinced that the student has complied with the prerequisite requirements for the course, `Course` object c finishes the job of registering the student (internal details omitted for now) and confirms the registration by responding with a value of `true` to the originator of the service request.

This example was overly simplistic; in reality, `Course` c may have had to speak to numerous other objects – a `Classroom` object (the room in which the course is to be held, to make sure that it has sufficient room for another student), a `DegreeProgram` object (the degree sought by the student, to make sure that the requested course is indeed required for the degree that the student is pursuing), and so forth – before sending a `true` response to indicate that the request to register `Student` s had been fulfilled. We'll see a slightly more complicated version of this message exchange later in the chapter.

Accessing Attributes via Dot Notation

Just as we use dot notation to formulate messages to be passed to objects, we can also use dot notation to refer to an object's attributes. For example, if we declare a reference variable x to be of type `Student`, we can refer to any of `Student` x's attributes via the notation:

> `x.attribute_name`

where the period ('dot') is used to prepend the name of the reference variable representing the object of interest to the name of the attribute of interest: `x.name`, `x.gpa`, and so forth.

Here are a few additional examples:

```
// Instantiate three objects.
Student x = new Student();
Student y = new Student();
Professor z = new Professor();

// We use dot notation to access attributes as variables.

// Set student x's name ...
x.name = "John Smith";

// ... and student y's name.
y.name = "Joe Blow";

// Set professor z's name to be the same as student x's name.
z.name = x.name;

// Compute the total of the two students' ages.
int i = x.age + y.age;
// Set the professor's age to be 40.
z.age = 40;
```

We will see later in this chapter that, although dot notation in theory allows us to directly manipulate the internal attributes of an object, there are other mechanisms at work that guard against this, to enable objects to protect the 'privacy' of their data.

Delegation

If a request is made of an object A and, in fulfilling the request, A in turn requests assistance from another object B, this is known as **delegation** by A to B. The concept of delegation among objects is exactly the same as delegation between people in the real world: if your 'significant other' asks you to mow the lawn while they are out running errands and you in turn hire a neighborhood teenager to mow the lawn then, as far as your partner is concerned, the lawn has been mowed. The fact that you delegated the activity to someone else is (hopefully!) irrelevant.

The fact that delegation has occurred between objects is often transparent to the initiator of a message, as well. In our previous message passing example, Course c delegated part of the work of registering Student s when c asked s to verify a prerequisite course. However, from the perspective of the originator of the registration request (c.register(s);) this seems like a simple interaction: namely, the requestor asked c to register a student, and it did so! All of the 'behind the scenes' details of what c had to do to accomplish this are hidden from the requestor.

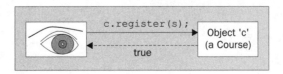

Access to Objects

The only way that an object A can pass a message to an object B is if A has access to a handle on B. This can happen in several different ways:

❑ **Object A might maintain a handle/reference to B as one of A's attributes;** for example, the example from Chapter 3 of a Student object having a Professor reference as an attribute:

```
class Student {
    // Attributes.
    String name;
    Professor facultyAdvisor;
    // etc.
```

❑ **Object A may be handed a reference to B as an argument of one of A's methods.** This is how Course object c obtained access to Student s in the preceding message passing example, when c's register() method was called:

```
c.register(s);
```

❑ **A reference to object B may be made 'globally available' to the entire application,** such that all other objects can access it. We'll discuss techniques for doing so in Part 3 of the book.

❑ **Object A may have to explicitly request a handle/reference to B by calling a method on some third object C.** Since this is potentially the most complex way for A to obtain a handle on B, we'll illustrate this with an example.

Going back to the example interaction between Course object c and Student object s from a few pages ago, we'll complicate the interaction a little bit by introducing a third object. A Transcript object t represents a record of all courses taken by Student object s. Furthermore, we'll assume that Student s maintains a handle on Transcript t as one of s's attributes (specifically, the 'transcript' attribute), and conversely, that Transcript t maintains a handle on its 'owner', Student s, as one of t's attributes.

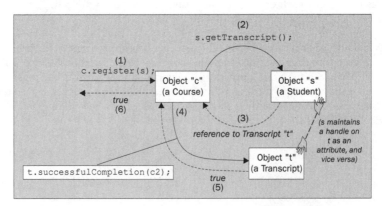

1. In this enhanced object interaction, the first step is exactly as previously described: namely, a Course object c receives the message:

```
c.register(s);
```

where s represents a Student object.

2. Now, instead of Course c sending the message s.successfullyCompleted(c2) to Student s as before, where 'c2' represents a prerequisite Course, Course object c instead sends the message:

```
s.getTranscript();
```

to the Student, because c wants to check s's transcript first-hand. This message corresponds to a method on the Student class whose signature is defined as follows:

```
Transcript getTranscript();
```

Note that the method is defined to return a Transcript object reference: specifically, a handle on the Transcript object t belonging to this student.

3. Because Student s maintains a handle on its Transcript object as an attribute, it is a snap for s to respond to this message by passing a handle on t back to Course object c.

4. Now that Course c has its *own* temporary handle on Transcript t, object c can talk directly to t. Object c proceeds to ask t whether t has any record of c's prerequisite course c2 having successfully been completed by Student s by passing the message:

```
t.successfulCompletion(c2);
```

This implies that there is a method defined for the Transcript class with the signature:

```
boolean successfulCompletion(Course c);
```

Note that it is not necessary for this message from c to t to mention Students in any way, because as we stated earlier, Transcript t maintains a handle on its owner as an attribute.

5. Transcript object t answers back with a response of true to Course c, indicating that Student s has successfully completed the prerequisite course in question. (Note that Student s is unaware that c is talking to t; object s knows that it was asked by c to return a handle to t in an earlier message, but s has no insights as to *why* c asked for the handle.)

6. Satisfied that the student has complied with its prerequisite requirements, Course object c finishes the job of registering Student s (internal details omitted for now) and confirms the registration by responding with a value of true to the originator of the registration request that first arose in Step 1. Now that c has finished with this transaction, it discards its (temporary) handle on t.

Note that, from the perspective of whoever sent the original message

```
c.register(s);
```

to Course c, this more complicated interaction appears identical to the earlier, simpler interaction; all the sender of the original message knows, is that the Course c eventually responded with a value of true to the request.

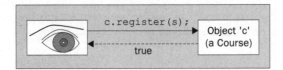

Objects as Clients and Servers/Agents

In the preceding example of message passing between a Course object and a Student object, we can consider Course object c to be a **client** of Student object s, because c is requesting (by initiating a message) that s perform one of its methods – namely, getTranscript() – as a *service* to c. This is identical to the 'real-world' concept of *you*, as a client, requesting the services of an accountant, or an attorney, or an architect. Similarly, c is a client of Transcript t when c asks t to perform its successfulCompletion() method.

We refer to code that invokes a method on an object A as **client code** relative to A because the code benefits from the service(s) performed by A. Let's look at a few examples of client code:

❑ The following code snippet, taken from the main() method of some application, instantiates two objects and invokes a method on one of them:

```
public static void main(String[] args) {
    Course c = new Course();
    Student s = new Student();

    // Details omitted.

    // Invoke a method on Course object c.
    c.register(s);

    // etc.
}
```

In this example, the main() method is considered to be client code relative to Course object c because it calls upon c to perform its register() method as a service.

❑ Let's now look at the code that implements the body of the register() method, inside of the Course class:

```
class Course {
  // details omitted ...

    public boolean register(Student s) {
        // Request a handle on Student s's Transcript object.
        Transcript t = s.getTranscript();

        // Now, request a service on that Transcript object.
        // (Assume that c2 is a handle on some prerequisite Course ...)
        if (t.successfullyCompleted(c2)) return true;
        else return false;
    }
  // etc.
}
```

We see that the register() method body is considered to be client code relative to both Student object s and Transcript object t because this code calls upon s and t to each perform a service.

Whenever an object A is a client of object B, object B in turn can be thought of as a **server** or **agent** of A. Note that the roles of client and server are not absolute between two objects; such roles are only relevant for the duration of a particular message passing event. If I ask you to pass me the butter, I am your client, and you are my server; and if a moment later you ask me to pass you the bread, then you are my client, and I am your server.

Information Hiding/Visibility

As we discussed earlier in this chapter, dot notation can be used, in theory, to access an object's attribute values, as in the following simple example:

```
Student x = new Student();
x.name = "Fred Schnurd";
System.out.println(x.name);
```

In reality, however, objects often restrict access to some of their features (attributes in particular). Such restriction is known as **information hiding**. In a well designed object-oriented application, an object publicizes what it can do – that is, the services it is capable of providing, or its method signatures – but *hides* the internal details both of *how* it performs these services and of the data (attributes) that it maintains in order to *support* these services.

We use the term **visibility** to refer to whether or not a particular feature of an object (attribute or method) can be accessed from client code by applying dot notation to the object's reference variable. In particular:

❑ **Public visibility** implies that the feature in question may indeed be accessed from client code using dot notation. For example, if we were to proclaim that the name attribute of the Student class were public, which we do by placing the reserved word 'public' just ahead of the attribute declaration, as follows:

```
class Student {
  public String name;
  // etc.
```

then it would be perfectly acceptable to write client code as follows:

```
class MyProgram {
  public static void main(String[] args){
  Student x = new Student();

  // Because name is a public attribute, we may access it via dot
  // notation from client code.
  x.name = "Fred Schnurd";

  // etc.
```

And, similarly, if we were to declare the isHonorsStudent() method of Student to be public, which we do by again placing the reserved word public ahead of the method signature:

```
class Student {
  // Attributes omitted.
  // Methods.
  public boolean isHonorsStudent() {
  // details omitted.
}

// etc.
```

it would then be perfectly acceptable to write client code as follows:

```
class MyProgram {
  public static void main(String[] args){
  Student x = new Student();

    // Because isHonorsStudent() is a public method, we may access it
    // via dot notation from client code.
    if (x.isHonorsStudent()) {
      // details omitted.
    }

// etc.
```

❑ **Private visibility**, on the other hand, implies that the feature in question may NOT be accessed via dot notation from client code. For example, if we were to proclaim that the ssn attribute of the Student class were private, as follows:

```
class Student {
  public String name;
  private String ssn;
  // etc.
```

then we could *not* use dot notation in our client code as follows:

```
class MyProgram {
  public static void main(String[] args){
  Student x = new Student();

    // Not permitted from client code!  ssn is private to the
    // Student class.
    x.ssn = "123-45-6789";
```

The same is true for method signature declared to be private. In fact, compilation errors will result if you attempt to access a private feature via dot notation from client code, as if the item never had been declared; the Java compilation error for the above example would be as follows:

Variable ssn in class Student not accessible from class MyProgram.

*There is a third type of visibility defined by Java – **protected** visibility – but we'll defer a discussion of this until Chapter 13 because there are a few more object concepts that we have to learn about first. For now, it is perfectly appropriate to think of visibility as coming in only two 'flavors' – public and private.*

Note that we can access all of a class's features, regardless of their visibility, from within any of the class's own method bodies; that is, public/private designations only affect access to a feature from client code. In the following example, the `Student` class's `printAllAttributes()` method is accessing the private `name` and `ssn` attributes of the `Student` class:

```
class Student {
  private String name;
  private String ssn;
  // etc.

  public void printAllAttributes() {
    System.out.println(name);
    System.out.println(ssn);
    // etc.
  }

  // etc.
}
```

Furthermore, we needn't use dot notation to access a feature of a class when we're inside the body of one of the class's own methods; it is automatically understood that the class is accessing one of its own features when dot notation is absent. These concepts are illustrated by the (abbreviated) `Student` class code below:

```
class Student {
  // A few private attributes.
  private double totalLoans;
  private double tuition;
  // other attributes omitted

  public boolean allBillsPaid() {
    // We can call upon another method that is defined within this
    // same class (see below) without using dot notation.
    double amt = moneyOwed();
    if (amt == 0.0) return true;
    else return false;
  }

  public double moneyOwed() {
    // We can access attributes of this class (totalLoans and
    // tuitionOwed) -- even though they are declared to be private! --
    // without using dot notation.
    return totalLoans + tuitionOwed;
  }
}
```

There is one exception to our comment about not needing to use dot notation when accessing a class's own attributes; we'll talk about this exception in Chapter 13, when we introduce the notion of the reserved word this.

As it turns out, method signatures of a class are typically declared public or 'visible' because an object (class) needs to publicize its services (as in a Yellow Pages ad!) so that client code may request these services. By contrast, most attributes are typically declared private or 'hidden', so that an object can maintain ultimate control over its data.

Although it is not explicitly declared as such, the internal code that implements each method (that is, the **method bodies**) is also implicitly private. When a client object A asks another object B to perform one of its methods, A doesn't need to know the 'behind the scenes' details of how B is doing what it is doing; A needs simply to trust that object B will perform the 'advertised' service.

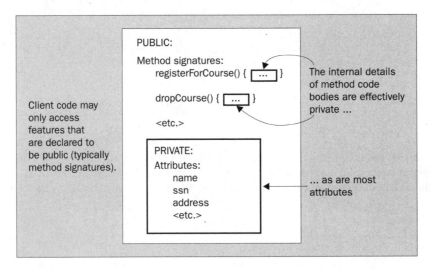

Accessor and Modifier Methods

If private attributes cannot be accessed outside of an object's own methods, how does client code manipulate them? Through public methods, of course! Good OO programming practice calls for providing public accessor and modifier methods by which clients of an object can effectively manipulate selected private attributes. These are informally known as 'get' methods and 'set' methods, respectively.

The following code, excerpted from the Student class, illustrates the accessor and modifier methods for the private name attribute:

```
class Student {
    // Attributes are typically declared to be private.
    private String name;
    // other attributes omitted ...
```

```
     // Provide public accessor and modifier methods for
     // manipulating the private 'name' attribute from client code.

     // Accessor.
     public String getName() {
       return name;
     }

     // Modifier.
     public void setName(String newName) {
       name = newName;
     }

     // etc.
   }
```

For an attribute declaration of the form:

> `visibility*` `attribute-type` `attributeName;`   *typically, but not always, `private`.

for example: `private String majorField;`

the recommended 'get' and 'set' method signatures are as follows:

❑   'get' method: `public` *attribute-type* `getAttributeName();`

For example,   `public String getMajorField();`

  ❑   We don't pass any arguments into a 'get' method, because all we want an object to do is to hand us back the value of one of its attributes; we don't typically need to tell the object anything more for it to know how to do this.

  ❑   Because we are expecting an object to hand back the value of a specific attribute, the return type of the 'get' method must match the type of the attribute of interest. If we are 'getting' the value of an `int` attribute, then the return type of the method must be `int`; if we're 'getting' the value of a `String` attribute, then the return type of the method must be `String`; and so forth.

❑   'set' method: `public void setAttributeName(`*attribute-type* `argumentname);`

For example,   `public void setMajorField(String major);`

  ❑   In the case of a 'set' method, we have to pass in the value that we want the object to use when setting its corresponding attribute value, and the type of the value that we are passing in must match the type of the attribute being set.

  ❑   However, since most 'set' methods perform their mission silently, without returning a value to the client, we typically declare 'set' methods to have a return type of `void`.

Note that we devise the names for both types of method by capitalizing the first letter in the attribute name and sticking either 'get' or 'set' in front of it.

> *Observing this 'get/set' method signature convention isn't mandatory, but it is strongly encouraged for the following reason. There is a way to structure your classes when you write them to make them maximally reusable with commercial Java-savvy applications; classes that are so designed are known as 'JavaBeans'. It turns out that one of the requirements for making your class behave like a 'Bean' is following these get/set method naming conventions (the other requirements for creating a Bean are beyond the scope of this book to address). So, even though you may not know enough about Beans – or Java, for that matter – to appreciate their versatility just yet, it can't hurt to set the stage for possibly taking advantage of JavaBeans later, all things being equal!*

There aren't any hard and fast rules concerning how to name the argument passed into a 'set' method, but there are several schools of thought:

❑   Use of a single letter that matches the type of the argument, as in:

```
public void setAdvisor(Professor p);
```

❑   Use of an argument that has the prefix 'new' tacked on to the front of the attribute name being set, as in:

```
public void setGpa(float newGpa);
```

❑   Use of an argument that exactly matches the name of the attribute being set, as in:

```
public void setName(String name);
```

and countless others. Pick whichever approach appeals to you, but then try to stick with it so that your code is consistent and hence easier to understand.

> *With this last form of argument name, there is something else we have to do internally to the method when working with this argument; it involves a special use of the reserved word 'this', which we will discuss in Chapter 13.*

There is one exception to this get/set method signature convention: when an attribute is of type `boolean`, it is recommended that you name the 'get' method starting with the verb 'is' instead of with 'get'. The 'set' method for a `boolean` attribute should follow the standard convention. For example:

```
class Student {
  private boolean honorsStudent;
  // other attributes omitted ...
  // Get method.
  public boolean isHonorsStudent() {
    return honorsStudent;
  }
  // Set method.
  public void setHonorsStudent(boolean x) {
    honorsStudent = x;
  }
  // etc.
}
```

All of the get/set method bodies that we've seen thus far are simple 'one liners': we're either returning the value of the attribute of interest with a simple return statement in a 'get' method, or copying the value of the passed-in argument to the internal attribute in a 'set' method so as to store it. This is not to imply that all get/set methods need be this simple. In fact, we often employ more complex logic in 'get' and 'set' methods – we'll see examples shortly.

In addition, because we haven't explicitly said so before, and because it may not be obvious to everyone, let us call attention now to the fact that an attribute's values persist as long as the object persists. That is, if we create a `Student` object in client code:

```
public static void main(String[] args) {
  Student s = new Student();
  s.setName("Fred");

  // etc.
}
```

then `Student` s's name attribute will remain set to the value 'Fred' until such time as the value is explicitly changed, or until such time as the object is destroyed and its memory is recycled (we'll talk about ways of destroying an object and recycling its memory in Chapter 13).

Exceptions to the Public/Private Rule

Even though it is generally true that:

❑ Attributes are declared to be private.

❑ Method signatures are declared to be public.

❑ Private attributes are teamed up with public get/set methods.

there are numerous exceptions to this rule.

1. **An attribute may be used by a class strictly for internal housekeeping purposes**. (Like the dishwashing detergent you keep under the sink, guests needn't know about it!). For such attributes, we needn't bother to create public accessor/modifier methods. One example for the `Student` class might be an attribute:

```
private int countOfDsAndFs;
```

This attribute might be used to keep track of how many poor grades a student has received in order to determine whether or not the student is on academic probation. We may provide a `Student` class method as follows:

```
public boolean onAcademicProbation() {
  // If the student received more than three substandard grades, they
  // will be put on academic probation.
  if (countOfDsAndFs > 3) return true;
  else return false;
}
```

This method uses the value of attribute `countOfDsAndFs` to determine whether a student is on academic probation, but no *client code* need ever know that there is such an attribute as `countOfDsAndFs`, and so there are no explicit get/set methods provided for this attribute. Such attributes are instead set as a 'side effect' of performing some other method, such as in the following example:

```
public void completeCourse(String courseName,
                           int creditHours,
                           char grade) {
  // Updating this private attribute is considered to be a
  // 'side effect' of completing a course.
  if (grade == 'D' || grade == 'F') countOfDsAndFs++;

  // Other processing details omitted.
}
```

2. **Some *methods* may be used strictly for internal housekeeping, as well, in which case these may also be declared private rather than public.** An example of such a `Student` class method might be `updateGpa()`, which recomputes the value of the `gpa` attribute each time a student completes another course and receives a grade. The only time that this method may ever need to be called is perhaps from within another method of `Student` – for example, the public `completeCourse()` method – as follows:

```
class Student {
  private double gpa;
  private int totalCoursesTaken;
  private int totalQualityPointsEarned;
  // other details omitted ...
```

```
  public void completeCourse(String courseName,
                             int creditHours,
                             char grade) {
    if (grade == 'D' || grade == 'F') countOfDsAndFs++;

    // Record grade in transcript.
    // details omitted ...

    // Update an attribute ...
    totalCoursesTaken = totalCoursesTaken + 1;

    // ... and call a private housekeeping method from within this
    // public method to adjust the student's GPA accordingly.
    updateGpa(creditHours, grade);
  }

  // The details of how the GPA gets updated are a deep, dark secret!
  // Even the SIGNATURE of what this method does is hidden from the
  // "outside world".
  private void updateGpa(int creditHours, char grade) {
    int letterGradeValue = 0;
```

```
        if (grade == 'A') letterGradeValue = 4;
        if (grade == 'B') letterGradeValue = 3;
        if (grade == 'C') letterGradeValue = 2;
        if (grade == 'D') letterGradeValue = 1;
        // For an 'F', it remains 0.

        int qualityPoints = creditHours * letterGradeValue;

        // Update two attributes.
        totalQualityPointsEarned = totalQualityPointsEarned + qualityPoints;
        gpa = totalQualityPointsEarned/totalCoursesTaken;
    }
}
```

Client code shouldn't be able to directly cause a `Student` object's GPA to be updated; this should only occur as a 'side effect' of completing a course. By making the `updateGpa()` method signature private, we've prevented any client code from intentionally invoking this method to manipulate this attribute's value.

3. **We needn't always provide both a 'set' and a 'get' method for private attributes**; if we provide only a 'get' method for an attribute, then that attribute is effectively read-only. We might do so, for example, with a student's ID number, which once set, should be unchanging. (We'll see how to initialize such an attribute a bit later in this chapter, when we talk about constructors.)

4. **Classes may occasionally declare public attributes as a convenience when such attributes are going to be accessed frequently.** Let's say that we were going to frequently need access to a `Student` object's student ID number, and so decided to declare the `studentId` attribute of the `Student` class to be public instead of private:

```
class Student {
  public String studentId;
  // etc.
```

This would enable us to streamline our client code; instead of having to call the 'get' method for this attribute:

```
// Client code.

Student s = new Student();
// Details omitted.
System.out.println(s.getStudentId());
```

we could instead access the attribute directly:

```
// Client code.

Student s = new Student();
// Details omitted.
// Note that, because the studentId attribute is declared to be public,
// we can access it directly via dot notation.
System.out.println(s.studentId);
```

However, in exchange for this slightly more convenient way of accessing the attribute, we have given up the object's ability to control how and when the attribute's value is altered. Therefore, it would now be possible for client code to inappropriately alter the value of this attribute, as follows:

```
s.studentId = "?";
```

The bottom line is that declaring attributes as public should only be done for the simplest of attributes i.e. those which do not require careful monitoring and maintenance. When in doubt, play it safe, and make all attributes private!

Encapsulation Revisited

We learned earlier that encapsulation is the mechanism that bundles together the state information (attributes) and behavior (methods) of an object. Now that we've gained some insights into public/private visibility, encapsulation warrants a more in-depth discussion.

It is useful to think of an object as a 'fortress' that 'guards' data – namely, the values of all of its attributes. Rather than trying to march straight through the walls of a fortress, which typically results in death and destruction (!), we ideally would approach the guard at the gate to ask permission to enter. Generally speaking, the same is true for objects: we cannot directly access the values of an object's privately-declared attributes without an object's permission and knowledge, that is, without using one of an object's publicly accessible methods to 'get' or 'set' the attribute's value.

Assume that you've just met someone for the first time, and wish to know their name. One way to determine his name would be to reach into his pocket, pull out his wallet, and look at his driver's license – essentially, accessing his private attribute values without his permission! The more 'socially acceptable' way would be to simply ask him for his name, and to allow him to answer – equivalent to using an object's getName() method.

By restricting access to an object's private attributes through public method calls, we can:

❑ **Prevent unauthorized access to the encapsulated data**. Some of the information that a Student object maintains about itself – say, the student's identification number – may be highly confidential. A Student object may choose to selectively pass along this information when necessary – for example, when registering for a course – but may not wish to hand out this information to any object that happens to casually ask for it. Simply by making the attribute private, and intentionally failing to provide a public getStudentId() method with which to request the attribute's value, there would be no way for another object to request the Student object's identification number.

❑ **Help to ensure data integrity**. As an example, let's say we have a Student method with signature:

```
boolean updateBirthdate(String d);
```

Our intention is to record birth dates in the format 'mm/dd/yyyy'. By providing a method to update the `birthdate` attribute (instead of permitting direct public access to the attribute), we can provide logic to validate the format of the new proposed date, and reject those that are invalid. There is no way for us to force the caller to pass in data conforming to this format – the single argument to the `updateBirthdate()` method as we've declared it is a `String` which can be of literally any format. However, what we *can* do is to provide logic within the method, which verifies and, if necessary, rejects the request to set the birthdate, as illustrated below:

```
class Student {
  private String birthdate;
  // details omitted

  public boolean updateBirthdate(String d) {
    // Perform appropriate validations.
    // Remember, italics represent pseudocode!
    if (date is not in the format mm/dd/yyyy )
      return false;
    else (if mm not in the range 01 to 12 )
      return false;
      // etc. for other validation tests
    else {
      // All is well with what was handed in to this
      // method, so we're calling our more 'rudimentary'
      // setBirthdate() method now, which does no validation
      // of its own.
      setBirthdate(d);
      return true;
    }
  }

  // The setBirthdate() method is fairly rudimentary.  We declare it
  // to be private in this example to force client code to use
  // the updateBirthdate() method instead.
  private void setBirthdate(String d) {
    birthdate = d;
  }
}
```

As we've written them above, the `updateBirthdate()` method serves as a public 'wrapper' around the private `setBirthdate()` method.

❑ Another huge benefit of encapsulation combined with information hiding, is that the hidden implementation details of a class can change without affecting how the object gets used by the outside world. As an example, let's say that we have a method on `Student` with the signature:

```
int getAge();
```

Internally to the `Student` class, the code for the `getAge()` method may:

❑ Simply pass back the student's age, which might be stored explicitly as an attribute – `int age` – that gets updated once a year on the student's birthday.

❑ Compute the student's age by subtracting their birthdate (an attribute) from today's date. This is an example of what I refer to as a **'pseudoattribute'** – to client code, the presence of a `getAge()` method implies that there is an attribute by the name of `age`, when in fact there may not be!

The beauty is that we don't care which of these approaches is used! If we are writing code to manipulate `Student` objects, we know that we can safely invoke the `getAge()` method for a particular student object, and that its age is guaranteed to be returned to us as an `int` value. So, if the developer of the `Student` class changes the internal implementation details of the `getAge()` method, none of the client code that we've written which calls that method will break!

> *The notion that a class is 'guaranteed' to do what it advertises that it is going, to do is often referred to as **programming by contract**; for more information, see Object-oriented Software Construction by Bertrand Meyer (Prentice Hall).*

```
// This client code is unaffected by the private details of how age is
// computed internally to the Student class. Such details can in fact
// change after this client code is written, and the client code
// will be unaffected.
Student s = new Student();
// details omitted ...
int i = s.getAge();
```

Such changes are said to be **encapsulated**, or limited to the internal code of the class only. (Of course, all bets are off if the developer of a class changes one of its public method signatures, because then all of the client code that passes messages to objects of this type using this method signature will have to change.)

As another example, let's look once again at the `updateBirthdate()` method that we discussed above. We can change the way that the date is stored internally to a `Student` object, if desired, to break it into three integers – `birthMonth`, `birthDay`, and `birthYear` – instead of storing it as a single `String` attribute, as was previously the case:

```
class Student {
  private int birthMonth;
  private int birthDay;
  private int birthYear;
  // etc.
```

The `updateBirthdate()` method's signature remains unchanged, as does the code body of this method:

```
// This method's signature is unchanged!
public boolean updateBirthdate(String date) {
  // Remember, italics represent pseudocode!
  if (date is not in the format mm/dd/yyyy )
    return false;
  else if (mm not in the range 01 to 12 )
    return false;
    // etc.
  else {
    setBirthdate(d);
    return true;
  }
}
```

and the *signature* of the `setBirthdate()` method also remains unchanged, but the internal details of how the method works, have been revised to accommodate the new attribute structure of this class:

```
// Adapted to the new attribute structure.
private void setBirthdate(String b) {
    // Parse out the month, day, and year from b.
    // Details omitted.

    // (A bit of pseudocode.)
    birthMonth = month, converted to an int value;
    birthDay = day, converted to an int value;
    birthYear = year, converted to an int value;
}
}
```

Because all we changed were the private details of the class – attributes and method body code, but not the public method signature(s) – then any client code that was previously written to call the `updateBirthdate()` method for a `Student` object will continue to work as intended; the client code will be blissfully ignorant that the internal details of the `Student` class have changed.

Accessing Attributes from within a Class's Own Methods

As we saw earlier in the chapter, there are no restrictions on directly accessing a class's attributes from within the bodies of that class's own methods. Both public and private attributes may be manipulated at will, without using the class's get/set methods and without using dot notation, as the following code example illustrates.

```
class Student {
    private String name;
    private String studentID;
    // etc.

    // Accessor and modifier methods.

    public String getName() {
        return name;
    }

    public void setName(String newName) {
        name = newName;
    }

    public void printAllAttributes() {
        // We're directly accessing the values of the attributes, because we
        // can!  We're not bothering to use the get and set methods provided
        // above.

        System.out.println(name);
        System.out.println(studentID);
        // etc.
    }

    // etc.
```

However, it is considered good practice to get into the habit of calling 'get' and 'set' methods, when available, even from within a class's own methods. This is because an attribute may be simple today, but may become complicated down the road. As an example, let's say that after we've programmed the `Student` class – including the `printAllAttributes()` method shown above – we decide that we want a student's name to always appear with the first name abbreviated as a single letter followed by a period; for example, 'John Smith' would always appear as 'J. Smith'. So, we change the internal logic of the `Student` class's `getName()` method to make it a bit more sophisticated, as follows:

```
class Student {
  private String name;
  private String studentID;
  // etc.

  // This version of getName() does more work.
  public String getName() {
    // Declare a few temporary variables.
    String firstInitial;
    String lastName;

    // Extract the first letter of the first name from the 'name'
    // attribute, and store the result in variable 'firstInitial'.
    // (Details omitted.)

    // Extract the last name from the 'name' attribute, and store
    // the result in variable 'lastName'.
    // (Details omitted.)

    return firstInitial + ". " + lastName;
  }

  public void setName(String newName) {
    name = newName;
  }

  // etc.
}
```

No longer does `getName()` simply return the value of the name attribute unaltered, as it used to. But, if from within our `printAllAttributes()` method we're still directly accessing the values of the attributes via dot notation:

```
public void printAllAttributes() {
    // We're still directly accessing the values of the attributes, and
    // so we're losing out on the logic of the newly crafted getName()
    // method.
    System.out.println(name);
    System.out.println(studentID);
    // etc.
  }
  // etc.
}
```

we circumvent the getName() method, which means that all of our hard work to restructure the name in the getName() method is being ignored. On the other hand, if we had originally written the printAllAttributes() method to invoke 'get' methods in the first place:

```
public void printAllAttributes() {
    // We're now using our own get methods.
    System.out.println(getName());
    System.out.println(getStudentID());
    // etc.
```

then we'd have automatically benefited from the change that we made to getName().

Constructors

When we talked about instantiating objects in the previous chapter, you may have been curious about the interesting syntax involved with the 'new' operator:

```
Student x = new Student();
```

In particular, you may have wondered why there were parentheses tacked onto the end of the statement. It turns out that when we instantiate an object via the new operator, we are actually invoking a special type of method called a constructor. A constructor literally constructs (instantiates) a brand new object by allocating enough program memory to house the object's attributes.

The signature for a constructor is a bit different from that of other methods:

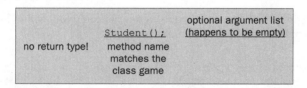

- ❑ The method name must be exactly the same as the name of the class for which you are constructing an object – you have no choice in the matter.

- ❑ You needn't specify a return type for a constructor, because by definition a constructor is returning an object reference of the type represented by the class. If constructors *were* to require a return type, it would be the same as the class name:

```
public Student Student();
```

However, since the return type for a constructor would always match the method name, which would always match the class name, it would be redundant to require programmers to do so.

As it turns out, you can actually define a method in Java with a signature of:

```
public Student Student();
```

However, it does not wind up being a constructor. It is instead a 'normal' method, which just so happens to have the same name as the class! This is admittedly a bit confusing, and can occasionally trip up new Java programmers.

❑   The argument list of a constructor may be used to specify which attributes you want to initialize, if any, at the time that an object is being instantiated. Instead of having to create a 'bare bones' object, and then calling the various 'set' methods defined for that class to pass in attribute values one-by-one as illustrated by this next snippet:

```
Student s = new Student();
s.setName("Fred Schnurd");
s.setSsn("123-45-6789");
s.setMajor("MATH");
// etc.
```

the initial values for selected attributes can all be passed in as a single step when the constructor is called, if desired:

```
Student s = new Student("Fred Schnurd", "123-45-6789", "MATH");
```

And, as with any method, constructor arguments can be used to provide general 'fuel' for controlling how the constructor behaves.

In order to pass arguments into a constructor, we have to learn how to define a constructor's method signature, which is a bit more involved than that of a normal method. We'll revisit constructors in much more detail in Chapter 13.

❑   One other 'oddity' with respect to constructors, as compared with other methods, is that invoking them does not involve dot notation:

```
// We are invoking the Professor class's constructor method, but are not
// using dot notation as we would have to with any other method.
Professor p = new Professor();
```

This is because we are not requesting a service of a particular object, but rather are requesting that a new object be crafted from 'thin air' by the programming environment.

Summary

In this chapter, we've learned:

❑ How to formally specify method signatures, the 'language' with which services may be requested of an object, and how to formulate messages to actually get an object to perform such services.

❑ That multiple objects often have to collaborate in carrying out a particular system function, such as registering a student for a course.

❑ That an object A can only communicate with another object B if A has a handle on B, and the various ways that such a handle can be obtained.

❑ How classes designate the public/private visibility of their features (attributes, methods), and how powerful a mechanism information hiding is in terms of protecting the integrity of an object's data as well as in 'bulletproofing' an application against change.

❑ How to declare and use accessor/modifier ('get'/'set') methods to gracefully access private attributes.

❑ How a special type of method called a constructor is specified and used to instantiate new objects.

Exercises

1. Given a class Book defined as having the following attributes:

```
Author author;
String title;
int noOfPages;
boolean fiction;
```

what should the signatures be for all of the 'get' and 'set' methods?

2. It is often possible to discern something about a class's structure based on the messages that are getting passed to objects in client code. Consider the following client code 'snippet':

```
Student s;
Professor p;
boolean b;
String x = "Math";

s.setMajor(x);
if (!(s.hasAdvisor()))
  b = s.designateAdvisor(p);
```

What method signatures had to have been defined for the Student class in order for this snippet to compile properly? Make sure to discuss any ambiguities that you might encounter.

3. What's wrong with the following code? Point out things that go against OO convention, based on what you've learned in this chapter, regardless of whether or not the compiler would 'complain' about them.

```
class Building {
  private String Address;
  public int numberOfFloors;

  void getnumberOfFloors() {
    return numberOfFloors;
  }

  private void setNumberOfFloors(float n) {
    numberOfFloors = n;
  }
}
```

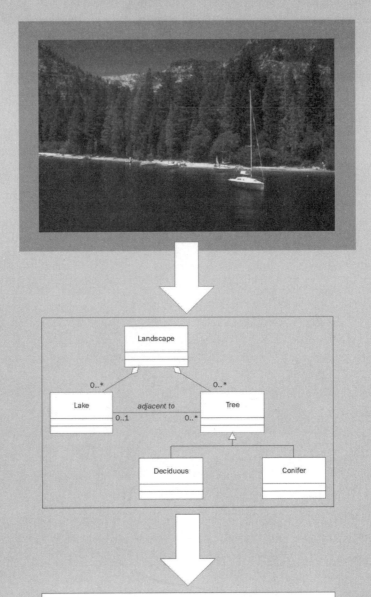

```
public class Tree {
    protected Landscape landscape;
    protected Lake nextTo;

    public void setNextTo(Lake l) {
        nextTo = l;
    }
    public Lake getNextTo() {
        return nextTo;
    }

    public abstract Color getLeafColor();
}
```

Relationships Between Objects

As we saw in Chapter 4, any two objects can have a 'fleeting relationship' based on the fact that they exchange messages, in the same way that two strangers passing on the street might say 'Hello!' to one another. We call such relationships between objects **behavioral relationships**, because they arise out of the behaviors, or actions, taken by one object 'X' relative to another object 'Y'. With behavioral relationships, object 'X' is either temporarily handed a reference to object 'Y' as an argument in a method call, or temporarily requests a handle on 'Y' from another object 'Z'. However, the emphasis is on *temporary*: when X is finished communicating with Y, object X often discards the reference to Y.

In the same way that you have significant and more lasting relationships with some people (family members, friends, colleagues, and so forth), there is also the notion of a more permanent relationship between objects. We refer to such relationships as **structural relationships** because, in order to keep track of such relationships, an object actually maintains lasting handles on its related objects in the form of attributes, a technique that we discussed in Chapter 3.

In this chapter, you will learn:

- ❑ The various kinds of structural relationships that may exist between classes and between individual objects, and how we characterize them.
- ❑ How through a powerful mechanism called **inheritance** we can derive new classes by describing only how they differ from existing classes.
- ❑ The rules for what we can and cannot do when deriving classes through inheritance.

Associations and Links

The formal name for a structural relationship that exists between classes is an **association.** With respect to the Student Registration System, some sample associations might be as follows:

- ❑ A Student *is enrolled in* a Course.
- ❑ A Professor *teaches* a Course.
- ❑ A Degree Program *requires* a Course.

Whereas an association refers to a relationship between *classes*, the term **link** is used to refer to a structural relationship that exists between two specific *objects* (*instances*.) Given the association 'a Student *is enrolled in* a Course', we might have the following links:

❑ Joe Blow (a particular `Student` object) is enrolled in Math 101 (a particular `Course` object).

❑ Fred Schnurd (a particular `Student` object) is enrolled in Basketweaving 972 (a particular `Course` object).

❑ Mary Smith (a particular `Student` object) is enrolled in Basketweaving 972 (a particular `Course` object; as it turns out, the *same* `Course` object that Fred Schnurd is linked to).

In the same way that an object is a specific instance of a class with its attribute values filled in, a link is a specific instance of an association with its member objects filled in:

Association:	_____	is enrolled in	_____
	(some student)		(some course)
Link:	James Conroy (a specific Student)	is enrolled in	Phys Ed 311 (a specific Course)

Another way to think of the difference between an association and a link is that:

❑ An association is a *potential* relationship between objects of a certain type/class.

❑ A link is an *actual* relationship between objects of those particular types.

Given any `Student` object X and any `Course` object Y, there is the *potential* for a link of type 'is enrolled in' to exist between those two objects *precisely because* there is an 'is enrolled in' association defined between the two classes that those objects belong to. In other words, associations facilitate or enable links.

Most of the time, we define associations between two different classes; such associations are known as **binary associations**. The 'is enrolled in' association, for example, is a binary association, because it interrelates two different classes – Student and Course. A **unary**, or **reflexive**, **association**, on the other hand, is between two instances of the same class; for example:

❑ A Course *is a prerequisite for* (another) Course.

❑ A Professor *supervises* (other) Professor(s).

Even though the two classes at either end of a reflexive association are the same, the objects are typically different instances of that class:

❑ Math 101 (a `Course` object) is a prerequisite for Math 202 (a different `Course` object).

❑ Professor Smith (a `Professor` object) supervises Professors Jones and Green (other `Professor` objects).

and so forth. However, although somewhat rare, there can be situations in which the same object can serve in both roles of a reflexive relationship.

Higher order associations are possible, but rare. A **ternary association**, for example, involves three classes; for example, a Student takes a Course from a particular Professor:

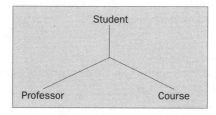

When describing associations, however, we usually decompose higher-order associations into an appropriate number of binary associations. We can, for example, represent the preceding three-way association as three binary associations instead:

❑   A Student *attends* a Course.

❑   A Professor *teaches* a Course.

❑   A Professor *instructs* a Student.

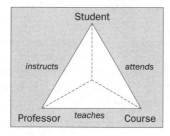

Given any two of these binary associations, we can derive the third. If we know, for example, that Mary Jones is attending Art 300 Section 3, and that Professor Smith is teaching Art 300 Section 3, we can easily determine that Professor Smith is instructing Mary Jones. So, we usually only bother to express the two associations (out of three) that we are most interested in.

Within a given association, each participant class is said to have a **role**. In the *advises* association (a Professor *advises* a Student), the role of the Professor might be said to be 'advisor', and the role of the Student might be said to be 'advisee'. We only bother to assign names to the roles at either end of an association if it helps to clarify the model. In the 'is enrolled in' association (a Student *is enrolled in* a Course), there is probably no need to invent role names for the Student and Course ends of the association, because they would not add significantly to the clarity of the abstraction of which this association is a part.

Multiplicity

For a given association type X between classes A and B, the term **multiplicity** refers to the number of objects of type A that may be associated with a given instance of type B. For example, a Student attends multiple Courses, but a Student has only one Professor in the role of advisor.

There are three basic categories of multiplicity:

One-to-one (1:1)

Exactly one instance of class A is related to exactly one instance of class B, no fewer, no more, and vice versa. For example:

❑ A Student has exactly one Transcript, and a Transcript belongs to exactly one Student.

❑ A Professor chairs exactly one Department, and a Department has exactly one Professor in the role of chairperson.

We can further constrain an association by stating whether the participation of the class at either end is optional or mandatory. For example, we can change the preceding association to read:

❑ A Professor *optionally* chairs exactly one Department, and it is *mandatory* that a Department has exactly one Professor in the role of chairperson.

This revised version of the association is a more realistic portrayal of real-world circumstances than the previous version because, while every department in a university typically does indeed have a chairperson, not every professor is a chairperson of a department – there aren't enough departments to go around! However, it is true that, *if* a professor happens to be a chairperson of a department, then they are chairperson of only *one* department.

One-to-many (1:m)

For a given single instance of class A, there can be many instances of class B related to it in a particular fashion; but, from the perspective of an object of type B, there can only be one instance of class A that is so related. For example:

❑ A Department employs many Professors, but a Professor (usually) works for exactly one Department.

❑ A Professor advises many Students, but a given Student has exactly one Professor as an advisor.

Note that 'many' in this case can be interpreted as either 'zero or more (optional)' or as 'one or more (mandatory)'. To be a bit more specific, we can refine the previous one-to-many associations as follows:

❑ A Department employs **one or more** ('many'; *mandatory*) Professors, but a Professor (usually) works for exactly one Department.

❑ A Professor advises **zero or more** ('many'; *optional*) Students, but a given Student has exactly one Professor as an advisor.

In addition, as with one-to-one relationships, the 'one' end of a one-to-many association may also be designated as mandatory or as optional. We may, for example, wish to 'fine tune' the previous association as follows:

❑ A Professor advises many (zero or more; *optional*) students, but a given Student may **optionally** have at most one advisor

if we are modeling a university setting in which students are not required to select an advisor.

Many-to-many (m:m)

For a given single instance of class A, there can be many instances of class B related to it, and vice versa. For example:

❑ A Student enrolls in many Courses, and a Course has many Students enrolled in it.

❑ A given Course can have many prerequisite Courses, and a given Course can in turn be a prerequisite for many other Courses. (This is an example of a many-to-many reflexive association.)

As with one-to-many associations, 'many' can be interpreted as *zero* or more (*optional*) or as *one* or more (*mandatory*); for example,

❑ A Student enrolls in **zero or more** (many; *optional*) Courses, and a Course has **one or more** (many; *mandatory*) Students enrolled in it.

Of course, the validity of a particular association – the classes that are involved, its multiplicity, and the optional or mandatory nature of participation in the association – is wholly dependent on the real-world circumstances being modeled. If you were modeling a university in which departments could have more than one chairperson, or where students could have more than one advisor, your choice of multiplicities would differ from those used in our examples above.

Multiplicity and Links

Note that the concept of multiplicity pertains to associations, but not to links. **Links always exist in pairwise fashion between two objects (or, in rare cases, between an object and itself).** Therefore, multiplicity in essence defines how many links of a certain association type can originate from a given object. This is best illustrated with an example.

Consider once again the many-to-many association:

'A Student enrolls in zero or more Courses, and a Course has one or more Students enrolled in it.'

A *specific* Student object X can have zero, one, or more *links* to Course objects, but any *one* of those links is between exactly *two* objects – Student X and a single Course object. In the diagram shown below, for example:

❑ Student X has one link (to Course A).

❑ Student Y has four links (to Courses A, B, C, and D).

❑ Student Z has no links to any Course objects whatsoever (Z is taking the semester off!).

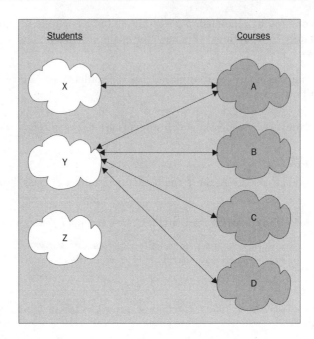

Conversely, a *specific* `Course` object A must have one or more links to `Student` objects to satisfy the mandatory nature and multiplicity of the association, but again, any *one* of those links is between exactly *two* objects -- Course A and a single `Student` object. In the diagram shown above, for example:

- ❑ `Course` A has two links (to `Students` X and Y).
- ❑ `Courses` B, C, and D each have one link (to the same `Student`, Y).

Note, however, that once again every link is between precisely two objects: a Student and a Course. This example scenario does indeed uphold the many-to-many 'is enrolled in' association between Student and Course; it is but one of an infinite number of possible scenarios that may exist between the classes in question.

Just to make sure that this concept is clear, let's look at another example, this time using the one-to-one association

'A Professor *optionally* chairs exactly one Department, and it is *mandatory* that a Department has exactly one Professor in the role of chairman.'

In the following diagram,

- ❑ Professor objects 1 and 4 each have one link, to Department objects A and B, respectively.
- ❑ Professor objects 2 and 3 have no such links.

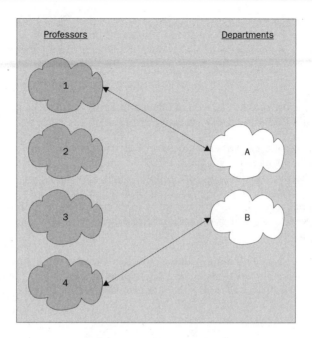

Moreover, from the Department objects' perspective, each Department does indeed have exactly one link to a Professor. Therefore, this example upholds the one-to-one 'chairs' association between Professor and Department, while further illustrating the optional nature of the Professor class's participation in such links. Again, it is but one of an infinite number of possible scenarios that may exist between the classes in question.

Aggregation

Aggregation is a special form of association, casually referred to alternatively as the 'contains', 'is composed of', 'is comprised of', 'is part of', or 'consists of' relationship. Like an association, an aggregation is used to represent a relationship between two classes A and B. But, with an aggregation, we are representing more than mere relationship: we are stating that an object belonging to a class A, known as an **aggregate class**, is composed of, or contains, **component objects** belonging to a class B.

Many authors also refer to aggregation as the 'has a' relationship, but I disagree with the latter, as it doesn't really convey composition or containment. It can be said that 'a Student has a Transcript', for example, but the Student doesn't 'contain' the Transcript.

For example, a car is composed of an engine, a transmission, four wheels, etc., so if Car, Engine, Transmission, and Wheel were all classes, then we could form the following aggregations:

- ❑ A Car *contains* an Engine.
- ❑ A Car *contains* a Transmission.
- ❑ A Car *is composed of* many (in this case, four) Wheels.

Or, as an example related to the SRS, we can say that:

❑ A University *is composed of* many Schools (the School of Engineering; the School of Law; etc.).

❑ A School *is composed of* many Departments.

One would not typically say, however, that a Department is *composed of* many Professors; instead, we'd probably state that a Department *employs* many Professors.

Note that these aggregation statements appear awfully similar to associations, where the name of the association just so happens to be 'is composed of' or 'contains'. That's because an aggregation *is* an association! So, why the fuss over trying to differentiate between aggregation and association? Do we even need to recognize that there is such a thing as an aggregation? It turns out that there are some subtle differences between aggregation and association that affect how an abstraction is rendered in code. Therefore, we'll defer further discussion of aggregation for now, but will return to discuss these subtleties in Chapter 14.

For now, use this simple rule of thumb: when you detect a relationship between two classes A and B, and the name you are inclined to give that association implies containment – 'contains', 'is composed of', 'is comprised of', 'consists of', and so forth – then it's probably really an aggregation that you are dealing with.

Inheritance

Let's assume that we have accurately and thoroughly modeled all of the essential features of students via our Student class, and that we have actually programmed the class in Java (as we'll learn to do in Part 3). A simplified version of the Student class is shown below:

```java
class Student {
  private String name;
  private String studentId;
  // etc.

  public String getName() {
    return name;
  }

  public void setName(String newName) {
    name = newName;
  }

  public String getStudentId() {
    return studentId;
  }

  public void setStudentId(String newId) {
    studentId = newId;
  }
  // etc.
}
```

In fact, let's further assume that our Student class code has been rigorously tested, found to be bug free, and is actually being used in a number of applications: our Student Registration System, for example, as well as perhaps a student billing system and an alumni relations system for the same university.

A new requirement has just arisen for modeling graduate students as a special type of student. As it turns out, the only features of a graduate student that we need to track above and beyond those that we've already modeled for a 'generic' student are:

❑ What undergraduate degree the student previously received before entering their graduate program of study.

❑ What institution they received the undergraduate degree from.

All of the other features necessary to describe a graduate student – attributes `name`, `studentId`, and so forth, along with all of the methods to manipulate these – are the same as those that we've already programmed for the `Student` class, because a graduate student *is* a student, after all.

How might we approach this new requirement for a `GraduateStudent` class? If we weren't well versed in object-oriented concepts, we might try one of the following approaches.

❑ Approach #1: We could add attributes to reflect undergraduate degree information to our definition of a `Student`, along with 'get' and 'set' methods to manipulate these, and simply leave these attributes empty when they are non-applicable: that is, for an undergraduate student who had not yet graduated.

```
class Student {
  private String name;
  private String studentId;
  private String undergraduateDegree;
  private String undergraduateInstitution;
  // etc.
```

Then, to keep track of whether these attributes were supposed to contain values or not for a given `Student` object, we'd probably also want to add a `boolean` attribute to note whether a particular student is a graduate student:

```
class Student {
  private String name;
  private String studentId;
  private String undergraduateDegree;
  private String undergraduateInstitution;
  boolean isGraduateStudent;
  // etc.
```

In any new methods that we subsequently write for this class, we'll have to take the value of this `boolean` attribute into account:

```
public void displayAllAttributes() {
  System.out.println(name);
  System.out.println(studentId);

  // If a particular student is NOT a graduate student, then the values
  // of the attributes 'undergraduateDegree' and
  // 'undergraduateInstitution' would be undefined, and so we would
  // only wish to print them if we are dealing with a graduate student.
  if (isGraduateStudent) System.out.println(undergraduateDegree);
  if (isGraduateStudent) System.out.println(undergraduateInstitution);
  // etc.
}
```

This results in convoluted code, which is difficult to debug and maintain.

❑   Approach #2: We could instead create a new GraduateStudent class by (a) making a duplicate copy of the Student class, (b) renaming the copy to be the GraduateStudent class, and (c) adding the extra features required of a Graduate Student to the copy.

```
class Student {
  // Attributes.

  private String name;
  private String studentId;
  private String birthdate;
  // etc.




  // Methods.

  public String getName() {
    return name;
  }

  public void setName(String n) {
    name = n;
  }

  // etc.
```

```
class GraduateStudent {
  // Student attributes DUPLICATED!

  private String name;
  private String studentId;
  private String birthdate;
  // etc.

  // Add the two new attributes.
  private String undergraduateDegree;
  private String
          undergraduateInstitution;


  // Student methods DUPLICATED!

  public String getName() {
    return name;
  }

  public void setName(String n) {
    name = n;
  }

  // etc.

  // Add get/set methods for the two
  // new attributes.
  // details omitted ...
```

This would be awfully inefficient, since we'd then have much of the same code in two places, and if we wanted to change how a particular method worked or how an attribute was defined later on – say, a change of the type of the 'birthdate' attribute from String to Date, with a corresponding change to the 'get' and 'set' methods for that attribute – then we'd have to make the same changes in both classes.

Strictly speaking, either of the above two approaches would work, but the inherent redundancy in the code would make the application difficult to maintain. In addition, where these approaches both really break down is when we have to add a third, or a fourth, or a fifth type of 'special' student. For example, consider how complicated the displayAllAttributes() method introduced in Approach #1 would become if we wanted to use it to represent a third type of student: namely, continuing education students, who do not seek a degree, but rather are just taking courses for continuing professional enrichment.

❏ We'd most likely need to add yet another `boolean` flag to keep track of whether or not a degree was being sought:

```
class Student {
    private String name;
    private String studentId;
    private String undergraduateDegree;
    private String undergraduateInstitution;
    private String degreeSought;
    boolean isGraduateStudent;
    boolean seekingDegree;
    // etc.
```

❏ We'd also have to now take the value of this `boolean` attribute into account in the `displayAllAttributes()` method:

```
public void displayAllAttributes() {
    System.out.println(name);
    System.out.println(studentId);

    if (isGraduateStudent) System.out.println(undergraduateDegree);
    if (isGraduateStudent) System.out.println(undergraduateInstitution);

    // If a particular student is NOT seeking a degree, then the values
    // of the attribute 'degreeSought' would be undefined, and so we
    // would only wish to print them if we are dealing with a degree-
    // seeking student.
    if (seekingDegree) System.out.println(degreeSought);
    else System.out.println("NONE");

    // etc.
}
```

This *worsens* the complexity issue!

We've had to introduce a lot of complexity in the logic of this one method to handle the various types of student; think of how much more 'spaghetti-like' the code might become if we had *dozens* of different student types to accommodate! Unfortunately, with non-OO languages, these convoluted approaches would typically be our only options for handling the requirement for a new type of object. It's no wonder that applications become so complicated and expensive to maintain as requirements inevitably evolve over time!

Fortunately, we do have an Alternative #3: with an object-oriented programming language, we can solve this problem by taking advantage of **inheritance**, a powerful mechanism for defining a new class by stating only the differences (in terms of features) between the new class and another class that we've already established. By use of the Java reserved word 'extends', we could therefore define a `Graduate Student` as a special type of `Student`, having two extra attributes – `undergraduateDegree` and `undergraduateInstitution` – that 'generic' `Students` do not have a need for, as shown on the following page:

```
class GraduateStudent extends Student {
  // Declare two new attributes above and beyond
  // what the Student class declares ...

  private String undergraduateDegree;
  private String undergraduateInstitution;

  // ... and a pair of accessor/modifier methods
  // for each of the new attributes ...

  public String getUndergraduateDegree() {
    return undergraduateDegree;
  }

  public void setUndergraduateDegree(String u) {
    undergraduateDegree = u;
  }

  public String getUndergraduateInstitution() {
    return undergraduateInstitution;
  }

  public void setUndergraduateInstitution(String u) {
    undergraduateInstitution = u;
  }
}
```

That's all we need to declare in our new GraduateStudent class: two attributes plus their get/set methods! There is no need to duplicate any of the attributes or methods of the Student class, because we are automatically inheriting these. It is as if we had 'plagiarized' the code for these attributes and methods from the Student class, and inserted it into GraduateStudent, but without the fuss of actually having done so.

When we take advantage of inheritance, the original class that we are starting from – Student, in this case – may be referred to as either the **base class**, **parent class**, **superclass**, or **supertype**; all of these terms are essentially interchangeable. The new class – GraduateStudent – may be referred to alternatively as either a **subclass** of Student, or as a **derived class**, or as a **subtype**.

> *Actually, the term 'parent class' has a slightly different connotation than the rest of the terms, which we'll explain when we talk about **class hierarchies** later in this chapter.*

Inheritance is often referred to as the 'is a' relationship between two classes, because if a class B (GraduateStudent) is derived from a class A (Student), then B truly **is a** special case of A. Anything that we can say about a superclass must also be true about all of its subclasses; that is,

- ❑ A Student attends classes, and so a GraduateStudent attends classes.

- ❑ A Student has an advisor, and so a GraduateStudent has an advisor.

- ❑ A Student pursues a degree, and so a GraduateStudent pursues a degree.

In fact, an 'acid test' for legitimate use of inheritance is as follows: if there is something that can be said about a superclass A that cannot be said about a proposed subclass B, then B really isn't a valid subclass of A.

Note, however, that the converse is not true: because a subclass is a special case of its parent class, it is possible to say things about the subclass that cannot be said about the parent class; for example,

❑ A GraduateStudent has already attended an undergraduate institution, whereas a 'generic' Student may *not* have done so.

❑ A GraduateStudent has already received an undergraduate degree, whereas a 'generic' Student may *not* have done so.

Because subclasses are special cases of their parent classes, the term **specialization** is used to refer to the process of deriving one class from another via inheritance. **Generalization**, on the other hand, is a term used to refer to the opposite process: namely, recognizing the common features of several existing classes and creating a new, common superclass for them all. Let's say we now wish to create the Professor class. Students and Professors have some features in common– name, birthdate, etc., and the methods that manipulate these. Yet, they each have unique features, as well; the Professor class might require the attributes title (a String) and worksFor (declared to be a reference to a Department), while the Student class's studentID, degreeSought, and majorField attributes are irrelevant for a Professor. Because each class has attributes that the other would find useless, neither class can be derived as a subclass from the other. Nonetheless, to duplicate their shared attribute declarations and method code in two places would be horribly inefficient. In such a circumstance, we may want to invent a new superclass called Person, consolidate the attributes and methods common to both Students and Professors in that class, and then have Student and Professor inherit these common features from Person. The resultant code in this situation appears below.

```
// Defining the superclass:
class Person {
  // Attributes common to Students and Professors.
  private String name;       // See note about use of 'private' visibility
  private String address;    // with inheritance after this code example.
  private String birthdate;

  public void setName(String newName) {
    name = newName;
  }

  public String getName() {
    return name;
  }
  // etc. for the other 'get' and 'set' methods.
}

// Creating one subclass of Person ...
class Student extends Person {
  // Attributes specific only to a Student.
  private String studentId;
  private String majorField;
  private String degreeSought;

  public void setStudentId(String newId) {
    studentId = newId;
  }
```

```
      public String getStudentId() {
        return studentId;
      }

      // etc. for the other 'get' and 'set' methods associated with
      // attributes majorField and degreeSought.
    }

    // ... and another subclass of Person!
    class Professor extends Person {
      // Attributes specific only to a Professor.
      private String title;
      private Department worksFor;

      public void setTitle(String newTitle) {
        title = newTitle;
      }

      public String getTitle() {
        return title;
      }

      // etc. for the other 'get' and 'set' methods associated with attribute
      // worksFor.
    }
```

We mentioned in Chapter 4 that there is a third type of visibility in Java known as 'protected' visibility. We'll learn in Chapter 13 that there are a few extra complexities about inheriting private features which we are temporarily 'glossing over', and how the protected visibility type comes into play. However, we haven't covered enough ground yet to do justice to such a discussion.

The Benefits of Inheritance

Inheritance is perhaps one of the most powerful and unique aspects of an OO programming language because:

❑ **Derived classes are much more succinct than they would be without inheritance**. Derived classes only contain the 'essence' of what makes them different from their ancestor class(es). We know from looking at the GraduateStudent class definition, for example, that a graduate student is 'a student who already holds an undergraduate degree from an educational institution'. As a result, the total body of code for a given application is significantly reduced as compared with the traditional non-OO approach to developing the same application.

❑ **Through inheritance, we can reuse and extend code that has already been thoroughly tested without modifying it.** As we saw, we were able to invent a new class – GraduateStudent – without disturbing the Student class code in any way. So, we can rest assured that any client code that relies on instantiating Student objects and passing messages to them will be unaffected by the creation of subclass GraduateStudent, and thus we avoid having to retest huge portions of our existing application. (Had we used a non-OO approach of 'tinkering' with the Student class code to try to accommodate graduate student attributes, we would have had to retest our entire existing application to make sure that nothing had 'broken'!)

❑ **Best of all, you can derive a new subclass from an existing class even if you don't own the source code for the latter!** As long as you have the compiled version of a class, the inheritance mechanism works just fine; you don't need the original source code of a class in order to extend it. This is one of the significant ways to achieve productivity with an object-oriented language: find a built-in class that does much of what you need, and create a subclass of that class, adding just those features that you need for your own purposes; or buy a third party library of classes written by someone else, and do the same.

❑ Finally, as we saw in Chapter 2, **classification is the natural way that humans organize information**; so, it only makes sense that we'd organize our software along the same lines, making it much more intuitive and hence easier to maintain and extend.

Class Hierarchy

Over time, we build up an inverted tree of classes that are interrelated through inheritance; such a tree is called a **class hierarchy**. One class hierarchy example is shown below. Note that arrows are used to point upward from each subclass to its superclass.

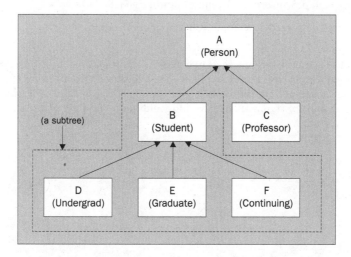

We refer to each class as a **node** in the hierarchy. Any given class in the hierarchy is said to be derived (directly or indirectly) from all of the **ancestor classes** above it in the hierarchy. The ancestor who is *immediately* above a class is considered its **parent class**. Conversely, all classes below a given class in the hierarchy are said to be its **descendant classes**. The class that sits at the top of the hierarchy is referred to as the **root class**. A **terminal class**, or **leaf node**, is one that has no subclasses. A **base class** is one that sits at the highest point in a tree or **subtree** of interest. Two classes that sit side by side in a hierarchy, and which descend from the same immediate parent(s), are known as **siblings**.

Applying this terminology to the example hierarchy above:

❑ Class A (Person) is the root class of the entire hierarchy.

❑ Classes B, C, D, E, and F are all said to be derived from class A, and are thus descendants of A.

❑ Classes D, E, and F can be said to be derived from class B.

- Classes D, E, and F are siblings; so are classes B and C.
- Class D thus has two ancestor classes, A and B.
- Class B (Student) is the base class of the subtree that is surrounded by a dotted line in the figure above.
- Classes C, D, E, and F are terminal classes, in that they don't have any classes derived from them (as of yet, at any rate).

In the Java language, a built-in class called Object *serves as the root class for all other classes, both user defined as well as those built into the language. We'll talk about the* Object *class in more depth in Part 3 of the book.*

As with any hierarchy, this one may evolve over time:

- It may widen with the addition of new siblings/branches in the tree.
- It may expand downward as a result of future specialization.
- It may expand upward as a result of future generalization.

Such changes to the hierarchy are made as new requirements emerge, or as our understanding of the existing requirements improves. For example, we may determine the need for MastersStudent and PhDStudent classes (as specializations of GraduateStudent) or of an Administrator class as a sibling to Student and Professor. This would yield the revised hierarchy shown below:

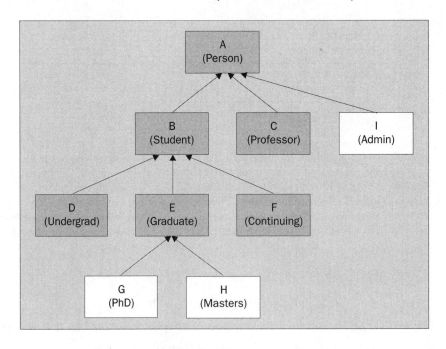

Is Inheritance Really a Relationship?

Association, aggregation, and inheritance are all said to be relationships between classes. Where inheritance differs from association and aggregation is at the object level.

As we have seen earlier in this chapter, association (and aggregation, as a special form of association) can be said to relate individual objects, in the sense that two different objects are linked to one another by virtue of the existence of an association between their respective classes. Inheritance, on the other hand, is a way of describing the properties of a single object. With inheritance, an object is simultaneously an instance of a (sub)class and all of its superclasses: a GraduateStudent is a Student that is a Person, all wrapped into one!

So, in looking once again at the hierarchy above, we see that:

- *All* classes in the hierarchy – class A (Person) as well as all of its descendants B through I – may be thought of as producing `Person` objects.

- Class B (Student), along with its descendants D through H, may all be thought of as producing `Student` objects.

This notion of an object having 'multiple identities' is a significant one that we'll revisit again and again throughout the book.

'Ripple Effects'

Once a class hierarchy is established and an application has been coded, changes to non-leaf classes (i.e., those classes which have descendants) will have 'ripple effects' down the hierarchy. For example, if after we have established the GraduateStudent class we go back and add a `minorField` attribute to the Student class, then GraduateStudent will automatically inherit this new attribute. Perhaps this is what we want; on the other hand, we may not have anticipated the derivation of a GraduateStudent class when we first conceived of Student, and so this may *not* be what we want!

As the developer of the Student class, it would be ideal if we could speak with the developers of all derived classes – GraduateStudent, MastersStudent, and PhDStudent – to obtain their approval for any proposed changes to Student. But, this isn't an ideal world, and often we may not even know that our class has been extended if, for example, our code is being distributed and reused on other projects or is being sold to clients. This points out a general rule of thumb:

Whenever possible, avoid having to add features to non-leaf nodes once they have been established in code in an application.

This is easier said than done! However, it reinforces the importance of spending as much time as possible on requirements analysis before diving into the coding stage of an application development project. This won't prevent new requirements from emerging over time, but we should avoid oversights regarding the current requirements.

Rules for Deriving Classes: The 'Do's'

When deriving a new subclass, we can do several things to specialize the base class that we are starting out with.

❑ We may **extend** the base class by **adding features**. In our GraduateStudent example, we added six features: two attributes – undergraduateDegree and undergraduateInstitution – and four methods/services – getUndergraduateDegree(), setUndergraduateDegree(), getUndergraduateInstitution(), and setUndergraduateInstitution().

❑ We may **specialize** the way that a subclass performs one or more of the **services** inherited from its parent class. For example, when a 'generic' student enrolls for a course, the student may first need to ensure that:

  ❑ He or she has taken the necessary prerequisite courses.

  ❑ The course is required for the degree that the student is seeking.

When a *graduate* student enrolls for a course, on the other hand, they may need to do both of these things as well as to:

  ❑ Ensure that their graduate committee feels that the course is appropriate.

Specializing the way that a subclass performs a service – that is, how it responds to a given message – as compared with the way that its parent class would have responded to the same message, is accomplished via a technique known as **overriding**.

Overriding

Overriding involves 'rewiring' how a method works internally, without changing the interface to/signature of that method. For example, let's say that we had defined a print() method for the Student class to print out all of a student's attribute values:

```
class Student {
  // Attributes.
  private String name;
  private String studentId;
  private String majorField;
  private double gpa;
  // etc.

  void print() {
    // We print out all the attributes that the Student class
    // knows about.
    System.out.println("Student Name:  " + name + "\n" +
                       "Student No.:   " + studentId + "\n" +
                       "Major Field:   " + majorField + "\n" +
                       "GPA:   " + gpa);
  }
}
```

By virtue of inheritance, all of the subclasses of Student will inherit this method. However, there is a problem: we added two new attributes to the GraduateStudent subclass – undergraduateDegree and undergraduateInstitution. If we take the 'lazy' approach of just letting GraduateStudent inherit the print() method of Student as is, then whenever we invoke the print() method for a GraduateStudent, all that will be printed are the values of the four attributes inherited from Student – name, studentId, major, and gpa – because these are the only attributes that the print() method has been explicitly programmed to print the values of. Ideally, we would like the print() method, when invoked for a GraduateStudent, to print these same four attributes *plus* the two additional attributes of undergraduateDegree and undergraduateInstitution.

With an object-oriented language, we are able to override, or replace, the Student version of the print() method that the GraduateStudent class has inherited by programming a new method for GraduateStudent with the exact same signature – void print() – as follows:

```
class GraduateStudent extends Student {
    String undergraduateDegree;
    String undergraduateInstitution;

    void print() {
        // We print the values of all the attributes that the
        // GraduateStudent class knows about:  namely, those that it
        // inherited from Student plus those that it explicitly declares.
        System.out.println("Student Name:  " + name + "\n" +
                        "Student No.:  " + studentId + "\n" +
                        "Major Field:  " + majorField + "\n" +
                        "GPA:  " + gpa + "\n" +
                        "Undergrad. Deg.:  " + undergraduateDegree + "\n" +
                        "Undergrad. Inst.:  " + undergraduateInstitution);
    }
}
```

The GraduateStudent class's version of print() thus overrides, or replaces, the version that would otherwise have been inherited from the Student class.

The above example is less than ideal because the first four lines of the print() method of GraduateStudent duplicate the code from the Student class's version of print(). You have probably started to sense that redundancy in an application is to be avoided, because redundant code represents a maintenance nightmare: when we have to change code in one place in an application, we don't want to have to remember to change it in countless other places or, worse yet, forget to do so, and wind up with inconsistency in our logic. We like to avoid code duplication and encourage code reuse in an application whenever possible, so our print() method for the GraduateStudent class would actually be written as follows:

```
class GraduateStudent extends Student {
    // details omitted ...

    void print() {
        // Reuse code by performing the print() method defined by the Student
        // superclass ...
        super.print();

        // ... and then go on to print this subclass's specific attributes.
        System.out.println("Undergrad. Deg.:  " + undergraduateDegree + "\n" +
                        "Undergrad. Inst.:  " + undergraduateInstitution);
    }
}
```

131

We use a special Java reserved word, super, as the prefix to a message:

    super.*methodname*(*arguments*);

when we wish to invoke the version of method *methodName* that was defined by a parent class.

Sometimes, in a complex inheritance hierarchy, we have occasion to override a method multiple times. In the hierarchy shown below,

- Root class A (Person) declares a method with signature

    ```
    public void print();
    ```

    that prints out all of the attributes declared for the Person class.

- Subclass B (Student) overrides this method, changing the internal logic of the method body to print not only the attributes inherited from Person but also those that were added by the Student class itself.

- Subclass E (GraduateStudent) overrides this method again, to print not only the attributes inherited from Student (which include those inherited from Person), but also those that were added by the GraduateStudent class itself.

Note that, in all cases, the method signature *must* remain the same – public void print(); – for overriding to take place.

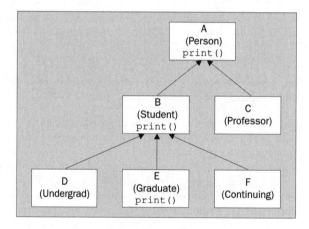

Under such circumstances, any class not specifically implementing/overriding a specific method signature itself will inherit the definition of that method from its most immediate ancestor. That is:

- Classes A, B, and E use their own forms of the print() method, specially tailored to suit their needs as discussed above.

- Class C inherits the print() method signature and body 'as is' from its nearest ancestor A; no overriding is taking place as far as C is concerned.

- Classes D and F inherit the print() method signature and body 'as-is' from their nearest ancestor B; no overriding is taking place as far as either D or F is concerned.

Rules for Deriving Classes: The 'Don'ts'

When deriving a new subclass, there are some things that you should <u>not</u> attempt to do. (And, as it turns out, OO languages will actually prevent you from successfully compiling programs that attempt to do most of these.)

- **You should not change the 'semantics' – i.e. the intention, or meaning – of a feature.** For example:

  - If the `print()` method of a base class such as `Student` is intended to display the values of all of an object's attributes on the computer screen, then the `print()` method of a subclass such as `GraduateStudent` should not, for example, be overridden so that it directs all of its output to a file instead.

  - If the `name` attribute of a base class such as `Person` is intended to store a person's name in 'last name, first name' order, then the `name` attribute of a subclass such as `Student` should be used in the same fashion.

- **You cannot 'override' an attribute.** Once an attribute is defined, its name and type cannot be changed in subclasses. Therefore, if the `Student` class defines the attribute `birthdate` to be of type `String`, for example, you cannot redefine the `birthdate` attribute to be of type `Date` in `GraduateStudent`.

- **You cannot physically eliminate features, nor should you effectively eliminate them by ignoring them.** To attempt to do so would break the spirit of the 'is a' hierarchy. By definition, inheritance requires that all features of all *ancestors* of a class 'A' must also apply to class A itself in order for A to truly be a proper subclass. If a `GraduateStudent` could eliminate the `degreeSought` attribute that it inherits from `Student`, for example, is a Graduate Student *really* a Student after all?

- **You cannot change the signature of a method** – i.e., the number and types of its arguments or its return type. For example, if the `print()` method inherited by the `Student` class from the `Person` class has the signature `void print();` where the return type of `void` signifies that the service will be carried out silently, without returning a result to the caller, then the `Student` class cannot try to change this method's signature to accept an argument, say, `void print(noOfCopies);`. To do so is to create a different method entirely, due to another (non-OO) language feature called **overloading**, discussed below.

Overloading

Overloading is a language mechanism supported by non-OO languages like C as well as by OO languages like Java and C++. Overloading is sometimes mistakenly confused with overriding because the two mechanisms have similar names, but in reality it is a wholly different concept.

Overloading allows two or more different methods belonging to the same class to have the *same* name as long as they have *different* argument signatures; neither the return type of the method nor the argument names enter into the picture with overloading. For example, the `Student` class may legitimately define the following five different `print()` method signatures:

```
void print(String fileName);  // a single argument
void print(int detailLevel);  // different argument type from above
void print(int detailLevel, String fileName);  // two arguments
int print(String reportTitle, int maxPages);  // two different argument types
boolean print();  // no arguments
```

and hence the `print()` method is said to be overloaded. Note that all five of the signatures differ in terms of their argument signatures:

❑   The first takes a single `String` as an argument.

❑   The second takes a single `int`.

❑   The third takes two arguments – an `int` and a `String`.

❑   The fourth takes two arguments – a `String` and an `int` (although these are the same argument types as in the previous signature, they are in a different order).

❑   The fifth takes no arguments at all.

So, all five of these represent valid, different methods, and all can coexist happily within the `Student` class without any complaints from the compiler! We can pick and choose among which of these five 'flavors' of `print()` method we'd like a `Student` object to perform based on what form of message we send to a `Student` object:

```
Student s = new Student();

// Calling the version that takes a single String argument.
s.print("output.rpt");

// Calling the version that takes a single int argument.
s.print(2);

// Calling the version that takes two arguments, an int and a String.
s.print(2, "output.rpt");

// etc.
```

The compiler is able to unambiguously match up which version of the `print()` method is being called in each instance based on the argument signatures of the respective messages.

This example also hints at why only the argument types and their order, and neither the *names* of the arguments nor the *return type* of the method, are relevant when determining whether a new method can be added: because these latter aspects of a method signature are not evident in a message. This is best illustrated with an example.

❑   We already know that we cannot, for example, introduce the following additional method as a sixth method of `Student`:

```
boolean print(int levelOfDetail);
```

because its argument signature – a single `int` – conflicts with the argument signature of existing method signature:

```
int print(int detailLevel);
```

in that they both take a single `int` argument, despite the fact that both the return type (`boolean` vs. `int`) and the argument names are different.

❑ Let's suppose for a moment that we *were* permitted to introduce the `boolean print(int levelOfDetail);` method signature as a sixth signature for the `Student` class. If the compiler were to then see a message in client code of the form:

```
s.print(3);
```

it would be unable to sort out which of these two methods was to be invoked, because all we see in a message like this is (a) the method name and (b) the argument type (an integer literal in this case).

So, to make life simple, the compiler prevents this type of ambiguity from arising by preventing classes from declaring like-named methods with identical argument signatures in the first place.

Note that there is no such thing as attribute overloading; that is, if a class tries to declare two attributes with the same name:

```
class SomeClass {
    private String foo;
    private int foo;
    // etc.
```

then the compiler will generate an error:

Duplicate variable declaration: int foo was String foo;

A Few Words About Multiple Inheritance

So far, the inheritance hierarchies we've looked at are known informally as 'single inheritance' hierarchies, because any particular class in the hierarchy may only have a single immediate ancestor (parent) class. In the hierarchy below, for example, classes marked B, C, and I all have the single parent class A; D, E, and F have the single parent B; and G and H have the single parent E.

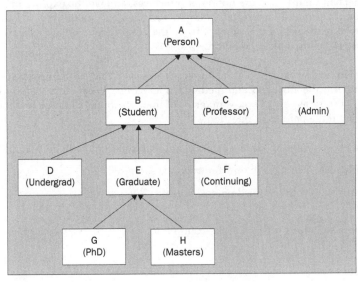

If you for some reason find yourself needing to meld together the characteristics of two different base classes to create a hybrid third class, **multiple inheritance** may seem be the answer. With multiple (as opposed to single) inheritance, any given class in a class hierarchy is permitted to have two or more classes as immediate ancestors. For example, we have a `Professor` class representing people who teach classes, and a `Student` class representing people who take classes. What might we do if we have a professor who wants to enroll in a class via the SRS? Or, a student – most likely a graduate student – who has been asked to teach an undergraduate level course? In order to accurately represent either of these two people as objects, we would need to be able to combine the features of the `Professor` class with those of the `Student` class – a hybrid '`ProfessorStudent`'. This might be portrayed in our class hierarchy as follows:

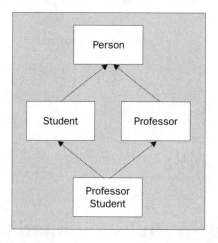

On the surface, this seems quite handy. However, there are many complications inherent with multiple inheritance; so many, in fact, that the Java language designers chose not to support multiple inheritance. Instead, they have provided an alternative mechanism for handling the requirement of creating an object with a 'split personality': that is, one that can behave like two or more different real-world entities. This mechanism involves the notion of **interfaces**, and will be explored in detail in Chapter 13. Therefore, if you are primarily interested in object concepts only as they pertain to the Java language, you may wish to skip the rest of this section. If, on the other hand, you are curious as to why multiple inheritance is so tricky, then please read on.

Here's the problem with what we've done above. We learned that, with inheritance, a subclass automatically inherits the attributes and methods of its parent. What about when we have two or more parents? If the parents have no overlaps in terms of their attribute names or method signatures, then we are fine. But, what if the parents in question:

❑   Have methods with the same signature, but with different code body implementations?

❑   Have identical attributes (name and type the same)?

❑   Have attributes with identical names, but with *different* types?

Let's explore these situations with a simple example.

First, say that we created a `Person` class that declares one attribute and one method, `getDescription()`, as shown below:

```
class Person {
  String name;

  public String getDescription() {
    return name;
    // e.g., "John Doe"
  }
}
```

Later on, we decide to specialize `Person` by creating two subclasses – `Professor` and `Student` – which each add a few attributes as well as overriding the `getDescription()` method to take advantage of their newly-added attributes, as follows:

```
class Student extends Person {
  // We add two attributes.
  String major;
  int id;  // a unique Student ID number

  // Override this method as inherited from Person.
  public String getDescription() {
    return name + " [" + major + "; " + id + "]";
    // e.g., "Mary Smith [Math; 10273]"
  }
}

class Professor extends Person {
  // We add two attributes; note that one has the same name, but a
  // different data type, as an attribute of Student.
  String title;
  String id;  // a unique Employee ID number

  // Override this method as inherited from Person.
  public String getDescription() {
    return name + " [" + title + "; " + id + "]";
    // e.g., "Harry Henderson [Chairman; A723]"
  }
}
```

Note that both subclasses happen to have added an attribute named 'id' but that in the case of the `Student` class, it is declared to be of type `int` and in `Professor`, of type `String`. Also, note that both classes have overridden the `getDescription()` method differently, to take advantage of each class's own unique attributes.

At some future point in the evolution of this system, we determine the need to represent a single object as both a `Student` and a `Professor` simultaneously, and so we create the hybrid subclass `ProfessorStudent` as a child of both `Student` and `Professor`. We don't particularly want to add any attributes or methods; we just want to meld together the characteristics of both parent classes, so we'd ideally like to declare `ProfessorStudent` as follows:

```
// * * * Important Note:  this is not permitted in java!!! * * *
class ProfessorStudent extends Professor and Student {
    // It's OK to leave a class body empty:  the class itself is not
    // really 'empty', because we are inheriting attributes and methods from
    // our parent(s).
}
```

But, we encounter several roadblocks to doing so.

❑ First, we have an attribute name 'clash'. If we were to simple-mindedly inherit all of the attributes of both `Professor` and `Student`, we'll wind up with:

Attribute	Notes
String name;	Inherited from `Student`, this in turn inherited it from `Person`.
String ssn;	Inherited from `Student`, this in turn inherited it from `Person`.
String major;	Inherited from `Student`.
int id;	Inherited from `Student`; this conflicts with the `String id` attribute inherited from `Professor` (the compiler won't allow both to coexist).
String name;	Inherited from `Professor`, which in turn inherited it from `Person`; a duplicate! the compiler won't allow this.
String ssn;	Inherited from `Professor`, which in turn inherited it from `Person`; another duplicate! the compiler won't allow this.
String title;	Inherited from `Professor`.
String id;	Inherited from `Professor`; this conflicts with the `int id` attribute inherited from `Student` (the compiler won't allow both to coexist).

Making a compiler intelligent enough to automatically resolve and eliminate true duplicates, such as the second copy of the `name` and `ssn` attributes, would not be too difficult a task; but, what about `int id` vs. `String id`? There is no way for the compiler to know which one to eliminate; and, indeed, we really shouldn't eliminate either, as they represent different information items. Our only choice would be to go back to either the `Student` class or the `Professor` class (or both) and rename their respective `id` attributes to be perhaps `studentId` and/or `employeeId`, to make it clear that the attributes represent different information items. Then, `ProfessorStudent` could inherit both without any problems. If we don't have control over the source code for at least one of these parent classes, however, then we are in trouble.

❑ Another problem we face is that the compiler will be confused as to which version of the `getDescription()` method we should inherit. Chances are that we'll want neither, because neither one takes full advantage of the other class's attributes; but even if we did wish to use one of the parent's versions of the method versus the other, we'd have to invent some way of informing the compiler of which one we wanted to inherit, or else we'd be forced to override `getDescription()` in the `ProfessorStudent` class.

This is just a simple example, but it nonetheless illustrates why multiple inheritance can be so cumbersome to take advantage of in an OO programming language.

Three Distinguishing Features of an Object-Oriented Programming Language, Take 2

We have now defined TWO of the three features required of a true OO language:

- ❑ **(Programmer creation of) Abstract Data Types (ADTs)**
- ❑ **Inheritance**
- ❑ Polymorphism

All that remains is to discuss **polymorphism**, one of the subjects of an upcoming chapter (Chapter 7, to be precise!). We're going to take a bit of a detour first, to discuss what we can do to gather up and organize groups of objects as we create them.

Summary

In this chapter, we've learned:

- ❑ That an association describes a relationship between classes – that is, a potential relationship between objects of two particular types/classes – whereas a link describes an actual relationship between two objects belonging to these classes.

- ❑ That we define the multiplicity of an association between classes X and Y in terms of how many objects of type X can be linked to a given object of type Y, and vice versa. Possible multiplicities are one-to-one (1:1), one-to-many (1:m), and many-to-many (m:m). In all of these cases, the involvement of the objects at either end of the relationship may be designated to be optional or mandatory.

- ❑ That an aggregation is a special type of association that implies containment.

- ❑ How to derive new classes based on existing classes through inheritance, and what the do's and don'ts are when deriving these new classes. Specifically, how we can extend a base class by adding features or specialize a base class by overriding behaviors.

- ❑ How class hierarchies develop over time, and what we can do to try to avoid 'ripple effects' to our application as the class hierarchy changes with evolving requirements.

- ❑ How overloading – a non-OO feature of programming languages – can be used to create multiple methods with the same name but with different argument signatures.

- ❑ Why multiple inheritances can be so troublesome to implement in an OO language.

Exercises

1. Given the following pairs of classes, what associations might exist between them from the perspective of the CRRS case study described in Appendix B?

   ❑ Employee – Conference Room

   ❑ Employee – Meeting

2. Go back to your solution for exercise No. 3 at the end of Chapter 2. For all of the classes you suggested, list the pairwise associations that you might envision occurring between them.

3. If the class `FeatureFilm` were defined to have the following method signatures:

```
public void update(Actor a, String title);
public void update(Actor a, Actor b, String title);
public void update(String topic, String title);
```

   which of the following additional signatures would be allowed by the compiler:

```
public boolean update(String category, String theater);
public boolean update(String title, Actor a);
public void update(Actor b, Actor a, String title);
public void update(Actor a, Actor b);
```

4. Given the following simplistic code, which illustrates overloading, overriding, and straight inheritance of methods:

```
class Vehicle {
  String name;

  public void fuel(String fuelType) {
    // details omitted ...
  }
  public boolean fuel(String fuelType, int amount) {
    // details omitted ...
  }
}


class Automobile extends Vehicle {
  public void fuel(String fuelType, String timeFueled) {
    // details omitted ...
  }
  public boolean fuel(String fuelType, int amount) {
    // ...
  }
}


class Truck extends Vehicle {
  public void fuel(String fuelType) {
    // ...
  }
}
```

```
class SportsCar extends Automobile {
  public void fuel(String fuelType) {
    // ...
  }
  public boolean fuel(String fuelType, String timeFueled) {
    // ...
  }
}


// Client code:

Truck t = new Truck();
SportsCar sc = new SportsCar();
```

How many different 'fuel' method signatures would each of the four classes recognize?

5. Given the following simplistic classes:

```
class FarmAnimal {
  String name;

  public void setName(String n) {
    name = n;
  }
  public void makeSound() {
    System.out.println(name + " makes a sound ...");
  }
}


class Cow extends FarmAnimal {
  public void makeSound() {
    System.out.println(name + " goes Moooooo ...");
  }
}


class Horse extends FarmAnimal {
  public void setName(String n) {
    name = n + " [a Horse]";
  }
}
```

what would be printed by the following client code?

```
Cow c = new Cow();
Horse h = new Horse();
c.setName("Elsie");
h.setName("Mr. Ed");
c.makeSound();
h.makeSound();
```

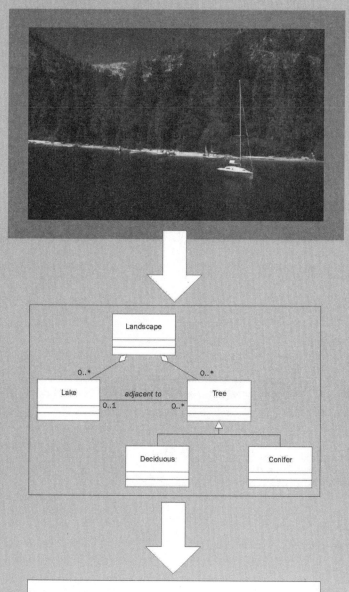

```java
public class Tree {
    protected Landscape landscape;
    protected Lake nextTo;

    public void setNextTo(Lake l) {
        nextTo = l;
    }
    public Lake getNextTo() {
        return nextTo;
    }

    public abstract Color getLeafColor();
}
```

Collections of Objects

We learned about the process of creating objects based on class definitions, a process known as instantiation, in Chapter 3. When we are only creating a few objects, we can afford to declare individualized reference variables for these objects: Students `s1`, `s2`, `s3`, perhaps, or Professors `profA`, `profB`, `profC`. But, at other times, individualized reference variables are impractical.

❑ Sometimes, there will be too many objects, as when creating `Course` objects to represent the hundreds of courses in a university's course catalog.

❑ Worse yet, we may not even *know* how many objects of a particular type there will be in advance. With our Student Registration System, for example, we may create a new `Student` object each time a new student logs on for the first time.

In this chapter, you will learn about:

❑ A special type of object called a **collection** that is used to hold and organize other objects.

❑ The properties and behaviors of some common collection types.

❑ How collections enable us to model very sophisticated real-world concepts or situations.

What are Collections?

We'd like a way to gather up objects as they are created so that we can manage them as a group and operate on them collectively, along with referring to them individually when necessary. For example:

❑ A `Professor` object may wish to step through all `Student` objects registered for a particular `Course` that the professor is teaching in order to compute their grades.

❑ The Student Registration System (SRS) application as a whole may need to step through all of the `Course` objects in the current schedule of classes to determine which of them do not yet have any students registered for them, possibly to cancel these courses.

We use a special type of object called a **collection** to group other objects. A collection object can hold/contain zero or more references to some other type of object. Think of a collection like an egg carton, and the objects it holds like the eggs!

Collections are implemented as objects; this implies that:

1. **Collections must be instantiated before they can first be used.** We cannot merely declare a collection:

```
Collection c;
```

because all this does is to tell the compiler that reference variable 'c' has the **potential** to be a reference to a Collection object. Until we 'hand' c a Collection object to refer to, c is said to have the value null. We have to take the distinct step of using the 'new' operator to actually create an empty Collection object in memory, as follows:

```
c = new CollectionType();
```

Think of the newly created Collection object as an **empty** egg carton, and the reference variable 'c' as the 'handle' that allows us to locate and access (reference) this 'egg carton' whenever we'd like.

Then, as we instantiate objects, we place **their** references into the various egg carton compartments.

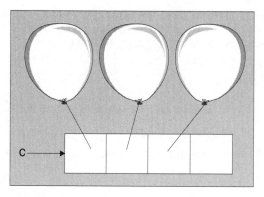

With certain OO languages – e.g. C++ – it is possible to actually stick objects as a whole into the collection;.

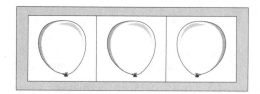

but in Java we always place references to objects in the collection

2. **Collections are defined by classes that in turn define methods for 'getting' and 'setting' their contents.** Here is a code snippet that illustrates the use of a collection in Java; we use a bit of pseudocode here because we don't wish to get into the 'nitty gritty' details of specific Java collection classes and their methods quite yet. We'll see a bit more detail later in this chapter, with a much more in-depth discussion of Java collection syntax in Chapter 13.

```
// Instantiate a collection object.
Collection x = new Collection();

// Create a few Student objects.
Student a = new Student();
Student b = new Student();
Student c = new Student();

// Store all three students in the collection by calling the appropriate
// method for adding objects to the collection ...
x.add(a);
x.add(b);
x.add(c);

// ... and then retrieve the first one.
x.retrieve(0); // we typically start counting at 0.
```

3. **By virtue of being objects, OO collections are encapsulated, and hence take full advantage of information hiding.** We don't need to know the private details of how object references are stored internally to a collection in order to use it properly; we only need to know a collection's public behaviors – its method signatures – in order to choose an appropriate collection type for a particular situation and to use it effectively.

*This is a tiny bit misleading: in the case of **huge** collections, it is helpful to know a little bit about the inner workings of various collection types so as to choose the one that is most efficient; we'll consider this matter further a bit later in this chapter.*

Virtually all collections, regardless of type and regardless of the programming language in which they are implemented, provide, at a minimum, methods for:

❏ Adding objects

❏ Removing objects

❏ Retrieving specific individual objects

❏ Iterating through the objects in some predetermined order

❏ Getting a count of the number of objects in the container

❏ Answering true/false question as to whether a particular object is in the container or not

*Throughout this chapter, we'll talk in short-hand terms about manipulating **objects** in collections, but please recall that, with Java, what we really mean is that we are manipulating object **references**.*

Arrays as Simple Collections

One simple type of collection that you may already be familiar with from your work with various programming languages is the **array**. We can think of an array as a series of compartments, with each compartment sized appropriately for whatever data type the array as a whole is intended to hold. Arrays typically hold items of like type: for example, int(eger)s, or char(acter)s, or, in an OO language, object references: Student objects, or Course objects, or Professor objects, etc.

Arrays are declared in Java in one of two ways:

❑ The official Java syntax for declaring that some variable x will serve as a reference to an array containing items of a particular data type is as follows:

```
datatype[] x;
```

e.g.

```
int[] x;
```

which is to be read 'int(eger) array x'.

❑ An alternative syntax, which is provided for backward compatibility for those folks who have programmed in C/C++, moves the square brackets to the end of the variable name:

```
datatype x[];
```

e.g.

```
int x[];
```

These two alternatives are equivalent; if possible, it's best to get accustomed to using the first syntax variation, as this is the newer syntax as introduced with Java.

Then, because Java arrays are objects, they must be instantiated using the new operator; we also specify how many items the array is going to hold, i.e. its size in terms of its number of compartments, when we first create the array. Here is a code snippet which illustrates the somewhat unusual syntax for constructing an array:

```
// Here, we are instantiating an array object that will be used to store 20
// int(eger) values, and are storing a 'handle' on the array object
// in reference variable x.
int[] x = new int[20];
```

This use of the new operator is unusual, in that we don't see a typical constructor call (with optional arguments being passed in via parentheses) following the new keyword the way we do when we are constructing other types of objects. Despite its unconventional appearance, however, this line of code is indeed instantiating a new Array object, just the same.

> *It turns out that there is another way to create an Array object in Java, but the code isn't 'pretty':*

```
Object x  = Array.newInstance(Class.forName("Integer"), 20);
```

> *To fully appreciate what this code is doing is beyond the scope of what we've learned about objects so far we'll revisit this code in Chapter 13, after we've learned quite a bit more about objects in general and the Java language in particular.*

Note that when we refer to individual items in an array based on their position, or **index**, relative to the beginning of the array, we start counting at 0. (As it turns out, the vast majority of collection types in Java as well as in other languages are **zero-based**.) So, the items stored in array int[] x above would be referenced as x[0], x[1], ..., x[19].

The contents of an array are initialized to their zero-equivalent values when the array is instantiated, so int[] x as declared above would be initialized to contain twenty zeroes (0's). Had we instead declared and constructed an array intended to hold references to objects, as in

```
Student[] studentBody = new Student[100];
```

then we'd wind up with an Array object containing 100 null values. If we think of an array as a simple type of collection, and we in turn think of a collection as an 'egg carton', then we've just created an empty egg carton with 100 egg compartments, but no 'eggs' (objects). To fill this Student array, we'd have to individually instantiate and store Student object references in the array, as follows:

```
studentBody[0] = new Student();
studentBody[1] = new Student();
// etc.
```

or:

```
Student s = new Student();
studentBody[0] = s;
// Reuse s!
s = new Student();
studentBody[1] = s;
```

In the latter example, note that we are 'recycling' the same reference variable, s, to create many different Student objects. This works because, after each instantiation, we store a handle on the newly created object in an array compartment, thus allowing s to let go of its 'handle' on that same object, as depicted below. This technique is used frequently, with **all** collection types, in virtually all OO programming languages.

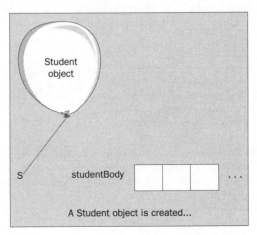

A Student object is created...

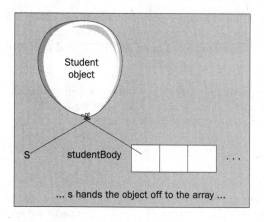
... s hands the object off to the array ...

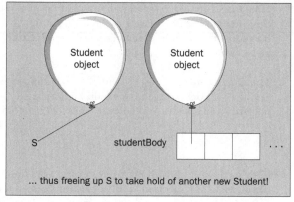
... thus freeing up S to take hold of another new Student!

When we've created an array to hold objects, as we did for the `studentBody` array above, then assuming we've populated the array with object references, an indexed reference to any populated compartment in the array may be thought of as an object reference, and can be used accordingly:

```
studentBody[0].getName();   // we're using dot notation to call a method on
                            // studentBody[0], the first Student object
                            // reference in the array.
```

The syntax of the message:

```
studentBody[0].getName();
```

may seem a bit peculiar at first, so let's study it a bit more carefully. Since `studentBody` is declared to be an array capable of holding `Student` object references, then '`studentBody[n]`' represents the contents of the nth compartment of the array – namely, a reference to a `Student` object! So, the 'dot' in the above message is separating an expression representing an object reference from the method call being made on that object, and is no different than any of the other 'dot notation' messages that we've seen up until now.

By using a collection such as an array, we don't have to invent a different variable name for each `Student` object, which means we can step through them all quite easily using a '`for`' loop. Here is the syntax for doing so with an array (we'll learn a more sophisticated way of stepping through collections in general in Chapter 13):

```
// Step through all 100 compartments of the array.
for (int i = 0; i <= 99; i++) {
  // Access the 'iᵗʰ' element of the array.
  System.out.println(studentBody[i].getName());
}
```

Note that we have to take care when stepping through an array to avoid 'landmines' due to empty compartments. That is, if we were executing the preceding '`for`' loop, but the array were not completely filled with `Student` objects, then our invocation of the `getName()` method would fail as soon as we hit the first empty compartment, because in essence we'd be trying to talk to an object that wasn't there! (We'll learn in Chapter 13 that this type of failure – namely, attempting to talk to a non-existent object – results in an **exception** being thrown.)

More Sophisticated Collection Types

In an OO language, there are typically many different types of collections available to us as programmers, arrays being perhaps the most primitive. There are several problems with using an array to hold a collection of objects:

❑ It is often hard for us to predict in advance the number of objects that a collection will need to hold – e.g. how many students are going to enroll this semester? However, arrays require that such a determination be made at the time they are first instantiated.

❑ Once sized, a 'classic' array cannot typically expand if you need it to hold more items than what it was originally declared to hold.

❑ We talked earlier about the 'landmine' issues inherent in arrays.

Fortunately, OO languages provide a wide variety of collection types besides arrays for us to choose from, each of which has its own unique properties and advantages.

The following are some basic collection types found in most OO languages; we use their 'generic' names here, but in Chapter 13 we'll illustrate some specific Java implementations of these collection types.

❑ **Ordered List:** An ordered list is similar to an array, in that items can be placed in the collection in a particular order and later retrieved in that same order. Specific objects can also be retrieved based on their position in the list; e.g. retrieve the 2nd item. One advantage of an ordered list over an array, however, is that its size does not have to be specified at the time that the collection object is first created; an ordered list will automatically grow in size as new items are added. (In fact, virtually all collections besides arrays have this advantage!)

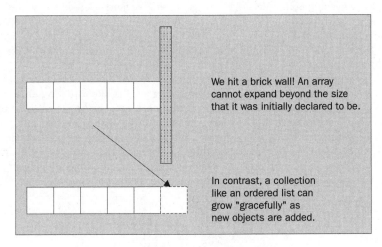

We hit a brick wall! An array cannot expand beyond the size that it was initially declared to be.

In contrast, a collection like an ordered list can grow "gracefully" as new objects are added.

By default, items are added at the end of an ordered list unless explicit instructions are given to insert a new item somewhere in the middle. When an item is removed from an ordered list, the 'hole' that would have been left behind is typically closed up:

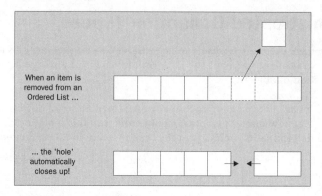

When an item is removed from an Ordered List ...

... the 'hole' automatically closes up!

This is actually true of most collection types other than arrays, and so we don't generally speaking encounter the 'landmine' problem with non-array collections.

An example of where we might use an ordered list in building our Student Registration System would be to manage a wait list for a course that had become full. Because the order with which Student objects are added to the list is preserved, we can be fair about selecting students from the wait list in first-come, first-served fashion should space later become available in the course.

❑ **Sorted Ordered List:** This is similar to an ordered list, except that when you add an object, the list automatically inserts the object at the appropriate location in the list to maintain some kind of sorted order instead of automatically adding the new object at the end of the list. With a sorted ordered list, you have to define on what basis the objects will be sorted: for example, you may wish to maintain a list of Course objects sorted by the value of each Course's courseNo attribute for purposes of displaying the SRS course catalog.

Note that you could accomplish the same goal using a plain ordered list, but then the burden of keeping things sorted properly is on you, the programmer, instead of on the collection object! That is, you'd have to step through the (unsorted) list, comparing the new item's value to the value of each object already in the list until you found the correct insertion point to preserve sorted order.

❑ **Set:** A set is an unordered collection, which means that there is no way to ask for a particular item by number once it has been inserted. Using a set is like throwing an assortment of differently colored marbles into a bag: we can reach into the bag to pull the marbles out one by one, but there is no rhyme or reason as to the order with which we pull them out. Similarly, with a set, we can step through the entire set of objects one-by-one to perform some operation on them; we just can't guarantee in what order the objects will be processed. We can also perform tests to determine whether a given specific object has been previously added to a set or not, just as we can answer the question 'Is the blue marble in the bag?'

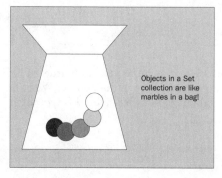

Objects in a Set collection are like marbles in a bag!

Note that duplicates are not allowed in a set. If we were to create a set of Student objects, and a particular Student object had already been placed in that set, then the same Student object could not be added to the same set a second time; the set would reject it. This is not true of collections in general: if we wanted to, we could add a reference to the same Student object to an ordered list, for example, multiple times.

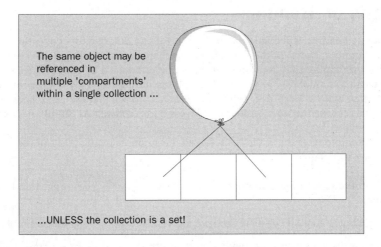

The same object may be referenced in multiple 'compartments' within a single collection ...

...UNLESS the collection is a set!

An example of where we might use sets in building our Student Registration System would be to group students according to the academic departments that they are majoring in. Then, if a particular course – say, Biology 216 – requires that a student be a Biology major in order to register, it would be a trivial matter to determine if a particular student is a member of the Biology Department set or not.

❑ **Dictionary:** A dictionary provides a means for storing each object reference along with a unique look-up key that can later be used to retrieve the object. The key is typically contrived based on one or more of the object's attribute values; for example, in our SRS, a Student object's ID number would make an excellent key, because it is inherently unique for each student. Items in a dictionary can then be quickly retrieved based on this key. Items can typically also be retrieved one by one in ascending key order.

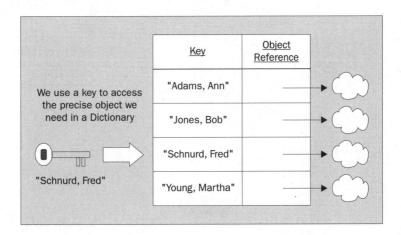

We use a key to access the precise object we need in a Dictionary

"Schnurd, Fred"

Key	Object Reference
"Adams, Ann"	
"Jones, Bob"	
"Schnurd, Fred"	
"Young, Martha"	

The SRS might use a dictionary, indexed on a unique combination of course number plus section number, to manage its course catalog. With so many courses to keep track of, being able to 'pluck' the appropriate `Course` object from a collection directly (instead of having to step through an ordered list one-by-one to find it) adds greatly to the efficiency of the application.

Collections of 'Handles'

As we mentioned earlier, when we talk about inserting an object into a collection, what we really mean more often than not (always, in the case of Java) is that we are inserting a reference to the object, not the object itself. This implies that the same object can be referenced by multiple collections simultaneously. Think of a person as an object, and his/her telephone number as a handle for reaching that person. Now, think of an address book as a collection: it is easy to see that the same person's phone number 'handle' can be recorded in many different address book 'collections' simultaneously.

Now, for an example relevant to the SRS. Given the students who are registered to attend a particular course, we may simultaneously maintain:

❑ An ordered list of these students for purposes of knowing who registered first for a follow-on course

❑ A dictionary that allows us to retrieve a given `Student` object based on his/her name

❑ Perhaps even a second SRS-wide dictionary that organizes *all* students at the university based on their student ID numbers

This is depicted conceptually in the figure below.

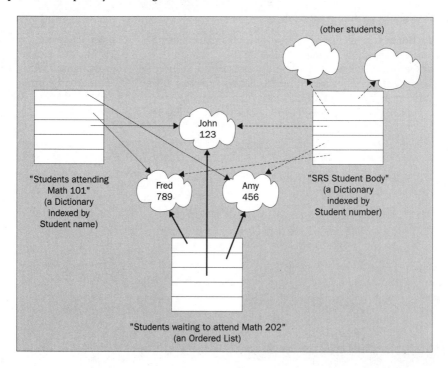

Inventing Your Own Collection Types

As mentioned earlier, different types of collections have different properties and behaviors. You must therefore familiarize yourself with the various built-in collection types available for your OO language of choice, and choose the one that is the most appropriate for what you need in a given situation. Or, if none of them suit you, invent your own! This is where we start to get a real sense of the power of an OO language: since we have the ability to invent our own abstract data types, we have free rein to define our own collection types, since these, after all, are merely classes.

There are several ways to create one's own collection type:

❏ **We can use the techniques that we learned in Chapter 5 to extend a built-in collection class**. In the following example, we extend the `Vector` class to create a collection class called `MyCollection`:

```
class MyCollection extends Vector {
  // We inherit all of the attributes and methods of a standard Vector
  // 'as-is', then add a few attributes and methods of our own.

  private String biggestItemInVector;
  public void sortIt() {
    // Logic required to sort the contents of the vector
    // (details omitted).
  }
}
```

This approach works well if you simply intend to add new features (attributes, methods), inheriting the methods and attributes of the parent class 'as is'. A problem arises with this approach, however, if you feel compelled to override any of the inherited methods in order to refine their behavior. To do so, you must be absolutely sure that you understand what the original methods were doing in great detail; this is not always practical.

```
class MyCollection extends Vector {
  private String biggestItemInVector;

  public void sortIt() {
    // Logic required to sort the contents of the vector
    // (details omitted).
  }

  // We're overriding an inherited method signature - we better be
  // darned sure we know what we're doing!
  public boolean add(Object o) {
    // GULP!  Do we know how the logic of the parent Vector
    // class's add() method works?
  }
}
```

❑ **We can create a brand new collection type from scratch.** This is typically quite a bit of work, although for certain simple collection types – say, a last-in, first-out stack, or a linked list – the programming involved isn't too onerous. However, most OO languages provide such a wide range of built-in collection types that it is difficult to think of a collection type that isn't already provided (this is certainly true for Java!).

❑ **We can create a 'wrapper' class that encapsulates one of the built-in collection types, to hide some of the details involved with manipulating the collection.** This is a nice compromise position, and we'll illustrate how one goes about doing this with a specific example.

Let's say we wanted to invent a new type of collection called an `EnrollmentCollection`, to be used by a `Course` object to manage all of its enrolled `Student` objects. We could take advantage of information hiding and encapsulation to 'hide' a standard container object – say, a Java `Vector`, which is Java's implementation of an ordered list collection – inside of our `EnrollmentCollection` class, as an attribute. We'd then provide:

❑ `enroll()` and `drop()` methods for adding or removing a `Student` from our `EnrollmentCollection`

❑ An `isEnrolled()` method, which will help us to determine if a particular `Student` object is already in the collection (we don't want the same `Student` to enroll twice in the same class)

❑ A `getTotalEnrollment()` method to determine how many students are enrolled at any given time

❑ A `getNthStudent()` method to allow us to pull a particular student from the collection

These methods' logic can be as sophisticated as we wish for it to be – the method bodies are ours to control! The following example uses heavy doses of pseudocode to give you a sense of what we might actually program these methods to do for us; you'll see plenty of real Java collection manipulation (`Vector`s in particular) in the SRS code examples in Part 3 of the book.

```
class EnrollmentCollection {
    // 'Hide' a standard Java collection object inside as a private attribute.
    // We'll be storing Student objects in this collection.
    private Vector students = new Vector();

    // Methods to add a student ...
    public boolean enroll(Student s) {
        // First, make sure that there is room in the class.
        if (total students exceeds course limit ) return false;

        // Next, make sure that this student isn't already enrolled
        // in this class.
        if (student is already enrolled ) return false;

        // Verify that the student in question has met
        // all necessary prerequisites.
        if (some prerequisite not satisfied ) return false;
```

```
        // If we made it to here, all is well!
        // Add the student to the Vector by calling the Vector class's method
        // for this purpose. (This is an example of delegation, a concept
        // that we discussed in Chapter 4.)
        students.add(s);
        return true;
    }

    // ... and to remove a student.
    public boolean unenroll(Student s) {
        // First make sure that the student in question
        // is actually enrolled.
        if (student is not enrolled ) return false;

        // Remove the student from the Vector by calling the Vector class's
        // method for this purpose.  (Another example of delegation.)
        students.remove(s);
        return true;
    }

    public int getTotalEnrollment() {
        // Access and return the size of the Vector.  (Delegation yet again!)
        return students.size();
    }
    public boolean isEnrolled(Student s) {
        // More delegation!
        if (students.contains(s)) return true;
        else return false;
    }

    public Student getNthStudent(int n) {
        // Details omitted.
    }
}
```

By taking advantage of information hiding to 'wrap' a standard collection type inside of one that we've invented, we've allowed for the flexibility to change the internal details of this implementation without disrupting the client code that takes advantage of this collection type. So, we may wish to switch from using a Vector to a different built-in (Java) collection type later on, and are free to do so, as long as we don't change the signatures of our existing public methods.

Now, how do we use this collection class that we've invented? Let's show it in action in the Course class.

```
class Course {
    // We declare an attribute to be a collection of type
    // EnrollmentCollection, and will use it to manage
    // all of the students who register for this course.
    private EnrollmentCollection enrolledStudents =
        new EnrollmentCollection();

    // Other simple attributes.
    String courseName;
    int credits;
    // etc.
```

```
    // details omitted ...

    public boolean enroll(Student s) {
      // All we have to do is to pass the Student reference
      // in to the collection's enroll method; the collection
      // does all of the hard work!  This is another example of
      // delegation.
      enrolledStudents.enroll(s);
    }

    public boolean unenroll(Student s) {
      // Ditto!
      enrolledStudents.unenroll(s);
    }

    // etc.
}
```

Collections as Method Return Types

Collections provide a way to overcome the limitation that we noted in Chapter 4 about methods only being able to return a single result. If we define a method as having a return type that is a collection type, we can hand back an arbitrary sized collection of object references to the client code that invokes the method. In the code snippet shown below for the Course class, we provide a getRegisteredStudents() method to enable client code to request a 'handle' on the entire collection of Student objects who have registered for a particular class:

```
class Course {
  private EnrollmentCollection enrolledStudents =
    new EnrollmentCollection();

  // other attribute/method details omitted ...

  // The following signature indicates that this method
  // returns a reference to an entire collection containing however
  // many students are registered for the course in question.
  EnrollmentCollection getRegisteredStudents() {
    return enrolledStudents;
  }
}
```

An example of how client code would then use such a method is as follows:

```
// Instantiate a course and several students.
Course c = new Course();
Student s1 = new Student();
Student s2 = new Student();
Student s3 = new Student();
```

```
// Enroll the students in the course.
c.enroll(s1);
c.enroll(s2);
c.enroll(s3);

// Now, ask the course to give us a handle on the collection of
// all of its registered students ...
EnrollmentCollection ec = c.getRegisteredStudents();

// ... and iterate through the collection, printing out a grade report for
// each Student.
// pseudocode
for (all Student objects in Collection ec) {
  Student s = ec.getNthStudent(i);
  s.printGradeReport();
}
```

Collections of Supertypes

We said earlier that arrays, as simple collections, contain items (either simple data types or objects) which are all of the same type: all int(egers), for example, or all (references to) Student objects. As it turns out, this is true of collections in general: we typically constrain them to contain similarly typed objects. However, the power of inheritance steps in to make collections quite versatile. It turns out that if we declare a collection to hold objects of a given supertype – e.g. Person – then we are free to insert into the collection objects explicitly declared to be of type Person or of *any* of the *subtypes* of Person – for example, UndergraduateStudent, GraduateStudent, and Professor. This is due to the 'is a' nature of inheritance: UndergraduateStudent, GraduateStudent, and Professor objects, as subclasses of Person, are simply special cases of Person objects. So, for example, our SRS could maintain a collection representing all users of the system – professors and students combined – as follows:

```
// Pseudocode 'snippet', taken perhaps from the main SRS driver program.

CollectionType srsUsers = new CollectionType();  // of Person objects

Professor p = new Professor();
UndergraduateStudent s1 = new UndergraduateStudent();
GraduateStudent s2 = new GraduateStudent();

// Add a mixture of professors and students in random order.
srsUsers.insert(s1);
srsUsers.insert(p);
srsUsers.insert(s2);
// etc.
```

As we'll see when we discuss Java collection types in more detail in Chapter 13, Java collections (other than Arrays) actually don't allow you to specify what type of object they will hold when you declare a collection, as illustrated below:

```
Vector v = new Vector();   // No type designated!
                           // Vectors hold generic Objects.
// versus
Student[] s = new Student[100];  // With arrays, we DO specify a
                                 // type (Student,in this case).
```

157

Most Java collections are automatically designed to hold objects of type `Object`, which as we learned in an earlier chapter is the superclass of all other classes in the Java language, user defined or otherwise. So, we can pretty much put whatever type of object we wish into a collection. But, it is still important that you, as the programmer, know what the intended supertype for a collection is going to be, so that you discipline yourself to only insert objects of the proper type in the collection. This will be important when you subsequently attempt to iterate through and process all of the objects in the collection: you'll need to know what general class of object they are, so that you'll know what methods they can be called upon to perform. We'll talk about this in more detail when we discuss **polymorphism** in Chapter 7.

Composite Classes, Revisited

You may recall that when we talked about the attributes of the `Student` class back in Chapter 3, we held off on assigning types to a few of these:

Attribute Name	Data Type
name	String
studentID	String
birthdate	Date
address	String
major	String
gpa	float
advisor	Professor
courseLoad	???
transcript	???

Armed with what we now know about collections, we can go back and assign types to attributes `courseLoad` and `transcript`.

The `courseLoad` attribute is meant to represent a list of all `Course` objects that the `Student` is presently enrolled in. So, it makes perfect sense that this attribute be declared to be simply a collection of `Course` objects!

The `transcript` attribute is a bit more challenging. What is a transcript, in real world terms? It's a list of all of the courses that a student has taken since he/she was first admitted to this school, along with the semester in which each course was taken and the letter grade that the student received for the course. If we think of each entry in this list as an object, we can define them via a `TranscriptEntry` class as follows:

```
class TranscriptEntry {
  private Course courseTaken;
  private String semesterTaken;  // e.g., "Spring 2000"
  private String gradeReceived;  // e.g., "B+"
```

```
    // Details omitted ...

    // Note how we 'talk to' the courseTaken object via its methods
    // to retrieve some of this information (delegation once again!).
    public void printTranscriptEntry() {
        // Reminder: \t is a tab character, \n is a newline.
        System.out.println(courseTaken.getCourseNo() + "\t" +
            courseTaken.getTitle() + "\t" +
            courseTaken.getCreditHours() + "\t" +
            gradeReceived);
    }

    // other methods TBD
}
```

Note that we are declaring one of the attributes of `TranscriptEntry` to be of type `Course`, which means that each `TranscriptEntry` object will maintain a handle on its corresponding `Course` object. By doing this, the `TranscriptEntry` object can avail itself of the `Course` object's title, course number, or credit hour value (needed for computing the GPA) – all privately encapsulated in the `Course` object as attributes – by calling the appropriate 'get' methods on that `Course` object as needed.

Back in the `Student` class, we can now define the `Student`'s `transcript` attribute to be a collection of `TranscriptEntry` objects! We can then add a `printTranscript()` method on the `Student` class, the pseudocode for which is as follows:

```
class Student {
    String name;
    String studentId;
    // etc.
    CollectionType transcript = new CollectionType ();    // of TranscriptEntry
                                                          // objects

    // Details omitted ...

    public void printTranscript(String filename) {
        // pseudocode
        for (each TranscriptEntry t in the transcript collection ) {
            t.printTranscriptEntry();
        }
    }
}
```

Alternatively, we could use the technique of creating a 'wrapper' class called `Transcript` to house some 'standard' collection type, as we did with `EnrollmentCollection` in an earlier example, and then declare the `transcript` attribute as follows:

```
class Student {
    String name;
    String studentId;
    // etc.
    Transcript transcript;   // an encapsulated collection of
                             // TranscriptEntry objects
    // etc.
```

This illustrates how we've taken full advantage of collections to round out our `Student` class definition.

Attribute Name	Data Type
name	String
studentID	String
birthdate	Date
address	String
major	String
gpa	Float
advisor	Professor
courseLoad	collection of `Course` objects
transcript	Either a collection of `TranscriptEntry` objects or `Transcript`

Summary

In this chapter, we've learned:

- ❏ That collections are a special type of object/class used to gather up and manage references to other objects.

- ❏ That arrays, as simple collections, have some limitations, but that we have other more powerful collection types to draw upon with OO languages, such as:
  - ❏ Ordered lists
  - ❏ Sorted ordered lists
  - ❏ Sets
  - ❏ Dictionaries

- ❏ That it is important to familiarize ourselves with the unique characteristics of whatever collection types are built into a particular OO language so as to make the most intelligent selection of which collection type to use for a particular circumstance.

- ❏ That we can invent our own collection types by creating 'wrapper classes' around any of the fundamental built-in collection classes.

- ❏ How we can work around the limitation that a method can only return one 'answer' by having that 'answer' be a collection of objects.

- ❏ How we can create very sophisticated composite classes through the use of collections as attributes.

Exercises

1. Given the following abstraction:

A book is a collection of chapters, which are each collections of pages.

sketch out the pseudocode for the Book, Chapter, and Page classes. Invent whatever attributes you think would be relevant, taking advantage of collections as attributes where appropriate. Include methods on the Book class for adding chapters and pages, and for determining how many chapters and how many pages the book contains.

2. What type of collection(s) might you use to represent each of the following abstractions? Explain your choices.

❏ A computer parts catalog.

❏ A poker hand.

❏ The letters of a foreign alphabet, to be used in translating English text to that language.

❏ Trouble calls logged by a technical help desk.

3. What collections do you think it would be important to maintain for the SRS?

4. What collections do you think it would be important to maintain for the Conference Room Reservation System (CRRS) described in Appendix B?

5. What collections do you think it would be important to maintain for the problem area that you described for exercise 3 in Chapter 2?

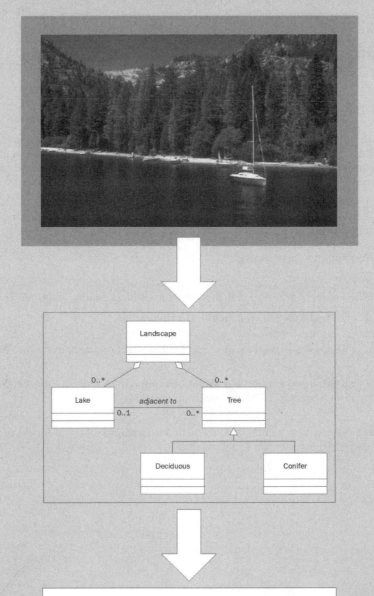

```
public class Tree {
    protected Landscape landscape;
    protected Lake nextTo;

    public void setNextTo(Lake l) {
        nextTo = l;
    }
    public Lake getNextTo() {
        return nextTo;
    }

    public abstract Color getLeafColor();
}
```

Some Final Concepts

By now, you've hopefully gained a solid appreciation for how powerful object-oriented languages are for modeling complex real-world situations. We can create our own abstract data types (ADTs), also known as classes, to represent objects of arbitrary complexity, particularly when we take advantage of collections, as we did when modeling the `transcript` attribute of the `Student` class in Chapter 6. As a matter of fact, these ADTs can get pretty darned sophisticated! And, we can arrange these data types into class hierarchies to take advantage of the inheritance mechanism of OO languages. Through encapsulation and information hiding, we can shield client code from changes that we make to the 'hidden' (private) implementation details of our classes.

You might wonder how there could be anything more to learn about object-oriented programming! However, as powerful as all of these OO language features are, there is one more essential feature which we have not yet spoken about, which ties them all together into an unbeatable package. That feature is known as **polymorphism**.

And, as with any technology, there are core concepts and then there are 'special topics': things that you don't necessarily need to know when you are first setting out to use the technology, but which are valuable to know as you become adept with the basics. If you buy an expensive, professional-calibre camera, for example, you may initially be able to use it only as a 'point and shoot' camera, letting the camera do all of the work of automatically determining how to adjust the lens to produce a quality picture. As your familiarity with the camera's features improves, however, you will find yourself able to command the camera to do some pretty amazing things!

Arming yourself with knowledge of the special object technology topics covered in this chapter – the 'icing' on the object 'cake' – will enhance the sophistication of the OO systems that you are able to build.

In this chapter, you will learn:

- ❏ How the same identical message can be responded to differently by different classes of objects.

- ❏ How a class can get away with specifying 'what' an object's mission should be without going to the trouble of specifying the details of 'how' an object is to carry out that mission, and why we'd want a class to do so.

- ❏ How an object can have a 'split personality' by exhibiting the behaviors of two or more different types of object.

- ❏ Creative ways for an entire class of objects to easily and efficiently share data without breaking the spirit of encapsulation.

What is Polymorphism?

The term **polymorphism** refers to the ability of two or more objects belonging to different classes to respond to exactly the same message (method call) in different class-specific ways. If we were instruct three different people – a surgeon, a hair stylist, and an actor – to 'cut!', then the surgeon would begin to make an incision; the hair stylist would begin to cut someone's hair; and the actor would abruptly stop acting out the current scene, awaiting directorial guidance. These three different professionals may be thought to be objects belonging to different professional 'classes'. Each was given the same message – 'cut!' – but knew the specific details of what this message meant to him/her by virtue of knowing the profession (class) that he/she is associated with.

Turning to a software example relevant to the SRS, assume that we have created an array called studentBody declared to hold references to Student objects. We then populate the array with Student object references – some graduate students and some undergraduate students, randomly mixed – as shown below. (Both GraduateStudent and UndergraduateStudent are assumed to be subclasses of Student.)

```
// Declare and instantiate an array.
Student[] studentBody = new Student[20];

// Instantiate various types of Student object.
UndergraduateStudent u1 = new UndergraduateStudent();
UndergraduateStudent u2 = new UndergraduateStudent();
GraduateStudent g1 = new GraduateStudent();
GraduateStudent g2 = new GraduateStudent();
// etc.

// 'Stuff' them into the array in random order.
studentBody[0] = u1;
studentBody[1] = g1;
studentBody[2] = g2;
studentBody[3] = u2;
// etc.
```

Since we are storing both GraduateStudent and UndergraduateStudent objects in this array, we declared the array to be of a supertype common to all objects that the array is intended to contain, namely, Student. Because an UndergraduateStudent object is a Student, and a GraduateStudent object is a Student, the compiler won't complain when we insert either type of object into the array. (The compiler would violently object, however, if we tried to insert a Professor object into the same array, because a Professor is not a Student, at least not in terms of the class hierarchy that we have defined for the SRS. If we wanted to include Professors in our array, we'd have to declare the array as holding a supertype common to both the Student and Professor classes, namely, Person, as we discussed in Chapter 6.)

In Chapter 5, we discussed the fact that a print() method as defined for the Student superclass would not suffice for printing the attribute values for a subclass such as GraduateStudent, because the code as written for the Student class would not know about any of the attributes that were added to the GraduateStudent subclass. So, we would override the print() method of Student to create special versions of the method for all of the subclasses. The code for doing so, which was first introduced in Chapter 5, is repeated again on the next page for convenience; we've added the UndergraduateStudent class code, and made a few minor enhancements to the print() method for the other two classes while we were at it.

```
class Student {
  // details omitted ...

  void print() {
    // We can only print the attributes that the Student class
    // knows about.
    System.out.println("Student Name:  " + name + "\n" +
      "Student No.:  "  +  studentId  + "\n" +
      "Major Field:  "  +  major  + "\n" +
      "GPA:   " + gpa);
  }
}

class GraduateStudent extends Student {
  // details omitted ...

  void print() {
    // Reuse code by performing the print() method of the
    // Student superclass ...
    super.print();

    // ... and then go on to print this subclass's specific attributes.
    System.out.println("Undergrad. Deg.:  "  +  undergraduateDegree +
      "\n" + "Undergrad. Inst.:  " +
      undergraduateInstitution + "\n" +
      "THIS IS A GRADUATE STUDENT ...");
  }
}

class UndergraduateStudent extends Student {
  // details omitted ...

  void print() {
    // Reuse code from the Student superclass ...
    super.print();

    // ... and then go on to print this subclass's specific attributes.
    System.out.println("High School Attended:  " + highSchool +
      "\n" + "THIS IS AN UNDERGRADUATE STUDENT ...");
  }
}
```

Now, back in our main SRS program, perhaps we want to print out the attributes of all of the students in our studentBody array. We'd like each Student object – whether it is a graduate student or an undergraduate student – to use the version of the print() method appropriate for its class. The following code will do the trick nicely:

```
// Step through the array (collection) ...
for (int i = 0; i < 20; i++) {
  // ... invoking the print() method of the i^th student object.
  studentBody[i].print();
}
```

As we step through a collection of objects, processing them one by one, each object will automatically know which version of the `print()` method it should execute, based on its own internal knowledge of its type/class (`GraduateStudent` or `UndergraduateStudent`, in this example), and we might wind up with a report similar to the following, where the highlighted lines emphasize the differences in output between the `GraduateStudent` and `UndergraduateStudent` `print()` methods:

```
Student Name:  John Smith
Student No.:  12345
Major Field:  Biology
GPA: 2.7
High School Attended:  Rocky Mountain High
THIS IS AN UNDERGRADUATE STUDENT ...

Student Name:  Paula Green
Student No.:  34567
Major Field:  Education
GPA: 3.6
Undergrad. Deg.: B.S. English
Undergrad. Inst.: UCLA
THIS IS A GRADUATE STUDENT ...

Student Name:  Fred Schnurd
Student No.:  98765
Major Field:  Computer Science
GPA: 4.0
Undergrad. Deg.: B.S. Computer Engineering
Undergrad. Inst.: Case Western Reserve University
THIS IS A GRADUATE STUDENT ...

Student Name:  James Roberts
Student No.:  82640
Major Field:  Math
GPA: 3.1
High School Attended:  James Ford Rhodes High
THIS IS AN UNDERGRADUATE STUDENT ...
```

The term **polymorphism** is defined in Merriam-Webster's dictionary as:

'The quality or state of being able to assume different forms'.

The line of code:

```
studentBody[i].print();
```

is said to be **polymorphic** because the method code performed in response to the message can take many different forms, depending on the class identity of the object.

Of course, this approach of iterating through a collection to ask objects one-by-one to each do something in its own class-specific way won't work unless all objects in the collection understand the message being sent.

That is, all objects in the `studentBody` array must have defined a `print()` method with the signature shown. But, since we constrained the array when we declared it to only hold objects of type `Student` (or subclasses thereof), we are *guaranteed* that they will all know what to do when asked to `print()`: by definition of inheritance, any subclass of `Student` will have either:

❑ Inherited the `Student`'s version of the `print()` method

❑ Overridden it with one of its own

for, as we learned in Chapter 5, there is no way for a subclass to *eliminate* a method defined for any of its ancestor classes. So, the bottom line is that all objects declared to be of type `Student` are guaranteed to be '`print()` savvy'!

Had we chosen a different Java collection type, we would not have been able to constrain the type of objects to be inserted when we declared the collection (Java arrays are somewhat unique in that regard, as we pointed out in Chapter 6). So, we'd have to take care when inserting objects into the collection to ensure that they all speak a common language in terms of messages that they understand.

Polymorphism Simplifies Code Maintenance

To appreciate the power of polymorphism, let's look at how we might have to approach this same challenge – namely, of handling different objects in different type-specific ways – with a non-OO programming language that doesn't support polymorphism.

In the absence of polymorphism, we'd typically handle all of the various scenarios having to do with different kinds of students using a series of '`if`' tests:

❑ One way would be to write different functions, with different names, for each of the different types of student, and to then call the appropriate function from our client code:

```
for (int i = 0; i < 20; i++) {
  // Process the iᵗʰ student.
  // (pseudocode)
  if (studentBody[i] is an undergraduate student)
    printAsUndergraduateStudent();
  else if (studentBody[i] is a graduate student)
    printAsGraduateStudent();
  else if ...
}
```

❑ Another way would be to have a single `print()` method, and to hide the details of such an '`if`' test within that method's code:

```
class Student {
  // details omitted ...

  public print() {
    if (this is an undergraduate student)
      print attributes relevant to an undergraduate student;
```

```
      else if (this is a graduate student)
        print attributes relevant to a graduate student;
      else if ...
    }
  }
```

With either approach, as the number of cases grows, so too does the 'spaghetti' nature of the resultant code! Maintenance of such code quickly becomes a nightmare.

Now, back to our polymorphic example. Because the same client code (for example our polymorphic array iteration above) can operate on a variety of objects without knowing specifically what subtype of object is involved, the client code is robust to change. Let's say that, long after our application has been coded and tested, we derive classes called `PhDStudent` and `MastersStudent` from `GraduateStudent`, each of which has its own 'flavor' of `print()` method. We can randomly insert `MastersStudent` and `PhDStudent` objects into the mix of `GraduateStudents` and `UndergraduateStudents` in the array, and our polymorphic array iteration:

```
// Step through the array (collection) ...
for (int i = 0; i < studentBody.size; i++) {
  // ... and invoke the print() method of the i^th student object.
  studentBody[i].print();
}
```

doesn't have to change! This is because the new object types – `MastersStudent` and `PhDStudent` – are, as derived subclasses of `Student`, guaranteed to understand the `print()` message, as well. But, the story is different with our non-polymorphic example. The code would indeed have to change to accommodate these new student types; we'd have to complicate our 'if' tests even further by adding additional cases:

```
class Student {
  // details omitted ...

  public print() {
    if (this is an undergraduate student)
      print attributes relevant to an undergraduate student;
    else if (this is a graduate student)
      print attributes relevant to a graduate student;
    else if (this is a PhD student)
      print attributes relevant to a PhD student;
    else if (this is a Masters student)
      print attributes relevant to a Masters student;
    else if ...
  }
}
```

causing the 'spaghetti pile' to grow ever taller.

If you are curious as to the mechanics of how polymorphism works behind the scenes, please take a look at Appendix F, which describes the underlying mechanism in some detail. However, you don't need to understand such details in order to make use of polymorphism in the applications that you develop any more than it is necessary to understand how an automobile engine works in order to drive a car. Because of this, reading Appendix F is strictly optional.

Three Distinguishing Features of an Object-Oriented Programming Language

We have now defined all three of the features required to make a language truly object-oriented:

- ❑   (Programmer creation of) Abstract Data Types (ADTs)
- ❑   Inheritance
- ❑   Polymorphism

We're in the home stretch! There are a few more 'bells and whistles' that we'd like to introduce to you – some of the finer points of objects – which we'll do in the remainder of this chapter.

Abstract Classes

We learned in Chapter 5 how useful it can be to consolidate shared features – attributes and methods – of two or more classes into a common superclass, a process known as generalization. We did this when we created the `Person` class as a generalization of `Student` and `Professor` and then moved the declarations of all of their common attributes (`name`, `address`, `birthdate`) and methods (the 'get' and 'set' methods for each of the shared attributes) into this superclass. By doing so, the `Student` and `Professor` subclasses both became simpler, and we eliminated a lot of redundancy that would otherwise have made maintenance of the SRS much more cumbersome.

There is one potential dilemma to be dealt with when creating a superclass after the fact: if all of the classes that are to be subclasses of this new superclass happen to have defined methods with the same signature, but with different logic, which version of the method, if any, should be propagated up to the parent? Let's use a specific example: say that long before it occurred to us to create a `Person` superclass, a requirement arose to devise a method for both the `Student` and `Professor` classes to compute their respective monthly salaries (we are assuming that students work for the university as teaching assistants or as research fellows). We decided that the signature of this method would be as follows:

```
public float computePaycheck(int hoursWorked);
```

- ❑   In the case of a professor, his/her salary is based on the number of hours worked in a given month multiplied by an hourly wage.
- ❑   In the case of a student, his/her salary is a fixed monthly stipend, but is only paid if the student worked more than a certain minimum number of hours during the month.

We then implemented the `computePaycheck()` methods for these two classes, the code for which is shown below:

```
class Professor {
   String name;
   String ssn;
   float hourlySalary;
   // etc.
```

```
      // Get/set methods omitted ...

    public float computePaycheck(int hoursWorked) {
      return hoursWorked * hourlySalary;
    }
  }

class Student {
  String name;
  String ssn;
  float monthlyStipend;
  int minimumRequiredHours;
  // etc.

  // Get/set methods omitted ...

  // Same signature as for the Professor class,
  // but different internal logic.
  public float computePaycheck(int hoursWorked) {
    if (hoursWorked > minimumRequiredHours)
      return monthlyStipend;
    else return 0.0;
  }
}
```

At some later point in time, we decide to generalize these two classes into a common superclass called Person. We can easily move the common attributes (name, ssn) and their get/set methods out of Student and Professor and into Person, but what should we do about the computePaycheck() method?

- We could provide a generic computePaycheck() method with the same exact signature in Person, and then allow the Professor and Student classes' specialized versions of the method to effectively override it. But, this raises the question, why even bother to code the internal processing details of a computePaycheck() method in Person if both Student and Professor have already in essence overridden it? The answer to this question depends on whether you plan on instantiating the Person class directly. That is:

    - If you plan on creating objects of generic type Person in your application – objects which are neither Students nor Professors – then the Person class may indeed need a computePaycheck() method of its own, to perform some sort of generic paycheck computation.

    - On the other hand, if you only plan on instantiating the Student and Professor classes, then going to the trouble of programming the internal processing details of a method for Person that will never get used, does indeed seem like a waste of time.

- If we know that we are not going to instantiate Person objects, then another option would be to leave the computePaycheck() method out of the Person class entirely. Both Student and Professor would then be adding this method as a new feature above and beyond what they inherit from Person, versus inheriting and overriding the method.

The shortcoming of this approach is that we lose the ability to *guarantee* that all future `Person` objects will understand the message for computing their paychecks. If another subclass of `Person` is created in the future (say, `AdministrativeStaffMember`), and the designer of that class isn't aware of the need to provide for a `computePaycheck()` method, then we'll wind up with a situation where some `Person` objects will understand a message like:

```
p.computePaycheck(40);
```

and others will not. We'll therefore lose the advantage of polymorphism: namely, being able to create a collection of all different types of `Person` objects, and to iterate through it to compute their paychecks, because even though an `AdministrativeStaffMember` is a `Person`, it doesn't know how to respond to a request to perform this service.

Before we try to make a final decision on how to approach the `computePaycheck()` method, let's consider a different set of circumstances.

The preceding example explored a situation where the need for generalization arose after the fact; now let's look at this problem from the opposite perspective. Say that we have the foresight to know that we are going to need various types of `Course` objects in our SRS: lecture courses, lab courses, independent study courses, etc. We want to start out on the right foot by designing the `Course` (super)class to be as versatile as possible to facilitate future specialization.

We might determine up front that all `Courses`, regardless of type, are going to need to share a few common attributes:

❑ `String courseName;`

❑ `String courseNumber;`

❑ `int creditValue;`

❑ `CollectionType enrolledStudents;`

❑ `Professor instructor;`

as well as a few common behaviors:

❑ `establishCourseSchedule()`

❑ `enrollStudent()`

❑ `assignInstructor()`

Some of these behaviors may be generic enough so that we can afford to program them in detail for the `Course` class, knowing that it is a pretty safe bet that any future subclasses of `Course` will inherit these methods 'as is' without needing to override them:

```
class Course {
   String courseName;
   String courseNumber;
   int creditValue;
   Collection enrolledStudents;
   Professor instructor;
```

```
   // Get/set methods omitted ...

   public boolean enrollStudent(Student s) {
     if (we haven't exceeded the maximum allowed enrollment yet)
       enrolledStudents.add (s);
   }

   public void assignInstructor(Professor p) {
     instructor = p;
   }
 }
```

However, other of the behaviors may be too specialized to enable us to come up with a useful generic version. For example, the rules governing how to schedule class meetings may differ for different types of courses:

❑   A lecture course may only meet once a week for 3 hours at a time.

❑   A lab course may meet twice a week for 2 hours each time.

❑   An independent study course may meet on a custom schedule agreed to by a given student and professor.

It would be a waste of time for us to bother trying to program a generic version of the establishCourseSchedule() method at this point in time. And yet we know that we'll need such a method to be programmed for all subclasses of Course that get created down the road. How do we communicate the requirement for such a behavior in all subclasses of Course and, more importantly, *enforce its future implementation?*

OO languages such as Java come to the rescue with the concept of **abstract classes**. An abstract class is used to enumerate the required behaviors of a class, without having to provide an explicit implementation of each and every such behavior. We program an abstract class in much the same way that we program a regular class, with one exception: for those behaviors for which we cannot (or care not to) devise a generic implementation – for example the establishCourseSchedule() method in our preceding example – we are allowed to specify method **signatures** without having to program the method **bodies**. We refer to a 'codeless', or signature-only, method specification as an **abstract method**.

> *Beginners often confuse the term 'abstract class' with 'abstract data type' because the terms sound the same. However, all classes – abstract or not – are abstract data types, whereas only certain classes are abstract classes.*

So, we can go back to our Course class definition, and add an abstract method as highlighted below:

```
class Course {
  String courseName;
  String courseNumber;
  int creditValue;
  CollectionType enrolledStudents = new CollectionType ();
  Professor instructor;
```

```
       public boolean enrollStudent(Student s) {
         if ( we haven't exceeded the maximum allowed enrollment yet )
           enrolledStudents.add(s);
       }

       public void assignInstructor(Professor p) {
         instructor = p;
       }
```

```
       // Note the use of the 'abstract' keyword.
       public abstract void establishCourseSchedule (String startDate,
                                                     String endDate);
     }
```

Note that the establishCourseSchedule() method signature has no curly braces following the closing parenthesis of the argument list. Instead, the signature ends with a semicolon (;) – in other words, it is missing its 'body', which normally contains the detailed logic of how the method is to be performed. The method signature is explicitly labeled as 'abstract', to notify the compiler that we didn't accidentally forget to program this method, but rather that we knew what we were doing when we intentionally omitted the body.

By specifying an abstract method, we have:

❑ Specified a service that objects belonging to this class (or one of its subclasses) must be able to perform.

❑ Detailed the means by which we will ask them to perform this service by providing a method signature, which as we learned in Chapter 4 controls the format of the message that we will pass to such objects, when we want them to perform the service.

❑ Facilitated polymorphism – at least with respect to a certain method – by ensuring that all subclasses of Course will indeed recognize a message associated with this method.

However, we have done so without pinpointing the private details of how the method will accomplish this behavior. That is, we've specified *what* an object belonging to this class needs to be able to do without pinning down *how* it is to be done.

Whenever a class contains one or more abstract methods, then the class as a whole is considered to be an abstract class. In Java, we designate that a class is abstract with the keyword 'abstract':

```
   abstract class Course {
     // details omitted
   }
```

It isn't necessary for all methods in an abstract class to be abstract; an abstract class can also contain 'normal' methods that have both a signature and a body, known as **concrete methods**.

Abstract Classes and Instantiation

There is one caveat with respect to abstract classes: they cannot be instantiated. That is, if we define `Course` to be an abstract class in the SRS, then we cannot ever instantiate generic `Course` objects in our application. This makes intuitive sense: if we *could* create an object of type `Course`, it would then be expected to know how to respond to a message to establish a course schedule, because the `Course` class defines a method signature for this behavior. But because there is no code *behind* that method signature, the `Course` object would not know *how* to behave in response to such a message.

The compiler comes to our assistance by preventing us from even writing code to instantiate an abstract object in the first place; if we were to try to compile the following code snippet:

```
Course c = new Course();  // Impossible!  The compiler will generate an error
                          // on this line of code.
// details omitted ...

c.establishCourseSchedule('01/10/2001', '05/15/2001');  // Behavior undefined!
```

we'd get the following compilation error on the first line:

class Course is an abstract class. It can't be instantiated.

While we are indeed prevented from instantiating an abstract class, we are nonetheless permitted to declare reference variables to be of an abstract type:

```
Course x;  // This is OK.
x = new Course();  // Error - Course is an abstract class!
```

Why would we even want to declare reference variables of type `Course` in the first place if we can't instantiate objects of type `Course`? It has to do with supporting polymorphism; we'll learn the importance of being able to define reference variables of an abstract type when we talk about Java collections in depth in Chapter 13.

Inheritance and Abstract Classes

An abstract class may be extended to create subclasses, in the same way that a 'normal' class can be extended. Having intentionally created `Course` as an abstract class to serve as a common 'template' for all of the various course types we envision needing for the SRS, we may later derive subclasses `LectureCourse`, `LabCourse`, and `IndependentStudyCourse`. Unless a subclass overrides **all** of the abstract methods of its abstract superclass with concrete methods, however, it will automatically be considered abstract, as well. That is, a subclass of an abstract class must provide an implementation for all inherited abstract methods in order to 'break the spell' of being abstract.

In the following code snippet, we show these three subclasses of `Course`; of these, only two – `LectureCourse` and `LabCourse` – provide implementations of the `establishCourseSchedule()` method, and so the third subclass – `IndependentStudyCourse` – remains an abstract class and hence cannot be instantiated.

```
class LectureCourse extends Course {
  // All attributes are inherited from the Course class; no new
  // attributes are added.

  public void establishCourseSchedule (String startDate, String endDate) {
    // Logic would be provided here for how a lecture course
    // establishes a course schedule; details omitted ...
  }
}

class LabCourse extends Course {
  // All attributes are inherited from the Course class; no new
  // attributes are added.

  public void establishCourseSchedule (String startDate, String endDate) {
    // Logic would be provided here for how a lab course establishes a
    // course schedule; details omitted ...
  }
}

class IndependentStudyCourse extends Course {
  // All attributes are inherited from the Course class; no new
  // attributes are added, and we don't override the
  // establishCourseSchedule() method in this subclass, either.
}
```

If we were to try to compile the above code, the Java compiler would force us to flag the IndependentStudyCourse class with the keyword 'abstract'; that is, we'd get the following compilation error:

class IndependentStudyCourse must be declared abstract. It does not define
void establishCourseSchedule (String, String) from class Course.

We've just hit upon how abstract methods serve to enforce implementation requirements! Declaring an abstract method in a superclass ultimately forces all derived subclasses to provide class-specific implementations of the abstract methods; otherwise, the subclasses cannot be instantiated.

Interfaces

Recall that a class, as an abstract data type, is an abstraction of a real world object from which some of the unessential details have been omitted. We can see that an abstract class is 'more abstract' than a 'normal' class because we've omitted the details for how one or more particular behaviors are to be performed.

Now, let's take this concept of abstraction one step further. With an abstract class, we are able to avoid programming the bodies of methods that are declared to be abstract. But what about the attributes of such a class? In our Course example, we went ahead and laid out the attributes that we thought would be needed generically by all types of courses: courseName; courseNumber; creditValue; enrolledStudents; and instructor. But, what if we only wanted to specify common behaviors, and not even bother with attributes? Attributes are, after all, typically declared to be private, and we may not wish to pin down what attributes a future class must use in order to achieve the desired public behaviors.

Say, for example, that we wanted to define what it means to teach at a university. Perhaps, in order to teach, an object would need to be able to provide the following services:

❑ Agree to teach a particular course

❑ Designate a textbook to be used for the course

❑ Define a syllabus for the course

❑ Approve the enrollment of a particular student in the course

Each of these behaviors could be formalized by specifying a method signature, representing how an object that is *capable of teaching* would be asked to perform each behavior:

```
public void agreeToTeach(Course c);
public void designateTextbook(TextBook b, Course c);
public Syllabus defineSyllabus(Course c);
public boolean approveEnrollment(Student s, Course c);
```

A set of method signatures such as these, which collectively define what it means to assume a certain role (such as teaching) in the grand scheme of an application, is known as an **interface**. Interfaces, like classes, are given names; so, let's call this the 'Teacher' interface.

Armed with this set of method signatures, we could set about designating various classes of objects as teachers. For example, we could deem Professors as being able to teach, or Students as being able to teach, or generic Person objects as being able to teach, simply by instructing the appropriate class to **implement** the Teacher interface using the syntax shown below:

```
class Professor implements Teacher {
    // details omitted ...
}
```

What exactly does it mean for a class to implement an interface? It means that the class must override all of the method signatures called for by the interface in question to provide them with method bodies. If we fail to do so, the Java compiler will generate an error; that is, if we were to code the Professor class as shown below, implementing three of the four method signatures called for by the Teacher interface but neglecting to code the fourth method:

```
class Professor implements Teacher {
    String name;
    String employeeId;
    // etc.

    // Get/set methods omitted.

    // We override three of the four method signatures called for by the
    // Teacher interface, to provide method bodies.

    public void agreeToTeach(Course c) {
        // Logic for the method body goes here; details omitted.
    }
```

```
    public void designateTextbook(TextBook b, Course c) {
      // Logic for the method body goes here; details omitted.
    }

    public Syllabus defineSyllabus(Course c) {
      // Logic for the method body goes here; details omitted.
    }

    // But, we've failed to provide an implementation of the
    // approveEnrollment() method!
  }
```

If we were to try to compile this class as is, we'd get the following compiler error:

class Professor must be declared abstract. It does not define
boolean approveEnrollment(Student, Course) from interface Teacher.

Implementing an interface is therefore virtually the same thing as having to 'flesh out' abstract methods when subclassing an abstract class. The only difference is that with an interface, we typically specify abstract behaviors only, whereas an abstract class specifies a data structure (attributes) as well as a mixture of abstract and concrete behaviors. So, in terms of the 'abstractness spectrum', an interface is even more abstract than an abstract class (which is in turn more abstract than a 'regular' class) because an interface leaves even more details out of the picture.

> *As we'll see in Chapter 13, an interface is also capable of defining constants.*

A class may be instructed to implement as many interfaces as desired. For example, if we were to invent a second interface called 'Administrator', which specified the following method signatures:

```
    public boolean approveNewCourse(Course c);
    public boolean hireProfessor(Professor p);
```

then we could instruct a class to implement both the Teacher and Administrator interfaces:

```
    class Professor implements Teacher, Administrator { ... }
```

in which case the class would need to override all of the method signatures called for by *both* of these interfaces.

When a class implements more than one interface, it effectively assumes multiple identities or roles, and its 'handle' can therefore be managed by various types of reference variables. Based on the preceding definition of a Professor as both a Teacher and an Administrator, the following code would be possible:

```
    // We instantiate a Professor object, and store its handle in a reference
    // variable of type Professor.
    Professor p = new Professor();
    Teacher t;
```

```
Administrator a;
t = p;   // We store a handle on the Professor in a reference variable of
         // type Teacher!
a = p;   // We store a handle on the Professor in a reference variable of
         // type Administrator!
```

as illustrated conceptually in the figure below.

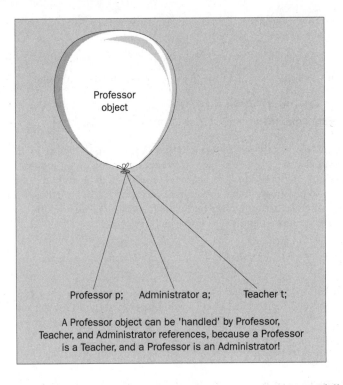

A Professor object can be 'handled' by Professor,
Teacher, and Administrator references, because a Professor
is a Teacher, and a Professor is an Administrator!

This is conceptually the same thing as you, as a person, being viewed as having different roles by different people: you are viewed as an employee by your manager, as a son or daughter to your parents, perhaps as a parent to your children, and so forth.

> *Note that not all OO languages embrace the notion of interfaces. For example, Java does, but C++ does not. It is Java's provision for a class to be able to implement multiple interfaces that justified the Java language designers from doing away with multiple inheritance, as we discussed in Chapter 5.*

Static Attributes

We've learned that whenever we create an object, we are creating an instance of the appropriate class template, which then gets filled in with attribute values specific to that object.

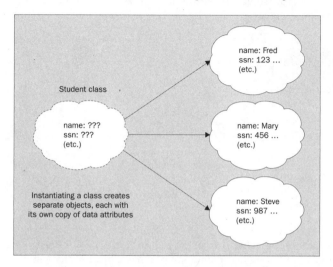

Suppose there were some piece of general information – say, the total student enrollment count at the university – that we wanted *all* Student objects to have shared access to. We could implement this as a 'standard' attribute of the Student class, totalStudents, along with methods for manipulating the attribute as shown below:

```
class Student {
    int totalStudents;

    // details omitted ...

    public int getTotalStudents() {
        return totalStudents;
    }

    public void incrementEnrollment() {
        totalStudents = totalStudents + 1;
    }

    // etc.
}
```

This would be inefficient for two reasons:

1. First of all, each object would be duplicating the same information. Although an int(eger) doesn't take up a lot of storage space, if we have thousands of Student objects in the system, this is still, in principle, a waste of storage. And, storage space aside, one of our 'quests' in adopting object technology is to avoid redundancy of data and/or code whenever possible.

2. Secondly, and perhaps more significantly, it would be cumbersome to have to call the `incrementEnrollment()` method on every `Student` object in the system each time a new `Student` were to be created.

Fortunately, there is a simple solution! We can declare `totalStudents` to be what is known as a **static attribute** of the `Student` class:

```
class Student {
  private static int totalStudents;

  // details omitted ...

  public int getTotalStudents() {
    return totalStudents;
  }

  public void incrementEnrollment() {
    totalStudents = totalStudents + 1;
  }
}
```

A static attribute is one whose value is shared by all instances of that class; it in essence belongs to the class as a whole instead of belonging to any one instance/object of that class.

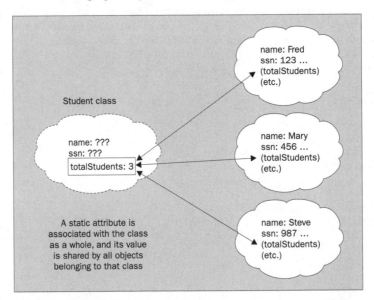

Each `Student` object can access and modify the shared `totalStudents` attribute just as if it were a regular (non-static) attribute; in the code above, the `getTotalEnrollment()` and `incrementEnrollment()` methods look no different than any other 'normal' method in terms of how they manipulate the `totalStudents` attribute. The difference is that the value of a static attribute is shared, so if we were to execute the following client code:

```
Student s1 = new Student();
s1.setName("Fred");
s1.incrementEnrollment();

Student s2 = new Student();
s2.setName("Mary");
s2.incrementEnrollment();

Student s3 = new Student();
s3.setName("Steve");
s3.incrementEnrollment();
```

then the resultant value of totalStudents would be affected as follows (assuming that it starts with a value of 0):

3. When s1 is passed the message s1.incrementEnrollment(), the shared value of totalStudents is incremented by 1 (from 0 to 1).

4. When s2 is passed the message s2.incrementEnrollment(), the shared value of totalStudents is incremented by 1 (from 1 to 2).

5. When s3 is passed the message s3.incrementEnrollment(), the shared value of totalStudents is incremented by 1 (from 2 to 3).

6. At any time thereafter, if any one of the three objects inspects the value of the totalStudents attribute, it will be equal to 3.

Accessing Static Attributes

Let's assume for the moment that totalStudents is declared to be a public static attribute of the Student class for convenience of access, rather than being declared private. We can therefore access the attribute from our client code using familiar dot notation in one of two ways:

❏   As an attribute of a Student object (like a 'normal', albeit public, attribute):

```
Student s1 = new Student();
s1.incrementEnrollment();
Student s2 = new Student();
s2.incrementEnrollment();
Student s3 = new Student();
s3.incrementEnrollment();
```

```
// Because totalStudents is public, we can access it directly without using
// an accessor ('get') method.
System.out.println("Total no. of students:  " + s1.totalStudents);
```

This would cause the following to print out:

Total no. of students: 3

Note that in formulating the `print` statement, we could have also accessed the `totalStudents` attribute using dot notation as an attribute of either object `s2` or `s3` rather than `s1` – the result would have been the same, because all three objects share the *same* value.

❏ Alternatively, we can access a static attribute **as an attribute of the class as a whole** by applying dot notation to the class name rather than applying it to an instance variable; the following code illustrates this technique, and accomplishes the same goal as the preceding code:

```
System.out.println("Total no. of students:  " + Student.totalStudents);
```

This would cause the same message to print out:

Total no. of students: 3

This illustrates that we can access a static attribute even if we **don't** have an instance (object) of the class handy.

In reality, we would most likely declare this attribute (like virtually all attributes) to be `private`, in which case we'd need to write public get/set methods for it, just like any other private attribute. However, by virtue of being a static attribute, we again have two options:

❏ We can create typical 'get' and 'set' methods:

```
class Student {
  private static int totalStudents;

  // details omitted

  public int getTotalStudents() {
    return totalStudents;
  }

  public void setTotalStudents(int t) {
    totalStudents = t;
  }

  public void incrementEnrollment() {
    totalStudents = totalStudents + 1;
  }
}
```

❏ Alternatively, we can create what are known as **static methods**, which are described below.

Static Methods

Just as static attribute values are thought to belong to the class as a whole versus belonging to a specific individual object, static methods may be invoked on the class as a whole. If we declare the `getTotalStudents()`, `setTotalStudents()`, and `incrementEnrollment()` methods to be static:

```
class Student {
  private static int totalStudents;
```

```
// details omitted

public static int getTotalStudents() {
    return totalStudents;
}

public static void setTotalStudents(int t) {
    totalStudents = t;
}

public static void incrementEnrollment() {
    totalStudents = totalStudents + 1;
}
}
```

then we may invoke them using dot notation in either of the following two ways:

❑ As methods of a Student object:

```
Student s1 = new Student();
s1.incrementEnrollment();
Student s2 = new Student();
s2.incrementEnrollment();
Student s3 = new Student();
s3.incrementEnrollment();
```

```
System.out.println("Total no. of students:  ", s1.getTotalStudents());
```

which, as before, produces the following output:

Total no. of students: 3

Note that we could have also invoked the getTotalStudents() method on either object s2 or s3 instead of on s1, and the result would have been the same.

❑ Alternatively, we can invoke a static method **on the class as a whole** by applying dot notation to the name of class versus to an instance variable:

```
System.out.println("Total no. of students:  ", Student.getTotalStudents());
```

which once again produces the output:

Total no. of students: 3

So, we see that we can invoke a static method even if we **don't** have an instance (object) of the class handy.

Static Methods and Static Attributes

Note that there is an important restriction on static methods: they may **only** access **static** attributes. If we tried to write a static method such as `print()` below that attempts to access the value of a non-static attribute such as name, the compiler would prevent us from doing so.

```
class Student {
  private String name;
  private static int totalStudents;

  public static void print() {
    // A static method may not access non-static attributes
    // such as 'name'.
    System.out.println(name + " is one of " + totalStudents + "
      students.");
  }
}
```

The compiler would generate the following error message:

Can't make a static reference to nonstatic variable name in class Student.

Why is this? The reason lies in the fact that we are permitted to invoke a static method on a class as a whole. As we learned in Chapter 3, classes are empty templates as far as 'normal' (non-static) attributes are concerned. If a static method is invoked on a class as a whole, and tries to access a non-static attribute, the value of that attribute will be undefined, as illustrated conceptually in the figure below.

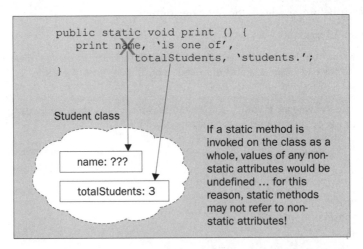

Of course, if the method were to be invoked on an object/instance instead, this problem wouldn't surface. But, the compiler cannot predict how a static method is going to be used over the lifetime of an application. So, in order to produce unambiguous results, a static method must be restricted to operate only on those attributes whose values will always be available, whether or not a specific instance of a class is involved.

Alternative Terminology

To differentiate between static attributes and 'normal' (non-static) attributes, some additional terminology has been introduced:

❏ The term **instance variable** is often used to refer to a 'normal' attribute, becuase such an attribute has value or meaning for an instance, or object.

❏ the term **class variable** is often used as a synonym for 'static attribute', because it belongs to the class as a whole

To round out this terminology, we use the term **local variable** to refer to a variable that is declared locally to a method, but is neither an instance variable nor a class variable:

```
// pseudocode
class Student {
    // Attributes
    String name;                 // an instance variable
    static int totalStudentCount; // a class variable

    // Methods
    public void someMethod
        int x;                   // a local variable
    }
}
```

Summary

Hooray - we did it! We have made it through all of the major object technology concepts that you'll need to know for the rest of the book (and have gotten a taste of Java syntax, to boot!). Make sure that you are comfortable with these concepts before proceeding to Part 2, as they will form the foundation of the rest of your object learning experience, because:

❏ These same concepts will be reinforced when you learn how to model a problem in Part 2.

❏ . They will be reinforced yet again when you learn how to render a model as Java code in Part 3.

Reflecting back on our home construction example in the Introduction to this book, we now know all about the unique properties of 'blue stars' (objects), and why they are superior construction materials. But, we still need how to layout a blueprint for how to use them effectively – we'll learn how to do so in Part 2!

We learned in this chapter that:

❏ Different objects can respond to the same exact message in different class specific ways, thanks to an OO language feature known as polymorphism.

❏ Abstract classes are useful if we want to prescribe common behaviors among a group of (sub)classes without having to go into details about those behaviors. We specify the 'what' that an object must do (the messages that an object must be able to respond to, also known as method signatures) without the 'how' (the method bodies) in the superclass.

❏ Interfaces are an even more abstract way to prescribe behaviors.

❏ Static attributes may be used to enable an entire class of objects to share data, and static methods enable us to manipulate such attributes, even if we don't have an instance of the appropriate class handy.

Exercises

1. Test yourself: run through the following list of OO terms, and see if you can define each in your own words without referring back through Part 1:

abstract class	feature	polymorphism
abstract data type	generalization	private visibility
abstract method	get method	public visibility
abstraction	handle	reference
accessor method	instance	reference variable
agent object	information hiding	reflexive association
aggregation	inheritance	root class
ancestor class	instance	server object
association	instance variable	service
attribute	instantiation	set
base class	interface	set method
behavioral relationship	leaf node class	sibling class
binary association	link	simple data type
built-in data type	message	sorted ordered list
class	method	specialization
class hierarchy	method signature	state
class variable	modeling	static attribute
classification	modifier method	static method
client object	multiple inheritance	structural relationship
collection class	multiplicity	subclass
composite class	object (in the software sense)	subtype
constructor	operation	superclass
delegation	ordered list	supertype
derived class	overloading	terminal class
dictionary	overriding	unary association
encapsulation	parent class	user-defined data type

2. Which attributes, belonging to which SRS classes, might be well suited to being declared as static?

3. Which attributes, belonging to which CRRS classes (as described in Appendix B), might be well suited to being declared as static?

4. It has been argued that the ability to declare and implement interfaces in the Java language alleviates the need for multiple inheritance support. Do you agree or disagree? Why?

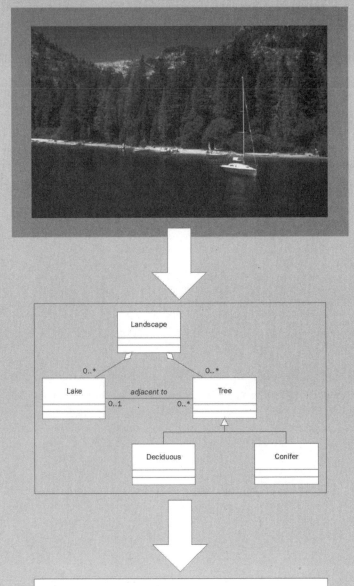

Part 2

Object Modeling:

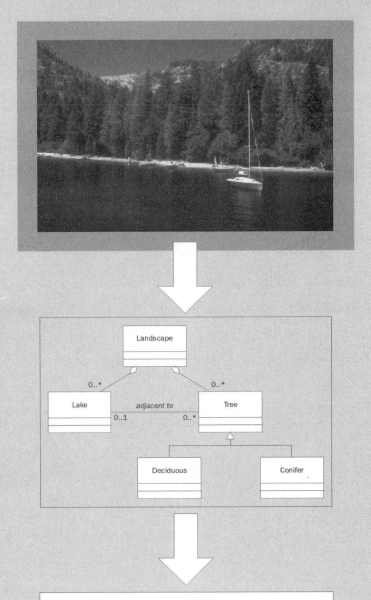

```
public class Tree {
    protected Landscape landscape;
    protected Lake nextTo;

    public void setNextTo(Lake l) {
        nextTo = l;
    }
    public Lake getNextTo() {
        return nextTo;
    }

    public abstract Color getLeafColor();
}
```

The Object Modeling Process in a Nutshell

Let's look in on the home builder whom we met in the Introduction to our book. He's just returned from a seminar entitled 'Blue Stars: A Builder's Dream Come True'. He now knows all about the unique properties of blue stars, and appreciates why they are superior construction materials – just as we've learned about the unique properties of software objects as application 'construction materials' earlier in the book. But, he is still inexperienced with actually using blue stars in a construction project: in particular, he doesn't yet know how to develop a blueprint suitable for a home that is to be built from blue stars. And, we still need to learn how to develop a 'blueprint' for a software system that is to be constructed from objects. This is the focus of Part 2 of this book.

In this chapter, you will learn:

- ❏ The goals and philosophy behind object modeling.

- ❏ How much flexibility we have in terms of selecting or devising a modeling methodology.

- ❏ The pros and cons of object modeling software tools.

The 'Big Picture' Goal of Object Modeling

Our goal in object modeling is to render a precise, concise, understandable object-oriented model, or 'blueprint', of the system to be automated. This model will serve as an important tool for communication:

- ❏ To the future users of the system that we are about to build, an object model communicates our understanding of the system requirements. Having the users review and 'bless' the model will ensure that we get off on the right foot with a project, for a mistake in judgement at the requirements analysis stage can prove much more costly to fix – by orders of magnitude – than if such a misunderstanding is found and corrected when the system is still just a 'gleam in the user's eye'.

❑ To the software development team, an object model communicates the structure and function of the software that needs to be built in order to **satisfy** those requirements. This benefits not only the software engineers themselves, but also the folks who are responsible for quality assurance, testing, and documentation.

❑ Long after the application is operational, an object model lives on as a 'schematic diagram' to help the myriad folks responsible for supporting and maintaining an application to understand its structure and function.

Of course, this last point is only true if the object model accurately reflects the system as it was actually built, not just as it was originally conceived. The design of complex systems invariably change during their construction, and so care should be taken to keep the object model up-to-date as the system is built.

Modeling Methodology = Process + Notation + Tool

Merriam-Webster's dictionary defines the term **methodology** as:

'A set of procedures used by a discipline to achieve a particular desired outcome'.

A modeling methodology, OO or otherwise, ideally involves three components:

❑ A **process**: the 'how to' steps for gathering the requirements and determining the abstraction to be modeled.

❑ A **notation**: a graphical 'language' for communicating the model.

❑ A **tool**: an automated way of rendering the notation, typically in 'drag and drop' fashion.

Although these constitute the ideal components of a modeling methodology, they are not all of equal importance. A sound process is certainly critical; however, we can get by with narrative text descriptions of many abstractions. And, when we do choose to use a graphical notation, it isn't mandatory that we use a specialized tool for doing so. In other words, the process is the most important, closely followed by the notation, and the tool is the least important of the three.

Many important contributions in the form of new processes, notations, and tools have been made in the OO methodology arena over the years by numerous well-known methodologists. In some sense, if you are just getting into objects for the first time now, you are fortunate, because you managed to avoid the 'methodology wars' that raged for many years as methodologists and their followers argued about what were in some cases esoteric details.

Here is a partial list of contributions made in the object methodology arena over the past few decades; the list is in no particular order:

❑ James Rumbaugh et al: the Object Modeling Technique (OMT)

❑ Grady Booch: The Booch Method

❑ Sally Schlaer and Stephen Mellor: emphasis on state diagrams

❑ Rebecca Wirfs-Brock et al: responsibility-driven design; 'Classes – Responsibilities – Collaborations' (CRC) cards

- ❑ Bertrand Meyer: the Eiffel programming language; the notion of programming by contract

- ❑ James Martin/James Odell: retooling of their functional decomposition methodologies for use with object-oriented systems

- ❑ Peter Coad/Edward Yourdon: as above

- ❑ Ivar Jacobsen: use cases as a means of formalizing requirements

- ❑ Derek Coleman et al (HP): the Fusion Method

- ❑ Erich Gamma, Richard Helm, Ralph Johnson, John Vlissides (the 'Gang of Four'): design pattern reuse

In recent years, there has been a major push in the industry to meld the best ideas of competing methodologies into a single approach, with particular emphasis being placed on coming up with a universal modeling notation. The resultant notation, known as the Unified Modeling Language (UML), represents the collaborative efforts of three of the leaders in the OO methodology field – James Rumbaugh, Grady Booch, and Ivor Jacobsen – and has become the industry standard object modeling notation. (You'll learn the basics of UML in Chapters 10 and 11.) Along with the UML, these three gentlemen – known affectionately in the industry as the 'Three Amigos' – have also contributed heavily to the evolution of an overall methodology known as the Rational Unified Process (RUP), a full-blown **software development methodology** encompassing modeling, project management, and configuration management workflows. But, we aren't going to dwell on the details of this particular methodology in this book, because as we mentioned in the Introduction, it is not our intention to teach you any one specific methodology in great detail. By teaching you a sound, **generic** process for object modeling, you will be armed with the knowledge you need to read about, evaluate, and select a specific methodology such as RUP, or to craft your own hybrid approach by mixing and matching the processes, notation, and tool(s) from various methodologies that make the most sense for your organization.

As for modeling tools, you don't need one, strictly speaking, to appreciate the material presented in this book. But, we've anticipated that many of you will want to get your 'hands dirty' with a modeling tool. Because of this, we've included a general discussion of tool pros and cons a bit later in this chapter.

It is important to keep in mind that a methodology is but a means to an end, and it is the **end** – a useable, flexible, maintainable, reliable, and functionally correct software system, along with thorough, clear supporting documentation – that we care most about when all is said and done.

To help illustrate this point, let's use a simple analogy. Say that our goal is to cheer people up. We decide to hand-draw (process) a smiley face (an abstraction of the desired behavior, rendered with a graphical notation) with a paintbrush (tool).

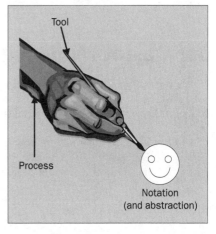

After we are done, we put our paintbrush away, hang our smiley face picture on the wall, and go about our business. A few days go by, and we note that people are indeed cheered up by our picture, and so our original goal has been achieved. In hindsight, we could have accomplished this same goal using:

- A variety of different 'processes' – hand drawing, rubber stamping, cutting pictures from a magazine.

- A variety of different 'notations' – the graphical notation of a smiley face or a cartoon, or the narrative text of a joke or sign.

- A variety of different 'tools' – a pen, a pencil, a paintbrush, a crayon.

Now, back to our homebuilding analogy. Long after the architect and construction crew have left a building site, taking their equipment and tools with them, the house that they have built will remain standing as a testimonial to the quality of the materials they used, how sound a construction approach was employed, and how elegant a blueprint they had to start with. The blueprint will come in handy later on when the time comes to remodel or maintain the home, so we certainly won't throw it away; but, the 'liveability' and ease/affordability of maintaining the home will be the primary measure of success.

The same is true for software development: the real legacy of a software development project is the resultant software system, which is, after all, the reason for using a methodology to produce a model in the first place. We must take care to avoid getting so caught up in debating the relative merits of one methodology versus another that we fail to produce useful software… there are **many** paths to the same destination.

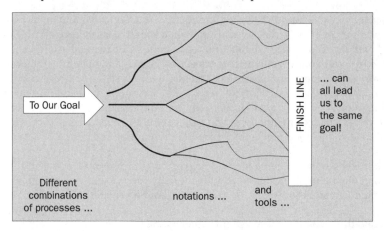

Our Object Modeling Process, in a Nutshell

We present here a basic preview of the modeling process that we advocate, and which we are going to illustrate in depth throughout the remainder of Part 2 of the book. Chapter references in square brackets […] indicate where each technique is covered in detail.

- Begin by obtaining or writing a narrative problem statement, similar to the Student Registration System (SRS) problem statement on page 8 or the alternative case studies included as Appendix B. (See also exercise 3 at the end of Chapter 2.) Think about the different categories of users that will be interacting with the system, and the various situations in which they will each use it, to make sure that you uncover any not-so-obvious requirements that may have been missed. [Chapter 9]

- ❏ Handle the data side of the application by identifying the different classes of 'real world' objects that your application will need to be concerned with, and determine how these interrelate. [Chapter 10]

- ❏ Handle the functional side of the application by studying how objects need to collaborate to accomplish the system's mission, determining what behaviors/responsibilities will be required of each class. [Chapter 11]

- ❏ Test the model to ensure that it does indeed meet all of the original requirements. [Chapter 12]

You'll see plenty of examples of each of these techniques in the chapters to follow, and will get an opportunity to practise these techniques based on the 'hands on' exercises suggested at the end of each chapter. Armed with a solid model of the SRS, you'll then be ready to render the model into Java code, which is the subject of Part 3 of the book.

Note that these process steps need not be performed in strictly sequential fashion. In fact, as you become comfortable with each of the steps, you may find yourself carrying some of them out in parallel, or in 'shuffled' order. For example, contemplating the behavioral aspects of a model may bring to light new data requirements. In fact, for all but the most trivial models, it is commonplace to iterate through these steps multiple times, 'dialing in' increased levels of understanding, and hence more detail in the model and supporting documentation, with each iteration.

It is also important to note that the formality of the process should be adjusted to the size of the project team and the complexity of the requirements. If we separate the *form* of using a methodology from the *substance* of what that methodology produces in the way of **artifacts** – models, documentation, code, and so on – then a good rule of thumb is that a project team should spend no more than 10 – 20 % of their time on form, 80 – 90 % on substance. If the team finds itself spending so much time on form that little or no progress is being made on substance, it is time to re-evaluate the methodology and its various components, to see where simplifying adjustments or improvements to efficiency may be made.

Thoughts Regarding Object Modeling Software Tools

It's worthwhile to spend a little bit of time talking about the pros and cons of using an object modeling software tool. For purposes of learning how to produce models, a generic drawing tool such as CorelDraw or PowerPoint may be good enough; for that matter, you may simply want to sketch your models using paper and pencil. But, getting some hands on experience with using a tool specifically designed for object modeling will better prepare you for your first 'industrial strength' project, and so you may wish to acquire one before embarking upon the next chapter. You'll find information about various object modeling software tools, including links to free and/or evaluation copies of software, on my web site: http://objectstart.com.

> *I make it a practice not to mention specific tools, vendors, versions, etc. in a book, as they change much too rapidly. Murphy's Law states that, as soon as a software product is mentioned in print, it will either change names, change vendors who market it, or go out of sight completely!*

Object modeling tools fall under the general heading of **Computer Aided Software Engineering**, or 'CASE', tools. The pros of CASE tools in general are as follows:

- ❏ CASE tools provide a quick drag and drop way to create visual models. Rather than trying to render a given notation with a generic drawing tool, where your basic drawing components are simple lines, arrows, text, boxes, and other geometric shapes, CASE tools provide one or more palettes of prefabricated graphical components specific to the supported notation. So, you can drag and drop the graphical representation for a class, for example, rather than having to painstakingly fabricate it from simpler drawing components.

❏ CASE tools produce 'intelligent' drawings that enforce the syntax rules of a particular notation. This is in contrast to a generic drawing package, which will pretty much let you draw whatever you like, whether it adheres to the notational syntax or not.

The controls imposed by a CASE tool can be a mixed blessing: on the plus side, they will prevent you from making syntactic errors, but as we discuss below, they may also prevent you from making desired adjustments to the notation.

❏ Information about the classes reflected in a diagram – their names, attributes, methods, and relationships – is typically stored in a repository that underlies the diagram. Most CASE tools provide documentation generation features based upon this repository, enabling you to automatically generate project documentation such as a data dictionary report, a type of report that we'll discuss in Chapter 10. Some tools even allow you to tap into this repository programmatically, should you find a need to do so.

❏ Most CASE tools provide code generation capabilities, enabling you to transition from a diagram to skeletal Java or C++ code with the push of a button. You may or may not wish to avail yourself of this feature, however, for the following reasons:

   ❏ Depending on how much control the CASE tool gives you as to the structure that the generated code takes, the code that is generated will potentially not meet team/corporate standards.

   ❏ With most tools, you are unable to edit the generated code externally to the tool, because the tool will then be 'unaware' of the changes that you've made, meaning that the next time the code is generated, your changes will be overwritten/obliterated.

   ❏ This has implications for reusing code from other projects, as well: make sure that your tool of choice allows you to import and introduce software components that did not originate within the tool.

It is sometimes better in the end to write your code from scratch, for even though it may take a bit longer at the outset, it often is much easier to manage such code over the lifetime of the project, and you avoid become 'enslaved' to a particular modeling tool for ongoing code maintenance. In the worst case scenario, the tool vendor goes out of business, and you're left with an unsupportable project.

❏ Many CASE tools provide some sort of version control, enabling you to maintain different generations of the same model. If you make a change to your model, but then after reviewing the change with your users decide that you'd prefer to return to the way things were previously, it's trivial to do if version control is in place.

❏ CASE tools often provide configuration management/team collaboration capabilities, to enable a group of modelers to easily share in the creation of a single model.

❏ Some CASE tools support multiple graphical notations, enabling you to initially create a diagram in one notation (say, OMT) but to then convert the diagram to another notation (such as UML) quickly and effortlessly.

This does not always occur flawlessly, however; things can get lost in the translation if the two notations don't have a one-for-one match in terms of notational components; it's not unusual to have to do some minor cleanup after the fact.

- ❑ Some tools even support customizable or 'do it yourself' notational paradigms, should you wish to either embellish a standard notation such as UML or to invent a new notation from scratch.

CASE tools are not without their drawbacks, however:

- ❑ CASE tools can be expensive; it's not unusual for a high-end CASE tool to cost hundreds or even thousands of dollars per 'seat'.

- ❑ CASE tools can sometimes be inflexible – we talk about adapting processes, notations, and tools to suit your own needs throughout Part 2 of the book, but tools don't always cooperate! We'll point out some specific examples in upcoming chapters of situations where you might want to bend the notation a little bit, if your CASE tool will accommodate it.

- ❑ A CASE tool can be difficult to adopt mid-cycle on a project, as existing software does not always import well.

- ❑ **It's easy to get caught up with form over substance!** This is true of any automated tool – even a word processor tends to lure people into spending more time on the cosmetics of a document than is warranted, long after the substantive content is rock solid.

Generally speaking, however, the pros of using an OO CASE tool significantly outweigh the cons – consider the cons 'words to the wise' on how to successfully apply a tool to your modeling efforts.

A Reminder

Although we've said it several times already in this book, it is important to remind you that the process of object modeling is language neutral. We presented Java syntax in Part 1 of the book because our ultimate goal is to make you comfortable with both object modeling and Java programming. In Part 2 of the book, however, we're going to drift away from Java, because we truly are at a point where the concepts you'll be learning are just as applicable to Java as they are to C++, or Smalltalk, or any other OO programming language. But, never fear – we'll return to Java 'big time' in Part 3!

Summary

By far, the most important lesson to take away from this chapter is:

> **Don't get caught up in form over substance! The model that you produce is only a means to an end... and the process, notation, and tools that you use to produce the model are but a *means* to the means to this end. If you get too hung up on which notation to use, or which process to use, or which tool to use, you may wind up spinning your wheels in 'analysis paralysis'. Don't lose sight of your ultimate goal: to build useable, flexible, maintainable, reliable, functionally correct software systems.**

Exercises

1. Briefly describe the methodology – process, notation, and tool(s) – that you used on a recent software development project. What aspects of this methodology worked well for you and your team mates, and what, in hindsight, do you think could have been approached more effectively?

2. Research one of the object modeling technologies/techniques mentioned in the 'Modeling Methodology = Process + Notation + Tool' section earlier in this chapter, and report briefly on the process, notation, and/or tools involved.

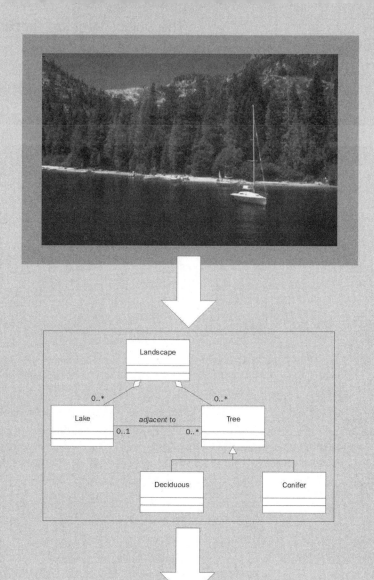

```
public class Tree {
    protected Landscape landscape;
    protected Lake nextTo;

    public void setNextTo(Lake l) {
        nextTo = l;
    }
    public Lake getNextTo() {
        return nextTo;
    }

    public abstract Color getLeafColor();
}
```

Formalizing Requirements through Use Cases

When you get ready to leave on a vacation, you may run through a mental or written checklist: Did you pack everything you need to take? Did you pack too much? Did you arrange to have the appropriate services (newspaper, mail delivery, etc.) stopped? Did you arrange for someone to water the plants and feed your pet rat? Once you depart on your trip, you want to enjoy yourself and know that when you arrive home again, you won't find any disasters waiting for you.

This is not unlike a software development project: we need to organize a checklist of the things that must be provided for by the system before we embark on its development, so that the project runs smoothly and so that we don't create a disaster (in the form of unmet requirements and dissatisfied customers/users) when the system is delivered.

The art and science of requirements analysis – for it truly is both! – is so extensive a topic that we could devote an entire book to this subject alone. There is one technique in particular for discovering and rounding out requirements known as **use case modeling** that is a cornerstone of the Rational Unified Process, and which warrants your consideration. Use cases are not strictly an artifact of OO methodologies; they can be prepared for any software system, regardless of the development methodology to be used. However, they made their debut within the software development community in the context of object systems, and have gained widespread popularity in that context.

In this chapter, you will learn:

- ❑ How we must anticipate all of the different roles that users will play when interacting with our future system

- ❑ That we must assume each of their viewpoints in describing the services that a software application as a whole is to provide

- ❑ How to prepare use cases as a means of documenting all of the above

We'll also give you enough general background about requirements analysis to provide an appropriate context for use case modeling.

What are Use Cases?

In determining what the desired functionality of a system is to be, we must seek answers to the following questions:

- ❏ **Who** will want to use our system?

- ❏ What **services** will the system need to provide in order to be of value to them?

- ❏ When a user interacts with the system for a particular purpose, what is his/her expectation as to the **desired outcome**?

Use cases are a natural way to express the answers to these questions. Each use case is a simple statement, narrative and/or graphical in fashion, that describes a particular goal or outcome of the system, and by whom that outcome is expected. For example, one goal of the SRS is to 'enable a student user to register for a course'; and thus we've just expressed our first use case! (Yes, use cases really are that straightforward. In fact, they **need** to be that straightforward, so that they are intelligible to the users/sponsors of the system, as we'll discuss further in a moment.)

Functional vs. Technical Requirements

The purpose of thinking through all of the use cases for a system is to explore the system's **functional requirements** thoroughly, so as to make sure that a particular category of user, or potential purpose for the system, isn't overlooked. We differentiate between functional requirements and technical requirements as follows:

- ❏ **Functional requirements** are those aspects of a system that have to do with how it is to operate or function from the perspective of someone using the system. Functional requirements may in turn be subdivided into:

  - ❏ **'Goal oriented' functional requirements:** these provide a statement of a system's purpose without regard to how the requirement will 'play out' from the user's vantage point; e.g. 'The system must be able to produce tailorable reports'. Avoid discussing implementation details when specifying goal oriented requirements.

  - ❏ **'Look and feel' requirements:** these requirements get a bit more specific in terms of what the user expects the system to look like externally (e.g. how the graphical user interface will be presented) and how they expect it to behave, again from the user's perspective. For example, we might have as a requirement 'The user will click a button on the main GUI, and a confirmation message will appear ...'. I often write a **concept of operations** document to serve as a 'paper prototype' describing how I envision the future system will look and behave, to stimulate discussion with intended users of the as-yet-to-be-built system before I even begin modeling.

  We emphasize *goal oriented* functional requirements when preparing use cases.

- ❏ **Technical requirements**, on the other hand, have more to do with how a system is to be built internally in order to **meet** the functional requirements, for instance: 'The system will use the TCP/IP protocol ...' or 'We will use a dictionary collection as the means for tracking students ...'. One can think of these as requirements for how programmers should tackle the **solution**, as contrasted with functional requirements, which are a statement of what the **problem** to be tackled actually is.

Technical requirements such as these do not play a role in use case analysis.

Although it is certainly conceivable that the users of our system may be technically sophisticated, it is best to express functional requirements in such a way that even a user who knows nothing about the inner workings of a computer will understand them. This helps to ensure that technical requirements don't 'creep into' the functional requirements statement, a common mistake made by many inexperienced software developers. When we allow technical requirements to color the functional requirements, they artificially constrain the solution to a problem too early in the development lifecycle.

Involving the Users

Because the intended users of a system are the ultimate experts in what they need the system to do, it is essential that they be involved in the use case definition process. If the intended users have not (as individuals) been specifically defined or recruited, as with a software product that is to be sold commercially, their anticipated needs nonetheless need to be taken into account by identifying people with comparable experience to serve as 'user surrogates'. Ideally, the users or 'user surrogates' will write some or all of the use cases themselves; at a minimum, you'll interview such people, write the use cases on their behalf, and then get their confirmation that what you've written is indeed accurate.

Use cases are one of the first deliverables/artifacts to emerge in a software development project's lifecycle, but also one of the last things to be put to good use in making sure that the system is a success.

❑   They turn out to be quite useful as a basis for writing testing scripts, to ensure that all functional threads are exercised during system and user acceptance testing.

❑   They also lend themselves to the preparation of a **requirements traceability matrix** – that is, a final checklist against which the users can verify that all of their initial requirements have indeed been met when the system is delivered. (Of course, a requirements traceability matrix must take into account all of the requirements for a system – functional as well as technical – of which use cases represent only a subset.)

Returning to the questions that we posed at the outset of this section, let's answer the first question – namely, 'Who will want to use our system?' – which in use case nomenclature is known as identifying **actors**.

Actors

Actors represent anybody or anything that will interact with the system after it is built; actors drive use cases. Actors generally fall into two broad categories:

❑   Human users

❑   Other computer systems

'Interaction' is generally defined to mean using the system to achieve some result, but can also be thought of as simply (a) providing/contributing information to the system and/or (b) receiving/consuming information from the system.

❑   By **providing** information, we mean whether or not the actor inputs substantive information that adds to the residual data stored by the system: for example, a Department Chair defining a new course offering, or a student registering his/her plan of study. This does not include the relatively trivial information that a user has to provide to look things up: for example, typing in a student ID to request his/her transcript.

❑ By **consuming** information, we mean whether or not the actor uses the system to obtain information/**knowledge**, for example: a Faculty user printing out a student roster for a course that he/she will be teaching, or a Student viewing his/her course schedule on-line.

We must create an actor for every different role that will be assumed by various categories of user relative to the system. To identify such roles, we typically turn first to the **narrative requirements specification**, if one exists: that is, a statement of the functional requirements, such as the Student Registration System specification. The only category of user explicitly mentioned by that specification is a student user. So, we would definitely consider Student to be one of the actor types for the SRS. If we think beyond the specification, however, it isn't difficult to come up with other potential categories of user who might also benefit from using the SRS:

❑ Faculty may wish to get a headcount of how many students are registered for one of the upcoming classes that they are going to be teaching, or may use the system to post final grades which in turn are reflected by a student's transcript.

❑ Department chairpersons may wish to see how popular various courses are or, conversely, whether or not a course ought to be cancelled due to lack of interest on the part of the student body.

❑ Personnel in the Registrar's Office may wish to use the SRS to verify that a particular student is projected to have met the requirements to graduate in a given semester.

❑ Alumni may wish to use the SRS to request copies of their transcripts.

❑ Prospective students – i.e. those who are thinking about applying for admission but who haven't yet done so – may wish to browse the courses that are going to be offered in an upcoming semester to help them determine whether or not the university has a curriculum that meets their interests.

and so on. Similarly, since we said that other computer systems can be actors, we might have to build interfaces between the SRS and other existing automated systems at the university, such as:

❑ The Billing System, so that students can be billed accurately based on their current course load.

❑ The Classroom Scheduling System, to ensure that classes to be taught are assigned to rooms of adequate capacity based on the student headcount.

❑ The Admissions System, so that the SRS can be notified when a new student has been admitted and is eligible to register for courses.

Of course, we have to make a decision early on as to what the scope of the system we are going to build should be, to avoid 'requirements inflation' or 'scope creep'. To try and accommodate all of the actors hypothesized above would result in a massive undertaking that may simply be too costly for the sponsors of the system. For example, does it make sense to provide for potential students to use the SRS to preview what the university offers in the way of courses, or is there a different system – say, an on-line course catalog of some sort – that is better suited to this purpose? Through in-depth interviews with all of the intended user groups, the scope of the system can be appropriately bounded, and some of the actors that we conceived of may be eliminated as a result.

In our particular case, we'll assume that the sponsors of the SRS have decided that we needn't accommodate the needs of alumni or prospective students in building the system; that is, that we needn't recognize Alumni or Prospective Students as actors. A key point here is that the sponsors decide such things, not the *programmers!* One responsibility of a software engineer is indeed to identify requirements, and certainly part of that responsibility may include suggesting functional enhancements that the software engineer feels will be of benefit to the user. But, the sponsors of the system rightfully have the final say in what actually gets built.

Many software engineers get into trouble because they assume that they 'know better' than their clients as to what the users really need. You may indeed have a brilliant idea to suggest, but think of it simply as that – a suggestion – and consider your task as one of either convincing the sponsors/users of its merit, or of graciously accepting their decision to decline your suggestion.

Note that the same user may interact with the system on different occasions in different actor's roles. That is, a professor who chairs a department may assume the role of a Department Chair actor when he or she is trying to determine whether or not a course should be cancelled. Alternatively, the same professor may assume the role of a Faculty user when he or she wishes to query the SRS for the student headcount for a particular course that he or she is teaching.

Once we've settled on what the actors for our system are, we may wish to optionally diagram them. UML notation calls for representing all actors – whether a human user or a computer system – as stick figures, then connecting these via straight lines to a box/rectangle representing the system.

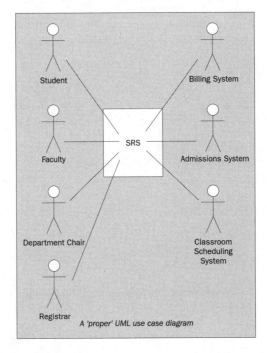

A 'proper' UML use case diagram

This figure appears rather simplistic, and yet, this is a legitimate diagram that might be produced for a project such as the SRS development effort.

I prefer to use a slightly modified version of the UML notation, as follows:

❑ I've extended the use of a box/rectangle to represent not only the core system but also all actors that are external systems, rather than representing the latter as human stick figures.

❑ I find that using arrowheads to reflect a directional flow of information – i.e. whether an actor provides or consumes information – is a bit more communicative. For example, in my amended version of the notation as follow, I reflect a Student as both providing and consuming information, whereas a Registrar only consumes information.

205

The Registrar does indeed provide information, but not to the SRS: he or she provides information to the Admissions System as to which students are registered at the university; this information then gets fed into the SRS by the Admissions System. So, the Admissions System is shown as providing information as an actor to the SRS; but, from the standpoint of the SRS, the Registrar is but a consumer.

With these slight changes in notation, the UML diagram becomes a much more communicative instrument, in my opinion.

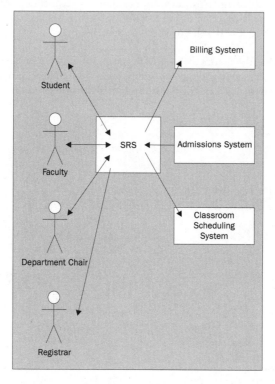

Of course, if you do decide to deviate from a widely understood notational standard such as UML, you'll need to:

❑ Reach consensus among your fellow software developers, to ensure that the team as a whole is speaking the same language.

❑ Document and communicate such deviations (along with the notation as a whole) to your customers/users, so that they, too, understand your particular 'dialect'.

❑ Make sure that such documentation is incorporated into the full documentation set for the project, so that future reviewers of the documentation will immediately understand your notational 'embellishments'.

If you make these enhancements intuitive enough, however, they may just speak for themselves!

Of course, as we pointed out in Chapter 8, you'll also need to consider whether the CASE tool you are using, if any, will support such alterations.

Time and again throughout Part 2 of this book, I'll remind you that it is perfectly acceptable to adapt or extend any process, notation, or tool that you care to adopt to best suit your company's or project's purposes; none of these methodology components is 'sacred'.

Specifying Use Cases

Having made a first cut at what the SRS actors are, we'll next enumerate in what ways the system will be used by these actors: in other words, the use cases themselves.

A use case represents a logical 'thread', or a series of cause and effect events, beginning with an actor's first contact with the system and ending with the achievement of that actor's goal for using the system in the first place. Note that an actor always initiates a use case; actions initiated by a system on its own behalf do not warrant the development of a use case (although they do warrant expression as either a functional or technical requirement, as defined earlier in the chapter).

Use cases emphasize 'what' the system is to do – functional requirements – without concern for 'how' such things will be accomplished internally, and are not unlike method signatures in this regard. In fact, you can think of a use case as a 'behavioral signature' for the system as a whole.

Some example high-level use cases for the Student Registration System might be:

- ❏ Register for a course
- ❏ Drop a course
- ❏ Determine a student's course load
- ❏ Choose a faculty advisor
- ❏ Establish a plan of study
- ❏ View schedule of classes
- ❏ Request a student roster for a given course
- ❏ Request a transcript for a given student
- ❏ Maintain course information (for example, change the course description, reflect a different instructor for the course, and so on)
- ❏ Determine a student's eligibility for graduation
- ❏ Post final semester grades for a given course

Remember that a use case is initiated by an actor, which is why we didn't list other functionality called out by the SRS requirements specification, such as 'Notify student by email', as use cases.

We may decompose any one of the use cases into steps, each one representing a 'sub use case'; for example, 'Register for a course ...' may be decomposed into:

- ❏ Verify that a student has met the prerequisites
- ❏ Check student's plan of study to ensure that this course is required

❏　　Check for availability of a seat in the course

❏　　(Optionally) Place student on a wait list

and so forth. These 'sub use cases' are often shared by multiple 'parent' use cases; for example, the 'Request a student roster ...' and 'Post final semester grades ...' use cases may both involve the 'Verify that professor is teaching the course in question' 'sub use case'.

> *The term 'sub use case' is a bit of a misnomer, since as we mentioned earlier, a true use case is an end-to-end thread through the system, whereas many of these 'sub use cases' are merely a step in such a process.*

Unfortunately, as is true of all requirements analysis, there is no magical formula to apply in order to determine whether or not you've identified all of the important use cases or all of the actors, and/or whether you've gone into sufficient depth in terms of sub use cases. The process of use case development is iterative; when subsequent iterations fail to yield substantial changes, you are probably finished! Copious interviews and reviews with users, along with periodic team walkthroughs of the use case set as a whole, go a long way in ensuring that nothing important has been missed.

Matching Up Use Cases with Actors

Another important step is to match up use cases with actors. The relationship between actors and use cases is potentially many-to-many, in that the same actor may initiate many different use cases, and a single use case may be relevant to many different actors. By cross-referencing actors with use cases, we ensure that:

❏　　We didn't identify an actor who, in the final analysis, really has no use for the system after all.

❏　　Conversely, that we didn't specify a use case that nobody really cares about after all.

For each use case–actor combination, it is useful to determine whether the actor consumes information and/or provides information. Another way to view this aspect of a system is whether actors need write access to the system's information resources (providing) versus having read-only access (consuming).

If the number of actors and/or use cases isn't prohibitive, a simple table can be used to summarize all of the above, as follows:

Initiating Actor ==> Use Case:	Student	Faculty	BillingSystem	(etc.)
Register for a course	provides info	N/A	N/A	
Post final grades	consumes info.	provides info.	N/A	
Request a transcript	consumes info.	consumes info.	N/A	
Determine a student's course load	consumes info.	consumes info.	consumes info.	
(etc.)				

To Diagram or Not to Diagram?

The use case concept is fairly straightforward, and hence simple narrative text as we've seen thus far in the chapter is often sufficient for expressing use cases. The UML does, however, provide a formal means for diagraming use cases and their interactions with actors. As mentioned earlier, actors (whether people or systems) are represented as stick figures; use cases are represented as ovals labeled underneath with a brief phrase describing the use case; and the box surrounding the oval(s) represent the system boundaries. A sample UML use case diagram follows; here, we depict three actors – Student, Faculty, and Registrar – as having occasion to participate individually in the Request Transcript use case.

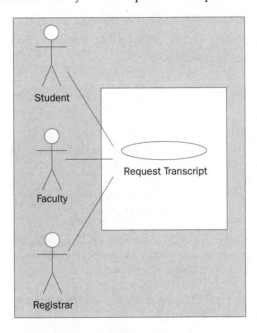

When deciding whether or not to go to the trouble of diagramming your use cases rather than merely expressing them in narrative form, think back to the rationale for producing use cases in the first place: namely, to think through, and to then communicate, the software development team's understanding of the system requirements to the users/sponsors in order to obtain consensus. It is up to you, your project team, and your users/sponsors to determine whether diagrams enhance this process or not. If they do, use them; if they don't, go with narrative use case documentation instead.

Once you have documented a system's actors and use cases, whether in text alone or with accompanying diagrams, these become part of the core documentation set defining the problem to be automated. In the next chapter, we'll learn how to use such documentation as a starting point for determining what classes we'll need to create and instantiate as our system 'building blocks'.

The UML spells out some additional formalism with regard to use case modeling; for more details on use case diagrams, including advanced diagraming techniques, please see our Recommended Reading list in Chapter 17.

Summary

In this chapter, we've learned that:

- ❑ Use case analysis is a simple yet powerful technique for making the requirements specification for a system more precise and complete.

- ❑ Use cases are based upon the goal oriented functional requirements for a system.

- ❑ Use cases are used to describe:

    - ❑ The desired behavior/functionality of the system to be built.

    - ❑ The external users or systems who avail themselves of these services (known as actors).

    - ❑ The interactions between the two.

Exercises

1. Determine the actors that might be appropriate for the Conference Room Reservation System (CRRS) case study discussed in Appendix B.

2. For the problem area whose requirements you defined for exercise no. 3 in Chapter 2, determine what the appropriate actors might be.

3. Based on the CRRS specification in Appendix B, list (a) the use cases that are explicitly called for by the specification, (b) any additional use cases that you suspect might be worth exploring with the future users of the system.

4. Repeat exercise 3 above, but in the context of the problem area whose requirements you defined for exercise no. 3 in Chapter 2.

5. Create a table mapping the actors you identified in exercise 1 above to the use cases you listed in exercise 3 above, indicating whether a particular actor's participation in a use case is as an information provider and/or consumer.

6. Create a table mapping the actors you identified in exercise 2 above to the use cases you listed in exercise 4 above, indicating whether a particular actor's participation in a use case is as an information provider and/or consumer.

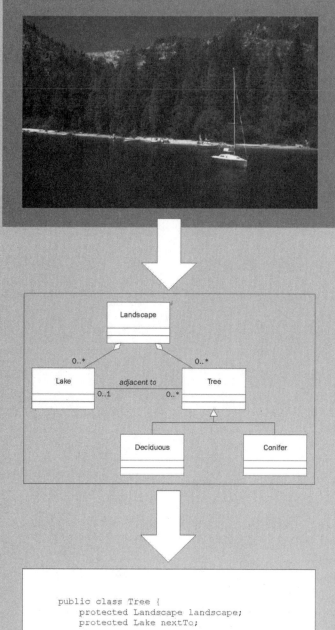

```
public class Tree {
    protected Landscape landscape;
    protected Lake nextTo;

    public void setNextTo(Lake l) {
        nextTo = l;
    }
    public Lake getNextTo() {
        return nextTo;
    }

    public abstract Color getLeafColor();
}
```

Modeling the Static/ Data Aspects of the System

Having employed use case analysis techniques in Chapter 9 to round out the SRS requirements specification, we're ready to tackle the next stage of modeling, which is determining how we're going to meet those requirements in an object-oriented fashion.

We learned in Part 1 of the book that objects form the building blocks of an OO system, and that classes are the templates used to define and instantiate objects. An OO model, then, must specify:

❑   **What classes of objects we are going to need to create and instantiate in order to represent the proper abstraction:** in particular, their attributes, methods, and structural relationships with one another. Because these elements of an object-oriented system, once established, are fairly static – in the same way that a house, once built, has a specific layout, a given number of rooms, a particular roofline, and so forth – we often refer to this process as preparing the **static model**.

We can certainly change the static structure of a house over time by undertaking remodeling projects, just as we can change the static structure of an OO software system as new requirements emerge by deriving new subclasses, inventing new methods for existing classes, and so forth. However, if a structure – whether a home or a software system – is properly designed from the outset, then the need for such changes should arise relatively infrequently over its lifetime and shouldn't be overly difficult to accommodate.

❑   **How these objects will need to collaborate in carrying out the overall requirements, or 'mission', of the system:** The ways in which objects interact can change literally from one moment to the next based upon the circumstances that are in effect. One moment, a Course object may be registering a Student object, and the next, it might be responding to a query by a Professor object as to the current student headcount. We refer to the process of detailing object collaborations as preparing the **dynamic model**. Think of this as all of the different day-to-day activities that go on in a home: same structure, different functions.

The static and dynamic models are simply two different sides of the same coin: they jointly comprise the blueprint that we'll work from in implementing an object-oriented Student Registration System (SRS) application in Part 3 of the book.

In this chapter, we'll focus on building the static model for the SRS, leaving a discussion of the dynamic model for Chapter 11. You will learn:

❑ A technique for identifying the appropriate classes and their attributes.

❑ How to determine the structural relationships that exist among these classes.

❑ How to graphically portray this information as a **class diagram** using the UML notation.

Identifying Appropriate Classes

Our first challenge in object modeling is to determine what classes we're going to need as our system building blocks. Unfortunately, the process of class identification is rather 'fuzzy'; it relies heavily on intuition, prior modeling experience, and familiarity with the subject area, or **domain**, of the system to be developed. So, how does an object-modeling novice **ever** get started? One tried and true (but somewhat tedious) procedure for identifying candidate classes is to use the 'hunt and gather' method: that is, to hunt for and gather a list of all nouns/noun phrases from the project documentation set and to then use a process of elimination to whittle this list down into a set of appropriate classes.

In the case of the SRS, our documentation set thus far consists of:

❑ The requirements specification

❑ The use case model that we prepared in Chapter 9

Noun Phrase Analysis

Let's perform noun phrase analysis on the requirements specification first, which was originally presented in the Introduction to the book, a copy of which is provided below. We've highlighted all noun phrases:

We have been asked to develop an **automated Student Registration System (SRS)** for the **university**. This **system** will enable **students** to register on-line for **courses** each **semester**, as well as tracking their **progress** toward **completion** of their **degree**.

When a **student** first enrolls at the **university**, he/she uses the **SRS** to set forth a **plan of study** as to which **courses** he/she plans on taking to satisfy a particular **degree program**, and chooses a **faculty advisor**. The **SRS** will verify whether or not the proposed **plan of study** satisfies the **requirements of the degree** that the **student** is seeking.

Once a **plan of study** has been established, then, during the **registration period** preceding each **semester**, **students** are able to view the **schedule of classes** on line, and choose whichever **classes** they wish to attend, indicating the **preferred section** (**day of the week** and **time of day**) if the **class** is offered by more than one **professor**. The **SRS** will verify whether or not the **student** has satisfied the necessary **prerequisites** for each **requested course** by referring to the **student**'s on-line **transcript** of **courses completed** and **grades received** (the **student** may review his/her **transcript** on-line at any time).

Assuming that (a) the **prerequisites** for the **requested course(s)** are satisfied, (b) the **course(s)** meet(s) one of the **student's plan of study requirements**, and (c) there is **room** available in each of the **class(es)**, the **student** is enrolled in the **class(es)**.

If (a) and (b) are satisfied, but (c) is not, the **student** is placed on a **first-come, first-served wait list**. If a **class/section that he/she was previously wait-listed for** becomes available (either because some other **student** has dropped the **class** or because the **seating capacity** for the **class** has been increased), the **student** is automatically enrolled in the **waitlisted class**, and an **email message** to that effect is sent to the **student**. It is his/her **responsibility** to drop the **class** if it is no longer desired; otherwise, he/she will be billed for the **course**.

Students may drop a **class** up to the **end** of the **first week of the semester in which the class is being taught**.

A simple spreadsheet serves as an ideal tool for recording our initial findings; just enter noun phrases as a single-column list in the order in which they occur in the specification. Don't worry about trying to eliminate duplicates or consolidating synonyms just yet; we'll do that in a moment. The resultant spreadsheet is shown in part below.

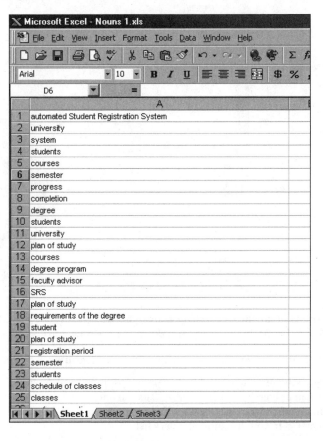

We're working with a very concise requirements specification (approximately 350 words in length), and yet this process is already proving to be very tedious! It would be impossible to carry out an exhaustive noun phrase analysis for anything but a trivially simple specification. If you are faced with a voluminous requirements specification, start by writing an 'executive summary' of no more than a few pages to paraphrase the system's mission, and then use your summary version of the specification as the starting point for your noun survey. Paraphrasing a specification in this fashion provides the added benefit of ensuring that you have read through and *understand* the 'big picture' concerning the system requirements. Of course, you'll need to review your summary narrative with your customers/users to ensure that you've accurately captured all key points.

After you've typed all of the nouns/noun phrases into the spreadsheet, sort the spreadsheet and eliminate duplicates; this includes eliminating plural forms of singular terms (e.g. eliminate 'students' in favor of 'student'). We want all of our class names to be singular in the final analysis, so if any plural forms remain in the list after eliminating duplicates (e.g. 'prerequisites'), make these singular, as well. In so doing, our SRS list shrinks to 38 items in length, as shown below.

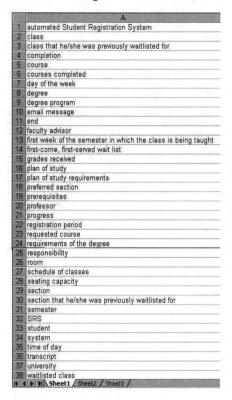

	A
1	automated Student Registration System
2	class
3	class that he/she was previously waitlisted for
4	completion
5	course
6	courses completed
7	day of the week
8	degree
9	degree program
10	email message
11	end
12	faculty advisor
13	first week of the semester in which the class is being taught
14	first-come, first-served wait list
15	grades received
16	plan of study
17	plan of study requirements
18	preferred section
19	prerequisites
20	professor
21	progress
22	registration period
23	requested course
24	requirements of the degree
25	responsibility
26	room
27	schedule of classes
28	seating capacity
29	section
30	section that he/she was previously waitlisted for
31	semester
32	SRS
33	student
34	system
35	time of day
36	transcript
37	university
38	waitlisted class

Remember, we're trying to identify physical or conceptual objects: as stated in Chapter 3, '*something mental or physical toward which thought, feeling, or action is directed*'. Let's now make another pass to eliminate:

❑ References to the system itself ('automated Student Registration System', 'SRS', 'system').

❑ References to the university. Because we are building the SRS within the context of a single university, the university in some senses 'sits outside' and 'surrounds' the SRS; we don't need to manipulate information about the university within the SRS, and so we may eliminate the term 'university' from our candidate class list.

Note, however, that if we were building a system that needed to span multiple universities – say, a system that compared graduate programs of study in information technology across the top 100 universities in the country – then we would need to model each university as a separate object, in which case we'd keep 'university' on our candidate class list.

❏ Other miscellaneous terms which don't seem to fit the definition of an object are 'completion', 'end', 'progress', 'responsibility', 'registration period' and 'requirements of the degree'. Admittedly, some of these are debatable, particularly the last two; to play it safe, you may wish to create a list of rejected terms to be revisited later on in the modeling lifecycle.

The list shrinks to 27 items as a result, as shown below – it's starting to get manageable now!

	A
1	class
2	class that he/she was previously waitlisted for
3	course
4	courses completed
5	day of week
6	degree
7	degree program
8	email message
9	faculty advisor
10	first-come, first-served wait list
11	grades received
12	plan of study
13	plan of study requirements
14	preferred section
15	prerequisites
16	professor
17	requested course
18	room
19	schedule of classes
20	seating capacity
21	section
22	section that he/she was previously waitlisted for
23	semester
24	student
25	time of day
26	transcript
27	waitlisted class

Sheet1 / Sheet2 / Sheet3 /

The next pass is a bit trickier. We need to group apparent synonyms, to choose the one designation from among each group of synonyms that is best suited to serving as a class name. Having a subject matter expert on your modeling team is important for this step, because determining the subtle shades of meaning of some of these terms so as to group them properly is not always easy.

We've grouped together terms which seem to be synonyms in the figure below, **bolding** the term in each synonym group that we are inclined to choose above the rest; italicized words represent those terms for which no synonyms have been identified.

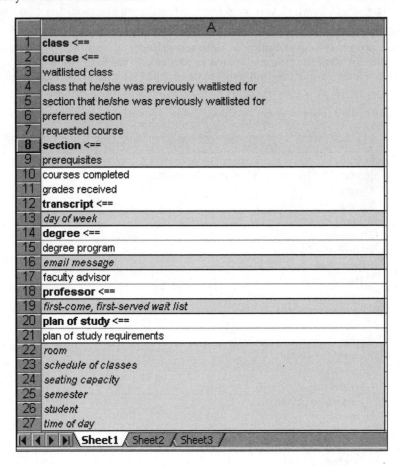

	A
1	**class <==**
2	**course <==**
3	waitlisted class
4	class that he/she was previously waitlisted for
5	section that he/she was previously waitlisted for
6	preferred section
7	requested course
8	**section <==**
9	prerequisites
10	courses completed
11	grades received
12	**transcript <==**
13	*day of week*
14	**degree <==**
15	degree program
16	*email message*
17	faculty advisor
18	**professor <==**
19	*first-come, first-served wait list*
20	**plan of study <==**
21	plan of study requirements
22	*room*
23	*schedule of classes*
24	*seating capacity*
25	*semester*
26	*student*
27	*time of day*

Sheet1 / Sheet2 / Sheet3 /

Let's review the rationale for our choices:

❑ We choose the shorter form of equivalent expressions whenever possible – **degree** instead of degree program and **plan of study** instead of plan of study requirements – to make our model more concise.

❑ Although they aren't synonyms as such, the notion of a **transcript** implies a record of 'courses completed' and 'grades received', so we'll opt to drop the latter two noun phrases for now.

❑ When choosing candidate class names, we should avoid choosing nouns that imply **roles** between objects. As we learned in Chapter 5, a role is something that an object belonging to class A possesses by virtue of its relationship to/association with an object belonging to class B. For example, a professor holds the role of 'faculty advisor' when that professor is associated with a student via an 'advises' association. Even if a professor were to lose all of his/her advisees, thus losing the role of faculty advisor, he/she would still be a professor by virtue of being employed by the university – it is inherent in the person's nature relative to the SRS.

If a professor were to lose his/her job with the university, one might argue that he/she is no longer a professor; but then, this person would have no dealings with the SRS, either, so it is a moot point.

For this reason, we prefer 'Professor' to 'Faculty Advisor' as a candidate class name, but make a mental note to ourselves that faculty advisor would make a good potential association when we get to considering such things later on.

❑   Regarding the notion of a course, we see that we have collected numerous noun phrases that all refer to a course in one form or another: 'class', 'course', 'preferred section', 'requested course', 'section', 'prerequisite', 'waitlisted class', 'class that they were previously waitlisted for', 'section that they were previously waitlisted for'. Within this grouping, several roles are implied:

   ❑   'waitlisted class' in its several different forms implies a role in an association between a Student and a Course

   ❑   'prerequisite' implies a role in an association between two Courses

   ❑   'requested course' implies a role in an association between a Student and a Course

   ❑   'preferred section' implies a role in an association between a Student and a Course

Eliminating all of these role designations, we are left with only three terms: 'class', 'course', and 'section'. Before we hastily eliminate all but one of these as synonyms, let's think carefully about what real-world concepts we're trying to represent.

❑   The notion that we typically associate with the term 'course' is that of a semester-long series of lectures, assignments, exams, etc. that all relate to a particular subject area, and which are a unit of education toward earning a degree. For example, Beginning Math is a course.

❑   The terms 'class' and 'section', on the other hand, generally refer to the offering of a particular course in a given semester on a given day of the week and at a given time of day. For example, the course Math 101 is being offered this coming Spring semester as three classes/sections:

   ❑   Section 1, which meets Tuesdays from 4 – 6 PM

   ❑   Section 2, which meets Wednesdays from 6 – 8 PM

   ❑   Section 3, which meets Thursdays from 3 – 5 PM

❑   There is a one-to-many association between Course and Class/Section. The same course is offered potentially many times in a given semester and over many semesters during the 'lifetime' of the course.

Therefore, 'course' and 'class/section' truly represent different abstractions, and we'll keep **both** concepts in our candidate class list. Since 'class' and 'section' appear to be synonyms, however, we need to choose one term and discard the other. Our inclination would be to keep 'class' and discard 'section', but in order to avoid confusion when referring to a class called Class (!) we'll opt for 'section' instead.

To make matters worse, there is also a built in Java class called `Class`*! We'll see it in use in Chapter 13.*

A list of candidate classes has begun to emerge from the fog! Here is our remaining 'short list' (please disregard the trailing symbols (*, +) for the moment – we will explain their significance shortly):

- ❑ course
- ❑ day of week*
- ❑ degree*
- ❑ email message+
- ❑ plan of study
- ❑ professor
- ❑ room*
- ❑ schedule of classes+
- ❑ seating capacity*
- ❑ section
- ❑ semester*
- ❑ student
- ❑ time of day*
- ❑ transcript
- ❑ (first-come, first-served) wait list

Not all of these will necessarily survive to the final model, however, as we're going to scrutinize each one very closely before deeming it worthy of implementation as a class. One classic test for determining whether or not an item can stand on its own as a class is to ask the questions:

- ❑ Can I think of any attributes for this class?
- ❑ Can I think of any services that would be expected of objects belonging to this class?

One example is the term 'room': we could invent a Room class as follows:

```
class Room {
  // Attributes.
  int roomNo;
  String building;
  int seatingCapacity;
  // etc.
}
```

or we could simply represent a room location as a `String` attribute of the `Section` class:

```
class Section {
  // Attributes
  Course offeringOf;
  String semester;
  char dayOfWeek;  // 'M', 'T', 'W', 'R', 'F'
  String timeOfDay;
  String classroomLocation; // building name and room name:  e.g.,
                            //   "Government Hall Room 105"
  // etc.
}
```

Which approach to representing a room is preferred? It all depends on whether or not a room needs to be a focal point of our application. If the SRS were meant to do 'double duty' as a Classroom Scheduling System, then we may indeed wish to instantiate Room objects so as to be able to ask them to perform such services as printing out their weekly usage schedules or telling us their seating capacities. However, since these services were not mentioned as requirements in the SRS specification, we'll opt for making a room designation a simple `String` attribute of the `Section` class. We reserve the right, however, to change our minds about this later on; it's not unusual for some items to 'flip flop' over the lifecycle of a modeling exercise between being classes on their own vs. being represented as simple attributes of other classes.

Following a similar train of thought for all of the items marked with an asterisk (*) in the candidate class list above, we'll opt to reflect them all as attributes rather than making them classes of their own:

❑ 'day of week' will be incorporated as either a `String` or `char` attribute of the `Section` class;

❑ 'degree' will be incorporated as a `String` attribute of the `Student` class;

❑ 'seating capacity' will be incorporated as an `int` attribute of the `Section` class;

❑ 'semester' will be incorporated as a `String` attribute of the `Section` class; and

❑ 'time of day' will be incorporated as a `String` attribute of the `Section` class.

When we are first modeling an application, we want to focus exclusively on functional requirements at the exclusion of technical requirements, as defined in Chapter 9; this means that we need to avoid getting into the technical details of how the system is going to function behind the scenes. Ideally, we want to focus solely on what are known as **domain classes** – that is, abstractions that an end user will recognize, and which represent 'real world' entities – and to avoid introducing any extra classes that are used solely as behind-the-scenes 'scaffolding' to hold the application together, known alternatively as **implementation classes** or **solution space classes**. Examples of the latter would be the creation of a collection object to organize and maintain references to all of the Professor objects in the system, or the use of a dictionary to provide a way to quickly find a particular Student object based on his/her student ID number. We will talk more about solution space objects in Part 3 of the book; for the time being, the items flagged with a plus sign (+) in the candidate class list above – email message, schedule of classes – seem arguably more like implementation classes than domain classes:

❑ An email message is typically a **transient** piece of data, not unlike a popup message that appears on the screen while using an application: it gets sent **out** of the SRS system, and after it is read by the recipient, we have no control over whether the email is retained or deleted. It is unlikely that the SRS is going to archive copies of all email messages that have been sent – there certainly was no requirement to do so – so we won't worry about modeling them as objects at this stage in our analysis.

Email messages will resurface in Chapter 11, when we talk about the behaviors of the SRS application, because **sending** an email message is definitely an important **behavior**; but, emails do not constitute an important **structural** piece of the application, so we don't want to introduce a class for them at this stage in the modeling process. When we actually get to programming the system, we might indeed create an `EmailMessage` class in Java, but it needn't be modeled as a domain class. (If, on the other hand, we were modeling an email messaging system in anticipation of building one, then `EmailMessage` would indeed be a key class in our model.)

❑ We could go either way with the schedule of classes – include it as a candidate class, or drop it from our list. The schedule of classes, as a single object, may not be something that the user will manipulate directly, but there will be some notion behind the scenes of a schedule of classes **collection** controlling which Section objects should be presented to the user as a GUI pick list when he/she registers in a given semester. We'll omit Schedule of Classes from our candidate class list for now, but can certainly revisit our decision as the model evolves.

Determining whether or not a class constitutes a domain class instead of an implementation class is admittedly a gray area, and either of the above candidate class 'rejects' could be successfully argued into or out of the list of core domain classes for the SRS. In fact, this entire exercise of identifying classes hopefully illustrates a concept that was first introduced in Chapter 2; because of its importance, we'll repeat it again:

'[...] developing an appropriate model for a software system is perhaps the most difficult aspect of software engineering, because:

There are an unlimited number of possibilities. Abstraction is to a certain extent in the eye of the beholder: several different observers working independently are almost guaranteed to arrive at different models. Whose is the best? Passionate arguments have ensued!

To further complicate matters, *there is virtually never only one 'best' or 'correct' model,* only 'better' or 'worse' models relative to the problem to be solved. The same situation can be modeled in a variety of different, equally valid ways. [...]

[...] There is no 'acid test' to determine if a model has adequately captured all of a user's requirements.'

As we continue along with our SRS modeling exercise, and particularly as we move from modeling to implementation in Part 3 of the book, we'll have many opportunities to rethink the decisions that we've made here. The key point to remember is that the model is not 'cast in stone' until we actually begin programming, and even then, if we've used objects wisely, the model can be fairly painlessly modified to handle most new requirements. Think of a model as being formed out of modeling clay: we'll continue to reshape it over the course of the analysis and design phases of our project until we're satisfied with the result.

Meanwhile, back to the task of coming up with a list of candidate classes for the SRS. The terms that have survived our latest round of scrutiny are as follows:

- Course
- Plan of Study
- Professor
- Section
- Student
- Transcript
- Wait List

Let's examine 'Wait List' one last time. There is indeed a requirement for the SRS to maintain a student's position on a first-come, first-served wait list. But, it turns out that this requirement can actually be handled through a combination of an association between the `Student` and `Section` classes, plus something known as an **association class** which we'll learn about later in this chapter. This would not be immediately obvious to a beginning modeler, and so we'd fully expect that the Wait List class might make the final cut as a suggested SRS class. But, we're going to assume that we have an experienced object modeler on the team, who convinces us to eliminate the class; we'll see that this was a suitable move when we complete the SRS class diagram at the end of the chapter.

So, we'll settle on the following list of classes, based on our noun phrase analysis of the SRS specification:

- Course
- Plan of Study
- Professor
- Section
- Student
- Transcript

Revisiting the Use Cases

One more thing that we need to do before we deem our class list good to go is to revisit our use cases – in particular, the actors – to see if any of them ought to be added as classes. You may recall that we identified seven potential actors for the SRS in Chapter 9:

- Student
- Faculty
- Department Chair

- ❏ Registrar
- ❏ Billing System
- ❏ Admissions System
- ❏ Classroom Scheduling System

Do any of *these* deserve to be modeled as classes in the SRS? Here's how to make that determination: if any user associated with any actor type 'A' is going to need to manipulate (access or modify) information concerning an actor type 'B' when 'A' is logged onto the SRS, then 'B' needs to be included as a class in our model. This is best illustrated with a few examples.

- ❏ When a student logs onto the SRS, might he or she need to manipulate information about faculty? Yes; when a student selects an advisor, for example, he/she might need to view information about a variety of faculty members in order to choose an appropriate advisor. So, the Faculty actor role must be represented as a class in the SRS; and, indeed, we have already designated a `Professor` class, so we're covered there. But, student users are not concerned with Department Chairs per se.

- ❏ Following the same logic, we'd need to represent the Student actor role as a class because when professors log onto the SRS, they will be manipulating `Student` objects when printing out a course roster or assigning grades to students, for example. Since Student already appears in our candidate class list, we're covered there, as well.

- ❏ When **any** of the actors – faculty, students, the Registrar, the Billing System, the Admissions System, or the Classroom Scheduling System – access the SRS, will there be a need for any of them to manipulate information about the Registrar? No, at least not according to the SRS requirements that we've seen so far. Therefore, we needn't model the Registrar actor role as a class.

- ❏ The same holds true for the Billing, Admissions, and Classroom Scheduling Systems: they require 'behind the scenes' access to information managed by the SRS, but nobody logging onto the SRS expects to be able to manipulate any of these three systems directly, so they needn't be represented by domain classes in the SRS.

    *Again, when we get to **implementing** the SRS in code, we may indeed find it appropriate to create 'solution space' Java classes to represent interfaces to these other systems; but, such classes don't belong in a **domain** model of the SRS.*

Therefore, our proposed candidate class list remains unchanged after revisiting all actor roles:

- ❏ Course
- ❏ Plan of Study
- ❏ Professor
- ❏ Section
- ❏ Student
- ❏ Transcript

Is this a perfect list? No – there is no such thing! In fact, before all is said and done, the list may – and in fact probably will – evolve in the following ways:

- ❏ We may add classes later on: terms we eliminated from the specification, or terms that don't even appear in the specification, but which we will unearth through continued investigation.

- ❏ We may see an opportunity to generalize – that is, we may see enough commonality between two or more classes' respective attributes, methods, and/or relationships with other classes to warrant the creation of a common superclass.

- ❏ In addition, as we mentioned earlier, we may rethink our decisions regarding representing some concepts as simple attributes (semester, room, etc.) instead of as full-blown classes, and vice versa.

The development of a candidate class list is, as we've tried to illustrate, fraught with uncertainty. For this reason, **it is important to have someone experienced with object modeling available to your team when embarking on your first object modeling effort.** Most experienced modelers don't use the rote method of noun phrase analysis to derive a candidate class list; such folks can pretty much review a specification and directly pick out significant classes, in the same way that a professional jeweler can easily choose a genuine diamond from among a pile of fake gemstones. Nevertheless, what does 'significant' really mean? That's where the 'fuzziness' comes in! It is impossible to define precisely what makes one concept significant and another less so. We've tried to illustrate some rules of thumb by working through the SRS example, but you ultimately need a qualified mentor to guide you until you develop – and trust – your own intuitive sense for such things.

The bottom line, however, is that even expert modelers can't really confirm the appropriateness of a given candidate class until they see its proposed use in the full context of a class diagram that also reflects associations, attributes, and methods, which we'll do later in this chapter.

Producing a Data Dictionary

Early on in our analysis efforts, it is important that we clarify and begin to document our use of terminology. A **data dictionary** is ideal for this purpose. For each candidate class, the data dictionary should include a simple definition of what this item means in the context of the model/system as a whole; include an example if it helps to illustrate the definition.

Here is our complete SRS data dictionary so far:

> **Course**: a semester-long series of lectures, assignments, exams, etc. that all relate to a particular subject area, and which are typically associated with a particular number of credit hours; a unit of study toward a degree. For example Beginning Objects is a required **course** for the Master of Science Degree in Information Systems Technology.
>
> **Plan of Study**: a list of the **courses** that a student intends to take to fulfill the **course** requirements for a particular degree.

Professor: a member of the faculty who teaches **sections** and/or advises **students**.

Section: the offering of a particular **course** during a particular semester on a particular day of the week and at a particular time of day (for example, **course** 'Beginning Objects' as taught in the Spring 2001 semester on Mondays from 1:00 – 3:00 PM).

Student: a person who is currently enrolled at the university and who is eligible to register for one or more **sections**.

Transcript: a record of all of the **courses** taken to date by a particular **student** at this university, including which semester each **course** was taken in, the grade received, and the credits granted for the **course**, as well as reflecting an overall total number of credits earned and the **student's** grade point average (GPA).

Note that it is permissible, and in fact encouraged, for the definition of one term to include one or more of the other terms; when we do so, we highlight the latter in **bold text**.

The data dictionary joins the set of other SRS narrative documents as a subsequent source of information about the model. As our model evolves, we will expand the dictionary to include definitions of attributes, associations, and methods.

It is a good idea to also include the dictionary definition of a class as a header comment in the Java code representing that class. Make sure to keep this in-line documentation in synch with the external dictionary definition, however.

Determining Associations Between Classes

Once we've settled on an initial candidate class list, the next step is to determine how these classes are interrelated. To do this, we go back to our narrative documentation set (which has grown to consist of the SRS requirements specification, use cases, and data dictionary) and study verb phrases this time. Our goal in looking at verb phrases is to choose those that suggest structural relationships, as were defined in Chapter 5 – associations, aggregations, and inheritance – but to eliminate or ignore those that represent (transient) actions or behaviors. (We'll focus on behaviors, but from the standpoint of use cases, in Chapter 11.)

❑   For example, the specification states that a student 'chooses a faculty advisor'. This is indeed an action, but the result of this action is a lasting structural relationship between a professor and a student, which can be modeled via the association 'a Professor *advises* a Student'.

❑   As a student's advisor, a professor also meets with the student, answers the student's questions, recommends courses for the student to take, approves their plan of study, etc. - these are behaviors on the part of a professor acting in the role of an advisor, but do not directly result in any new relationships being formed between objects.

Let's try the verb phrase analysis approach on the requirements specification. We've highlighted all relevant verb phrases below (note that we omitted such obviously irrelevant verb phrases as 'We have been asked to develop an automated SRS ...'):

We have been asked to develop an automated Student Registration System (SRS) for the university. This system will **enable students to register** on-line **for courses** each semester, as well as **tracking their progress toward completion of their degree**.

When a student first **enrolls at the university**, he/she uses the SRS to **set forth a plan of study** as to which **courses he/she plans on taking** to **satisfy a particular degree program**, and **chooses a faculty advisor**. The SRS will **verify whether or not the proposed plan of study satisfies the requirements of the degree that the student is seeking**.

Once a **plan of study has been established**, then, during the registration period preceding each semester, students are able to **view the schedule of classes** on line, and **choose whichever classes he/she wishes to attend, indicating the preferred section** (day of the week and time of day) if the **class is offered by more than one professor**. The SRS will **verify whether or not the student has satisfied the necessary prerequisites** for each requested course by **referring to the student's on-line transcript** of courses completed and grades received (the **student may review his/her transcript** on-line at any time).

Assuming that (a) the **prerequisites for the requested course(s) are satisfied**, (b) the **course(s) meet(s) one of the student's plan of study requirements**, and (c) **there is room available** in each of the class(es), the **student is enrolled in the class(es)**.

If (a) and (b) are satisfied, but (c) is not, the **student is placed on a first-come, first-served wait list**. If a **class/section that he/she was previously wait-listed for becomes available** (either because some other **student has dropped the class** or because the **seating capacity for the class has been increased**), the **student is automatically enrolled in the waitlisted class**, and an **email message** to that effect **is sent** to the student. It is his/her responsibility to **drop the class** if it is no longer desired; otherwise, **he/she will be billed for the course**.

Students may drop a class up to the end of the first week of the semester in which the **class is being taught**.

Let's scrutinize a few of these:

❑ 'students [...] register [...] for courses': although the act of registering is a behavior, the end result is that a static relationship is created between a Student and a Section, as represented by the association 'a Student *registers* for a Section'. (Note that the specification mentions registering for 'courses', not 'sections', but as we stated in our data dictionary, a Student registers for concrete Sections as embodiments of Courses. Keep in mind when reviewing a specification that the English language is imprecise, and that as a result we have to read between the lines as to what the author really meant in every case. (If we are going to be the ones to write the specification, here is an incentive to keep the language as clear and concise as possible!)

- ❏ '[students track] their progress toward completion of their degree': again, this is a behavior, but it nonetheless implies a structural relationship between a Student and a Degree. However, recall that we didn't elect to represent Degree as a class – we opted to reflect it as a simple `String` attribute of the `Student` class – and so this suggested relationship is immaterial with respect to the candidate class list that we've developed.

- ❏ 'student first enrolls at the university': this is a behavior that results in a static relationship between a Student and the University; but, we deemed the notion of 'university' to be external to the system and so chose not to create a University class in our model. So, we disregard this verb phrase, as well.

- ❏ '[student] sets forth a plan of study': this is a behavior that results in the static relationship 'a Student *pursues/observes* a Plan of Study'.

- ❏ 'students are able to view the schedule of classes on-line': this is strictly a transient behavior of the SRS; no lasting relationship results from this action, so we disregard this verb phrase.

and so on.

Another complementary technique for both determining and recording what the relationships between classes should be is to create an n x n **association matrix**, where n represents the number of candidate classes that we've identified. Label the rows and the columns with the names of the classes, as shown for the empty matrix below.

	Section	Course	Plan of Study	Professor	Student	Transcript
Section						
Course						
Plan of Study						
Professor						
Student						
Transcript						

Then, complete the matrix as follows:

- ❏ In each cell of the matrix, list all of the associations that you can identify between the class named at the head of the row and the class named at the head of the column. For example, in the cell highlighted in the diagram on the next page at the intersection of the Student 'row' and the Section 'column', we have listed three potential associations:

  - ❏ A Student is waitlisted for a Section.

  - ❏ A Student is registered for a Section (this could be alternatively phrased as 'a Student is currently attending a Section').

  - ❏ A Student has previously taken a Section: this third association is important if we plan on maintaining a history of all of the classes that a student has ever taken in their career as a student, which we must do if we are to prepare a student's transcript on-line.

    (As it turns out, we'll be able to get by with a single association that does 'double duty' for the latter two of these, as we'll see later on in this chapter.)

❑ Mark a cell with an '✗' if there are no known relationships between the classes in question, or if the potential relationships between the classes are irrelevant. For example, we've marked the cells representing the intersection between Professor and Course with an '✗', even though there is an association possible – 'a Professor *is qualified to teach* a Course' – because it isn't relevant to the mission of the SRS.

❑ We mentioned in Chapter 4 that all associations are inherently bidirectional. This implies that if a cell in row *j*, column *k* indicates one or more associations, then the cell in row *k*, column *j* should reflect the reciprocal of these relationships. E.g. since the intersection of the Plan of Study 'row' and the Course 'column' indicates that 'a Plan of Study *calls for* a Course', then the intersection of the Course 'row' and the Plan of Study 'column' must indicate that 'a Course *is called for by* a Plan of Study'.

It's not always practical to state the reciprocal of an association; for example, our association matrix shows that 'a Student *plans to take* a Course', but to try to state its reciprocal – 'a Course *is planned to be taken* by a Student' – is quite awkward. In such cases where a reciprocal association would be awkward to phrase, simply indicate its presence with a '✓'.

	Section	Course	Plan of Study	Professor	Student	Transcript
Section	✗	instance of	✗	is taught by	✓	included in
Course	✓	prerequisite for	is called for by	✗	✓	✗
Plan of Study	✗	calls for	✗	✗	observed by	✗
Professor	teaches	✗	✗	✗	advises; teaches	✗
Student	registered for; waitlisted for; has previously taken	plans to take	observes	is advised by; studies under	✗	owns
Transcript	includes	✗	✗	✗	belongs to	✗

We'll be portraying these associations in graphical form shortly! For now, we'd want to go back and extend our data dictionary to explain what each of these associations means; here's one such example:

'**calls for** (a Plan of Study calls for a Course): In order to demonstrate that a **student** will satisfy the requirements for his/her chosen degree program, the **student** must formulate a **plan of study**. This **plan of study** lays out all of the **courses** that a **student** intends to take, and possibly specifies in which semester the **student** hopes to complete each **course**.'

Identifying Attributes

To determine what the attributes for each of our domain classes should be, we make yet another pass through the requirements specification looking for clues. We already stumbled upon a few attributes earlier, when we weeded out some nouns/noun phrases from our candidate class list:

❑   For the Section class, we identified 'day of week', 'room', 'seating capacity', 'semester', and 'time of day' as attributes

❑   For the Student class, we identified 'degree' as an attribute

We can also bring any prior knowledge that we have about the domain into play when assigning attributes to classes. Our knowledge of the way that universities operate, for example, suggests that all Students will need some sort of student ID number as an attribute, even though this is not mentioned anywhere in the SRS specification. We can't be sure whether this particular university assigns an arbitrary student ID number, or whether the default is to use a student's social security number (SSN) as his/her ID; these are details that we'd have to go back to our end users for clarification on.

Finally, we can also look at how similar information has been represented in existing legacy systems for clues as to what a class's attributes should be. For example, if a Student Billing System already exists at the university based on a relational database design, we might wish to study the structure of the relational database table housing Student information. The columns that have been provided in that table – name, address, birthdate, etc. – are logical attribute choices.

UML Notation: Modeling the Static Aspects of an Abstraction

Now that we have a much better understanding about the static aspects of our model, we're ready to portray these in graphical fashion to complement the narrative documentation that we've developed for the SRS. We'll be using the Unified Modeling Language (UML) to produce a **class diagram**; here are the rules for how various aspects of the model are to be portrayed.

Classes, Attributes, and Methods

We represent classes as rectangles. When we first conceive of a class – before we know what any of its attributes or methods are going to be – we simply place the class name in the rectangle, for example:

An *abstract* class is denoted by presenting the name in italics, for example:

When we are ready to reflect the attributes and/or methods of a class, we divide the class rectangle into three **compartments** – the class name compartment, the attributes compartment, and the operations compartment – as shown below. Note that we prefer the nomenclature of 'operations' versus 'methods' to reinforce the notion that the diagram that we are producing is intended to be programming language independent.

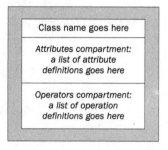

Some CASE tools automatically portray all three compartments when a class is first created, even if we haven't specified any attributes or methods yet:

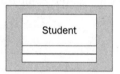

As we begin to identify what the attributes and/or operations need to be for a particular class, we can add these to the diagram in as much or as little detail as we care to.

❑ We may choose simply to list attribute names:

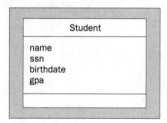

or we may specify their names along with their types:

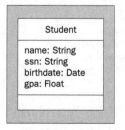

We may even wish to specify an initial starting value for an attribute, as in:

```
gpa : Float = 0.0
```

although this is less commonplace.

❑ Static attributes are identified as such by underlining them:

❑ We may choose simply to list method names (typically with the suffix '()' attached to imply their nature as methods) in the operations compartment of a class rectangle:

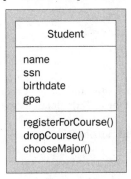

or we may optionally choose to use an expanded form of operation definition as we have for the `registerForCourse()` method below:

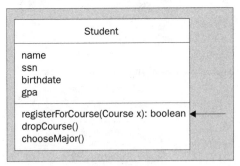

Note that the formal syntax for operation specifications in a UML class diagram:

methodName(optional argument list) : returnType

differs from the syntax that we are used to seeing for Java method signatures:

returnType methodName(optional argument list);

Here is a situation where using a CASE tool may restrict your flexibility. The rationale for making these operation definitions generic instead of representing them as language specific method signatures is so that the same model may be rendered in any of a variety of target programming languages. It can be argued, however, that there is nothing inherently better or clearer about the first form versus the second. Therefore, if you know that you are going to be programming in Java, it might make sense to reflect standard Java method signatures in your class diagram, if your object modeling tool will accommodate this.

It is often impractical to show all of the attributes and methods of every class in a class diagram, because the diagram will get so cluttered that it will lose its 'punch' as a communications tool. Consider the data dictionary to be the official, complete source of information concerning the model, and only reflect in the diagram those attributes and methods that are particularly important in describing the mission of each class. In particular, 'get' and 'set' methods are implied for all attributes, and should not be explicitly shown.

Also, just because the attribute or operation compartment of a class is empty, don't assume that there are no features of that type associated with a class; it may simply mean that the model is still evolving.

Relationships Between Classes

In Chapter 4, we defined several different types of structural relationship that may exist between classes – associations, aggregations (a specific type of association), and inheritance. Let's explore how each of these relationship types is represented graphically.

❑   Binary associations – in other words relationships between two different classes – are indicated by drawing a line between the rectangles representing the participating classes, and labeling the line with the name of the association. Role names can be reflected at either end of the association line if they add value to the model, but should otherwise be omitted.

We also mark each end of the line with the appropriate **multiplicity indicator**, to reflect whether the relationship is one-to-one, one-to-many, or many-to-many; we'll talk about how to do this a bit later in the chapter.

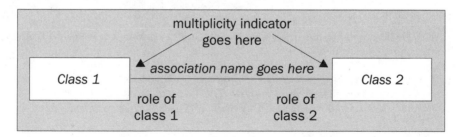

All associations are assumed to be bidirectional at this stage in the modeling effort, and it doesn't matter in which order the participating classes are arranged in a class diagram. So, to depict the association 'a Professor advises a Student', the following graphical notations are all considered equivalent:

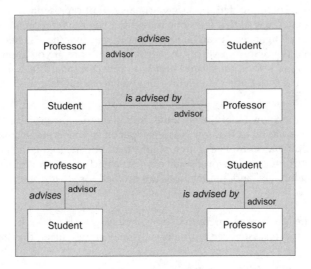

With OMT, the precursor notation to UML, we were instructed to label associations so that their names made sense when reading a diagram from left to right, top to bottom. There was thus an incentive to arrange classes in our diagram in whatever way would make association names less 'awkward'. In the examples above, placing the `Professor` class above or to the left of `Student` simplifies the association name. Achieving an optimal placement of classes for purposes of simplifying all of the association names in a diagram is often not possible in an elaborate diagram, however. Therefore, UML has introduced the simple convention of using a small arrowhead (▸) to reflect the direction in which the association name is to be interpreted, giving us a lot more freedom in how we place our class rectangles in a diagram:

With UML, no matter how the above two rectangles are situated, we can still always label the association 'advises'.

It is easy to get caught up in the trap of trying to make diagrams 'perfect' in terms of how classes are positioned, to minimize crossed lines, etc. Try to resist the urge to do so early on, because the diagram will inevitably get changed many times before the modeling effort is finished.

❑ Unary (reflexive) associations – i.e. relationships between two different objects belonging to the same class – are drawn with an association line that loops back to the same class rectangle from which it originates. For example, to depict the association 'a Course *is a prerequisite for* a (different) Course', we'd use the notation shown below:

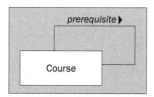

❑ Aggregation, which as we learned in Chapter 5 is really just an association that happens to imply containment, is differentiated from a 'normal' association by placing a diamond at the end of the association line that touches the 'containing' class. For example, to portray the fact that a University is comprised of Schools – the School of Engineering, School of Law, School of Medicine, etc. – we'd use the following notation:

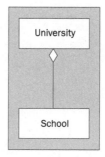

An aggregation relationship can actually be oriented in any direction, as long as the diamond is properly anchored on the 'containing' class:

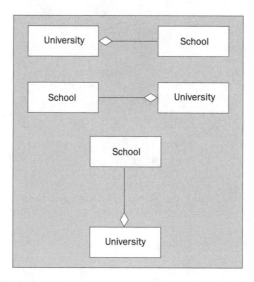

As we mentioned when we first introduced aggregation in Chapter 5, however, you can get by without ever using aggregation! To represent the above concept, we could have just created a simple association between the University and School classes, and labeled it 'is comprised of':

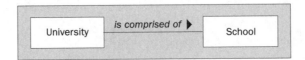

The decision of whether to use aggregation vs. plain association is subtle, because it turns out that both can be rendered in code in essentially the same way, as we'll see in Part 3 of the book.

Unlike association lines, which should always be labeled with the name of the association that they represent, aggregation lines are typically not labeled, since an aggregation by definition implies containment. However, if you wish to optionally label an aggregation line with a phrase such as 'consists of', 'is comprised of', 'contains', etc. you may certainly do so.

When two or more different classes represent 'parts' of some other 'whole', each 'part' is involved in a separate aggregation with the 'whole', as shown below:

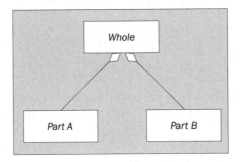

However, we often join such aggregation lines into a single structure that looks something like an organization chart, as follows:

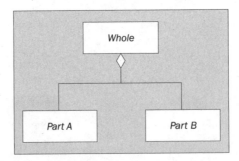

Doing so is not meant to imply anything about the relationship of *Part A* to *Part B*; it is simply a way to clean up the diagram.

❑ Inheritance (generalization/specialization) is illustrated by connecting a subclass to its parent class with a line, and then marking the line with a triangle that touches the base class.

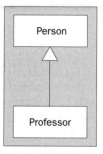

As with aggregation, the classes involved in an inheritance relationship can be portrayed with any orientation, as long as the triangle points to the superclass.

Unlike association lines, which must always be labeled, and aggregation lines, which needn't be labeled (but can be if you desire), inheritance lines should **not** be labeled, as they unambiguously represent the 'is a' relationship.

As with aggregation, when two or more different classes represent subclasses of the same parent class, each subclass is involved in a separate inheritance relationship with the parent:

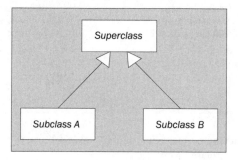

but we often join the inheritance lines into a single structure, as follows:

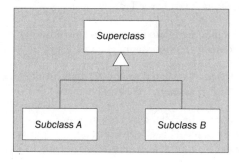

Doing so is not meant to imply anything different about the relationship of *Subclass A* to *Subclass B* as compared with the previous depiction – these classes are considered to be sibling classes with a common parent class in both cases. It is simply a way to clean up the diagram.

Reflecting Multiplicity

We learned in Chapter 5 that for a given association type X between classes A and B, the term 'multiplicity' refers to the number of instances of objects of type A that must/may be associated with a given instance of type B, and vice versa. When preparing a class diagram, we mark each end of an association line to indicate what its multiplicity should be from the perspective of an object belonging to the class at the other end of the line: in other words,

❑   We mark the number of instances of 'B' that can relate to a single instance of 'A' at *B*'s end of the line

❑   We mark the number of instances of 'A' that can relate to a single instance of 'B' at *A*'s end of the line

This is depicted in the figure below.

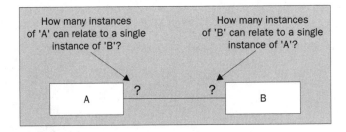

By way of review, given a single object belonging to class 'A', there are four different scenarios for how object(s) of type 'B' may be related to it:

❑   The 'A' type object may be related to **exactly one** instance of a 'B' type object (**mandatory**), as in the situation 'a Student (A) has a Transcript (B)'.

❑   The 'A' type object may be related to **at most one** instance of a 'B' type object (**optional**), as in the situation 'a Professor (A) optionally chairs a Department (B)'.

❑   The 'A' type object may be related to **one or more** instances of a 'B' type object (**mandatory**), as in the situation 'a Department (A) employs many (one or more) Professors (B)'.

❑   The 'A' type object may be related to **zero or more** instances of a 'B' type object (**optional**), as in the situation 'a Student (A) is attending many (zero or more) Sections (B)'. (At our hypothetical university, a Student is permitted to take a semester off.)

With UML notation, multiplicity markings are as follows:

- 'Exactly one' is represented by the notation '1'.

- 'At most one' is represented by the notation '0..1', which is alternatively read as 'zero or one'.

- 'One or more' is represented by the notation '1..*'.

- 'Zero or more' is represented by the notation '0..*'.

- We use the notation '*' when we know that the multiplicity should be 'many' but we are not certain (or we don't care to specify) whether it should be 'zero or more' or 'one or more'.

- It is even possible to represent an arbitrary range of explicit numerical values $x..y$, such as using '3..7' to indicate, for example, that 'a Department employs no fewer than three, and no more than seven, Professors'.

Here are some UML examples:

- 'A Student has exactly one Transcript, and a Transcript belongs to exactly one Student.'

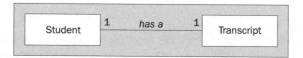

- 'A Professor works for exactly one Department, but a Department has many (one or more) Professors as employees.'

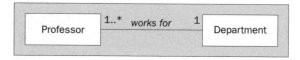

- 'A Professor optionally chairs at most one Department, while a Department has exactly one Professor in the role of chairman.'

- 'A Student attends many (zero or more) Sections, and a Section is attended by many (zero or more) Students.'

A Section which continues to have zero students signed up to attend will most likely be cancelled; nonetheless, there is a period of time after a Section is first made available for enrollment via the SRS that it will have zero Students enrolled.

❑   'A Course is a prerequisite for many (zero or more) Courses, and a Course can have many (zero or more) prerequisite Courses.'

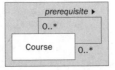

We reflect multiplicity on aggregations as well as on simple associations. For example, the following UML notation would be interpreted as follows: 'A (Student's) Plan of Study is comprised of many Courses; any given Course can be included in many different (Students') Plans of Study.'

It makes no sense to reflect multiplicity on inheritance relationships, however, because as we discussed in Chapter 4, inheritance implies a relationship between classes, but not between objects. That is, the notation:

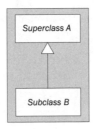

implies that any object belonging to *Subclass B* is also simultaneously an instance of *Superclass A* by virtue of the 'is a' relationship. If we wanted to illustrate some sort of relationship between different objects of types 'A' and 'B', e.g. 'a Person is married to a Student', we'd need to introduce a separate association between these classes independent of their inheritance relationship, as follows:

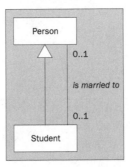

Object Diagrams

When describing how objects can interact, we sometimes find it helpful to sketch out a scenario of specific objects and their linkages, and for that we create an **object diagram**. An instance, or object, looks much the same as a class in UML notation, the main differences being that:

❑ We typically provide both the name of the object and its type, separated by a colon. We underline the text to emphasize that this is an object, not a class.

❑ The object's type may be omitted if it is obvious from the object's name; for example, the name 'student x' implies that the object in question belongs to the Student class.

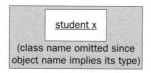

❑ Alternatively, the object's name may be omitted if we want to refer to a 'generic' object of a given type; such an object is known as an **anonymous object**. Note that we must precede the class name with a colon (:) in such a situation.

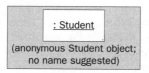

Therefore, if we wanted to indicate that Dr. Brown, a Professor, is the advisor for three students, we could create the following object diagram:

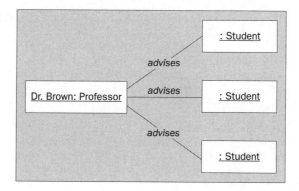

or, to reflect that a Student by the name of Joe Blow is attending two classes this semester, one of which is also attended by a Student named Mary Green:

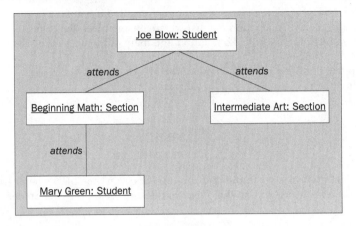

Associations as Attributes

Given the following diagram of the association 'a Course is offered as a Section':

we see that a `Course` object can be related to many different `Section` objects, but that any one `Section` object can only be related to a single `Course` object. What does it mean for two objects to be related? It means that they maintain 'handles' on one another so that they can easily find one another to communicate and collaborate, a concept that we talked about in detail in Chapter 4. If we were to sketch out the attributes of the `Course` and `Section` classes based solely on the above diagram, we'd need to allow for these handles as reference variable attributes, as follows:

```
class Section {
  // Attributes.
  private Course represents;    // A 'handle' on a single related Course
                                // object.

  // etc.
}

class Course {
  // Attributes.
  private Collection offeredAs;    // A collection of related Section
                                   // object 'handles'.
  // etc.
}
```

So we see that the presence of an association between two classes A and B in a class diagram implies that class A *potentially* has an attribute declared to be either:

- ❑ A reference to a single object of type B
- ❑ A collection of references to many objects of type B

depending on the multiplicity involved, and vice versa. We say 'potentially' because, when we get to the point of actually programming this application, we may or may not wish to code this relationship bidirectionally, even though at the analysis stage all associations are presumed to be bidirectional. We'll talk about the pros and cons of doing so in Chapter 14.

Because the presence of an association line implies attributes as handles in both related classes, it is inappropriate to additionally list such attributes in the attribute compartment of the respective classes.

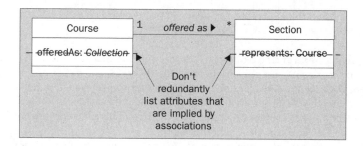

This is a mistake commonly made by beginners. The biggest resultant problem with doing so arises when using the code generation capability of a CASE tool: if the attribute is listed explicitly in a class's attributes compartment, and also implied by an association, it may appear in the generated code twice:

```
class Course {
  Collection offeredAs;    // by virtue of an explicit attribute
  Collection offered_as;   // by virtue of the association
  // etc.
}
```

Information 'Flows' Along the Association 'Pipeline'

Beginning modelers also tend to make the mistake of introducing undesired redundancy when it comes to attributes in general. In the following association diagram, we see that the 'name' attribute of the Professor class is inappropriately mirrored by the 'chairmanName' attribute of the Department class.

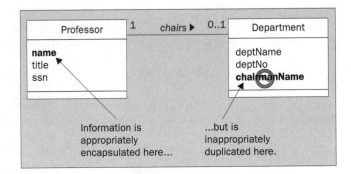

While it is true that a Professor object needs to know the name of the Professor object that chairs that Department, it is inappropriate to explicitly create a chairmanName attribute to reflect this information. Because the Department object maintains a reference to its associated Professor object as an attribute, the Department has ready access to this information any time it needs it, simply by invoking the Professor object's getName() method. This piece of information is rightfully encapsulated in the Professor class, where it belongs, and should not be duplicated anywhere else. A corrected version of the preceding diagram is shown below, with the redundancy eliminated.

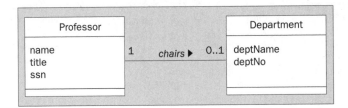

In essence, whenever we see an association/aggregation line in a diagram, we can think of this as a conceptual 'pipeline' across which information can 'flow' between related objects as needed.

> *At the analysis stage, we don't worry about the visibility (public, private) of attributes, or of the directionality of associations; we'll assume that the values of all of the attributes reflected in a diagram are obtainable by calling the appropriate 'get' methods on an object.*

Sometimes, this 'pipeline' extends across multiple objects, as illustrated by the next example.

Here, we have a diagram involving three classes:

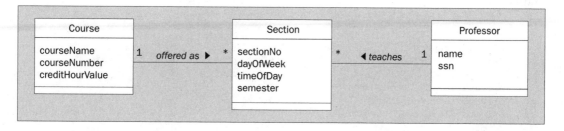

Let's say that someone wishes to obtain a list of all of the Professors who have ever taught the Course entitled 'Beginning Objects'. Because each `Course` object maintains a handle on all of its `Section` objects, past and present, the `Course` object representing 'Beginning Objects' can ask each of its `Section` objects the name of the `Professor` who previously taught, or is currently teaching, that `Section`. The `Section` objects, in turn, each maintain a handle on the `Professor` object who taught/teaches the `Section`, and can use the `Professor` object's `getName()` method to retrieve the name. So, information flows along the association 'pipeline' from the `Professor` objects to their associated `Section` objects and from there back to the `Course` object that we started with.

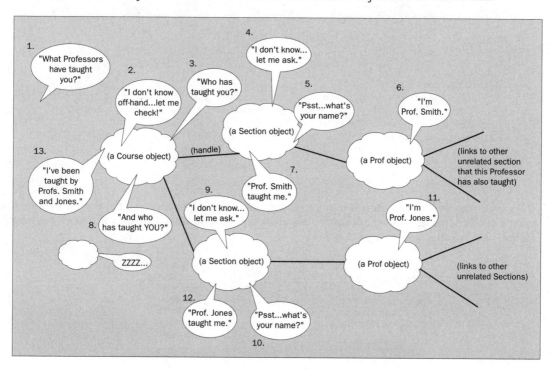

We'll learn a formal, UML-appropriate way to analyze and depict such 'object conversations' in Chapter 11.

We've modeled these three classes' attributes in code below, highlighting all of the association-driven attributes:

```
class Course {
  // Attributes.
  private Collection offeredAs;        // a collection of Section object
                                       // 'handles'
  private String courseName;
  private int courseNumber;
  private float creditHourValue;
  // etc.
}

class Section {
  // Attributes.
  private Course represents;    // a 'handle' on the related Course
                                // object
  private int sectionNo;
  private String dayOfWeek;
  private String timeOfDay;
  private String semester;
  private Professor taughtBy;   // a 'handle' on the related Prof. object

  // etc.
}

class Professor {
  private Collection sectionsTaught; // a collection of Section obj.
                                     // 'handles'
  private String name;
  private String ssn;

  // etc.
}
```

If we knew that the Course class was going to regularly need to know who all the Professors were that ever taught the course, we might decide to introduce the redundant association 'a Professor has taught a Course' into our diagram, as illustrated below:

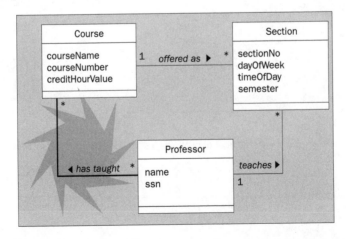

This has the advantage of improving the speed with which a `Course` object can determine who has ever taught it. `Course` objects can now talk directly to `Professor` objects without using `Section` objects as go-betweens – but the cost of this performance improvement is that we've just introduced additional complexity to our application, reflected by the highlighted additions to the code below:

```
class Course {
   // Attributes.
   private Collection offeredAs;       // a collection of Section object
                                       // 'handles'
   private String courseName;
   private int courseNumber;
   private float creditHourValue;
   private Collection professors;      // a collection of Professor obj.
                                       // 'handles'
   // etc.
}

class Section {
   // Attributes.
   private Course represents;     // a 'handle' on the related Course
                                  // object
   private int sectionNo;
   private String dayOfWeek;
   private String timeOfDay;
   private String semester;
   private Professor taughtBy;    // a 'handle' on the related Prof. object

   // etc.
}

class Professor {
   private Collection coursesTaught;    // a collection of Course obj.
                                        //'handles'
   private Collection sectionsTaught;   // a collection of Section obj.
                                        // 'handles'
   private String name;
   private String ssn;

   // etc.
}
```

By adding the redundant association, we now have extra work to do in terms of maintaining referential integrity: that is, if a different Professor is assigned to teach a particular Section, we have two links to update rather than one: the link between the Professor and the Section, and the link between the Professor and the Course.

We'll talk more in Part 3 of the book about the implications, from a coding standpoint, of making such tradeoffs. The bottom line, however, is that deciding which associations to include, and which to eliminate as derivable from others, is similar to the decision of which web pages you create a bookmark for in your web browser: you bookmark those that you visit frequently, and type out the URL long-hand for those that you only occasionally need to access. The same is true for object linkages: the decisions of which to implement depends on which 'communication pathways' through the application we're going to want to use most frequently. We'll get a much better sense of what these communication patterns are when we move on to modeling behaviors in Chapter 11.

'Mixing and Matching' Relationship Notations

It is possible to intertwine the various relationship types in some rather sophisticated ways. To appreciate this fact, let's study the following model to see what it is telling us:

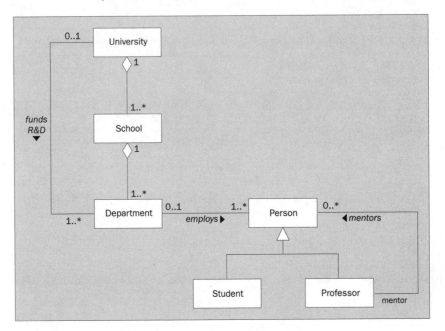

❏   First of all, we see some familiar uses of aggregation and inheritance.

   ❏   The use of aggregation in the upper left hand corner of the diagram – a two-tier aggregation – communicates the facts that a University is comprised of one or more Schools, and that a School is comprised of one or more Departments, but that any one Department is only associated with a single School and any one School is only associated with a single University.

   ❏   The use of inheritance in the lower right hand corner of the diagram indicates that Person is the common superclass for both Student and Professor. Alternatively, stated another way: that a Student is a Person, and a Professor is a Person.

❏   The first interesting use of the notation that we observe is that an association can be used to relate classes at differing levels in an aggregation, as in the use of the *funds R&D (Research & Development)* association used to relate the University and Department classes. This indicates that the University funds one or more Departments for research and development purposes, but that a given Department may or may not be funded for R&D.

❏   Next, we note the use of the *employs* association to relate the Department and Person classes, indicating that a Department employs one or more Persons, but that a given Person may work for only one Department, if indeed they work for any Department at all.

   Because Person is a superclass to both the Student and Professor subclasses, then by virtue of the 'is a' relationship, anything we can say about a Person must also be true of its subclasses.

Therefore, a given Student may optionally work for one Department, perhaps as a teaching assistant, and a given Professor may optionally work for one Department. Thus, associations/aggregations that a superclass participates in are inherited by its subclasses. (This makes sense, because we now know that associations are really rendered as attributes.)

❑ Also, because we can deduce (via the aggregation relationship) which School and University a given Department belongs to, the fact that a Person works for a given Department also implies which School and University the Person works for.

❑ Finally, we note that an association can be used to relate classes at differing levels in an inheritance hierarchy, as in the use of the **mentors** association to relate the Person and Professor classes. Here, we are stating that a Professor optionally mentors many Persons – Students and/or Professors – and conversely that a Person – either a Student or a Professor – is mentored by optionally many Professors. We label the end of the association line closest to the Professor class with the role designation 'mentor' to emphasize that Professors are mentors at the University, but that Persons in general (i.e. Students) are not.

What if we instead wanted to reflect the fact that both Students and Professors may hold the role of mentor? We could substitute a unary/reflexive association on the Person class, as follows:

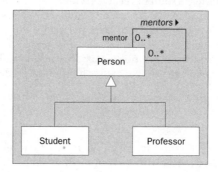

which, by virtue of inheritance, actually implies four relationship possibilities:

❑ A Professor mentoring a Student

❑ A Professor mentoring another Professor

❑ A Student mentoring another Student

❑ A Student mentoring a Professor (which is not very likely!)

If we wanted to reflect that only the first three of these are possible, we'd have to resort to the rather more complex version shown below, where the three relationships of interest are all reflected as separate association lines (two reflexive, one binary):

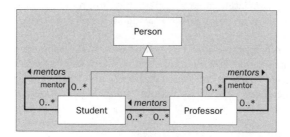

249

As cumbersome as it is to change the diagram to reflect these refinements in our understanding, it would be orders of magnitude more painful to change in the software once the application had been coded.

Association Classes

We sometimes find ourselves in a situation where we identify an attribute that is critical to our model, but which doesn't seem to nicely fit into any one class. As an example, let's revisit the association 'a Student attends a Section'. (Note that we are using the 'generic' **many** multiplicity adornment this time, a single asterisk (*), at each end of the association line.)

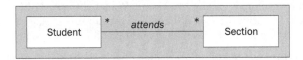

At the end of every semester, a student receives a letter grade for every section that he/she attended during that semester. We decide that the grade should be represented as a `String` attribute (e.g. 'A-', 'C+'). However, where does the 'grade' attribute belong?

❑ It's not an attribute of the `Student` class, because a student doesn't get a single overall grade for all of his/her coursework, but rather a different grade for each course attended.

❑ It's not an attribute of the `Section` class, either, because not all students attending a section typically receive the same letter grade.

If we think about this situation for a moment, we realize that the grade is actually an attribute of the *pairing* of a given `Student` object with a given `Section`; that is, it is an attribute of the **link** that exists between these two objects.

With UML, we create a separate class, known as an **association class**, to house the attribute(s) belonging to the link between objects, and attach it with a dashed line to the association line as shown below.

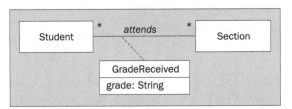

Any time you see an association class in a class diagram, realize that there is an alternative equivalent way to represent the same situation **without** using an association class.

❑ In the case of a many-to-many association involving an association class, you may split the many-to-many association into two one-to-many associations, inserting what was formerly the association class as a 'normal' class between the other two classes. Doing this for the preceding *attends* association, we wind up with the following equivalent alternative:

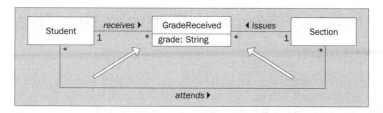

One important point to note is that the 'many' ends of these two new associations reside with the newly inserted class, because a Student *receives* many grades and a Section *issues* many grades.

❏ If we happen to have an association class for a one-to-many association, as in the *works for* association between Professor and Department:

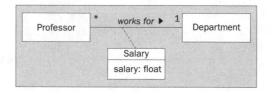

then the association class's attribute(s) can, in theory, be 'folded into' the class at the 'many' end of the association instead, and we can do away with the association class completely:

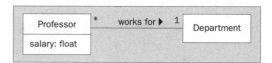

(With a one-to-one association, we can fold the association class's attributes into either class.)

That being said, this practice of folding in association class attributes into one end of a one-to-many or one-to-one association is discouraged, however, because it reduces the amount of information communicated by the model. In the preceding example, the only reason that a Professor has a salary is because he/she works for a Department; knowledge of this 'cause and effect' connection between employment and salary is lost if the association class is eliminated as such from the model.

Note that association classes are 'normal' classes that may themselves participate in relationships with other classes. In the diagram to the right, for example, we show the association class 'Role' participating in a one-to-many association with the class 'U.S. President'; an example illustrating this model would be that 'Film Star Anthony Hopkins starred in the movie 'Nixon' in the role of Richard M. Nixon, thus portraying the **real** former U.S. President Richard M. Nixon'.

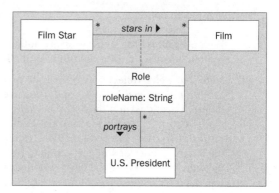

Our 'Completed' Student Registration System Class Diagram

Applying all that we've learned in this chapter about static modeling, we produce the UML class diagram for the SRS shown below. Of course, as we've said repeatedly, this is not the only correct way to model the requirements, nor is it necessarily the 'best' model that we could have produced; but it is an accurate, concise, and correct model of the static aspects of the problem to be automated.

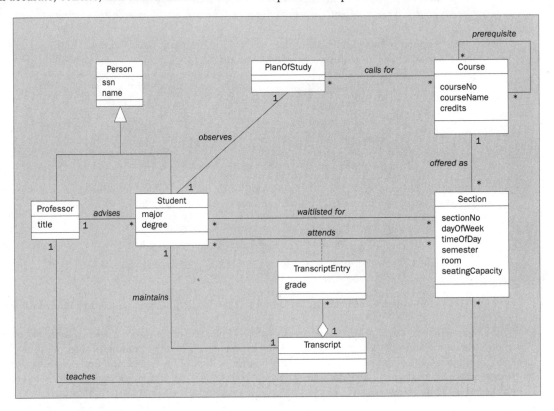

A few things worth noting:

❏ We opted to use the 'generic' *many* notation (* for UML) rather than specifying 0..* or 1..*; this is often adequate during the initial modeling stages of a project.

❏ Note that we've reflected two separate many-to-many associations between the Student and Section classes: *waitlisted for* and *attends*. A given Student may be waitlisted for many different Sections, and they may be registered for/attending many other sections. What this model doesn't reflect is the fact that a Student may not simultaneously be attending and waitlisted for the *same* Section. Constraints such as these can be reflected as textual notes on the diagram, enclosed in curly braces, or can be omitted from the diagram but spelled out in the data dictionary. In the following diagram excerpt, we use the annotation '{ xor }' to represent an 'exclusive or' situation between the two associations: a Student can either be waitlisted for or attending a Section, but not both.

❑ As mentioned earlier in this chapter, we are able to get by with a single *attends* association to handle both the Sections that a Student is currently attending, as well as those that they have attended in the past. The date of attendance – past or present – is reflected by the 'semester' attribute of the `Section` class; also, for any courses that are currently in progress, the value of the 'grade' attribute of the `TranscriptEntry` association class would be as of yet undetermined.

❑ We could have also reflected an association class on the *waitlisted for* association representing a given Student's position in the wait list for a particular Section, and then could have gone on to model the notion of a `WaitList` as an aggregation of `WaitListEntry` objects:

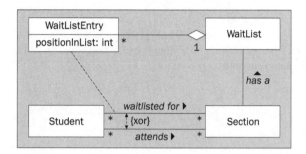

Since we are going to want to use the object model to gain user confirmation that we understand their primary requirements, we needn't clutter the diagram with such behind-the-scenes implementation details just yet.

❑ We also renamed the association class for the *attends* relationship; it was introduced earlier in this chapter as `GradeReceived`, but is now called `TranscriptEntry`. We've also introduced an aggregation relationship between the `TranscriptEntry` class and another new class called `Transcript`.

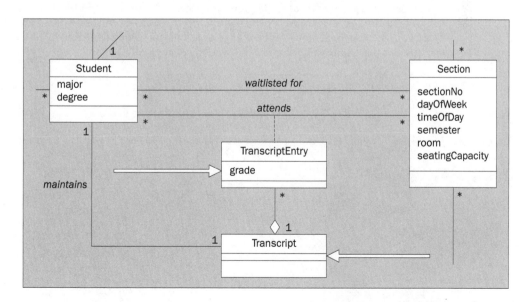

Let's explore how all of this evolved.

❑   When we first introduced the *attends* association earlier in this chapter, we portrayed it as follows:

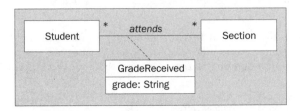

❑   We then learned that it could equivalently be represented as a pair of one-to-many associations *issues* and *receives*:

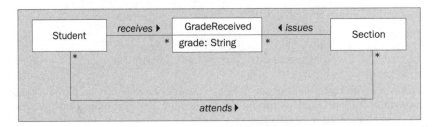

❑   In this alternative form, it is clear that any individual `GradeReceived` object maintains one handle on a `Student` object and another handle on a `Section` object, and can ask either of them for information whenever necessary. The `Section` object, in turn, maintains a handle on the `Course` object that it represents by virtue of the *offered as* association. It is a trivial matter, therefore, for the `GradeReceived` object to request the values of attributes `'semester'`, `'courseNo'`, `'courseName'`, and `'credits'` from the `Section` object (which would in turn have to ask its associated `Course` object for the last three of these four values); this is illustrated conceptually below.

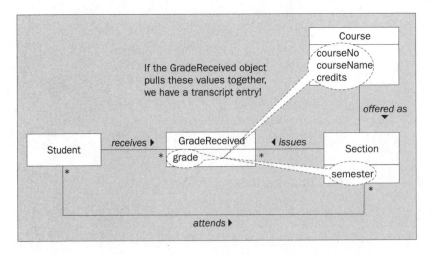

❑ If the `GradeReceived` object pulls these values together, we have everything that we need for a line item entry on a student's transcript:

Transcript For: Joe Blow				Semester: Spring 2000
Course No.	Credits	Course Name	Grade Received	Credits Earned*
MATH 101	3	Beginning Math	B	9
OBJECTS 101	3	Intro to Objects	A	12
ART 200	3	Clay Modelling	A	12

* 'Credits Earned' is computed by multiplying the credit value of a course - say, 3 - by 4 if the student earned an A grade, 3 if he/she earned a B, and so forth.

Therefore, we see that renaming the association class from `GradeReceived` to `TranscriptEntry` makes good sense.

❑ It was then a natural step to aggregate these into a `Transcript` class.

❑ The diagram is a little 'light' in terms of attributes; we've only reflected those which we'll minimally need when we build an automated SRS in Part 3.

Of course, we need to go back to the data dictionary to capture definitions of all of the new attributes, relationships, and classes that we've identified in putting together this model. Here is our revised SRS data dictionary:

Classes

Course: a semester-long series of lectures, assignments, exams, etc. that all relate to a particular subject area, and which are typically associated with a particular number of credit hours; a unit of study toward a degree. For example, Beginning Objects is a required **course** for the Master of Science Degree in Information Systems Technology.

Person: a human being associated with the university.

PlanOfStudy: a list of the **courses** that a student intends to take to fulfill the **course** requirements for a particular degree.

Professor: a member of the faculty who teaches **sections** and/or advises **students**.

Section: the offering of a particular **course** during a particular semester on a particular day of the week and at a particular time of day (For example, **course** 'Beginning Objects' as taught in the Spring 2001 semester on Mondays from 1:00 – 3:00 PM).

Student: a person who is currently enrolled at the university and who is eligible to register for one or more **sections**.

Transcript: a record of all of the **courses** taken to date by a particular **student** at this university, including which semester each **course** was taken in, the grade received, and the credits granted for the **course**, as well as reflecting an overall total number of credits earned and the **student's** grade point average (GPA).

TranscriptEntry: one line item entry from a **transcript**, reflecting the **course** number and name, semester taken, value in credit hours, and grade received.

Relationships

*advises: a **professor** advises a **student**:* A professor is assigned to oversee a student's academic pursuits for the student's entire academic career, leading up to his/her attainment of a degree. An advisor counsels his/her advisees regarding course selection, professional opportunities, and any academic problems the student might be having.

*attends: a **student** attends a **section**:* A student registers for a section, attends class meetings for a semester, and participates in all assignments and examinations, culminating in the award of a letter grade representing the student's mastery of the subject matter.

*calls for: a **plan of study** calls for a **course**:* A student may only take a course if it is called out by his/her plan of study. The plan of study may be amended, with a student's advisor's approval.

*maintains: a **student** maintains a **transcript**:* Each time a student completes a course, a record of the course and the grade received is added to the student's transcript.

*observes: a **student** observes a **plan of study**:* See notes for the *calls for* association, above.

*offered as: a **course** is offered as a **section**:* The same course can be taught numerous times in a given semester, and of course over numerous semesters for the 'lifetime' of a course – that is, until such time as the subject matter is no longer considered to be of value to the student body, or there is no qualified faculty to teach the course.

*prerequisite: a **course** is a prerequisite for another **course**:* If it is determined that the subject matter of a course 'A' is necessary background to understanding the subject matter of a course 'B', then 'A' is said to be a prerequisite of 'B'. A student typically may not take 'B' unless he/she has either successfully completed 'A', or can otherwise demonstrate mastery of the subject matter of 'A'.

*teaches: a **professor** teaches a **section**:* A professor is responsible for delivering lectures, assigning thoughtful homework assignments, examining students, and otherwise ensuring that a quality treatment of the subject matter of a course is made available to students.

*waitlisted for: a **student** is waitlisted for a **section**:* If a section is 'full' – for example the maximum number of students have signed up for the course based on either the classroom capacity or the student group size deemed effective for teaching – then interested students may be placed on a waitlist, to be given consideration should seats in the course subsequently become available.

(aggregation between Transcript and TranscriptEntry)
(specialization of Person as Professor)
(specialization of Person as Student)

Attributes

Person.ssn: The unique social security number (SSN) assigned to an individual.

Person.name: The person's name, in 'last name, first name' order.

Professor.title: The rank attained by the professor, e.g. 'Adjunct Professor'.

Student.major: A reflection of the department in which a student's primary studies lie, for example Mathematics. (We assume that a student may only designate a single major.)

Student.degree: The degree that a student is pursuing, e.g. Master of Science Degree.

TranscriptEntry.grade: A letter grade of A, B, C, D, or F, with an optional +/- suffix, such as 'A+' or 'C-'.

Course.courseNo: A unique ID assigned to a course, consisting of the department designation plus a unique numeric ID within the department, for example: 'MATH 101'.

Course.courseName: A full name describing the subject matter of a course, for example 'Beginning Objects'.

Course.credits: The number of units or credit hours a course is worth, roughly equating to the number of hours spent in the classroom in a single week (typically, 3 credits for a full semester lecture course).

Section.sectionNo: A unique number assigned to distinguish one section/offering of a particular course from another offering of the same course in the same semester, for example MATH 101 section no. 1.

Section.dayOfWeek: The day of the week on which the lecture course meets.

Section.timeOfDay: The time (range) during which the course meets, for example 2 – 4 PM.

Section.semester: An indication of the scholastic semester in which a section is offered, for example 'Spring 2000'.

Section.room: The building and room number where the section will be meeting, for example 'Government Hall Room 105'.

Section.seatingCapacity: The maximum number of students permitted to register for a section.

Metadata

One question that is often raised by beginning modelers is why we don't use an inheritance relationship to relate the `Course` and `Section` classes, rather than using a simple association as we have chosen to do. On the surface, it does indeed seem tempting to want `Section` to be a subclass of `Course`, because all of the attributes listed for a `Course` – courseNo, courseName, and credits – also pertain to a `Section`; so, why wouldn't we want `Section` to **inherit** these, in the same way that `Student` and `Professor` inherit all of the attributes of `Person`? A simple example should quickly illustrate why inheritance isn't appropriate.

Let's say that, because 'Beginning Object Concepts' is such a popular course, the university is offering three sections of the course for the Spring 2001 semester. So, we instantiate one `Course` object and three `Section` objects. If `Section` were a subclass of `Course`, then all four objects would reflect courseNo, courseName, and credits attributes. Filling in the attribute values for these four objects, as follows:

Attribute Name	Value for the Course Object
courseName	"Beginning Object Concepts"
courseNumber	"OBJECTS 101"
creditValue	3

Attribute Name	Value for Section Object #1	Value for Section Object #2	Value for Section Object #3
courseName	"Beginning Object Concepts"	"Beginning Object Concepts"	"Beginning Object Concepts"
courseNumber	"OBJECTS 101"	"OBJECTS 101"	"OBJECTS 101"
creditValue	3	3	3
studentsRegistered	(to be determined)	(to be determined)	(to be determined)
instructor	reference to professor X	reference to professor Y	reference to professor Z
semesterOffered	Spring 2001	Spring 2001	Spring 2001
dayOfWeek	Monday	Tuesday	Thursday
timeOfDay	7:00 PM	4:00 PM	6:00 PM
classroom	Hall A, Room 123	Hall B, Room 234	Hall A, Room 345

we see that there is quite a bit of repetition in the attribute values across these four objects: we've repeated the same courseName, courseNumber, and creditValue four times! That's because the information contained within a `Course` object is common to, and hence describes, **numerous** `Section` objects. To reduce redundancy and promote encapsulation, we should eliminate inheritance of these attributes, and instead create only one instance of a `Course` object for *n* instances of its related `Section` objects. We can then have each `Section` object maintain a handle on the common `Course` object so as to retrieve these shared values whenever necessary. This is precisely what we have modeled via the one-to-many *offered as* association.

Whenever an instance of some class 'A' encapsulates information that describes numerous instances of some other class 'B' (such as Course does for Section), we refer to the information contained by the 'A' object (Course) as **metadata** relative to the 'B' objects (Sections).

Comparing UML and OMT Notations

We mentioned in the Introduction to the book that UML notation is remarkably similar to OMT (which stands for 'Object Modeling Technique') notation because UML is based to a great extent on OMT. To illustrate how similar the UML and OMT notations are, we present the same model in OMT notation below; note that the only differences are:

1. The change in position of the triangle for the inheritance relationship (it no longer touches the bottom of the superclass).

2. The use of solid circles instead of asterisks to represent the 'many' ends of relationships.

3. The use of a loop instead of a dashed line for the association class (which is called a 'link attribute' in OMT nomenclature).

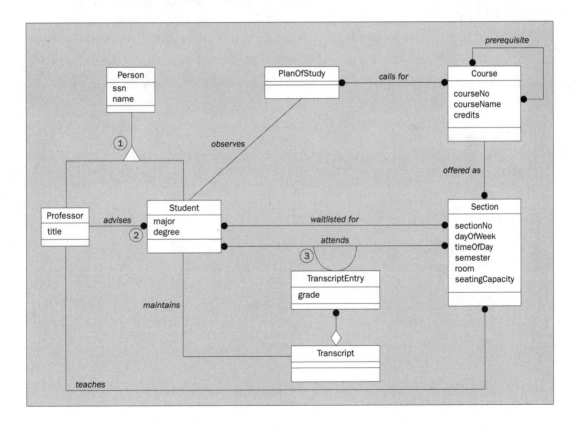

Summary

Our object model has started to take shape! We have a good idea of what the static structure needs to be for the SRS – the classes, their attributes and relationships with one another – and are able to communicate this knowledge in a concise, graphical form. There are many more embellishments to the UML notation than we haven't covered in this chapter, but we've presented the core concepts that will suffice for most 'industrial strength' modeling projects. Once you've mastered these, you can explore the Recommended Reading section of the book if you'd like to learn more about these notations.

There is an obvious 'hole' in our class diagram, however: all of our classes have empty operations compartments. We'll address this deficiency by learning some complementary modeling techniques for determining the dynamic behavior of our intended system in Chapter 11.

In this chapter, we've learned:

- ❑ The noun phrase analysis technique for identifying candidate domain classes.

- ❑ The verb phrase analysis technique for determining potential relationships among these classes.

- ❑ That coming up with candidate classes is a bit subjective, and hence that we have to remain flexible, and willing to revisit our model, through many iterations until we – and our users – are satisfied with the outcome.

- ❑ The importance of producing a data dictionary as part of a project's documentation set.

- ❑ How to graphically portray the static structure of our model as a class diagram using UML.

- ❑ How important it is to have an experienced object modeling mentor available to a project team.

Exercises

1. Come up with a list of candidate classes for the Conference Room Reservation System (CRRS) case study presented in Appendix B, as well as an association matrix.

2. Develop a class diagram for the CRRS case study, using UML notation. Reflect all significant attributes and relationships among classes, including the appropriate multiplicity. Ideally, you should use an object modeling software tool if you have one available to you.

3. Prepare a data dictionary for the CRRS, to include definitions of all classes, attributes, and associations.

4. Devise a list of candidate classes for the problem area whose requirements you defined for exercise No. 3 in Chapter 2, as well as an association matrix.

5. Develop a class diagram for the problem area whose requirements you defined for exercise No. 3 in Chapter 2, using UML notation. Reflect all significant attributes and relationships among classes, including the appropriate multiplicity. Ideally, you should use an object modeling software tool if you have one available to you.

6. Prepare a data dictionary for the problem area whose requirements you defined for exercise No. 3 in Chapter 2, to include definitions of all classes, attributes, and associations.

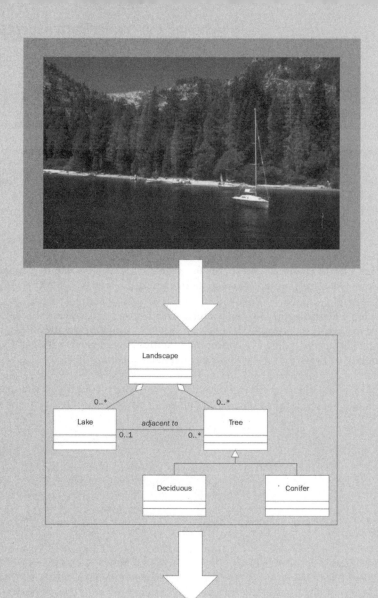

Modeling the Dynamic/Behavioral Aspects of the System

Thus far, we have been focused on the **static structure** of the problem being modeled – the floor plan for our custom home, as it were. As we learned in Chapter 10, this static structure is communicated via a class diagram plus supporting documentation. The building blocks of a class diagram are:

- ❑ Classes.

- ❑ Associations/aggregations.

- ❑ Attributes.

- ❑ Generalization/specialization hierarchies (also known as inheritance relationships).

- ❑ Operations/methods. **These are conspicuously absent from our class diagram.** Why? Because they are not part of the static structure, so we haven't discussed how to determine these yet; this will be the focus of this chapter.

As we've said many times already, an OO software system is a set of collaborating objects, each with a 'life' of its own. If each object went about its own business without regard to what any other object needed it to do, however, utter chaos would reign! The only way that objects can collaborate to perform some overall system mission, such as registering a student for a course, is if each class defines the appropriate methods, or services, that will enable its instances to fulfill their respective roles in the collaboration.

In order to determine what these methods/services must be, we must complement our knowledge of the static structure of the system to be built by also modeling the **dynamic** aspects of the situation: that is, the ways in which concurrently active objects interact over time (that is, their **behaviors**), and how these interactions affect each object's state. Producing a dynamic model to complement the static model will not only enable us to determine the methods required for each class, but will also give us new insights into ways to improve upon the static structure.

In this chapter, you will learn about the building blocks of a **dynamic model**:

❏ Events

❏ Scenarios

❏ Sequence diagrams

❏ Collaboration diagrams

and how to use the knowledge gleaned from these to identify the operations/methods that are needed to complete our class diagram.

How Behavior Affects State

Back in Chapter 3, we defined the **state** of an object as the collective set of all of the object's attribute values at a given point in time; this includes:

❏ The values of all of the 'simple' attributes for that object – in other words, attributes that do not represent other domain objects.

❏ The values of all of the reference variable attributes representing links to other domain objects.

We've repeated the list of the `Student` class attributes from Chapter 6, adding a column to indicate which category each attribute falls into.

`Student` Class Attributes

Attribute Name	Data Type	Represents Link(s) to Another SRS Domain Object?
name	String	no
studentID	String	no
birthdate	Date	no
address	String	no
major	String	no
gpa	Float	no
advisor	Professor	yes
courseLoad	collection of Course objects	yes
transcript	collection of TranscriptEntry object s – or – Transcript	yes

In Chapter 10, we learned about UML object diagrams as a way to portray a 'snapshot' of the links between specific individual objects. Let's use an object diagram to reflect the state of a few hypothetical objects within the SRS 'domain'.

Here, we see that Dr. Smith (a Professor) works for the Math Department, Dr. Green (another Professor) works for the Science Department, and that Bill and Mary, both Students, are majoring in Math and Science, respectively.

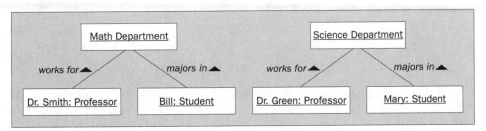

Bill is dissatisfied with his choice of majors, and calls Dr. Green, a professor whom he admires, to make an appointment. Bill wants to discuss the possibility of transferring to the Science Department. After meeting with Dr. Green and discussing his situation, Bill indeed decides to switch majors. We've informally reflected these object interactions using arrows on the object diagram, below; as this chapter progresses, you'll learn the 'official' way to portray object interactions in UML notation.

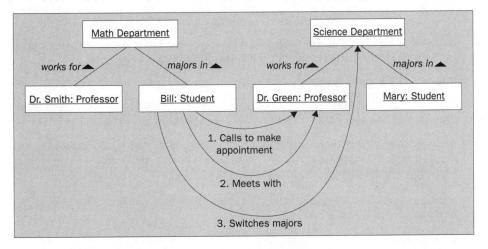

When the dust settles from all of this activity, we see that the resultant state of the system has changed, as reflected in the following revised object diagram 'snapshot'. In particular:

- Bill's state has changed, because his link to the Math Department object has been replaced with a link to the Science Department object.

- The Math Department object's state has changed, because it no longer has a link to Bill.

- The Science Department's state has changed, because it now has an additional link (to Bill) that wasn't previously there.

Note, however, that although Dr. Green collaborated with Bill in helping him to make his decision to switch majors, the state of the 'Dr. Green' (Professor) object **has not changed** as a result of the collaboration.

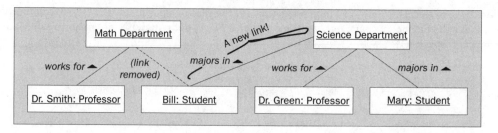

So, we see that objects' dynamic activities can result in changes to the **static structure of a system** – that is, the collective states of all of its objects – but that such activities needn't affect the state of *all* objects involved in a collaboration.

Events

We learned in Chapter 4 that object collaborations are triggered by events. By way of review, an **event** is an external stimulus to an object, signaled to the object in the form of a **message**. An event can be:

❑ User initiated (for example, the result of clicking a 'button' on a GUI).

❑ Initiated by another computer system (such as the arrival of information being transferred from the Student Billing System to the Student Registration System).

❑ Initiated by another object within the same system (a `Course` object requesting some service of a `Transcript` object, for example).

When an object receives notification of an event via a message, it may react in a variety of ways:

❑ **An object may change its state** (the values of its 'simple' attributes and/or links to other objects), as in the case of a `Professor` object receiving a message to take on a new `Student` advisee, illustrated by the following code snippet:

```
Professor p = new Professor();
Student s = new Student();
// details omitted
p.addAdvisee(s);
```

Let's look at the code for the `Professor` class's `addAdvisee()` method to see how the `Professor` will respond to this message. We see that the `Professor` object is 'stuffing' the reference to `Student` object s that it is being handed as an argument into a `Collection` of `Student` object references called 'advisees':

```
class Professor {
  // Attributes.
  Collection advisees;  // Holds Student object references.
  // details omitted

  public void addAdvisee(Student s) {
    // Insert s into the advisees collection.
    // (pseudocode)
    advisees.insert(s);
  }
}
```

In so doing, `Professor` object p will have formed a new link of type *advises* with `Student` object s.

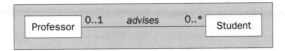

Typical 'set' methods fall into this category of event response.

❏ **An object may direct an event (message) toward another object** (including, perhaps, the sender of the original message), as in the case of a `Section` object receiving a message to register a `Student`, illustrated by the following code snippet:

```
Section x = new Section();
Student s = new Student();
// details omitted
x.register(s);
```

If we next look at the method code for the `Section` class's `register()` method to see how it will respond to this message, we see that the `Section` object in turn fires a message at the `Student` to be enrolled, to verify that the `Student` has completed a necessary prerequisite course:

```
class Section {
  // details omitted

  boolean register(Student s) {
    // Verify that the student has completed a necessary
    // prerequisite course.
    // (pseudocode)
    boolean completed = s.successfullyCompleted(some prerequisite );
    if (completed) register the student and return a value of true;
      else return a value of false to signal that the registration
        request has been rejected;
  }
}
```

This happens to be an example of delegation, which we discussed in Chapter 4: namely, another object (a `Student`, in this case) helping to fulfill a service request originally made of the `Section` object.

❏ **An object may return a value**; the returned value may be:

❏ The value of one of the object's private attributes

❏ Some computed value (that is, a 'pseudoattribute', as we discussed in Chapter 4)

❏ A value that was obtained from some **other** object through delegation

❏ A status code (as in `true`/`false` responses, signaling success or failure of `boolean` methods)

Typical 'get' methods fall into this category of event response.

❑ **An object may react with the external boundaries of a system**: that is, it may display some information on a GUI, or cause information to be printed to a printer. As we'll learn in Chapters 15 and 16 of the book, however, what appears to be an external system boundary is often implemented in Java code as yet another object.

❑ Finally, **an object may seemingly ignore an event**, as would be the case if a `Professor` object received the message to add an advisee:

```
Student s = new Student();
Professor p = new Professor();
// details omitted
p.addAdvisee(s);
```

but determined that the `Student` whom it was being asked to take on as an advisee was **already** an advisee. Let's look a slightly different version of the `addAdvisee()` method than what we saw previously:

```
class Professor {
  Collection advisees;  // Holds Student object references.
  // details omitted

    public void addAdvisee(Student s) {
      // Only insert s into the 'advisees' collection IF IT
      // ISN'T ALREADY IN THERE.
      // (pseudocode)
      if ( s is already in collection ) return;  // do nothing
      else advisees.insert (s);
    }
}
```

Actually, to say that the `Professor` object is doing nothing is an oversimplification: at a minimum, the object is executing the appropriate method code, which is performing some internal state checks ('Is this student already one of my advisees?'). It's just that, when the dust settles, the `Professor` object has neither changed state nor fired off any messages to other objects, so it **appears** as if nothing has happened.

Of course, these various object responses to an event may occur in combination, as well.

Scenarios

Events originating externally to a system occur randomly: we cannot predict, for example, when a user is going to click a button on a GUI. In order for a system to perform useful functions, however, the **internal** events that arise in **response** to these external events – in other words, the messages that objects exchange in carrying out some system function – cannot be left to occur randomly. Rather, they must be orchestrated in such as way as to lead, in cause-and-effect fashion, to some desired result. In the same way that a musical score indicates which notes must be played by various instruments to produce a melody, a **scenario** prescribes the sequence of internal messages (events) which must occur in carrying out some system function from beginning to end.

We introduced use cases in Chapter 9 as a way to specify all of the goals for a system from the standpoint of external actors – users and/or other computer systems. Merriam-Webster's dictionary defines the term scenario as:

> *'[...] a sequence of events, especially when imagined; an account or synopsis of a projected course of action or events.'*

which is precisely how the term is used in the object modeling sense.

A scenario is one hypothetical instance of how a particular use case might play out. Just as an object is an instance of a class, and a link is an instance of an association, a scenario may be thought of as an instance of a use case. Or, stated another way, just as a class is a template for creating objects, and an association is a template for creating links, a use case is a template for creating scenarios.

A single use case thus inspires many different scenarios, in the same way that planning a driving trip from one city to another can involve many different routes.

We describe scenarios in narrative fashion, as a series of steps observed from the standpoint of a hypothetical observer who is able to see not only what is happening outwardly as the system carries out a particular request, but also what is going on behind the scenes, internally to the system. (Note, however, that even though we are now concerned with internal system processes, we are still only interested in functional requirements as defined in Chapter 9, not in the 'bits and bytes' of how the computer works.)

The following is a sample scenario representing the 'Register for a course' use case, one of several use cases that we identified for the SRS in Chapter 9.

Scenario #1 for the 'Register for a Course' Use Case:

1. Fred, a student, logs onto the SRS.

2. He views the schedule of classes for the current semester to determine which section(s) he wishes to register for.

3. Fred requests a seat in a particular section of a course entitled 'Beginning Objects', course no. OBJ101, section 1.

4. Fred's plan of study is checked to ensure that the requested course is appropriate for his overall degree goals. (We assume that students are not permitted to take courses outside of their plans of study.)

5. His transcript is checked to ensure that he has satisfied all of the prerequisites for the requested course, if there are any.

6. Seating availability in the section is confirmed.

7. The section is added to Fred's current course load.

From Fred's vantage point (sitting in front of a computer), here's what he perceives to be occurring: after logging on to the SRS, he indicates that he wishes to register for OBJ101, section 1 by choosing it from the 'Course Catalog' list, and then clicks the Add button.

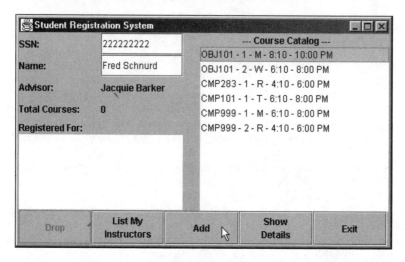

'Fred's View of Things', Part 1

A few moments later, Fred receives a confirmation message.

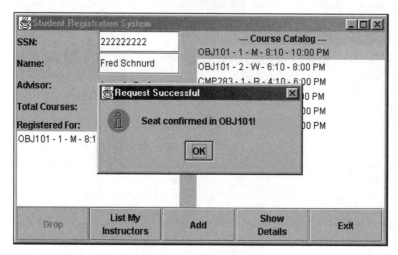

'Fred's View of Things', Part 2

He's unaware (for the most part) of all of the 'behind the scenes' processing steps that are taking place on his behalf!

The preceding scenario represents a 'best case' scenario, where everything goes smoothly and Fred ends up being successfully registered for the requested course. But, as we know all too well, things don't always work out this smoothly, as evidenced by the following alternative scenario for the **same** use case. Everything is the same between Scenarios #1 and #2 except for the steps that are shown in **bold** below:

Scenario #2 for the 'Register for a course' Use Case:

1. Fred, a student, logs onto the SRS.

2. Fred views the schedule of classes for the current semester to determine which section(s) he wishes to register for.

3. Fred requests a seat in a particular section of a course entitled 'Beginning Objects', course no. OBJ101, section 1.

4. Fred's plan of study is checked to ensure that the requested course is appropriate for his overall degree goals.

5. His transcript is checked to ensure that he has satisfied all of the prerequisites for the requested course, if any.

6. Seating availability in the section is checked, but the section is found to be full.

7. Fred is asked if he/she wishes to be put on a first come, first served wait list.

8. Fred elects to be placed on the wait list.

With a little imagination, you can think of numerous other scenarios for this use case, involving such circumstances as Fred having requested a course that is not called for by his plan of study, or a course for which he hasn't met the prerequisites. And, there are many other *use cases* to be considered, as well, as were discussed in Chapter 9.

Are there practical limits to the number of alternative scenarios that one should consider for a given use case? As with all requirements analysis, the criteria for when to stop are somewhat subjective: we stop when it appears that we can no longer generate **significantly different** scenarios; trivial variations are to be avoided.

When devising scenarios, it is often helpful to observe the future users of the system that we are modeling as they go about performing the same business functions today. In the case of student registration, for example, what manual or automated steps does a student have to go through presently to register for a class? What steps does the university take before deeming a student eligible to register? Whether the registration process is 100% manual at present, or is based on an automated system that you are going to be replacing or augmenting, a historical transcript of the steps that are involved in carrying out some business goal, can serve as the basis for one or more useful scenarios.

Scenarios, once written, should be added to our project's use case documentation; generally, we pair all scenarios with their associated use cases in that document.

Why are scenarios so important? Because they are the means by which we start to gain insight into the **behaviors** that will be required of our objects. We'll need a way to formalize these scenarios so that the actual methods needed for each of our classes become apparent; UML **sequence diagrams** are the means by which we do so.

Sequence Diagrams

Sequence diagrams are one of two types of UML **interaction diagrams** (we'll explore the second type, **collaboration diagrams**, a bit later in this chapter). Sequence diagrams are a way of graphically portraying how messages should flow from one object to another in carrying out a given scenario.

To prepare a sequence diagram, we must first determine:

❑ Which classes of objects (from among those that we specified in our static model (class diagram) in Chapter 10) are involved in carrying out a particular scenario

❑ Which external actors are involved

Looking back at Scenario #1 for the 'Register for a Course' use case, we determine that the following objects are involved:

❑ One Student object (representing Fred)

❑ One Section object (representing the course entitled 'Beginning Objects' - course number 'OBJ101', section number 1)

❑ One PlanOfStudy object, belonging to Fred

❑ One Transcript object, also belonging to Fred

The scenario also mentions that the student 'views the schedule of classes for the current semester to determine which section(s) he wishes to register for'. You may recall that when we were determining what our candidate classes should be back in Chapter 10, we debated whether or not to add ScheduleOfClasses as a candidate class to our model, and elected to leave it out at that time. In order to fully represent the details of Scenario #1, we're going to reverse that decision, and retrofit ScheduleOfClasses into our class diagram now as follows:

❑ We'll show ScheduleOfClasses participating in a one-to-many aggregation with the Section class because one ScheduleOfClasses object will be instantiated per semester to represent all of the sections that are being taught that semester. (It's an abstraction of the paper or on-line schedule that students look at in choosing which classes they wish to register for in a given semester.)

❑ We'll also transfer the 'semester' attribute from the Section class to ScheduleOfClasses. Since each Section object will now be maintaining a handle on its associated ScheduleOfClasses object by virtue of the aggregation relationship between them, a Section object will be able to request semester information whenever it is needed.

The results of these changes to our class diagram are highlighted below.

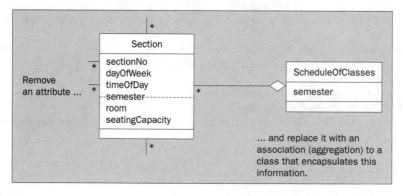

Acknowledging ScheduleOfClasses as a class in our model allows us to now reference a ScheduleOfClasses object in our sequence diagram, as we'll see in a moment. **Scenarios often unearth new classes, attributes, and relationships, thus contributing to our structural 'picture' of the system; this is a common occurrence, and is *desirable*.**

Of course, we must remember to add a definition of ScheduleOfClasses to our data dictionary!

> **Schedule of Classes:** a list of all classes/**sections** that are being offered for a particular semester; **students** review the **schedule of classes to** determine which **sections** they wish to register for.

Finally, since the scenario explicitly mentions interactions between the student user and the system, we'll reflect Fred the **actor** separately from Fred the **object**. Doing so will allow us to reflect the SRS interacting externally with the user, as well as showing the system's internal object-to-object interactions. We refer to an object that represents an abstraction of an actor as an instance of a **boundary class**.

Our adjusted list of object/actor participants is now as follows:

- ❏ One Student object (representing Fred)
- ❏ One Section object (representing the course entitled 'Beginning Objects'; course number 'OBJ101', section number 1)
- ❏ One PlanOfStudy object, belonging to Fred
- ❏ One Transcript object, also belonging to Fred
- ❏ One ScheduleOfClasses object
- ❏ One Student actor (Fred again!)

To prepare a sequence diagram for Scenario #1:

- ❏ We draw vertical dashed lines, one per object or actor that participates in the scenario; these are referred to as the objects' **lifelines**. Note that the objects/actors can be listed in any order from left to right in a diagram, although it is common practice to place the external user/actor at the far left.

- ❏ At the top of each lifeline, as appropriate, we place either an **instance icon** – that is, a box containing the (optional) name and class of an object participant – or a stick figure symbol to designate an actor. (For rules governing how an instance icon is to be formed, please refer back to the section on creating object diagrams in Chapter 10).

- ❏ Then, for each event called out by our scenario, we reflect its corresponding message as a horizontal **solid-line** arrow drawn from the lifeline of the sender to the lifeline of the receiver.

- ❏ Responses back from messages (in other words, return values from methods, or simple 'return;' statements in the case of methods declared to have a void return type) are shown as horizontal **dashed-line** arrows drawn from the lifeline of the **receiver** of the original message **back to** the lifeline for the **sender** of the message.

- ❏ Message arrows appear in chronological order from top to bottom in the diagram.

The completed sequence diagram for Scenario #1 is shown below.

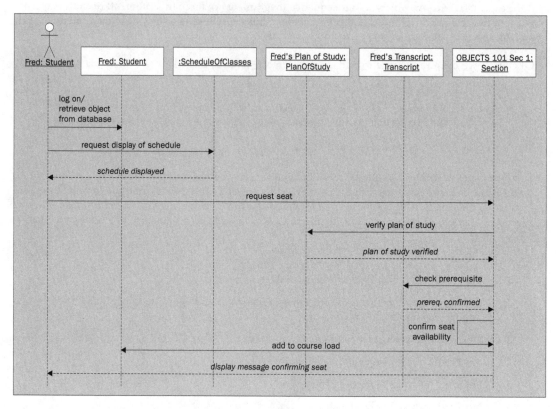

*Note that we've omitted one element of sequence diagram notation from this example: namely, the use of what are known as **focus of control bars** to illustrate the period of time over an object's lifeline that the object is actually engaged in processing a request. For more details on sequence diagram notation, please see the Recommended Reading suggestions in Chapter 17.*

Let's step through the diagram to make sure that we understand all of the activities that are reflected in the diagram.

1. When Fred logs onto the system, his 'alter ego' as an object is activated. (Presumably, information representing each Student – in other words, the Student object's attribute values – is maintained off-line in **persistent storage** such as a database or file until such time as he/she logs on, at which time the information is used to instantiate a Student object in memory, mirroring the user who has just logged on. We'll talk about reconstituting objects from persistent storage in Chapter 15.)

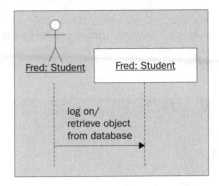

2. When Fred the user/actor requests that the semester class schedule be displayed, we reflect the message 'request display of schedule' being sent to an anonymous ScheduleOfClasses object. The dashed-line-arrow response from the ScheduleOfClasses object indicates that the schedule is being displayed to the user; strictly speaking, via a GUI.

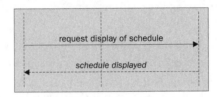

We've chosen to label our response arrows with italic instead of regular font, a slight departure from official UML notation.

3. The next message shown in our diagram is a message from the user to the Section object, requesting a seat in the class.

*This message is shown originating from the user; in reality, it originates from a **GUI component object** of the SRS graphical user interface (GUI), but we aren't worrying about such implementation details at this stage in the analysis effort. We'll talk about the object-oriented aspects of graphical user interface design and event processing in depth in Chapter 16.*

Note that there is no immediate reply to this message; that's because the Section object has a few other objects that it needs to consult with before it can grant a seat to this student, namely:

❏ The Section sends a message to the object representing Fred's plan of study, asking that object to confirm that the course that Fred has requested is one of the courses required of Fred in completing his degree program.

❏ The Section next sends a message to the object representing Fred's transcript, asking that object to confirm that a prerequisite course – say COMP 001 – has been satisfactorily completed by this student.

4. Assuming that both of these other objects respond favorably, as they are expected to do by virtue of how this scenario was written, the `Section` object then performs some internal processing to verify that there is indeed room for Fred in this section. We reflect internal processing within a single object as an arrow that loops back to the same lifeline that it starts with:

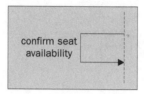

Of course, if we were to reflect **all** of the internal processing that is performed by every one of the objects in our sequence diagram, it would be **flooded** with such loops! The only reason that we have chosen to show this particular loop, is because it is explicitly called out as a step in Scenario #1; if we had omitted it from our diagram, it might appear that we had accidentally overlooked this step.

5. Finally, with all checks having been satisfied, the `Section` object has two remaining responsibilities:

- ❑ First, it fires off a new message to the 'Fred' `Student` object, requesting that the `Student` object add this `Section` to Fred's course load.

- ❑ Next, the `Section` object sends a response back to Fred the user/actor (via the GUI) confirming his seat in the section. **This is the response to the original 'request seat' message that was sent by the user toward the beginning of the scenario!** All of the extra 'behind the scenes' processing necessary to fulfill the request – involving a `Section` object collaborating with a `PlanOfStudy` object, a `Transcript` object, and a `Student` object – is invisible to the user. As we saw earlier in the chapter, Fred merely selected a section from the schedule of classes that was displayed on the SRS GUI, and clicked the **Add** button; and, a few moments later, saw a confirmation message appear on his screen.

Of course, as with all modeling, this particular sequence diagram isn't necessarily the best, or only, way to portray the selected scenario. And, for that matter, one can argue the relative merits of one scenario as compared with another. It is important to keep in mind that preparing sequence diagrams is but a means to an end: namely, discovering the dynamic aspects of the system to be built – that is, the methods – to complement our static/structural knowledge of the system. Recall that our *ultimate* goal for Part 2 of the book is to produce an object-oriented blueprint that we can use as the basis for coding the SRS as a Java application in Part 3. But, as we've already pointed out, the class diagram that we created in Chapter 10 had a noticeable deficiency: all of its classes' operations compartments were empty. Fortunately, sequence diagrams provide us with the missing pieces of information.

Using Sequence Diagrams to Determine Methods

Now that we've prepared a sequence diagram, how do we put the information that it contains to good use? In particular, how do we 'harvest' information from such diagrams concerning the methods that the various classes need to implement?

The process is actually quite simple. We step through the diagram, one lifeline at a time, and study all arrows pointing into that line.

❑ Arrows representing a new request being made of an object – solid-line arrows – signal methods that the receiving object must be able to perform. For example, we see a solid line arrow labeled 'check prerequisite' pointing into the lifeline representing a `Transcript` object. This tells us that the `Transcript` class needs to define a method that will allow some client object to pass in a particular course object reference, and receive back a response indicating whether or not the `Transcript` contains evidence that the course was successfully completed.

We are free to name our methods in whatever intuitive way makes the most sense, consistent with the method naming conventions discussed in Chapter 4. We are using the method in this particular scenario to check completion of a prerequisite course, so we could define the method signature as follows:

```
boolean checkPrerequisite(Course c);
```

but this name is unnecessarily restrictive; what we're **really** doing with this method is checking the successful completion of some `Course c`; the fact that it happens to be a prerequisite of some other course is immaterial to how this method will perform. So, by naming the method

```
boolean verifyCompletion(Course c);
```

instead, we'll be able to use it anywhere in our application that we need to verify successful completion of a course – for example, when we check whether a student has met all of the course requirements necessary to graduate. (Of course, we could have still used the method in this fashion even if it **had** been named `checkPrerequisite()`, but then our code would be less accurately self-documenting.)

❑ Arrows representing responses from an operation that some other object has performed – dashed line arrows – do not get modeled as methods/operations. These do, however, hint at the return type of the method from which this response is being issued. For example, since the response to the 'verify plan of study' message is 'plan of study verified', this would imply that the method is returning a `boolean` result, and hence we'd define a method signature for the `PlanOfStudy` class as follows:

```
boolean verifyPlan(Course c);
```

❑ Loops also represent method calls, performed by an object on itself; these may either represent private 'housekeeping' methods or public methods that other client objects may avail themselves of.

In looking at our sequence diagram for Scenario #1 from a few pages back, we note the following arrows:

Arrow Labeled:	Drawn Pointing into Class 'X':	A New Request or a Response to a Previous Request?	Method to be Added to Class 'X':
log on	Student	request	(a method to reconstitute this object from persistent storage, such as a file or database; perhaps a special form of constructor – we'll discuss this in Part 3 of the book)
request display of schedule	Schedule OfClasses	request	`display()`
schedule displayed	Student	response	N/A
request seat	Section	request	`boolean enroll(Student s)`
verify plan of study	PlanOfStudy	request	`boolean verifyPlan (Course c)`
plan of study verified	Section	response	N/A
check prerequisite	Transcript	request	`boolean verifyCompletion(Course c)`
prereq. Confirmed	Section	response	N/A
confirm seat availability	Section	request	`boolean confirmSeatAvailability()` (perhaps a private housekeeping method)
add to course load	Student	request	`void addSection(Section s)`
display message confirming seat	(actor/user)	response	N/A (will eventually involve calling upon some method of a user interface object – we'll worry about this in Part 3 of the book)

and thus we have identified six new 'standard' methods plus one constructor that will need to be added to our class diagram; we'll do so shortly.

Repeating this process of sequence diagram production and analysis for various other use case/scenario combinations will flush out most of the methods that we'll need to implement for the SRS. **Despite our best efforts, however, a few methods may not surface until we have begun to program our classes; this is to be expected.**

Collaboration Diagrams

The UML notation introduced a second type of interaction diagram, called a **collaboration diagram**, as an alternative to sequence diagrams; both types of diagram present more or less the same information, but portrayed in a different manner.

In a collaboration diagram, we eliminate the lifelines used to portray objects and actors. Rather, we lay out instance icons representing objects and stick figures representing actors in whatever configuration is most visually appealing. We then use lines and arrows to represent the flow of messages and responses back and forth between these objects/actors. Because we lose the top-to-bottom chronological sense of message flow that we had with the sequence diagrams, we compensate by numbering the arrows in the order that they would occur during execution of a particular scenario.

The following collaboration diagram is equivalent to the sequence diagram that we produced for Scenario #1.

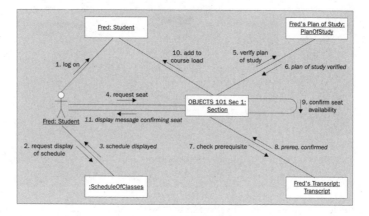

Again, from Fred's vantage point, he observes only a few of these actions.

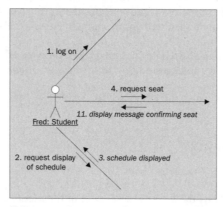

Because the sequence and collaboration diagrams reflect essentially the same information, many object modeling software tools automatically enable you to produce one diagram from the other with the push of a button.

Revised SRS Class Diagram

Going back to the SRS class diagram that we produced in Chapter 10, let's reflect all of the new insights – some behavioral, some structural – that we've gained from analyzing one scenario/sequence diagram.

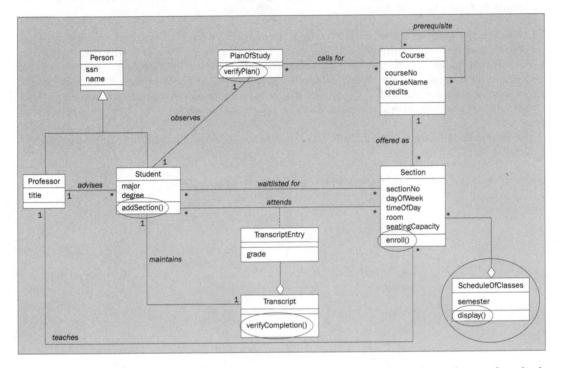

Note that we've decided not to reflect the `confirmSeatAvailability()` 'housekeeping' method at this time, as we suspect that it will be a private method, and therefore don't wish to clutter our diagram. The decision of whether to reflect private methods on a class diagram – or, for that matter, to reflect *any* feature of a class – is up to the modeler, because again, the purpose of the diagram is to communicate, and too much detail can actually lessen a diagram's effectiveness in this regard.

We must remember to update the SRS data dictionary any time we add classes, attributes, relationships, or methods to our model. Here's a suggested format for how we might wish to describe a method in the dictionary:

Method: `enroll()`

Defined for class: `Section`

Signature: `boolean enroll(Student s);`

Description: This method enrolls the designated person in the section, unless (a) the section is already full, (b) the student's plan of study doesn't call for this course, or (c) the student has not met the prerequisites. It returns a `boolean` value to indicate success (`true`) or failure (`false`) of the enrollment.

Summary

In this chapter, we've learned how the process of dynamic modeling is a complementary technique to static modeling that enriches our overall understanding of the problem to be automated, hence enabling us to improve our object 'blueprint', also known as a class diagram. In particular, we've learned:

❑   How events trigger state changes.

❑   How to develop scenarios, based on use cases.

❑   How to represent these as UML interaction diagrams: sequence diagrams or, alternatively, collaboration diagrams.

❑   How to glean information from sequence diagrams concerning the behaviors expected of objects – that is, the methods that our classes will need to implement – so as to round out our class diagram.

❑   How sequence diagrams can also yield additional knowledge about the structural aspects of a system.

Exercises

1. Prepare a sequence diagram for Scenario #2 as presented earlier in this chapter.

2. Prepare a sequence diagram to represent the following scenario for the SRS case study:

- Mary, a student, logs onto the SRS.
- She indicates that she wishes to drop ART 222, Section 1.
- ART 222, Section 1 is removed from Mary's course load.
- The system determines that Joe, another student, is waitlisted for this section.
- The section is added to Joe's current course load.
- A email is sent to Joe notifying him that ART 222 has been added to his course load.

3. Provide a list of all of the method signatures that you would add to each of your classes based on the sequence diagram that you prepared for problem 2. Also, note any new classes, attributes, or relationships that would be needed.

4. Prepare a second sequence diagram for the SRS case study, representing a scenario of your own choosing based upon any of the SRS use cases identified in Chapter 9. This scenario should be significantly different from those presented in this chapter and from the scenario in exercise 2 above. You must also narrate the scenario as was done for exercise 2.

5. Provide a list of all of the method signatures that you would add to each of your classes based on the sequence diagram that you prepared for exercise 4. Also, note any new classes, attributes, or relationships that would be needed.

6. Prepare a sequence diagram to represent the following scenario for the Conference Room Reservation System (CRRS) case study presented in Appendix B:

- Employee Fred Schnurd attempts to reserve Conference Room 123, which he knows to be the largest room at XYZ Corporation in terms of seating capacity, for the afternoon of March 5th. He plans on holding a meeting with 50 participants, and that room's capacity is 60; unfortunately, the next largest room can only hold 40 people. (Assume that no A/V resources will be needed other than those built into the room.)
- Fred learns from the CRRS that the room is already booked by Joe Blow for that same afternoon; Fred elects to be put on a wait list for that room.
- The system automatically sends a courtesy email to Joe, to let him know that Fred is waitlisted for the room.
- Joe realizes that he doesn't need such a big room after all, and so Joe agrees to release his reservation for room 123. (Don't worry about what Joe subsequently does; let's focus on Fred for the remainder of the scenario.)
- The system temporarily reserves the room for Fred, and an email is automatically sent to Fred giving him 24 hours to either confirm or reject the reservation.
- Fred confirms the reservation before the 24 hour deadline has elapsed.

7. Devise an 'interesting' scenario, and prepare the corresponding sequence diagram, for the problem area whose requirements you defined for exercise no. 3 in Chapter 2.

8. Provide a list of all of the method signatures that you would add to each of your classes based on the sequence diagram that you prepared for exercise 7. Also, note any new classes, attributes, or relationships that would be needed.

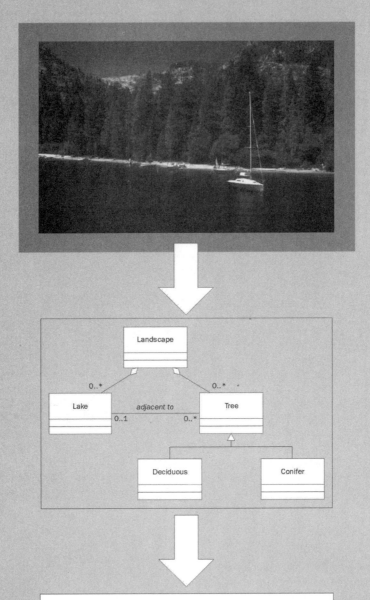

```
public class Tree {
    protected Landscape landscape;
    protected Lake nextTo;

    public void setNextTo(Lake l) {
        nextTo = l;
    }
    public Lake getNextTo() {
        return nextTo;
    }

    public abstract Color getLeafColor();
}
```

Wrapping Up Our Modeling Efforts

Having used the techniques for static and dynamic modeling presented in Chapters 10 and 11, respectively, we've arrived at a fairly thorough object model of the SRS – or, so it seems! Before we embark upon implementing our class diagram as Java code in Part 3 of the book, however, we need to make sure that our model is as accurate and representative of the goal system as possible.

In this chapter, we'll:

❑ Explore some simple techniques for testing our model.

❑ Talk about the notion of reusing models.

Testing Your Model

Testing a model does not involve 'rocket science'; rather, it calls for some common-sense measures designed to identify errors and/or omissions.

❑ First of all, revisit all requirements-related project documentation – the original problem statement and the supporting use cases – to ensure that no requirements were overlooked. We'll do so for our SRS model in a moment.

❑ Conduct a minimum of two separate formal 'walk-throughs' of the model: one with the development team members, and a second with the future users of the system. Prior to each walk-through, make sure to distribute copies of the following documentation to each of the participants far enough in advance to allow them adequate time to review these, if they so desire:

  ❑ 'Executive summary' problem statement, if available

  ❑ Class diagram

  ❑ Data dictionary

  ❑ Use case documentation

  ❑ Significant scenarios and corresponding message trace diagrams

Be prepared to discuss significant aspects of these at the meeting, however, in case they haven't reviewed them.

By this stage in the project, you will have hopefully already educated your users on how to read UML diagrams, and they will have informally seen numerous iterations of the evolving models. If any of the participants in the upcoming walk-throughs are not familiar with any of the notation, however, take time in advance to tutor them in this regard. (The information contained in Chapters 10 and 11 of this book should be more than adequate as the basis for such a tutorial.)

When conducting the walk-through, designate someone to be the narrator and discussion leader, and a different person to be responsible for recording significant discussion content, particularly changes that need to be made. Having one person trying to do both is too distracting, and important notes may be missed as a result. If appropriate, you may even arrange to tape record the discussion.

Remain open-minded throughout the review process. It is human nature to want to defend something that we've worked hard on putting together, but remember that it is far better to find and correct shortcomings now, when the SRS is still a paper skeleton, than after it has been rendered into code.

A Shortcoming in our Model

In revisiting the SRS case study problem statement, we find that we have indeed missed one requirement, namely:

'The SRS will verify whether or not the proposed plan of study satisfies the requirements of the degree that the student is seeking.'

We didn't model Degree as a class – recall that we debated whether or not to do so back in Chapter 10, and ultimately decided against it. Nor, for that matter, do we reflect the requirements of a particular degree program in our model. Let's look at what it would take to do so properly at this time.

Researching the way in which our university specifies degree program requirements, we learn the following:

❑ Every degree program specifies five 'core' courses – that is, courses that a student *must* take. For example, for the degree of Master of Science in Information Technology, students are required to complete the following five core courses:

   ❑ Analysis of Algorithms
   ❑ Application Programming Design
   ❑ Computer Systems Architecture
   ❑ Data Structures
   ❑ Information Systems Project Management

❑ Secondly, students are expected to select an area of specialization within their degree program known as a concentration. For the MS in IT degree, our university offers three different concentrations:

   ❑ Object Technology
   ❑ Database Management Systems
   ❑ Networking and Communications

- ❑ Each concentration in turn specifies three mandatory, concentration-specific courses; for the MS in IT with a concentration in Object Technology, the required concentration-specific courses are:

  - ❑ Object Methods for Software Development
  - ❑ Advanced Java Programming
  - ❑ Object Database Management Systems

- ❑ Finally, the student must take two additional electives to bring his/her course total to 10.

Phew! To model all of these interdependencies would require a fairly complex class diagram structure, as shown below:

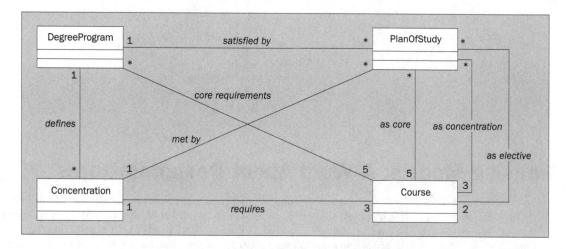

We go back to our project sponsors – the future users of the SRS – and break the news to them that we've just uncovered a previously missed requirement that is going to significantly increase the complexity and cost of our automation effort. The sponsors decide that having the SRS verify the correctness of a student's plan of study is too ambitious a goal; they've instead decided that a student will use the SRS to submit a proposed plan, but that his/her advisor will then be responsible for *manually* verifying and approving it. So, all we wind up having to do to correct our class diagram is to add one attribute to the PlanOfStudy class, reflecting the date on which it was approved, and a new *approves* association connecting the Professor class to the PlanOfStudy class, and we're good to go!

Note that we don't need to add an approvePlan() method to the PlanOfStudy class, because as discussed in Chapter 10 we may assume the presence of 'set' methods for all attributes; the setDateApproved() method would suffice for marking a plan as approved. And, the *approves* association between the PlanOfStudy and Professor classes assures us that each PlanOfStudy object will maintain a handle on the Professor object who actually approved the plan on the date indicated.

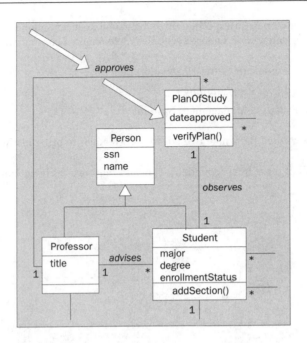

Reusing Models: A Word About Design Patterns

As we discussed in Chapter 2, when learning about something new, we automatically search our 'mental archive' for other abstractions/models that we've previously built and mastered, to look for similarities that we can build upon. This technique of comparing features to find an abstraction that is similar enough to be reused effectively is known as **pattern reuse**. As it turns out, pattern reuse is an important technique for object oriented software development.

Let's say that after we finish up our SRS class diagram, we are called upon to model a system for a small travel agency, Wild Blue Yonder (WBY). As a brand new travel agency, they wish to offer a level of customer service above and beyond their well-established competitors, so they decide to enable their customers to reserve accommodations on-line via the Web. For any given travel package – let's say a 10 day trip to Ireland – WBY offers numerous trips throughout the year. Each trip has a maximum client capacity, so if a client cannot get a confirmed seat for one of the trips, he/she may request a position on a first-come, first-served wait list.

In order to keep track of each client's overall experience with WBY, the travel agency plans on following up with each client after a trip to conduct a satisfaction survey, and will ask the client to rate his/her experience for that trip on a scale of 1 – 10, with 10 being outstanding. By doing so, WBY can determine which trips are the most successful, so as to offer them more frequently in the future, as well as perhaps eliminating those which are less popular. WBY will also be able to make more informed recommendations for future trips that a given client is likely to enjoy by studying that client's travel satisfaction history.

In reflecting on the requirements for this system, we experience déjà vu! We recognize that many aspects of the WBY system requirements are similar to those of the SRS.

In fact, we are able to reuse the overall structure, or *pattern*, of the SRS object model by making the following class substitutions:

- ❏ Substitute `TravelPackage` for `Course`
- ❏ Substitute `Trip` for `Section`
- ❏ Substitute `Client` for `Student`
- ❏ Substitute `TripRecord` for `TranscriptEntry`
- ❏ Substitute `TravelHistory` for `Transcript`

Note that all of the relationships among these classes – their names, types, and even their multiplicities – remain unchanged from the SRS class diagram.

Such an exact match is exceptionally rare when reusing design patterns; don't be afraid to change some things (eliminate classes or associations; change multiplicities; and so forth) in order to facilitate reuse.

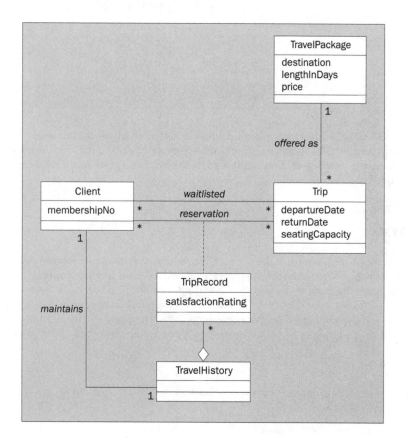

Having recognized the similarities between these two designs, we are poised to take advantage of quite a bit of re-use with regard to the code of these two systems, as well. In fact, had we anticipated the need for developing these two systems prior to developing either one, we could haven taken steps up front to develop a generic pattern that could have been used as the basis for both systems, as well as any future reservation systems we might be called upon to model:

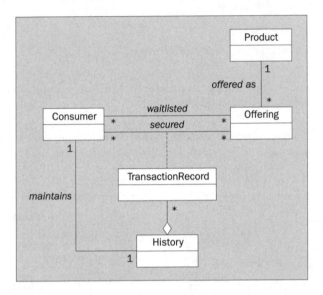

Many useful, reusable patterns have been studied and documented; before embarking on a new object modeling project, it's worth exploring whether any of these may be a suitable starting point. Our Recommended Reading section at the end of the book suggests some references that you might wish to explore on this topic.

Summary

Learning to model a problem from the perspective of objects is a bit like learning to ride a bicycle. You can read all the books ever published on the subject of successful bicycle riding, but until you actually sit on the seat, grab the handlebars and start pedaling, you won't get a real sense of what it means to ride. You will probably wobble at first, but with a bit of a boost from training wheels or a friendly hand to steady you, you'll be riding off on your own with time. The same is true of object modeling: with practice, you'll get an intuitive feel for what makes a good candidate class, a useful scenario, and so on.

In this chapter, we:

❑   Discussed some common-sense techniques for verifying the accuracy and completeness of your class diagram.

❑   Looked at how object models can be reused/adapted to other problems with similar requirements.

Exercises

1. Conduct a walk through of one of the class diagrams that you prepared as an exercise for Chapter 10 – either the Conference Room Reservation System (CRRS) case study presented in Appendix B or the problem area whose requirements you defined for exercise no. 3 in Chapter 2 – with a classmate or coworker. Report on any insights that you gained as a result of doing so.

2. Think of two other problem areas where the Reservation pattern that we identified for the Wild Blue Yonder travel agency might also apply. What adjustments, if any, would you need to make to the Reservation pattern in order to use it in those situations?

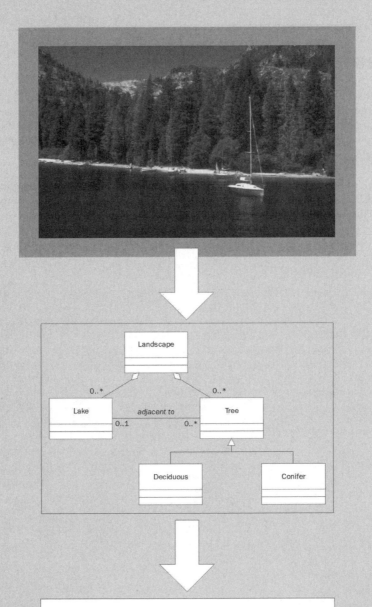

```
public class Tree {
    protected Landscape landscape;
    protected Lake nextTo;

    public void setNextTo(Lake l) {
        nextTo = l;
    }
    public Lake getNextTo() {
        return nextTo;
    }

    public abstract Color getLeafColor();
}
```

Part 3

Translating an Object 'Blueprint' into Java Code

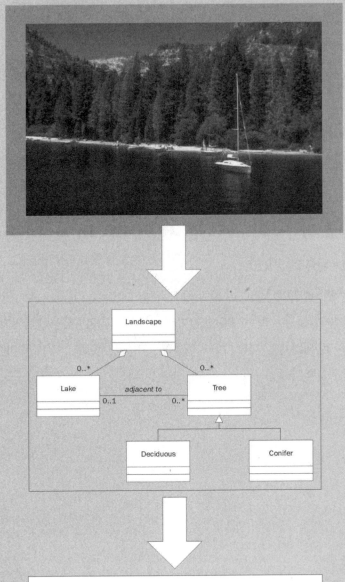

A Deeper Look At Java

Before we dive into the specifics of coding the Student Registration System (SRS), it's important that you feel comfortable with basic Java syntax. You received an introductory taste of Java in Chapter 1, and have seen some fairly simple Java code 'snippets' throughout Parts 1 and 2 of the book. But, there was a lot to Java that we couldn't easily show you back then, because we had to first introduce some object concepts. We're now ready to delve into Java in much more depth.

One must realize, though, that we can't do justice to all of Java in just one chapter; Java is an extremely rich language, and most good Java references are 1000+ pages long! Our goal is not to duplicate the hard work that has gone into existing Java language books, but rather to complement them by showing you how to bridge the gap between producing an object model and turning it into live Java code, something that few, if any, other books do. So we're going to be selective in terms of what aspects of the Java language we introduce in this chapter: namely, those that are most critical to understanding the Student Registration System coding examples that follow in Chapters 14 through 16. Nonetheless, you'll have a very respectable working knowledge of Java by the time we're finished.

Even if you have already been programming in Java for a while, and feel that you have a fairly good grasp of the language syntax, we encourage you to at least skim this chapter before moving on to Chapter 14, because we mention a few things along the way with regard to how we'll be approaching the SRS.

In this chapter, you will learn about:

- ❑ The anatomy of a real-world Java program, consisting of many separate classes driven by one 'official' `main()` method.

- ❑ The Java notion of **packages**, and how we must import packages if we wish to make use of the classes that they contain.

- ❑ An in-depth look at the anatomy of a Java class, including a discussion of how various types of visibility at both the class and attribute/method levels affect an object's 'useability'.

- ❑ The object nature of `Strings`, and some of the methods provided to manipulate them.

- ❑ How we can form highly complex expressions by chaining messages.

❑ The object nature of `Arrays` in a bit more depth.

❑ Some subtleties of variable initialization.

❑ How Java exceptions arise, and how to gracefully handle them.

❑ How to read input from the command line when a Java application is invoked, as well as how to prompt the user for keyboard inputs, useful techniques when running a command-line driven application testing program.

❑ Using a special keyword, `this`, to self-reference an object from within one of its methods.

❑ Using constructors to initialize an object's attributes at the time that the object first comes into being.

❑ How dynamically created objects are deleted so as to 'recycle' their memory, and the role that the Java garbage collector plays in this recycling.

❑ Inheritance in the Java language: in particular, how the visibility of a feature affects the way in which a subclass can utilize that feature; how to reuse superclass behaviors via the `super` keyword; and all of the complexities concerning constructors and inheritance.

❑ How to use two of Java's collection classes, `Vector` and `Hashtable`; the need for casting objects retrieved from a collection; and the use of `Enumeration` objects to iterate through the contents of a collection.

❑ How to use 'wrapper' classes, such as `Integer`, to turn simple data types into true objects.

❑ Use of the `final` keyword to make a variable, method, or class immutable.

❑ A review of abstract classes and interfaces as they are implemented in the Java language.

❑ A review of static attributes and methods as they are implemented in the Java language.

❑ The nature of object identities in Java; how to discover the true class that an object belongs to; and how to test the equality of two Java objects.

❑ The importance of overriding the `toString()` method for all user-defined classes.

❑ The form and function of inner classes.

Setting Up a Java Programming Environment

As we embark upon our in-depth studies of the Java language in Part 3 of the book, it's important that you have access to a Java programming environment so that you can get hands on experience with the concepts and code that we'll present. The good news is that everything you'll need to get started programming in Java on various platforms – Solaris, Windows, Linux – is available for free with Sun Microsystem's Java 2 Software Developer's Kit (SDK), which is available as a download from Sun's web site at http://java.sun.com – see Appendix C for helpful tips on what you'll need to do to get the Java SDK downloaded and installed properly on your computer. We strongly advise that you take the time now to establish your Java development environment, so that you'll be prepared to experiment with the language as you learn.

Note that the Java 2 SDK is a command-line driven toolkit, which means that on a Windows platform you'll be opening up an MS-DOS Prompt window, from which you'll be doing all of your work (Unix and Linux are naturally command-line oriented). Of course, there are also numerous Java Integrated Development Environments (IDE's) to choose from, some of which are available on a free trial basis as Web downloads. However, my personal bias is that if you first learn Java from the ground up, writing all of your code from scratch using only Sun's SDK and your favorite text editor, you'll gain a much better understanding of Java language fundamentals than if you rely too heavily on an IDE, particularly those that provide drag and drop GUI building capabilities and automated code generation. You can always consider graduating to an IDE after you've mastered the language, to take advantage of their debugging and code/project management features, among others.

Anatomy of a Java Program, Revisited

In Chapter 1, we introduced the anatomy of a trivially simple Java program, which consisted of a `main()` method, containing the logic of our program, inside of a class 'wrapper':

```
// Simple.java
//
// A trivially simple example for illustrating the anatomy
// of a (non-OO) Java program.
//
// Written by Jacquie Barker.
```
introductory comment

```
public class Simple {

    public static void main(String[] args) {
        System.out.println("Wheee!!!!");
    }
}
```
class 'wrapper'
main method

Such a class would reside in a file by the name of *classname*.`java`; `Simple.java`, in this example.

IMPORTANT NOTE: the external name of the file containing the source code of a Java class must *exactly* match the name given to the class *inside* of the file, *including the same use of upper/lower case*, with `.java` tacked on at the end. Java is a case sensitive language, even on operating systems like DOS that are traditionally case insensitive in most respects.

A common error for beginners is to assume that case doesn't matter, and to name the file for our example program `simple.java` or `SIMPLE.java`, or some other variation. This leads to compilation problems, as we'll see in a moment.

A non-trivial Java application consists of *many* such `.java` files, because the source code for each class comprising your application typically (but not always) resides in its own `*.java` file.

❑ You'll have one .java file for each of the domain classes that you defined in your object model: for the SRS application, for example, we'll have eight:

```
Course.java
Person.java
Professor.java
ScheduleOfClasses.java
Section.java
Student.java
Transcript.java
TranscriptEntry.java
```

❑ You'll also typically have a separate .java file for each of the primary 'windows' comprising the graphical user interface of your application, if any. For the SRS application, we'll have two:

```
MainFrame.java
PasswordPopup.java
```

(We'll talk about graphical user interfaces in depth in Chapter 16.)

❑ You'll typically have a separate .java file that contains the 'official' main() method which serves as the application driver. One of the primary responsibilities of this driver class's main() method is to instantiate the core objects needed to fulfill a system's mission; of course, actions taken by the these objects as well as by the user will cause additional objects to come to life over time, as the application executes. The main() method is also responsible for displaying the start-up window of the graphical user interface of an application, if any. (We'll see in a later chapter that other classes can have main() methods, too, used for testing purposes; but only one of these main() methods is considered to be the 'official' main() method that jump-starts the application.)

We'll name the driver class for our Student Registration System application SRS, so of course it will need to be stored in a file named `SRS.java`.

❑ Finally, you'll quite possibly have other 'helper' classes necessary for behind the scenes application support; with the SRS, we'll have a need for three such classes:

```
CollectionWrapper.java
CourseCatalog.java
Faculty.java
```

All told, by the time we reach the end of Chapter 16, we will have programmed a total of 14 classes, integrating them into a single SRS application with a GUI front-end and a way to persist data from one SRS application session to the next.

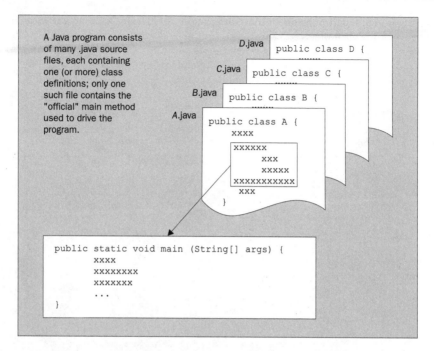

A Java program consists of many .java source files, each containing one (or more) class definitions; only one such file contains the "official" main method used to drive the program.

```
D.java    public class D {
          ........
C.java    public class C {
          ........
B.java    public class B {
          ........
A.java    public class A {
             xxxx
             xxxxxx
                   xxx
                   xxxxx
             xxxxxxxxxxx
                   xxx
          }
```

```
public static void main (String[] args) {
        xxxx
        xxxxxxxx
        xxxxxx
        ...
}
```

Assuming that you have properly installed Sun's Java 2 SDK as discussed in Appendix C, a Java source code file (.java file) can be compiled at the command line via the command:

```
javac classname.java
```

e.g.

```
javac Simple.java
```

Again, pay close attention to match upper/lower case usage; if you were to name your class Simple (upper case 'S'), but store it in a file named simple.java (lower case 's'), the Java compiler would generate the following compilation error:

Public class Simple must be defined in a file called 'Simple.java'.

Please see the section entitled 'Troubleshooting Your Installation' in Appendix D for suggestions on what to do to remedy various other compilation errors that arise as a result of an improper Java installation.

Note that you can compile multiple files in a single step:

```
javac file1.java file2.java ... filen.java
```

or

```
javac *.java
```

Assuming that no compilation errors occur, compilation produces *at least one classname*.class file for every .java file; for example, Simple.class for our example program. (We'll see later in this chapter why more than one .class file might be produced from a single .java file.) As discussed in Chapter 1, the *.class files contain platform-independent Java **byte code** that can be run on any platform for which there is a Java Virtual Machine available.

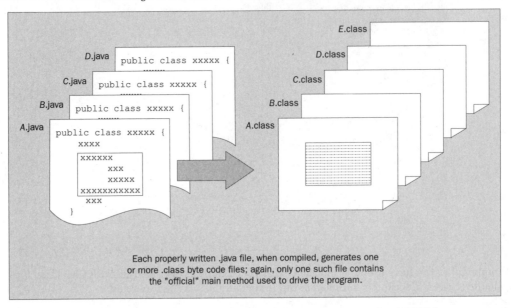

Each properly written .java file, when compiled, generates one or more .class byte code files; again, only one such file contains the "official" main method used to drive the program.

To run a Java program from the command line, type the following to invoke the JVM:

```
java MainClassName
```

e.g.

```
java Simple
```

or

```
java SRS
```

where *MainClassName* is the name of the class file (minus the .class suffix) containing the compiled byte code version of the 'official' main() driver method for your application.

The JVM loads the byte code for whatever class you've named, and if it discovers within that byte code a main() method with the proper signature (recall that the name of the argument being passed into the main() method – *args*, in this case – is the only thing that is flexible in the signature):

```
public static void main(String[] args)
```

then the JVM executes that main() method to jump start your application. From that point on, the JVM will load additional classes – either classes that you've written and compiled, or classes built into the Java language – as needed, when referenced by your application. That is, the first time the SRS application has occasion to refer to the Person class, the byte code for the Person class will be loaded into the JVM, and so forth.

It is important that you not type the `.class` suffix when attempting to run a program, as you'll get an error if you do:

```
java Simple.class
```

Exception in thread "main" java.lang.NoClassDefFoundError: Simple/class

which is, to say the least, not very intuitive! This particular error message arises because the Java compiler interprets the name `Simple.class` as being the name of a class called `'class'`, to be found within a package called `'Simple'`; we'll be talking about packages shortly. (Please see the section entitled 'Troubleshooting Your Installation' in Appendix D for suggestions on what to do to remedy various other execution errors that arise as a result of an improper Java installation.)

Why must the `main()` method of an application be declared `static`? At the moment that the JVM first loads whatever class you've told it to load to jump-start your application, no objects exist yet, because the `main()` method hasn't yet executed; and, it's the `main()` method that will start the process of instantiating your application's objects, as we'll see in Chapter 14. So, at that very moment of application startup, all the JVM has at its disposal is a class; and, as we learned in Chapter 7, a `static` method is a type of method that can be invoked on a class as a whole, even if we don't have an instance of that class handy.

One final note about program structure: we said that the source code for each class comprising your application *typically* resides in its own `.java` file. It is actually permissible to place the source code for two or more Java classes back to back in the same physical `.java` file. We don't generally do so, however, for it's much easier to manage Java source code when there is a one-to-one correspondence between the external file name and the internal Java class name. If we were to combine multiple class definitions back-to-back in a single `.java` file, however, they would each produce their own `.class` file when compiled.

Importing Packages

When we originally discussed Java class/program anatomy in Chapter 1, we skipped one key element: **import statements**. We've revised the anatomy figure from Chapter 1 to include these:

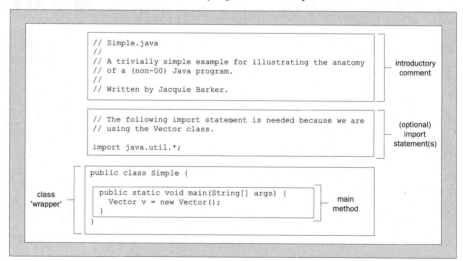

To appreciate import statements, we first must understand the notion of Java **packages**.

Because the Java language is so extensive, its various built-in classes are organized into logical groupings called packages. For example, we have:

- ❑ `java.sql` – the package that contains classes related to communicating with Object Database Connectivity(ODBC)-compliant relational databases

- ❑ `java.io` – the package that contains classes related to file input/output

- ❑ `java.util` – the package that contains a number of utility classes, such as the Java collection classes that we'll be learning about in this chapter

- ❑ `java.awt` – one of the packages that contains classes related to GUI development

and so forth. Most built-in Java package names start with `java`, but there are some that start with other prefixes, like `javax`; and, if we acquire Java classes from a third party, they typically come in a package that starts with `com.`*companyname*, e.g. `com.xyzcorp.stuff`.

The package named `java.lang` contains the absolute core of the Java language, and the classes contained within that package are always available to us whenever we write Java programs, so we needn't worry about **importing** `java.lang`; but if we wish to instantiate a `Vector` (one of Java's built in collection classes) as an attribute inside one of *our* classes, for example, then we must import the `java.util` package, as the following example illustrates:

```
// Simple.java

// Our class needs to instantiate a Vector, and so we must import the package
// that defines what a Vector is.

import java.util.*;

public class Simple {
  public static void main(String[] args) {
    Vector v = new Vector();
  }
}
```

The asterisk (*) at the end of the import statement above is a **wildcard** character; it informs the Java compiler that we wish to import *all* of the classes contained within the `java.util` package. As an alternative, we can import individual classes from a package:

```
// ImportExample.java

// We can import individual classes, to better document where each class
// that we are using originates.

import java.util.Enumeration;
import java.util.Vector;
import java.util.Date;
import java.io.PrintWriter;

// etc.
```

This of course requires more typing, but it serves as better documentation of where each class that we are using in our program originates.

If we were to attempt to reference the `Vector` class in one of our classes *without* this `import` statement, we'd get the following compilation error when compiling that particular class:

Class Vector not found.

This is because `Vector` is not in the **name space** of our class: that is, it is not one of the names that the Java compiler recognizes in the context of that class. Generally speaking, the name space for a given class contains the following categories of names, among others:

- ❏ The name of the class itself
- ❏ The names of all of the attributes of the class
- ❏ The names of all of the methods of the class
- ❏ The names of any local variables declared within a method of a class
- ❏ The names of all classes belonging to the package that the class in question belongs to
- ❏ The names of all `public` classes in any other package that has been imported (we'll learn what constitutes a `public` class later in this chapter)
- ❏ The names of all `public` features (attributes, methods) of any of the classes whose names are in the name space
- ❏ The names of all `public` classes in `java.lang`

and so forth.

We could work around the failure to import a package by **fully qualifying** the names of any classes, methods, etc. that we use from such a package; that is, we can prefix the name of the class, method, etc. with the name of the package from which it originates, as shown in the next example:

```
// Simple2.java

// no import statement

public class Simple {
  public static void main(String[] args) {
    java.util.Vector v = new java.util.Vector();
  }
}
```

This, of course, requires a lot more typing, and impairs the readability of the code.

Although most built-in Java packages have names that consist of two terms separated by periods – for example, `java.awt` – some built-in Java packages have three – e.g. `java.awt.event`; and, as far as packages developed by third party organizations are concerned, there's really no limit to the number of terms that can be concatenated to form a package name. (The package name is a reflection of the directory hierarchy used to store `.class` files, but understanding the details of how this works is somewhat complex, and is not necessary for the work that we're going to do in this book.) The important point to note about all of this is that the statement:

`import nameA.nameB.*;`

will only import classes in the *nameA.nameB* package; it will *not* import classes in the *nameA.nameB.someothername* package. That is, the wildcard pertains to **class names** only.

It's also important to note that importing a package is only effective for the particular `.java` file in which the import statement resides. If you have three different classes of your own that all need to manipulate `Vectors`, for example, then all three of their `.java` files must include an `import` statement for `java.util`.

Java also provides programmers with the ability to logically group their *own* classes into packages. For example, if we wanted to, we could invent a package such as `com.objectstart.srs` to house our SRS application. Then, anyone else wishing to incorporate our SRS classes within an application that they were going to write could include the statement

```
import com.objectstart.srs;
```

in their code, and even though our compiled class files are kept *physically* separated from their application's compiled class files, our classes would become *logically* combined with theirs, assuming a few other environmental details had been taken care of.

Going into a detailed discussion of how to create our own packages is beyond the scope of this book to address. But, as it turns out, if you do nothing in particular to take advantage of programmer-defined packages, then as long as all of the compiled `.class` files for your code reside in the same directory on your computer system, they are automatically considered to be in the same package, known as the **default package**. All of the code that we write for the SRS application will be housed in the same directory, and hence will fall within the same default package. This is what enables us to write code such as:

```
public class SRS {
    public static void main(String[] args) {
        Student s = new Student();
        Professor p = new Professor();
        // etc.
    }
}
```

without using import statements: because `Student`, and `Professor`, and `SRS`, and all of the other classes comprising our SRS applications are within the same default package.

The bottom line is that import statements as a building block of a `.java` source code file are optional; they are only needed if we are using classes that are neither found in package `java.lang` nor in our own (default) package. Throughout our work on the SRS, we will point out specifically which Java language packages we need to import for the various built-in classes that we'll be using.

Anatomy of a Java Class

We've seen one trivial use of a Java class as a 'wrapper' for a `main()` method, which in turn is used to serve as a driver for a program. Let's now turn our attention to a more conventional use of classes in Java: namely, to define abstract data types. As we know from our discussions in Part 1 of the book, a (Java) class is a definition, or template, for creating objects belonging to that class: e.g. `Student` objects, or `Professor` objects, or whatever type of abstract data we care to define.

The formal syntax of a basic Java class definition is shown below; angle brackets `< ... >` indicate optional items, and reserved words are shown in **boldface**.

```
<access> class classname <extends classname> <implements interface, ...,
                                              interface> {
    // Declare all attributes of the class as follows:
    <access> datatype attributeName;

    // Define all methods as follows:
    <access> returntype methodName(optional_argument_list) {
    code to implement the method; i.e., the method body
    }
}
```

where `<access>` for a class that stands alone in a `.java` file can be omitted or declared `public`, and `<access>` for a class feature – i.e. an attribute or a method – can either be omitted or declared `public`, `private`, or `protected`. We'll discuss the implications of these `access` designations shortly.

This definition looks rather intimidating, but as it turns out you've seen many class definitions throughout earlier chapters that conform to this definition; here's a trivially simple example:

```
public class Professor extends Person {
  private String name;

  public String getName() {
    return name;
  }

  public void setName(String n) {
    name = n;
  }
}
```

Now, let's explore what it means to assign `public`, `private`, or `protected` access to a feature.

❑   As we already know from our discussion of visibility in Chapter 4, **public** access of a feature (i.e. an attribute or a method) means that the feature so marked is accessible not only within the object/class that it is declared for, but to all other objects/classes in the application, as well, via dot notation.

```
public class Person {
  public String name;
  // etc.
```

❑ And, as we also know from that discussion, **private** access means that a feature is not accessible outside of the object itself – and, as it turns out, not even directly accessible to a subclass that inherits it! We'll revisit this issue a bit later in this chapter when we talk about inheritance as implemented in Java.

```
public class Person {
    public String name;
    private String ssn;
    // etc.
```

❑ Another access type that we didn't previously discuss is **protected** access, which means that a feature is generally `private` from the standpoint of classes that are *outside* of the package, but `public` to classes within the *same* package. (There is one exception, dealing with inheritance situations, that we'll discuss when we speak about visibility and inheritance a bit later in this chapter.) For single-package applications like the SRS, declaring something as `protected` is essentially the same as declaring it to be `public`.

We'll also see later in this chapter that `protected` access has a special purpose in inheritance situations.

```
public class Person {
    public String name;
    private String ssn;
    protected String address;
    // etc.
```

❑ If the access type for a given feature is omitted entirely, as in the following example:

```
public class Person {
    public String name;
    private String ssn;
    protected String address;
    int age;    // this attribute has not specified an access type
    // etc.
```

then the default is for that feature to be visible/accessible to all classes within the same package, and so is alternatively said to be **package visible**. For single-package applications like the SRS, this is the same thing as making it `public`.

So for same-package classes such as those that we'll be developing for the SRS, the bottom line is that if we don't explicitly declare something to be `private`, then it essentially becomes `public`, whether it is declared to be `public`, `protected`, or the access specification is omitted entirely:

```
public class Person {
    // This first attribute is truly private.
    private String ssn;

    // But, all the rest of these attributes are effectively public from the
    // perspective of other classes in the same package.
    public String name;
    protected String address;
    int age;

    // etc.
}
```

As to *class* visibility, we stated that there are only *two* visibility options:

❑   If we declare a class as a whole to be `public`:

```
public class Person {...}
```

this simply means that if the package that the class belongs to is imported into code belonging to some *other* package, then this class, and all of its public attributes and methods, can be referenced, instantiated, etc. from within client code in the *other* package. As an example, the fact that we are able to import `java.util.*` to use the `Vector` class means that the `Vector` class must be designated `public` in the `java.util` package.

Note that making a *class* `public` does not have any direct effect on the visibility of its *features*: `private` features are still private, `protected` features are still protected, and so forth.

❑   If, on the other hand, we leave the access designation off of a class declaration completely:

```
class Animal { ... }
```

then it is said to be 'package visible', meaning that we can refer to the class, instantiate objects of that type, and so forth, from within the code of any of the other classes that belong to the *same* package, but that the class effectively does not exist outside of the package, and cannot be referenced or instantiated from client code within another package.

In a sense, you can think of class visibility as it pertains to classes in a package as being analogous to attribute visibility as it pertains to attributes in a single class: that is, if we think of both a package and a class as a type of container of information, then

❑   A `public` class is analogous to a `public` attribute, in that it can be 'seen' from outside of its 'container', and

❑   A 'package visible' class is analogous to a `private` attribute, in that it cannot be 'seen' from outside of its 'container'.

Class visibility, therefore, constitutes a form of encapsulation at the package level.

We spoke in an earlier section about the ability to bundle two or more classes back to back in a single `.java` file; there is one limitation, however: if more than one class is placed within the same `.java` file, only one of these classes may be a `public` class, and as we stated earlier, its name must match the name of the external file. Should we choose to place additional class definitions in the same `.java` file (a practice that is to be discouraged for the most part), these classes must all be package visible – that is devoid of any specific visibility designation – but can therefore be named independently of the `.java` file as the following simple example illustrates:

```
// Bundle.java

// Assume that the definitions of the following three classes are all colocated
// in the same 'Bundle.java' file; only one of these may be
// declared public, and MUST be named 'Bundle'.

public class Bundle {
```

```
    // details omitted
}

// This class is package visible, and can be named freely.
class Whatever {
  // details omitted
}

// The same is true of this class.
class Anything {
  // details omitted
}

// end of the Bundle.java file
```

Again, since all of the classes that we develop for the SRS application will reside in the same default package, we needn't concern ourselves too much with class-level visibility; we'll declare all of our SRS classes to be `public`, and place each of them in their own `.java` file, but even if we left the `public` designation off, they'd still be visible to one another.

As we discussed in Chapter 4, we need to provide a `public` accessor ('get') and modifier/mutator ('set') method for virtually every `private` attribute (except for `private` housekeeping attributes) – otherwise, the `private` attribute is effectively 'walled in' to the object – i.e. encapsulated – and the outside world cannot do anything with it.

And, by way of review, for an attribute declaration of the form:

visibility attribute-type attributeName;

(for example, `private String majorField;`) the recommended signatures for `get` and `set` methods are as follows:

❑   A `get` method's return type must match the type of the attribute being 'gotten', and the method takes no arguments:

```
public attribute-type getAttributeName();
```

For example:

```
public String getMajorField();
```

❑   A `set` method typically has a return type of `void`, and takes a single argument of the same type as the attribute being set:

```
public void setAttributeName(attribute-type argument-name);
```

For example:

```
public void setMajorField(String major);
```

❑   We'll ignore the `extends` and `implements` keywords in our class template for the time being – we'll talk about these later in this chapter when we discuss inheritance and interfaces, respectively.

Let's look at a simple example of one of the classes that is required for the SRS application; namely, the Student class. (Note that this version of Student does not include all of the attributes and methods that will ultimately be required for the SRS; we'll round it out in Chapter 14.)

```java
// Student.java

public class Student {
  // Declare the attributes.

  private String name;
  private String ssn;
  private Professor facultyAdvisor;

  // We provide public 'get' and 'set' methods for all of the private
  // attributes.

  public void setName(String n) {
    name = n;
  }

  public String getName() {
    return name;
  }

  public void setSsn(String s) {
    ssn = s;
  }

  public String getSsn() {
    return ssn;
  }

  public void setFacultyAdvisor(Professor p) {
    facultyAdvisor = p;
  }

  public Professor getFacultyAdvisor() {
    return facultyAdvisor;
  }
}
```

Here is a simplistic definition of the Professor class; again, we'll flesh it out in Chapter 14:

```java
// Professor.java

public class Professor {
  // Declare the attributes.

  private String name;

  // We provide public 'get' and 'set' methods for all of the private
  // attributes.

  public void setName(String n) {
    name = n;
  }

  public String getName() {
    return name;
  }
}
```

And, here is a third class called `MyProgram`, which serves as the 'wrapper' for the `main()` driver method of an application that manipulates `Student` and `Professor` objects:

```java
public class MyProgram {
  public static void main(String[] args) {
    // Declare and instantiate one Professor object.

    Professor p = new Professor();
    p.setName("Dr. Oompah");

    // Declare and instantiate an array of Student object references.
    // Recall that this does not create the Student objects themselves; it
    // merely creates an array full of null values - an 'empty egg carton'
    // of sorts - which can later be filled with handles on Student objects
    // ('eggs') after we create them.

    Student[] students = new Student[2];

    // Now, let's create two student objects and stuff handles on these
    // objects into the array. While we're at it, we'll use various 'set'
    // methods to initialize their attribute values.

    students[0] = new Student();
    students[0].setName("Fred");
    students[0].setSsn("123-45-6789");
    students[0].setFacultyAdvisor(p);

    students[1] = new Student();
    students[1].setName("Mary");
    students[1].setSsn("987-65-4321");
    students[1].setFacultyAdvisor(p);

    // Finally, step through the array and print out all
    // of the Student information.

    for (int i = 0; i < students.length; i++) {
      System.out.println("Student Information:");
      System.out.println("\tName:    " + students[i].getName());
      System.out.println("\tSSN:     " + students[i].getSsn());
      System.out.println("\tAdvisor: " +
        students[i].getFacultyAdvisor().getName());
      System.out.println("* * * End of Information * * *");
    }
  }
}
```

If we compile all three source files and then run `MyProgram` from the command line:

```
javac Student.java Professor.java MyProgram.java
java MyProgram
```

then the following output will be produced:

```
Student Information:
  Name:  Fred
  SSN:   123-45-6789
  Advisor: Dr. Oompah
* * * End of Information * * *
Student Information:
  Name:  Mary
  SSN:   987-65-4321
  Advisor: Dr. Oompah
* * * End of Information * * *
```

Strings as Objects

In Chapter 1, we introduced the following 'built-in' Java data types: byte, short, int, long, float, double, char, boolean, and String. What we *didn't* make clear at the time is that Strings are *objects*, while all of the other types that we mentioned in Chapter 1 can be thought of as **primitive** – that is, non-object – data types. The structural and behavioral characteristics of String objects are, naturally, defined by the built-in String class.

A sample String declaration and instantiation follow:

```
// Declare a reference variable to a FUTURE String - the String object itself
// doesn't exist yet (recall our discussion of object instantiation in
// Chapter 3).

String s;

// Now, we'll instantiate an actual String object by invoking a String class
// constructor via the 'new' operator. (Recall our discussion of
// constructors in Chapter 4 - we'll talk about them in more depth later
// in this chapter.)

// A 'handle' on the String object is stored in reference variable s.

s = new String("I am a string!");
```

Note that we used the new operator above to create a String object, just as we would any other object. Because creating Strings is such a fundamental operation, however, we learned in Chapter 1 that Java also provides a shorthand way of instantiating a String object without having to explicitly use the new operator with a constructor; this is the syntax that was introduced in Chapter 1:

```
// Declare and instantiate a String object in one step.
String aString = "I am a string!";
```

Actually, this latter form of instantiation without the 'new' keyword is the preferred String construction technique in most cases. This has to do with the fact that Strings created in this fashion are stored in a literal pool which allows them to be shared, so that if you have occasion to use the same String literal in several different places in your code, memory overhead will be reduced. With the 'new' keyword form of instantiation, on the other hand, a new String object is created every time, even if there is a preexisting String object with the same literal value already in existence in your application. The details of how this all works are beyond the scope (or requirements) of this book to address.

As we saw in Chapter 1, the plus sign (+) operator concatenates `Strings`:

```
String x = "foo";
String y = "bar";
String z = x + y + "!";  // z now equals "foobar!"
```

But now that we appreciate the object nature of `Strings`, we can also take advantage of the numerous methods that are available for manipulating `Strings`:

❑   `int length()` – this method, when applied to a `String` object, returns its length as an integer value:

```
int len = z.length();  // continuing the above example,
                       // len now equals 7
```

❑   `boolean startsWith(String)` – returns `true` if the `String` to which this method is applied starts with the `String` provided as an argument, `false` otherwise:

```
// This will evaluate to true.
String s = "foobar";
if (s.startsWith("foo")) ...
```

❑   `boolean endsWith(String)` – returns `true` if the `String` to which this method is applied ends with the `String` provided as an argument, `false` otherwise:

```
// This will evaluate to true.
String s = "foobar";
if (s.endsWith("bar")) …
```

❑   `int indexOf(String)` – returns a non-negative integer indicating the starting character position (counting from 0) at which the `String` provided as an argument is found within the `String` to which this method is applied, or a negative value if the `String` argument is not found:

```
String s = "foobar";
int i = s.indexOf("bar");  // i will equal 3
int j = s.indexOf("cat");  // j will be less than 0, because
                           // "cat" is not found in "foobar"
String t = "oo";
int k = s.indexOf(t);      // k will equal 1
```

❑ `String replace(char old, char new)` – creates a new `String` object in which all instances of the `old` character are replaced with the new character– the original `String` remains unaffected:

```
String s = "o1o2o3o4";
// Note use of single quotes around characters
// vs. double quotes around Strings.
String p = s.replace('o', 'x');   // p now equals "x1x2x3x4", and
                                   // s remains "o1o2o3o4"
```

❑ `String substring(int)` – creates a new `String` object by taking a substring of an existing `String` object starting at the position indicated by the `int` argument through the end of the existing `String`:

```
String s = "foobar";
String p = s.substring(3); // p now equals "bar"
```

❑ `String substring(int, int)` – creates a new `String` by taking a substring of an existing `String` object starting at the position indicated by the first `int` argument and stopping just *before* the position indicated by the second `int` argument; we begin counting with 0 as the first character position:

```
String s = "foobar";
String p = s.substring(1, 4);  // p now equals "oob";
```

Strings are **immutable**: that is, when you seem to be modifying a `String` via the concatenation operator, you are actually creating a *new* `String` object with the desired content:

```
String x = "Foo";         // This results in a String object with the value
                          // "Foo" being created somewhere in memory.
```

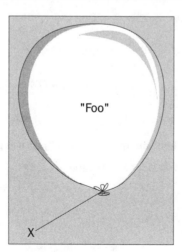

```
x = x + "bar!";    // This results in a SECOND String object with the value
                   // "Foobar!" getting created somewhere else in memory;
                   // the original "Foo" String is still out there, but
                   // like a balloon whose String we've released, it is
                   // no longer directly accessible to us by reference.
```

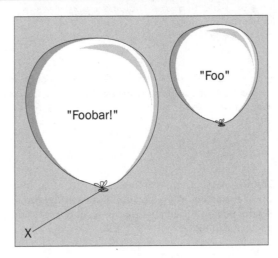

Java Expressions, Revisited

When we defined the term **simple expression** in Chapter 1, there was one form of expression that we omitted, because we hadn't yet talked about objects: namely, messages. We've repeated our list of what constitutes expressions below, and highlighted the previously missing items with boldface:

- ❑   A constant: 7

- ❑   A `String` literal: `"foo"`

- ❑   A variable declared to be of either a simple or abstract data type: `myString, x,` `facultyAdvisor`

- ❑   Any two of the above that are combined with one of the Java binary operators (+, -, *, /, etc.): `z.length() + 2`

- ❑   Any one of the above that is modified by one of the Java unary operators (++, --, !, etc.): `q++`

- ❑   **A message (that is, a method call applied to an object using dot notation): `z.length()`**

- ❑   **A 'chain' of 2 or more messages, concatenated by dots (`.`)**

In Java, it is quite commonplace to form complex expressions by nesting or concatenating method calls. We evaluate such expressions from innermost to outermost parentheses, left to right. So, given the following code 'snippet':

```
Student s = new Student() ;
s.setName("Fred") ;
Professor p = new Professor() ;
p.setName("John") ;
Course c = new Course() ;
c.setName("Math") ;
s.setFacultyAdvisor(p) ;
p.setCourseTaught(c) ;
Course c2 = new Course() ;
```

let's evaluate the expression:

```
c2.setName("BEGINNING " + (s.getFacultyAdvisor().getCourseTaught().getName()));
```

1. Looking for the deepest level of nested parentheses, we see that part of the expression is two sets of parentheses deep, so we evaluate the leftmost deepest subexpression first:

    `s.getFacultyAdvisor()`   which returns a reference to `Professor p`

2. Next, we apply the `getCourseTaught()` method to this `Professor`:

    `p.getCourseTaught()`   which returns a reference to `Course c`

3. Next, we apply the `getName()` method to this `Course`:

    `c.getName()`   which returns the `String` object `"Math"`

4. We've now completed evaluating the expression enclosed within the innermost set of parentheses, effectively giving us the intermediate expression:

    `c2.setName("BEGINNING " + "Math");`

So, we see in the final analysis that the outcome of the complex expression is to assign the name `"BEGINNING Math"` to `Course` object c2.

We'll see many such concatenated method calls in the SRS code.

Printing to the Screen, Revisited

As we learned in Chapter 1, we invoke a special type of method on a special purpose object built into the Java language to print text messages to the command line window, as follows:

System.out.println("*the String expression to be printed*");

We glossed over the syntax when this was first introduced; now that we know a lot more about objects, let's revisit this syntax in more depth:

❑ System is a class built into the core Java language (i.e. it is defined within the java.lang package).

❑ out is a public static attribute of the System class, declared to be of type PrintStream. So, System.out refers to a special object of type PrintStream.

❑ The PrintStream class defines a println() (typically pronounced 'print line') method, which accepts a String expression of arbitrary complexity as an argument and displays it to the standard output window – i.e. the command line window from which you invoked the program.

The System.out.println() and System.out.print() methods can accept very complex expressions, and do their best to ultimately turn these into a single String, which then gets displayed. As it turns out, *any* expression that is capable of producing a String value, including complex method calls, can be passed in as an argument to this method, as illustrated by the following code snippet:

```
Course c = new Course();
// details omitted
System.out.println(c.getProfessor().getAdvisee().getName() +
                   " is an advisee of " + c.getProfessor().getName());
```

Arrays, Revisited

When we introduced arrays in Chapter 6, we alluded to the fact that they are objects in the Java language. As such, the size of an Array – i.e. the number of cells that it has been declared to consist of – may be determined by referring to its length attribute, which is a *public* static attribute of the Array class, meaning we can access it using dot notation. Note that this is in contrast with Strings, which use a length() *method* to determine their length.

The following snippet shows the length attribute in use for an array:

```
int x[] = new int[20];
int y = x.length; // y now equals 20

// details of array content initialization omitted ...

// Step through the array.
// Stop BEFORE i equals x.length!!!!
for (int i = 0; i < x.length; i++) {
  System.out.println(x[i]);
}
```

Because arrays are zero-based, we need to always stop just short of the length when using it as an upper bound in a `for` loop, as the preceding example illustrates.

Note that the length of an array does not reflect how many cells you have explicitly *filled* with values because, technically speaking, even if you store nothing explicitly in an array, it will be automatically filled with zero-equivalent values, as we mentioned in Chapter 6. Rather, the length of an array simply represents the total capacity of the array in terms of the number of items that it *can* hold; the capacity is fixed when an array is first declared, and cannot be changed thereafter. (We'll talk about some other Java collection types later in this chapter which can 'grow gracefully' as needed.)

Also, just to emphasize an array's `Object` nature, let's compare some Java code that creates and manipulates an array using conventional notation:

```
// Conventional:

public class ArrayExample {
  public static void main(String[] args) {
    Student s1 = new Student("Fred Schnurd");
    Student s2 = new Student("Joe Blow");
    Student s3 = new Student("John Smith");

    Student[] students = new Student[3];

    students[0] = s1;
    students[1] = s2;
    students[2] = s3;

    for (int i = 0; i < students.length; i++) {
      System.out.println(students[i].getName());
    }
  }
}
```

with some relatively obscure looking Java code that nonetheless does exactly the same thing! Don't worry too much about what each line of code is doing; some of these things are beyond the scope of this book to address. This is simply an effective way to emphasize that `Arrays` are indeed objects!

```
// An "unconventional" way to manipulate arrays, which clearly demonstrates
// their object nature.

import java.lang.reflect.Array;

public class ArrayExample2 {
  public static void main(String[] args) {
    Student s1 = new Student("Fred Schnurd");
    Student s2 = new Student("Joe Blow");
    Student s3 = new Student("John Smith");

    Object students = null;
```

```
    try {
      // Student[] students = new Student[3];
      students = Array.newInstance(Class.forName("Student"), 3);
    }
    catch (ClassNotFoundException e) {
      System.out.println("DRAT!  Student class not found!");
      System.exit(0);
    }

    // students[0] = s1;
    Array.set(students, 0, s1);

    // students[1] = s2;
    Array.set(students, 1, s2);

    // students[2] = s3;
    Array.set(students, 2, s3);

    // for (int i = 0; i < students.length; i++) {
    for (int i = 0; i < Array.getLength(students); i++) {
      // System.out.println(students[i].getName());
      Student s = (Student) Array.get(students, i);
      System.out.println(s.getName());
    }
  }
}
```

Initializing Variables, Revisited

We said in Chapter 1 that when primitive (i.e. non-object) variables are declared, their values are not automatically initialized; trying to access such variables without explicitly initializing them will result in a compilation error. For example, this next bit of code:

```
1    public static void main(String[] args) {
2        // Declare several local variables within the main() method.
3        int i;  // not automatically initialized
4        int j;  // ditto
5        j = i;  // compilation error!
6    }
```

was shown to produce the following compilation error on line 5:

> Variable i may not have been initialized.

We also stated in Chapter 3 that reference variables – i.e. variables defined to refer to objects, such as Strings, or Students, or Vectors – are considered to have a value of null if they haven't been explicitly initialized. This was a bit of an oversimplification, however, which we'd like to correct now.

To properly understand the notion of initialization in Java, we must differentiate between **local variables** -- that is, variables declared *within a method*, and whose scope was therefore only for the duration of that method (recall our discussion of the scope of a variable in Chapter 1) and attributes of a class, sometimes referred to as **instance variables** that are declared as part of an instance (object). As it turns out:

- *All local variables*, whether declared to be of a primitive data type or of an abstract data type, are considered by the compiler to be *uninitialized* until they have been *explicitly initialized* within a program.

- *All instance variables*, on the other hand, whether declared to be of a primitive data type or of an abstract data type, are *automatically initialized*. That is, in the following code snippet:

```
public class Student {
    int age;
    boolean isHonorsStudent;
    Professor myAdvisor
    // etc.
}
```

the attributes in question are initialized to the appropriate 'zero equivalent' values in Java: that is, booleans are initialized to `false`, numerics to either 0 or 0.0, abstract data types are initialized to `null`, and so forth.

So, to make sure that this is clear, here's a hypothetical example illustrating these initialization rules once again:

```
public class Student {
    // Attributes (aka instance variables) are automatically initialized when
    // an object is instantiated.

    // Primitive data types are initialized to their zero-equivalent values ...

    private int age;                // automatically initialized to 0

    private boolean honorsStudent;  // automatically initialized to false

    // ... and reference variables, aka variables defined to be of an
    // abstract data type, aka object references, are initialized to null.

    private String name;            // automatically initialized to null

    private Professor facultyAdvisor; // automatically initialized to null

    // etc.

    // Methods.
    public void someMethod() {
        // Any variables declared within a method, on the other hand, aka
        // local variables, are considered to be uninitialized by the Java
        // compiler unless they are explicitly initialized within the program.
        // This is true regardless of whether they are a primitive or an
        // abstract data type.

        int x;       // a primitive data type - NOT INITIALIZED!
        String y;    // a built-in abstract data type - NOT INITIALIZED!
        Professor p; // a user defined abstract data type - NOT INITIALIZED!

        // etc.
    }
}
```

Now, a few words about initializing array values.

You may declare, instantiate, and initialize an array in a single step by enclosing the items to be placed into the array inside a set of curly braces, separated by commas; in doing so, Java counts the elements for you, so you needn't declare an explicit size for the array. Here are a few examples:

```
// With the following statement, we declare, instantiate, and initialize an int
// array to contain 3 entries.
int[] x = { 7, 4, 8 };

// The following String array is initialized to contain 5 String objects.
String[] words = { "foo", "bar", "whatever", "done", "yahoo!" };

// The following String array is initialized to contain 3 String objects;
// this is a technique that we'll see used in Chapter 16, when we formulate
// messages for our GUI.
String[] message = { "You are already enrolled in a section of ",
                     "this course; please try again.",
                     " " };

// We declare and instantiate a Student array to hold 2 Student objects,
// creating these on the fly as well. Note that we are calling a Student class
// constructor which accepts a single argument representing the name of the
// Student; we'll talk more about constructors later in this chapter.
Student[] studentBody = { new Student("Bob"), new Student("Alice") };
```

Note that this style of initialization can only be done as a single statement in combination with an array declaration; that is, we may not break such statements into two:

```
int[] x;

// The following line won't compile:
x = {7, 4, 8 };
```

Java Exception Handling

Exceptions are a way for the JVM to signal that a serious error condition has arisen during program execution, one that could potentially cause your program to crash. One such situation would be trying to access a non-existent object, as in the following example:

```
// We declare two Student object references, but only instantiate one of these;
// s2 is given a value of null, indicating that it isn't presently holding
// onto any object.
Student s1 = new Student();
Student s2 = null;

// This line of code is fine.
s1.setName("Fred");

// This next line of code throws a NullPointerException at run time, because we
// are trying to invoke a method on a non-existent object:
s2.setName("Mary"); // throws an exception
```

Exception handling enables a programmer to gracefully anticipate and handle such exceptions by providing a way for a program to transfer control from within the block of code where the exception arose – known as the **try** block – into a special error handling code block known as the **catch** block. The basics of exception handling are as follows:

- ❑ We place code that is likely to throw an exception inside of a pair of curly braces, thereby turning it into a code block. We then place the keyword `try` just ahead of the opening curly brace for that block to signal the fact that we intend to catch exceptions thrown within that block.

- ❑ A `try` block must be immediately followed by one or more `catch` blocks. Each `catch` block declares which category of exception it will catch, and then provides the 'recovery' code which is to be executed upon occurrence of that exception.

Going back to our previous example, here's a revised version of the code that employs exception handling:

```java
// We declare two Student object references, but only instantiate one of these;
// s2 has a default value of null, indicating that it isn't presently holding
// onto any object.
Student s1 = new Student();
Student s2;
```

```java
// Exception handling is now in place.
try {
  s1.setName("Fred");

    // This next line of code throws a NullPointerException at run time ...
    s2.setName("Mary"); // throws an exception
    // ... and as soon as the exception is detected by the JVM, we automatically
    // jump out of the middle of the try block - none of the remaining code in
    // this try block will be executed - and into the catch block for NullPointer
    // Exception
    s1.setMajor("MATH");
    s2.setMajor("SCIENCE");
} // end of try block
catch (UnrelatedException e) { ... }
catch (NullPointerException e2) {
  // Here's where we write the code for what the program should do if
  // a null pointer exception occurred.
  System.out.println("Darn - we forgot to initialize all of the students!");

  // Even though we have a return statement here, which normally causes an
  // immediate return to the calling code, the finally block will still
  // get executed first.
  return;
}
catch (Exception e3) { ... } // note: Exception is a 'catch-all'
finally {
  // This code gets executed whether or not an exception occurred.
  System.out.println("Finally ...");
}
```

Catch clauses are examined in order from top to bottom. The JVM compares the type of exception that has been thrown with the exception type declared to be caught for each catch clause until it finds a match, and then executes the code enclosed in the curly braces immediately following the catch clause; only the first such match is executed. The 'mother of all exception types', the generic Exception class, can be used as the exception type in the last catch block (as shown above) to literally serve as a 'catch-all' if desired.

Once a given catch block's code is executed, control passes beyond all remaining catch blocks associated with that same try block. If no exceptions occur – that is, if the try block's code runs to completion, then control passes beyond all of the catch blocks. Either way, control passes to either the finally block, if one is present, or to the first line of code following the closing curly brace of the last catch block in the group.

The finally block, if present, will always execute whether or not an exception has been caught (i.e. whether or not a catch block was executed). This is where we place code that must always be executed – for example, clean-up code such as file close statements.

Note that you need do nothing to explicitly transfer control from the try block to the appropriate catch block – the JVM handles this automatically for you as needed.

Reading Data from the Command Line

Now that we've learned about Java Strings and arrays, we can appreciate how to pass data into a Java program when invoking the program from the command line. For this, we'll go back to study the main() method's signature a bit more closely.

We saw earlier that, when running a Java program from the command line, we typically only type the command java (to invoke the JVM) followed by the name of the class containing the main() method, e.g. java Simple.

It is possible to control certain aspects of the JVM's behavior by passing it command-line parameters – such parameters go between the keyword java and the name. For example, to control how much memory is allocated to the JVM when running a program, we could type:

java –Xms*memsize* Simple

However, if we want to initialize our *own* program by passing in some command-line information when we invoke it, we can do so by typing this data *after* the name of the program on the command line; for example:

java Simple ABC 123

Such data gets handed to the main() method of the Java program as a String array of **command-line arguments** called args (or whatever else we wish to name it), as indicated by the main() method signature's argument list:

```
public static void main(String[] args) {
  // details omitted
}
```

Inside the `main()` method, we can do with `args` whatever we'd do with any other array; for example, determine its length, manipulate individual `String` items within the array, and so forth. The program below shows some examples:

```java
// FruitExample.java

// This nonsensical program is intended to illustrate command line argument
// passing.

public class FruitExample {
    // The signature of the main() method always needs to
    // declare one argument, which happens to be a String array
    // named 'args'. (You can name the array whatever you'd like,
    // but 'args' is the standard name that most people use.)
    //
    // This array is automatically initialized when the program is run
    // from the DOS or Unix command line with whatever (space-separated)
    // values ('arguments') you've typed on the command line
    // after the program name.
    //
    // For example, if the compiled program is run from the DOS
    // command line as follows:
    //
    //      java FruitExample apple banana cherry
    //
    // then the args array will be automatically initialized with
    // three String values "apple", "banana", and "cherry" which
    // will be stored in array 'cells' args[0], args[1], and
    // args[2], respectively (remember that arrays start counting at 0).

    public static void main(String[] args) {
        // Let's print out a few things.
        System.out.println("The args array contains " + args.length +
                        " entries." );

        // Only execute this next block of code if the array isn't empty.
        if (args.length > 0) {
            int i = args.length - 1;
            System.out.println("The last array entry is: " + args[i]);

            // Note the use of parentheses to invoke the length() method
            // on an individual String object, versus the lack of parentheses
            // above when accessing the length attribute of the array as a
            // whole.
            System.out.println("It is " + args[i].length() +
                        " characters long.");
        }

        // etc.
    }
}
```

When this program is run from the command line as:

java FruitExample apple banana cherry

it produces the following output:

The args array contains 3 entries.
The last array entry is: cherry
It is 6 characters long.

Accepting Keyboard Input

Most applications receive information either directly from users via the application's graphical user interface, or by reading information from a file or database. But, until you have learned how to program such things in Java, it's handy to know how to prompt for textual inputs from the command line window.

Just as Java provides a special OutputStream stream called System.out, which in turn provides both println() and print() methods for displaying messages to the command line window one line at a time, Java also provides a special InputStream object called System.in to read inputs from the command line as typed by a user via the keyboard. There is only one minor problem: the primary method provided by the InputStream class for doing so, read(), only reads one character at a time, and this character is actually returned to the code invoking System.in.read() as an int(eger) value. Not to worry! We simply encapsulate (hide) these details in a class of our own making, called KeyboardInput, as follows:

```java
// KeyboardInput.java

// I discovered that you can only read one character from the keyboard
// at a time, so I created this little class to hide the 'ugliness'.
//
// To use it, do the following in your main program:
//
//          KeyboardInput k = new KeyboardInput();
//          k.readLine();
//
// then, use the method call:
//
//          k.getKeyboardInput();
//
// which returns a String representing a line's worth of input
// (up until the user pressed the Enter key).

import java.io.*;

public class KeyboardInput {
  // Whatever the user last typed gets saved in this String.
  private String keyboardInput;

  public String readLine() {
    char in;
```

```
            // Clear out previous input.
            keyboardInput = "";

            try {
                // Read one integer, and cast it into a character.
                in = (char) System.in.read();

                // Keep going until we hit a newline character, which is
                // generated when a user presses the Enter key on the keyboard.
                while (in != '\n') {   //  \n is a newline character
                keyboardInput = keyboardInput + in;
                in = (char) System.in.read();
            }
        }
    catch (IOException e) {
        // We may want to do some error reporting ... details omitted.
        // Reset the input.
        keyboardInput = "";
    }

    // Strip off any leading/trailing whitespace.
    keyboardInput = keyboardInput.trim();

    // Return the complete String.
    return keyboardInput;
}

public String getKeyboardInput() {
    return keyboardInput;
}
```

Then, here's an example of how to put the KeyboardInput class to use:

```
// KeyboardInputTest.java

import java.util.*;
import java.io.*;

// A sample main program that prompts the user for command-line keyboard input.
public class KeyboardInputTest {
    public static void main(String args[]) {
        // Instantiate a KeyboardInput object.
        KeyboardInput k = new KeyboardInput();

        // Gather input from the keyboard.

        // Prompt the user (note use of print() vs. println()).
        System.out.print("Enter your name: ");

        // Read one line's worth of input (up until user presses the Enter key).
        k.readLine();

        // Display the input back as a test.
        System.out.println("You typed: |" + k.getKeyboardInput() + "|");
    }
}
```

Running this program from the DOS/Unix command line would produce the following results (**bolded** text reflects that which was typed by the user):

C:\> **java KeyboardInputTest**
Enter your name: **Jacquie**
You typed: IJacquieI

Using Constructors

We learned in Chapter 4 that when we instantiate a brand new object with the new operator, we are creating a 'bare bones' object with essentially empty attributes (each attribute will be initialized to 0, null, or whatever is appropriate for a given attribute type, as we discussed earlier). We also learned that if we want to create an object in a more intelligent fashion – that is, to do more elaborate things when the object is first created – we create a special type of a method called a **constructor**. A constructor:

❑ Has the same name as the class.

❑ Has no explicit return type, because it really has a *default* return type of the class that it is defined for – a constructor returns a brand new object of that type.

> *This is a very important fact to remember! If you accidentally declare a constructor signature with a return type, for example,* public **void** Student (...), *the compiler will not report an error, because what you have just done is to declare a **legitimate, non-constructor method** which just happens to have the same name as the default constructor signature* public Student () has; *i.e. you have overloaded the method name* 'Student'! *This can be a particularly frustrating problem to debug.*

❑ Can take any number or variety of arguments.

Here's one simple example of a constructor for the Student class:

```
public class Student {
  // Attributes.
  private String name;
  // other details omitted

  // A constructor. (Note: no return type!)
  // This constructor passes in a String value representing the name that is
  // to be assigned to the Student object when it is first instantiated.
  public Student(String n) {
    name = n;
  }

  // etc.
}
```

We can create many different constructors for the same class which take different combinations of arguments – this is known as **overloading**, a concept that we discussed in Chapter 5. As long as each constructor has a different 'pattern' of argument types, it is considered to be a different constructor:

```
// One argument, a String.
public Student(String name) {
  // details omitted ...
}

// Two String arguments; this is OK!
public Student(String name, String ssn) {
  // details omitted ...
}

// One int, one string; this is also OK!
public Student(String name, int id) {
  // details omitted ...
}

// This last constructor signature would be rejected by the compiler,
// since there is already another constructor with two String arguments -
// the fact that the argument names are different is immaterial.
public Student(String firstName, String lastName) {
  // details omitted ...
}
```

It turns out that if you don't explicitly declare any constructors for a class, Java automatically provides a default constructor with no arguments for that class. So, even though we may have designed a class with no constructors whatsoever:

```
public class Student {
  // Attributes.

  private String name;
  // other details omitted

  // Methods (but NO EXPLICIT CONSTRUCTORS!).

  public String getName() {
    return name;
  }

  public void setName(String n) {
    name = n;
  }

  // etc.
}
```

we are still able to have client code as follows:

```
Student s1 = new Student();  // calling the default constructor
```

because we are using the default constructor with no arguments, also referred to as the default 'no args' constructor.

327

There is one very important caveat about default constructors in Java: if we invent *any* of our own constructors for a class, with any number of arguments, then the default 'no args' constructor is *not* automatically provided. This is by design, because it is assumed that if we've gone to the trouble to program any constructors whatsoever, then we must have some special initialization requirements for our class that the Java default constructor could not possibly anticipate. So, if we want or need a constructor that accepts no arguments for a particular class *along with* other versions of constructors that *do* take arguments, we must program a 'no args' constructor. Generally speaking, it is considered good practice to always explicitly provide a 'no args' constructor if you are providing any constructors at all.

Here is another version of a `Student` class, this time with multiple constructors provided; note that here we are indeed replacing the 'no args' constructor:

```java
// Student.java

public class Student {
  private String name;
  private String ssn;
  private Professor facultyAdvisor;

  // Constructors.

  // This version takes three arguments.
  public Student(String n, String s, Professor p) {
    name = n;
    ssn = s;
    facultyAdvisor = p;
  }

  // This "flavor" takes two arguments.
  public Student(String n, String s) {
    name = n;
    ssn = s;

    // Since we aren't getting a Professor object handed in to us in
    // this version, we set this attribute to null for the time being.

    facultyAdvisor = null;
  }

  // We must explicitly provide the "default" constructor (if we want
  // to be able to use it) if we have created ANY other constructors.
  public Student() {
    // Note here that we've decided to invent some "placeholder"
    // values for the name and ssn attributes in the case where
    // specific values are not being passed in.

    name = "???";
    ssn = "???-??-????";
    facultyAdvisor = null;
  }
```

```
public String getName() {
  return name;
}

// etc. for other get/set method pairs

public String getFacultyAdvisorName() {
  // Note: since some of our constructors initialize facultyAdvisor with
  // a Professor object, and others do not, we cannot assume that the
  // attribute has been initialized to a Professor "handle" when the
  // getFacultyAdvisorName() method is invoked. To avoid the possibility
  // of throwing a NullPointerException, we check to make sure that the
  // facultyAdvisor attribute is NOT null before proceeding.
  if (facultyAdvisor != null) {
    return facultyAdvisor.getName();
  }
  else return "TBD";
}
}
```

Here is a simplistic version of a Professor class, to use in testing:

```
// Professor.java

public class Professor {
  // Declare the attributes.

  private String name;

  // We provide public 'get' and 'set' methods for all of the private
  // attributes.

  public void setName(String n) {
    name = n;
  }

  public String getName() {
    return name;
  }
}
```

and, here is a revised version of our main class, MyProgram, which shows the various constructors in use:

```
public class MyProgram {
  public static void main(String[] args) {
    Student[] students = new Student[3];
    Professor p;

    p = new Professor();
    p.setName("Dr. Oompah");
```

```
        // We'll try out the various constructor signatures.
        students[0] = new Student("Joe", "123-45-6789", p);
        students[1] = new Student("Bob", "987-65-4321");
        students[2] = new Student();

        System.out.println("Advisor Information\n");
        for (int i = 0; i < students.length; i++) {
          System.out.println("Name:  " + students[i].getName() +
            "      Advisor:   " +
            students[i].getFacultyAdvisorName());
        }
      }
    }
```

The preceding program produces the following output when run at the command line:

Advisor Information

Name: Joe   Advisor: Dr. Oompah
Name: Bob   Advisor: TBD
Name: ???   Advisor: TBD

There are some additional complexities that you need to be aware of when it comes to constructors and inheritance – we'll discuss these later.

Using the 'this' Keyword for Object Self-Referencing

In client code, such as the `main()` method of a program, we declare reference variables in which to store handles on objects:

```
Student s = new Student();  // s is a reference variable of type Student.
```

and can then conveniently access the objects that these reference variables refer to by manipulating the reference variables themselves:

```
s.setName("Fred");
```

When we are executing the code that comprises the body of one of an object's own methods, we sometimes need the object to be able to refer to itself – i.e. to **self-reference**, as in this next bit of code:

```
public class Student {
  Professor facultyAdvisor;
  // other details omitted

  public void selectAdvisor(Professor p) {
    // We're down in the 'bowels' of the selectAdvisor() method,
    // executing this method for a particular Student object.
```

```
        // We save the handle on our new advisor as one of our attributes …
        facultyAdvisor = p;

        // … and now we want to turn around and tell this Professor object to
        // add us as one of its (Student) advisees. The Professor class has a
        // method with signature
        //
        //        public void addAdvisee(Student s);
        //
        // so, all we need to do is call this method on our advisor object
        // and pass in a reference to ourselves; but who the heck are we?
        // That is, how do we refer to ourself?
        p.addAdvisee(???);
    }
}
```

Within the body of a method, when we need a way to refer to the object whose method we are executing, we use the reserved word this to 'self reference'. So, in our example above, the following line of code would do the trick:

```
    p.addAdvisee(this);    // passing a reference to THIS Student
```

Specifically, it would pass a reference to *this* Student – the Student object whose method we are executing – as an argument of the addAdvisee() method, to Professor p.

Using this to refer to an object from within one of its own methods is like referring to yourself as 'me'!

Another rather trivial use for the this keyword has to do with variable scope. We mentioned in Chapter 4 that one of the possible ways to name arguments being passed into a 'set' method is to use the exact same name as is used for the attribute being set. In the following example, for instance, we have declared a method signature

```
    void setSsn(String ssn)
```

to be used to set the value of Student attribute ssn. We *cannot*, however, write the method as follows:

```
    public class Student {
      String ssn;

      // details omitted

      public void setSsn(String ssn) {
        ssn = ssn;  // this line will confuse the compiler!
      }

      // etc.
    }
```

This is because the second (inner) declaration of ssn – namely, the argument to the setSsn() method – will mask the first (outer) declaration of ssn, and as a result, we won't wind up updating our ssn attribute. The line of code

```
    ssn = ssn;
```

is simply copying the value of the locally scoped version of ssn back onto itself, and the version of ssn that 'lives' at the class level remains untouched.

The this keyword comes to our rescue, as follows:

```
public class Student {
    String ssn;

    // details omitted

    void setSsn (String ssn) {    // This declaration of 'ssn'
                                   // overshadows the previous
        this.ssn = ssn;            // declaration ...
                                   // ... but using 'this', we can get
                                   // at the outermost scoped 'ssn'
```

We use the same name – ssn – for both the attribute at the class level and the argument being passed into the method, so we use the expression this.ssn to refer to the 'outer scoped' instance of ssn.

If we don't care to follow this programming style, we'd have to invent a different name for the argument being passed in, so that the compiler doesn't get confused:

```
void setSsn(String s) {
  ssn = s;  // no problem!
}
```

We discussed several alternative argument naming conventions for 'set' methods in Chapter 4.

One last noteworthy use of the this keyword has to do with reusing constructor code. If we have a class which declares more than one form of constructor, and we wish to reuse the code from one constructor in the body of another constructor, we can use the expression

this(*optional arguments*);

as a shorthand way of running one constructor from within another. This is best illustrated by a short example.

```
// Student.java

public class Student {
  private String name;
  private String ssn;
  private Transcript transcript;
```

```java
    // Constructors.

    // This version takes one argument.
    public Student(String n) {
      name = n;
      transcript = new Transcript();
      // pseudocode
      do some other complicated things ...
    }

    // This "flavor" takes two arguments.  But, we want to reuse the logic
    // from the preceding constructor, without having to retype the same code.
    public Student(String n, String s) {
      // We include - as the FIRST line of code in this constructor -
      // a line of code which indicates that we want to reuse the
      // logic of a different constructor for this same class:  i.e.
      // the constructor that takes a single String argument, to
      // be precise (because we're passing in a String)!
      this(n);

      // Now, go on to do other things that this version of the constructor
      // needs to take care of.
      ssn = s;
    }

    // etc.
  }
```

(We'll see a similar use for the super keyword when we talk about constructors and inheritance a bit later in this chapter.)

Object Deletion and Garbage Collection

In the C++ language, there is a 'delete' operator that allows the programmer to explicitly control when a dynamically-allocated object is no longer needed, and its memory can therefore be recycled. This is both a blessing and a curse! It is a blessing, because it gives a C++ programmer very tight control over his/her memory resources in a program. But, if a C++ programmer forgets to recycle his/her objects, the program can literally run out of memory – this is known as a 'memory leak'.

With Java, however, there is no delete operator: anything dynamically created – i.e. everything but simple data types – is a candidate for Java **garbage collection** when all references to it (handles) have been eliminated. Like the 'object as a helium balloon' example that we discussed in Chapter 3, when we let go of all strings on a balloon, it essentially floats away. Garbage collection is an automatic function performed by the JVM; when an object is garbage collected, the memory that was allocated to that object is recycled and added back to the pool of memory that is available to the JVM for new object creation.

By way of review, there are several ways to release handles on objects in Java so as to make them candidates for garbage collection, as the following example illustrates:

```
// Declare two reference variables to hold on to future
// (as of yet to be created) Student objects.
Student s1;
Student s2;

// Instantiate a Student object, and store a handle on this object in s1.
s1 = new Student();

// Copy the handle into s2, so that we now have two handles on the same object.
s2 = s1;

// Let's now look at two different ways to 'drop' an object reference.

// We can reset a variable previously holding a handle to the value null ...
s1 = null;  // (We still have one of two handles left on the object.)

// ... or we can hand a variable some OTHER object's handle,
// causing it to drop the first handle. Here, by creating a
// second Student object and handing it to s2, s2 drops the
// only remaining handle on the first Student object.
s2 = new Student( );  // No more handles on the original student remain!
```

We have eliminated all obvious references to the original instance of a Student; if there are no remaining references to an object, it becomes a *candidate* for garbage collection. We emphasize the word 'candidate' in the previous sentence, however, because the garbage collector doesn't immediately recycle the object. Rather, the garbage collector runs whenever the JVM determines that there is a need for some recycling to be done – e.g. when the application is getting low on free memory necessary to allocate new objects. So, for some period of time, the 'orphaned' Student object will still exist in memory – we merely won't have any handles with which to reach it.

There is a way for a programmer to make a request of the JVM to perform garbage collection explicitly:

```
Runtime.getRuntime().gc();  // nothing to import - the Runtime class is
                            // defined in java.lang
```

but even then the precise moment of *when* garbage collection occurs is out of the programmer's control, as is which and how many of the eligible objects will be collected.

The inclusion of garbage collection in Java has virtually eliminated memory leaks. Note that it is still possible for the JVM to run out of memory, however, if you maintain too many handles on too many objects; so, a Java programmer cannot be totally oblivious to memory management – it is just less error prone than with C/C++.

Inheritance and Java

From our discussion of inheritance in Chapter 5, we learned that:

❏ Inheritance is used to derive a new class definition from an existing class when the new class is perceived to be a special case of the existing class.

❏ The derived class automatically inherits the properties/attributes and behaviors/methods of the base class.

❏ Java uses the `extends` keyword to signal that one class is derived from another:

```
public class Person {
   String name;

   public String getName() { return name; }
   public void setName(String name) { this.name = name; }
}
```

```
// We derive the Student class from Person.
public class Student extends Person {
   // If we define nothing in the body of this class, it will still have
   // one attribute - name - and two methods - getName() and setName()
   // - because these are inherited from Person!
}
```

Although we mastered the basics of inheritance in that chapter, it turns out that there are a lot of important subtleties about inheritance in Java that we haven't yet discussed; we'll do so now.

Visibility/Accessibility of Inherited Components

By virtue of inheritance, everything defined in a base class is automatically present in a derived class – inheritance is an 'all or nothing' proposition. However, some inherited features (attributes/methods) may not be directly accessible by the derived class, depending on their access permissions as assigned in the base class.

Consider the following base class:

```
public class Person {
   <access> int age;
   // details omitted
}
```

`<access>` for a feature, as we learned earlier in this chapter, can be one of:

❏ `private`

❏ `public`

❏ `protected`

❏ unspecified or omitted, known as package visibility

and as we said earlier, for same-package classes such as we will have for the SRS, the latter three are all, in effect, public.

Suppose that we derive the Student class from Person as follows:

```
public class Student extends Person {
  // The age attribute is inherited from the superclass...
  // here, we add a method which manipulates this attribute.
  public boolean isOver65( ) {
    if (age > 65) return true;
    else return false;
  }
}
```

Now, what will happen when we try to compile this Student class? The answer to this question depends on how the access has been defined for the age attribute of Person.

If we declare age to be either protected or public in Person, or if we omit the access declaration entirely, then this means that the attribute is both inherited and visible/accessible to Student, and the Student class shown above will compile without error.

If, on the other hand, age is declared to be private in Person:

```
public class Person {
  private int age;
```

then we will get a compilation error on the highlighted line of the Student class:

```
public class Student extends Person {
  // The age attribute is inherited from the superclass...
  // here, we add a method which manipulates this attribute.
  public boolean isOver65( ) {
    if (age > 65) return true;
    else return false;
  }
}
```

The error message will be:

Undefined variable: age

That's because the age attribute is indeed inherited – it is part of the data structure comprising a Student object – but it is nonetheless 'invisible' to the Student! It's like your heart: it is part of your physical body, but you cannot see or access it directly.

If our inclination is to make all attributes private, how can a subclass *ever* manipulate its privately inherited attributes? The answer is quite simple: through the public accessor/mutator methods that it has also inherited from its parent. We've revised the previous example program to illustrate this technique.

First, we make sure that the parent `Person` class provides a `public getAge()` method (good programming practice would always call for this anyway):

```
public class Person {
  private int age;
  // details omitted

  // We provide an accessor method for subclasses to inherit.
  public int getAge() { // this method could also be declared
                        // as a protected method, if we only want
                        // subclasses to access it.
    return age;
  }
}
```

Then, we use the *inherited* `getAge()` method from within the `Student`'s `isOver65()` method, and we're back in business. `Student` compiles without error.

```
public class Student extends Person {
  public boolean isOver65( ) {
    // Even though the age attribute per se is 'invisible',
    // the getAge() method that we inherit from Person
    // allows us to access the value of age.
    if (getAge() > 65) return true;
    else return false;
  }
}
```

As we mentioned back in Chapter 4, it is generally considered good practice to always use 'get' and 'set' methods to access the values of attributes, even from within a class's own methods, so as to take advantage of any special processing that the get/set method might provide relative to that attribute.

Reusing Base Class Behaviors: The 'super' Keyword

As we learned in Chapter 5, if we provide a method in a derived class whose signature matches that of a base class method (identical method name and argument type sequence) then we are said to have **overridden**, or 'masked', the base class behavior. When would we want/need to do this? When the derived class needs to do something slightly more specialized in response to a message, as in the following example:

```
public class Person {
  private String name;
  private String ssn;

  public String getName() {
    return name;
  }

  public String getSsn() {
    return ssn;
  }

  // etc.
```

```
    // Have a Person object describe itself.
    public String getDescription() {
      return getName() + " (" + getSsn() + ")";
      // e.g., "John Doe (123-45-6789)"
    }
  }

public class Student extends Person {
  private String major;

  public String getMajor() {
    return major;
  }

  // etc.

  // We want a Student object to return a description of itself
  // differently from the way its parent class (Person) does so.
  // So, we equip this subclass with a method having the exact
  // same signature as was defined for its parent class; this
  // version of the method overrides (masks) the inherited version.
  public String getDescription() {
    return getName() + " (" + getSsn() + ") [" + getMajor() + "]";
    // e.g., "Mary Smith (987-65-4321) [Math]"
  }
}
```

We also mentioned back in Chapter 5 that if we wanted to do everything that the parent's version of a method did, plus something extra, there was a way to invoke the parent's version of the method from within the child's version. In Java, this is accomplished by using the super keyword as follows:

```
public class Student extends Person {
  String major;

  // etc.

  // Exact same method signature as was defined for Person - so, this
  // method overrides (masks) the inherited version.
  public String getDescription() {
    // Notice, however, that we are now calling the parent class's version
    // of the method so as to reuse that code.
    String parentDesc = super.getDescription();
    return parentDesc + " [" + getMajor() + "]";
    // e.g., "Mary Smith (123-45-6789) [Math]"
  }
}
```

Just as this is a keyword used to generically refer to an object from within one of its methods, super is used when we want to generically refer to the parent class of some object from within one of its methods.

Another important use of the super keyword has to do with constructors, which we'll learn about momentarily.

Inheritance and Constructors

Constructors are not inherited the way other methods are. This raises some interesting complications that are best illustrated via an example.

Let's start by declaring a constructor for the `Person` class which takes two arguments:

```
public class Person {
   String name;
   String ssn;

   public Person(String n, String s) {
     name = n;
     ssn = s;
   }
}
```

We know from an earlier discussion that the `Person` class now only recognizes one constructor signature – one which takes two arguments – because the default constructor with no arguments has been eliminated.

Now, say that we extend the `Person` class to create the `Student` class, and furthermore that we want the `Student` class to define two constructors – one which takes two arguments and one which takes three arguments. Unfortunately, because constructors are not inherited, we cannot take advantage of the fact that the `Person` class has already gone to the trouble to define a constructor with two arguments; we have to recode one ourselves, as follows:

```
public class Student extends Person {
   String major;

   // Constructor with two arguments.
   public Student(String n, String s) {
     // Note the redundancy of logic between this constructor and
     // the parent constructor - we'll come back and fix this in a
     // moment.
     name = n;  // redundant
     ssn = s;  // redundant
     major = null;
   }

   // Constructor with three arguments.
   public Student(String n, String s, String m) {
     // More redundancy.
     name = n;  // redundant
     ssn = s;  // redundant
     major = m;
   }
}
```

As a result of having declared explicit constructors, the `Student` class has also lost its default 'no args' constructor.

339

Fortunately, there is a way to reuse a parent class's constructor code without having to duplicate its logic in the derived class's constructor. We accomplish this via the same super keyword we discussed a moment ago for the reuse of standard methods. If you wish to explicitly reuse a particular parent class's constructor, you refer to it as super(...), and pass in whatever arguments it needs, as the following revised version of the Student class illustrates:

```
public class Student extends Person {
    String major;

    // Constructor with two arguments.
    public Student(String n, String s) {
        // We'll explicitly invoke the Person constructor with two
        // arguments, passing in the values of n and s.
        super(n, s);

        // By doing this, we can eliminate the next two lines...
        // name = n;
        // ssn = s;
        // ... and can concentrate on only those things that need be done
        // uniquely for a Student.
        major = null;
    }

    // Constructor with three arguments.
    public Student(String n, String s, String m) {
        // See comments above.
        super(n, s);
        major = m;
    }
}
```

One important thing to note is that if you explicitly call a base class constructor from a derived class constructor, the call *must* be the *first* statement in the derived class constructor; that is, the following constructor would fail to compile:

```
public Student(String n, String s, String m) {
    major = m;

    // This won't compile, because the call to the parent's
    // constructor must come first in the derived class's constructor.
    super(n, s);
}
```

This arises by virtue of the 'is a' nature of inheritance. When we create a Student object, we are in reality simultaneously creating a Person and a Student, for a Student is both. So, whether we *explicitly* call a parent class's constructor from the subclass's constructor using the super(...) convention or not, the fact is that Java will always attempt to execute constructors for all of the ancestor classes for a given class, from most general to most specific in the class hierarchy, before launching into that given class's constructor code.

❑ If you are instantiating a `Student`, for example, then a `Person` constructor will be executed first, followed by a `Student` constructor.

❑ If you have in turn derived the `GraduateStudent` class from the `Student` class, then whenever you instantiate a `GraduateStudent`, a `Person` constructor will be executed first, followed by a `Student` constructor, followed at last by the `GraduateStudent` class's constructor code.

This makes intuitive sense, because we said that inheritance represents the 'is a' relationship – a `Student` is a `Person` – so whatever we have to do when we create a `Person` will most likely make sense to do when we create a `Student`. The question is, *which* base class constructor gets called if you've defined more than one? There are several different scenarios that we must explore in answering this question.

Case #1: The Derived Class Declares No Constructors of its Own

If we derive a class such as `Student`, but don't bother to define any consrtuctors for the derived class, then Java will attempt to provide us with a default 'no args' constructor for that derived class. When we create a new object of the derived class, the default constructor with no arguments for each of the ancestor class(es) automatically gets called first, then the default constructor of the derived class. So, if we have derived a class B from class A, the *parent* class A must have also defined a constructor with no arguments.

The following example won't compile:

```
public class Person {
  String name;

  // A constructor with one argument - by having created this,
  // we've lost Person's default constructor with no arguments.
  public Person(String n) {
    name = n;
  }
}

public class Student extends Person {
  String major;

  // No constructors defined here!
}
```

When we try to compile `Student`, we'll get the error message:

No constructor matching Person() found in class Person

This is because the Java compiler is trying to create a default constructor with no arguments for the `Student` class but, in order to do so, it knows that it is going to need to be able to call the default constructor for a `Person` from within the `Student` default constructor – but, no such default constructor for `Person` exists!

The only way around this dilemma is to either:

- ❑ Explicitly program a constructor with no arguments for the Person class, to replace the 'lost' default Person constructor, for the compiler to take advantage of when creating a default Student class constructor (this is the *preferred* approach); or

- ❑ Always use a constructor for the Student class that *explicitly* invokes a *particular* Person constructor.

This latter option is explored in the next case.

Case #2: The Derived Class Explicitly Declares One or More Constructors

This can actually be split into two subcases:

Subcase #2A

If you do not explicitly call a base class constructor from the derived class constructor, the default base class constructor with no arguments will still be called, as in Case #1. The following code won't compile:

```
public class Person {
  String name;

  // A constructor with one argument - by having created this,
  // we've lost Person's default constructor with no arguments.
  public Person(String n) {
    name = n;
  }
}

public class Student extends Person {
  String major;

  // We declare a Student constructor, but don't explicitly invoke a
  // particular Person constructor from within it.
  public Student(String n, String m) {
    name = n;
    major = m;
  }
}
```

When we try to compile Student, we'll get the error message:

No constructor matching Person() found in class Person

for the same reasons cited earlier.

Subcase #2B

The derived class constructor explicitly calls a particular parent class constructor:

```java
public class Person {
  String name;

  // A constructor with one argument - by having created this,
  // we've lost Person's default constructor with no arguments.
  public Person(String n) {
    name = n;
  }
}

public class Student extends Person {
  String major;

  // Constructor.
  public Student(String n, String m) {
    // We'll explicitly invoke the Person constructor with one
    // argument, passing through the value of n.
    super(n);
    major = m;
  }
}
```

All is well when this code is compiled!

Java's Collection Classes

We learned in Chapter 6 that we need a convenient way to collect references to objects as we create them, so that we may iterate over them, retrieve a particular object on demand, and so forth. In an application, it is often impossible to anticipate how many of a given object type we are going to create as the application is running, and so using fixed-size arrays to store varying numbers of objects is inefficient. The Java language defines several different alternative collection classes that can be used to store object collections – two of the more commonly used classes in this regard are Vector and Hashtable, although there are many more.

The Vector Class

The Vector class, a simple container, allows us to store a varying number of items without having to worry about properly sizing the container. To use a Vector, we must import the class (which belongs to the java.util package) into our application. There are two ways to do so:

```java
import java.util.*;        // This makes ALL of the classes defined in the
                           // java.util package available to this program
```

or

```
import java.util.Vector;       // This imports only the Vector class
```

Note that there is no advantage in terms of execution efficiency with using one versus the other form of import, since the JVM only loads those classes at runtime that your application actually uses. The only slight advantage of the second version over the first is with regard to documentation – it clarifies which class(es) we are using from this package – but this is a fairly minor advantage, and typically programmers use the 'wildcard' (*) form of the import statement instead.

To use a Vector, we must instantiate the Vector class using one of several alternative constructors. The simplest form of constructor is the default constructor with no arguments:

```
Vector coursesTaken = new Vector();  // We've just created an 'egg carton'!
```

Once we've created a Vector, we can instantiate objects and add them to the Vector using the appropriate method:

```
// Create 'eggs'!
Course c1 = new Course("Math 101");
Course c2 = new Course("Physics 250");
Course c3 = new Course("Management 283");
// Insert 'eggs' into the 'carton'!
coursesTaken.add(c1);
coursesTaken.add(c2);
coursesTaken.add(c3);
```

We use the size() method to determine how many items have been added:

```
System.out.println("Student has taken " + coursesTaken.size() + " courses.");
```

This syntax is at odds with the length attribute of an array and the length() method of a String ... Java is clearly being developed by committee!

Vectors and Casting

One significant difference between a Java Array and a Vector is as follows:

❑ With an Array, you declare it to hold items (objects references or simple data types) of a certain type – e.g. if you wanted to hold onto a group of Person objects, you'd declare an array as follows:

```
Person[] people = new Person[20];
```

and then you would be limited by the compiler to only storing items of that type (or, by virtue of inheritance, of any subtype of that type – for example Person, Student, or Professor references) in the array.

❑ With a Vector, on the other hand, there is no indication in its declaration of what type of object references the Vector will hold! This is because Vectors hold arbitrary Object references and return them as generic Object references.

In the Java language, a core language class called `Object` (defined in the `java.lang` package) is the parent class to all other classes, whether built-in or programmer-defined – in other words, `Object` is at the root of the entire Java inheritance hierarchy. So, although you didn't realize it before, whenever we declare a class, such as:

```
public class Person {
  // details omitted
}
```

it is as if we are declaring it as follows:

```
public class Person extends Object {
  // details omitted
}
```

We'll talk later in this chapter about some of the implications of having all Java objects descended from the `Object` class.

Meanwhile, back to `Vectors`: because a `Vector` treats everything that is inserted as a generic `Object` reference, we as programmers must remember what class of object reference we are storing in a given `Vector` so that we may cast these references back to the correct class when we retrieve them. Here's an example, continuing from above:

```
Vector coursesTaken = new Vector();   // We've just created an 'egg carton'!

Course c1 = new Course("Math 101");
Course c2 = new Course("Physics 250");
Course c3 = new Course("Management 283");

// Insert Course object references into the Vector, which treats them as generic
// Object references.
coursesTaken.add(c1);
coursesTaken.add(c2);
coursesTaken.add(c3);
```

```
// Let's now pull them back out!
for (int i = 0; i < coursesTaken.size(); i++) {
  // Cast a generic Object reference back into a Course reference.
  Course c = (Course) coursesTaken.elementAt(i);

  // We now can invoke the methods of a Course on c.
  System.out.println(c.getName());
}
```

Later in this chapter, we'll dig a little deeper to see what casting is really all about.

Suggestion: add a comment to your `Vector` declarations to help you remember what sort of object references you intended to store there:

```
Vector coursesTaken; // of Course object references
```

You can mix object reference types in a `Vector`, but then you may have trouble casting them properly when you retrieve them! We'll talk later about determining an object's identity, and will revisit this issue then. Note, however, that we often store object references of different subtypes in a `Vector` when they all have a common supertype, as for example, if we wanted to create a `Vector` to hold references to all `Person` objects – either `Students` or `Professors` – who are employed by the university.

As a class, `Vector` defines a lot of very interesting behaviors:

❏ `add(Object)` – adds an object reference to the end of the `Vector`, automatically expanding the `Vector` if need be to accommodate the reference (note that it can be a reference to any type of object, as they are all descended from the Java `Object` class).

❏ `add(int, Object)` – adds the specified object reference to the position in the `Vector` indicated by the `int` argument (where counting starts with 0, as in an `Array`), shifting everything in the `Vector` over by one location to accommodate the new item.

❏ `set(int, Object)` – replaces the nth object reference with the specified object reference.

❏ `elementAt(int)` – retrieves the nth object reference as type `Object` – a cast is needed to 'restore' the object reference's 'true identity'.

❏ `removeElementAt(int)` – takes out the nth reference and 'closes up'/'collapses' the resultant 'hole'.

❏ `remove(Object)` – hunts for existence of the object reference in question and, if found, removes the (first) occurrence of that reference from the `Vector`, closing up the 'hole'.

❏ `indexOf(Object)` – hunts for the existence of a specific object reference (e.g. a particular `Student`) and, if found, returns an integer indicating what the (first) postion is of this reference in the `Vector` (starting with 0).

❏ `contains(Object)` – hunts for existence of the object reference in question and, if found, returns the value `true`, otherwise `false`.

❏ `isEmpty()` – returns `true` if the `Vector` is empty, `false` otherwise.

❏ `clear()` – empties out the `Vector`.

and there are more!

Hashtables

A Java `Hashtable` is another way to store collections of object references in Java. A `Hashtable` is a bit more sophisticated than a `Vector` because it gives us direct access to a given object based on a unique key value; it is an implementation of the dictionary collection type that we defined in Chapter 6. Both the key and the object itself can be of any object type.

To use a `Hashtable`, we must import the `java.util` package as we did for a `Vector`. We then instantiate a `Hashtable` object:

```
Hashtable students = new Hashtable();  // creating an 'egg carton'!
```

Then we create the objects to be inserted:

```
// Create several Student objects ('eggs').
Student s1 = new Student("123-45-6789", "John Smith");
Student s2 = new Student("987-65-4321", "Mary Jones");
Student s3 = new Student("654-32-1987", "Jim Green");
```

and insert their handles into the `Hashtable`. Note that we must specify a key value that will be used to retrieve the items later on; the key may be of any object type, but we'll use simple `String` objects for this example – in particular, the students' social security numbers:

```
// Store their handles in the hash table.
students.put(s1.getSsn(), s1);
students.put(s2.getSsn(), s2);
students.put(s3.getSsn(), s3);
```

Now, to retrieve an item from the `Hashtable`, we specify the key value of the object of interest:

```
// Note that we have to recast the object when we retrieve it,
// just as we must do with Vectors.
Student s = (Student) students.get("123-45-6789');  // retrieves the object
                              // reference representing Student John Smith
```

Some of the more commonly used method signatures for `Hashtable` objects are as follows:

- ❏ `Object put(Object key, Object value)` – inserts the second `Object` reference (represented by argument `value`) into the table with a retrieval key represented by the first `Object` reference (represented by argument `key`). If there already was something stored at that key location, it is silently overwritten and returned by this method, otherwise the method returns `null`. So, it is important to first verify that the key we are about to use isn't already in use in the table, using the next method:

- ❏ `boolean containsKey(Object key)` – returns `true` if designated key is found in the `Hashtable`, otherwise returns `false`.

  Here's how we'd use this method in concert with the `put()` method to make sure we weren't accidentally overwriting an entry in the `Hashtable`:

  ```
  Student s1 = new Student("111-11-1111", "Arnold Brown");
  if (students.containsKey(s1.getSsn()) {
    // Whoops! This is a duplicate; we need to decide what to do!
    // details omitted
  }
  else students.put(s1.getSsn(), s1);  // OK; no duplicate detected
  ```

- ❏ `Object get(Object key)` – looks for the designated key, and returns the `Object` associated with that key if found, otherwise returns `null`.

- ❏ `Object remove(Object key)` – deletes the **reference** to the object represented by the given key from the `Hashtable`; note that the object itself, as it exists outside of the `Hashtable`, is unaffected.

- ❏ int size() – returns a count of the number of key-object pairs currently stored in the Hashtable.
- ❏ void clear() – empties out the Hashtable to its original state, as if it had just been newly instantiated.
- ❏ boolean isEmpty() – returns true if the Hashtable contains no entries, otherwise returns false.

Stepping Through a Collection with an Enumeration Object

When we create collections of objects, we often have a need to step through the entire collection to process it in some fashion. For example, we may want to step through a Vector of Student object references to compute final grades for the semester. One way to step through a Vector is to use a for loop, as we've previously seen:

```
Vector enrollment = new Vector();   // of Student references

// Populate the Vector … details omitted.

// Step through the Vector, and process all Students' grades.
for (int i = 0; i < enrollment.size(); i++) {
  Student s = (Student) enrollment.elementAt(i);
  s.computeFinalGrade();
}
```

Processing all items in a Vector in this fashion is possible because we have a means for referring to a particular element in the Vector by its index, via the elementAt() method. However, with a Hashtable, objects don't have a relative position, so we can't use a for loop to iterate through them numerically. There is an alternative way of stepping through all of the elements in a Hashtable, however, via a method with signature:

```
Enumeration elements();
```

The return type of this method, Enumeration, is a type of object defined by the java.util package. An Enumeration is a special type of temporary collection, used specifically to step through another collection of object references one by one in exhaustive fashion, pulling the references out of the Enumeration until it is empty. The handles in the original collection remain unaffected.

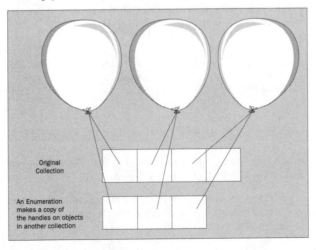

Original Collection

An Enumeration makes a copy of the handles on objects in another collection

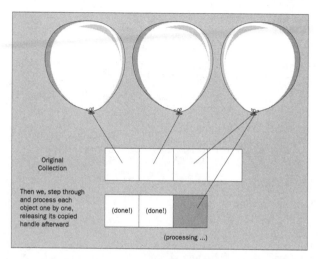

Original
Collection

Then we, step through
and process each
object one by one,
releasing its copied
handle afterward

(done!)   (done!)

(processing ...)

An Enumeration object, in turn, recognizes the following methods:

- boolean hasMoreElements() – returns false if the Enumeration has been exhausted (emptied), true otherwise.

- Object nextElement() – returns the next element of this Enumeration as a generic Object reference if this Enumeration is not yet empty, requiring that we cast the reference to the appropriate type.

Here's a simple example to illustrate how to put all of this to use. We'll use this simple version of the Student class:

```java
// Student.java

public class Student {
  private String name;
  private String ssn;

  // Constructor.

  public Student(String n, String s) {
    name = n;
    ssn = s;
  }

  public Student() {
    name = "???";
    ssn = "???-??-????";
  }

  public String getName() {
    return name;
  }

  public String getSsn() {
    return ssn;
  }

  // etc. for set method pairs
}
```

This program will serve as the driver:

```java
import java.util.*;

public class HashTableTest {
  public static void main(String[] args) {
    // We will create a hash table to store references to Student
    // objects, using their student ID number as the retrieval key.
    Hashtable students = new Hashtable();

    // Create several student objects.
    Student s1 = new Student("John Smith", "123456789");
    Student s2 = new Student("Mary Jones", "987654321");
    Student s3 = new Student("Jim Green", "654321987");

    // Store their handles in the hash table.
    students.put(s1.getSsn(), s1);
    students.put(s2.getSsn(), s2);
    students.put(s3.getSsn(), s3);

    // Iterate through the entire table.
    // Note the use of an Enumeration object to step through
    // the hash table from beginning to end.
    System.out.println("\nContents of the student hash table:");
    Enumeration e = students.elements();
    while (e.hasMoreElements()) {
      Student s = (Student) e.nextElement();
      System.out.println("\t" + s.getName() + " - " + s.getSsn());
    }
    System.out.println("Total of " + students.size() + " students.");
  }
}
```

This program, when run, produces as output:

Contents of the student hash table:
  John Smith - 123456789
  Mary Jones - 987654321
  Jim Green - 654321987
Total of 3 students.

There is a second `Hashtable` method with signature:

```java
Enumeration keys();
```

This works in a similar fashion to the `elements()` method, except that it retrieves an `Enumeration` containing references to the *key* objects from the `Hashtable`. Using this method would change our `while` loop as follows:

```java
Enumeration e = students.keys();
while (e.hasMoreElements()) {
  // Since we used String objects as our keys for this Hashtable,
  // we must cast references as Strings.
  String key = (String) e.nextElement();

  // Now, we use the key to look up the Student.
  Student s = (Student) students.get(key);

  System.out.println("\t" + s.getName() + " - " + s.getSsn());
}
```

Note that the `Vector` class also defines an `elements()` method, which works in exactly the same fashion as it does for `Hashtables`.

'Wrapper' Classes to the Rescue

We have a dilemma! Can we use a `Vector` or a `Hashtable` to store simple data types, like `int`, `double`, or `boolean`? Strictly speaking, no. This is because `Vectors` and `Hashtables` hold `Objects`, and simple data types are not `Objects`. There is a way around this problem, however, through the use of some of the other Java utility classes.

Java defines utility classes `Boolean`, `Integer`, `Float`, `Double`, etc. to correspond one-to-one with the simple data types. These classes can be used as object 'wrappers' around simple data types. Here is an example of how we'd use a `Vector` to store simple `int`(eger)s:

```
import java.util.*;

public class VectorTest {
  public static void main(String[] args) {
    Vector v = new Vector(); // of Integers

    // Let's store the integers 0 through 9 in a Vector.
    for (int i = 0; i < 10; i++) {
      // First, we must build an object wrapper around each int value
      // by calling the Integer class's constructor.
      Integer intWrapper = new Integer(i);

      // Add the object wrapper to the vector versus
      // the int itself.
      v.add(intWrapper);
    }

    // Now, let's pull them back out.
    for (int i = 0; i < v.size(); i++) {
      // Remember to (re)cast the object!
      Integer intWrapper = (Integer) v.elementAt(i);

      // Pull the int back out of its wrapper.
      int j = intWrapper.intValue();

      System.out.println(j);
    }
  }
}
```

In addition to serving as object wrappers for simple data types, the wrapper utility classes have some static methods which are useful when you need to do data type conversions. (Recall from our discussion in Chapter 7 that a static method is a method that can be invoked on the class as a whole versus on an individual object.) For example, the `Integer` class defines a static method with signature:

```
int Integer.parseInt(String);
```

Pass in a `String`, and the `Integer` class will convert it to an `int`(eger) for you if it represents a valid integer, or will throw a `NumberFormatException` if it is not. Here's an example of how this method can be put to use:

```java
public class IntegerTest {
  public static void main(String[] args) {
    String[] ints = { "123", "456", "foobar", "789" };
    int i = 0;

    try {
      for (i = 0; i < ints.length; i++) {
        int test = Integer.parseInt(ints[i]);
        System.out.println(test + " converted just fine!");
      }
    }
    catch (NumberFormatException e) {
      System.out.println(ints[i] + " is an invalid integer.");
    }
  }
}
```

This program, when run, produces the following output:

```
123 converted just fine!
456 converted just fine!
foobar is an invalid integer.
```

Here's another `static` method defined on the `Integer` class:

```java
String Integer.toString(int);
```

which will do the reverse: namely, turn an integer into a `String`, as the following example illustrates:

```java
int j = 4;
int i = 3 * j;
String s = Integer.toString(i);     // s equals "12"
```

There is a shortcut way for doing the same thing, however:

```java
int j = 4;
int i = 3 * j;
String s = "" + i;     // Here, we concatenate an empty string with the numeric
                       // variable i; because the String concatenation operator
                       // tries its best to convert everything to a String, it
                       // saves us some work!
```

After you've mastered the Java language, take time to explore all of the Java wrapper classes in more depth.

The 'final' Keyword

If we wish to assign to variable x a value that cannot ever be changed – i.e. to make x a constant – we do so by declaring the variable with the keyword `final`, as follows:

```
final int x = 3;   // x's value may never be changed
```

Attempting to subsequently change the value of x as follows:

```
x = 4; // will produce a compilation error
```

will result in the following compilation error:

Can't assign a value to a final variable: x

The `final` keyword can be used in other circumstances, as well.

First, if we wish to prevent a subclass from overriding a method that it inherits from a base class, we can declare the method as `final` in the base class:

```
public class Person {
  // details omitted

    final void printDescription() {
      // details omitted
    }
}
```

```
public class Student extends Person {
  // The following attempt to override the printDescription()
  // method will result in a compilation error:
  void printDescription() {
    // details omitted
  }
}
```

Second, if we wish to prevent a class from being specialized as a subclass, we can declare an entire class to be `final`:

```
// No subclasses of Student may now be created!
  public final class Student {
  // details omitted
}
```

Third, if we wish for a class 'X' to be able to publish a list of valid values for use by client code as arguments to one of X's methods, we typically do so having X declare `public static final` attributes as constants; for example:

```
public class SomeClass {
  // This class needs to be handed a value of 1, 2, or 3
  // for the first argument to this method:
  public void someMethod(int x) {
    // pseudocode
    if (x == 1) do something
    else if (x == 2) do something else
    else if (x == 3) do something still different
    // details omitted
  }

  // and so we declare a few public static final attributes of
  // the class to represent these values.
  public static final int FIRST_CHOICE = 1;
  public static final int SECOND_CHOICE = 2;
  public static final int THIRD_CHOICE = 3;
  // Note that these would typically be found at the top of the
  // class definition, but it doesn't really matter to the compiler.

  // etc.
}
```

Then, any client code wanting to use this method is able to refer to these descriptive, symbolic names when passing arguments to this method:

```
// Client code.
SomeClass sc = new SomeClass();
sc.someMethod(SomeClass.FIRST_CHOICE);
```

Note that the programming convention is to assign names to constants in all UPPER CASE letters.

Static Attributes and Methods, Revisited

We introduced the notion of attributes and methods which belong to a class as a whole, versus to an individual object – i.e. static attributes and methods – in Chapter 7. By way of review:

❑ A static attribute is one whose value is shared across all instances of a class; in essence it belongs to the class as a whole instead of belonging to any one instance/object of that class.

```
public class Student {
  public static int totalStudentCount = 0;   // note optional
                                             // initialization, which
                                             // occurs when the class is
                                             // first loaded into the JVM
```

❑ When any one of the objects belonging to such a class modify the value of a static attribute, all other objects see that same value:

```
Student s1 = new Student();
Student s2 = new Student();
```

```
s1.totalStudentCount++;      // totalStudentCount is now equal to 1, as seen by
                             // both Students

s2.totalStudentCount++;      // totalStudentCount is now equal to 2, as seen by
                             // both Students
```

❑ We can also access the value of a `static` attribute by applying dot notation to the class as a whole:

```
Student.totalStudentCount++;
System.out.println(Student.totalStudentCount);
```

❑ A `static` method is one which may be invoked on either an instance or a class as a whole:

```
public class Student {
  public static int totalStudentCount;

  public static void incrementTotalCount() {
    totalStudentCount++;
  }
}

// In our main program:

Student.incrementTotalCount();

// or

Student s1 = new Student();
s1.incrementTotalCount();
```

❑ Finally, a `static` method may only access `static` attributes, due to the fact that it may be invoked on the class as a whole, for which the values of non-static attributes are undefined.

❑ Now that we've discussed the concept of the `this` keyword for object self-referencing, we can also make another statement about `static` methods: namely, that the `this` keyword has no meaning within a `static` method, because we cannot be guaranteed that there will be an instance of an object to self-reference.

Some of the common uses of `static` attributes are:

❑ To define constants, in combination with the `final` keyword, as we've seen a moment ago; and

❑ To make data globally available to an application, as we'll do with various collections of objects in the SRS application later in the book

Static methods are commonly used to provide utility methods; one such example is the `Runtime.getRuntime()` method, which enables us to obtain information about the runtime environment of an application (memory usage, for example).

As mentioned in Chapter 7, just as we introduced the term 'instance variable' as a synonym for 'attribute' earlier in the chapter, the term **'class variable'** is often used as a synonym for 'static attribute'.

Abstract Classes and Interfaces, Revisited

As we learned in Chapter 7, abstract classes are useful if we want to prescribe common behaviors among a group of (sub)classes without having to go into details about all of those behaviors. With an abstract class, we specify the 'what' that an object must do – i.e. the messages that an object must be able to respond to, a.k.a. method signatures – without necessarily specifying the 'how' – for example, the method bodies. A method without a body is known as an *abstract method*; a method with a body is known as a *concrete method*.

In Java, the keyword `abstract` is used to designate a class and/or a method as abstract:

```
public abstract class Person {
    String name;
    String ssn;

    public abstract void paySalary(int hoursWorked);
    public void setName(String n) { name = n; } // concrete method

    // etc.
}
```

If the Java compiler detects the presence of one or more abstract methods in a class, then the compiler forces us to declare the containing class as an abstract class as well.

We also learned in Chapter 7 that an interface is another more abstract way in Java to specify 'what' without 'how'. Recall that an interface is a way to describe an object in terms of the methods that the object must implement in order to be considered an instance of that interface. An interface is similar to an abstract class, except that it may only declare:

- ❑ method signatures
- ❑ `final static` data items, which serve as constant values

but cannot specify:

- ❑ traditional attributes – i.e. those to which instance-specific values may be assigned
- ❑ method bodies

To create an interface in Java, we use the keyword `interface` rather than `class` in the definition:

```
public interface Trigonometry {
    public double sine(double d);
    public double cosine(double d);
    public double sqrt(double d);
}
```

Note that it is understood that all methods in an interface are essentially abstract, and so no special keyword is required in their signatures.

Once we've created an interface, we can specify that a class is to implement the interface via the implements keyword:

```
public class MyComputation implements Trigonometry {
    // details omitted
}
```

Doing so in the above example forces the programmer to provide method bodies in the class MyComputation for all of the method signatures called for by the Trigonometry interface.

A class may implement as many interfaces as necessary to achieve some desired behavioral profile.

Here's another example to help illustrate how interfaces work; the following code would be found in three separate .java files:

```
// TaxPayer.java

public interface TaxPayer {
    // This interface defines a few constants.
    public static final int TAXYEAR = 2000;
    public static final double TAXRATE = 0.40;

    // No attributes - only method signatures.
    public float fileTaxes();
    public void displayTaxReturn(int year);
}
```

```
// FamousPerson.java

public interface FamousPerson {
    public void listStageNames();
    public boolean starredIn(String film);
}
```

```
// Person.java

// Enforce the implementation of these two interfaces on
// the Person class.

public class Person implements TaxPayer, FamousPerson {
    // The Person class may define whatever attributes and methods are
    // appropriate, as usual.
    protected String name;
    public void setName(String name) { this.name = name; }
    // etc.

    // Additionally, this class must provide implementations of all of
    // the methods called for by both the TaxPayer and FamousPerson
    // interfaces; otherwise, the class won't compile (unless we declare
    // it to be abstract).

    public void listStageNames() { provide body code - details omitted }
    public boolean starredIn(String film) { provide body code }
    public float fileTaxes() { provide body code }
    public void displayTaxReturn(int year) { provide body code }
    // etc.
}
```

Through the introduction of interfaces, Java was able to eliminate the need for true multiple inheritance. An object can simultaneously have any one of numerous 'identities' by implementing multiple interfaces. Such an object can then be 'plugged in' to any situation where any of its 'identities' is appropriate. For example, let's say we have a `Film` class with a method that has the following signature:

```
public void castActorInFilm(FamousPerson p);
```

Any object belonging to a class that implements the `FamousPerson` interface can be passed in as an argument to this method, because if an object implements an interface, then it *is* an object of that type.

Object Identities

When we discussed Java collection classes – `Vectors` and `Hashtables` – earlier, we spoke briefly about the need to cast an `Object` reference back into the appropriate reference type when extracting an object from one of these collections. This may lead one to believe that an object somehow 'forgets' what class it belongs to, but this is not true. An object always retains its class identity; it is simply that we can *refer* to an object with various different reference variables, which may be declared to be of different types, and it is this phenomenon that affects what messages the compiler believes that an object is capable of responding to. To help illustrate this point, let's use an example.

If we create a `Professor` object, which is a type of `Person`, which, as we learned earlier, is therefore a type of `Object`, we can think of the `Professor` object as being allocated in memory as follows:

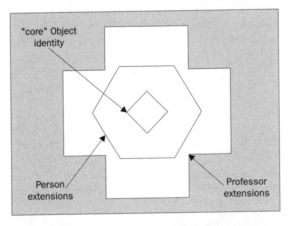

We can then create reference variables of varying types (namely, any of the types in this object's derivation chain) to store handles on this `Object/Person/Professor`; each reference refers to a different 'rendition' of the object:

```
// Create a Professor object, and maintain three handles on it of varying types.
Professor pr = new Professor();
Person p = pr;
Object o = pr;
```

If we refer to this `Professor` object by its `Object` reference o, then, as far as the compiler is concerned, the only aspects of the object that exist are its `Object` 'core'; the 'Person-ness' and 'Professor-ness' of the object is in question. So, the compiler will reject any attempts to access the `Professor`- or `Person`- defined features of o:

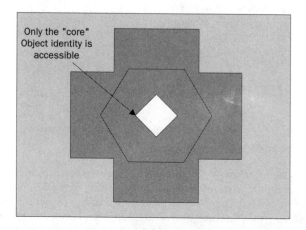

Only the "core" Object identity is accessible

```
// The compiler would reject this attempt to invoke the addAdvisee() method,
// declared for the Professor class, on this object, because even though WE
// know from the code above that it is really a Professor whose handle is
// stored as an Object, the compiler cannot be certain of this.
o.addAdvisee();  // compiler error

// However, we can invoke any of the methods that this Professor inherited
// from the Object class:
o.toString();
```

If we now refer to the `Professor` object by its `Person` reference p, then, as far as the compiler is concerned, the only aspects of the object that exist are its `Object` 'core' and its `Person` 'extensions'; the 'Professor-ness' of the object is in question:

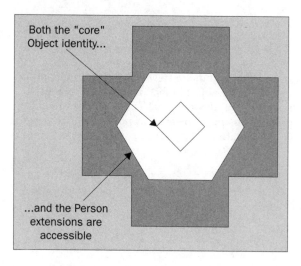

Both the "core" Object identity...

...and the Person extensions are accessible

```
// The compiler would again reject this attempt to invoke the addAdvisee()
// method, declared for the Professor class, on this object, because even
// though WE know from the code above that it is really a Professor whose
// handle is stored as a Person, the compiler cannot be certain of this.
p.addAdvisee();  // compiler error

// However, we can invoke any of the methods that this Professor inherited
// from either the Object class ...
p.toString();

// ... or the Person class:
p.getName();
```

❑ Only if we refer to the object by its `Professor` handle `pr` will the compiler allow us to access `Professor`-specific features of the object.

Now, back to casting: when a reference to an object like a `Professor` is stored in a `Vector`, it gets stored in the `Vector` as an `Object` reference. When this `Object` reference is subsequently retrieved from the `Vector`, the compiler has no way to be certain that the object referred to by the reference is anything but a generic `Object`. Because we, as programmers, know that the object is in reality a `Professor`, we can reassure the compiler that it is so by performing a cast:

```
Professor p1 = new Professor();
Professor p2 = new Professor();
Vector v = new Vector();
v.add(p1);
v.add(p2);

for (int i = 0; i < v.size(); i++) {
  // Cast the Object reference that was stored in the
  // Vector back into a Professor reference.
  Professor pr = (Professor) v.elementAt(i);

  // We may now manipulate the reference as a true Professor.
  pr.listAdvisees();

  // etc.
}
```

What would happen if we tried to cast the retrieved object to an inappropriate type? For example, if we placed a reference to a `Professor` object in the `Vector`, but then tried to cast it to be a `Student` reference when we retrieved it from the `Vector`? The compiler would trust that we knew what we were doing, and would not produce an error; however, at *runtime*, a `ClassCastException` would be thrown, for there is no way to 'mutate' a `Professor` object into a `Student` object via a simple cast.

Determining the Class That an Object Belongs To

By virtue of being descended from the Java `Object` class, every object inherits a method with the signature:

```
Class getClass()
```

which, when invoked on an object, returns an object of type `Class` representing the class that an object belongs to. The `Class` class, in turn, defines a method with signature:

```
String getName()
```

Putting these two methods together, we can ask an object reference to identify which class the object it holds onto belongs to, as follows:

```
reference.getClass().getName();
```

For example:

```
Professor pr = new Professor();
System.out.println(pr.getClass().getName());  // this would print "Professor"
```

Even if an object has 'temporary amnesia' from being 'stuffed' into a `Vector`, it still can be asked to identify its true identity with this method call, as the following example illustrates:

```java
import java.util.*;

public class CastingExample {
  public static void main(String[] args) {
    Student s = new Student();
    Professor p = new Professor();
    Vector v = new Vector();
    v.add(s);
    v.add(p);
    for (int i = 0; i < v.size(); i++) {
      // Note that we are not casting the objects here!
      // We're pulling them out as generic objects.
      Object o = v.elementAt(i);
      System.out.println(o.getClass().getName());
    }
  }
}
```

This program produces as output:

Student
Professor

This illustrates that the objects themselves really do remember their roots!

Another way to test whether a given object reference belongs to a particular class is via the `instanceof` operator. This is a boolean operator which allows us to determine if some reference variable X is an object/instance of class/type Y. Here is a simple code snippet to illustrate this concept.

```
// x is declared to be of type Person (an abstract supertype), but we are
// actually instantiating a Student object.  (We could have also instantiated
// a Professor object and handed its reference to x, because both Students and
// Professors are subclasses of Person.)
Person x = new Student();

if (x instanceof Student) System.out.println("x is a Student");
else if (x instanceof Professor) System.out.println("x is a Professor");
```

The preceding code would produce the following as output:

x is a Student

Testing the Equality of Objects

Java provides two ways to compare objects for equality: the double equal sign operator (==) and the `boolean equals()` method, which is inherited by all objects from the `Object` class. Both of these mechanisms, as defined for `Objects` generically, test to see if two references refer to exactly the same object.

Here's some example code to illustrate how these function:

```
public class EqualsTest {
  public static void main(String[] args) {
    // We'll create one Person object ...
    Person p1 = new Person("222-22-2222", "Fred");

    // ... and maintain two handles on it (p1 and p2).
    Person p2 = p1;

    // We'll create a second different Person object with exactly the same
    // attribute values as the first Person object that we created, and will
    // use variable p3 to maintain a handle on this second object.
    Person p3 = new Person("222-22-2222", "Fred");
```

The picture so far is as follows:

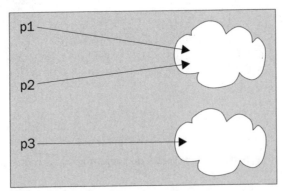

Now, when we execute the following code:

```
if (p1 == p2) System.out.println("p1 == p2 is true");
if (p1.equals(p2)) System.out.println("p1.equals(p2) is true");

if (p1 == p3) System.out.println("p1 == p3 is true");
if (p1.equals(p3)) System.out.println("p1.equals(p3) is true");
```

the following output results:

p1 == p2 is true
p1.equals(p2) is true

This is because `p1` and `p2` are truly referring to exactly the same object, whereas `p3` is referring to a different object with exactly the same attribute values, which does not satisfy either of the equality tests.

Note, however, that some classes in Java have overridden the `equals()` method as inherited from `Object` so that it returns a value of `true` even if the objects are different, as long as they have the same attribute values. One such example is the `String` class; if we repeat the same test as above, but change all `Person` references to be `String` references instead, we'll get a different result than before:

```
public class EqualsTest {
  public static void main(String[] args) {
    // Create two String objects with exactly the same value; maintain
    // two handles on one, and one handle on the other.
    String s1 = new String("foobar");
    String s2 = s1;
    String s3 = new String("foobar");

    if (s1 == s2) System.out.println("s1 == s2 is true");
    if (s1.equals(s2)) System.out.println("s1.equals(s2) is true");

    if (s1 == s3) System.out.println("s1 == s3 is true");
    if (s1.equals(s3)) System.out.println("s1.equals(s3) is true");
  }
}
```

This code produces the following output:

s1 == s2 is true
s1.equals(s2) is true
s1.equals(s3) is true

We see that `s1` and `s3` are deemed equal via the `equals()` method, but not by the `==` operator, because their values are the same, but they truly are two distinct objects.

Several other classes built into the Java language have overridden the `equals()` method in a similar fashion: the 'wrapper' classes (`Boolean`, `Integer`, `Float`, etc.); `Date`; and a few others. And, of course, we can override the `equals()` method for our own classes. Let's say we want the `equals()` method to return a value of `true` if two `Person` objects have the same value for their `ssn` attribute; we'd simply program the method as follows:

```
public class Person {
  private String name;
  private String ssn;

  // Constructor.
  public Person(String s, String n) {
    ssn = s;
    name = n;
  }

  public String getSsn() {
    return ssn;
  }

  // details omitted

    // Overriding the equals() method that we inherited from Object
    public boolean equals(Object o) {
      if (o instanceof Person) {
      //Cast the Object reference into a Person reference
      Person p = (Person) 0;
      //compare ssns
      if (this.getSsn().equals(p.getSsn()))
        return true;
        else return false;
      }
      else return false;
    }
}
```

Then, in our main program:

```
public class ComparePeople {
  public static void main(String[] args) {
    // We create two different Person objects with the same ssn.
    Person p1 = new Person("222-22-2222", "Joe");
    Person p2 = new Person("222-22-2222", "Sam");
    System.out.println(p1.equals(p2));  // This would print the value "true"
  }
}
```

The toString() Method

If we were to try to print out the value of an object reference, we'd get a cryptic looking result that represents an internal object ID, as the following example illustrates:

```
Student s1 = new Student();
s1.setName("Harvey");
System.out.println(s1);
```

The preceding code would produce printed output similar to the following:

```
Student@71f71130
```

Recall that the `println()` method expects to be handed a `String` expression, or something that can be used to produce a `String` expression, such as a method call. The reason that the `println()` method even works at *all* when we pass it a `Student` object reference is because all objects inherit a method from the Java `Object` class with signature:

```
String toString();
```

What we probably meant to do was to print one of the `Student` object's attributes as a *representation* of the object; e.g. the student's name. We could do this by inserting a call to the `getName()` method in the `println()` call:

```
System.out.println(s1.getName());
```

Alternatively, we could override the `toString()` method for the `Student` class to define what it is that we wish to have printed when a `Student` object reference is passed as an argument to `println()`; e.g. the `Student` class may define the method:

```
public String toString() {
   return getName();
}
```

and, in so doing, the following code:

```
Student s1 = new Student();
s1.setName("Harvey");
System.out.println(s1);
```

would now produce the following printed output:

Harvey

as desired.

It's a good idea to override the `toString()` method for all classes that you create from scratch.

Inner Classes

An inner class is a class that is wholly defined within the boundaries of another class, and which is instantiated only internally to that class. For example, we may wish to define a class called `BirthCertificate` which will only be used internally to the `Person` class. So, we declare the `BirthCertificate` class wholly within the `Person` class, and are then free to declare variables of type `BirthCertificate`, and to instantiate them, as shown in the simple example below.

```
// Person.java

public class Person {
   // Attributes.
```

```
     private String ssn;

  // Instead of storing the Person's name as an attribute, we may wish
  // to encapsulate the name as an attribute of this Person's
  // birth certificate instead.

  // private String name; COMMENTED OUT

  // Instead of storing age as an attribute, we may wish to
  // compute the person's age as the difference between the
  // date on his/her birth certificate and the current system
  // date.

  // private int age; COMMENTED OUT

  // We declare a new attribute of type BirthCertificate, where this type is
  // defined below as an inner class of Person.

  private BirthCertificate bc;

  //-----------------------------------------------------------
  // A class within a class! (AKA an 'inner class'.)

  class BirthCertificate {
    // Attributes for the inner class.

    private String nameOnCertificate;
    private String cityIssued;
    private String dateIssued;

    // Constructor for the inner class.

    public BirthCertificate(String n) {
      setNameOnCertificate(n);
    }

    // Methods for this inner class.

    public void setNameOnCertificate(String name) {
      nameOnCertificate = name;
    }

    public String getNameOnCertificate() {
      return nameOnCertificate;
    }

    // and so on for the other attributes ...
  }
  //---------- end of the inner class definition ------------

  // Person constructor.

  public Person(String s, String name) {
    ssn = s;
```

```
    // Instantiate a birth certificate for this person.
    // (Note that we are passing through the name.)

    bc = new BirthCertificate(name);
  }

  public String getName() {
    // Behind the scenes, we retrieve the Person's name
    // from his/her birth certificate.

    return bc.getNameOnCertificate();
  }

  public int getAge() {
    int age = 0;

    // We'd compute and return the age as the differnce
    // between the current system date and the date on
    // the birth certificate (details omitted).

    return age;
  }

  // etc.
}
```

When the `Person.java` class is compiled:

javac Person.java

two `.class` files are produced:

```
Person.class
Person$BirthCertificate.class
```

Here we see that the inner class, `BirthCertificate`, produces its own class file
(`Person$BirthCertificate.class`).

This example illustrates one common use of inner classes: namely, the creation and encapsulation of a complex data structure that will never be directly used by others. We'll see a second use of inner classes when we talk about GUI event handling in Chapter 16.

Note that the syntax for an inner class as shown above is:

```
public class A {
  // details omitted

  class B {
    // details omitted
  }
}
```

This is distinctly different from the circumstance described earlier in the chapter wherein two class definitions are contained with a single .java file, but are not nested one within the other:

```
public class A {
  // details omitted
}

class B {
  // details omitted
}
```

The latter is not an example of inner classes.

Summary

We've just been on a whirlwind tour of the Java language! Although there is a lot more to learn about Java, you have been armed with all of the essential information that you'll need in order to understand – and experiment with – the sample SRS application that we'll build in the remaining chapters of the book.

In particular, we discussed:

- ❑ The anatomy of a real-world Java program, consisting of many separate classes driven by one 'official' `main()` method.

- ❑ The Java notion of packages, and how we must import packages if we wish to make use of the classes that they contain.

- ❑ An in-depth look at the anatomy of a Java class, including a discussion of how various types of visibility at both the class and attribute/method levels affect an object's 'useability'.

- ❑ The object nature of `Strings`, and some of the methods provided to manipulate them.

- ❑ How we can form highly complex expressions by chaining messages.

- ❑ The object nature of `Arrays` in a bit more depth.

- ❑ Some subtleties of variable initialization.

- ❑ How Java exceptions arise, and how to gracefully handle them.

- ❑ How to read input from the command line when a Java application is invoked, as well as how to prompt the user for keyboard inputs, useful techniques when running a command-line driven application testing program.

- ❑ Using a special keyword, `this`, to self-reference an object from within one of its methods.

- ❑ Using constructors to initialize an object's attributes at the time that the object first comes into being.

- ❑ How we delete dynamically created objects so as to 'recycle' their memory, and the role that the Java garbage collector plays in this recycling.

❏ Inheritance in the Java language: in particular, how the visibility of a feature affects the way in which a subclass can utilize that feature; how to reuse superclass behaviors via the `super` keyword; and all of the complexities concerning constructors and inheritance.

❏ How to use two of Java's collection classes, `Vector` and `Hashtable`; the need for casting objects retrieved from a collection; and the use of `Enumeration` objects to iterate through the contents of a collection.

❏ How to use 'wrapper' classes, such as `Integer`, to turn simple data types into true objects.

❏ Use of the `final` keyword to make a variable, method, or class immutable.

❏ A review of `abstract` classes and interfaces as they are implemented in the Java language.

❏ A review of `static` attributes and methods as they are implemented in the Java language.

❏ The nature of object identities in Java; how to discover the true class that an object belongs to; and how to test the equality of two Java objects.

❏ The importance of overriding the `toString()` method for all user-defined classes.

❏ The form and function of inner classes.

With all of the Java knowledge at our fingertips, we are now ready to proceed to building the SRS application.

> **Now is a good time to download the code associated with the remaining chapters from the Wrox website, if you haven't already done so; please see Appendix D for instructions.**

Exercises

1. Follow the instructions included in Appendix C to get the latest version of Sun's Java Software Development Kit (SDK) running on your computer.

2. Write a Java program that will print out the integers from 1 to 10 in reverse order.

3. Write a Java program that will accept a series of individual characters, separated by one or more spaces, as command line input, and will then 'glue' them together to form a word. For example, if we were to invoke the program as follows:

java Glue B A   N A N   A

then the program should output:

BANANA

with no spaces.

4. Advanced exercise: Write a Java program that accepts a sentence as command line input, and outputs statistics about this sentence. For example, if we were to invoke the program as follows:

java SentenceStatistics this is my sample sentence

then the program should output the following results:

> number of words: 5
>
> longest word(s):   sentence
>
> length of longest word(s): 8
>
> shortest word(s):   is my
>
> length of shortest word(s): 2

(To keep things simple, do not use any punctuation in your sentence.)

Hint: see the section entitled 'Reading Data from the Command Line' for ideas on how to approach this.

5. Advanced Exercise: Write a Java program that accepts strings as command line arguments, and outputs these strings in sorted order. For example, if we were to invoke the program as follows:

java StringSorter dog cat bird fish

then the program should output the following results:

bird

cat

dog

fish

In writing this program, use the bubble sort algorithm, which is a simple way to sort a list of items by comparing them in pairwise fashion.

❑ Start by comparing the first string to the second and, if the second is less than the first, swap their positions; then, compare the second to the third, etc.

❑ Keep making passes through the entire list from beginning to end, comparing them in pairwise fashion, until you are able to get through the list without having to make any 'swaps'.

Then, have your program print out the results.

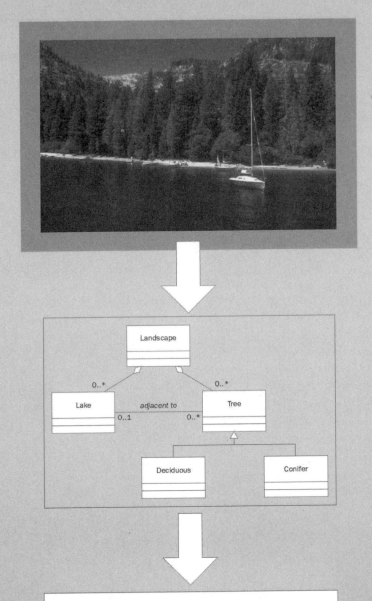

```
public class Tree {
    protected Landscape landscape;
    protected Lake nextTo;

    public void setNextTo(Lake l) {
        nextTo = l;
    }
    public Lake getNextTo() {
        return nextTo;
    }

    public abstract Color getLeafColor();
}
```

Transforming Your Model into Java Code

It's now time to turn our attention back to the class diagram that we produced in Part 2 of the book in order to develop a Java application based on that object-oriented blueprint. We'll step through all of the Java code necessary to automate a simple command-line version of the SRS application first, so that we may focus solely on what it takes to accurately model the SRS domain information in an OO programming language. Then, in the next two chapters, we'll round out our application by adding a means of persisting data from one session to another and a graphical user interface, respectively.

In this chapter, you will learn how to represent all of the following object-oriented constructs in Java code:

- ❑ Associations of varying multiplicities (one-to-one, one-to-many, and many-to-many), including aggregations
- ❑ Inheritance relationships
- ❑ Association classes
- ❑ Reflexive associations
- ❑ Abstract classes
- ❑ Metadata
- ❑ Static attributes and methods

along with practical guidelines as to when to use these various constructs. We also cover a technique for testing your core classes via a command-line driven application.

Suggestions for Getting the Maximum Value out of This and Subsequent Chapters

Our primary goal for this book is to show you how to take the same Student Registration System case study through a complete object lifecycle, from requirements definition via use cases, to object modeling, and from there into Java code as a working application. To do so, however, required us to develop a non-trivial application that was complex enough to be able to demonstrate as many 'real world' issues surrounding OO development as possible within the scope of a single book.

The code that we've written for the SRS application is sizeable; to have included the full listings for each and every Java class intact in every chapter would have been prohibitive. So, to make this as effective a learning experience as possible for you, we've chosen to feature just those portions of code in each chapter that are particularly critical to your understanding of object concepts as they translate into the Java language.

Of course we realize that you will need access to the complete source code to round out your understanding of the SRS application as we've implemented it, so we are making an electronic softcopy of the SRS source code files available for download from the Apress]website, http://www.apress.com.

One of the best ways to master a language is to start with code that works, and to experiment with it; we'd like you to get some hands on experience with Java by actually compiling and running the SRS application; studying it, so as to familiarize yourself with the techniques that we've used; and finally, modifying it yourself. Exercises provided at the end of each chapter provide specific suggestions for experiments that you may wish to try. Therefore, before you dive into this chapter:

> We encourage you to download the Java source code for this chapter from the Apress website if you haven't already done so; instructions for doing so are included in Appendix D. You'll also want to install Sun's free Java software development kit (SDK) if you haven't already done so; please see Appendix C for details.

The SRS Class Diagram, Revisited

Let's turn our attention back to the SRS class diagram that we produced in Part 2 of the book. In speaking with our sponsors for the SRS system, we learn that they've decided to cut back on a few features in the interest of reducing development costs:

- First of all, they have decided not to automate students' Plans of Study via the SRS. Instead, it will be up to each student to make sure that the courses that they register for are appropriate for the degree that they are seeking.

- Since automated Plans of Study are being eliminated, there will no longer be a need to track who a student's faculty advisor is. The only reason for modeling the *advises* relationship between the `Professor` and `Student` classes in the first place was so that a student's advisor could be called upon to approve a tentative Plan of Study when a Student had first posted it via the SRS.

- Finally, our sponsors have decided that maintaining a wait list for a section once it becomes full is a luxury that they can live without, since most students, upon learning that a section is full, immediately choose an alternative course anyway.

Therefore, we've pared down the SRS class diagram accordingly, to eliminate these unnecessary features; also, to keep the diagram from getting too cluttered, we didn't reflect attribute types or full method signatures. The resultant diagram is shown below.

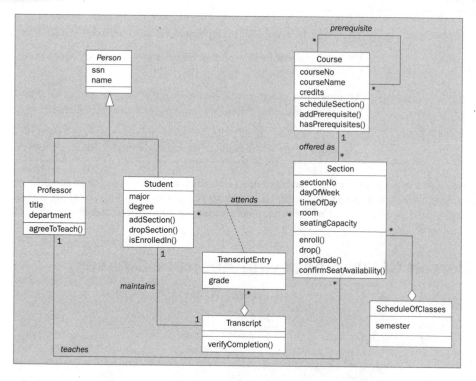

Fortunately for us, the resultant model still provides examples of all of the key object-oriented elements that we need to learn how to program, as listed below.

OO Feature:	Embodied in the SRS Class Diagram As Follows:
Inheritance	The `Person` class serves as the base class for the `Student` and `Professor` subclasses.
Aggregation	We have two examples of this: the `Transcript` class represents an aggregation of `TranscriptEntry` objects, and the `Schedule OfClasses` class represents an aggregation of `Section` objects.
One-to-One Association	The *maintains* association between the `Student` and `Transcript` classes.
One-to-Many Association	The *teaches* association between `Professor` and `Section`; the *offered as* association between `Course` and `Section`.
Many-to-Many Association	The *attends* association between `Student` and `Section`; the *prerequisite* (reflexive) association between instances of the `Course` class.
Association Class	The `TranscriptEntry` class is affiliated with the *attends* association.

Table continued on following page

OO Feature:	Embodied in the SRS Class Diagram As Follows:
Reflexive Association	The *prerequisite* association between instances of the Course class.
Abstract Class	The Person class will be implemented as an abstract class.
Metadata	Each Course object embodies information that is relevant to multiple Section objects.
Static Attributes	Although not specifically illustrated in the class diagram, we'll take advantage of static attributes when we code the Section class.
Static Methods	Although not specifically illustrated in the class diagram, we'll take advantage of static methods when we code the TranscriptEntry class.

As mentioned earlier, we're going to implement a command-line driven version of the SRS in this chapter; in particular, we're going to code the eight classes illustrated in the class diagram along with a ninth 'driver' class that will house the main() method necessary to run the application. In Chapter 16, we'll explain why it was useful to do so.

The Person Class (Specifying Abstract Classes)

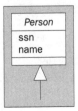

Let's start with writing the code for the Person class. The first thing that we notice in the class diagram is that the name of the class is italicized, which we learned in Chapter 10 means that Person is to be implemented as an abstract class. By including the keyword 'abstract' in the class declaration, we prevent client code from ever being able to instantiate a Person object directly.

```
// We are making this class abstract because we do not wish for it
// to be instantiated.

public abstract class Person {
```

Attributes of Person

The Person class icon specifies two simple attributes; we'll make **all** of our attributes private throughout the SRS application unless otherwise stated:

```
//------------
// Attributes.
//------------

private String name;
private String ssn;
```

Person Constructors

We'll provide a constructor for the `Person` class that accepts two arguments, so as to initialize these two attributes:

```
//----------------
// Constructor(s).
//----------------

public Person(String name, String ssn) {
    setName(name);
    setSsn(ssn);
}
```

Note that we use the `Person` class's own 'set' methods to set the values of the 'name' and 'ssn' attributes as was recommended in Chapter 4.

And, because the creation of any constructor for a class eliminates that class's default constructor as we discussed in Chapter 13, we'll program a replacement for the default constructor, as well.

```
public Person() {
    setName("?");
    setSsn("???-??-????");
}
```

Person Get/Set Methods

Next, we provide get/set methods for all of the attributes, observing the proper method signature syntax as reviewed in Chapter 13:

```
//----------------
// Get/set methods.
//----------------

public void setName(String n) {
    name = n;
}

public String getName() {
    return name;
}

public void setSsn(String ssn) {
    this.ssn = ssn;
}

public String getSsn() {
    return ssn;
}
```

toString()

We'd like for all subclasses of the `Person` class to implement a `toString()` method, but we don't want to bother coding the details of such a method for `Person`; we'd prefer to let each subclass handle the details of how the `toString()` method will work in its own class-appropriate way. The best way to enforce this requirement for a `toString()` method is to declare an *abstract method signature* for this method in `Person`, as we discussed in Chapters 7 and 13:

```
//----------------------------
// Miscellaneous other methods.
//----------------------------

// We'll let each subclass implement how it wishes to be
// represented as a String value.

public abstract String toString();
```

display()

We also want all subclasses of `Person` to implement a `display()` method, to be used for printing the values of all of an object's attributes to the command line window; we'll be using the `display()` method solely for testing our application, to verify that an object's attributes have been properly initialized. But, rather than making this method abstract, as well, we'll go ahead and actually program the body of this method, since we know how we'd like the attributes of `Person` to be displayed when these are inherited, at a minimum.

```
// Used for testing purposes.

public void display() {
   System.out.println("Person Information:");
   System.out.println("\tName:   " + getName());
   System.out.println("\tSoc. Security No.:   " + getSsn());
}
```

This way, we enable subclasses of `Person` (`Student`, `Professor`) to use the `'super'` keyword to recycle this logic in their own `display()` methods. As an example, here is a preview excerpt from the `Student` class's `display()` method:

```
public void display() {
   // First, let's display the generic Person info.

   super.display();

   // etc.
```

Again, note that we are invoking the `Person` class's 'get' methods from with the `println()` calls, versus accessing attributes directly.

That's all there is to programming the `Person` class – pretty straightforward!

We'll tackle the `Student` and `Professor` subclasses of `Person` next.

The Student Class (Reuse through Inheritance; Extending Abstract Classes; Delegation)

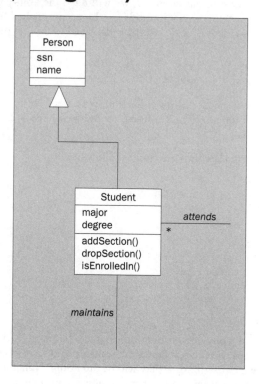

We indicate that Student is a subclass of Person through the extends keyword:

```
public class Student extends Person {
```

Attributes of Student

There are two attributes indicated for the Student class in our class diagram – major and degree – but we learned in Chapter 10 that we must also encode associations as attributes. Student participates in two associations:

❏   *attends*, a many-to-many association with the Section class

❏   *maintains*, a one-to-one association with the Transcript class

and so we must allow for each Student to maintain handles on one Transcript object and on many Section objects. Of the Java collection types that we learned about in Chapters 6 and 13 – Arrays, Vectors, and Hashtables – a Vector seems like the best choice for managing multiple Section handles:

❏   An Array is a bit too rigid; we'd have to size the Array in advance to be large enough to accommodate references to all of the Sections that a Student will ever attend over the course of their studies at the university. A Vector, on the other hand, can start out small and automatically grow in size as needed.

❑ The decision of whether to use a Vector versus a Hashtable to manage a collection comes down to whether or not we'll need to retrieve an object reference from the collection based on some key value. We don't anticipate the need for such a lookup capability as it pertains to the Sections that a Student has attended; we will need the ability to verify if a Student has taken a particular Section or not, but this can be accomplished by using the Vector class's contains() method: that is, if attends is declared to be of type Vector, then we can use the statement:

```
if (attends.contains(someSection)) { ... }
```

For most other uses of the attends collection, we'll need to step through the entire collection anyway, as when printing out the Student's course schedule. So, a Vector should serve our purposes just fine.

The attributes for the Student class thus turn out as follows:

```
//------------
// Attributes.
//-----------

private String major;
private String degree;
private Transcript transcript;
private Vector attends; // of Sections
```

Student Constructors

We'll provide a constructor for convenience of initializing attributes; note, though, that we are not trying to initialize the attends Vector via the constructor, because a Student object will most likely come into existence before we know which Sections they will be attending. Nonetheless, we must instantiate collection attributes such as the attends Vector so that we have an empty 'egg carton' ready for us when it is time to add 'eggs'.

```
//---------------
// Constructor(s).
//---------------

public Student(String name, String ssn, String major, String degree) {
  // Reuse the code of the parent's constructor.

  super(name, ssn);

  setMajor(major);
  setDegree(degree);

  // Create a brand new Transcript.

  setTranscript(new Transcript(this));

  // Note that we must instantiate an empty Vector.

  attends = new Vector();
}
```

In the code above, note that we create a brand new `Transcript` object on the fly by calling the `Transcript` constructor, passing a reference to *this* `Student` in as the lone argument to the constructor. Since we haven't discussed the structure of the `Transcript` class yet, the signature of its constructor may seem a bit puzzling, but will make sense once we get a chance to review the `Transcript` class in its entirety later in this chapter.

We choose to overload the `Student` constructor by providing a second constructor signature, to be used if we wish to create a `Student` object for whom we don't yet know the major field of study or degree sought. We take advantage of the `'this'` keyword (introduced in Chapter 13) to reuse the code from the first constructor, passing in the `String` value `'TBD'` to serve as a temporary value for both the `'major'` and `'degree'` attributes.

```java
// A second form of constructor, used when a Student has not yet
// declared a major or degree.

public Student(String name, String ssn) {
    // Reuse the code of the other Student constructor.

    this(name, ssn, "TBD", "TBD");
}
```

Student Get/Set Methods

We provide get/set methods for all of the simple (non-collection attributes):

```java
//------------------
// Get/set methods.
//------------------

public void setMajor(String major) {
    this.major = major;
}

public String getMajor() {
    return major;
}

public void setDegree(String degree) {
    this.degree = degree;
}

public String getDegree() {
    return degree;
}

public void setTranscript(Transcript t) {
    transcript = t;
}

public Transcript getTranscript() {
    return transcript;
}
```

For the `attends` collection attribute, we will provide methods `addSection()` and `dropSection()` in lieu of traditional get/set methods, to be used for adding and removing `Section` objects from the `Vector`; we'll talk about these methods momentarily.

display() method

As we did for Person, we choose to provide a display() method for Student for use in testing our command-line version of the SRS. Because a Student is a Person, and because we've already gone to the trouble of programming a display() method for the attributes inherited from Person, we'll reuse that method code by making use of the 'super' keyword before going on to additionally display attribute values specific to a Student object:

```
public void display() {
    // First, let's display the generic Person info. by invoking the parent
    // class's version of the display() method.

    super.display();

    // Now, display Student-specific attribute values.

    System.out.println("Student-Specific Information:");
    System.out.println("\tMajor:   " + getMajor());
    System.out.println("\tDegree:   " + getDegree());
    displayCourseSchedule();
    printTranscript();
}
```

Note that we are calling two of the Student class's other methods, displayCourseSchedule() and printTranscript(), from within the Student's display() method. We chose to program these as separate methods versus incorporating their code into the body of the display() method to keep the display() method from getting too cluttered.

printTranscript()

The printTranscript() method is a straightforward example of delegation: we use the Student's getTranscript() method to retrieve a handle on the Transcript object that belongs to this Student, and then invoke the display() method for that Transcript object:

```
public void printTranscript() {
    getTranscript().display();
}
```

Note that we could have accomplished this with two lines of code instead of one:

```
public void printTranscript() {
    Transcript t = getTranscript();
    t.display();
}
```

but it is commonplace to string together one method call after another in a single Java statement when each subsequent method call is a message being passed to the object that was returned by the previous method call, as we discussed in Chapter 13.

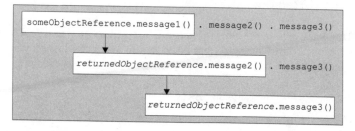

There is no point in going to the trouble of declaring a variable 't' to serve as a handle on a Transcript object if we're only going to reference the variable one time, and then discard it when it goes out of scope as soon as the method exits.

displayCourseSchedule()

The displayCourseSchedule() method is a more complex example of delegation; we'll defer a discussion of this method until we've discussed a few more of the SRS classes.

toString()

By extending an abstract class, as we did with the Person class when we created the Student subclass, we implicitly agree to round out any abstract method signature(s) specified by the parent class with concrete method bodies. In the case of the Person class, we have one such method, toString():

```
// We are forced to program this method because it is specified
// as an abstract method in our parent class (Person); failing to
// do so would render the Student class abstract, as well.
//
// For a Student, we wish to return a String as follows:
//   Joe Blow (123-45-6789) [Master of Science - Math]

public String toString() {
  return getName() + " (" + getSsn() + ") [" + getDegree() +
    " - " + getMajor() + "]";
}
```

addSection()

When a Student enrolls in a Section, this method will be used to deliver a handle on that Section object to the Student object so that it may be stored in the attends Vector:

```
public void addSection(Section s) {
  attends.addElement(s);
}
```

dropSection()

When a `Student` withdraws from a `Section`, this method will be used to pass a handle on that `Section` object to the `Student` object, so that it can use the `Vector` class's `remove()` method to seek and remove that specific `Section` reference from the `attends Vector`:

```
public void dropSection(Section s) {
    attends.remove(s);
}
```

isEnrolledIn()

This method is used to determine whether a given `Student` is already enrolled in a particular `Section` – that is, whether that `Student` is already maintaining a handle on the `Section` in question – by taking advantage of the `Vector` class's `contains()` method:

```
public boolean isEnrolledIn(Section s) {
    if (attends.contains(s)) return true;
    else return false;
}
```

isCurrentlyEnrolledInSimilar()

Although not specified by our model, we've added another version of the `isEnrolledIn()` method called `isCurrentlyEnrolledInSimilar()`, because we found a need for such a method when we coded the `Section` class (coming up later in this chapter). No matter how much thought you put into object modeling, you will inevitably determine the need for additional attributes and methods for your classes once coding is underway, because coding causes you to think at a much more finely-grained level of detail about the 'mechanics' of your application.

Because this method is so complex, we'll show the method code in its entirety first, followed by an in-depth explanation.

```
// Determine whether the Student is already enrolled in ANOTHER
// Section of this SAME Course.

public boolean isCurrentlyEnrolledInSimilar(Section s1) {
    boolean foundMatch = false;
    Course c1 = s1.getRepresentedCourse();
    Enumeration e = getEnrolledSections();
    while (e.hasMoreElements()) {
        Section s2 = (Section) e.nextElement();
        Course c2 = s2.getRepresentedCourse();
        if (c1 == c2) {
            // There is indeed a Section in the attends()
            // Vector representing the same Course.
            // Check to see if the Student is currently
            // enrolled (i.e., whether or not he has
            // yet received a grade). If there is no
            // grade, he/she is currently enrolled; if
            // there is a grade, then he/she completed
            // the course some time in the past.
```

```
        if (s2.getGrade(this) == null) {
          // No grade was assigned!  This means
          // that the Student is currently
          // enrolled in a Section of this
          // same Course.
          foundMatch = true;
          break;
        }
      }
    }

    return foundMatch;
  }
```

The details of this method are as follows.

❑　In coding the enroll() method of the Section class, we realized that we needed a way to determine whether a particular Student is enrolled in any Section of a given Course. That is, if a Student is attempting to enroll for Math 101 Section 1, we want to reject this request if they are already enrolled in Math 101 Section 2. We chose to pass in a Section object reference as an argument to this method, although we could have alternatively declared the argument to this method to be a Course reference.

```
// Determine whether the Student is already enrolled in another
// Section of this same Course.

public boolean isCurrentlyEnrolledInSimilar(Section s1) {
```

We initialize a flag to 'false', with the intention of resetting it to 'true' later on if we do indeed discover that the Student is currently enrolled in a Section of the same Course.

```
boolean foundMatch = false;
```

We obtain a handle on the Course object that the Section of interest represents, and then step through an Enumeration of all of the Sections that this Student is either currently enrolled in or has enrolled in in the past, using variable 's2' to maintain a temporary handle on each such Section one by one.

```
Course c1 = s1.getRepresentedCourse();
Enumeration e = getEnrolledSections();
while (e.hasMoreElements()) {
  Section s2 = (Section) e.nextElement();
```

We obtain a handle on a second Course object – the Course object that Section s2 is a Section of – and test the equality of the two Course objects. If we find a match, we're not quite done yet, however, because the attends Vector for a Student holds onto all Sections that the Student has ever taken. To determine if Section s2 is truly a Section that the Student is currently enrolled in, we must check to see if a grade has been issued for this Section; a missing grade – that is, a grade value of null – indicates that the Section is currently in progress. As soon as we have found the first such situation, we can break out of the enclosing 'while' loop and return a value of true to the caller.

```
        Course c2 = s2.getRepresentedCourse();
        if (c1 == c2) {
          // There is indeed a Section in the attends()
          // Vector representing the same Course.
          // Check to see if the Student is currently
          // enrolled (i.e., whether or not he has
          // yet received a grade). If there is no
          // grade, they are currently enrolled; if
          // there is a grade, then they completed
          // the course some time in the past.
          if (s2.getGrade(this) == null) {
            // No grade was assigned! This means
            // that the Student is currently
            // enrolled in a Section of this
            // same Course.
            foundMatch = true;
            break;
          }
        }
      } // end of previous while

      return foundMatch;
    } // end of method
```

getEnrolledSections()

The getEnrolledSections() method used in the above is a simple one-liner:

```
    public Enumeration getEnrolledSections() {
      return attends.elements();
    }
```

Next, we'll turn our attention to the Professor class.

The Professor Class (Bi-directionality of Relationships)

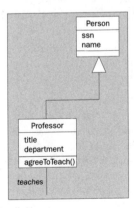

Because the code that is necessary to implement the `Professor` class is so similar to that of `Student`, we'll only comment on those features of `Professor` that are particularly noteworthy. We encourage you to look at the full code of the `Professor` class, however, to reinforce your ability to read and interpret Java syntax.

To indicate that the `Professor` is a subclass of `Person`, we use the extends keyword:

```
public class Professor extends Person {
```

Professor Attributes

The `Professor` class is involved in one association – the one-to-many *teaches* association with the `Section` class – and so we must provide a means for a `Professor` object to maintain multiple `Section` handles, which we do by creating a `teaches` attribute of type `Vector`:

```
//------------
// Attributes.
//------------

private String title;
private String department;
private Vector teaches; // of Sections
```

agreeToTeach()

Our class diagram calls for us to implement an `agreeToTeach()` method. This method accepts a `Section` object reference as an argument, and begins by storing this handle in the `teaches` `Vector`:

```
public void agreeToTeach(Section s) {
  teaches.addElement(s);

  // We need to link this bi-directionally.
  s.setInstructor(this);
}
```

Associations, as modeled in a class diagram, are assumed to be bi-directional. When implementing associations in code, however, we must think about whether or not bi-directionality is important.

- ❑ Can we think of any situations in which a `Professor` object would need to know which `Sections` it is responsible for teaching? Yes, as, for example, when we ask a `Professor` object to print out its teaching assignments.

- ❑ How about the reverse: that is, can we think of any situations in which a `Section` object would need to know who is teaching it? Yes, as, for example, when we print out a `Student`'s course schedule.

So, not only must we store a handle on the `Section` object in the `Professor`'s `teaches` `Vector`, but we must also make sure that the `Section` object is somehow notified that this `Professor` is going to be its instructor. We accomplish this by invoking the `Section` object's `setInstructor()` method, passing in a handle on the `Professor` object whose method we are in the midst of executing:

```
public void agreeToTeach(Section s) {
  teaches.addElement(s);

  // We need to link this bi-directionally.
  s.setInstructor(this);
}
```

We'll explore the implications of bi-directionality, and the various options for implementing bi-directional relationships, in more depth a bit later in this chapter.

We'll turn our attention next to the Course class.

The Course Class (Reflexive Relationships; Unidirectional Relationships)

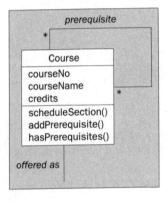

Course Attributes

Referring back to the SRS class diagram, we see that Course has three simple attributes and participates in two associations:

❑ *offered as*, a one-to-many association with the Section class, and

❑ *prerequisite*, a many-to-many reflexive association.

for a total of five attributes:

```
//------------
// Attributes.
//------------

private String courseNo;
private String courseName;
private double credits;
private Vector offeredAsSection; // of Section object references
private Vector prerequisites;    // of Course object references
```

Note that a reflexive association is handled in exactly the same way that any other association is handled: we provide the Course class with a Vector attribute called prerequisites that enables a given Course object to maintain handles on other Course objects. We have chosen not to encode this reflexive association bi-directionally. That is, a given Course object X knows which other Course objects A, B, C, ... serve as *its* prerequisites, but does not know which Course objects L, M, N, ... consider X to be one of *their* prerequisites.

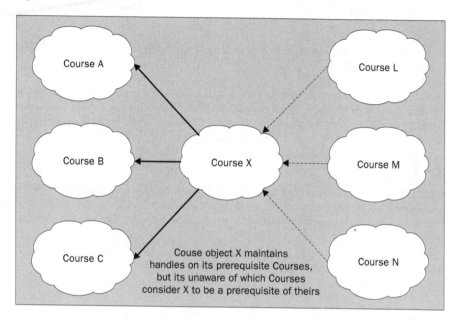

Had we wanted this association to be bi-directional, we would have had to include a second Vector as an attribute in the Course class:

```
private Vector prerequisites;  // of Course object references
private Vector prerequisiteOf; // of Course object references
```

so that Course object X could hold on to this latter group of Course objects separately.

Course Methods

Most of the Course class methods use techniques that should already be familiar to you, based on our discussions of the Person, Professor, and Student classes. We'll highlight a few of the more interesting Course methods here, and leave it for you as an exercise to review the rest.

hasPrerequisites()

This method inspects the size of the prerequisites Vector to determine whether or not a given Course has any prerequisite Courses:

```
public boolean hasPrerequisites() {
  if (prerequisites.size() > 0) return true;
  else return false;
}
```

getPrerequisites()

This method returns an `Enumeration` object as a convenient way for client code to step through the collection of prerequisite `Course` objects:

```
public Enumeration getPrerequisites() {
    return prerequisites.elements(); // returning an Enumeration
}
```

We see this method in use within the `Course display()` method, and we'll also see it in use by the `Section` class a bit later on.

Because we are returning an object reference of type `Enumeration` from this method call, we are essentially hiding the details of what type of collection we've chosen for the implementation of the `prerequisites` attribute. As we discussed in Chapter 13, many of the Java collection types – including both `Vectors` and `Hashtables` – are able to produce `Enumerations` of their elements.

scheduleSection()

This method illustrates several interesting techniques. First, note that this method invokes the `Section` class constructor to fabricate a new `Section` object on the fly, storing one handle on this `Section` object in the `'offeredAsSection'` `Vector` before returning a second handle on the object to the client code:

```
public Section scheduleSection(char day, String time, String room,
    int capacity) {

    // Create a new Section (note the creative way in
    // which we are assigning a section number) ...

    Section s = new Section(offeredAsSection.size() + 1,
        day, time, this, room, capacity);

    // ... and then remember it!
    offeredAsSection.addElement(s);

    return s;  //return handle to client code
}
```

Secondly, we are generating the first argument to the `Section` constructor – representing the Section number to be created – as a 'one up' number by adding 1 to the size of the `'offeredAsSection'` `Vector`. The first time that we invoke the `scheduleSection()` method for a given `Course` object, the `Vector` will be empty, and so the expression

```
offeredAsSection.size() + 1
```

will evaluate to 1, and hence we'll be creating `Section` number 1. The second time that this method is invoked for the same `Course` object, the `Vector` will already contain a handle on the first `Section` object that was created, so the expression

```
offeredAsSection.size() + 1
```

will evaluate to 2, and hence we'll be creating `Section` number 2, and so forth.

There is one flaw with this approach: if we were to create, then delete, `Section` objects, the size of the `Vector` would expand and contract, and we could wind up with duplicate Section numbers. We remedy this flaw in Chapter 15.

Now, let's turn our attention to the `Section` class.

The Section Class (Representing Association Classes; Public Static Final Attributes)

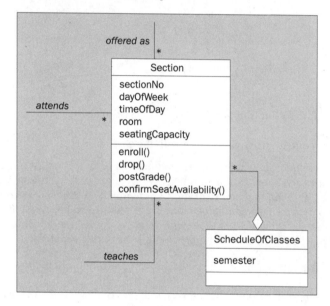

Section Attributes

The `Section` class participates in numerous relationships with other classes:

- ❑ *offered as*, a one-to-many association with `Course`

- ❑ an unnamed, one-to-many aggregation with `ScheduleOfClasses`

- ❑ *teaches*, a one-to-many association with `Professor`

- ❑ *attends*, a many-to-many association with `Student`

The *attends* association is in turn affiliated with an association class, `TranscriptEntry`. We learned in Chapter 10 that an association class can alternatively be depicted in a class diagram as having direct relationships with the classes at either end of the association, as follows:

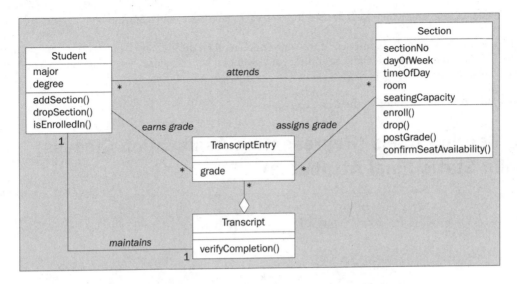

and so we'll encode a fifth relationship for the `Section` class, namely,

❑ *assigns grade*, a one-to-many association with the `TranscriptEntry` class.

(You may be wondering whether we should now go back and adjust the `Student` class to reflect the *earns grade* association with the `TranscriptEntry` class as a `Student` class attribute. The decision of whether or not to implement a particular relationship in code depends in part on what we anticipate our usage patterns to be, as we discussed in Chapter 10. We'll defer the decision of what to do with *earns grade* until we talk about the `TranscriptEntry` class in a bit more depth later in this chapter.)

We'll represent these five relationships in terms of `Section` attributes as follows:

❑ A `Section` object need only maintain a handle on one other object for those one-to-many relationships in which `Section` occupies the 'many' end, namely:

```
private Course representedCourse;
private ScheduleOfClasses offeredIn;
private Professor instructor;
```

❑ For the two situations in which `Section` needs to maintain handles on *collections* of objects – `Students` and `TranscriptEntries` – we are going to employ `Hashtables` instead of `Vectors` this time. We do so because it is conceivable that we'll have a frequent need to 'pluck' a given item from the collection directly, and `Hashtable` provides a key-based lookup mechanism that is ideal for this purpose.

    ❑ For the `Hashtable` of `Student` object references, we'll use a `String` representing the `Student`'s social security number (`ssn`) as a key for looking up a `Student`.

```
// The enrolledStudents Hashtable stores Student object references,
// using each Student's ssn as a String key.

private Hashtable enrolledStudents;
```

❑   For the `Hashtable` of `TranscriptEntry` object references, on the other hand, we'll use a `Student` object as a whole as a key for looking up that particular `Student`'s `TranscriptEntry` as issued by this `Section`.

```
// The assignedGrades Hashtable stores TranscriptEntry object
// references, using a reference to the Student to whom it belongs
// as the key.

private Hashtable assignedGrades;
```

Public Static Attributes as Constants

In the `Section` class, we encounter our first use of `public static final` attributes, which as we learned in Chapter 13 are an excellent means of defining constant values. In this particular situation, we want to define some status codes that the `Section` class can use when signaling the outcome of an enrollment attempt.

```
public static final int SUCCESSFULLY_ENROLLED = 0;
public static final int SECTION_FULL = 1;
public static final int PREREQ_NOT_SATISFIED = 2;
public static final int PREVIOUSLY_ENROLLED = 3;
```

Let's look at how these are put to use by studying the `enroll()` method of `Section`.

enroll()

This is a very complex method; we'll list the code in its entirety first without discussing it, and will then proceed to 'dissect' it afterward.

```
public int enroll(Student s) {
  // First, make sure that this Student is not already
  // enrolled for this Section, and that he/she has
  // never taken and passed the course before.

  Transcript transcript = s.getTranscript();

  if (s.isEnrolledIn(this) ||
    transcript.verifyCompletion(this.getRepresentedCourse()))
    return PREVIOUSLY_ENROLLED;

  // If there are any prerequisites for this course,
  // check to ensure that the Student has completed them.

  Course c = getRepresentedCourse();
  if (c.hasPrerequisites()) {
    Enumeration e = c.getPrerequisites();
    while (e.hasMoreElements()) {
      Course pre = (Course) e.nextElement();

      // See if the Student's Transcript reflects
      // successful completion of the prerequisite.
      if (!transcript.verifyCompletion(pre))
        return PREREQ_NOT_SATISFIED;
    }
  }
```

```
    // If the total enrollment is already at the
    // the capacity for this Section, we reject this
    // enrollment request.

    if (!confirmSeatAvailability()) return SECTION_FULL;

    // If we made it to here in the code, we're ready to
    // officially enroll the Student.

    // Note bidirectionality:  this Section holds
    // onto the Student via the Hashtable, and then
    // the Student is given a handle on this Section.

    enrolledStudents.put(s.getSsn(), s);
    s.addSection(this);
    return SUCCESSFULLY_ENROLLED;
}
```

❑   We begin by verifying that the Student seeking enrollment (represented by argument 's') hasn't already enrolled for this Section, and furthermore that they have never taken and successfully completed this Course (any Sections) in the past. We obtain a handle on the Student's transcript and store it in a locally-declared reference variable called 'transcript', because we are going to need to consult with the Transcript object twice in this method.

```
public int enroll(Student s) {
    // First, make sure that this Student is not already
    // enrolled for this Section, and that they have
    // never taken and passed the course before.

    Transcript transcript = s.getTranscript();
```

We then use an 'if' statement to test for either of two conditions: (a) is the Student currently enrolled in this Section or another Section of the same Course, and/or (b) does their Transcript indicate successful prior completion of the Course that is represented by this Section?

Because we only have need to use this Course object once in this method, we don't bother to save the handle returned to us by the getRepresentedCourse() method in a variable; we just nest the invocation of this method within the call to verifyCompletion(), so that the Course object can be retrieved by the former and immediately passed along as an argument to the latter.

```
    if (s.isCurrentlyEnrolledInSimilar(this) ||
        transcript.verifyCompletion(this.getRepresentedCourse()))
        return PREVIOUSLY_ENROLLED;
```

Whenever we encounter a 'return' statement midway through a method as we have here, the method will immediately terminate execution without running to completion.

Note our use of PREVIOUSLY_ENROLLED, one of the public static final attributes declared by Section, as a return value. Declaring and using such standardized values is a great way to communicate status back to client code, as this sample pseudocode invocation of the enroll() method illustrates:

```
// Client code (pseudocode).

Section sec = new Section(…);
Student s = new Student(…);
…
int status = sec1.enroll(s1);
if (status == Section.PREVIOUSLY_ENROLLED) {
  take appropriate action
}
if (status == Section.PREREQ_NOT_SATISFIED) {
  take appropriate action
}
else if (status == Section.SECTION_FULL) {
  take appropriate action
}
// etc.
```

Thus, both the client code and the Section object's method code are using the same symbolic names to communicate.

❏ Next, we check to see if the Student has satisfied the prerequisites for this Section, if there are any. We use the Section's getRepresentedCourse() method to obtain a handle on the Course object that this Section represents, and then invoke the hasPrerequisites() method on that Course object; if the result returned is true, then we know that there are prerequisites to be checked.

```
// If there are any prerequisites for this course,
// check to ensure that the Student has completed them.

Course c = getRepresentedCourse();
if (c.hasPrerequisites()) {
```

If there are indeed prerequisites for this Course, we use the getPrerequisites() method defined by the Course class to obtain an Enumeration object of all prerequisite Courses.

```
Enumeration e = c.getPrerequisites();
```

Then, we iterate through the Enumeration; for each Course object reference 'pre' that we extract from the Enumeration, we invoke the verifyCompletion() method on the Student's Transcript object, passing in the prerequisite Course object reference 'pre'. We haven't taken a look at the inner workings of the Transcript class yet, so for now, all we need to know about verifyCompletion() is that it will return a value of true if the Student has indeed successfully taken and passed the Course in question, or a value of false otherwise. We want to take action in situations where a prerequisite was **not** satisfied, so we use the unary negation operator (!) in front of the expression to indicate that we want the 'if' test to succeed if the method call returns a value of false:

```
while (e.hasMoreElements()) {
  Course pre = (Course) e.nextElement();

  // See if the Student's Transcript reflects
  // successful completion of the prerequisite.
```

397

```
        if (!t.verifyCompletion(pre))
          return PREREQ_NOT_SATISFIED;
      }
    } // end if
```

❑   If we make it through the prerequisite check without triggering the 'return' statement, the next
     step in this method is to verify that there is still available seating in the Section; we return
     the status value SECTION_FULL value if there is not.

```
    // If the total enrollment is already at the
    // the capacity for this Section, we reject this
    // enrollment request.

    if (!confirmSeatAvailability()) return SECTION_FULL;
```

❑   Finally, if we've made it through both of the above tests unscathed, we're ready to officially
     enroll the Student. We use the Hashtable class's put() method to insert the Student
     reference into the 'enrolledStudents' Hashtable, invoking the getSsn() method on
     the Student to retrieve the String value of its 'ssn' attribute, which we pass in as the key
     value. To achieve bi-directionality of the link between a Student and a Section, we then
     turn around and invoke the addSection() method on the Student object reference,
     passing it a handle on this Section.

```
    // Note bi-directionality: this Section holds
    // onto the Student via the Hashtable, and then
    // the Student is given a handle on this Section.

    enrolledStudents.put(s.getSsn(), s);
    s.addSection(this);
    return SUCCESSFULLY_ENROLLED;
  }
```

drop()

The drop() method of Section performs the reverse operation of enroll(). We start by verifying
that the Student in question is indeed enrolled in this Section, since we cannot drop a Student who
isn't enrolled in the first place:

```
    public boolean drop(Student s) {
        // We may only drop a student if they are enrolled.

        if (!s.isEnrolledIn(this)) return false;
```

and, if they truly are enrolled, then we use the Hashtable class's remove() method to locate and delete
the Student reference, again via its 'ssn' attribute value, and in the interest of bi-directionality, we
invoke the dropSection() method on the Student, as well, to get rid of the handles at *both* ends of the
the link.

```
  else {
    // Find the student in our Hashtable, and remove it.

    enrolledStudents.remove(s.getSsn());

    // Note bi-directionality.

    s.dropSection(this);
    return true;
  }
}
```

postGrade()

The postGrade() method is used to assign a grade to a Student by creating a TranscriptEntry object to link the two. To ensure that we aren't inadvertently trying to assign a grade to a given Student more than once, we first check the 'assignedGrades' Hashtable to see if already contains an entry for this Student. If the get() method call on the Hashtable returns anything but null, then we know a grade has already been posted for this Student, and we terminate execution of the method.

```
public boolean postGrade(Student s, String grade) {
  // Make sure that we haven't previously assigned a
  // grade to this Student by looking in the Hashtable
  // for an entry using this Student as the key. If
  // we discover that a grade has already been assigned,
  // we return a value of false to indicate that
  // we are at risk of overwriting an existing grade.
  // (A different method, eraseGrade(), can then be written
  // to allow a Professor to change their mind.)

  if (assignedGrades.get(s) != null) return false;
```

Assuming that a grade was not previously assigned, we invoke the appropriate constructor to create a new TranscriptEntry object. As we will see when we study the inner workings of the TranscriptEntry class, this object will maintain handles on both the Student to whom a grade has been assigned and on the Section for which the grade was assigned. To enable this latter link to be bi-directional, we also store a handle on the TranscriptEntry object in the Section's Hashtable for this purpose.

```
  // First, we create a new TranscriptEntry object. Note
  // that we are passing in a reference to THIS Section,
  // because we want the TranscriptEntry object,
  // as an association class ..., to maintain
  // "handles" on the Section as well as on the Student.
  // (We'll let the TranscriptEntry constructor take care of
  // "hooking" this TranscriptEntry to the correct Transcript.)

  TranscriptEntry te = new TranscriptEntry(s, grade, this);

  // Then, we "remember" this grade because we wish for
  // the connection between a T.E. and a Section to be
  // bi-directional.

  assignedGrades.put(s, te);

  return true;
}
```

confirmAvailability()

The confirmSeatAvailability() method called from within enroll() is an internal 'housekeeping' method; by declaring it to have private versus public visibility, we restrict its use so that only other methods of the Section class may invoke it.

```
private boolean confirmSeatAvailability() {
  if (enrolledStudents.size() < getSeatingCapacity())
    return true;
  else return false;
}
```

Delegation, Revisited

In discussing the Student class, we briefly mentioned the displayCourseSchedule() method as a complex example of delegation, and promised to come back and discuss it further.

What are the 'raw materials' – data – available for an object to use when it is responding to a service request by executing one of its methods? By way of review, an object has at its disposal the following data sources:

- ❏ Simple data and/or object references (handles) that have been encapsulated as attributes within the object itself

- ❏ Simple data and/or object references that are passed in as arguments in the method signature

- ❏ Data that is made available globally to the application as public static attributes of some other class (we saw this technique demonstrated earlier in the chapter when we defined various status codes for the Section class, and will see this technique used again several more times within the SRS)

- ❏ Data that can be requested from any of the objects that this object has a handle on, a process that we learned in Chapter 3 is known as delegation

It is this last source of data – data available by collaborating with other objects and delegating part of a task to them – that is going to play a particularly significant role in implementing the displayCourseSchedule() method for the Student class.

Let's say we want the displayCourseSchedule() method to display the following information for each Section that a Student is currently enrolled in:

Course No.:
Section No.:
Course Name:
Meeting Day and Time:
Room Location:
Professor's Name:

For example:

```
Course Schedule for Fred Schnurd
   Course No.: CMP101
   Section No.: 2
   Course Name:  Beginning Computer Technology
   Meeting Day and Time Held:  W - 6:10 - 8:00 PM
   Room Location:  GOVT202
   Professor's Name:  John Smith
   -----
   Course No.: ART101
   Section No.: 1
   Course Name:  Beginning Basketweaving
   Meeting Day and Time Held:  M - 4:10 - 6:00 PM
   Room Location:  ARTS25
   Professor's Name:  Snidely Whiplash
   -----
```

Let's start by looking at the attributes of the Student class, to see which of this information is readily available to us. Student inherits from Person:

```
private String name;
private String ssn;
```

and adds:

```
private String major;
private String degree;
private Transcript transcript;
private Vector attends; // of Sections
```

Let's begin to write the method; by stepping through the 'attends' Vector, we can gain access to Section objects one by one:

```
public void displayCourseSchedule() {
   // Display a title first.

   System.out.println("Course Schedule for " + getName());

   // Step through the Vector of Section objects,
   // processing these one by one.

   for (int i = 0; i < attends.size(); i++) {
      Section s = (Section) attends.elementAt(i);

      // Now what goes here????
      // We must create the rest of the method...

   }
}
```

Now that we have the beginnings of the method, let's determine how to fill in the gap in the above code.

Looking at all of the method signatures declared for the Section class as evidence of the services that a Section object can perform, we see that several of these can immediately provide us with useful pieces of information relative to our mission of displaying a Student's course schedule:

```
public void setSectionNo(int no);
public int getSectionNo();
public void setDayOfWeek(char day);
public char getDayOfWeek();
public void setTimeOfDay(String time);
public String getTimeOfDay();
public void setInstructor(Professor prof);
public Professor getInstructor();
public void setRepresentedCourse(Course c);
public Course getRepresentedCourse();
public void setRoom(String r);
public String getRoom();
public void setSeatingCapacity(int c);
public int getSeatingCapacity();
public void setOfferedIn(ScheduleOfClasses soc);
public ScheduleOfClasses getOfferedIn();
public String toString();
public int enroll(Student s);
public boolean drop(Student s);
public int getTotalEnrollment();
public void display();
public void displayStudentRoster();
public String getGrade(Student s);
public boolean postGrade(Student s, String grade);
public boolean successfulCompletion(Student s);
public boolean isSectionOf(Course c);
```

Let's put these four methods to use, and where we cannot yet fill the gap completely, we'll insert '???' as a place holder:

```
public void displayCourseSchedule() {
  // Display a title first.

  System.out.println('Course Schedule for ' + getName());

  // Step through the Vector of Section objects,
  // processing these one by one.

  for (int i = 0; i < attends.size(); i++) {
    Section s = (Section) attends.elementAt(i);

      // Since the attends Vector contains Sections that the
      // Student took in the past as well as those for which
      // the Student is currently enrolled, we only want to
      // report on those for which a grade has not yet been
      // assigned.
```

```
            if (s.getGrade(this) == null) {
                System.out.println("\tCourse No.:   " + ???
                System.out.println("\tSection No.:   " + s.getSectionNo());
                System.out.println("\tCourse Name:   " + ???
                System.out.println("\tMeeting Day and Time Held:   " +
                    s.getDayOfWeek() + " - " + s.getTimeOfDay());
                System.out.println("\tRoom Location:   " + s.getRoom());
                System.out.println("\tProfessor's Name:   " + ???

                // Print out a separator.

                System.out.println("\t-----");
            }
        }
    }
```

Now what about the remaining 'holes'?

Two of the Section class methods:

```
public Professor getInstructor();
public Course getRepresentedCourse();
```

will each hand us yet another object that we can 'talk to': the Professor who teaches this Section, and the Course that this Section represents – let's now look at what these objects can perform in the way of services.

❑   A Professor object can perform the following services (those marked with an asterisk (*) are inherited from Person):

```
public void setName(String n);   // *
public String getName();         // *
public void setSsn(String ssn);  // *
public String getSsn();          // *
public void display();
public void setTitle(String title);
public String getTitle();
public void setDepartment(String dept);
public String getDepartment();
public void display();
public String toString();
public void displayTeachingAssignments();
public void agreeToTeach(Section s);
```

❑   A Course object can perform these services:

```
public void setCourseNo(String cNo);
public String getCourseNo();
public void setCourseName(String cName);
public String getCourseName();
public void setCredits(double c);
public double getCredits();
```

```
public void display();
public String toString();
public void addPrerequisite(Course c);
public boolean hasPrerequisites();
public Enumeration getPrerequisites();
public Section scheduleSection(char day, String time, String room,
   int capacity);
```

If we bring all of the highlighted methods to bear, we can wrap up the displayCourseSchedule() method of the Student class as follows:

```
public void displayCourseSchedule() {
  // Display a title first.

  System.out.println("Course Schedule for " + getName());

  // Step through the Vector of Section objects,
  // processing these one by one.

  for (int i = 0; i < attends.size(); i++) {
    Section s = (Section) attends.elementAt(i);

    // Since the attends Vector contains Sections that the
    // Student took in the past as well as those for which
    // the Student is currently enrolled, we only want to
    // report on those for which a grade has not yet been
    // assigned.

    if (s.getGrade(this) == null) {
      System.out.println("\tCourse No.:   " +
        s.getRepresentedCourse().getCourseNo());
      System.out.println("\tSection No.:   " + s.getSectionNo());
      System.out.println("\tCourse Name:   " +
        s.getRepresentedCourse().getCourseName());
      System.out.println("\tMeeting Day and Time Held:   " +
        s.getDayOfWeek() + " - " + s.getTimeOfDay());
      System.out.println("\tRoom Location:   " +
        s.getRoom());
      System.out.println("\tProfessor's Name:   " +
        s.getInstructor().getName());
      System.out.println("\t-----");
    }
  }
}
```

Note that we are invoking the getRepresentedCourse() method on each Section object twice; we could instead call this method once, retrieving a Course object reference and holding on to it, as follows:

```
for (int i = 0; i < attends.size(); i++) {
  Section s = (Section) attends.elementAt(i);
  Course c = s.getRepresentedCourse();
  Professor p = s.getInstructor();

  // ...
  if (s.getGrade(this) == null) {
    System.out.println("\tCourse No.:   " + c.getCourseNo());
    System.out.println("\tSection No.:   " + s.getSectionNo());
    System.out.println("\tCourse Name:   " + c.getCourseName());
    System.out.println("\tMeeting Day and Time Held:   " +
      s.getDayOfWeek() + " - " + s.getTimeOfDay());
    System.out.println("\tRoom Location:   " + s.getRoom());
    System.out.println("\tProfessor's Name:   " + p.getName());
    System.out.println("\t-----");
  }
 }
}
```

This method is a classic example of delegation:

❑   We start out asking a Student object to do something for us – namely, to display the
     Student's course schedule.

❑   The Student object in turn has to talk to the Section objects representing sections that the
     student is enrolled in, asking each of them to perform some of their services (methods).

❑   The Student object also has to ask those Section objects to hand over references to the
     Professor and Course objects that the Section objects know about, in turn asking them
     to perform some of their services.

This multi-tiered collaboration is depicted conceptually in the following diagram:

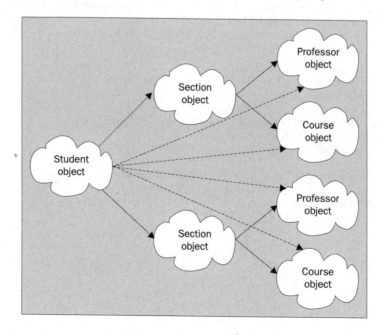

The ScheduleOfClasses Class

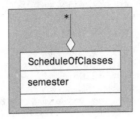

ScheduleOfClasses Attributes

The ScheduleOfClasses class is a fairly simple class that serves as an example of how we might wish to encapsulate a collection object within some other class. It consists of only two attributes: a simple String representing the semester for which the schedule is valid (for example 'SP2001' for the Spring 2001 semester), and a Hashtable used to maintain handles on all of the Sections that are being offered that semester.

```
private String semester;

// This Hashtable stores Section object references, using
// a String concatenation of course no. and section no. as the
// key, for example, "MATH101 - 1".

private Hashtable sectionsOffered;
```

addSection()

Aside from a simple constructor, a display() method, and get/set methods for the semester attribute, the only other feature that this class provides is a method for adding a Section object to the Hashtable, then bi-directionally connecting the ScheduleOfClasses object back to the Section:

```
public void addSection(Section s) {
    // We formulate a key by concatenating the course no.
    // and section no., separated by a hyphen.

    String key = s.getRepresentedCourse().getCourseNo() +
                 " - " + s.getSectionNo();
    sectionsOffered.put(key, s);

    // Bi-directionally hook the ScheduleOfClasses back to the Section.

    s.setOfferedIn(this);
}
```

The TranscriptEntry Association Class (Static Methods)

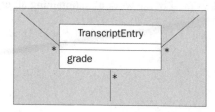

TranscriptEntry Attributes

As we saw earlier in this chapter, the `TranscriptEntry` class has one simple attribute, `'grade'`, and maintains associations with three other classes:

❑ *earns grade*, a one-to-many association with `Student`;

❑ *assigns grade*, a one-to-many association with `Section`; and

❑ an unnamed, one-to-many aggregation with the `Transcript` class.

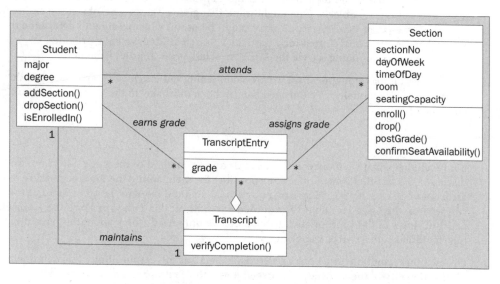

`TranscriptEntry` is at the 'many' end of all of these associations, and so it only needs to maintain a single handle on each type of object; no collection attributes are required:

```
private String grade;
private Student student;
private Section section;
private Transcript transcript;
```

TranscriptEntry Constructor

The constructor for this class does most of the work of maintaining all of these relationships.

- Via the call to setStudent(), it stores the associated Student object's handle in the appropriate attribute.

```
//----------------
// Constructor(s).
//----------------

public TranscriptEntry(Student s, String grade, Section se) {
  setStudent(s);
```

Note that we have chosen *not* to maintain the *earns grade* association bi-directionally; that is, we have provided no code in either this or the Student class to provide the Student object with a handle on this TranscriptEntry object. We have made this decision based upon the fact that we don't expect a Student to ever have to manipulate TranscriptEntry objects directly. Every Student object has an indirect means of reaching all of its TranscriptEntry objects, via the handle that a Student object maintains on its Transcript object, and the handles that the Transcript object in turn maintains on its TranscriptEntry objects. One might think that giving a Student object the ability to directly pull a given TranscriptEntry might be useful when wishing to determine the grade that the Student earned for a particular Section, but we have provided an alternative means of doing so, via the Section class's getGrade() method.

- Even though it may not appear so, we are maintaining the *assigns grade* association with Section bi-directionally. We only see half of the 'handshake' in the TranscriptEntry constructor:

```
setSection(se);
```

but recall that when we looked at the postGrade() method of the Section class, we discussed the fact that Section was responsible for maintaining the bi-directionality of this association. When the Section's postGrade() method invokes the TranscriptEntry constructor, the Section object is returned a handle on this TranscriptEntry object, which it stores in the appropriate attribute. So, we only need worry about the second half of this 'handshake' in TranscriptEntry.

- On the other hand, the TranscriptEntry object has full responsibility for maintaining the bi-directionality of the association between it and the Transcript object:

```
// Obtain the Student's transcript ...

Transcript t = s.getTranscript();

// ... and then hook the Transcript and the TranscriptEntry
// together bidirectionally.

setTranscript(t);
t.addTranscriptEntry(this);
}
```

validateGrade(), passingGrade()

The `TranscriptEntry` class provides our first SRS example of public static methods: it declares two methods, `validateGrade()` and `passingGrade()`, that may be invoked as utility methods on the `TranscriptEntry` class from anywhere in the SRS application:

❑   The first is used to validate whether a particular string, – say, "B+" – is a valid grade or not.

```java
//These next two methods are declared to be static, so that they
// may be used as utility methods.

public static boolean validateGrade(String grade) {
  boolean outcome = false;

  if (grade.equals("F") ||
    grade.equals("I")) outcome = true;

  if (grade.startsWith("A") ||
    grade.startsWith("B") ||
    grade.startsWith("C") ||
    grade.startsWith("D")) {
      if (grade.length() == 1) outcome = true;
      else if (grade.length() > 2) outcome = false;
      else {
        if (grade.endsWith("+") ||
          grade.endsWith("-")) outcome = true;
        else outcome = false;
      }
  }

  return outcome;
}
```

❑   The second is used to determine whether a particular string, – say "D+" – is a *passing* grade or not.

```java
public static boolean passingGrade(String grade) {
  // First, make sure it is a valid grade.

  if (!validateGrade(grade)) return false;

  // Next, make sure that the grade is a D or better.

  if (grade.startsWith("A") ||
    grade.startsWith("B") ||
    grade.startsWith("C") ||
    grade.startsWith("D")) return true;

  else return false;
}
```

As we discussed in Chapters 7 and 13, public static methods can be invoked on the hosting class as a whole – in other words, an object needn't be instantiated in order to use these methods.

We'll see actual use of the `passingGrade()` method in a moment, when we discuss the `Transcript` class.

The Transcript Class

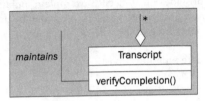

Transcript Attributes

The Transcript class participates in two relationships:

- ❏ *maintains*, a one-to-one association with Student, and
- ❏ an unnamed, one-to-many aggregation with TranscriptEntry.

The SRS class diagram does not call out any other attributes for the Transcript class, so we only encode these two:

```
private Vector transcriptEntries; // of TranscriptEntry object references
private Student studentOwner;
```

verifyCompletion()

The Transcript class has one particularly interesting method, verifyCompletion(), which is used to determine whether or not the Transcript contains evidence that a particular Course requirement has been satisfied. This method steps through the Vector of TranscriptEntries maintained by the Transcript object:

```
public boolean verifyCompletion(Course c) {
  boolean outcome = false;

  // Step through all TranscriptEntries, looking for one
  // which reflects a Section of the Course of interest.

  for (int i = 0; i < transcriptEntries.size(); i++) {
    TranscriptEntry te = (TranscriptEntry)
      transcriptEntries.elementAt(i);
```

For each entry, it obtains a handle on the Section object represented by this entry, and then invokes the isSectionOf() method on that object to determine whether or not that Section represents the Course of interest.

```
    Section s = te.getSection();

    if (s.isSectionOf(c)) {
```

Assuming that the `Section` is indeed relevant, the method next uses the static `passingGrade()` method of the `TranscriptEntry` class to determine whether the grade earned in this `Section` was a passing grade or not. If it was a passing grade, we can terminate the loop immediately, since we only need find one example of a passing grade for the `Course` of interest in order to return a `true` outcome from this method.

```
    // Ensure that the grade was high enough.

    if (TranscriptEntry.passingGrade(te.getGrade())) {
      outcome = true;

      // We've found one, so we can afford to
      // terminate the loop now.

      break;
    }
  }
}

return outcome;
  }
}
```

The SRS 'Driver' Program

Now that we've coded all of the classes called for by our model of the SRS, we need a way to test these. We could wait to put our application through its paces until we've built a GUI front-end; however, it would be nice to know sooner rather than later that our core classes are working properly. One very helpful technique for doing so is to write a command-line driven program to instantiate objects of varying types and to invoke their critical methods, displaying the results to the command-line window for us to inspect.

We've developed just such a program by creating a class called `SRS` with a `main()` method that will serve as our test 'driver'.

Public Static Attributes

We are going to instantiate some `Professor`, `Student`, `Course`, and `Section` objects in this program, so we need a way to organize handles on these objects; we'll create collection objects as attributes of the SRS class to hold each of these different object types. While we're at it, we'll declare them to be public static attributes, which means that we are making the main object collections globally available to the entire application.

```
    // We can effectively create "global" data by declaring
    // public static attributes in the main class.

    // Entry points/"roots" for getting at objects.

    public static ScheduleOfClasses scheduleOfClasses =
      new ScheduleOfClasses("SP2001");
```

```
// Note that we could encapsulate the rest of these, the way that we
// did for the ScheduleOfClasses ...

public static Vector faculty; // of Professors
public static Vector studentBody; // of Students
public static Vector courseCatalog; // of Courses
```

The SRS ScheduleOfClasses class serves as a collection point for Section objects; for the other types of objects, we use simple Vectors, although we could go ahead and design classes comparable to ScheduleOfClasses to serve as encapsulated collections, perhaps named Faculty, StudentBody, and CourseCatalog, respectively. (We'll actually do so in Chapter 15.) We don't need a collection for Transcript objects – we'll get to these via the handles that Student objects maintain – or for TranscriptEntry objects – we'll get to these via the Transcript objects themselves.

main()

We'll now dive into the main() method for the SRS class; we'll start by declaring reference variables for each of the four main object types:

```
public static void main(String[] args) {
    Professor p1, p2, p3;
    Student s1, s2, s3;
    Course c1, c2, c3, c4, c5;
    Section sec1, sec2, sec3, sec4, sec5, sec6, sec7;
```

and we'll then use their various constructors to fabricate object instances, storing handles in the appropriate collections (in Chapter 15, we'll explore how we can instantiate objects by reading data from a file instead of 'hard coding' attributes as we have here):

```
// -----------
// Professors.
// -----------

p1 = new Professor("Jacquie Barker", "123-45-6789",
                    "Adjunct Professor", "Information Technology");
p2 = new Professor("John Smith", "567-81-2345",
                    "Full Professor", "Chemistry");

p3 = new Professor("Snidely Whiplash", "987-65-4321",
                    "Full Professor", "Physical Education");

// Add these to the appropriate Vector.

faculty = new Vector();
faculty.add(p1);
faculty.add(p2);
faculty.add(p3);

// ---------
// Students.
// ---------

s1 = new Student("Joe Blow", "111-11-1111", "Math", "M.S.");
```

```
s2 = new Student("Fred Schnurd", "222-22-2222",
                  "Information Technology", "Ph. D.");

s3 = new Student("Mary Smith", "333-33-3333", "Physics", "B.S.");

// Add these to the appropriate Vector.

studentBody = new Vector();
studentBody.add(s1);
studentBody.add(s2);
studentBody.add(s3);

// --------
// Courses.
// --------

c1 = new Course("CMP101", "Beginning Computer Technology", 3.0);

c2 = new Course("OBJ101", "Object Methods for Software Development",
                  3.0);

c3 = new Course("CMP283", "Higher Level Languages (Java)", 3.0);

c4 = new Course("CMP999", "Living Brain Computers", 3.0);

c5 = new Course("ART101", "Beginning Basketweaving", 3.0);

// Add these to the appropriate Vector.

courseCatalog = new Vector();
courseCatalog.add(c1);
courseCatalog.add(c2);
courseCatalog.add(c3);
courseCatalog.add(c4);
courseCatalog.add(c5);
```

We use the `addPrerequisite()` method of the `Course` class to interrelate some of the `Courses`, so that c1 is a prerequisite for c2, c2 for c3, and c3 for c4. The only `Courses` that do not specify prerequisites in our test case are c1 and c5.

```
// Establish some prerequisites (c1 => c2 => c3 => c4).

c2.addPrerequisite(c1);
c3.addPrerequisite(c2);
c4.addPrerequisite(c3);
```

To create `Section` objects, we take advantage of the `Course` class's `scheduleSection()` method which, as you may recall, contains an embedded call to a `Section` class constructor. Each invocation of `scheduleSection()` returns a handle to a newly-created `Section` object, which we store in the appropriate collection.

```
// ---------
// Sections.
// ---------
```

```
// Schedule sections of each Course by calling the
// scheduleSection method of Course (which internally
// invokes the Section constructor).

sec1 = c1.scheduleSection('M', "8:10 - 10:00 PM", "GOVT101", 30);

sec2 = c1.scheduleSection('W', "6:10 - 8:00 PM", "GOVT202", 30);

sec3 = c2.scheduleSection('R', "4:10 - 6:00 PM", "GOVT105", 25);

sec4 = c2.scheduleSection('T', "6:10 - 8:00 PM", "SCI330", 25);

sec5 = c3.scheduleSection('M', "6:10 - 8:00 PM", "GOVT101", 20);

sec6 = c4.scheduleSection('R', "4:10 - 6:00 PM", "SCI241", 15);

sec7 = c5.scheduleSection('M', "4:10 - 6:00 PM", "ARTS25", 40);

// Add these to the Schedule of Classes.

scheduleOfClasses.addSection(sec1);
scheduleOfClasses.addSection(sec2);
scheduleOfClasses.addSection(sec3);
scheduleOfClasses.addSection(sec4);
scheduleOfClasses.addSection(sec5);
scheduleOfClasses.addSection(sec6);
scheduleOfClasses.addSection(sec7);
```

Next, we use the agreeToTeach() method declared for the Professor class to assign Professors to Sections:

```
// Recruit a professor to teach each of the sections.

p3.agreeToTeach(sec1);
p2.agreeToTeach(sec2);
p1.agreeToTeach(sec3);
p3.agreeToTeach(sec4);
p1.agreeToTeach(sec5);
p2.agreeToTeach(sec6);
p3.agreeToTeach(sec7);
```

We then simulate student registration by having Students enroll in the various Sections using the enroll() method. Recall that this method returns one of a set of predefined status values – either SUCCESSFULLY_ENROLLED, SECTION_FULL, PREREQ_NOT_SATISFIED, or PREVIOUSLY_ENROLLED – and so in order to display which status is returned in each case, we created a reportStatus() method solely for the purpose of formatting an informational message:

```
System.out.println("Student registration has begun!");
System.out.println("");

// Students drop/add courses.
```

```
System.out.println("Student " + s1.getName() +
  " is attempting to enroll in " + sec1.toString());

int status = sec1.enroll(s1);

// Note the use of a special method to interpret
// and display the outcome of this enrollment request.
// (We could have included the code in-line here, but
// since (a) it is rather complex and (b) it will need
// to be repeated for all subsequent enrollment requests
// below, it made sense to turn it into a reusable method
// instead.)

reportStatus(status);
```

The reportStatus() method is discussed separately below.

```
// Try enrolling the same Student in a different Section
// of the same Course!

System.out.println("Student " + s1.getName() +
  " is attempting to enroll in " + sec2.toString());
status = sec2.enroll(s1);
reportStatus(status);

System.out.println("Student " + s2.getName() +
  " is attempting to enroll in " + sec2.toString());
status = sec2.enroll(s2);
reportStatus(status);

System.out.println("Student " + s2.getName() +
  " is attempting to enroll in " + sec3.toString());
status = sec3.enroll(s2);
reportStatus(status);

System.out.println("Student " + s2.getName() +
  " is attempting to enroll in " + sec7.toString());
status = sec7.enroll(s2);
reportStatus(status);

System.out.println("Student " + s3.getName() +
  " is attempting to enroll in " + sec1.toString());
status = sec1.enroll(s3);
reportStatus(status);

System.out.println("Student " + s3.getName() +
  " is attempting to enroll in " + sec5.toString());
status = sec5.enroll(s3);
reportStatus(status);

// Skip a line.
System.out.println("");
```

```
// When the dust settles, here's what folks wound up
// being registered for:
//
// sec1:   s1, s3
// sec2:   s2
// sec7:   s2
```

Next, we simulate the assignment of grades at the end of the semester by invoking the postGrade() method for each Student – Section combination:

```
// Semester is finished (boy, that was quick!). Professors
// assign grades.

sec1.postGrade(s1, "C+");
sec1.postGrade(s3, "A");
sec2.postGrade(s2, "B+");
sec7.postGrade(s2, "A-");
```

Finally, we put our various display() methods to good use by displaying the internal state of the various objects that we created – in essence, an 'object dump':

```
// Let's see if everything got set up properly
// by calling various display methods!

System.out.println("====================");
System.out.println("Schedule of Classes:");
System.out.println("====================");
System.out.println("");
scheduleOfClasses.display();

System.out.println("======================");
System.out.println("Professor Information:");
System.out.println("======================");
System.out.println("");
p1.display();
System.out.println("");
p2.display();
System.out.println("");
p3.display();
System.out.println("");

System.out.println("====================");
System.out.println("Student Information:");
System.out.println("====================");
System.out.println("");
s1.display();
System.out.println("");
s2.display();
System.out.println("");
s3.display();
}
```

Here is the `reportStatus()` housekeeping method that we mentioned earlier:

```
public static void reportStatus(int status) {
  if (status == Section.SUCCESSFULLY_ENROLLED)
    System.out.println("outcome:  SUCCESSFULLY_ENROLLED");
  else if (status == Section.PREREQ_NOT_SATISFIED)
    System.out.println("outcome:  PREREQ_NOT_SATISFIED");
  else if (status == Section.PREVIOUSLY_ENROLLED)
    System.out.println("outcome:  PREVIOUSLY_ENROLLED");
  else if (status == Section.SECTION_FULL)
    System.out.println("outcome:  SECTION_FULL");
}
```

When compiled and run, the SRS program produces the following command-line window output:

Student registration has begun!

Student Joe Blow is attempting to enroll in CMP101 - 1 - M - 8:10 - 10:00 PM
outcome: SUCCESSFULLY_ENROLLED
Student Joe Blow is attempting to enroll in CMP101 - 2 - W - 6:10 - 8:00 PM
outcome: PREVIOUSLY_ENROLLED
Student Fred Schnurd is attempting to enroll in CMP101 - 2 - W - 6:10 - 8:00 PM
outcome: SUCCESSFULLY_ENROLLED
Student Fred Schnurd is attempting to enroll in OBJ101 - 1 - R - 4:10 - 6:00 PM
outcome: PREREQ_NOT_SATISFIED
Student Fred Schnurd is attempting to enroll in ART101 - 1 - M - 4:10 - 6:00 PM
outcome: SUCCESSFULLY_ENROLLED
Student Mary Smith is attempting to enroll in CMP101 - 1 - M - 8:10 - 10:00 PM
outcome: SUCCESSFULLY_ENROLLED
Student Mary Smith is attempting to enroll in CMP283 - 1 - M - 6:10 - 8:00 PM
outcome: PREREQ_NOT_SATISFIED

=====================
Schedule of Classes:
=====================

Schedule of Classes for SP2001

Section Information:
  Semester: SP2001
  Course No.: CMP101
  Section No: 2
  Offered: W at 6:10 - 8:00 PM
  In Room: GOVT202
  Professor: John Smith
  Fred Schnurd
Total of 1 students enrolled.

Section Information:
 Semester: SP2001
 Course No.: CMP101
 Section No: 1
 Offered: M at 8:10 - 10:00 PM
 In Room: GOVT101
 Professor: Snidely Whiplash
 Mary Smith
 Joe Blow
Total of 2 students enrolled.

Section Information:
 Semester: SP2001
 Course No.: CMP283
 Section No: 1
 Offered: M at 6:10 - 8:00 PM
 In Room: GOVT101
 Professor: Jacquie Barker
Total of 0 students enrolled.

Section Information:
 Semester: SP2001
 Course No.: CMP999
 Section No: 1
 Offered: R at 4:10 - 6:00 PM
 In Room: SCI241
 Professor: John Smith
Total of 0 students enrolled.

Section Information:
 Semester: SP2001
 Course No.: OBJ101
 Section No: 2
 Offered: T at 6:10 - 8:00 PM
 In Room: SCI330
 Professor: Snidely Whiplash
Total of 0 students enrolled.

Section Information:
 Semester: SP2001
 Course No.: OBJ101
 Section No: 1
 Offered: R at 4:10 - 6:00 PM
 In Room: GOVT105
 Professor: Jacquie Barker
Total of 0 students enrolled.

Section Information:
 Semester: SP2001
 Course No.: ART101
 Section No: 1
 Offered: M at 4:10 - 6:00 PM
 In Room: ARTS25
 Professor: Snidely Whiplash
 Fred Schnurd
Total of 1 students enrolled.

=======================
Professor Information:
=======================

Person Information:
 Name: Jacquie Barker
 Soc. Security No.: 123-45-6789
Professor-Specific Information:
 Title: Adjunct Professor
 Teaches for Dept.: Information Technology
Teaching Assignments for Jacquie Barker:
 Course No.: OBJ101
 Section No.: 1
 Course Name: Object Methods for Software Development
 Day and Time: R - 4:10 - 6:00 PM

 Course No.: CMP283
 Section No.: 1
 Course Name: Higher Level Languages (Java)
 Day and Time: M - 6:10 - 8:00 PM

Person Information:
 Name: John Smith
 Soc. Security No.: 567-81-2345
Professor-Specific Information:
 Title: Full Professor
 Teaches for Dept.: Chemistry
Teaching Assignments for John Smith:
 Course No.: CMP101
 Section No.: 2
 Course Name: Beginning Computer Technology
 Day and Time: W - 6:10 - 8:00 PM

 Course No.: CMP999
 Section No.: 1
 Course Name: Living Brain Computers
 Day and Time: R - 4:10 - 6:00 PM

Person Information:
 Name: Snidely Whiplash
 Soc. Security No.: 987-65-4321
Professor-Specific Information:
 Title: Full Professor
 Teaches for Dept.: Physical Education
Teaching Assignments for Snidely Whiplash:
 Course No.: CMP101
 Section No.: 1
 Course Name: Beginning Computer Technology
 Day and Time: M - 8:10 - 10:00 PM

 Course No.: OBJ101
 Section No.: 2
 Course Name: Object Methods for Software Development
 Day and Time: T - 6:10 - 8:00 PM

 Course No.: ART101
 Section No.: 1
 Course Name: Beginning Basketweaving
 Day and Time: M - 4:10 - 6:00 PM

====================
Student Information:
====================

Person Information:
 Name: Joe Blow
 Soc. Security No.: 111-11-1111
Student-Specific Information:
 Major: Math
 Degree: M.S.
Course Schedule for Joe Blow
Transcript for: Joe Blow (111-11-1111) [M.S. - Math]
 Semester: SP2001
 Course No.:   CMP101
 Credits: 3.0
 Grade Received: C+

Person Information:
 Name: Fred Schnurd
 Soc. Security No.: 222-22-2222
Student-Specific Information:
 Major: Information Technology
 Degree: Ph. D.
Course Schedule for Fred Schnurd
Transcript for: Fred Schnurd (222-22-2222) [Ph. D. - Information Technology]
 Semester: SP2001
 Course No.:   CMP101
 Credits: 3.0
 Grade Received: B+

```
Semester:      SP2001
Course No.:    ART101
Credits:       3.0
Grade Received: A-
-----

Person Information:
 Name: Mary Smith
 Soc. Security No.: 333-33-3333
Student-Specific Information:
 Major: Physics
 Degree: B.S.
Course Schedule for Mary Smith
Transcript for: Mary Smith (333-33-3333) [B.S. - Physics]
 Semester:      SP2001
 Course No.:    CMP101
 Credits:       3.0
 Grade Received:  A
 -----
```

thus demonstrating a successful test! Of course, the SRS driver program could be extended to test various other scenarios; some of the exercises at the end of this chapter suggest ways that you might wish to try doing so.

Debugging Tip

One of the most frequent problems that the new Java programmer encounters when testing an application is a NullPointerException. This is a run time error caused when a programmer has forgotten to initialize a reference, but then tries to access it as though it were a real object. As an example, let's look at a simplified version of the Section class:

```java
public class Section {
  private int sectionNo;
  private Professor instructor;
  // etc.
  // Constructor.
  public Section(int sNo) {
    setSectionNo(sNo);

    // A Professor has not yet been identified.
    setInstructor(null);
  }

  public Professor getInstructor() {
    return instructor;
  }

  // Used for testing purposes.
  public void display() {
    System.out.println("\tSection No.:  " + getSectionNo());
    System.out.println("\tProfessor:  " + getInstructor().getName());
  }

  // etc.
}
```

Now, in our main program, we'll try to instantiate, then display, a `Section` object:

```
public class NullPointerExample {
  public static void main(String[] args) {
    Section s = new Section(1);
    // We forgot to set the instructor attribute, so when we call
    // the display() method, we're in trouble!
    s.display();
  }
}
```

We get the following runtime error message:

```
Section No.: 1
Exception in thread "main" java.lang.NullPointerException
  at Section.display(Section.java:17)
  at NullPointerExample.main(NullPointerExample.java:6)
```

This is known as an **exception trace** – it lists the line of code on which the error occurred (line 17 in the `Section.java` file, in the `display` method), and then shows where that line was called from (line 6 in the `NullPointerExample.java` file, in the `main` method). By going to line 17 in the `Section.java` file, we see that the line on which the exception was thrown was:

```
System.out.println("\tProfessor:  " + getInstructor().getName());
```

A null pointer exception means that some reference variable, instead of pointing to an object, points to **nothing**! In this line of code, the `getInstructor()` method is returning the value of the 'instructor' attribute of the `Section` object, which was set to the value `null` by the constructor and then never updated. So, the attempt to invoke `getName()` is what actually raised the exception – we cannot get the name of a non-existent object!

If it is likely that we'll want to display information about a `Section` object that does not have a `Professor` assigned to teach it, we could alter the 'offending' line of code to read as follows:

```
public void display() {
   System.out.println("\tSection No.:  " + getSectionNo());
   Professor p = getInstructor();
   if (p != null) System.out.println("\tProfessor:  " + p.getName());
}
```

Sometimes, the JVM does not tell you exactly what line the exception was thrown on:

```
Exception in thread "main" java.lang.NullPointerException
  at MyProgram.main(Compiled code)
```

In such a case, rerun your program using the following JVM command-line option:

```
java –Djava.compiler=NONE MyProgram
```

which will force line numbers to be reported, then try to recreate the conditions that led to the exception.

Summary

You've now seen Java in action! We've built a command-line driven version of the SRS application; although this is not typically how most applications are invoked – most 'industrial strength' application have GUI front-ends – developing such a version is a crucial step in testing your 'core' classes to ensure that all methods are working properly. And, aside from the various `display()` methods that we encoded for testing purposes, all of the code that we've written for the command-line version of the application will carry forward intact when we round the application out in the next chapter.

Exercises

All of the following exercises involve making modifications/extensions to the SRS code presented in this chapter. If you have not already done so, please download the code from the Apress website in preparation for these exercises; see Appendix D for details.

1. Expand the `SRS.java` class's `main()` method to represent a second semester's worth of course registrations. (Hint: this will require a second instantiation of the `ScheduleOfClasses` class.)

   ❑ Change the grades received by some Students in the first semester to failing grades, then attempt to register the Student for a course in the second semester requiring successful completion in a previous semester.

   ❑ Try registering a Student for a course in the second semester that they have already successfully completed in the first semester.

2. Improve the logic of the `addPrerequisite()` method of the `Course` class to ensure that a `Course` cannot accidentally be assigned as its own prerequisite.

3. Improve the logic of the `agreeToTeach()` method of the `Professor` class so that a Professor cannot accidentally agree to teach two different Sections which meet at the same day/time.

4. Implement a `cancelSection()` method for the `Course` class, and then correct the erroneous logic of the `scheduleSection()` method having to do with the manner in which Section numbers are assigned. (Hint: introduce a static attribute to the `Course` class for this purpose.)

5. The `enroll()` method of the `Section` class does not take into account the fact that a `Student` may simultaneously be registered for a course and its prerequisite. Modify this method to allow for this possibility.

6. The `postGrade()` method of the `Section` class makes mention of the need for an `eraseGrade()` method, in the event that a Professor wishes to change their mind about the grade that has been issued to a Student; create the `eraseGrade()` method.

Advanced Exercises

7. Modify the `scheduleSection()` method of the `Course` class to prevent two Sections from being scheduled for the same classroom at the same day/time.

8. The `display()` method of the `ScheduleOfClasses` class doesn't presently list Sections in alphabetically sorted order by course name; make whatever changes are necessary to do so.

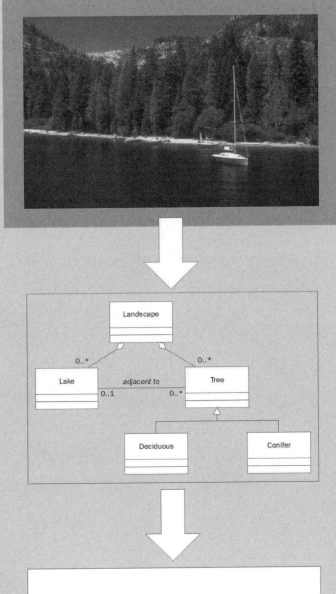

```
public class Tree {
    protected Landscape landscape;
    protected Lake nextTo;

    public void setNextTo(Lake l) {
        nextTo = l;
    }
    public Lake getNextTo() {
        return nextTo;
    }

    public abstract Color getLeafColor();
}
```

Rounding Out Your Application, Part 1: Adding File Persistence

In Chapter 14, we built our first version of the SRS: a command-line driven version that focused on the domain classes called out by our model: Person, Professor, Student, Course, Section, ScheduleOfClasses, Transcript, and TranscriptEntry. The main() method of the SRS 'driver' class was written simply to instantiate objects of the various types and to put them through their paces, as a means of testing that we have implemented the logic of their methods correctly. But, the SRS application as written is not useful as a 'real world' application because:

1. It 'hard codes' all of its data.

2. It provides no means of saving the state of the objects from one invocation of the application to the next, a process known as **persisting data**.

3. Most 'industrial strength' information systems requiring significant user interaction rely on a graphical user interface (GUI) for such interaction.

In essence, we've developed the core of our application by creating the classes that represent the domain model. In this chapter, we are going to revise our SRS application to provide a means for reading/writing data to/from files so that we can remedy the first two of these shortcomings; then, in Chapter 16, we'll remedy the third deficiency by adding a graphical user interface front end.

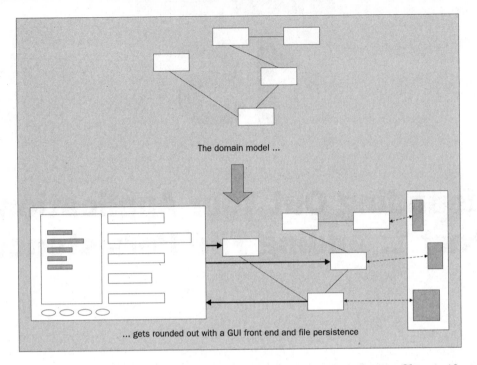

The domain model ...

... gets rounded out with a GUI front end and file persistence

In this chapter, you will get to apply much of what you've learned about Java in Chapter 13, and to actually see it in action in the SRS. You will also learn the following techniques:

- How we approach file Input/Output in Java.

- An approach for parsing tab delimited ASCII records to initialize an object's state, or to initialize a collection of objects.

- A means of persisting an object's state in an ASCII file.

- How to prepare a 'test scaffold' `main()` method for testing isolated classes.

- A technique for encapsulating collections.

- How proper encapsulation streamlines client code (for example the SRS `main()` method).

What is File Persistence?

Whenever we run a program such as the SRS, any objects (or simple data types, for that matter) that we declare and instantiate 'live' in memory. When the program terminates, all of the memory allocated to the program is released back to the operating system, and the internal states of all of the objects created by the application are lost unless they have been saved – **persisted** – in some fashion.

Using various APIs, Java provides a wealth of options with regard to persisting data.

1. Using the Java Database Connectivity (JDBC) API, we can save data to an ODBC-compliant relational database.

2. We can output whole objects in a special binary form known as a Java **serialized** object, ideal for distributing objects over a network.

3. We can also save information in a fairly straightforward, 'human readable' ASCII data format, as either:

    a. Hierarchically arranged data, such as with the emerging eXtensible Markup Language (XML) format standard, in which we intersperse information – 'content' – with 'tags' that describe how the information is to be interpreted, such as this simple example illustrating a `Professor` object with two `Student` advisees:

```
<Professor>
  <name>Dr. Irving Smith</name>
  <ssn>123-45-6789</ssn>
  <title>Associate Professor</title>
  <advisee>
     <type>Student</type>
     <sname>Joe Blow</sname>
     <sssn>987-65-4321</sssn>
  </advisee>
  <advisee>
     <type>Student</type>
     <sname>Mary Jones</sname>
     <sssn>999-88-7777</sssn>
  </advisee>
</Professor>
```

    b. Simple tab- or comma- delimited record oriented data.

We'll be illustrating the most basic form of data persistence – record-oriented ASCII file persistence – in our SRS application code; but many of the same design issues are applicable to these other forms of persistence, as well, such as:

❑ Hiding the details of how we persist an object by encapsulating them within an object's methods, so that client code doesn't have to get bogged down with the details.

❑ Ensuring that whatever approach we take to persisting an object today is flexible, so that we can swap out one approach and swap in another without making dramatic changes to our entire application.

❑ Proper and graceful error handling when something goes amiss: since persistence involves interacting with an external file system, database management system, and/or network, there are a lot of potential points of failure that are outside of the immediate program's control.

and so forth.

Of course there are two sides to file persistence: reading and writing! We'll talk briefly about a Java approach for each.

Reading from a File

The basic Java approach that we're going to use for reading records one-by-one from an ASCII file involves two special types of Java object.

1. First, we'll create an object of type `FileReader`, a type of Java object that knows how to open a file and read data from the file one byte at a time.

2. Next, we'll pass that `FileReader` object as an argument to the constructor for a `BufferedReader`, a more sophisticated type of object that effectively encapsulates the `FileReader`. The `BufferedReader`'s `readLine()` method knows how to internally collect up, or **buffer**, individual characters as read by the `FileReader` until an end of line character is detected, at which point the `BufferedReader` hands back a complete line/record of data to the client code.

Both the `FileReader` and `BufferedReader` classes are defined in the `java.io` package.

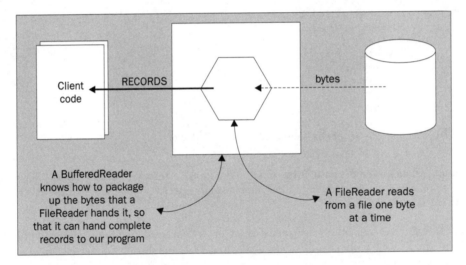

Here is pseudocode to illustrate the general process of reading from a file; we've left out some details, but will see this carried out in earnest in the various SRS classes that we'll be reviewing in this chapter.

```
// Pseudocode

FileReader fr = new FileReader("data.dat");
BufferedReader bIn = new BufferedReader(fr);

// Read the first line from the file.
line = bIn.readLine();

// As long as the line isn't null, keep going!
while (line != null) {
  process the most recently read line

  // Read another line (will be set to null when
```

```
      // the file has been exhausted)
      line = bIn.readLine();
  }

bIn.close();
```

Writing to a File

The basic Java approach that we'll be using for writing records to an ASCII file is similar, but in reverse!, to what it takes to read from a file.

1. We first create an object of type `FileOutputStream`, an object that knows how to open a file and write data to the file one byte at a time. (Note that if we attempt to open a `FileOutputStream` to a file that doesn't previously exist, the `FileOutputStream` object will *create* the file, and if we attempt to open a `FileOutputStream` to a file that does previously exist, we will *overwrite* the file.)

2. Then, we pass that `FileOutputStream` object as an argument to the constructor for a `PrintWriter`, a more sophisticated type of object that encapsulates the `FileOutputStream`. The `PrintWriter`'s `println()` method knows how to pass an entire record/line's worth of data one character at a time to its encapsulated `FileOutputStream` object, which then outputs the data one byte at a time to the file.

The `PrintWriter` class's version of `println()` works in a similar fashion to the `System.out.println()` method call that you are already familiar with, the only difference being that the former causes text to be written to a file whereas the latter causes text to be displayed in the command line window.

`PrintWriter` also defines a `print()` method which works exactly like the `System.out.print()` method.

Both the `FileOutputStream` and `PrintWriter` classes are defined in the `java.io` package, as well.

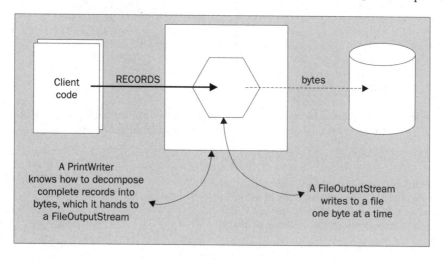

431

We will see this carried out in earnest in the Student class, which we'll be reviewing in this chapter.

```
FileOutputStream fos = new FileOutputStream("data.dat");
PrintWriter pw = new PrintWriter(fos);

while (still want to print more) {
  pw.println(whatever String data we wish to output);
}

pw.close();
```

We'll use this basic approach when we persist the results of a student registration session to a file; this will be discussed in detail toward the end of the chapter.

Populating the Main SRS Collections

In Chapter 14, we introduced the ScheduleOfClasses class as a means of encapsulating a collection of Section objects, but all of the work necessary to populate this collection was performed in the main() method of the SRS class. By way of review,

❑ We instantiated a ScheduleOfClasses object as a public static attribute of the SRS class:

```
public static ScheduleOfClasses scheduleOfClasses =
    new ScheduleOfClasses("SP2001");
```

❑ We called the scheduleSection() method on various Course objects named 'c1' through to 'c5' from the SRS main() method to instantiate seven Section objects named 'sec1' through to 'sec7', using hard coded attribute values; that code is repeated below:

```
// Schedule sections of each Course by calling the
// scheduleSection method of Course (which internally
// invokes the Section constructor).

sec1 = c1.scheduleSection('M', "8:10 - 10:00 PM", "GOVT101", 30);
sec2 = c1.scheduleSection('W', "6:10 - 8:00 PM", "GOVT202", 30);
sec3 = c2.scheduleSection('R', "4:10 - 6:00 PM", "GOVT105", 25);
sec4 = c2.scheduleSection('T', "6:10 - 8:00 PM", "SCI330", 25);
sec5 = c3.scheduleSection('M', "6:10 - 8:00 PM", "GOVT101", 20);
sec6 = c4.scheduleSection('R', "4:10 - 6:00 PM", "SCI241", 15);
sec7 = c5.scheduleSection('M', "4:10 - 6:00 PM", "ARTS25", 40);
```

❑ We then invoked the addSection() method on the scheduleOfClasses object numerous times to add these Sections to its encapsulated collection:

```
// Add these to the Schedule of Classes.

scheduleOfClasses.addSection(sec1);
scheduleOfClasses.addSection(sec2);
scheduleOfClasses.addSection(sec3);
scheduleOfClasses.addSection(sec4);
```

```
scheduleOfClasses.addSection(sec5);
scheduleOfClasses.addSection(sec6);
scheduleOfClasses.addSection(sec7);
```

Ideally, rather than hard-coding the information about these `Sections` in the `main()` method of the SRS class, we'd like to acquire this information dynamically from an ASCII file. In fact, while we are at it, it would be preferable to acquire *all* of the data needed to initialize the SRS application's primary object collections from ASCII files. This includes:

❑   The Schedule of Classes itself.

❑   The Course Catalog: that is, a list of Courses on which the Schedule of Classes is based, along with information about which Course is a prerequisite of which other(s).

❑   The Faculty Roster, along with information regarding which Professor is scheduled to teach which Section(s).

These latter two collections haven't appeared in our object model before, because they weren't necessary for fulfilling the use cases that we came up with for the SRS back in Chapter 9. These collections represent what we've spoken of before as **implementation classes**; looking ahead, we know that we're going to need these when the time comes to build our SRS user interface, so we'll go ahead and implement them now. (We're not worrying about creating a Student Body collection to house `Student` objects, for reasons that will become apparent later.)

We'll define five data files to 'feed' these three collections, as follows:

❑   `CourseCatalog.dat`: this file contains records consisting of three tab-delimited fields: a course number, a course title, and the number of credits that the course is worth, represented as a floating point number.

In other words, this data file represents the attributes of the `Course` class in our domain model. It will 'feed' the `CourseCatalog` collection.

Here are the test data contents of the file that we will use for all of the work that we will do in this chapter; '`<tab>`' represents the presence of an otherwise invisible tab character.

```
CMP101 <tab> Beginning Computer Technology <tab> 3.0

OBJ101 <tab> Object Methods for Software Development <tab> 3.0

CMP283 <tab> Higher Level Languages (Java) <tab> 3.0

CMP999 <tab> Living Brain Computers <tab> 3.0

ART101 <tab> Beginning Basketweaving <tab> 3.0
```

❑   `Faculty.dat`: this file contains records consisting of four tab-delimited fields, representing a professor's name, SSN, title, and the department that they work for, all as `Strings`.

In other words, this file represents the attributes of the `Professor` class in our domain model. It will 'feed' the `Faculty` collection.

Here is the test data that we will use:

```
Jacquie Barker <tab> 123-45-6789 <tab> Adjunct Professor <tab> Information
    Technology

John Smith <tab> 567-81-2345 <tab> Full Professor <tab> Chemistry

Snidely Whiplash <tab> 987-65-4321 <tab> Full Professor <tab> Physical
    Education
```

❏ SoC_SP2001.dat: this file contains the Schedule of Classes (SoC) information for the Spring 2001 (SP2001) semester; each tab-delimited record consists of six fields representing the course number, section number, day of the week, time of day, room, and seating capacity for the section in question.

This file represents the attributes of the Section class, *combined with* the courseNo attribute of Course, which the Section class is able to 'pull' by virtue of its one-to-many association with Course (recall our discussion of 'data flowing along an association line' from Chapter 10). In other words, it simultaneously represents Section objects as a whole as well as *links* that Section objects maintain to Course objects. It will 'feed' the ScheduleOfClasses collection.

Here is the test data that we will use:

```
CMP101 <tab> 1 <tab> M <tab> 8:10 - 10:00 PM <tab> GOVT101 <tab> 30

CMP101 <tab> 2 <tab> W <tab> 6:10 - 8:00 PM <tab> GOVT202 <tab> 30

OBJ101 <tab> 1 <tab> R <tab> 4:10 - 6:00 PM <tab> GOVT105 <tab> 25

OBJ101 <tab> 2 <tab> T <tab> 6:10 - 8:00 PM <tab> SCI330 <tab> 25

CMP283 <tab> 1 <tab> M <tab> 6:10 - 8:00 PM <tab> GOVT101 <tab> 20

CMP999 <tab> 1 <tab> R <tab> 4:10 - 6:00 PM <tab> SCI241 <tab> 15

ART101 <tab> 1 <tab> M <tab> 4:10 - 6:00 PM <tab> ARTS25 <tab> 40
```

❏ Prerequisites.dat: this file contains information about which Course, listed in the first column, is a prerequisite for which other Course, listed in the second column.

In other words, this file represents the reflexive *prerequisite* association that exists on the Course class, and the records themselves represent links between specific Course objects. It will also 'feed' the CourseCatalog collection.

Here is the test data that we will use:

```
CMP101 <tab> OBJ101

OBJ101 <tab> CMP283

CMP283 <tab> CMP999
```

- ❑ TeachingAssignments.dat: this file pairs up a Professor (whose ssn is reflected in the first column) with the Course/Section number that the professor is going to be teaching (listed in the second column).

    In other words, this file represents the *teaches* association between a Professor and a Section. It will also 'feed' the Faculty collection.

    Here is our test data:

    ```
    987-65-4321 <tab> CMP101 - 1
    567-81-2345 <tab> CMP101 - 2
    123-45-6789 <tab> OBJ101 - 1
    987-65-4321 <tab> OBJ101 - 2
    123-45-6789 <tab> CMP283 - 1
    567-81-2345 <tab> CMP999 - 1
    987-65-4321 <tab> ART101 - 1
    ```

All five of these data files are provided with the accompanying SRS code for download from the Apress web site.

Persisting Student Data

One key difference between the way that we plan on handling Student data as compared with data for the other classes mentioned above is that we are going to store each Student object's data in its own separate file, versus lumping all of the data about all Students into a single StudentBody.dat file. This will enable us to retrieve the information for just one student at a time – namely, whichever student is currently 'logged on' to the SRS – and to easily save any changes that occur to that Student's information during their SRS session when they log off. (We'll see how a student logs on in Chapter 16, when we add a GUI to our application.)

- ❑ The naming convention for a student's data file will be to use the student's Social Security Number (ssn) with a suffix of '.dat'; for example, '111-11-1111.dat'.

- ❑ At a minimum, a student's data file will contain a single *primary* record, comprised of four tab-delimited fields representing the student's ssn, name, major department, and degree sought. In other words, this record represents the attributes of the Student class in our object model.

- ❑ If the student has already registered for one or more sections in a previous SRS session, then the student's data file will also contain one or more *secondary* records, each consisting of a single field representing the **full section number** (that is, the course number followed by a hyphen, followed by the section number as an integer) of a section that the student is currently enrolled in. In other words, a secondary record represents the *attends* association in our object model, and any one record implies a link between this Student and a Section object.

We'll simulate three students in this fashion:

- ❑ 111-11-1111.dat: this student will be simulated as already having enrolled in two sections; the contents of this data file are as follows:

    ```
    111-11-1111   <tab> Joe Blow <tab> Math <tab> M.S.
    CMP101 - 1
    ART101 - 1
    ```

❏ 222-22-2222.dat: this student will be simulated as not yet having enrolled in any sections; the contents of this data file are as follows:

```
222-22-2222 <tab> Fred Schnurd <tab> Information Technology <tab> Ph. D.
```

❏ 333-33-3333.dat: this student will also be simulated as not yet having enrolled in any sections; the contents of this data file are as follows:

```
333-33-3333 <tab> Mary Smith <tab> Physics <tab> B.S.
```

As with the previous data files, all three of these are provided with the accompanying SRS code for download from the Apress web site.

Why Aren't We Going to Persist Other Object Types?

We're not worried about persisting information about any other object type besides Student, because we assume that the rest of the data is 'static': that is, during a particular login session, the user will not be able to alter Professor or Course information; all the student user will be able to do is to choose classes (sections) from the ScheduleOfClasses to register for, and/or to drop classes (sections); this merely changes the status of the *links* between a Student and various Section objects, which are stored as *secondary* records in the student's data file. In fact, we aren't even giving student users the ability to change their *primary* information: name, ssn, etc.

CollectionWrapper (Encapsulating Collections; Reading from an ASCII File)

The UML diagram below illustrates the design approach that we're going to take with regard to populating the CourseCatalog, Faculty, and ScheduleOfClasses collections.

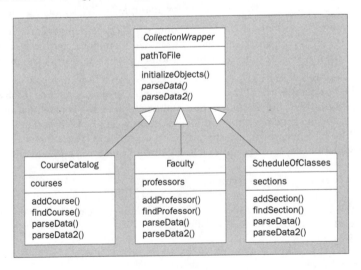

We'll first create an abstract base class called `CollectionWrapper`.

- ❏ `CollectionWrapper` will define a single attribute: namely, a `String` that holds onto the full path to the file that is currently being read, for example: `"C:\SRS\Faculty.dat"`

- ❏ It will also prescribe three behaviors:

  - ❏ The ability to read a generic ASCII file using a combination of a `BufferedReader` and a `FileReader`.

  - ❏ Two different flavors of 'parse' methods, to allow for the fact that at least two of the three subclasses will need to read two separate data files, as we've just discussed.

  - ❏ As we'll see in a moment, the `initializeObjects()` method will be a concrete method, whereas the `parseData()` and `parseData2()` method signatures will be abstract.

The three subclasses will each extend this abstract class as follows:

- ❏ They will each encapsulate a `Collection` of their own choosing:

  - ❏ The `CourseCatalog` class will call its collection `'courses'`, and will use it to store handles on `Course` objects as these are instantiated from the appropriate data file.

  - ❏ The `Faculty` class will call its collection `'professors'`, and will use it to store handles on `Professor` objects as these are instantiated from the appropriate data file.

  - ❏ The `ScheduleOfClasses` class already had a collection attribute as of the Chapter 14 version that we built, called `'sections'`, used to store handles on `Section` objects as these are instantiated from the appropriate data file.

- ❏ They will all inherit the `initializeObjects()` method 'as is', because it will be generic enough to handle routine file I/O.

- ❏ They will all need to override the `parseData()` and `parseData2()` methods in order to provide concrete method bodies; otherwise, as we learned in Chapters 7 and 13, we wouldn't be able to instantiate these three classes.

We'll step through each of these four classes, reviewing significant aspects of their class structure and method logic. We encourage you, however, to download the full set of Java source files for all of these classes from the Apress web site (http://www.apress.com) if you haven't already done so; please refer to Appendix D for the instructions on how to do this.

Since we started out this discussion talking about the `CollectionWrapper` class, let's proceed with a discussion of its methods.

initializeObjects()

We'll declare a method called `initializeObjects()` which accepts a value for, and initializes, the `pathToFile` attribute (the file path is determined and handed in to this method from the client code; that is, from the SRS class's `main()` method). The purpose of this method will be to step through the data file of interest, processing its contents one record at a time until the end of the file is reached.

We'll present the full code of the method first, and then we'll talk through it in detail:

```java
public boolean initializeObjects(String pathToFile, boolean primary) {
  this.pathToFile = pathToFile;
  String line = null;
  BufferedReader bIn = null;
  boolean outcome = true;

  try {
    // Open the file.
    bIn = new BufferedReader(new FileReader(pathToFile));

        line = bIn.readLine();
        while (line != null) {
            if (primary) parseData(line);
            else parseData2(line);
          line = bIn.readLine();
    }

    bIn.close();
  }
  catch (FileNotFoundException f) {
    outcome = false;
  }
  catch (IOException i) {
    outcome = false;
  }

  return outcome;
}
```

The method signature expects two arguments: the second of these is a `boolean` flag, to indicate whether we are going to read a primary file or a secondary file: in other words, whether we should invoke `parseData()` or `parseData2()`.

```java
public boolean initializeObjects(String pathToFile, boolean primary) {
  this.pathToFile = pathToFile;
  String line = null;
  BufferedReader bIn = null;
  boolean outcome = true;
```

After initializing a few temporary variables, we attempt to open the file with the technique of using a combination `BufferedReader/FileReader` as discussed earlier in the chapter. Note that we must wrap this code in a 'try – catch' block, because there are many environmental issues that can pose problems when accessing a computer's file system (the file may not exist; it may exist, but be locked against the attempted access; etc.).

```java
try {
  // Open the file.
  bIn = new BufferedReader(new FileReader(pathToFile));
```

We use the readLine() method of the BufferedReader class to successively read in one line/record's worth of data at a time. The readLine() method will set the value of String variable 'line' to null as a signal when the end of the file has been reached, so we use a 'while' loop to check for this condition. Within the 'while' loop, we make a call to one of two 'flavors' of parse method – either parseData() or parseData2() – depending on whether the value of primary, passed in as an argument when the initializeObjects() method was called, is set to true or false. We'll talk about what the parseData() and parseData2() methods need to do shortly.

```
line = bIn.readLine();
while (line != null) {
  if (primary) parseData(line);
  else parseData2(line);
  line = bIn.readLine();
}
```

After the end of file has been reached, the 'while' loop will automatically terminate. We then close the BufferedReader (which closes the FileReader, which closes the file itself) with the command:

```
bIn.close();
}
```

It is important to remember to close a BufferedReader when we are finished with a file for several reasons:

❑ So that the file will not remain open/locked to subsequent access.

❑ So that the application as a whole doesn't exceed the (platform dependent) maximum allowable open file limit.

❑ For the general good of freeing up unused objects so that they will be subject to garbage collection.

Our error handling in this example is not very sophisticated! We simply print out an error message, then set the 'outcome' flag to false to signal that something went wrong, so that we may return this news to whatever client code invoked the initializeObjects() method in the first place. In an industrial strength application with a GUI, for example, we might pop-up a window containing a more elaborate error message; we might record such an error in an error log file; or we might have some alternative means of recovering 'gracefully'. (An exercise at the end of Chapter 16 will request that you enhance error handling for the GUI version of the SRS application.)

```
catch (FileNotFoundException f) {
  System.out.println("FILE NOT FOUND:  " + pathToFile);
  outcome = false;
}
catch (IOException i) {
  System.out.println("IO EXCEPTION:  " + pathToFile);
  outcome = false;
}
```

Finally, we return a true/false status just prior to exiting. Note that outcome was initialized to the value true when this method first started, and will still have a true value unless something went wrong, such that an exception was triggered.

```
        return outcome;
    }
```

parseData() and parseData2()

Now, back to the `parseData()` and `parseData2()` methods. What do these methods need to do in order to process a record from a data file? Generally speaking, for each record, we'll need to

1. Break apart the record along tab-separated boundaries.

2. Call one or more constructor(s) to construct the appropriate object(s) whose attributes have been parsed from the record.

3. Create links between objects, if appropriate.

4. Finally, insert the newly created object(s) into the appropriate encapsulated collection.

The details of how these steps take place will differ widely from one data file to the next, however:

❑   In the case of the `CourseCatalog.dat` file, for example, we need to break each record into three different values – two `String` values and a `double` numeric value – along tab boundaries. Then, we'll use those values as inputs to the `Course` class constructor. Finally, we'll insert the newly created `Course` object into the `courses` collection, an attribute of the `CourseCatalog` class.

❑   For the `Faculty.dat` file, we need to break each record into four different `String` values. Then, we'll use those values to construct a `Professor` object. Finally, we'll insert the newly created `Professor` object into the `professors` collection of the `Faculty` class.

and so forth for the other three files. Since we cannot easily write a universal parsing method that can handle all of the different permutations and combinations of record formats and desired outcomes – at least not based on the amount of Java technology that we've learned so far in this book – we'll instead declare two abstract methods with the following signatures:

```
public abstract void parseData(String line);
public abstract void parseData2(String line);
```

and leave the job of working out the details of these two methods to the various classes that extend the `CollectionWrapper` class. Let's tackle these classes next.

CourseCatalog

We'll start with the `CourseCatalog` class. As mentioned earlier, we'll treat it as an encapsulated collection by adding one feature, an attribute `'courses'` declared to be a `Hashtable` that will hold `Course` object references.

```
import java.util.*;
import java.io.*;
```

```
public class CourseCatalog extends CollectionWrapper {
  //------------
  // Attributes.
  //------------

  // This Hashtable stores Course object references, using
  // the (String) course no. of the Course as the key.

  private Hashtable courses;
```

Constructor

The constructor for this class is fairly trivial:

```
public CourseCatalog() {
  // Instantiate a new Hashtable.

  courses = new Hashtable();
}
```

and there are no conventional get/set methods.

display()

We create a display() method for testing purposes, which uses an Enumeration object to step through the table, a technique that we discussed in Chapter 13.

```
// Used for testing purposes.

public void display() {
  System.out.println("Course Catalog:");
  System.out.println("");

  // Step through the Hashtable and display all entries.

  Enumeration e = courses.elements();

  while (e.hasMoreElements()) {
    Course c = (Course) e.nextElement();
    c.display();
    System.out.println("");
  }
}
```

addCourse()

We also create an addCourse() 'housekeeping' method which is used to insert a Course object reference into the encapsulated collection:

```
public void addCourse(Course c) {
  // We use the course no. as the key.
```

```
        String key = c.getCourseNo();
        courses.put(key, c);
    }
```

parseData()

In order to be able to instantiate the CourseCatalog class, we must make it concrete by providing a method body for the abstract parseData() and parseData2() methods that we've inherited from CollectionWrapper. We'll start with parseData(), which will be used to read the CourseCatalog.dat file.

Because this is such a complex method, we'll present the code in its entirety first, and will then narrate it after the fact.

```
public void parseData(String line) {
    // We're going to parse tab-delimited records into
    // three attributes -- courseNo, courseName, and credits --
    // and then call the Course constructor to fabricate a new
    // course.

    // First, make a copy of the record.

    String restOfLine = line;

    // Use the indexOf() method to search for the first
    // occurrence of a tab character. The variable "index"
    // will contain an integer pointing to the character
    // position in the record (starting with 0 for the first
    // position) of where the first tab character sits.

    int index = restOfLine.indexOf("\t");

    // We subdivide the line into two segments:  the portion
    // which precedes the tab ...

    String courseNo = restOfLine.substring(0, index);

    // ... and the portion which follows it (note that by
    // adding 1 to the value of index we have jumped past
    // the first tab character).

    restOfLine = restOfLine.substring(index+1);

    // We now search the REST of the line for the NEXT
    // tab character, and once again subdivide the
    // remainder of the record into two segments.

    index = restOfLine.indexOf("\t");
    String courseName = restOfLine.substring(0, index);
    String creditValue = restOfLine.substring(index+1);

    // We have to convert the last value into a number,
```

```
    // using a static method on the Double class to do so.

    double credits = Double.parseDouble(creditValue);

    // Finally, we call the Course constructor to create
    // an appropriate Course object, and store it in our
    // collection.

    Course c = new Course(courseNo, courseName, credits);
    addCourse(c);
  }
```

We'll now narrate selected portions of the code.

We use the indexOf() method defined by the String class to search for the first occurrence of a tab character in the record. The int variable 'index' will contain an integer value pointing to the character position in the record (counting from 0) where the first tab character sits, or a value less than zero if no tab character is found.

```
    int index = restOfLine.indexOf("\t");   // \t is a tab character
```

So, if the record that we're reading is:

```
    CMP101<tab>Beginning Computer Technology<tab>3.0
    012345   6
```

then the value of 'index' will be equal to 6.

Once we know where the tab character sits, we can use a combination of two forms of the substring() method to split the record into two pieces. The first invocation of substring(), which takes two integer arguments:

```
    String courseNo = restOfLine.substring(0, index);
```

copies everything from the beginning of the record up to, but **not** including, the 6th character position – that is, up to but not including the tab character:

```
    CMP101│<tab>Beginning Computer Technology<tab>3.0
    012345   6
```

The String variable 'courseNo' now contains the value 'CMP101', which is indeed the course number.

The second invocation of substring(), which takes only one integer argument, jumps past the tab character by adding 1 to the value of 'index', and pulls everything from that 7th character position to the end of the line:

```
    restOfLine = restOfLine.substring(index+1);
```

```
    CMP101 <tab>│Beginning Computer Technology<tab>3.0
    012345   6   7
```

so the result of this call is to copy the value `'Beginning Computer Technology<tab>3.0'` into `String` variable `'restOfLine'`.

We repeat the process a second time, looking for the next tab character in `restOfLine`:

```
index = restOfLine.indexOf("\t");
```

which occurs at position 29.

```
Beginning Computer Technology<tab>3.0
012345 ...                         29
```

Again, using the appropriate calls to `substring()`, we split the remainder of the record into two pieces, the result being that `String` variable `'courseName'` receives a copy of the `String` value `'Beginning Computer Technology'`, and `'creditValue'` receives the `String` value `'3.0'`.

```
String courseName = restOfLine.substring(0, index);
String creditValue = restOfLine.substring(index+1);
```

We now have three `String` variables – `courseNo`, `courseName`, and `creditValue` – correctly parsed. But, there's one small problem: the method signature for the `Course` constructor, shown below:

```
public Course(String cNo, String cName, double credits) { ... }
```

expects to be handed a `double` value for the credit value of the course, not a `String` value! So, we have to convert the `String` stored in variable `'creditValue'` into a `double`, using the static `parseDouble()` method of the `Double` class (one of the wrapper classes we learned about in Chapter 13) to do so:

```
double credits = Double.parseDouble(creditValue);
```

We're finally ready to call the `Course` constructor to create an appropriate `Course` object, and to store it in our collection by calling the `addCourse()` method.

```
      Course c = new Course(courseNo, courseName, credits);
      addCourse(c);
    }
```

Please note that we provided virtually no error checking in the `parseData()` method. We are assuming that the `CourseCatalog.dat` file is perfectly formatted, which is a risky assumption! One of the exercises at the end of this chapter will give you a chance to make this code more robust.

findCourse()

We also provide a convenience method, `findCourse()`, to enable client code to easily retrieve a particular `Course` object from this collection based on its course number. If the requested course number is not found, the value `null` will be returned by this method:

```
  public Course findCourse(String courseNo) {
    return (Course) courses.get(courseNo);
  }
```

Providing such a method hides the fact that the collection is implemented as a `Hashtable`: client code simply invokes the method and gets handed back a `Course` object, without any idea as to what is happening behind the scenes, as simulated by the following hypothetical client code 'snippet':

```
// Sample client code

CourseCatalog courseCatalog = new CourseCatalog();
// ...
Course c = courseCatalog.findCourse("ART101");
```

parseData2()

We're not quite done yet. We must read a second file, `Prerequisites.dat`, which defines course prerequisites, so that we may properly link our newly created `Course` objects together. (We have to do this as a separate second step after all `Course` objects have been created via the `parseData()` method so that we don't wind up with a 'chicken or egg' situation – namely, needing to hook together two `Course`s that don't both exist yet.)

So, let's now provide a body for the abstract `parseData2()` method. Because the logic of the `parseData2()` method is so similar to the `parseData()` method, we won't discuss all of its logic in detail, but *will* point out one interesting 'twist' below:

```
public void parseData2(String line) {
    // We're going to parse tab-delimited records into
    // two values, representing the courseNo "A" of
    // a course that serves as a prerequisite for
    // courseNo "B".

    // First, make a copy of the record.

    String restOfLine = line;
    int index = restOfLine.indexOf("\t");
    String courseNoA = restOfLine.substring(0, index);
    String courseNoB = restOfLine.substring(index+1);
```

Because we wish to link together two preexisting `Course` objects via the `addPrerequisite()` method of the `Course` class, we have to obtain handles on these objects. We do so by using our `findCourse()` method to look up the two course numbers that we've just parsed. Only if we are successful in finding both `Course`s in our internal `Hashtable` – that is, only if both `Course` references 'a' and 'b' have non-`null` values – will we invoke the `addPrerequisite()` method on 'b', passing in a reference to 'a':

```
    // Look these two courses up in the CourseCatalog.

    Course a = findCourse(courseNoA);
    Course b = findCourse(courseNoB);
    if (a != null && b != null) {
      b.addPrerequisite(a);
    }
}
```

Adding a 'Test Scaffold' main() Method

In Chapter 13, we discussed the fact that the Java Virtual Machine (JVM) looks for a method with a particular signature:

```
public static void main(String[] args)
```

in whatever class we designate on the command line when we start up the application. As an example, to run the SRS application we'd type:

java SRS

and the JVM would invoke the main() method contained within the SRS.class file. It is permissible, however, to have more than one main() method sprinkled throughout an application's classes; only one of these will serve as the 'official' main method for purposes of driving the application, however. So, what would we use the other main() methods for? As testing drivers, or 'scaffolds', for putting a single class through its paces.

As an example, if we now wish to test the CourseCatalog class to ensure that it:

❑ Properly parses the CourseCatalog.dat and Prerequisites.dat files

❑ Instantiates all Course objects correctly

❑ Links prerequisites appropriately

❑ Stores them all in the 'courses' Hashtable encapsulated within the CourseCatalog class

We *could* run the full-blown SRS application. However, we'd have to jump ahead and modify the SRS class's main() method to take advantage of the CourseCatalog class and all of its various methods in order to do this. A simpler approach is to provide the CourseCatalog class with its *own* main() method, as follows:

```
// Test scaffold.

public static void main(String[] args) {

    // We instantiate a CourseCatalog object ...

    CourseCatalog cc = new CourseCatalog();

    // ... cause it to read both the CourseCatalog.dat and
    // Prerequisites.dat files, thereby testing both
    // the parseData() and parseData2() methods internally
    // to the initializeObjects() method ...

    cc.initializeObjects("CourseCatalog.dat", true);
    cc.initializeObjects("Prerequisites.dat", false);
```

```
        // ... and use its display() method to demonstrate the
        // results!

        cc.display();
    }
```

With the addition of this main() method to class CourseCatalog, we can now compile CourseCatalog.java, and run it from the command line as:

```
java CourseCatalog
```

The following output would be produced as a result of the invocation of cc.display():

Course Catalog:

Course Information:
  Course No.: CMP101
  Course Name: Beginning Computer Technology
  Credits: 3.0
  Prerequisite Courses:
   (none)
  Offered As Section(s):

Course Information:
  Course No.: CMP283
  Course Name: Higher Level Languages (Java)
  Credits: 3.0
  Prerequisite Courses:
   OBJ101: Object Methods for Software Development
  Offered As Section(s):

Course Information:
  Course No.: CMP999
  Course Name: Living Brain Computers
  Credits: 3.0
  Prerequisite Courses:
   CMP283: Higher Level Languages (Java)
  Offered As Section(s):

Course Information:
  Course No.: ART101
  Course Name: Beginning Basketweaving
  Credits: 3.0
  Prerequisite Courses:
   (none)
  Offered As Section(s):

Course Information:
  Course No.: OBJ101
  Course Name: Object Methods for Software Development
  Credits: 3.0

Prerequisite Courses:
   CMP101: Beginning Computer Technology
Offered As Section(s):

thus demonstrating that our code does indeed work!

Note that there is no harm in leaving this main() method in the CourseCatalog class even after our testing is finished – in fact, it is a handy thing to keep around in case we change the details of how any of these methods work later on, and want to retest it.

Faculty

Next, we'll create the Faculty class, which is used to populate a Hashtable with Professor objects by reading their pertinent information from two data files:

❑   Faculty.dat, the primary file used as the basis for creating the Professors.

❑   TeachingAssignments.dat, a secondary file used for linking Professor objects to the Section objects that they are assigned to teach, and vice versa.

Since the structure and behaviors of the Faculty class are so similar to that of CourseCatalog, we won't explain the Faculty class in detail, but will point out one interesting nuance regarding the parseData2() method.

parseData2()

```
// This next version is used when reading in the file that defines
// teaching assignments.

public void parseData2(String line) {
    // We're going to parse tab-delimited records into
    // two values, representing the professor's SSN
    // and the section number that they are going to teach.

    // First, make a copy of the record.

    String restOfLine = line;
    int index = restOfLine.indexOf("\t");
    String ssn = restOfLine.substring(0, index);

    // The full section number is a concatenation of the
    // course no. and section no., separated by a hyphen;
    // for example, "ART101 - 1".

    String fullSectionNo = restOfLine.substring(index+1);
```

Just as we did in the parseData2() method of CourseCatalog, we are linking together two objects here, and so we need to first verify that both objects do indeed exist, and obtain handles on them. But, unlike the parseData2() method of CourseCatalog, where both objects were Courses, and hence both objects were stored in the Hashtable internal to the CourseCatalog class, here we have a situation where one of the objects (a Professor) is stored in our own internal 'professors'

Hashtable, but the other object (a Section) is stored in a collection elsewhere in our application: namely, in the scheduleOfClasses collection that we have defined as an attribute of the main SRS class. However, by declaring that collection to be a public static attribute of the SRS class, we have in essence made it globally visible/accessible to the entire application, which enables us to reference it as highlighted below:

```
// Look these two objects up in the appropriate collections.
// Note that having made scheduleOfClasses a public
// static attribute of the SRS class helps!

Professor p = findProfessor(ssn);
Section s = SRS.scheduleOfClasses.findSection(fullSectionNo);
if (p != null && s != null) p.agreeToTeach(s);
}
```

Adding a 'Test Scaffold' main() Method

Just as we did for CourseCatalog, we also provide a test scaffold main() method for the Faculty class. We are a bit constrained with regard to testing the full functionality of Faculty in this manner, however: because the parseData2() method expects to access the SRS.scheduleOfClasses collection object, and because we won't have instantiated that object through our test scaffold, we cannot put the parseData2() method through its paces without running the full-blown SRS application. Nonetheless, we'll go ahead and test our code for reading the primary file, 'Faculty.dat'.

```
// Test scaffold.
public static void main(String[] args) {
  Faculty f = new Faculty();
  f.initializeObjects("Faculty.dat", true);

  // We cannot test the next feature, because the code
  // of parseData2() expects the SRS.scheduleOfClasses
  // collection object to have been instantiated, but
  // it will not have been if we are running this test
  // scaffold instead.
  // f.initializeObjects("TeachingAssignments.dat", false);

  f.display();
}
```

Revamping ScheduleOfClasses

Next, we'll retrofit the ScheduleOfClasses class that we developed in Chapter 14 with this same ability to 'self-initialize' from an ASCII file. To do so, we'll start by indicating that we want ScheduleOfClasses to extend CollectionWrapper:

```
public class ScheduleOfClasses extends CollectionWrapper {
```

By doing so, we will inherit the initializeObjects() method of CollectionWrapper, which will give us all of the generic file manipulation capability that we need. Note that we can do so after the fact without disturbing any of the code that we've already written and tested for ScheduleOfClasses from Chapter 14!

Next, we must provide a method body for the abstract `parseData()` method that we inherited; since it is so similar to the `parseData()` methods of both the `Faculty` and `CourseCatalog` classes, we won't discuss it in detail, but simply present its code here.

parseData()

```java
public void parseData(String line) {
    // We're going to parse tab-delimited records into
    // six attributes -- courseNo, sectionNo, dayOfWeek,
    // timeOfDay, room, and capacity. We'll use courseNo to
    // look up the appropriate Course object, and will then
    // call the scheduleSection() method to fabricate a
    // new Section object.

    // First, make a copy of the record.

    String restOfLine = line;
    int index = restOfLine.indexOf("\t");
    String courseNo = restOfLine.substring(0, index);
    restOfLine = restOfLine.substring(index+1);
    index = restOfLine.indexOf("\t");

    // We have to parse the next value as a number.

    String sectionNumber = restOfLine.substring(0, index);
    int sectionNo = Integer.parseInt(sectionNumber);
    restOfLine = restOfLine.substring(index+1);

    index = restOfLine.indexOf("\t");
    String dayOfWeek = restOfLine.substring(0, index);
    restOfLine = restOfLine.substring(index+1);
    index = restOfLine.indexOf("\t");
    String timeOfDay = restOfLine.substring(0, index);
    restOfLine = restOfLine.substring(index+1);
    index = restOfLine.indexOf("\t");
    String room = restOfLine.substring(0, index);

    // We have to parse the last value as a number.

    String capacityValue = restOfLine.substring(index+1);
    int capacity = Integer.parseInt(capacityValue);

    // Look up the Course object in the Course Catalog.
    // Having made courseCatalog a public static attribute
    // of the SRS class comes in handy!

    Course c = SRS.courseCatalog.findCourse(courseNo);

    // Schedule the Section.

    Section s = c.scheduleSection(sectionNo, dayOfWeek.charAt(0),
                timeOfDay, room, capacity);
    addSection(s);
}
```

parseData2()

There is one minor flaw in our application design. Unlike both the CourseCatalog and Faculty classes, which each required us to read both a primary and a secondary data file when initializing their respective Hashtables, we do not have a need at present to read and parse a secondary file when loading the ScheduleOfClasses Hashtable; all of the information that we need to process is contained within the SoC_SP2001.dat file, which is handled by the parseData() method. So, we really don't have a need for a parseData2() method in the ScheduleOfClasses class. But, because we have chosen to extend the CollectionWrapper class, we are forced to implement such a method; otherwise, the ScheduleOfClasses class will be deemed abstract by the compiler, and we won't be able to instantiate it in the main() method of the SRS class.

To work around this dilemma, we 'stub out' a parseData2() method with an empty method body, as follows:

```
public void parseData2(String line) { }
```

This makes the compiler happy and, since we have no intention of ever calling this method anyway, no serious harm is done. However, this breaks (or at least severely bends!) the spirit of the 'is a' relationship of inheritance. Strictly speaking, if the ScheduleOfClasses class has no need for a parseData2() method, then we shouldn't declare it to be a subclass of CollectionWrapper. But, if we didn't inherit the methods of CollectionWrapper, we'd then have to code an initializeObjects() method for the ScheduleOfClasses class from scratch to replace the one that it is no longer inheriting from CollectionWrapper, which would complicate our application in a different way, by introducing code redundancy. So, doing what we have done by extending CollectionWrapper and 'stubbing out' the parseData2() method seems like a reasonable compromise.

> *There is also an advanced Java technique that involves passing a method as an argument to another method; using such a technique, we could modify the* initializeObjects() *method of* CollectionWrapper *so that there would be no need for any of our collection classes to declare a* parseData2() *method. Discussing such a technique is beyond the scope of this book to address.*

findSection()

As we did for the CourseCatalog and Faculty classes, we provide ScheduleOfClasses with a convenience method for looking up a particular Section based upon the full section number, which is defined here as being a concatenation of course number and section number, separated by a hyphen; for example, 'ART101 – 1':

```
public Section findSection(String fullSectionNo) {
  return (Section) sections.get(fullSectionNo);
}
```

Test Scaffolding?

We cannot provide a simple test scaffold main() method for the ScheduleOfClasses class as we did for CourseCatalog and Faculty; this is due to the fact that the parseData() method of the ScheduleOfClasses object will attempt to access the SRS.courseCatalog, which will not have been initialized.

Course Modifications

There is only one minor change to be made to the Course class to accommodate our new file persistence scheme.

Because we are now reading in a *predetermined* section number from the SoC_SP2001.dat file, we must modify the scheduleSection() method of the Course class so that it no longer automatically assigns a 'one-up' section number to each Section.

Here is the original code for the scheduleSection() method from Chapter 14; the highlighted code shows that we were automatically determining how many sections had already been created and stored in the offeredAsSection collection (an attribute of Course), and bumping that up by one to create a section number on the fly.

```
public Section scheduleSection(char day, String time, String room,
    int capacity) {
    // Create a new Section (note the creative way in
    // which we are assigning a section number) ...
    Section s = new Section(offeredAsSection.size() + 1,
        day, time, this, room, capacity);

    // ... and then remember it!
    offeredAsSection.addElement(s);

    return s;
}
```

In our new, modified version of this method, shown below, we've added an argument, secNo, to enable us to simply hand in the section number as read in from the data file.

```
public Section scheduleSection(int secNo, char day, String time,
    String room, int capacity) {
    // Create a new Section (note that we're now assigning
    // the section number by passing it in).
    Section s = new Section(secNo, day, time, this, room, capacity);

    // ... and then remember it!
    offeredAsSection.addElement(s);

    return s;
}
```

The Student Class (Dynamic Data Retrieval; Persisting Object State)

Aside from a minor change to the scheduleSection() method of the Course class that we just discussed, and the 'refurbishing' of the ScheduleOfClasses class that we previously discussed, the only other domain class that we wish to enhance among those that we created in Chapter 14 is the Student class. To demonstrate the techniques of dynamic data retrieval and data persistence, we are going to:

❑   Modify the `Student` class's constructor to read data from a student's data file, to be used in initializing attributes.

❑   Add a `persist()` method that can be called from the `SRS main()` method when a student logs off, to persist the student's state back to his/her data file.

Much of the `Student` class's code remains unchanged from the way that it was presented in Chapter 14, so we'll only touch upon the significant changes that we've made to the class here.

Initializing a Student's State

The first significant change that we've made is in the `Student` class constructor. Because this code is fairly involved, we'll present the constructor here in its entirety first, and will then narrate it.

```
//----------------
// Constructor(s).
//----------------

public Student(String ssn) {
  // First, construct a "dummy" Student object. Then,
  // attempt to pull this Student's information from the
  // appropriate file (ssn.dat:  e.g., 111-11-1111.dat).
  // The file consists of a header record, containing
  // the student's basic info. (ssn, name, etc.), and
  // 0 or more subsequent records representing a list of
  // the sections that he/she is currently registered for.

  this();

  String line = null;
  BufferedReader bIn = null;
  boolean outcome = true;

  // Formulate the file name.

  String pathToFile = ssn + ".dat";

  try {
    // Open the file.

    bIn = new BufferedReader(new FileReader(pathToFile));

    // The first line in the file contains the header
    // information, so we use parseData() to process it.

    line = bIn.readLine();
    if (line != null) parseData(line);

    // Remaining lines (if there are any) contain
    // section references. Note that we must
    // instantiate an empty vector so that the
    // parseData2() method may insert
    // items into the Vector.
```

```
      attends = new Vector();

      line = bIn.readLine();

      // If there were no secondary records in the file,
      // this "while" loop won't execute at all.

      while (line != null) {
        parseData2(line);
        line = bIn.readLine();
      }

      bIn.close();
    }
    catch (FileNotFoundException f) {
      // Since we are encoding a "dummy" Student to begin
      // with, the fact that his/her name will be equal
      // to "???" flags an error. We have included
      // a boolean method successfullyInitialized()
      // which allows client code to verify the success
      // or failure of this constructor (see code below).
      // So, we needn't do anything special in this
      // "catch" clause!
    }
    catch (IOException i) {
      // See comments for FileNotFoundException above;
      // we needn't do anything special in this
      // "catch" clause, either!
    }

    // Create a brand new Transcript.
    // (Ideally, we'd read in an existing Transcript from
    // a file, but we're not bothering to do so in this
    // example).

    setTranscript(new Transcript(this));
  }
```

Before we discuss the preceding constructor in depth, let's take a look at the 'no args' constructor that we have created for the student class, because as we learned in Chapter 13, if we overload the constructor signature for a class, then the default 'no args' constructor is lost unless we explicitly replace it.

All of the attributes are set to the value '???' in this constructor; as we'll see later, if these never get overwritten with the proper values from a Student's file, then we'll be able to detect that an error has occurred.

```
    // A second form of constructor, used when a Student's data
    // file cannot be found for some reason.

    public Student() {
      // Reuse the code of the parent's (Person) constructor.
```

```
        // Question marks indicate that something went wrong!

        super("???", "???");

        setMajor("???");
        setDegree("???");

        // Placeholders for the remaining attributes (this
        // Student is invalid anyway).

        setTranscript(new Transcript(this));
        attends = new Vector();
    }
```

Let's walk through the first constructor. Now, rather than simply passing in hard coded attributes via the constructor method signature, we are going to attempt to read these from the appropriate student data file. Therefore, the constructor signature now expects only one argument: the Student-to-be-constructed's ssn, which will be used to formulate the data file name (*ssn*.dat)

```
        public Student(String ssn) {
```

We'll start by constructing a 'dummy' Student object, using the 'no args' Student constructor. Recall that the keyword 'this' allows us to self-reference when running another of our constructors, a concept that was discussed in Chapter 13.

```
        this();
```

Next, we'll attempt to open and read the appropriate data file, using a technique very similar to the technique used in the initializeObjects() method of CollectionWrapper. (If we were to have made Student a subclass of CollectionWrapper, then we could have simply inherited initializeObjects(); but, such inheritance would truly compromise the 'is a' relationship – far more severely than we did with the ScheduleOfClasses class (when we knew it didn't need to parse two files, but extended CollectionWrapper anyway) – because a Student is clearly not a collection! So, we resist the urge to 'misuse' inheritance, and instead write code that looks remarkably similar to the initializeObjects() method.)

```
        String line = null;
        BufferedReader bIn = null;
        boolean outcome = true;

        // Formulate the file name.
        String pathToFile = ssn + ".dat";

        try {
          // Open the file.

          bIn = new BufferedReader(new FileReader(pathToFile));
```

Note that we use two different methods once again – parseData() and parseData2() – but back to back in this case, because although we are only reading one student data file, there are two different record formats within a single file: the primary record containing student information, and zero or more secondary records containing section numbers for which the student has registered.

```
        // The first line in the file contains the header information,
        // so we use parseData() to process it.

        line = bIn.readLine();
        if (line != null) parseData(line);

        // Remaining lines (if there are any) contain section references.
        // Note that we must instantiate an empty vector so that the
        // parseData2() method may insert items into the Vector.

        attends = new Vector();

        line = bIn.readLine();

        // If there were no secondary records in the file, this
        // "while" loop won't execute at all.

        while (line != null) {
            parseData2(line);
            line = bIn.readLine();
        }

        bIn.close();
    }
```

If anything goes wrong while attempting to read the student's data file (the file isn't found; or cannot be accessed; or it contains incorrectly formatted data), then one or the other of the 'catch' clauses will be invoked. But, since we've already gone to the trouble of executing the generic constructor (with no arguments) as the first step of this constructor, then we have a 'bare bones' (albeit somewhat useless) Student object full of '???'.

There really isn't any way for a constructor to return an error flag (say, a boolean true/false) – by definition, a constructor returns an object (of type Student, in this case) – so we have to devise an alternative way for the client code to detect whether or not the Student object initialization succeeded or failed. We'll do so by creating a separate method called studentSuccessfullyInitialized() in a moment.

```
        catch (FileNotFoundException f) {
            // Since we are encoding a "dummy" Student to begin
            // with, the fact that their name will be equal
            // to "???" flags an error. We have included
            // a boolean method studentSuccessfullyInitialized()
            // which allows client code to verify the success
            // or failure of this constructor (see code below).
            // So, we needn't do anything special in this catch
            // clause!
        }
        catch (IOException i) {
            // See comments for FileNotFoundException above;
            // we needn't do anything special in this catch
            // clause, either!
        }
```

```
    // Create a brand new Transcript.
    // (Ideally, we'd read in an existing Transcript from
    // a file, but we're not bothering to do so in this
    // example).

    setTranscript(new Transcript(this));
}
```

studentSuccessfullyInitialized()

We were concerned about how to return failure status from a constructor. This turns out to be a rather simple matter: since we have created a 'dummy' Student to begin with, the fact that the student's name will be equal to '???' constitutes an error. So, we provide a boolean method, studentSuccessfullyInitialized(), to allow client code to verify the success or failure of this constructor after the fact.

```
    // Used after the constructor is called to verify whether or not
    // there were any file access errors.

    public boolean studentSuccessfullyInitialized() {
      if (getName().equals("???")) return false;
      else return true;
    }
```

Here is an example of how the preceding method would be used in client code (say, in the main() method of the SRS application):

```
    // Excerpt from the main() method of SRS:

    String ssn;

    // Obtain an ssn value as a user input when they log on (details omitted; we'll
    // see how this is done via a GUI in Chapter 16).

    // Invoke the new form of Student constructor, which will attempt to read the
    // appropriate data file behind the scenes.

    Student s = new Student(ssn);

    // Now, check to see if the Student's data was successfully retrieved!

    if (s.studentSuccessfullyInitialized()) {
      // Success! Do whatever is appropriate in this case ...
    }
    else {
      // Failure! Do whatever is appropriate in this case ...
    }
```

parseData()

Because the logic of the parseData() and parseData2() methods of Student is so similar to the parseData() and parseData2() methods that we've discussed for these other classes, we won't review them in detail here, but merely present their code:

457

```
public void parseData(String line) {
    // We're going to parse tab-delimited records into
    // four attributes -- ssn, name, major, and degree.

    // First, make a copy of the record.

    String restOfLine = line;
    int index = restOfLine.indexOf("\t");
    setSsn(restOfLine.substring(0, index));
    restOfLine = restOfLine.substring(index+1);
    index = restOfLine.indexOf("\t");
    setName(restOfLine.substring(0, index));
    restOfLine = restOfLine.substring(index+1);
    index = restOfLine.indexOf("\t");
    setMajor(restOfLine.substring(0, index));
    setDegree(restOfLine.substring(index+1));
}
```

parseData2()

```
public void parseData2(String line) {
    // The full section number is a concatenation of the
    // course no. and section no., separated by a hyphen;
    // for example, "ART101 - 1".

    String fullSectionNo = line.trim();
    Section s = SRS.scheduleOfClasses.findSection(fullSectionNo);

    // Note that we are using the Section class's enroll()
    // method to ensure that bidirectionality is established
    // between the Student and the Section.
    s.enroll(this);
}
```

We've now provided all of the code necessary to dynamically retrieve a student's information whenever they log on to the SRS. We'll demonstrate how to simulate a logon in order to test this code when we talk about changes to the SRS class's main() method in a few moments. Before we do so, however, there is one more important enhancement that we wish to make to the Student class, having to do with persisting the results of a student's registration session.

Persisting the State of a Student

During the course of an SRS session, the student will presumably be registering for sections and/or perhaps dropping sections. So, the state of the Student object representing that student – namely the attribute values of the Student object and all links maintained by that Student object with other objects (in particular, with Section objects in which the student is enrolled) – is likely to change.

We must provide a way for the SRS to 'remember' these changes from one logon session to the next; otherwise, the SRS system will be of no practical value. So, we are going to provide a method to persist a Student object's state whenever the student logs off: specifically, we are going to write information about this Student back out to the same data file that we originally used to initialize the Student object's state in the constructor.

```
// This method writes out all of the student's information to
// their ssn.dat file when they log off.

public boolean persist() {
```

We use the approach discussed earlier in the chapter of using a `FileOutputStream` and `PrintWriter` object combination to write to the student's data file.

```
FileOutputStream fos = null;
PrintWriter pw = null;
try {
  // Attempt to create the ssn.dat file. Note that
  // the FileOutputStream will overwrite one if it already
  // exists, which is what we want to happen.

  fos = new FileOutputStream(getSsn() + ".dat");
  pw = new PrintWriter(fos);

  // First, we output the header record as a tab-delimited
  // record.

  pw.println(getSsn() + "\t" + getName() + "\t" +
      getMajor() + "\t" + getDegree());

  // Then, we output one record for every Section that
  // the Student is enrolled in.

  for (int i = 0; i < attends.size(); i++) {
    Section s = (Section) attends.elementAt(i);
    pw.println(s.getFullSectionNo());
  }
  pw.close();
}
```

It is important to remember to close the `PrintWriter` when we are finished with the file (which in turn closes the `FileOutputStream`, which in turn closes the file itself) for several reasons:

- So that the file will not remain open/locked to subsequent access.

- So that the application as a whole doesn't exceed the (platform dependent) maximum allowable open file limit.

- For the general good of freeing up unused objects so that they will be subject to garbage collection.

If anything went wrong during the persistence process (such as the file could not be opened or written to), the following 'catch' block is triggered. In this case, we'll return a `boolean` value of `false` to signal to the client code that something went wrong, and will allow the client code to determine what needs to be done as a result (whether some error message needs to be displayed to the user, or whether some alternative recovery mechanism needs to be engaged):

```
      catch (IOException e) {
        // Signal that an error has occurred.

        return false;
      }

      // All is well!
      return true;
    }
```

Revisiting the SRS Class

Having encapsulated so much functionality into the ScheduleOfCourses, CourseCatalog, and Faculty classes allows us to *dramatically* simplify the main() method for the SRS 'driver' class; let's revisit that class to see how it should be changed to accommodate all that we've done in this chapter.

First, in addition to the public static 'scheduleOfClasses' attribute that we provided in Chapter 14, we now will provide two more such attributes: 'faculty' and 'courseCatalog':

```
  // SRS.java

  // A main driver for the command-line driven version of the SRS, with
  // file persistence added.

  import java.util.*;

  public class SRS {
    // We can effectively create "global" data by declaring
    // public static attributes in the main class.

    // Entry points/"roots" for getting at objects.

    public static Faculty faculty = new Faculty();

    public static CourseCatalog courseCatalog = new CourseCatalog();

    public static ScheduleOfClasses scheduleOfClasses =
        new ScheduleOfClasses("SP2001");

    // We don't create a collection for Student objects, because
    // we're only going to handle one Student at a time -- namely,
    // whichever Student is logged on.
```

In the main() method, we take advantage of our initializeObjects() method to read data from the various ASCII files that we've provided, automatically initializing the 'faculty', 'courseCatalog' and 'scheduleOfClasses' collections with the appropriate objects.

```
    public static void main(String[] args) {
      // Initialize the key objects by reading data from files.
      // Setting the second argument to true causes the
      // initializeObjects() method to use the parseData()
```

```
         // method instead of parseData2().

         faculty.initializeObjects("Faculty.dat", true);
         courseCatalog.initializeObjects("CourseCatalog.dat", true);
         scheduleOfClasses.initializeObjects("SoC_SP2001.dat", true);
```

We'll handle the students differently: that is, rather than loading them all in at application outset, we'll pull in the data that we need just for one Student when that Student logs on, as we saw when we reviewed the 'new and improved' Student class constructor earlier in this chapter. Because we do not yet have a mechanism to allow a user to log on – we'll provide that in Chapter 16 – we'll temporarily create a few Student objects by hard-coding calls to the Student constructor, to simulate Students logging on. This enables us to exercise and test the enhanced Student class constructor. Note that only the first of these Students has 'preregistered' for courses based on the content of their *ssn*.dat file, as discussed earlier.

```
         // Let's temporarily create Students this way as a test,
         // to simulate Students logging on. Note that only the
         // first Student has "preregistered" for courses based
         // on the content of their ssn.dat file (see Student.java
         // for details).

         Student s1 = new Student("111-11-1111");
         Student s2 = new Student("222-22-2222");
         Student s3 = new Student("333-33-3333");
```

We invoke the initializeObjects() method a second time for the CourseCatalog and Faculty classes, respectively, to enable us to read their respective supplemental data files:

```
         // Establish some prerequisites (c1 => c2 => c3 => c4).
         // Setting the second argument to false causes the
         // initializeObjects() method to use the parseData2()
         // method instead of parseData().
```

```
         courseCatalog.initializeObjects("Prerequisites.dat", false);
```

```
         // Recruit a professor to teach each of the sections.
         // Setting the second argument to false causes the
         // initializeObjects() method to use the parseData2()
         // method instead of parseData().
```

```
         faculty.initializeObjects("TeachingAssignments.dat", false);
```

Now, we'll simulate having Student 's2' enroll in a Section, so that we may exercise and test the persist() method. We use the findSection() convenience method of the ScheduleOfClasses class to obtain a handle on a Section object based on a particular course and section number, and then use the enroll() method of the Section class to bidirectionally enroll Student 's2' in that Section:

```
         // Let's have one Student try enrolling in something, so
         // that we can simulate their logging off and persisting
         // the enrollment data in the ssn.dat file (see Student.java
```

```
// for details).

Section sec = scheduleOfClasses.findSection("ART101 - 1");
sec.enroll(s2);
```

Now, we invoke the `persist()` method on `Student` object s2.

```
s2.persist();  // Check contents of 222-22-2222.dat!
```

Before running the SRS application, the contents of the `222-22-2222.dat` file consisted of a single record as follows:

```
222-22-2222 <tab> Fred Schnurd <tab> Information Technology <tab> Ph. D.
```

because this student was not enrolled in any sections. After running the SRS application, if we inspect the contents of the `222-22-2222.dat` file, we find that a record has been added to persist the fact that this student is now enrolled in ART101 section 1:

```
222-22-2222 <tab> Fred Schnurd <tab> Information Technology <tab> Ph. D.
ART101 - 1
```

so the `persist()` method is indeed working!

To round out our testing, we include a few calls to the `display()` methods of our various collection objects:

```
// Let's see if everything got initialized properly
// by calling various display methods!

System.out.println("====================");
System.out.println("Course Catalog:");
System.out.println("====================");
System.out.println("");
courseCatalog.display();

System.out.println("====================");
System.out.println("Schedule of Classes:");
System.out.println("====================");
System.out.println("");
scheduleOfClasses.display();

System.out.println("======================");
System.out.println("Professor Information:");
System.out.println("======================");
System.out.println("");
faculty.display();

System.out.println("====================");
System.out.println("Student Information:");
System.out.println("====================");
```

```
        System.out.println("");
        s1.display();
        System.out.println("");
        s2.display();
        System.out.println("");
        s3.display();
    }
}
```

The output produced by running this program is as follows:

```
====================
Course Catalog:
====================

Course Catalog:

Course Information:
 Course No.: CMP101
 Course Name: Beginning Computer Technology
 Credits: 3.0
 Prerequisite Courses:
  (none)
 Offered As Section(s): 1 2

Course Information:
 Course No.: CMP283
 Course Name: Higher Level Languages (Java)
 Credits: 3.0
 Prerequisite Courses:
  OBJ101: Object Methods for Software Development
 Offered As Section(s): 1

Course Information:
 Course No.: CMP999
 Course Name: Living Brain Computers
 Credits: 3.0
 Prerequisite Courses:
  CMP283: Higher Level Languages (Java)
 Offered As Section(s): 1

Course Information:
 Course No.: ART101
 Course Name: Beginning Basketweaving
 Credits: 3.0
 Prerequisite Courses:
  (none)
 Offered As Section(s): 1

Course Information:
 Course No.: OBJ101
 Course Name: Object Methods for Software Development
```

Credits: 3.0
Prerequisite Courses:
  CMP101: Beginning Computer Technology
Offered As Section(s): 1 2


```
===================
```
Schedule of Classes:
```
===================
```

Schedule of Classes for SP2001

Section Information:
  Semester: SP2001
  Course No.: CMP101
  Section No: 2
  Offered: W at 6:10 - 8:00 PM
  In Room: GOVT202
  Professor: John Smith
  Total of 0 students enrolled.

Section Information:
  Semester: SP2001
  Course No.: CMP101
  Section No: 1
  Offered: M at 8:10 - 10:00 PM
  In Room: GOVT101
  Professor: Snidely Whiplash
  Total of 1 students enrolled, as follows:
    Joe Blow

Section Information:
  Semester: SP2001
  Course No.: CMP283
  Section No: 1
  Offered: M at 6:10 - 8:00 PM
  In Room: GOVT101
  Professor: Jacquie Barker
  Total of 0 students enrolled.

Section Information:
  Semester: SP2001
  Course No.: CMP999
  Section No: 1
  Offered: R at 4:10 - 6:00 PM
  In Room: SCI241
  Professor: John Smith
  Total of 0 students enrolled.

Section Information:
  Semester: SP2001
  Course No.: OBJ101
  Section No: 2

Offered: T at 6:10 - 8:00 PM
In Room: SCI330
Professor: Snidely Whiplash
Total of 0 students enrolled.

Section Information:
 Semester: SP2001
 Course No.: OBJ101
 Section No: 1
 Offered: R at 4:10 - 6:00 PM
 In Room: GOVT105
 Professor: Jacquie Barker
 Total of 0 students enrolled.

Section Information:
 Semester: SP2001
 Course No.: ART101
 Section No: 1
 Offered: M at 4:10 - 6:00 PM
 In Room: ARTS25
 Professor: Snidely Whiplash
 Total of 2 students enrolled, as follows:
  Fred Schnurd
  Joe Blow

=======================
Professor Information:
=======================

Faculty:

Person Information:
 Name: John Smith
 Soc. Security No.: 567-81-2345
Professor-Specific Information:
 Title: Full Professor
 Teaches for Dept.: Chemistry
Teaching Assignments for John Smith:
 Course No.: CMP101
 Section No.: 2
 Course Name: Beginning Computer Technology
 Day and Time: W - 6:10 - 8:00 PM

 Course No.: CMP999
 Section No.: 1
 Course Name: Living Brain Computers
 Day and Time: R - 4:10 - 6:00 PM

Person Information:
 Name: Jacquie Barker
 Soc. Security No.: 123-45-6789
Professor-Specific Information:

Title: Adjunct Professor
Teaches for Dept.: Information Technology
Teaching Assignments for Jacquie Barker:
Course No.: OBJ101
Section No.: 1
Course Name: Object Methods for Software Development
Day and Time: R - 4:10 - 6:00 PM

Course No.: CMP283
Section No.: 1
Course Name: Higher Level Languages (Java)
Day and Time: M - 6:10 - 8:00 PM

Person Information:
Name: Snidely Whiplash
Soc. Security No.: 987-65-4321
Professor-Specific Information:
Title: Full Professor
Teaches for Dept.: Physical Education
Teaching Assignments for Snidely Whiplash:
Course No.: CMP101
Section No.: 1
Course Name: Beginning Computer Technology
Day and Time: M - 8:10 - 10:00 PM

Course No.: OBJ101
Section No.: 2
Course Name: Object Methods for Software Development
Day and Time: T - 6:10 - 8:00 PM

Course No.: ART101
Section No.: 1
Course Name: Beginning Basketweaving
Day and Time: M - 4:10 - 6:00 PM

====================
Student Information:
====================

Person Information:
Name: Joe Blow
Soc. Security No.: 111-11-1111
Student-Specific Information:
Major: Math
Degree: M.S.
Course Schedule for Joe Blow
Course No.: CMP101
Section No.: 1
Course Name: Beginning Computer Technology
Meeting Day and Time Held: M - 8:10 - 10:00 PM

Room Location: GOVT101
Professor's Name: Snidely Whiplash

Course No.: ART101
Section No.: 1
Course Name: Beginning Basketweaving
Meeting Day and Time Held: M - 4:10 - 6:00 PM
Room Location: ARTS25
Professor's Name: Snidely Whiplash

Transcript for: Joe Blow (111-11-1111) [M.S. - Math]
(no entries)

Person Information:
 Name: Fred Schnurd
 Soc. Security No.: 222-22-2222
Student-Specific Information:
 Major: Information Technology
 Degree: Ph. D.
Course Schedule for Fred Schnurd
 Course No.: ART101
 Section No.: 1
 Course Name: Beginning Basketweaving
 Meeting Day and Time Held: M - 4:10 - 6:00 PM
 Room Location: ARTS25
 Professor's Name: Snidely Whiplash

Transcript for: Fred Schnurd (222-22-2222) [Ph. D. - Information Technology]
(no entries)

Person Information:
 Name: Mary Smith
 Soc. Security No.: 333-33-3333
Student-Specific Information:
 Major: Physics
 Degree: B.S.
Course Schedule for Mary Smith
 (none)
Transcript for: Mary Smith (333-33-3333) [B.S. - Physics]
(no entries)

In summary, here is how our Chapter 14 version of the SRS had to be modified to achieve file persistence:

Class	Modifications
CollectionWrapper	New
CourseCatalog	New
Course	Yes: we changed the signature on the scheduleSection() method to accept an explicit section number as an argument, because we are now reading it from a file

Table continued on following page

Class	Modifications
Faculty	New
Person	No
Professor	No
Section	No
ScheduleOfClasses	Yes: it now extends the CollectionWrapper class; we implemented the parseData() and parseData2() methods; and we added a findSection() method
SRS	Yes: it was revamped – and streamlined! – to take advantage of all of the new collections that we've created
Student	Yes: we did a lot! We revamped the constructor to do dynamic data loading at login from a student's private data file by using a version of parseData() and parseData2() written specifically for Student; we created a studentSuccessfullyInitialized() method; we created a persist() method that will record the state of a student's registration situation when he/she logs off
Transcript	No
TranscriptEntry	No

This concludes the work that we are going to do with respect to persistence in the SRS application. We'll finish rounding out the SRS application by adding a graphical user interface in Chapter 16.

Summary

In this chapter, we've learned:

- How we approach file I/O in Java, using the FileReader, BufferedReader, FileOutputStream, and PrintWriter classes of the java.io package.

- An approach for parsing tab delimited ASCII records to initialize an object's state, or a collection of objects.

- A means of persisting an object's state in an ASCII file.

- How to prepare a 'test scaffold' main() method for testing isolated classes.

- A technique for encapsulating collections.

- How proper encapsulation streamlines client code (for example, the SRS main() method).

We're also getting quite an opportunity to apply the Java language skills that we covered in Chapter 13. We encourage you to work with the SRS code, and to attempt some of the exercises that follow, to reinforce your learning experience.

Exercises

1. Review all of the code associated with the SRS as produced in this chapter, and cite all cases where error handling could be improved.

2. Use the test scaffold provided in the `CourseCatalog` class to test the `parseData()` and `parseData2()` methods of that class against all of the following error situations in either the `CourseCatalog.dat` or `Prerequisites.dat` files (edit these files to introduce the following problems one by one, then run the code to see what happens):

   a. The course name is missing from one of the records in `CourseCatalog.dat` (i.e. the record only contains two fields instead of three).

   b. The value for credits (third field in a record) in `CourseCatalog.dat` is a non-numeric value, such as 'X'.

   c. The `Prerequisites.dat` file refers to a course that was not defined in the `CourseCatalog.dat` file.

   d. The `Prerequisites.dat` file is empty.

   e. The `Prerequisites.dat` file contains a record with only one field in it.

   Describe what happens in each case, and discuss what coding changes you'd have to make, if any, to handle each of the above situations 'gracefully'.

3. Follow up Exercise 2 by actually making the necessary changes to the `CourseCatalog.java` file, and then retest (Hint: this will involve exception handling).

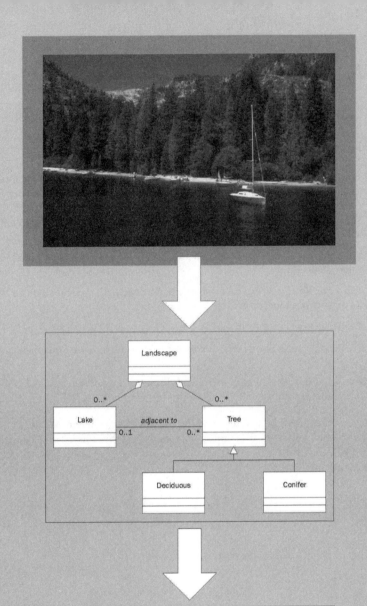

```
public class Tree {
    protected Landscape landscape;
    protected Lake nextTo;

    public void setNextTo(Lake l) {
        nextTo = l;
    }
    public Lake getNextTo() {
        return nextTo;
    }

    public abstract Color getLeafColor();
}
```

Rounding Out Your Application, Part 2: Adding a Graphical User Interface

In Chapter 15, we greatly improved the usefulness of the SRS application by providing a means for persisting the state of Student objects – in particular, their enrollment status in various classes – from one SRS invocation to the next. However, we still haven't provided a means by which a student user can interact with the SRS. As it is currently implemented, we launch the application from the command line via the command:

```
java SRS
```

and from then on, the application runs to completion without any further user input, relying solely on ASCII files and/or hardcoded information as its 'fuel'/data.

In this chapter, we are going to enhance our latest version of the SRS application once again by retrofitting a graphical user interface (GUI) front-end. With the GUI that we add, we'll provide hypothetical students with the capability to:

❑   Log on to the SRS

❑   View the schedule of sections available for registration in the current semester

❑   View and modify their individual course load by dropping and adding sections of courses which they are eligible to attend

❑   Save these changes to a file before logging off again

In this chapter, you will learn:

- ❑ The basics of Java GUI composition and event handling.

- ❑ What the two primary Java GUI application programming interfaces (APIs) – the Abstract Windowing Toolkit (AWT) and Swing – have to offer.

- ❑ Details about a number of AWT and Swing components – the 'building blocks' of GUIs.

- ❑ A recommended architecture for GUI applications.

- ❑ The importance of developing a concept of how the GUI is to look, operate, and 'flow' before any code is written.

- ❑ How to retrofit a GUI to an existing application, using our SRS application from Chapter 15 as an example.

Java GUIs: a Primer

Components

The fundamental approach to graphical user interface programming with virtually any programming language, Java or otherwise, is to assemble graphical building blocks called **components**. We assemble components in specific ways to provide the 'look', or presentation, that we desire for an application, and then program their 'behind the scenes' logic to enable them to do useful things. Users interact with these components – push buttons, text fields, lists, and so on – to provide information to the system and/or to obtain information from the system in order to achieve some worthwhile goal; in other words, to fulfill the use cases that we identified in Chapter 9.

Moreover, because it is objects that actually carry out the mission of an object-oriented system, a GUI enables us to create and interact with objects. In the case of the SRS, we'll be:

- ❑ **Instantiating objects**: for example, when a student user logs onto the system, we'll instantiate a Student object as an abstraction of that user.

- ❑ **Invoking their methods**: as we do when we invoke the validatePassword() method on a Student object to ensure that the password a user has keyed in is valid.

- ❑ **Changing their state:** by modifying attribute values and/or creating new links between them: for example, when a student successfully enrolls in a course, we will form a link between the appropriate Student and Section objects.

In fact, the GUI *itself* consists of objects! All Java GUI components are created as objects, and hence:

- ❏ Are described by classes
- ❏ Are instantiated via the 'new' operator, using an appropriate constructor method
- ❏ Have attributes (that are typically private) and methods (that are typically public) that we access via dot notation
- ❏ Communicate via messages
- ❏ Participate in inheritance hierarcies
- ❏ Are referenced by reference variables, when we wish to maintain named 'handles' on them
- ❏ Maintain handles on *other* objects – GUI as well as non-GUI objects
- ❏ Collaborate with other objects – GUI as well as non-GUI objects – to accomplish the mission of the overall system

Therefore, all of the techniques that you've learned about creating and communicating with objects in general throughout this book will apply to GUI component objects in particular. Through user interactions with the SRS GUI, the GUI's component objects will be requested to perform services, which in many cases, lead them to collaborate behind the scenes with the domain objects – Students, Professors, Courses, Sections, and so on – to carry out a particular user-requested service such as registering for a course.

Containers

A **container** is a special type of component that is used to organize, manage, and present other components. We may depict the relationship between components and containers via a UML diagram, as follows:

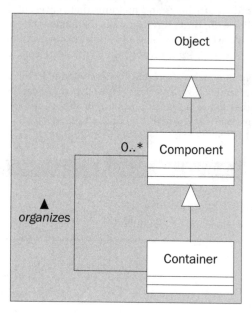

We learn from this diagram that:

- A container is a component, but a component is not necessarily a container.

- Since a container can contain components, and a container *is* a component, then a container may contain other containers. In fact, this is the way that we build up complex GUIs – by layering components/containers, a technique that we'll explore in depth in this chapter.

- By way of analogy, a container is like a directory on your computer system, whereas a component is like an item placed within that directory.

  - Just as any one file has only one 'home' directory, any one component instance can be placed in only one container instance.

  - Conversely, a container may contain many components – including other containers – just as a directory may contain many files and/or other directories.

With Java, when components are added to a container, they are typically positioned through the help of a **layout manager,** a Java-specific concept that we'll learn more about later in this chapter.

Separating the Model from the View

A technique known as **separating the model from the view** is an important design approach when developing a graphically-oriented application. This concept relates to the **Model–View–Controller (MVC) paradigm**, which was popularized as a formal concept with the Smalltalk language, but is equally applicable to all OO languages, including Java.

MVC is a way of thinking of an application as being subdivided into three parts:

- The **model** embodies the abstract domain knowledge of the application: that is, the objects/classes and their attributes and methods that represent the real-world items/issues that the users are familiar with, often referred to as the **business logic** of the application. Up until this point in the book, we've been focusing almost exclusively on these so-called **domain classes**: Person, Student, Professor, Course, Section, and the like.

- The **view** is the way in which we present this knowledge to the user – typically, although not exclusively, via a graphical user interface. Note that there can be many different views of the same model, in either the same or different applications. For example, with respect to the SRS GUI, we could represent the Students enrolled in a particular Section as a list of their names and student ID numbers:

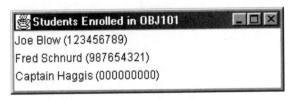

Or as photographs:

Or as a diagram:

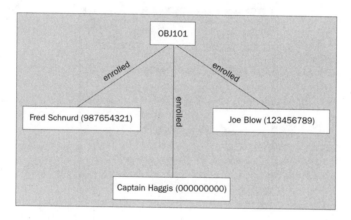

Or in any number of other forms.

- ❑ The **controller** is the automatic mechanism by which the user interface is displayed, and by which events are communicated back and forth between the model and the view. In the case of Java, this is handled by the Java Virtual Machine (JVM) in conjunction with the underlying windowing mechanism of your particular computer system.

As OO developers, we must:

- ❑ Develop and program the **model**, as we did throughout Part 2 of the book and in Chapter 14, respectively.

- ❑ Design and program the **view(s)**. In Java, this is accomplished through the use of **Java's Abstract Windowing Toolkit (AWT)** and **Swing APIs,** which provide the graphical user interface 'building blocks' that we'll focus our attention on for much of this chapter.

- ❑ Understand how the **controller** works, in order to take advantage of the mechanism for 'hooking' the model and view together. This involves learning Java's approach to **event handling**, which we will introduce later in this chapter as well.

When designing and programming an application, if we take care to cleanly separate and insulate the code for the model from the code for the view, then it becomes much easier to:

- **Add or change a view, if need be, without disturbing the underlying model**; that, in essence, is what we'll be doing when we add a GUI 'view' to the SRS application later in this chapter. As you'll see, the domain classes that we've already programmed will remain, for the most part unchanged by our addition of a GUI.

- **Provide multiple alternative views of the same underlying model**. Sometimes, we provide different views for different categories of user; for example, a Professor using the SRS may see different windows and options than a Student would see. We may even give a single user the ability to switch among multiple views; a familiar example of this can be found within the Microsoft Windows operating system. With Windows, users are able to view the contents of a folder as either large icons:

Or as a detailed list:

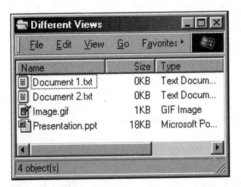

Or as an HTML page:

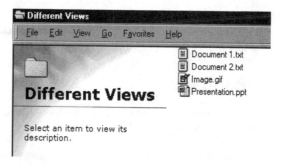

Or even as a DOS window:

```
.                   <DIR>        06-30-00  7:32p .
..                  <DIR>        06-30-00  7:32p ..
DOCUME~1 TXT              0       06-30-00  7:32p Document 1.txt
IMAGE    GIF            796       06-30-00  7:34p Image.gif
DOCUME~2 TXT              0       06-30-00  7:32p Document 2.txt
PRESEN~1 PPT         18,432       04-07-00  1:42p Presentation.ppt
         4 file(s)           19,228 bytes
         2 dir(s)        25,133,056 bytes free
```

Regardless of the view chosen, however, the underlying model in our Windows example is the same: we have a directory entitled 'Different Views' on our file system, and it contains four files: two text documents, a GIF image, and a PowerPoint presentation.

The model should, in essence, be 'view free': just as we can change the appearance of a sofa by adding a slipcover without changing its underlying structure or general functionality, so too can we change the appearance of an application without changing its underlying structure.

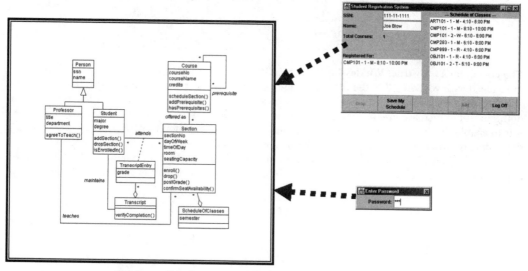

With model view separation, the model is insulated from
the view; the view can 'see' the model, but not vice versa.

477

One way to help ensure that the model and view are logically separated is to develop the model first, without regard for the view. In theory, if we do a proper job of developing the model, based on the analysis techniques of Part 2, then virtually any view relevant to the original goals (use cases) set forth for the system should be attainable. Moreover, we'll prove that theory by retroactively adding a GUI to the model that we automated in Chapter 14.

AWT vs. Swing Components

In order for the Java language to truly achieve platform independence, designers of the language had to provide a way for building platform independent GUIs.

With many programming languages that preceded Java, GUI components (buttons, text fields, windows, etc.), regardless of the language that they are written in, typically look different on Windows platforms than they do on X-Windows based Unix machines or than they do on Macintosh computers. For example, here is a comparison of a pop-up dialog displayed by Microsoft Word on a Macintosh computer:

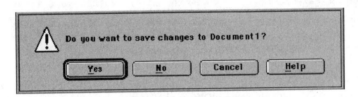

and the same pop-up as it would appear on a Windows PC:

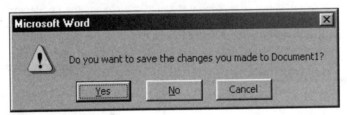

The goal of Java's **Abstract Windowing Toolkit (AWT)** application programming interface (API), introduced with version 1.0 of the Java language, was to emphasize compatibility with the graphical look and feel standard for each platform on which a Java application might possibly run. The thinking was that doing so would increase users' comfort level with a Java application's GUI. The intention with the AWT was to enable the same Java application to automatically take on different platform-specific 'looks' depending on where it was being executed. On a Windows PC, the Java application's GUI would automatically look like other Windows applications; on a Mac, it would automatically look like other Mac applications; and on a Unix platform, it would automatically look like other X-Windows applications.

To accomplish this goal, platform-specific versions of all the GUI components were programmed (typically, in the C language) by the developers of the various platform-specific 'flavors' of the Java Virtual Machine; these were then bundled into the JVM. These so-called component **peers** did all of the actual work of displaying themselves graphically and interacting with the user. If we, as Java programmers, wrote an application that called for the creation of an AWT Button object, for example, then *our* Button object talked (without our explicit knowledge) to a ButtonPeer object; and thanks to some magic performed by the JVM, it was the ButtonPeer object that actually appeared on the screen for the user to interact with. Because running Java applications written using the AWT thus involved the invocation of native C code, the AWT components were nicknamed 'heavyweight' components because of this extra code 'baggage'.

Because the same Java AWT GUI application *intentionally* looked different when run on different platforms, it therefore became important to test such applications on every platform that they were ever expected to run on to make sure that the various GUI components lined up properly, that the fonts were suitable such that no labels got truncated, and so on. Sun's official motto of 'Write once, run anywhere' informally became 'Write once, test everywhere, run anywhere'.

The Java Swing API became available as an optional add-on API to the Java language with release 1.1, and was officially incorporated into the core Java language as of Java release 1.2 (also known simply as 'Java 2'). With the Swing API, a new set of GUI components was introduced to complement the AWT components. Swing components do not attempt to *automatically* assume a platform-specific 'look'; their default is to assume the same generic Java-specific look no matter which computer they are being used on. In fact, Swing components have been re-engineered so that most of them no longer need to rely on native peers as did the AWT components, and hence they are known as 'lightweight' components.

Swing's top level window components, however, do still rely on 'native' windows to host them, and hence are still heavyweight.

It is possible to control the look of your GUI components so that if you wish to have them assume a particular platform specific look – for example, a Windows look – it is possible to do so. This is known as assigning a 'pluggable look and feel'; we won't be discussing how to do this in this chapter, as it isn't relevant to building the SRS GUI.

Many (but not all) AWT components named 'xxx' have Swing counterparts named 'Jxxx'; for example, the AWT Frame class has a Swing counterpart called JFrame; the AWT Button class has a JButton counterpart, and so on. It is recommended that the Swing version of a component be used in lieu of its AWT version whenever the former is available, as the Swing components generally provide faster performance with less overhead; we'll do so in building the SRS GUI.

The Swing API also introduces more advanced GUI components for which there were no AWT equivalents, such as:

- ❑ JTable, a component for displaying data in a rows-and-columns tabular format, ideal for displaying data that has been returned from a relational database query.

- ❑ JTree, a way of displaying and navigating hierarchical information similar to the way that Windows Explorer facilitates directory navigation.

and others. We won't be discussing these more elaborate Swing components in this book, however, as we won't need to make use of them for building the SRS GUI.

The Swing components are in most cases specialized subclasses derived from the AWT `Component` class. The following diagram illustrates the derivation hierarchy of all of the AWT and Swing component classes that we'll need to concern ourselves with in building the GUI for the SRS; asterisks (*) indicate the specific classes that we will instantiate. Note that there are many more AWT and Swing classes than we've reflected in this diagram. All components – like all other Java objects – are ultimately descended from the `java.lang.Object` class.

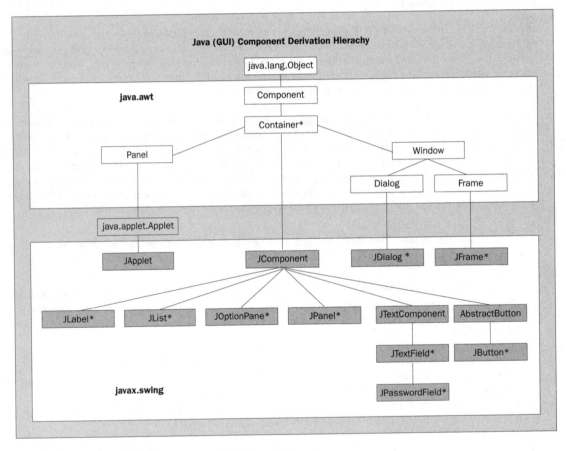

The AWT and Swing components reside in four packages:

- ❏ `java.awt` – AWT components.
- ❏ `javax.swing` – Swing components (note the 'x' at the end of the first part of this package name; that's a vestige of the fact that Swing was originally released as an optional Java language eXtension).
- ❏ `java.awt.event` – classes related to AWT event handling.
- ❏ `javax.swing.event` – classes related to Swing event handling.

When we import the entire AWT component set into an application, via the statement

```
import java.awt.*;
```

the wildcard at the end often lulls programmers into thinking that the `java.awt.event` package will also be imported. This is not the case; if you want `java.awt.event` classes to be available to your application, you must import the package separately:

```
import java.awt.*;
import java.awt.event.*;
```

The same is true for the two Swing-related packages.

Even when using Swing, we still rely on many classes from the AWT, particularly when it comes to GUI event handling, which we'll learn about later in this chapter. Swing doesn't replace the AWT component set, it *extends* it.

In contrast to Java, C++ has no integrated GUI mechanism. As we discussed in Chapter 1, we typically have to use platform-specific windowing technologies such as Motif or Microsoft's Foundation Classes to build a GUI for a C++ application, which compromises an application's portability.

The AWT is an **event driven** system where each visual component can generate a number of events based on a user's interaction with that component. For example, clicking a button (either an AWT `Button` or a Swing `JButton`), pressing the `Enter` key after typing in a text field, or clicking on an item in a list to select it, all generate events. We'll learn more about Java GUI event handling later in this chapter. But first, we'll learn about the various components and techniques used in producing the visual appearance of a GUI; i.e. its 'look' or presentation.

JFrames

A `JFrame` is a top-level container/component that serves as a stand-alone window; it may not be contained by or attached to any other type of component. A `JFrame` has a title bar and window controls imposed by the native windowing system, and may optionally be equipped with a menu bar.

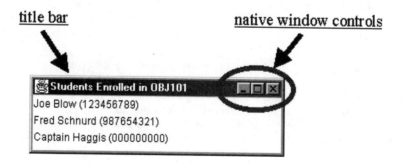

When building a free-standing Java application (as contrasted with an applet), you must create a single JFrame to hold the components necessary to provide the desired GUI appearance and functionality. Non-trivial GUI applications typically consist of multiple free-standing windows – one main JFrame and multiple other JFrames and/or transient pop-up windows called JDialogs, which we'll talk about later in this chapter after we've explored event handling a bit.

In contrast with an application, a Java applet has no main window of its own. Instead, the browser window (for example, Netscape) serves as the top-level container, and we attach the applet as a type of component – a subclass of java.awt.Panel, actually – to the browser 'frame'.

Let's build our first JFrame. We'll create a program/class called FrameTest, and within the main() method of that class we'll perform the bare minimum steps necessary to create and display a JFrame:

> **Note: All code examples in this chapter were compiled using version 1.2.2 of the Java compiler, and should be forwardly compatible with later versions of the Java language.**

```
// FrameTest.java
```

❑ First, we'll import the Swing package, so that the Java compiler will know what a JFrame is:

```
import javax.swing.*;

public class FrameTest {
  public static void main(String[] args) {
```

❑ Secondly, we'll instantiate a JFrame object by using one of the JFrame class's constructor methods, passing in a title for the frame; we'll hold onto the reference to the newly created object in a reference variable named 'theFrame':

```
JFrame theFrame = new JFrame("Whee!!!");
```

❑ Next, we need to set the size of the frame to be something reasonable. We express the width and height of GUI components in **pixels**; a pixel is the smallest addressable graphical unit on a display screen. The default JFrame size is zero pixels wide by zero pixels high, which is too small to be seen.

```
theFrame.setSize(200, 200);    // width, height in pixels
```

❑ Finally, we must explicitly make the frame appear by invoking its setVisible() method, passing in a value of true. A JFrame is by default invisible when it is first created, to give us time to assemble all of the components that we wish to attach to the frame before 'unveiling' it. (In this example, we aren't attaching any components to the frame, however.)

```
theFrame.setVisible(true);
  }
}
```

(Note that a `JFrame` *can also be made invisible again by calling* `setVisible()` *with an argument of* `false`.*)*

Here is the code again, in its entirety:

```
// FrameTest.java
import javax.swing.*;

public class FrameTest {
  public static void main(String[] args) {
    // Create the frame by calling the appropriate constructor
    // (we are passing in a title to the frame).

    JFrame theFrame = new JFrame("Whee!!!");

    // Set the size to something reasonable (the default JFrame
    // size is 0 pixels wide by 0 pixels high, which isn't visible).

    theFrame.setSize(200, 200);  // width, height in pixels

    // Make the frame appear on the screen.

    theFrame.setVisible(true);
  }
}
```

Reminder: the full code for all of the examples in this chapter are available as a download from the Wrox website; see Appendix D for details.

When we subsequently compile, then run, the program by typing :

```
javac FrameTest.java
java FrameTest
```

at the DOS or Unix command line, we see the following window (frame) appear on the screen in the upper left hand corner:

Of course, Java programs may also be launched through other means, e.g. from a desktop graphical icon. Because the instructions for setting such icons up are operating system dependent and are not Java related, we don't discuss such details in this book.

There is one slight problem with this program: if we click the 'close' button (**X**) located in the upper right corner of the frame, the window does indeed close, but our program continues to run! That is, the command line in the DOS or Unix window from which we launched the program remains 'locked up'. We'll have to do something explicitly in our code to enable the application to exit gracefully when the 'close' button is clicked; we'll learn how to do this when we cover **event handling** later in the chapter. For now, to regain control of the command line, you'll need to do the following:

❑ Click anywhere in the window from which you typed the 'java FrameTest' command, to get the window's attention (that is, to cause that window to **gain focus**).

❑ Press the 'Ctrl' and 'C' keys simultaneously in the command line window to 'kill' the program.

> You'll need to do this for a number of the example programs that we'll discuss in this chapter; we'll abbreviate these instructions from now on as simply 'regain the focus of the window from which you launched the program, and press 'Ctrl C' to kill it.'

Positioning a Frame on the Screen

As you develop a GUI, think of the monitor surface as an x-y grid, with the **origin** – a point with (x, y) coordinates of (0, 0) – located in the upper left corner of the screen. As you move to the right, the x coordinates of the points increase; and as you move downward, the y coordinates increase. Points correspond one-to-one with pixels; the lower right hand corner of the monitor has coordinates (*maxX*, *maxY*), depending on the resolution of the monitor in pixels. On a monitor with a pixel resolution of 800 pixels wide by 600 pixels high, the (x, y) coordinate values of the lower right hand corner of the screen would be (799, 599).

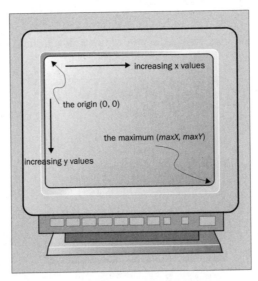

increasing x values

the origin (0, 0)

the maximum (*maxX*, *maxY*)

increasing y values

When we created our first frame with the `FrameTest.java` program, we didn't explicitly tell the program where we wanted to position the frame, so its upper left hand corner was **anchored** at (0, 0) by default, as illustrated in the following figure.

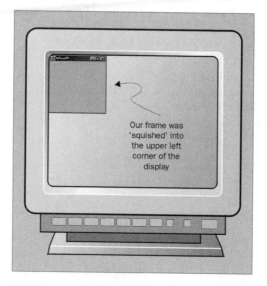

Our frame was 'squished' into the upper left corner of the display

If we wish to explicitly anchor a frame somewhere else, we can use its `setLocation()` method to do so. `setLocation()` is actually a useful method not only for positioning a `JFrame` on the screen, but also for positioning `Components` onto `Containers`; the method takes two integer arguments, representing the x and y coordinate of the upper left hand corner of the component relative to the surface it is being attached to (the screen surface, in the case of a `JFrame`). Here is a simple example to illustrate this technique:

```
// FrameTest1.java
import javax.swing.*;

public class FrameTest1 {
  public static void main(String[] args) {
    // Create the frame by calling the appropriate constructor
    // (we are passing in a title to the frame).

    JFrame theFrame = new JFrame("Whee!!!");

    // Set the size to something reasonable (the default JFrame
    // size is 0 pixels wide by 0 pixels high, which isn't visible).

    theFrame.setSize(200, 200);  // width, height in pixels

    // Position the upper left hand corner of the frame
    // at the coordinate (300, 400).

    theFrame.setLocation(300, 400);

    // Make the frame appear on the screen.

    theFrame.setVisible(true);
  }
}
```

Centering a Frame on the Screen

Often, we would like to center a new frame in the middle of the computer screen when it first appears. We will look at a particular example to help us determine the calculation that needs to be made.

❑ Let's say that we have a frame of size 200 by 200 pixels that we wish to center on a screen of size 800 by 600 pixels. The center of the screen is located at (800/2, 600/2) = (400, 300).

❑ In order to set the location of the frame's upper left hand corner so that the frame's *center* coincides with the center of the screen, half of the frame's width, or 100 pixels, must fall to the left of center, and half of the frame's height, or 100 pixels, must fall above the center. The upper left hand corner of the frame must therefore be positioned at (400 − 100, 300 − 100) = (300, 200), as shown in the figure that follows.

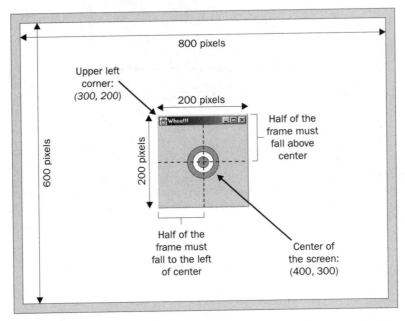

Because different screens have different physical dimensions and different pixel resolutions, we need a way to *dynamically* determine a particular computer's screen size wherever the Java program is run, so that the frame in question will be centered no matter what computer it is run on. Fortunately, the AWT provides a `Toolkit` class that enables us to make such a determination. Let's talk through how it works conceptually first, and then we'll see it in use in code.

❑ First, we invoke a static method, `getDefaultToolkit()`, on the `Toolkit` class to obtain a handle on the AWT `Toolkit` object for this platform.

❑ We then invoke that `Toolkit` object's `getScreenSize()` method, which returns an object of type `Dimension`. A `Dimension` object happens to have two *public* int attributes – `width` (in pixels) and `height` (in pixels).

❑ We 'string' together these two method calls because we don't want to hold onto the `Toolkit` object for very long: we just want to use it momentarily to retrieve the screen's `Dimension` object:

```
Dimension screenSize = Toolkit.getDefaultToolkit().getScreenSize();
```

and so we don't bother to assign the handle on the `Toolkit` object to a reference variable.

❑ We also use the `getSize()` method on the frame object itself, to get its size, again as a `Dimension` object.

Armed with all of this size information, we perform the calculation discussed previously, as illustrated by the following sample program:

```
// FrameTest2.java
import javax.swing.*;

// Import a few classes from the AWT API.
import java.awt.Dimension;
import java.awt.Toolkit;

public class FrameTest2 {
  public static void main(String[] args) {
    // Create the frame by calling the appropriate constructor
    // (we are passing in a title to the frame).

    JFrame theFrame = new JFrame("Whee!!!");

    // Set the size to something reasonable (the default JFrame
    // size is 0 pixels wide by 0 pixels high, which isn't visible)

    theFrame.setSize(200, 200); // width, height in pixels

    // Technique for centering a frame on the screen.

    // First, obtain the size of the frame to be centered. Invoking
    // the getSize() method on a Component returns a Dimension
    // object which in turn has two public int attributes:
    // width(in pixels) and height (in pixels).

    Dimension frameSize = theFrame.getSize();

    // Now, invoke the static getDefaultToolkit() method on the
    // Toolkit class to obtain a handle on the AWT Toolkit object
    // for this platform, and then invoke its getScreenSize()
    // method to obtain a second Dimension object.

    Dimension screenSize = Toolkit.getDefaultToolkit().getScreenSize();

    // Compute the center point of the screen as (centerX, centerY).

    int centerX = screenSize.width/2;
    int centerY = screenSize.height/2;
```

```
        // We want half of the frame to be to the left of center,
        // and half to be above center.

        int halfWidth = frameSize.width/2;
        int halfHeight = frameSize.height/2;
        theFrame.setLocation(centerX - halfWidth, centerY - halfHeight);

        // Make the frame appear on the screen.

        theFrame.setVisible(true);
    }
}
```

Now, when we run the program, the frame will indeed appear centered on the screen.

It turns out that there is a shorter calculation that achieves the same result:

```
        // Technique for centering a frame on the screen.

        Dimension frameSize = theFrame.getSize();
        Dimension screenSize = Toolkit.getDefaultToolkit().getScreenSize();

        // "Split the difference" between the screen size
        // and the frame size.

        theFrame.setLocation((screenSize.width - frameSize.width)/2,
                             (screenSize.height - frameSize.height)/2);
```

We'll use this more condensed version for centering a frame from now on.

Adding Components to a JFrame

To add Components to a JFrame, we must first obtain a handle on the JFrame's **content pane**, which is a type of Container.

```
    Container contentPane = theFrame.getContentPane();
```

We then use the add() method on that Container to add Components one by one.

If we modify our FrameTest2 program to include the lines highlighted below:

```
    // FrameTest3.java

    import javax.swing.*;
    import java.awt.*;

    public class FrameTest3 {
      public static void main(String[] args) {
        // Create the frame by calling the appropriate constructor
        // (we are passing in a title to the frame).
```

```
        JFrame theFrame = new JFrame("Whee!!!");

        // Set the size to something reasonable (the default JFrame
        // size is 0 pixels wide by 0 pixels high, which isn't visible).

        theFrame.setSize(200, 200);   // width, height in pixels

        // Technique for centering a frame on the screen.

        Dimension frameSize = theFrame.getSize();
        Dimension screenSize = Toolkit.getDefaultToolkit().getScreenSize();
        theFrame.setLocation((screenSize.width - frameSize.width)/2,
                (screenSize.height - frameSize.height)/2);

        // Let's create and add a component.

        Container contentPane = theFrame.getContentPane( );
        JLabel stuff = new JLabel("I am a label");
        contentPane.add(stuff);

        // Make the frame appear on the screen.

        theFrame.setVisible(true);
    }
}
```

we cause a JLabel to appear on the frame with the text 'I am a label':

The positioning of the label isn't very interesting – we will learn how to control this shortly through the intelligent use of layout managers.

Note that we had to use two import statements – for javax.swing.* and java.awt.* – for this example. We'll do this frequently, because we do indeed use a combination of the two APIs for most GUI development:

❑ Classes Container, Toolkit, and Dimension were introduced with the AWT API, and are still used heavily because the Swing API did not improve upon these.

❑ On the other hand, classes JFrame and JLabel are new in Swing.

As an option, we can import individual classes, rather than using the wildcard (*) form of import, to better document where each class that we are using originates, as illustrated below. (We discussed this technique in Chapter 13.)

```
// FrameTest3B.java
// We can import individual classes, to better document where each
// class that we are using originates.

import javax.swing.JFrame;
import javax.swing.JLabel;
import java.awt.Container;
import java.awt.Toolkit;
import java.awt.Dimension;

// etc.
```

JPanels

A JPanel is a Container (Component) that does not have an obvious border. It cannot stand alone, the way a JFrame can – it *must* be placed on/in another Container, and is used as a convenient way to group multiple other graphic Components, such as buttons, lists, slide bars, radio buttons, text fields, check boxes, and so on. We'll see several creative uses of JPanel later in the chapter.

JPanels do not make use of a content pane the way JFrames do; to add a Component to a JPanel, simply invoke the add() method on the JPanel directly, as this snippet illustrates:

```
// Contrast the method for adding a Component to a JFrame ...
Container contentPane = aFrame.getContentPane();
contentPane.add(button1);

// ... with that for a JPanel.
aPanel.add(button2);
```

Common Component Properties and Behaviors

Because all of the AWT and Swing components are descended from a common ancestor class, java.awt.Component, they all share a number of attributes and methods inherited from Component:

Color:

In Java, colors are implemented as objects belonging to the class java.awt.Color. The Color class defines a handful of static attributes, representing the following built-in colors: black, blue, cyan, darkGray, gray, green, lightGray, magenta, orange, pink, red, white, and yellow. All displayable colors are derived by blending three primary colors – red, green, and blue – in varying intensities from 0 (none) to 255 (maximum), as illustrated for the built-in Java colors in the following table.

Color:	RED intensity :	GREEN intensity:	BLUE intensity :
Color.black	0	0	0
Color.blue	0	0	255
Color.cyan	0	255	255
Color.darkGray	64	64	64
Color.gray	128	128	128
Color.green	0	255	0
Color.lightGray	192	192	192
Color.magenta	255	0	255
Color.orange	255	200	0
Color.pink	255	175	175
Color.red	255	0	0
Color.white	255	255	255
Color.yellow	255	255	0

You can also easily invent your own colors by calling the Color class's constructor, specifying the intensity of the red, green, and blue values that make up the desired color in the range 0 (darkest) to 255 (brightest). For example:

```
Color limeGreen = new Color(50, 205, 50);
```

All components have both a default background color and a default foreground color. For example:

- ❏ For a JFrame, the default background color is a medium gray color with red/green/blue intensities of (204, 204, 204), and the default foreground color is black.

- ❏ For a JTextField, the default background color is white, and the default foreground color, used for displaying the text within the text field, is black.

- ❏ For a JLabel, the default background color is the same as for a JFrame, while the default foreground color is a purplish-blue with red/green/blue intensities of (102, 102, 153).

To alter the colors assigned to a component, use the setForeground(Color) and setBackground(Color) methods, respectively, as in the following 'snippet':

```
// (Assume that 'theFrame' was declared to be a JFrame, and has
// been properly instantiated, sized, etc.)

// Use a standard color ...
theFrame.setBackground(Color.magenta);

// ... or, invent a color on the fly!
theFrame.setForeground(new Color(20, 30, 40));
```

491

Note the previous technique of creating an object 'on the fly' and passing it on to another object without maintaining a named 'handle' (reference) to it – we could have instead written:

```
Color myColor = new Color(20, 30, 40);
theFrame.setForeground(myColor);
```

but if we have no further use for this particular color, then there is no need to go to the trouble of creating a reference called 'myColor' so as to maintain a named handle on this Color object. We'll use this technique of 'on the fly' object creation a lot with GUI development.

Enablement:

A Component is **enabled** by default when it is created, meaning that it can respond to user input and generate events. Enabled Components provide visual cues to indicate that they have been selected: for example, a JButton has a three-dimensional appearance:

and appears to become pushed in when it is clicked:

A Component may be explicitly enabled or disabled by calling its setEnabled(*boolean*) method, as demonstrated by the following code snippet:

```
JFrame f = new JFrame("Whee");
// other details regarding JFrame set up have been omitted ...

JButton b1 = new JButton("Foo!");
f.getContentPane().add(b1);
b1.setEnabled(false);
```

> **Important note:** when we show isolated code 'snippets' in this chapter without showing you the full program/class that they originate from, this is usually because the program as a whole is too complex to introduce at that point in the chapter. For example, to create a GUI that supports two buttons, as these figures represent, requires the use of a layout manager, a concept that we won't be talking about until later in the chapter. In order to avoid overwhelming readers with too much complexity too soon, we postpone such examples until all of the details are either relevant to the discussion at hand, or have been previously discussed. So, when you see 'snippets' but not the full-blown program that they come from, please view them as instructional examples only; do not try to type them and run them as a program in isolation, because they simply won't work.

A disabled `Component` ignores user interactions: a `JButton` that has been disabled, for example, will not appear to be pushed in when it is clicked. To signal to the user that a `Component` has been disabled, the `Component` appears to be greyed out in some fashion, as illustrated by the 'Foo!' button below (the 'Bar ...' button, in contrast, is enabled):

It is common practice to disable `Components` whenever having a user interact with them would be meaningless given the state of an application. For example, if a user is expected to enter data into a GUI 'form', but hasn't yet done so, then the OK button used to confirm their data entry on that form might be temporarily disabled/'greyed out'. We'll use this approach with `JButtons` for the SRS.

Visibility

We've already seen the use of the `setVisible()` method to make a `JFrame` appear on the screen. Visibility is a characteristic of all `Components`, as it turns out; some `Components` are automatically visible when created, and other `Components` by default take the visibility of the `Container` to which they are attached. For example, if we create a `JButton` and add it to a `JFrame`, then as long as the `JFrame` is invisible, the `JButton` will remain invisible, and when we make the `JFrame` visible, then the `JButton` will automatically become visible.

We can, however, explicitly make an individual `Component` invisible while keeping the `Container` as a whole visible by passing the message `setVisible(false)` to the `Component`:

```
// Create a frame and add two buttons.

JFrame f = new JFrame("Whee");
JButton b1 = new JButton("Foo!");
JButton b2 = new JButton("Bar ...");

// Details of attaching the buttons to the frame are intentionally
// omitted from this 'snippet' ... DO NOT TRY TO RUN THIS CODE!

// Conditionally hide the first button.
if (some condition) b1.setVisible(false);
```

As a result of the above, the 'Foo!' button no longer appears on the frame:

This is an alternative technique to disabling individual Components whenever using them would be meaningless given the state of an application.

These aren't *all* of the shared properties of Components, but rather those that we need to know about for building the SRS.

Layout Fundamentals

We can use a special type of object known as a **layout manager** to automatically arrange how Component objects are positioned when they are added to a Container object. We either use the default layout manager that is associated with a container such as a JFrame or JPanel, or explicitly assign a specific layout manager to a container using the container's setLayout() method. Then as we add components to the container, the components will be positioned relative to one another, and to the container as a whole, according to the rules of the governing layout manager.

There are a number of different layout managers defined in the core Java language. It is also possible to invent your own layout manager, but this is not trivial! We'll be using two of the built-in layout manager types – BorderLayout and GridLayout – to produce the SRS GUI, and so we'll talk about these in some depth. BorderLayout happens to be the default layout manager for JFrames. FlowLayout is another commonly used built-in layout manager. Although we aren't taking advantage of FlowLayout with the SRS application, it happens to be the default layout manager for JPanels, and so it is worth knowing a little bit about how this layout manager behaves, as well.

BorderLayout

The BorderLayout subdivides a Container into five regions, as shown below for a JFrame:

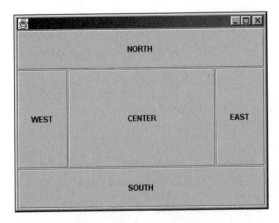

The preceding figure was produced by compiling and running program BorderLayoutLayout.java, which is available as part of the code download from the Wrox website. We aren't providing the code of this particular program here because it is a somewhat 'nonsensical' program: we inserted five labels, named 'NORTH', 'SOUTH', etc. into the five regions of a BorderLayout in order to produce this figure.

❑ The **NORTH** region extends across the entire top of the Container. Its height varies, depending on what sort of Component is inserted into this region.

❑ The **SOUTH** region extends across the entire bottom of the Container. Its height also varies, depending on what sort of Component is inserted into this region.

❑ The **WEST** region extends from the bottom of the NORTH region to the top of the SOUTH region, along the left-hand side of the Container. Its width varies, depending on what sort of Component is inserted into this region.

❑ The **EAST** region extends from the bottom of the NORTH region to the top of the SOUTH region, along the right-hand side of the Container. Its width also varies, depending on what sort of Component is inserted into this region.

❑ The **CENTER** region occupies all remaining space in the center of the Container.

If the JFrame above is resized by 'grabbing' and dragging an edge of the window with the mouse, the regions change size/shape but still maintain their relative positions, as shown below:

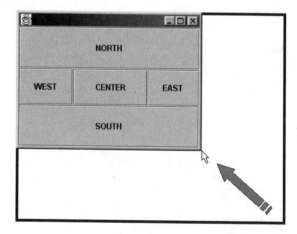

When using this layout manager, any of the five regions can be left empty; other non-empty regions are then able to expand into the space that has been effectively vacated by the empty region(s). For example, if we were to leave the NORTH region empty in a JFrame, the other regions would expand to consume the available space as follows:

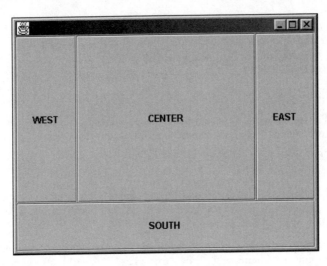

Note that any one region in a BorderLayout-controlled Container may only contain a single Component. Does this mean that a BorderLayout-controlled Container may only contain a total of five Components? The answer is yes – and no! If any one of these five Components happens to be a Container itself, such as a JPanel, then *that* Container can contain as many Components as *its* layout manager allows. In this fashion, we can build up arbitrarily complex GUIs by layering Containers and Components. We'll see several examples of how this is done a bit later in this chapter.

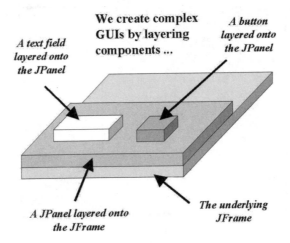

Meanwhile, we can modify our FrameTest3 program from a few pages back to place the label that we attached in the NORTH region of the layout simply by changing the add() method call to accept a second argument, as follows:

```
contentPane.add(stuff, BorderLayout.NORTH);
```

where BorderLayout.NORTH is one of five *public static final* attributes (that is, constants) defined by the BorderLayout class, the other four being BorderLayout.SOUTH, BorderLayout.WEST, BorderLayout.EAST, and BorderLayout.CENTER.

```
// FrameTest4.java

import javax.swing.*;
import java.awt.*;

public class FrameTest4 {
  public static void main(String[] args) {
    // Create the frame by calling the appropriate constructor
    // (we are passing in a title to the frame).

    JFrame theFrame = new JFrame("Whee!!!");

    // Set the size to something reasonable (the default JFrame
    // size is 0 pixels wide by 0 pixels high, which isn't visible).

    theFrame.setSize(200, 200);  // width, height in pixels

    // Technique for centering a frame on the screen.

    Dimension frameSize = theFrame.getSize();
    Dimension screenSize = Toolkit.getDefaultToolkit().getScreenSize();
    theFrame.setLocation((screenSize.width - frameSize.width)/2,
                         (screenSize.height - frameSize.height)/2);

    // Let's add a component.

    Container contentPane = theFrame.getContentPane( );
    JLabel stuff = new JLabel("I am a label");
    contentPane.add(stuff, BorderLayout.NORTH);

    // Make the frame appear on the screen.

    theFrame.setVisible(true);
  }
}
```

We see the following effect of doing so:

The label is now at the top of the frame, but it's *still* not centered! It turns out that centering a label is a responsibility of the JLabel component itself, not of the layout manager. If we want to center the label at the top of the JFrame, we must build a label that is *inherently* centered by changing one more line of code in our example; namely, by passing a second argument in to the JLabel constructor:

```
JLabel stuff = new JLabel("I am a label", JLabel.CENTER);
```

where JLabel.CENTER is one of three possible public static attributes defined by the JLabel class, the other two being JLabel.RIGHT and JLabel.LEFT (which is the default justification when none is specified).

```java
// FrameTest5.java
import javax.swing.*;
import java.awt.*;

public class FrameTest5 {
    public static void main(String[] args) {
        // Create the frame by calling the appropriate constructor
        // (we are passing in a title to the frame).

        JFrame theFrame = new JFrame("Whee!!!");

        // Set the size to something reasonable (the default JFrame
        // size is 0 pixels wide by 0 pixels high, which isn't visible).

        theFrame.setSize(200, 200);  // width, height in pixels

        // Technique for centering a frame on the screen.

        Dimension frameSize = theFrame.getSize();
        Dimension screenSize = Toolkit.getDefaultToolkit().getScreenSize();
        theFrame.setLocation((screenSize.width - frameSize.width)/2,
                             (screenSize.height - frameSize.height)/2);

        // Let's add a component.

        Container contentPane = theFrame.getContentPane( );
        JLabel stuff = new JLabel("I am a label", JLabel.CENTER);
        contentPane.add(stuff, BorderLayout.NORTH);

        // Make the frame appear on the screen.

        theFrame.setVisible(true);
    }
}
```

The result of this code change is shown below:

The AWT and Swing component classes make ample use of public static final attributes to define constant values, such as JLabel.CENTER, BorderLayout.NORTH, Color.pink, and so on. Note that some classes use all capital letters to name their static attributes, while others (for example, Color) do not. The generally accepted convention is to name public static final attributes with all capital letters, so do use this convention when creating public static final attributes of your own, as we've done for the SRS.

Note that we don't have to explicitly tell a JFrame that we wish for it to succumb to a BorderLayout, because BorderLayout is the default layout manager for a JFrame. For other Containers (like JPanel) which do not automatically default to a BorderLayout, we can instruct them to adopt such a layout via the setLayout() method, as the following snippet shows:

```
// Create a panel ...

JPanel p = new JPanel();

// ... and set its layout manager to be a Border Layout. (Otherwise, it
// would retain FlowLayout as its default layout manager.) We create a
// new BorderLayout object "on the fly", but don't maintain a named
// handle on it - we simply pass the layout manager object in as an
// argument to the setLayout() method, and then forget about it!
```

```
p.setLayout(new BorderLayout());  // passing in a BorderLayout object
```

GridLayout

GridLayout arranges a Container into a row/column layout, or grid. The number of rows and columns is determined when the GridLayout is first created; for example:

```
contentPane.setLayout(new GridLayout(3, 2));  // 3 rows, 2 cols.
```

Components are then added to the Container in ascending row by column order: the first component added goes into row 1 column 1, the second, into row 1 column 2, and so forth until the first row is filled; then, the next component goes into row 2 column 1, etc. until all components have been added.

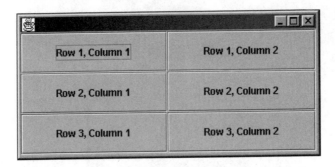

The preceding figure was produced by compiling and running program GridLayoutLayout.java, which is available as part of the code download from the Wrox website. We aren't providing the code of this particular program here because it is a somewhat 'nonsensical' program: we inserted six non-functioning buttons into the six cells of a GridLayout to create this figure.

Here is another version of our `FrameTest` program, modified to illustrate the use of a `GridLayout`:

```java
// FrameTest6.java
import javax.swing.*;
import java.awt.*;

public class FrameTest6 {
    public static void main(String[] args) {
        // Create the frame by calling the appropriate constructor
        // (we are passing in a title to the frame).

        JFrame theFrame = new JFrame("Whee!!!");

        // Set the size to something reasonable (the default JFrame
        // size is 0 pixels wide by 0 pixels high, which isn't visible).

        theFrame.setSize(400, 400);  // width, height in pixels

        // Technique for centering a frame on the screen.

        Dimension frameSize = theFrame.getSize();
        Dimension screenSize = Toolkit.getDefaultToolkit().getScreenSize();
        theFrame.setLocation((screenSize.width - frameSize.width)/2,
                             (screenSize.height - frameSize.height)/2);

        // Assign a grid layout to the frame.

        Container contentPane = theFrame.getContentPane( );
        contentPane.setLayout(new GridLayout(3, 2));  // 3 rows, 2 cols.

        // Create some components to attach.

        JLabel l = new JLabel("Name:");
        JLabel l2 = new JLabel("Address:");
        JLabel l3 = new JLabel("SSN:");
```

```
    // This next component, a text area, is a multi-line
    // text component; we're asking for it to be six lines
    // "tall" vs. 20 characters wide.

    JTextArea t = new JTextArea("This is a MULTI-LINE text area, " +
                                "which can contain a lot of text." +
                                "  We've asked it to wrap along " +
                                "word boundaries.",
                                6, 20);

    // Turn on line wrapping ...

    t.setLineWrap(true);

    // ... along word boundaries.

    t.setWrapStyleWord(true);

    // Creating two single-line text fields.

    JTextField t2 = new JTextField("This is a SINGLE LINE text field.");
    JTextField t3 = new JTextField("Another text field.");

    // Add in ascending row, then column, order.

    contentPane.add(l);         // row 1, col. 1
    contentPane.add(t);         // row 1, col. 2
    contentPane.add(l2);        // row 2, col. 1 (etc.)
    contentPane.add(t2);
    contentPane.add(l3);
    contentPane.add(t3);

  theFrame.setVisible(true);
 }
}
```

The result of running the above program is as follows:

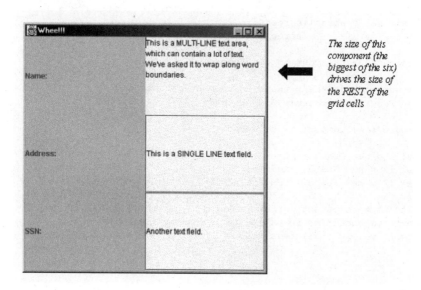

The size of this
component (the
biggest of the six)
drives the size of
the REST of the
grid cells

One problem with the GridLayout apparent in the example above is that the size of all of the cells in a container is driven by the preferred size of the *biggest* component that you are placing on the grid, which can make for an odd looking interface. In this example, we added six components: three JLabels, two single-line JTextFields, and one multi-line JTextArea. The text area is the largest component (when we called the JTextArea constructor, we indicated that we wanted it to be capable of showing up to 6 lines of 20 characters each), which drives all other cells to be that same size. When we tackle the SRS GUI, we'll learn a technique for the creative use of GridLayouts in combination with layered JPanels that enables us to work around this shortcoming.

Note that 'funny' things happen if you try to add too many Components to a GridLayout-managed Container. If we modify our FrameTest6 program to add *seven* items to the 3 x 2 grid (please see highlighted lines of code below):

```
// FrameTest6B.java

import javax.swing.*;
import java.awt.*;

public class FrameTest6B {
  public static void main(String[] args) {
    // Create the frame by calling the appropriate constructor
    // (we are passing in a title to the frame).

    JFrame theFrame = new JFrame("Whee!!!");

    // Set the size to something reasonable (the default JFrame
    // size is 0 pixels wide by 0 pixels high, which isn't visible).

    theFrame.setSize(400, 400);  // width, height in pixels

    // Technique for centering a frame on the screen.

    Dimension frameSize = theFrame.getSize();
    Dimension screenSize = Toolkit.getDefaultToolkit().getScreenSize();
    theFrame.setLocation((screenSize.width - frameSize.width)/2,
                         (screenSize.height - frameSize.height)/2);

    // Assign a grid layout to the frame.

    Container contentPane = theFrame.getContentPane( );
    contentPane.setLayout(new GridLayout(3, 2));  // 3 rows, 2 cols.

    // Create some components to attach.

    JLabel l = new JLabel("Name:");
    JLabel l2 = new JLabel("Address:");
    JLabel l3 = new JLabel("SSN:");

    // This next component, a text area, is a multi-line
    // text component; we're asking for it to be six lines
    // "tall" vs. 20 characters wide.
```

```
JTextArea t = new JTextArea("This is a MULTI-LINE text area, " +
                            "which can contain a lot of text." +
                            " We've asked it to wrap along " +
                            "word boundaries.",
                            6, 20);

// Turn on line wrapping ...

t.setLineWrap(true);

// ... along word boundaries.

t.setWrapStyleWord(true);

// Creating two single-line text fields.

JTextField t2 = new JTextField("This is a SINGLE LINE text field.");
JTextField t3 = new JTextField("Another text field.");

// Add in ascending row, then column, order.

contentPane.add(l);    // row 1, col. 1
contentPane.add(t);    // row 1, col. 2
contentPane.add(l2);   // row 2, col. 1 (etc.)
contentPane.add(t2);
contentPane.add(l3);
contentPane.add(t3);

// Create ONE TOO MANY component!

JTextField t4 = new JTextField("ONE TOO MANY! :op");

// Add it, even though there really is no more room.

contentPane.add(t4);

    theFrame.setVisible(true);
  }
}
```

then the GridLayout, in an attempt to accommodate seven instead of only six components, adds an extra column (for a total of 3 rows x 3 columns, or nine grid cells), and then adds the seven components to the grid in row-first order as shown next – this is not at all what we were hoping for!

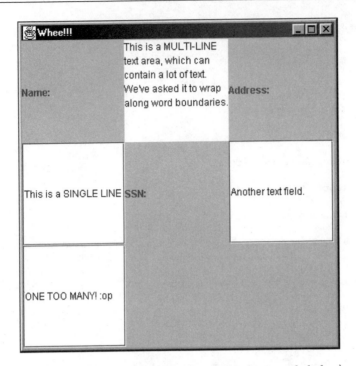

You may use blank labels to 'pad' a grid if need be (see highlights in code below):

```
// FrameTest6C.java
import javax.swing.*;
import java.awt.*;

public class FrameTest6C {
  public static void main(String[] args) {
      // Create the frame by calling the appropriate constructor
      // (we are passing in a title to the frame).

      JFrame theFrame = new JFrame();

      // Set the size to something reasonable (the default JFrame
      // size is 0 pixels wide by 0 pixels high, which isn't visible).

      theFrame.setSize(300, 300);  // width, height in pixels

      // Technique for centering a frame on the screen.

      Dimension frameSize = theFrame.getSize();
      Dimension screenSize = Toolkit.getDefaultToolkit().getScreenSize();
      theFrame.setLocation((screenSize.width - frameSize.width)/2,
                           (screenSize.height - frameSize.height)/2);

      // Assign a grid layout to the frame.
```

```
Container contentPane = theFrame.getContentPane( );
contentPane.setLayout(new GridLayout(3, 2));   // 3 rows, 2 cols.

// Create some components to attach.

JLabel l1 = new JLabel("Name:");
JLabel l2 = new JLabel("Fred");
JLabel l3 = new JLabel("SSN:");
JLabel l4 = new JLabel("123-45-6789");

// Add in ascending row, then column, order.

contentPane.add(l1);          // row 1, col. 1
contentPane.add(l2);          // row 1, col. 2

// Create two blank labels "on the fly", and add them
// to the 2nd row.

contentPane.add(new JLabel(""));   // row 2, col. 1
contentPane.add(new JLabel(""));   // row 2, col. 2

contentPane.add(l3);          // row 3, col. 1
contentPane.add(l4);          // row 3, col. 2

theFrame.setSize(200, 200);
theFrame.setVisible(true);
    }
}
```

The result is shown below:

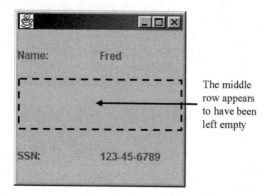

The middle row appears to have been left empty

FlowLayout

Like a `GridLayout`, a `FlowLayout` adds `Components` to the `Container` that it manages from left to right, top to bottom. Whereas a `GridLayout` divides a `Container` into rows of equal numbers of evenly-sized cells, a `FlowLayout` is much more unstructured: it simply fits as many `Components` across the `Container` as it can from left to right to form a row, allowing each `Component` to retain its preferred size, and then 'wraps' to start a new row when a given row is full. (This is similar to the way that sentences of differing lengths wrap along word boundaries in a word processor.)

Here is a revised version of our `FrameTest` program, modified to use a `FlowLayout` (see highlights in code below):

```
// FrameTest7.java
import javax.swing.*;
import java.awt.*;

public class FrameTest7 {
  public static void main(String[] args) {
    // Create the frame by calling the appropriate constructor
    // (we are passing in a title to the frame).

    JFrame theFrame = new JFrame("Whee!!!");

    // Technique for centering a frame on the screen.

    Dimension frameSize = theFrame.getSize();
    Dimension screenSize = Toolkit.getDefaultToolkit().getScreenSize();
    theFrame.setLocation((screenSize.width - frameSize.width)/2,
                         (screenSize.height - frameSize.height)/2);

    // Override the default layout manager.

    Container contentPane = theFrame.getContentPane();
    contentPane.setLayout(new FlowLayout());

    // Create several labels.

    JLabel l1 = new JLabel("A short label");
    JLabel l2 = new JLabel("A rather long label");
    JLabel l3 = new JLabel("Another fairly long label");

    // Play with the colors.

    l1.setBackground(Color.cyan);
    l1.setForeground(Color.black);
    l2.setBackground(Color.white);
    l2.setForeground(Color.black);
    l3.setBackground(Color.yellow);
    l3.setForeground(Color.black);

    // Make the labels opaque (the default is transparent)
    // so that their background colors show up.
```

```
11.setOpaque(true);
12.setOpaque(true);
13.setOpaque(true);

// Add them to the GUI.

contentPane.add(l1);
contentPane.add(l2);
contentPane.add(l3);

// Set the size to something reasonable (the default is 0 x 0,
// which isn't visible).

theFrame.setSize(200,200);  // width, height

// Make the frame appear on the screen.

theFrame.setVisible(true);
  }
}
```

When this frame is first displayed, it appears as follows:

The first two labels are able to fit side-by-side in the frame, but the third slips down into a second row by itself.

If we resize the frame by grabbing and dragging an edge of the window with the mouse so that it is wide enough for all three labels to fit side by side, the FlowLayout manager automatically moves them all into the same row:

If we then make the frame narrow enough by grabbing and dragging an edge of the window with the mouse, each label will instead show up on its own separate line:

Note that we had to explicitly set the JFrame's layout manager to be a FlowLayout object in this case, because as we learned earlier, the JFrame's default layout manager is BorderLayout; we did so with the method call:

```
contentPane.setLayout(new FlowLayout());
```

JLabels

As we've already learned, JLabels are a simple type of Component used to display a single line of text, which can be left justified, centered, or right justified. A JLabel may also be used to display an image, or a combination of text and an image, but we won't be availing ourselves of that capability in building the SRS.

As is true of so many of the Swing components, the Java language defines many different forms of constructor for JLabels; the only forms of JLabel constructor that we'll be using in building the SRS GUI are:

❑   JLabel(String text, int horizontalAlignment), where horizontalAlignment can assume one of the three different public static final attribute values JLabel.LEFT, JLabel.CENTER, or JLabel.RIGHT.

❑   JLabel(String text), where left-justified alignment is the default.

A JLabel is not meant to be editable by the user directly, but we can programmatically affect what a label says in response to what a user does by making use of the setText() method:

```
// Pseudocode.
JLabel l = new JLabel("");  // blank for now
// Intervening details omitted ...
if (user chose option X ) l.setText("Option X selected ...");
else l.setText("Option X was NOT selected!");
```

JTextFields and JPasswordFields

A `JTextField` displays a single line of text that is either typed into the field by a user or supplied automatically by the program. We have numerous constructors to choose from for `JTextFields`; the two that we'll be focusing on are:

- ❏ `JTextField(int columns)`, where `columns` sizes the text field by describing the number of visible character positions. For proportional fonts – that is, fonts in which not all characters are the same width – the width of the letter 'm' is used as the standard character size/column width.

   Note that it is possible to assign specific fonts to a text component, but since we have no need to do so in building the SRS, we will not discuss the details for doing so in this book.

- ❏ `JTextField()` – this version creates an empty text field, but doesn't try to mandate its size – in this case, the layout manager of whatever `Container` the field is attached to will decide an appropriate size.

Either way, text fields are scrollable, which means that if a user types in more text than can visibly fit into a field, the text will simply scroll off to the left. In the `JTextField` shown below, the user has typed `'If I type too much text, the field will scroll.'` Note that there is no visual cue given to the user: for example, no scroll bar appears to signal the user that this has happened.

Using the left arrow (cursor) key on the keyboard, we can scroll back to the beginning of the text in this field:

Two of the more frequently used methods defined by the `JTextField` class are:

- ❏ `String getText()` - returns a `String` containing the text currently in the `JTextField` (that is, the text that a user has typed in). If the field is empty, this method returns an empty string (`" "`).

- ❏ `void setText(String s)` - allows us to programmatically populate a field with the text specified by `s`.

Two other useful properties that we often manipulate with `JTextFields` is whether or not a field is editable and whether or not it is enabled. We talked about the enablement of `Components` in general earlier in this chapter; the editability of `JTextFields` is controlled in much the same way, via the `setEditable(boolean)` method. If a field's editability is set to `false`, a user cannot modify what is displayed in the text field: it *looks* like a text field, but behaves more like a label. To truly be editable, a `JTextField` must be *both* editable and enabled.

In the sample GUI code below, we create four `JTextFields`, and experiment with various settings for the editability and enablement of each field:

```java
// EditableExample.java
import java.awt.*;
import javax.swing.*;

public class EditableExample {
  public static void main(String args[]) {
    JFrame theFrame = new JFrame("");
    Container contentPane = theFrame.getContentPane( );
    contentPane.setLayout(new GridLayout(4, 1));

    JTextField l1 = new JTextField("Editable and Enabled");
    l1.setEditable(true);
    l1.setEnabled(true);
    JTextField l2 = new JTextField("Editable and Disabled");
    l2.setEditable(true);
    l2.setEnabled(false);
    JTextField l3 = new JTextField("Not Editable and Enabled");
    l3.setEditable(false);
    l3.setEnabled(true);
    JTextField l4 = new JTextField("Not Editable and Disabled");
    l4.setEditable(false);
    l4.setEnabled(false);

    contentPane.add(l1);
    contentPane.add(l2);
    contentPane.add(l3);
    contentPane.add(l4);

    theFrame.setSize(300, 200);
    theFrame.setVisible(true);
  }
}
```

The resultant GUI is shown below. Only the first of the four of these text fields can actually be modified by the user, yet note the differing appearances of the other three.

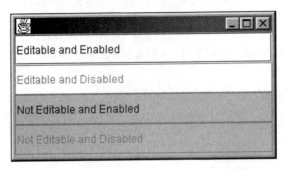

`JPasswordField`, a subclass of `JTextField`, is used when we want to provide security with respect to information being typed in. As a user types data into a `JPasswordField`, each character that is typed is reflected as an **echo character**; in the following figure, the user typed '123' as a password, but it appeared instead as '***':

To set the echo character to something other than the default of '*', use the `setEchoCharacter(char c)` method as shown in the following snippet:

```
JPasswordField passwordField = new JPasswordField();
passwordField.setEchoCharacter('#');        // note use of single vs.
                                            // double quotes
```

As mentioned in Chapter 1, we must use *single quotes* to enclose a `char` (character) constant; this has a very different meaning from `"#"`, which is actually a `String` of length 1.

We have to do a little bit of extra work to retrieve the value that has been typed into a `JPasswordField`, since the `getText()` method inherited from `JTextField` is *deprecated* for the `JPasswordField` class, which means that although the `getText()` method still works as of Java version 1.2.2, it is not guaranteed to work in a future release of Java. The preferred alternative to using `getText()` is as follows:

❑   We first declare and instantiate a password field:

```
JPasswordField passwordField = new JPasswordField();

// details omitted ... assume that the password field has been attached
// to a JFrame, the JFrame has been displayed, and the user has typed in a
// password.
```

❑   Retrieving the value as typed by a user is a two step process: first, we use the `getPassword()` method, which returns an array of `char`(acters) rather than a `String`:

```
char[] pw = passwordField.getPassword();
```

❑   Then, we pass this `char`(acter) array in as an argument to a form of `String` constructor that knows how to turn the contents of the array into a `String`:

```
String password = new String(pw);
```

When we get to working with the SRS code, we'll look at an application of this technique in the SRS `PasswordPopup` class.

JButtons

`JButtons` allow the user to initiate an action by 'clicking' what appears to be a three-dimensional button on the GUI. We have to program an **event listener** to define what we actually want the button to do when it is clicked (we'll learn about event listeners later in the chapter), but the button is inherently 'clickable' just by virtue of creating it – it appears to move in and out of the computer screen as we illustrated earlier in the chapter.

There are several `JButton` constructors; the one that we'll use for the SRS is:

```
JButton(String text)
```

where `text` is used as the button's label. (As with `JLabels`, a button may also carry an image, or a combination of an image and text.)

JLists

A `JList` is used for presenting a list of choices to a user. These choices can be text, images, or literally any GUI component: for example, a list of `JButtons`, each of which may be clicked to trigger a different action! We'll be working with simple, text-oriented lists in developing the SRS GUI.

There are various `JList` constructors; the ones that we'll be focusing on are as follows:

❑ `JList()` – creates an empty `JList`.

❑ `JList(Vector listData)` – this is a very interesting constructor! We hand in a `Vector` containing whatever type of `Object` we like, and the `JList` in turn displays a list of textual items by invoking the `toString()` method on each of the `Objects` contained within the `Vector`. (Recall our discussion from Chapter 13 of the importance of programming a `toString()` method for all of the classes that we invent).

Let's look at a simple program that demonstrates the latter form of `JList` constructor; we're going to display a list of student names based on a `Vector` of `Student` objects. In order for this to work, we must have programmed a `toString()` method for the `Student` class; we'll use the following simplified version of `Student`, rather than the more elaborate one we've developed for the SRS, to support this `JList` example:

```
// Student.java

// * * * * * * * * * * * * * * * * * * * * * * * * * * * * *
// THIS IS AN ABBREVIATED VERSION OF THE Student CLASS,
// FOR USE WITH THE VARIOUS VERSIONS OF JListDemo.
// * * * * * * * * * * * * * * * * * * * * * * * * * * * * *

import java.util.*;

public class Student {
```

```
//-----------
// Attributes.
//-----------

private String name;
private String ssn;

//----------------
// Constructor(s).
//----------------

public Student(String ssn, String name) {
  this.ssn = ssn;
  this.name = name;
}

public String toString() {
  return name + " (" + ssn + ")";
}

public String getName() {
  return name;
}
}
```

❑ We start with the basics:

```
// JListDemo.java

import java.util.*;
import javax.swing.*;
import java.awt.*;

public class JListDemo {
  public static void main(String[] args) {
    JFrame theFrame = new JFrame("Sample JList");
    Container contentPane = theFrame.getContentPane();
```

❑ Next, we create a Vector and populate it with a few Student objects:

```
Vector v = new Vector();        // of Students
v.add(new Student("123456789", "Joe Blow"));
v.add(new Student("987654321", "Fred Schnurd"));
v.add(new Student("000000000", "Englebert Humperdink"));
```

❑ Now, we'll create a new JList object called 'myList', passing in the Student vector:

```
JList myList = new JList(v);
```

❏ Finally, we round out the program:

```
            contentPane.add(myList);
            theFrame.setSize(300, 90);        // width, height
            theFrame.setVisible(true);
        }
    }
```

Here is the code, in its entirety:

```
// JListDemo.java
import java.util.*;
import javax.swing.*;
import java.awt.*;

public class JListDemo {
    public static void main(String[] args) {
        JFrame theFrame = new JFrame("Sample JList");
        Container contentPane = theFrame.getContentPane( );

        // Create a vector of students.

        Vector v = new Vector(); // of Students
        v.add(new Student("123456789", "Joe Blow"));
        v.add(new Student("987654321", "Fred Schnurd"));
        v.add(new Student("000000000", "Captain Haggis"));

        // Create a list based on this vector. The reason that
        // we can do this is because the Student class inherits
        // a toString() method from its parent Person class;
        // the method is defined as follows:
        /*
          public String toString() {
            return name + " (" + ssn + ")";
          }
        */
        // which causes each Student object to be rendered
        // in terms of its name and SSN in the list.

        JList myList = new JList(v);
        contentPane.add(myList);

        theFrame.setSize(300, 90);   // width, height
        theFrame.setVisible(true);
    }
}
```

The preceding program, when run, produces the following GUI as expected:

Had we failed to program a toString() method for the Student class, this example would still work, because as we discussed in Chapter 13, all objects inherit the toString() method of the Object class; however, the list wouldn't be nearly as readable, since the default toString() method of the Object class returns an internal ID for each object:

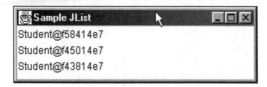

Calculator Example, Take 1

Let's put all that we've learned about GUI components so far into practice by building a simple little calculator GUI which, when finished, will look as follows:

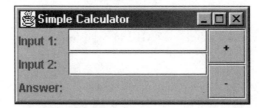

❑ The calculator provides two input text fields labeled 'Input 1:' and 'Input 2:'.

❑ To operate the calculator, the user types a numeric value into each field, and then clicks either the plus (+) or minus (-) button, depending on whether they wish to add or subtract the two values.

❑ The sum or difference of the two values, as appropriate, will be displayed as a non-editable value next to the label 'Answer:'.

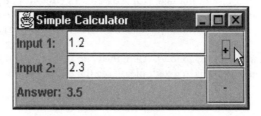

The components that comprise this GUI are visually grouped into three clusters of similarly sized components:

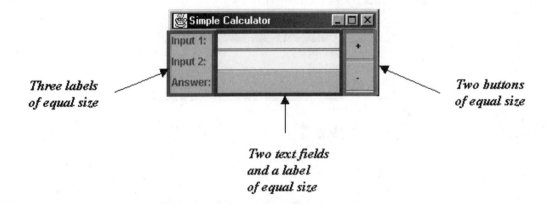

Three labels of equal size

Two buttons of equal size

Two text fields and a label of equal size

Whenever you are able to visually subdivide a GUI into clusters of similarly-sized components, think GridLayout-managed JPanels!

Actually, once you become proficient with Java in general and with GUIs in particular, you may wish to investigate the use of GridBagLayout instead. Even knowing how to use GridBagLayout, however, I still find GridLayout quite useful for the technique I am about to describe.

For our calculator, we'll create three JPanels:

❑   For each of the leftmost and center panels, we'll create a GridLayout with three rows and one column; and, for the rightmost panel, we'll create a GridLayout with two rows and one column.

❑   Then, since the default layout manager for a JFrame's content pane is a BorderLayout, we can add the leftmost panel to the WEST region of the JFrame, the center panel to the CENTER region, and the rightmost panel to the EAST region to achieve the desired look.

The code used to produce this GUI is as follows. All of the code that we use in this example should by now be familiar to you, so we won't discuss it in detail; please see the in-line comments included with the code.

```
// Calculator1.java

import java.awt.*;
import javax.swing.*;

public class Calculator1 {
  public static void main(String[ ] args) {
    JFrame aFrame = new JFrame("Simple Calculator");
    Container contentPane = aFrame.getContentPane();
    aFrame.setSize(250, 100);
```

```java
// We don't need to set the layout manager for
// a JFrame's content pane - it is automatically a
// BorderLayout by default!

// Technique for centering a frame on the screen.

Dimension frameSize = aFrame.getSize();
Dimension screenSize = Toolkit.getDefaultToolkit().getScreenSize();
aFrame.setLocation((screenSize.width - frameSize.width)/2,
                   (screenSize.height - frameSize.height)/2);

// Let's create the leftmost panel. Note that we use names
// for our components that are somewhat self-documenting.

JPanel leftPanel = new JPanel();

// We'll assign the panel a GridLayout (it would otherwise
// default to FlowLayout).

leftPanel.setLayout(new GridLayout(3, 1));

// We'll create three labels on the fly and hand them
// to the panel; there's no need to bother maintaining
// a named handle on any of these labels.

leftPanel.add(new JLabel("Input 1: "));
leftPanel.add(new JLabel("Input 2: "));
leftPanel.add(new JLabel("Answer: "));

// Now, we'll attach the panel to the frame.

contentPane.add(leftPanel, BorderLayout.WEST);

// Repeat the process with the center panel.

JPanel centerPanel = new JPanel();
centerPanel.setLayout(new GridLayout(3, 1));
JTextField input1TextField = new JTextField(10);
JTextField input2TextField = new JTextField(10);

// We use a JLabel to display the answer of the
// calculation, although we could have also used
// a non-editable JTextField instead.

JLabel answerLabel = new JLabel();
centerPanel.add(input1TextField);
centerPanel.add(input2TextField);
centerPanel.add(answerLabel);
contentPane.add(centerPanel, BorderLayout.CENTER);

// The third, and final, panel.
```

517

```
        JPanel buttonPanel = new JPanel();
        buttonPanel.setLayout(new GridLayout(2, 1));
        JButton plusButton = new JButton("+");
        JButton minusButton = new JButton("-");
        buttonPanel.add(plusButton);
        buttonPanel.add(minusButton);
        contentPane.add(buttonPanel, BorderLayout.EAST);

        aFrame.setVisible(true);
    }
}
```

Note that there is no limit to the 'depth' of layering that you can achieve with JPanels – in the sketch below, we show three levels of JPanel being attached to an underlying JFrame, with varying GridLayout configurations. Be creative! We'll see an example of how to do this with the SRS GUI's main window, class MainFrame, later in this chapter.

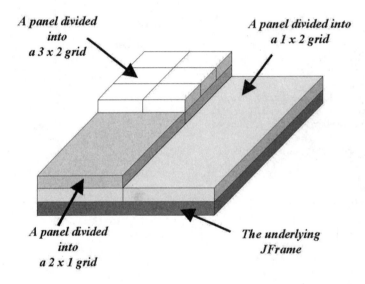

A panel divided into a 3 x 2 grid

A panel divided into a 1 x 2 grid

A panel divided into a 2 x 1 grid

The underlying JFrame

Meanwhile, back to our calculator. As currently programmed, it doesn't do anything interesting yet because we haven't programmed any event handling; a user can type values into the 'Input 1:' and 'Input 2:' fields, but clicking either of the two buttons will not cause any computation to occur. Nonetheless, the buttons do reflect movement when clicked.

We'll add functionality to the calculator in just a moment, after we look at ways to restructure our calculator code to conform to a more 'typical' Java software architecture.

Application Architecture with GUIs

The simple GUI examples that we've seen thus far all involve a single class whose main() method instantiates a JFrame, creates and add components to the frame, and finally displays the frame; this basic skeletal structure is summarized below:

```
// Pseudocode.

public class GUIClass {
    public static void main(...) {
    // Create a frame ...

    JFrame f = new JFrame();

    // ... create and add components ...

    JButton b = new JButton("Foo");
    f.getContentPane().add(b);

    // etc.

    // ... and make the frame appear!

    f.setSize(...);
    f.setVisible(true);
    }
}
```

This is not an appropriate architecture for anything but trivial applications, however. A better architecture for a GUI application is to create a minimum of two classes:

❑ A class, derived from JFrame, which defines the appearance (and behavior) of the main GUI window:

  ❑ All components to be attached to the frame become *attributes* of this class.

  ❑ The components are instantiated and attached in the *constructor* for this class.

❑ An application 'driver' class, which:

  ❑ Instantiates an instance of the main window in its main() method.

  ❑ Handles any other application initialization steps – for example, establishing database connectivity, perhaps with a log-on dialog.

  ❑ Houses any 'global data' (as public static attributes), constants (as public static final attributes), or convenience methods (as public static methods) for the application as a whole.

❑ If more than one window is needed for the GUI (as will be the case for the SRS GUI), additional classes are created, each of which define the appearance and behavior of some other key window (usually either another JFrame or a JDialog). Some simplistic dialogs – error message pop-ups, 'confirm/cancel' questions, and the like – can be created on the fly, and don't necessarily need their own separate classes; we'll see examples of this with the SRS GUI.

Let's take another look at our calculator example, rearchitected as suggested above.

❑ First, we'll create a class called `Calculator2`, in a file named `'Calculator2.java'`, to represent the main window – namely, the calculator itself! We've moved most of the code from the `main()` method of `Calculator1.java` into the constructor for `Calculator2`.

❑ We declare all of the `Component` 'building blocks' of the GUI as attributes of this class, which serves to make them visible throughout all of the methods of the class. This is not particularly critical for the `Calculator2` example, because there are no methods besides the constructor; but, for more complex GUIs, this will prove to be a valuable technique.

By now, most of the code which follows should be familiar to you, so we'll keep our 'interruptions' to a minimum:

```
// Calculator2.java
import java.awt.*;
import javax.swing.*;

public class Calculator2 extends JFrame {
    // Components are treated as attributes, so that they will be
    // visible to all of the methods of the class.

    private Container contentPane;

    // Use descriptive names for components where possible; it makes
    // your job easier later on!

    private JPanel leftPanel;
    private JPanel centerPanel;
    private JPanel buttonPanel;
    private JTextField input1TextField;
    private JTextField input2TextField;
    private JLabel answerLabel;
    private JButton plusButton;
    private JButton minusButton;

    // Constructor.
    // The constructor is where we create and attach all of the
    // Components to the underlying JFrame.

    public Calculator2() {
        // Invoke the generic JFrame constructor.
        super("Simple Calculator");

// The content pane container is now declared to be an
        // attribute.  Note that the use of "this." is unnecessary;
        // we could have simply written:
        // contentPane = getContentPane();
        contentPane = this.getContentPane();
        this.setSize(250, 100);
```

One important thing to note: since we are now doing things from *within* the JFrame class that we used to do *externally* to the JFrame *instance* from within the main() method – for example, getting a handle on the content pane, setting the size of the frame – we use the 'this' prefix to clarify that the frame in question is *this* frame.

```
        // Technique for centering a frame on the screen.
        Dimension frameSize = this.getSize();
        Dimension screenSize = Toolkit.getDefaultToolkit().getScreenSize();
        this.setLocation((screenSize.width - frameSize.width)/2,
                         (screenSize.height - frameSize.height)/2);

        leftPanel = new JPanel();
        leftPanel.setLayout(new GridLayout(3, 1));
        leftPanel.add(new JLabel("Input 1:  "));
        leftPanel.add(new JLabel("Input 2:  "));
        leftPanel.add(new JLabel("Answer:  "));
        contentPane.add(leftPanel, BorderLayout.WEST);

        centerPanel = new JPanel();
        centerPanel.setLayout(new GridLayout(3, 1));
        input1TextField = new JTextField(10);
        input2TextField = new JTextField(10);
        answerLabel = new JLabel();
        centerPanel.add(input1TextField);
        centerPanel.add(input2TextField);
        centerPanel.add(answerLabel);
        contentPane.add(centerPanel, BorderLayout.CENTER);

        buttonPanel = new JPanel();
        buttonPanel.setLayout(new GridLayout(2, 1));
        plusButton = new JButton("+");
        minusButton = new JButton("-");
        buttonPanel.add(plusButton);
        buttonPanel.add(minusButton);
        contentPane.add(buttonPanel, BorderLayout.EAST);

        this.setVisible(true);

        // We still need to add behaviors!
    }
}
```

❑   Next, we'll create the 'driver' class, CalculatorDriver, in a separate file called 'CalculatorDriver.java'. For this example, the driver's main() method is a trivially simple 'one-liner' – it needs merely to create an instance of the Calculator2 class by invoking the Calculator2 constructor. The constructor (shown above) does all of the work of creating and displaying the GUI!

```
// CalculatorDriver.java
public class CalculatorDriver {
    // If this program were to require any "global" data (as public static
    // attributes of the CalculatorDriver class), these would be declared here:
    // ***
    // but this example doesn't require any.

    public static void main(String[] args) {
        // Instantiate the main window -- the Calculator class
        // does the rest of the work!

        new Calculator2();
    }

    // If this program were to require any "convenience" methods (as public
    // static methods of the CalculatorDriver class), these might be
    // declared here:
    // ***
    // but this example doesn't require any.
}
```

To invoke this new calculator application, we compile *both* classes, and then we pass the name of the *driver* class to the JVM on the command line:

```
javac CalculatorDriver.java Calculator2.java
java CalculatorDriver
```

This combination of two classes produces the same calculator GUI as before.

We'll use this approach of separating the main window from the application driver when we develop the SRS GUI later in this chapter.

The 'Look of a GUI', In Review

Despite the fact that we've covered a lot of ground so far in this chapter, we've barely scratched the surface with regard to Java GUI components! We've covered the basics of what you'll need to know from the AWT and Swing API perspectives as it pertains to the 'look' of the SRS GUI in order to appreciate the SRS solution code later in this chapter. But, you'll almost certainly want to go on to learn more about GUI programming with Java; see the Recommended Reading section in Chapter 17.

We'll now turn our attention away from how a GUI looks to how it behaves, that is, event handling.

Java Event Handling

Now that we have gotten a sense of how to build a GUI – that is, a 'view' – we still have to learn how to recognize events – i.e. users' interactions with the GUI/view – and how to control how the application responds to them.

Events - Basic Concepts

GUI events are generated when the user interacts with a component on the GUI: for example, clicks a button, types in a field, and so on. As with virtually everything else in Java, events are objects! There are many different types of event, each represented by its own `Event` class; we'll learn about several of these shortly.

When we create a GUI component, it automatically has the ability to generate events whenever a user interacts with it - we need do nothing to get this phenomenon to occur. What we *do* need to explicitly deal with, however, is programming how the GUI should react to the *subset* of events that we are interested in (known as **event handling**).

In order to handle events, we need to do two things when programming a GUI:

1. We must instantiate a special type of object called a `Listener` that is capable of 'hearing' and responding to the appropriate type of event. We must then program the Listener object's methods with whatever behavior that we want it to react with when it *hears* such an event.

For example, we may create an `ActionListener`, a type of listener that is capable of listening to `ActionEvents`, the type of event that is generated, for example, when a `JButton` is clicked.

2. We must **register** the `Listener` object with the *specific* Component object(s) that we want the listener to listen to. Just because a listener can react to button presses, for example, doesn't mean that we want a *particular* `Listener` object to listen and respond to *all* button presses in our application; we may instead want a different `Listener` object to react to each different `JButton` object, or to have one `Listener` object assigned to listen to all of the `JButtons` on a given `JFrame`. If we try to make any one listener listen to too many components, however, the behavioral code of that listener will become 'bloated' and complex, making it difficult to maintain.

The following figures illustrate how event handling works conceptually.

- ❑ Whenever a user interacts with a component on a Java graphical user interface, the component generates numerous events of various types. For example, if the cursor is moved over a `JButton`, the `JButton` is 'clicked', and the cursor is then moved off the button, the following events are generated:

  - ❑ A 'mouse entered' event is generated when the cursor enters the JButton.
  - ❑ Numerous 'mouse moved' events are generated as the cursor moves from pixel to pixel within the boundaries of the JButton.
  - ❑ Three events – a 'mouse pressed' event, a 'mouse clicked' event, and an 'action' event – are generated when the mouse button is depressed.
  - ❑ A 'mouse released' event is generated when the mouse button is released.

In addition:

❑ A 'focus gained' event is generated for a JButton when the window (JFrame) that the JButton is attached to gains focus.

❑ A 'focus lost' event is generated when the cursor moves outside of the boundaries of the JButton.

This is depicted in the figure below, where the letters 'A', 'B', 'C', and 'D' represent four different types of events that are generated by interacting with a component – specifically, a JButton labeled 'Foo!'. Note, however, that if no listeners have been created, then these events are not detected (just like a tree falling in the woods when there is nobody around to hear it!).

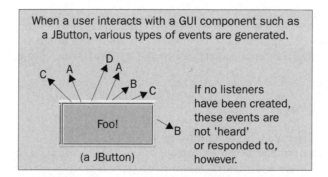

When a user interacts with a GUI component such as a JButton, various types of events are generated.

Foo!

(a JButton)

If no listeners have been created, these events are not 'heard' or responded to, however.

❑ In the next figure, we create three different types of listener, capable of listening to event types 'A', 'B', and 'C', respectively. We purposely ignore event type 'D', as we are not interested in knowing when such events occur.

As mentioned before, simply creating the listeners is not sufficient, however; the listeners won't react to any events unless the listeners are specifically registered with one or more components capable of generating such events. In our example, the listeners would have to explicitly be registered to listen to the 'Foo!' button in order to hear any of its events.

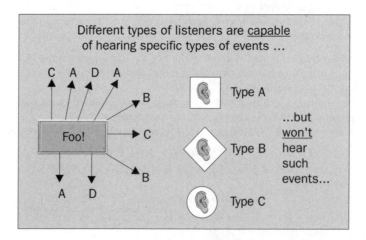

Different types of listeners are <u>capable</u> of hearing specific types of events ...

Foo!

Type A

Type B

Type C

...but <u>won't</u> hear such events...

❑   In the third and final figure, we have registered the 'A' and 'B' type listeners to listen to button 'Foo!' for 'A' and 'B' type events, respectively. However, since we've neither registered the 'C' type listener on this component nor created a 'D' type listener, then the 'C' and 'D' events that Foo! generates continue to be ignored.

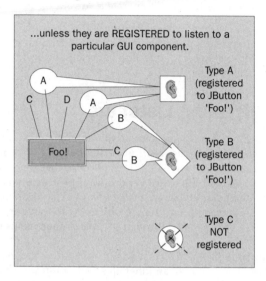

Note that it is also possible for non-GUI objects to generate events. We won't be covering this aspect of event handling in this book because the SRS application doesn't make use of such a capability, but it is nonetheless a very powerful feature of the Java language. For further information, research Java Beans and PropertyChangeListeners; *see Chapter 17 for some recommendations. In addition, as a 'freebie', we've included four files in the downloadable code for Chapter 16 –* BeanExample.java, ListeningObject.java, ListenedToObject.java, *and* SomeObject.java *– to give you a taste of how* PropertyChangeListeners *work.*

Basic Event Types

There are many different types of GUI events, and therefore many different types of listeners! Some event types were defined by the AWT API, while others have been added with the Swing API.

We are only going to be dealing with a few types of events and listeners in building the SRS; these are summarized in the table below.

Type of Events That We Care About in the SRS GUI:	We'll Be Listening to These as Generated in the SRS GUI by Components of Type:	Type of Listener Required for Listening to this Event Type:	Defined in Which API/Package?
ActionEvent	JButton, JTextField	ActionListener	java.awt.event
WindowEvent	JFrame, JDialog	WindowListener	java.awt.event
ListSelectionEvent	JList	ListSelectionListener	javax.swing.event

Two important points to note:

❏ The components listed in the second column of the table above are capable of generating many more event types than those which we are interested in listening for and responding to. For example, all of these components generate MouseEvents and FocusEvents, but we aren't going to bother to listen for them.

❏ Other components (beyond those listed in the second column) are capable of generating these same event types: for example, JLists also generate ActionEvents, but we aren't going to bother to listen for them.

Creating and Registering Listeners

In my experience with teaching Java, I have found that one of the most overwhelming aspects of learning Java event handling for most students is understanding all of the many ways that Java provides for creating Listener objects. There are Listener *interfaces* that we may implement, and/or Adapter *classes* that we may extend; there are various ways to structure and organize the listener objects once we instantiate them; and there are various ways to associate listeners to the components that they'll listen to. To keep things manageable, we are going to focus on only one approach for creating Listeners in this book: namely, through the use of **anonymous inner classes**.

By way of review, we learned in Chapter 13 that an *inner class* is a class that is wholly defined within the boundaries of another class. The syntax of an inner class definition was shown to be as follows:

```
// Pseudocode.
public class OuterClass {
  define the outer class's attributes

  class InnerClass {
    define the inner class's attributes and methods
  }

  public void methodOfOuterClass () {
    // Instantiate an object of type InnerClass. The compiler
    // understands what an 'InnerClass' is, by virtue of the
    // declaration of class InnerClass above.
    InnerClass x = new InnerClass();
    // etc.
  }

  declare other methods of the outer class
}
```

We also learned in Chapter 13 that when a class containing an inner class definition is compiled, we wind up with *two* .class files, named *OuterClass*.class and *OuterClass$InnerClass*.class, respectively. Because the inner class in our example has an explicit name – 'InnerClass' – we actually refer to it as a **named inner class**.

What does this have to do with creating and registering listeners? We're going to use a special technique for creating listeners in terms of what are known as **anonymous inner classes**. An anonymous inner class is conceptually the same as a named inner class – that is, a class that is wholly defined within the bounds of another class – but the syntax for creating such a class differs from what we presented above for a named inner class, which we'll see shortly.

Since our ultimate short term goal is to add behavior to our calculator application, let's talk about the specific type of listener that the calculator will be making use of: an `ActionListener`. To create an `ActionListener` object, we must implement an interface called `ActionListener` (recall our discussion of Java interfaces in Chapters 7 and 13). This interface specifies only one method, the `actionPerformed()` method, with the following signature:

```
void actionPerformed(ActionEvent e)
```

The body of this method will need to be programmed to contain the logic of how this listener is going to react when it hears an `ActionEvent`. Note that the method takes one argument, which will be an object reference of type `ActionEvent`. This event object has several methods that can prove extremely useful for discovering information about the source of the event; we'll see the use of one such method when we program a future version of the calculator program (`Calculator4`).

The `actionPerformed()` method is going to need to be able to manipulate the components on our calculator GUI – in particular, it needs to read the values of the two input text fields and output the answer to a third label component. If we declared the action listeners as separate external classes, which we certainly could do, as illustrated in the following pseudocode:

```
// pseudocode
  // Contents of file #1:
public class Calculator3 extends JFrame {
  // Attributes (components) are declared here.
  private JTextField input1TextField;
  // etc.

  // other details omitted
}
  // Contents of file #2:
public class PlusButtonListener implements ActionListener {
  public void actionPerformed(...) {
    // The private components of Calculator3 (e.g. input1TextField)
    // are not visible to PlusButtonListener!
  }
}

  // Contents of file #3:
public class MinusButtonListener implements ActionListener {
  public void actionPerformed(...) {
    // Ditto!
  }
}
```

then we see that the listeners don't have ready access to the GUI components of the calculator. We'd have to go to a lot of extra work to make these *private, encapsulated* attributes of *Calculator3* visible/accessible to the listeners. Therefore, there is a definite advantage to defining the listeners as inner classes: namely, that they'll be within the private scope of the outer class's attributes, and can easily 'see'/manipulate the desired components.

See Calculator3B.java, which is included in the code download from the Wrox website, for an example of what all we'd have to go through to make the preceding scenario of using external listener classes work.

Instead of declaring the `ActionListeners` as *named* inner classes, however, we're going to take advantage of a special 'shortcut' syntax that lets us create a new 'flavor' of `ActionListener` on the fly, implementing the `actionPerformed()` method without going through the full formalities of creating a separate named inner class. The syntax is as follows:

```
// pseudocode

ActionListener l = new ActionListener() {
  public void actionPerformed(ActionEvent e) {
    program whatever action we want to occur here …
  }
};  Note ending semicolon!
```

This syntax has a very strange feature: note the ending semicolon (;) after the closing curly brace on this complex statement! We don't normally see semicolons following curly braces; but, this is a special use of curly braces, and the semicolon is needed to terminate the *single* statement that begins with 'ActionListener l = ...'.

It turns out that, although it doesn't look like one, we've just created an inner class – what's known as an **anonymous inner class**, to be precise, because we haven't named the class, only the instance variable 'l' that will hold onto the listener object that is returned from instantiating this inner class.

Adding Behavior to our Calculator

We're now ready to go back and add some event handling to the `Calculator2` class/GUI from earlier in this chapter. In this next revision to the class, we'll instantiate two anonymous inner class `ActionListeners` – one for the 'plus' button and one for the 'minus' button – and register these listeners with their respective buttons. Here are the highlights of the approach that we are going to take:

❏ First, we'll use the new technique that we just learned for creating anonymous inner classes on the fly to create a listener object to respond to the 'plus' button:

```
ActionListener l = new ActionListener() {
  public void actionPerformed(ActionEvent e) {
    // Get the value the user entered in the JText field and
    // convert it to a double ...
    double d1 =
      new Double(input1TextField.getText()).doubleValue();
    double d2 =
      new Double(input2TextField.getText()).doubleValue();
    answerLabel.setText("" + (d1 + d2));
  }
};
```

Note the unusual syntax of the statement:

```
double d1 = new Double(input1TextField.getText()).doubleValue();
```

What exactly are we doing here? We're using the message `input1TextField.getText()` to retrieve the value that the user typed into the `input1TextField` as a `String` (because that's the only way that `JTextFields` know how to report their contents); then, we're creating a `Double` 'wrapper' object based on that text string (we talked about wrapper classes for primitive data types in Chapter 13); and then we use the `doubleValue()` method of the `Double` class to pull out a simple `double` value.

❑ We'll then need to register this listener with the plus button:

```
plusButton.addActionListener(l);
```

❑ We'll then do the same two things for the minus button; note that we are 'recycling' reference variable `l` here, in essence dropping our handle on the first listener object so as to grab onto the second listener object. (This is OK, because as it turns out the `plusButton` is still holding onto a reference to the first listener. That's what the `addActionListener()` method does: it gives a component a way to receive and maintain a handle on a `Listener` object, so that the listener won't prematurely get 'garbage collected'.)

```
l = new ActionListener() {
  public void actionPerformed(ActionEvent e) {
    double d1 =
      new Double(input1TextField.getText()).doubleValue();
    double d2 =
      new Double(input2TextField.getText()).doubleValue();
    answerLabel.setText("" + (d1 - d2));
  }
};

minusButton.addActionListener(l);
```

❑ We must import a new package, `java.awt.event`, because the `ActionListener` class is defined therein. (Recall from an earlier discussion that importing `java.awt.*` doesn't also 'grab' `java.awt.event` classes.) Note that although we are using Swing components (`JButtons`), we are using AWT listeners to listen to them, because Swing didn't see the need to make any improvements to the `ActionListener` class.

The full code of the revised calculator example follows:

```
// Calculator3.java
import java.awt.*;
import javax.swing.*;
import java.awt.event.*; // added for event handling

public class Calculator3 extends JFrame {
  // Components are treated as attributes, so that they will be
  // visible to all of the methods of the class.

  private Container contentPane;

  // Use descriptive names for components where possible; it makes
  // your job easier later on!
```

```
      private JPanel leftPanel;
      private JPanel centerPanel;
      private JPanel buttonPanel;
      private JTextField input1TextField;
      private JTextField input2TextField;
      private JLabel answerLabel;
      private JButton plusButton;
      private JButton minusButton;

      // Constructor.
      public Calculator3() {
        // Invoke the generic JFrame constructor.
        super("Simple Calculator");

        // The content pane container is now declared to be an
        // attribute.  Note that the use of "this." is unnecessary;
        // we could have simply written:
        // contentPane = getContentPane();
        contentPane = this.getContentPane();
        this.setSize(250, 100);

        // Technique for centering a frame on the screen.
        Dimension frameSize = this.getSize();
        Dimension screenSize = Toolkit.getDefaultToolkit().getScreenSize();
        this.setLocation((screenSize.width - frameSize.width)/2,
                         (screenSize.height - frameSize.height)/2);

        leftPanel = new JPanel();
        leftPanel.setLayout(new GridLayout(3, 1));
        leftPanel.add(new JLabel("Input 1:   "));
        leftPanel.add(new JLabel("Input 2:   "));
        leftPanel.add(new JLabel("Answer:   "));
        contentPane.add(leftPanel, BorderLayout.WEST);

        centerPanel = new JPanel();
        centerPanel.setLayout(new GridLayout(3, 1));
        input1TextField = new JTextField(10);
        input2TextField = new JTextField(10);
        answerLabel = new JLabel();
        centerPanel.add(input1TextField);
        centerPanel.add(input2TextField);
        centerPanel.add(answerLabel);
        contentPane.add(centerPanel, BorderLayout.CENTER);

        buttonPanel = new JPanel();
        buttonPanel.setLayout(new GridLayout(2, 1));
        plusButton = new JButton("+");
        minusButton = new JButton("-");
        buttonPanel.add(plusButton);
        buttonPanel.add(minusButton);
        contentPane.add(buttonPanel, BorderLayout.EAST);
```

```java
    // Add behaviors! Note the use of anonymous inner classes.

    // First, we create a listener object to respond to
    // the "plus" button ...

    ActionListener l = new ActionListener() {
      public void actionPerformed(ActionEvent e) {
        double d1 = new Double(input1TextField.getText()).doubleValue();
        double d2 = new Double(input2TextField.getText()).doubleValue();
        answerLabel.setText("" + (d1 + d2));
      }
    };

    // ... and then we register this listener with the appropriate
    // component.

    plusButton.addActionListener(l);

    // We do the same for the minus button.

    l = new ActionListener() {
      public void actionPerformed(ActionEvent e) {
        double d1 = new Double(input1TextField.getText()).doubleValue();
        double d2 = new Double(input2TextField.getText()).doubleValue();
        answerLabel.setText("" + (d1 - d2));
      }
    };

    minusButton.addActionListener(l);

    // We set the frame to be visible after adding the listeners,
    // as a bug in 1.2.2 occasionally makes a listener
    // "dysfunctional" if it is added after the frame has been
    // made visible.

    this.setVisible(true);
  }
}
```

Due to a 'quirk' with Java version 1.2.2, the setVisible(true); *method call should always come last in the constructor, after you've attached your various listeners; under some circumstances, if the* setVisible(true); *method call is made before listeners are created and registered, the listeners don't work for some reason.*

When Calculator3.java is compiled, each anonymous inner class produces its own separate .class file, and so a total of three .class files are produced. Because these are *anonymous* inner classes – they don't have an explicit class name – their class files are given rather 'cryptic' names by the compiler:

❑ Calculator3.class

❑ Calculator3$1.class (corresponding to the plusButton listener)

❑ Calculator3$2.class (corresponding to the minusButton listener)

We need to make a minor modification to the `CalculatorDriver` class, to reference `Calculator3` instead of `Calculator2`:

```
public class CalculatorDriver {
  public static void main(String[] args) {
    // Instantiate the main window -- the Calculator class
    // does the rest of the work!

    new Calculator3();
  }
}
```

Every time we introduce a new version of the `Calculatorn` class from now on, we'll remind you to make such a corresponding change to the `CalculatorDriver` class with the simple statement 'remember to update the CalculatorDriver class to refer to this new version of the calculator GUI.'

When this version of the program is run:

java CalculatorDriver

we now find that we have the ability to use the calculator as originally intended: if we type in two legitimate numbers in the 'Input 1:' and 'Input 2:' fields, and click the plus (+) button, we do indeed see the answer displayed in the 'Answer:' field:

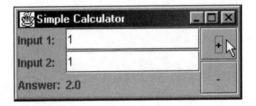

We haven't done any exception handling, though, so typing non-numeric input values such as 'ABC' or leaving either input field blank results in various run time exceptions being thrown. We have included an exercise at the end of this chapter to give you a chance to remedy this shortcoming of the calculator.

Here is another slightly different version of our calculator; in this version, we use a *single* `ActionListener` object to listen to *both* buttons. Since most of the code for this version of the `Calculator` is the same as the previous version, we'll only discuss significant changes (see highlighted code passages):

```
// Calculator4.java
import java.awt.*;
import javax.swing.*;
import java.awt.event.*; // added

public class Calculator4 extends JFrame {
    // Components are treated as attributes, so that they will be
    // visible to all of the methods of the class.
```

```
      private Container contentPane;

      // Use descriptive names for components where possible; it makes
      // your job easier later on!

      private JPanel leftPanel;
      private JPanel centerPanel;
      private JPanel buttonPanel;
      private JTextField input1TextField;
      private JTextField input2TextField;
      private JLabel answerLabel;
      private JButton plusButton;
      private JButton minusButton;

   // Constructor.
   public Calculator4() {
      // Invoke the generic JFrame constructor.
      super("Simple Calculator");

      // The content pane container is now declared to be an
      // attribute. Note that the use of "this." is unnecessary;
      // we could have simply written:
      // contentPane = getContentPane();
      contentPane = this.getContentPane();
      this.setSize(250, 100);

      // Technique for centering a frame on the screen.
      Dimension frameSize = this.getSize();
      Dimension screenSize = Toolkit.getDefaultToolkit().getScreenSize();
      this.setLocation((screenSize.width - frameSize.width)/2,
                       (screenSize.height - frameSize.height)/2);

      leftPanel = new JPanel();
      leftPanel.setLayout(new GridLayout(3, 1));
      leftPanel.add(new JLabel("Input 1:  "));
      leftPanel.add(new JLabel("Input 2:  "));
      leftPanel.add(new JLabel("Answer:   "));
      contentPane.add(leftPanel, BorderLayout.WEST);

      centerPanel = new JPanel();
      centerPanel.setLayout(new GridLayout(3, 1));
      input1TextField = new JTextField(10);
      input2TextField = new JTextField(10);
      answerLabel = new JLabel();
      centerPanel.add(input1TextField);
      centerPanel.add(input2TextField);
      centerPanel.add(answerLabel);
      contentPane.add(centerPanel, BorderLayout.CENTER);

      buttonPanel = new JPanel();
      buttonPanel.setLayout(new GridLayout(2, 1));
      plusButton = new JButton("+");
      minusButton = new JButton("-");
      buttonPanel.add(plusButton);
      buttonPanel.add(minusButton);
      contentPane.add(buttonPanel, BorderLayout.EAST);

      // Add behaviors!  This time we use the SAME
      // listener object to listen to BOTH buttons.
```

```
ActionListener l = new ActionListener() {

  public void actionPerformed(ActionEvent e) {
    double d1 = new Double(input1TextField.getText()).doubleValue();
    double d2 = new Double(input2TextField.getText()).doubleValue();
```

Up until now, we've ignored the lone argument to the `actionPerformed()` method – an `ActionEvent` object reference named e – but we're now going to put it to use. An `Event` object (`ActionEvent` is a subclass of `Event`) is created automatically by the JVM whenever an interaction occurs with a GUI component. The purpose of the `Event` object is to carry with it some useful information about the circumstances of the event – think of it as a sort of 'eye witness'. Using various methods defined for that `Event` object, we can gain additional insight into the circumstances of the event. The `getSource()` method, when invoked on an `ActionEvent` object, returns a reference to the GUI component that served as the origin for the event. By retrieving the source of the event and testing its identity, we can determine where the event originated, and act accordingly: if the source was the `plusButton`, we add the two input values that we've retrieved; otherwise, we subtract one from the other.

```
    if (e.getSource() == plusButton)
      answerLabel.setText("" + (d1 + d2));
    else answerLabel.setText("" + (d1 - d2));
  }
};
```

Then, we register the same listener object with both buttons:

```
plusButton.addActionListener(l);
minusButton.addActionListener(l);

  this.setVisible(true);
  }
}
```

This version of the `Calculator` behaves exactly as the earlier version did. (Remember that `CalculatorDriver.java` must be revised to refer to 'Calculator4' wherever it previously referred to 'Calculator3'.)

Closing a Window

When we click the 'Close' button located in the upper right corner of the `Calculator3` frame (and, for that matter, for `Calculator1` and `Calculator2` as well), the window does indeed close:

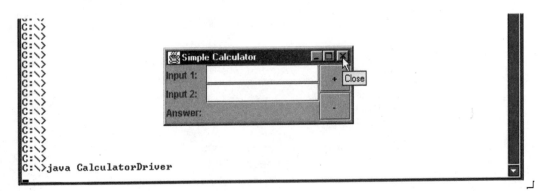

but our program continues to run! It's not doing anything useful, but nonetheless the JVM is waiting for additional user input via the GUI. The problem is that *there is no GUI*, because we've closed it down! So, the command line remains tied up, and program resources remain allocated. As we discussed earlier in the chapter, the only way to regain control of the command line if this happens is to press the 'Ctrl' and 'C' keys simultaneously in the command line window to 'kill' the program.

We would really like to be able to respond to user-initiated requests to terminate a GUI-oriented application, either by:

- ❏ Clicking on the main application window's **Close (X)** button
- ❏ Clicking some other button that we've provided for this purpose, for example, an '**Exit**' button
- ❏ Choosing **File => Exit** from an application's menu bar

In order to do this, we must once again employ event handling techniques: specifically, we must:

- ❏ Create a new type of listener called a `WindowListener` object
- ❏ Register it as a listener to the `JFrame` to be closed as a whole
- ❏ Program the `windowClosing()` method of the listener so that it terminates the program via the command:

```
System.exit(0);
```

`System` *is a built-in Java class; the method* `public static void exit(int status)`

is a static method of the `System` *class used to terminate the currently running Java Virtual Machine. The* `status` *argument serves as a status code to the operating system; by convention, a status code of 0 traditionally signals error-free termination.*

We'll illustrate what it takes to do this with yet another version of our calculator GUI; again, because so much of this code is identical with the previous version of the calculator, please focus on the highlighted code, relevant to the window closing operation.

```java
// Calculator5.java

import java.awt.*;
import javax.swing.*;
import java.awt.event.*;

public class Calculator5 extends JFrame {
    // Components are treated as attributes, so that they will be
    // visible to all of the methods of the class.

    private Container contentPane;

    // Use descriptive names for components where possible; it makes
    // your job easier later on!
```

```
private JPanel leftPanel;
private JPanel centerPanel;
private JPanel buttonPanel;
private JTextField input1TextField;
private JTextField input2TextField;
private JLabel answerLabel;
private JButton plusButton;
private JButton minusButton;

// Constructor.
public Calculator5() {
  // Invoke the generic JFrame constructor.
  super("Simple Calculator");

  // The content pane container is now declared to be an
  // attribute.  Note that the use of "this." is unnecessary;
  // we could have simply written:
  // contentPane = getContentPane();
  contentPane = this.getContentPane();
  this.setSize(250, 100);

  // Technique for centering a frame on the screen.
  Dimension frameSize = this.getSize();
  Dimension screenSize = Toolkit.getDefaultToolkit().getScreenSize();
  this.setLocation((screenSize.width - frameSize.width)/2,
                   screenSize.height - frameSize.height)/2);

  leftPanel = new JPanel();
  leftPanel.setLayout(new GridLayout(3, 1));
  leftPanel.add(new JLabel("Input 1:  "));
  leftPanel.add(new JLabel("Input 2:  "));
  leftPanel.add(new JLabel("Answer:   "));
  contentPane.add(leftPanel, BorderLayout.WEST);
  centerPanel = new JPanel();
  centerPanel.setLayout(new GridLayout(3, 1));
  input1TextField = new JTextField(10);
  input2TextField = new JTextField(10);
  answerLabel = new JLabel();
  centerPanel.add(input1TextField);
  centerPanel.add(input2TextField);
  centerPanel.add(answerLabel);
  contentPane.add(centerPanel, BorderLayout.CENTER);

  buttonPanel = new JPanel();
  buttonPanel.setLayout(new GridLayout(2, 1));
  plusButton = new JButton("+");
  minusButton = new JButton("-");
  buttonPanel.add(plusButton);
  buttonPanel.add(minusButton);
  contentPane.add(buttonPanel, BorderLayout.EAST);

  // Add behaviors!
```

```
        ActionListener l = new ActionListener() {
          public void actionPerformed(ActionEvent e) {
            double d1 =
              new Double(input1TextField.getText()).doubleValue();
            double d2 =
              new Double(input2TextField.getText()).doubleValue();
            if (e.getSource() == plusButton)
              answerLabel.setText("" + (d1 + d2));
            else answerLabel.setText("" + (d1 - d2));
          }
        };

        plusButton.addActionListener(l);
        minusButton.addActionListener(l);

        // We want to use a WindowListener to terminate the
        // application when the user closes the window.  Create the
        // listener as an instance of an anonymous inner class ...

        WindowListener w = new WindowAdapter() {
          public void windowClosing(WindowEvent e) {
          // Note the need to preface "this." with
          // the name of the outer class.
          Calculator5.this.dispose();  // see notes after the code
          System.exit(0);
          }
        };

        // ... and register it with the frame, since it will be the JFrame
        // object that generates the window closing event.

        this.addWindowListener(w);

        this.setVisible(true);
        }
    }
```

(Remember that `CalculatorDriver.java` must be revised to refer to 'Calculator5' wherever it previously referred to 'Calculator4'.)

Note the syntax '*outerclassname*.this' – for example `Calculator5.this.dispose();` – to refer to the instance of the JFrame that we wish to dispose of in the `windowClosing()` method. Had we instead tried to refer to the frame as follows:

```
public void windowClosing(WindowEvent e) {
    this.dispose();
    System.exit(0);
}
```

then the compiler would have complained with the following rather 'cryptic' error message:

Method dispose() not found in local class Calculator5. 2.

because the keyword 'this' in this case refers to the instance of the enclosing *anonymous inner class* that we've just created (referred to as 'Calculator5. 2' by the compiler in its error message), not of the outer class Calculator5; but, it's the instance of the Calculator5 (JFrame) object that we wish to dispose of. This issue of scoping is illustrated in the figure below.

```
//Pseudocode
class Outer {
    public void someMethod() {

        ActionListener 1 = new ActionListener() {
            this.something...
            Outer.this.something...
        };
    }
}
```

The scope of the 'this' keyword can be altered by prefixing it with the name of the outer class

Selecting an Item from a JList

Similar to the other components that we have seen, we can register a listener – a ListSelectionListener, to be specific – with a JList component, to automatically react whenever a selection is made by clicking on an item in the JList:

click!

Let's look at a sample program to illustrate the use of a ListSelectionListener. We're once again going to display a list of student names based on a Vector of Student objects, and we'll reuse the simplified version of class Student that we introduced earlier in this chapter; the code is repeated below for your convenience.

```
// Student.java

// * * * * * * * * * * * * * * * * * * * * * * * * * * * * * *
// THIS IS AN ABBREVIATED VERSION OF THE Student CLASS,
// FOR USE WITH THE VARIOUS VERSIONS OF JListDemo.
// * * * * * * * * * * * * * * * * * * * * * * * * * * * * * *

import java.util.*;

public class Student {
    //------------
    // Attributes.
    //------------
```

```
    private String name;
    private String ssn;

    //----------------
    // Constructor(s).
    //----------------

    public Student(String ssn, String name) {
      this.ssn = ssn;
      this.name = name;
    }

    public String toString() {
      return name + " (" + ssn + ")";
    }

    public String getName() {
      return name;
    }
  }
```

Now, on to the actual program (please see highlighted lines):

```
// JListDemo3.java

import java.util.*;
import java.awt.*;
import javax.swing.*;
import javax.swing.event.*;   // added for ListSelectionListener/Event
```

❑   The `ListSelectionListener` and `ListSelectionEvent` classes were newly added with the Swing API – they didn't exist in the AWT – and so we must import the `javax.swing.event` package in order for the compiler to recognize these types.

```
public class JListDemo3 {
  public static void main(String[] args) {
    JFrame theFrame = new JFrame("Sample JList");
    Container contentPane = theFrame.getContentPane();
    Vector v = new Vector(); // of Students
    v.add(new Student("123456789", "Joe Blow"));
    v.add(new Student("987654321", "Fred Schnurd"));
    v.add(new Student("000000000", "Captain Haggis"));
```

❑   Note that we must declare `myList` to be a `final` variable; otherwise, the compiler will complain when we try to access `myList` from the inner class that we create as a `ListSelectionListener` later on.

```
    final JList myList = new JList(v);
    contentPane.add(myList);
```

The need to use 'final' in the above example has to do with the fact that a variable defined in a method of an outer class 'A' is not available to the methods of an inner class 'B'; basically, it is a scoping problem. Later on, when we are accessing components as attributes of outer classes from within inner class methods, as we do with the SRS for example, the problem will go away.

❑ We instantiate a `ListSelectionListener` object to immediately react whenever an item is selected in the `JList`, and program its `valueChanged()` method:

```
ListSelectionListener lsl = new ListSelectionListener() {
    public void valueChanged(ListSelectionEvent e) {
        // Whenever an item is selected (clicked!) in this list,
        // display it at the command line.
```

❑ We invoke the `getSelectedValue()` method on `myList` to obtain a handle on the `Object` that the selected list entry represents. A `JList` is zero-based, meaning that it counts the items in the list starting with 0:

❑ If we click the first entry in the list, we obtain a handle on the first (0th) object in the `Vector` that was used to populate the `JList`.

❑ If we click the second entry in the list, we obtain a handle on the second object from the original `Vector`, and so forth.

Because `getSelectedValue()` returns a generic `Object` reference, we must cast the reference back to a `Student` reference so that we may subsequently invoke its `getName()` method:

```
        Student s = (Student) myList.getSelectedValue();
        System.out.println("Selected " + s.getName());
    }
};
```

This is typical; many built in Java classes deal in generic Objects for versatility.

In this example, we simply print out a message to the command line window to verify that we have indeed retrieved the desired `Student`.

❑ As always, we must register the listener with the object being listened to (in this case, the `JList`):

```
    myList.addListSelectionListener(lsl);
    theFrame.setSize(300, 90);
    theFrame.setVisible(true);
  }
}
```

Here is the uninterrupted code:

```
// JListDemo3.java

import java.util.*;
import java.awt.*;
import javax.swing.*;
import javax.swing.event.*; // added
```

```
public class JListDemo3 {
  public static void main(String[] args) {
    JFrame theFrame = new JFrame("Sample JList");
    Container contentPane = theFrame.getContentPane();

    // Create a vector of students.

    Vector v = new Vector(); // of Students
    v.add(new Student("123456789", "Joe Blow"));
    v.add(new Student("987654321", "Fred Schnurd"));
    v.add(new Student("000000000", "Englebert Humperdink"));

    // Create a list based on this vector.  (We must declare
    // myList to be a final variable; otherwise, the compiler
    // will complain when we try to access it from the inner
    // class that we create as a listener below.)

    final JList myList = new JList(v);
    contentPane.add(myList);

    // Add a listener to note when an item has been selected.

    ListSelectionListener lsl = new ListSelectionListener() {
      public void valueChanged(ListSelectionEvent e) {
        // When an item is selected (clicked!) in this
        // list, display it at the command line.

        Student s = (Student) myList.getSelectedValue();
        System.out.println("Selected " + s.getName());
      }
    };

    myList.addListSelectionListener(lsl);

    theFrame.setSize(300, 90);  // width, height
    theFrame.setVisible(true);
  }
}
```

An interesting observation is that when we click an entry in the list, the `itemStateChanged()` method fires twice – once when the mouse button is depressed, and once again when it is released – causing our printed message to appear twice at the command line:

Selected Joe Blow
Selected Joe Blow

If we wish to remedy this, we can take advantage of another method of `JList` – `boolean getValueIsAdjusting()` – as shown in the code snippet below:

```
// Excerpt from program JListDemo3B.java - available as part of
// the Wrox code download.
```

```
ListSelectionListener lsl = new ListSelectionListener() {
  public void valueChanged(ListSelectionEvent e) {
    // When an item is selected (clicked!) in this
    // list, display it at the command line.

    // To eliminate the "double display"
    // of this message, perform an initial
    // test.
    if (!myList.getValueIsAdjusting()) {
      Student s = (Student) myList.getSelectedValue();
      System.out.println("Selected " + s.getName());
    }
  }
};
```

We don't necessarily have to connect a listener directly to a JList in order to process a selection from the list. If we don't want to react immediately when an item is clicked, we can forego the use of a ListSelectionListener, and can instead have a separate JButton that, when clicked, retrieves the selected value from the JList and manipulates it in some fashion. The next example program (a variation of the previous program) demonstrates this alternative approach.

❑ The program starts out in the same way that the previous program begins: we still create and populate a Vector of Students to be used as the basis for creating the JList, etc.

```
// JListDemo4.java

import java.util.*;
import java.awt.*;
import javax.swing.*;
import java.awt.event.*;

public class JListDemo4 {
  public static void main(String[] args) {
    JFrame theFrame = new JFrame("Sample JList");
    Container contentPane = theFrame.getContentPane();

    // Create a vector of students.

    Vector v = new Vector(); // of Students
    v.add(new Student("123456789", "Joe Blow"));
    v.add(new Student("987654321", "Fred Schnurd"));
    v.add(new Student("000000000", "Captain Haggis"));

    // Create a list based on this vector.
    final JList myList = new JList(v);
```

❑ In this example, we want to add two components to the JFrame – a JList and a JButton – and so we attach the JList to the CENTER region of the JFrame's default BorderLayout:

```
contentPane.add(myList, BorderLayout.CENTER);
```

and we then create a JButton labeled 'Select' that will pull the selected entry from the JList when the button is clicked, and add it to the SOUTH region of the BorderLayout:

```
    JButton selectButton = new JButton("Select");
    contentPane.add(selectButton, BorderLayout.SOUTH);
```

❑ Now, instead of creating and adding a ListSelectionListener to the JList as we did in the previous example program, we instead create and add an ActionListener to the JButton. Note that the internal logic of the actionPerformed() method is identical to the internal logic of the valueChanged() method in our previous example: we want the exact same behavior to result; we just want it to be **triggered** in a different way.

```
    ActionListener listener = new ActionListener() {
      public void actionPerformed(ActionEvent e) {
        // Pull the selected Student from the list when the
        // button is clicked.

        Student s = (Student) myList.getSelectedValue();
        System.out.println("Selected " + s.getName());
      }
    };

    selectButton.addActionListener(listener);

    theFrame.setSize(300, 120);  // width, height
    theFrame.setVisible(true);
  }
}
```

Here is the complete, uninterrupted code:

```
// JListDemo4.java

import java.util.*;
import java.awt.*;
import javax.swing.*;
import java.awt.event.*; // added

public class JListDemo4 {
  public static void main(String[] args) {
    JFrame theFrame = new JFrame("Sample JList");
    Container contentPane = theFrame.getContentPane();

    // Create a vector of students.

    Vector v = new Vector(); // of Students
    v.add(new Student("123456789", "Joe Blow"));
    v.add(new Student("987654321", "Fred Schnurd"));
    v.add(new Student("000000000", " Captain Haggis"));

    // Create a list based on this vector.  (We must declare
    // myList to be a final variable; otherwise, the compiler
    // will complain when we try to access it from the inner
    // class that we create as a listener below.)

    final JList myList = new JList(v);
```

```
        contentPane.add(myList, BorderLayout.CENTER);

        // Create a button that will pull the selected entry
        // from the list when the button is clicked.

        JButton selectButton = new JButton("Select");
        contentPane.add(selectButton, BorderLayout.SOUTH);

        // Add a listener to the button.

        ActionListener listener = new ActionListener() {
          public void actionPerformed(ActionEvent e) {
            Student s = (Student) myList.getSelectedValue();
            System.out.println("Selected " + s.getName());
          }
        };

        selectButton.addActionListener(listener);

      theFrame.setSize(300, 120);  // width, height
      theFrame.setVisible(true);
    }
  }
```

When we compile and run this version of the program, selecting an entry in the list in and of itself doesn't trigger any action on the part of the GUI. A `ListSelectionEvent` is indeed still being generated at that moment, as it was in our previous example; but, since we haven't programmed a listener to listen for it this time around, it is simply ignored. In fact, the user can change his/her mind numerous times, clicking alternative entries in the `JList`, but no action is taken in response to each individual click. Clicking the 'Select' button, on the other hand, generates an `ActionEvent`, which we are listening for:

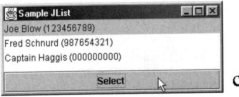

This triggers the `actionPerformed()` method for that button, which 'grabs' the user's most recent selection from the `JList` ('Joe Blow', in this case), which in turn results in the following output being displayed in the command line window:

Selected Joe Blow

We'll illustrate both of these types of `JList` manipulation – direct manipulation via `ListSelectionListeners` and indirect manipulation via `JButtons` – in the upcoming SRS example.

More Container Types: JDialog and JOptionPane

Dialogs are 'pop-up' windows that are typically used to force the user into making a decision or providing some input. Although we can certainly create pop-up dialog windows by extending the JFrame class, it is often preferable to extend the Swing JDialog class instead, because JDialog enables us to create pop-up windows that are **modal**. A modal window is one that the user cannot ignore: once a modal dialog has been displayed, a user cannot interact with any other window belonging to that same GUI application until he/she responds to and dismisses the dialog. This behavior is known as the dialog holding the **focus** of the application.

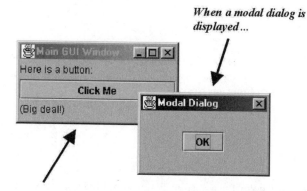

When a modal dialog is displayed …

… then the user cannot interact with any of that application's OTHER windows until he/she reacts to the modal dialog window, and the application then dismisses it.

There are a number of different JDialog constructor signatures; the one that we'll be using with the SRS is:

```
JDialog(Frame owner, String title, boolean modal)
```

where:

- ❑ owner is a reference to the AWT Frame or Swing JFrame from which the JDialog was spawned;

- ❑ title is whatever text we wish to have appear as a title on the JDialog;

- ❑ modal can be set to true if we want the JDialog to be modal, and false otherwise.

When we create a JDialog, we follow the same general steps that we followed when creating an application's main frame (such as Calculator4) by extending the JFrame class. That is, we:

- ❑ Invent a class that extends JDialog.

- ❑ Declare and add whatever components we want the JDialog to display as attributes of the class, optionally changing the JDialog's layout manager from the default BorderLayout if desired.

- ❑ Create and register listeners on selected components, just as we would in creating a frame.

Here's a simple example of a class that can be used to produce the following simplistic JDialog:

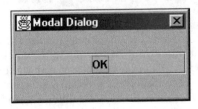

```
// MyDialog.java

import java.awt.*;
import javax.swing.*;
import java.awt.event.*;
```

❏   We declare all components to be attached to the dialog (only one button, in this case) as attributes of the class, so that they are 'visible' throughout all of the methods we write (including methods of inner classes):

```
public class MyDialog extends JDialog {
    // Components as attributes.

    JButton okButton;
```

❏   Note that the constructor for a custom dialog should take at least one argument, either of type Frame or JFrame, which will be a reference to the (J)Frame from which this dialog is being launched. We need to provide the dialog with such a reference because the constructor for the parent JDialog class, which is invoked as the first line of code from within this constructor, expects this reference to be passed in as an argument.

  Note that we're also making this dialog modal.

```
    // Constructor.

    // We need to pass in a reference to the "parent" frame from
    // which this dialog was launched, because we will need to
    // hand it, in turn, to the generic JDialog constructor
    // (see the first line of code inside of the constructor).

    public MyDialog(JFrame parent) {
        // Let's make this dialog modal by invoking the generic
        // JDialog constructor with a value of "true" for the
        // final argument.  We're also passing through the
        // reference to our parent frame, as the first argument.

        super(parent, "Modal Dialog", true);

        okButton = new JButton("OK");
```

❑   We're using the 'padding' technique introduced earlier to get this single button to appear in the middle of the dialog:

```
this.getContentPane().setLayout(new GridLayout(3, 1));
this.getContentPane().add(new Label(""));
this.getContentPane().add(okButton);
this.getContentPane().add(new Label(""));

this.setSize(200, 100);
```

❑   We're attaching an `ActionListener` to the `okButton`, as we've seen done before for other `JButtons`. The `actionPerformed()` method is doing a few unusual things, however.

❑   It's closing the dialog as a whole by sending the message `setVisible(false)` to the dialog instance (referred to as 'MyDialog.this' from within the inner class's method).

❑   When we previously created a `WindowListener` for use with our `Calculator5` program, we used its `windowClosing()` method to `dispose()` of the `JFrame` followed by a call to `System.exit(0)` in order to terminate our application. Typically, we don't want to bring our application to a screeching halt when we close a `JDialog`, however! So, we simply call the `dispose()` method on the dialog instance to get the JVM to 'recycle' the resources (including memory) that have been allocated to the dialog.

```
// Attach an ActionListener to the button, so that
// when it is clicked, the dialog will close.

okButton.addActionListener(new ActionListener() {
  public void actionPerformed(ActionEvent e) {
    // Close the dialog.
    System.out.println("OK clicked");
    MyDialog.this.setVisible(false);
    MyDialog.this.dispose();

    // Note that we don't call System.exit(0),
    // because if we did, then the whole
    // application will come to a screeching
    // halt when the dialog is closed.
    // System.exit(0);
  }
});
```

❑   If we also want to be able to close the dialog via the 'close' button at the upper right hand corner of the dialog, we have to provide a `WindowListener`, as well:

```
WindowListener w = new WindowAdapter() {
  public void windowClosing(WindowEvent e) {
    // Note the need to preface "this." with
    // the name of the outer class.
    MyDialog.this.setVisible(false);
    MyDialog.this.dispose();
```

```java
                // Note that we don't call System.exit(0),
                // because if we did, then the whole application
                // will come to a screeching halt when the
                // dialog is closed.
                // System.exit(0);
            }
        };

        this.addWindowListener(w);


        // Always make the setVisible call the LAST call in
        // the constructor.  For some strange reason, if you
        // don't, then the listeners don't always work
        // properly.

        this.setVisible(true);
    }
}
```

Here's the 'uninterrupted' code in its entirety:

```java
// MyDialog.java

import java.awt.*;
import javax.swing.*;
import java.awt.event.*;

public class MyDialog extends JDialog {
    // Components as attributes.

    JButton okButton;

    // Constructor.

    // We need to pass in a reference to the "parent" frame from
    // which this dialog was launched, because we will need to
    // hand it, in turn, to the generic JDialog constructor
    // (see the first line of code inside of the constructor).

    public MyDialog(JFrame parent) {
        // Let's make this dialog modal by invoking the generic
        // JDialog constructor with a value of "true" for the
        // final argument.  We're also passing through the
        // reference to our parent frame, as the first argument.

        super(parent, "Modal Dialog", true);

        okButton = new JButton("OK");

        this.getContentPane().setLayout(new GridLayout(3, 1));
        this.getContentPane().add(new Label(""));
        this.getContentPane().add(okButton);
        this.getContentPane().add(new Label(""));
```

```
      this.setSize(200, 100);

      // Attach an ActionListener to the button, so that
      // when it is clicked, the dialog will close.

      okButton.addActionListener(new ActionListener() {
        public void actionPerformed(ActionEvent e) {
          // Close the dialog.
          System.out.println("OK clicked");
          MyDialog.this.setVisible(false);
          MyDialog.this.dispose();

          // Note that we don't call System.exit(0),
          // because if we did, then the whole
          // application will come to a screeching
          // halt when the dialog is closed.
          // System.exit(0);
        }
      });

      // If we also want to be able to close the dialog via
      // the "close" button at the upper right hand corner
      // of the dialog, we have to provide a WindowListener,
      // as well.
      WindowListener w = new WindowAdapter() {
        public void windowClosing(WindowEvent e) {
          // Note the need to preface "this." with
          // the name of the outer class.
          MyDialog.this.setVisible(false);
          MyDialog.this.dispose();

          // Note that we don't call System.exit(0),
          // because if we did, then the whole application
          // will come to a screeching halt when the
          // dialog is closed.
          // System.exit(0);
        }
      };

      this.addWindowListener(w);

      // Always make the setVisible call the last call in
      // the constructor.  For some strange reason, if you
      // don't, then the listeners don't always work
      // properly.

      this.setVisible(true);
    }
  }
```

Now, we need some way to display this dialog; here's a trivially simple driver program that can be used to create and display an instance of `MyDialog`:

```
// DialogDriver.java

import javax.swing.*;

public class DialogDriver {
   public static void main(String[] args) {
      // Create a frame to serve as the parent for the dialog.
      JFrame theFrame = new JFrame("Daddy Frame");
      theFrame.setSize(200, 200);  // width, height in pixels
      theFrame.setVisible(true);

      // Now, create and display our custom dialog!
      // Because the dialog's constructor contains the
      // logic to make the dialog visible, we needn't do
      // so in this program.
      MyDialog theDialog = new MyDialog(theFrame);
   }
}
```

This program is not very representative of how a dialog would really be used, because all it does is display the dialog; under normal circumstances, we'd only display a dialog conditionally, when certain circumstances had arisen in our program requiring that we communicate with the user. We'll demonstrate a more conventional use of `JDialogs` when we introduce the `PasswordPopup` class as part of our SRS GUI solution a bit later in the chapter.

One Step Dialogs with JOptionPane

We often need a very simple, standard form of dialog to ask the user a quick question, or to convey a message. Rather than having to go through the trouble of extending `JDialog` to invent a custom dialog class from scratch for this purpose, the Swing API introduced a convenience class called `JOptionPane` which provides a simple way to create various types of standardized dialogs with a minimum of effort.

Recall from Chapter 7 that a static method is one that may be invoked on a class as a whole, without having an instance of that class handy. By calling static methods provided by the `JOptionPane` class, we can instantiate and display various types of dialog:

Static Method:	Produces a dialog that:
`JOptionPane.showConfirmDialog(...)`	Asks a confirming question, like 'OK/Cancel?'
`JOptionPane.showInputDialog(...)`	Prompts the user for some 'free form' textual input, such as his/her name; automatically provides 'OK' and 'Cancel' buttons for dismissing the dialog.
`JOptionPane.showMessageDialog(...)`	Displays a message informing the user of the outcome of some operation or of the state of the application; automatically provides an 'OK' button for dismissing the dialog.
`JOptionPane.showOptionDialog(...)`	Provides the user with a number of programmer-specified options in the form of multiple buttons, then returns the user's choice to the client code.

The only type of JOptionPane that we are going to be using in the SRS application is a message dialog. The JOptionPane.showMessageDialog() method is overloaded, which as we discussed in Chapter 5 means that there is more than one form of showMessageDialog(), each having a different argument signature. We are interested in using the following form of the method:

```
public static void showMessageDialog(Component parentComponent,
                                     Object message,
                                     String title,
                                     int messageType);
```

where arguments are defined as follows:

- ❏ parentComponent: The first argument is a reference to the component that is considered to be responsible for 'sponsoring' this dialog (typically, but not always, a JFrame). This Component is informally referred to as the dialog's 'parent', but not in the inheritance sense of the word. The message dialog will be centered relative to its parent component on the screen; if this argument is set to null, then the dialog will instead be centered relative to the screen as a whole.

- ❏ message: We can pass any arbitrary Object as the second argument to this method; the Object's toString() method will be used to produce an object-appropriate textual message. Of course, since all classes in Java are descended from Object, one of the most common types of Object to be passed in for this argument is a simple String representing the message itself: for example, 'Operation completed.'

- ❏ title: a String representing the dialog's desired title.

- ❏ message type: this argument determines the default icon to be displayed along with the message text; JOptionPane provides a handful of **final static attributes** (that is, constant values) to be used for this argument. For our upcoming example, we'll use JOptionPane.INFORMATION_MESSAGE, which displays an exclamation point (!) in a blue circle:

but other choices include JOptionPane.ERROR_MESSAGE:

JOptionPane.WARNING_MESSAGE:

JOptionPane.QUESTION_MESSAGE:

and JOptionPane.PLAIN_MESSAGE (no icon).

Here's a simple class/program which demonstrates the use of the JOptionPane.showMessageDialog() method; the main() method consists of only one single 'line' of Java code, but because it is so long, we've broken it up into multiple physical lines of text and attached comments to help make it easier to understand.

```java
// JOptionPaneDemo.java - Chapter 16 example.

import javax.swing.*;

public class JOptionPaneDemo {
  public static void main(String[] args) {
    // We'll demo only one of the flavors of JOptionPane:
    // namely, a message dialog, which simply displays a
    // message, and automatically provides an "OK" button
    // for dismissing the dialog.

    JOptionPane.showMessageDialog(
        null, // no parent; center dialog on the screen
        "Click this dialog when you are ready.", // message
        "Whenever", // title
        JOptionPane.INFORMATION_MESSAGE); // type of icon to be used

  }
}
```

These particular argument values cause the following dialog to appear when the program is run:

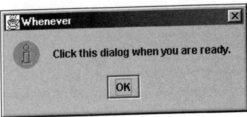

When the OK button is clicked, the dialog is automatically dismissed.

If we wish to display a multi-line message on a message dialog, here is a code snippet that illustrates how this is done:

```java
// Create a String array of TWO lines of message text plus a blank line.
String[] message = { "Line 1.", "Line 2.", " "};

// Then, we can just hand the String array in to the showMessageDialog()
// call.
JOptionPane.showMessageDialog(null, message, "Multiple Lines",
    JOptionPane.INFORMATION_MESSAGE);
```

We'll see JOptionPane at work in the SRS application later in this chapter.

SRS, Take 3: Adding a GUI

We've now learned enough about Java GUIs to be able to retrofit a GUI to our SRS application from Chapter 15. In particular, we need to integrate a GUI 'view' to our 'model' – that is, our domain objects Student, Professor, Course, Section, and so on. As we said earlier, the model will for the most part be unaware that we are doing so; the classes in the *view* will assume the lion's share of the effort of presenting the information encapsulated by the classes in the *model*. By insulating the model classes from the view, we facilitate replacing the view and/or adding additional views in the future.

Concept of Operations

Before we dive into the code required to automate the GUI, let's quickly talk through how we envision that the GUI will operate. Sketching out the functional flow of a graphical user interface through pictures and accompanying narrative – a technique informally known as **storyboarding** – is a great way to come to agreement with the future users of a system on how the application should look and behave before development begins. And, if the application truly evolves as we envisioned that it would, then the document that we've prepared to describe the storyboard *before* developing the application, known as a **concept of operations document**, can be used as the basis for a user's guide and/or on-line tutorial *after* the application is finished. The 'story' that is told by the concept of operations document is presented from the external viewpoint of a user; it is, in essence, a pictorial representation of how the various use cases for the application will be fulfilled.

Because the code for the SRS was already developed before this chapter was written, we had the luxury of using actual screen snapshots as illustrations; but, in a real life situation, we'd start by informally sketching our ideas, perhaps with pen or paper or on a whiteboard, so as to 'test drive' them with colleagues and the sponsors and/or future users of the system. Once we felt we were on the right track, then, depending on what tools we have available, we might either render our conceptualized GUI with a conventional drawing tool, such as PowerPoint, or even create a GUI 'shell' using an IDE.

> As I've said elsewhere in the chapter, however, I don't advocate using a drag and drop GUI builder to actually fabricate the GUI code when you are just beginning to learn the Java language.

Our concept of operations begins when Joe Blow, a student user, launches the SRS application. The GUI that first appears, shown on the next page, presents a list of all sections offered this semester entitled 'Schedule of Classes', along with a number of empty fields labeled 'SSN:', 'Name:', and 'Total Courses:'. A number of buttons appear at the bottom of the window labeled 'Drop', 'Save My Schedule', 'Add', and 'Log Off', but these are all greyed out initially to signal that they are disabled; until a user logs on, none of the functions provided by these buttons is relevant.

(We recognize that the SSN and Name fields are JTextFields by their white backgrounds, whereas the 'field' labeled 'Total Courses:' is actually a non-editable JLabel.)

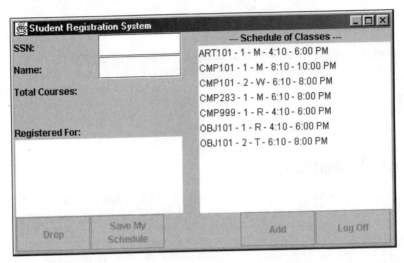

Joe logs onto the SRS by typing his social security number, '111-11-1111', in the field labeled 'SSN:', and then presses the Enter key. A small dialog window pops up to request that he enter his password to complete the logon process:

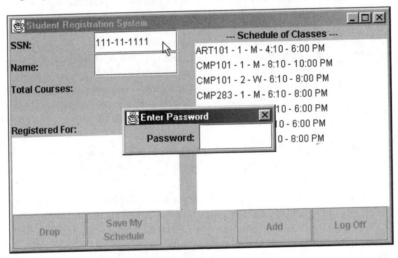

As Joe types in his password (which happens to be '111', the first three digits of his social security number), asterisks (*) appear in place of the characters that he types, to ensure his privacy.

After typing in his password, Joe presses the Enter key. Unfortunately, Joe has mistyped his password, and so the following popup message appears:

After Joe clicks the 'OK' button on this popup to dismiss it, he must click anywhere in the 'SSN:' field to give that field focus, and then presses the Enter key again to redisplay the password popup a second time (he needn't retype his SSN, however). Assuming that he types his password correctly this time, he receives confirmation of a successful logon:

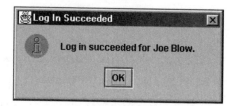

After clicking 'OK' on this confirmation popup, Joe sees that the 'Name:', 'Total Courses:', and 'Registered For:' components on the main GUI window have been filled in with his current registration information. (Although Joe doesn't know it, this information was read in behind-the-scenes from file '111-11-1111.dat'.) We see that Joe had previously used the SRS to register for section 1 of course number CMP101. Notice that two of the buttons at the bottom of the GUI – 'Save My Schedule' and 'Log Off' – have now become enabled and selectable.

Note that there are three data files supplied with the SRS code download from Wrox that support this application, and which represent three different students' data: 111-11-1111.dat, 222-22-2222.dat, and 333-33-3333.dat.

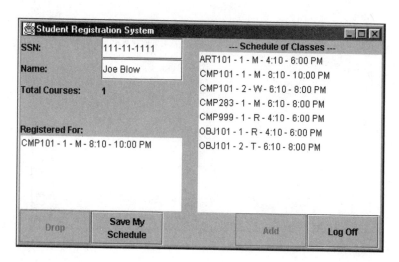

Joe decides to try to enroll in course CMP101 – 2. He selects this section from the Schedule of Classes list, which causes the 'Add' button at the bottom of the screen to automatically become active. (Until he had selected a section in the Schedule of Classes list, it made no sense for the Add button to be selectable.) Joe clicks the 'Add' button.

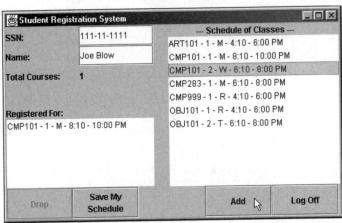

Because Joe is already registered for a different section of that same course (CMP101 – 1), the system notifies him via a pop-up message that he may not register for CMP101 - 2. (Had Joe's transcript reflected successful prior completion of any section of CMP101, his request would have also been rejected.)

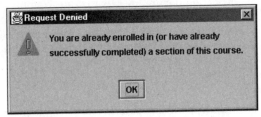

Joe clicks OK to dismiss the dialog. He next selects CMP999 – 1 from the Schedule of Classes, and again clicks the Add button.

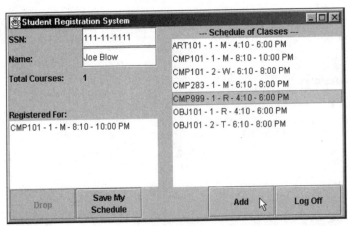

Unfortunately, Joe strikes out again! Course CMP999, 'Living Brain Computers', requires that students have successfully completed the prerequisite course CMP283, 'Higher Level Languages (Java)'. Since Joe's transcript (which is checked behind-the-scenes) does not show evidence that he has previously completed CMP283, the system once again rejects his registration request with a pop-up explanation:

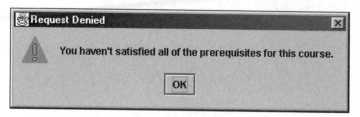

After clicking OK to dismiss this popup, Joe selects ART101 − 1 from the Schedule of Classes list, and clicks the Add button yet again.

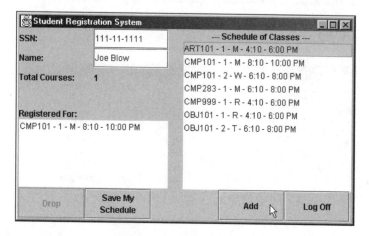

Success at last! ART101 has no prerequisites to satisfy, and Joe is neither currently registered for, nor has ever successfully completed, a section of this course. Joe receives confirmation that he has been registered in ART 101.

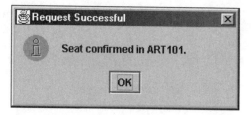

After Joe dismisses the confirmation popup, he sees the newly-added section reflected in the 'Registered For:' list on the main SRS window, with the 'Total Courses:' field reflecting the correct new total. Joe's selection in the Schedule of Classes list has also been cleared, and the Add button is no longer enabled.

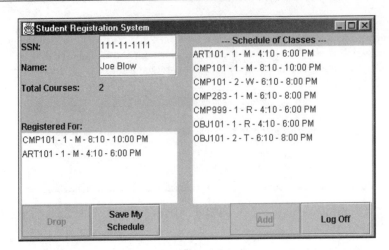

Next, Joe decides that he wishes to drop CMP101. He clicks on that entry in his 'Registered For:' list, at which point the 'Drop' button becomes enabled and selectable. He then clicks the Drop button:

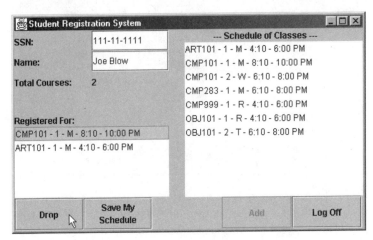

and, in response, the SRS displays a confirmation popup that the course has been dropped from his course load.

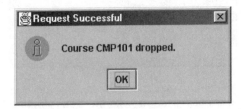

When the popup is dismissed, Joe's course load information has once again been properly updated, and the 'Drop' button has been disabled.

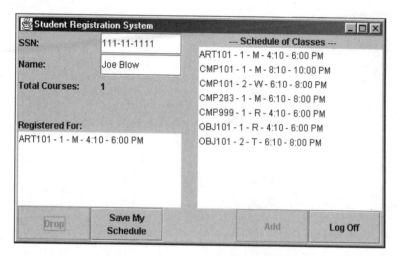

Satisfied with his new schedule, Joe decides to persist this information by clicking the 'Save My Schedule' button:

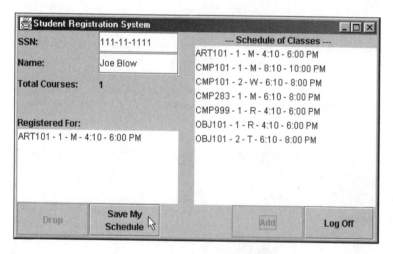

The system confirms this operation. (Behind the scenes and unbeknownst to Joe, his updated course load information has been persisted to file `111-11-1111.dat`, replacing the information that was previously in that file.)

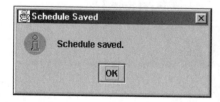

Finally, Joe clicks the 'Log Off' button, and the screen is cleared of all of Joe's student-specific information, ready for a different student to log on.

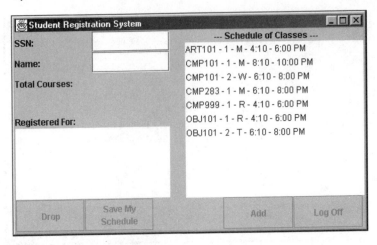

Planning the 'Look' of the GUI: Getting Creative With GridLayout

Looking at the desired layout for the SRS GUI, we can visually decompose it into various regions of more or less evenly sized and spaced components; as we mentioned earlier in the chapter, if we can do this, then the use of layered JPanels with GridLayouts is in order!

❑ We see a row of evenly spaced and sized buttons at the bottom, which we can tackle through the creation of a button panel with a grid layout of 1 row x 5 columns, place in the SOUTH region of the frame's BorderLayout.

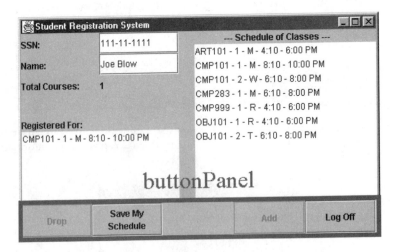

❑ The remainder of the GUI can be split in half, with the left half being represented by one JPanel and the right by another. We can place the left panel in the JFrame's WEST region, and the right panel in the JFrame's EAST region.

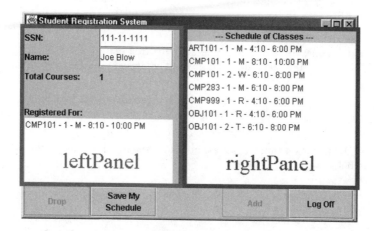

❑ Focusing on the left panel for a moment, we see that if we manage the left panel with a 2 row x 1 column GridLayout, the panel can in turn be subdivided vertically into two equally-sized smaller panels.

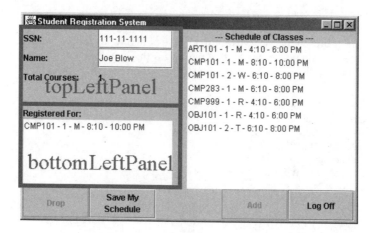

❑ And, that the topmost of these can be managed by a 1 x 2 GridLayout to be subdivided into two even smaller panels.

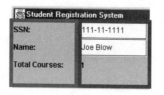

❑ Each of these smallest panels – one to contain static labels, and the other to contain data (either input by the user or provided by the system) – can be managed by a 4 x 1 GridLayout. (We could also use a 3 x 1 GridLayout for each of these, but we want to place some 'white space' at the bottom of each, to visually separate it from the list entitled 'Registered For:' which falls below this area on the GUI.)

Armed with these decisions, we're now ready to code the first half – i.e. the 'look' – of class MainFrame, which is to be the main application window, based on a JFrame container.

Reminder: if you haven't already done so, please consider downloading and printing a copy of the MainFrame.java file, to follow along with and to jot notes on during our discussion.

We'll import all of the packages that we'll need both for creating the 'look' of the GUI now as well as for implementing the behavior a bit later on.

```java
// MainFrame.java

import java.awt.*;
import java.awt.event.*;
import javax.swing.*;
import javax.swing.event.*;
import java.util.*;

public class MainFrame extends JFrame {
```

We define all of the components that we're going to be attaching to the MainFrame as attributes of this class; note that we strive to choose descriptive names for them so that when we see them referenced in the code further down, we'll remember what purpose each one serves.

```java
    private JPanel leftPanel;
    private JPanel topLeftPanel;
    private JPanel labelPanel;
    private JPanel fieldPanel;
    private JPanel bottomLeftPanel;
    private JPanel rightPanel;
    private JPanel buttonPanel;
    private JTextField ssnField;
    private JTextField nameField;
    private JLabel totalCoursesLabel;
    private JButton dropButton;
    private JButton addButton;
    private JButton logoffButton;
    private JButton saveScheduleButton;
    private JLabel l1;
    private JLabel l2;
    private JLabel l3;
    private JLabel l4;
    private JList studentCourseList;
    private JList scheduleOfClassesList;
```

We are going to use reference variable `currentUser` to maintain a handle on whichever `Student` object represents the `Student` who is currently logged in; a value of `null` for this variable signifies that nobody is officially logged on.

```
private Student currentUser;
```

Most of the code comprising the constructor for our `MainFrame` class should by now be familiar, so we'll only explain those items that are particularly clever or unusual.

```
// Constructor

public MainFrame() {
  // Initialize attributes.

  currentUser = null;

  // Note that using "this." as a prefix is unnecessary -
  // any method calls that stand alone (without a dot notation
  // prefix) are understood to be invoked on this object.

  this.setTitle("Student Registration System");
  this.setSize(500, 300);
  Container contentPane = this.getContentPane();

  // Technique for centering a frame on the screen.

  Dimension frameSize = this.getSize();
  Dimension screenSize = Toolkit.getDefaultToolkit().getScreenSize();
  this.setLocation((screenSize.width - frameSize.width)/2,
    (screenSize.height - frameSize.height)/2);

  // Create a few panels.

  leftPanel = new JPanel();
  leftPanel.setLayout(new GridLayout(2, 1));

  topLeftPanel = new JPanel();
  topLeftPanel.setLayout(new GridLayout(1, 2));

  labelPanel = new JPanel();
  labelPanel.setLayout(new GridLayout(4, 1));

  fieldPanel = new JPanel();
  fieldPanel.setLayout(new GridLayout(4, 1));

  bottomLeftPanel = new JPanel();
  bottomLeftPanel.setLayout(new BorderLayout());
```

The only panel that we don't assign a `GridLayout` to is the `rightPanel`:

```
rightPanel = new JPanel();
rightPanel.setLayout(new BorderLayout());

buttonPanel = new JPanel();
buttonPanel.setLayout(new GridLayout(1, 4));

// We'll allow the main frame's layout to remain the
// default BorderLayout.
```

Note that we are adding labels without maintaining permanent handles on them! That's because we won't ever need to communicate with them as objects again, once they've been attached to the GUI. We do use a temporary handle `l`, however, to hold onto each label object just long enough to invoke its `setForeground()` method (the default color for a label's text, or foreground, is a bluish-gray color, but we'd prefer it to be black).

```
JLabel l = new JLabel("SSN:  ");
l.setForeground(Color.black);
labelPanel.add(l);
l = new JLabel("Name:  ");
l.setForeground(Color.black);
labelPanel.add(l);
l = new JLabel("Total Courses:  ");
l.setForeground(Color.black);
labelPanel.add(l);

// Add an empty label for padding/white space.

l = new JLabel("");
labelPanel.add(l);
```

We do maintain named references to the text fields, however, so that we can later go back and read their contents (whatever the user has typed in) by name.

```
ssnField = new JTextField(10);
nameField = new JTextField(10);
```

Because this next 'field' is not going to be editable by the user, we are making it a `JLabel`. We could have alternatively made it a non-editable `JTextField`, but we wanted it to *look* like a label.

```
totalCoursesLabel = new JLabel();
totalCoursesLabel.setForeground(Color.black);
fieldPanel.add(ssnField);
fieldPanel.add(nameField);
fieldPanel.add(totalCoursesLabel);

// Add an empty label for padding/white space.

l = new JLabel("");
fieldPanel.add(l);
```

```
// Create the buttons and add them to their panel. Again,
// note use of descriptive names.

dropButton = new JButton("Drop");
addButton = new JButton("Add");
logoffButton = new JButton("Log Off");
```

Here's an interesting technique for creating a multi-line button label!

❑ Normally, when we create a `JButton`, we assign its label in one step – for example `JButton b = new JButton(label);` – but this doesn't afford us an easy way to separate the label onto two or more lines.

❑ But, because the `JButton` class is a subclass of `JComponent`, which in turn is a subclass of `Container`, a `JButton` may itself serve as a container for other components – in particular, of `JLabel`s!

❑ If instead we set the layout manager for a `JButton` to be a 2 x 1 `GridLayout`, we can then add two different labels to the same button and have them appear one above the other:

```
saveScheduleButton = new JButton();
saveScheduleButton.setLayout(new GridLayout(2, 1));
l1 = new JLabel("Save My", JLabel.CENTER);
l1.setForeground(Color.black);
l2 = new JLabel("Schedule", JLabel.CENTER);
l2.setForeground(Color.black);
saveScheduleButton.add(l1);
saveScheduleButton.add(l2);

buttonPanel.add(dropButton);
buttonPanel.add(saveScheduleButton);
buttonPanel.add(new JLabel("")); // white space padding
buttonPanel.add(addButton);
buttonPanel.add(logoffButton);
```

In creating the `JList` used to display all of the `Section`s that a `Student` has registered for, it is necessary to use the `setFixedCellWidth()` method to explicitly assign a width to the list entries, because the list will sometimes be empty; without a fixed width assignment, the list will shrink to a width of 0, which would effectively make this component invisible on the GUI.

```
studentCourseList = new JList();
studentCourseList.setFixedCellWidth(200);
bottomLeftPanel.add(studentCourseList, BorderLayout.CENTER);

l = new JLabel("Registered For:");
l.setForeground(Color.black);
bottomLeftPanel.add(l, BorderLayout.NORTH);

l = new JLabel("--- Schedule of Classes ---", JLabel.CENTER);
l.setForeground(Color.black);
rightPanel.add(l, BorderLayout.NORTH);
```

You may recall from Chapter 14 that we declared scheduleOfClasses to be a public static attribute of the SRS driver class, so that it would be visible to/globally accessible from all of the other classes in our application. We now take advantage of this fact to instantiate the scheduleOfClassesList, a JList.

❑ As we saw demonstrated earlier in this chapter, we may pass a Vector object reference in as an argument to a JList constructor, and the JList will automatically use the toString() method of the objects contained within the JList to render them as textual entries in the list that is displayed.

❑ SRS.scheduleOfClasses, however, is declared to be a static attribute of type ScheduleOfClasses, which is a special type of class that we've invented, not a Vector! So, how do we get around this dilemma?

❑ Our solution is to invent a new method for the ScheduleOfClasses class with signature:

```
public Vector getSortedSections()
```

This method will formulate and hand back a Vector for us, based on the contents of the ScheduleOfClasses object, so that we may in turn hand that Vector to the JList constructor.

❑ We use the technique of 'stringing together' method calls, separated by 'dots', to accomplish this in a single line of code:

```
scheduleOfClassesList = new JList(SRS.scheduleOfClasses.getSortedSections());
```

❑ We'll see the code for the getSortedSections() method later in the chapter, when we discuss the ScheduleOfClasses class.

As we did for the studentCourseList, it is necessary to use the setFixedCellWidth() method to explicitly assign a width to the scheduleOfClassesList entries, to ensure that this component remains visible even if for some reason the list of available classes were empty.

```
scheduleOfClassesList.setFixedCellWidth(250);
rightPanel.add(scheduleOfClassesList, BorderLayout.EAST);
```

The next line of code is a call to method resetButtons(), which is defined for the MainFrame class, but later down in the class. This method is responsible for making sure that the various buttons on the GUI are properly enabled or disabled, depending on the student's registration situation, or state, at any given time. We'll defer explaining what this method does in detail until a bit later in this chapter, when we discuss the behaviors of the MainFrame class.

```
// Initialize the buttons to their proper enabled/disabled state.

resetButtons();
```

Finally, we assemble the various panels by layering them onto one another and then onto the underlying `contentPane` of the `MainFrame`.

```
// Finally, attach all of the panels to one another
// and to the frame.
// Add in ascending row, then column, order.

topLeftPanel.add(labelPanel);
topLeftPanel.add(fieldPanel);
leftPanel.add(topLeftPanel);
leftPanel.add(bottomLeftPanel);
contentPane.add(leftPanel, BorderLayout.WEST);
contentPane.add(rightPanel, BorderLayout.CENTER);
contentPane.add(buttonPanel, BorderLayout.SOUTH);

// -----------------
// Add all behaviors ... to be discussed later in the chapter!
// -----------------
```

We've yet to finish off our `MainFrame` class definition; in particular, we are going to need to provide listeners for each of the following GUI components, as these are the components that the user will be interacting with:

❑ We'll need the GUI to recognize when a user has typed his/her student ID number into the `ssnField` as a signal that he/she wishes to log on.

❑ We'll need to program the logic for what is to happen behind the scenes when each of the four buttons at the bottom of the GUI -- `addButton`, `dropButton`, `saveScheduleButton`, and `logoffButton` – is clicked.

❑ We'll need to recognize when a user has made a selection in either the `studentCourseList` or `scheduleOfClassesList`.

❑ We'll also want to provide a `WindowListener` to enable us to close down the application as a whole 'gracefully' if the user clicks the window close button at the upper right hand corner of the window.

We'll provide all of these behaviors a bit later in this chapter, after we've learned a bit more about the other classes/components that these behaviors will be reliant upon.

Successful Model - View Separation

Many of the classes used in the Chapter 15 version of the SRS application remain unchanged in the solution to Chapter 16 – that's the beauty of separating the model from the view! Because the model is, for the most part, blissfully ignorant that there even is a view (the view knows about the model, but the model doesn't know about the view), the model classes needn't change to accommodate it. So, the following classes (as presented in Chapter 15) are unaltered in the GUI version of the SRS:

❑ `CollectionWrapper.java`

❑ `Course.java`

❑ `CourseCatalog.java`

- ❑ Faculty.java
- ❑ Person.java
- ❑ Professor.java
- ❑ Transcript.java
- ❑ TranscriptEntry.java

and therefore we won't revisit any of these classes in this chapter.

The following classes have been modified from the version used in Chapter 15 so as to add a method or two in support of the GUI; we'll study their code in detail one by one:

- ❑ ScheduleOfClasses.java: we've added a single method, getSortedSections(), to support our use of JLists, as we mentioned briefly when discussing the 'look' of the MainFrame.

- ❑ Student.java: we've added a single attribute – String password – to handle the requirement for a user to log on to the SRS system, and then made a few changes to the Student methods to recognize this new attribute. We also added a few other data retrieval methods needed to support the GUI; we'll discuss all of these changes in depth shortly.

- ❑ Section.java: we made only one minor change, which as it turns out wasn't related to the GUI at all, but rather was simply an improvement in the logic from that used in Chapter 15.

- ❑ And, of course, we had to significantly revamp the main SRS.java 'driver' code to accommodate the newly added GUI. As it turns out, we were able to significantly streamline this code, as you will soon see.

Despite the fact that we did go back to make a few enhancements to the domain classes to accommodate the GUI, these were still done in such a way as to keep the model loosely coupled from the view; that is, we could easily swap out the SRS GUI that we are building and add a completely new GUI down the road, and our domain classes would remain intact. In the worst case, they would have a few methods (those that we added for use by the first GUI) that would no longer get used.

Finally, the following two GUI classes are brand new as of the solution presented in Chapter 16:

- ❑ MainFrame.java, a type of JFrame, used as our main application window.

- ❑ PasswordPopup.java, a type of JDialog, used when logging a student on to the SRS.

and we'll discuss these in depth, as well.

Recommendation: if you haven't already done so, please consider downloading and printing a copy of all of the SRS program files related to Chapter 16, so that you have them handy to refer to when following along with the discussion that follows. Download instructions are provided in Appendix D.

The ScheduleOfClasses Class (Harnessing the Power of JLists)

The only change that we had to make to the `ScheduleOfClasses` class as originally presented in Chapter 15 is related to our decision to use a `JList` to display the 'Schedule of Classes' in our SRS GUI.

❏ We learned earlier in this chapter that a `Vector` can be passed in as an argument to a `JList` constructor so that the contents of the `Vector` will be used to initialize the `JList`.

❏ However, as originally designed, the `ScheduleOfClasses` class maintains information on what sections are available for student registration as a `Hashtable` of `Section` objects. In the section entitled *'Stepping Through a Collection with an Enumeration Object'* in Chapter 13, we learned how to use an `Enumeration` object to step one-by-one through all of the objects contained within a collection such as a `Vector` or a `Hashtable`. But, the `Section` objects are stored in no particular order in the `Hashtable` – the nature of `Hashtables` does not guarantee sorted ordering, but simply that you can retrieve a specific object from the table based on its key – and so stepping through the `Hashtable` with an `Enumeration` wouldn't yield an **alphabetically sorted** list of `Sections`. All things being equal, we would prefer to display the schedule of classes sorted in order by course number.

❏ By adding a single method, `getSortedSections()`, to return an alphabetically sorted `Vector` of `Section` objects based on this `Hashtable`, we were then able to use this method from within `MainFrame.java` to construct the `scheduleOfClassesList`, as shown earlier:

```
scheduleOfClassesList = new JList(
    SRS.scheduleOfClasses.getSortedSections());
```

First, we'll present the new `getSortedSections()` method in its entirety; then, we'll review what the new method does in depth. (Because the code for the entire `ScheduleOfClasses` class is rather lengthy, and because you've seen much of the class code in previous chapters, we're only going to present those chunks of code that are new as of the Chapter 16 version. Again, we encourage you to have a printed copy of the complete class available for comparison purposes.)

```java
// This next method was added to the ScheduleOfClasses class
// for use with the SRS GUI.

// Convert the contents of the Hashtable into a Vector
// that is sorted in alphabetical order.

public Vector getSortedSections() {
  Vector sortedKeys = new Vector();
  Vector sortedSections = new Vector();

  // Note that we can pull the keys as an Enumeration as
  // well as the objects themselves.

  Enumeration e = sections.keys();
  while (e.hasMoreElements()) {
    boolean inserted = false;
    String key = (String) e.nextElement();
    for (int i = 0; i < sortedKeys.size(); i++) {
      String val = (String) sortedKeys.elementAt(i);
```

```
        // The compareTo() method compares two Strings,
        // returning a negative value if "key" comes
        // alphabetically before "val", zero if
        // they are equal, and a positive value if
        // "key" comes alphabetically after "val".

        if (key.compareTo(val) <= 0) {
          sortedKeys.insertElementAt(key, i);
          inserted = true;
          break;
        }
      }

      // If it hasn't been inserted yet, stick it at the end
      // of the "sortedKeys" Vector.

      if (!inserted) sortedKeys.add(key);
    }

    // Now that "sortedKeys" Vector contains all of the keys in
    // alphabetic order, we'll step through that Vector and use
    // it to pull the Section objects themselves out of the
    // Hashtable and into another Vector "sortedSections".

    for (int i = 0; i < sortedKeys.size(); i++) {
      String key = (String) sortedKeys.elementAt(i);
      Section s = (Section) sections.get(key);
      sortedSections.add(s);
    }

    return sortedSections;
  }
```

Let's step through the code for this new method:

```
// This next method was added to the ScheduleOfClasses class
// for use with the SRS GUI.

// Convert the contents of the Hashtable into a Vector
// that is sorted in alphabetical order.

public Vector getSortedSections() {
```

We begin by creating a few empty Vectors, which will be used to store the intermediate results of our sorting efforts:

```
    Vector sortedKeys = new Vector();
    Vector sortedSections = new Vector();
```

We'll put Enumerations to good use now. Using the keys() method defined for Hashtable objects, we are able to obtain an Enumeration object representing all of the key objects from the 'sections' Hashtable. (Recall that we used String objects to serve as keys in that Hashtable.)

```
    Enumeration e = sections.keys();
```

Stepping through this `Enumeration` until it is exhausted, we cast each key as it is retrieved back to its `String` representation.

```
while (e.hasMoreElements()) {
    boolean inserted = false;
    String key = (String) e.nextElement();
```

Then, stepping one-by-one through the `sortedKeys` Vector (which will be empty the first time we process the `while` loop), we use the `compareTo()` method as defined by the `String` class to compare the key that we've just retrieved from the `Enumeration` against each of the `String` objects in the `sortedKeys` Vector. When we find the position in the `sortedKeys` Vector where the key that we are processing belongs alphabetically, we'll insert it.

Let's illustrate this approach with a simple example before we look at the code:

❑   Assume that the `scheduleOfClasses` Hashtable contains the following entries in this physical order:

The Contents of the scheduleOfClasses Hashtable:

Key: a reference to	Value: a reference to
The `String` object 'CMP101 – 1'	The `Section` object representing CMP101 –1
The `String` object 'OBJ101 – 1'	The `Section` object representing OBJ101 – 1
The `String` object 'ART101 – 1'	The `Section` object representing ART101 – 1
The `String` object 'CMP283 – 1'	The `Section` object representing CMP283 – 1

and that the `sortedKeys` Vector is currently empty, because we are just getting started with the sorting effort.

The Contents of the sortedKeys Vector:

'Cell' in the Vector	Contents: a reference to
empty	

❑   We pull the first key value from the `Hashtable`, which is the `String` 'CMP101 – 1'.

❑   Since the `sortedKeys` Vector is empty, we insert a reference to this `String` object in the `Vector`, which now looks like this:

The Contents of the sortedKeys Vector:

'Cell' in the Vector	Contents: a reference to
0	the String object 'CMP101 – 1'

❑ We pull the second key value from the Hashtable, which is the String 'OBJ101 – 1'.

❑ We compare this String to the first (0th) element in the Vector. Since 'OBJ101 – 1' is alphabetically greater than 'CMP101 – 1', we step to the next element in the Vector. But, there *is* no next element in the Vector! So, we know that we must insert this key at the end of the Vector, which now looks like this:

The Contents of the sortedKeys Vector:

'Cell' in the Vector	Contents: a reference to
0	the String object 'CMP101 – 1'
1	the String object 'OBJ101 – 1'

❑ We pull the third key value from the Hashtable, which is the String 'ART101 – 1'.

❑ We compare this String to the first (0th) element in the Vector. Since 'ART101 – 1' is alphabetically less than 'CMP101 – 1', we know that we must insert this key ahead of 'CMP101 – 1' in the Vector, which now looks like this:

The Contents of the sortedKeys Vector:

'Cell' in the Vector	Contents: a reference to
0	the String object 'ART101 – 1'
1	the String object 'CMP101 – 1'
2	the String object 'OBJ101 – 1'

❑ We pull the fourth and final key value from the Hashtable, which is the String 'CMP283 – 1'.

❑ We compare this String to the first (0th) element in the Vector. Since 'CMP283 – 1' is alphabetically greater than 'ART101 – 1', we know that we must insert this key somewhere later in the Vector.

❑ We advance to the next cell in the Vector, and do another comparison. Since 'CMP283 – 1' is alphabetically greater than 'CMP101 – 1', we know that we must insert this key somewhere later in the Vector.

❑ We advance to the next cell in the Vector, and do yet another comparison. Since 'CMP283 – 1' is alphabetically less than 'OBJ101 – 1', we know that we must insert this key ahead of 'OBJ101 – 1' in the Vector, which now looks like this:

Contents of the sortedKeys Vector:

'Cell' in the Vector	Contents: a reference to
0	the String object 'ART101 – 1'
1	the String object 'CMP101 – 1'
2	the String object 'CMP283 – 1'
3	the String object 'OBJ101 – 1'

❑ We see that the `sortedKeys` `Vector` does indeed now contain references to all of the keys of the `Hashtable` in alphabetically sorted order!

Let's now look at the code necessary to accomplish this.

❑ The `key.compareTo(val)` method call compares two `String` objects represented by reference variables `key` and `val`, returning a *negative* value if 'key' comes alphabetically before `val`, zero if they are equal, and a *positive* value if 'key' comes alphabetically after `val`.

❑ As soon as this method call returns a *negative* value, then we know that we've reached the point in the `sortedKeys` `Vector` where the key that we're processing needs to be inserted.

```
for (int i = 0; i < sortedKeys.size(); i++) {
  String val = (String) sortedKeys.elementAt(i);

  // The compareTo() method compares two Strings,
  // returning a negative value if "key" comes
  // alphabetically before "val", zero if
  // they are equal, and a positive value if
  // "key" comes alphabetically after "val".

  if (key.compareTo(val) <= 0) {
```

❑ We insert the key that we've retrieved from the `Hashtable` into the ith 'cell' of the `Vector`:

```
    sortedKeys.insertElementAt(key, i);
```

and, as soon as we've performed the insertion, we (a) set a boolean flag (previously set to `false`) to `true` to keep track of the fact that we have indeed inserted the key into the `Vector`, and (b) use the 'break' statement to terminate the `for` loop, because there's no need in looking through the rest of the `sortedKeys` array if we've already inserted the key of interest.

```
    inserted = true;
    break;
  }
}
```

❑ We now check the `boolean` flag, because if we've gotten through the entire `Vector` without inserting this key yet, that means that the key is to be inserted at the end of the `Vector`, as the last entry.

```
  // If it hasn't been inserted yet, stick it at the end
  // of the "sortedKeys" Vector.

  if (!inserted) sortedKeys.add(key);
}
```

❑ Now that 'sortedKeys' `Vector` contains all of the *keys* in alphabetic order, we'll step through this `Vector` and use it to pull the `Section` objects themselves out of the `Hashtable` in sorted order! As we pull them out of the `Hashtable`, we'll stick them into a second `Vector` called 'sortedSections'.

```
      for (int i = 0; i < sortedKeys.size(); i++) {
        String key = (String) sortedKeys.elementAt(i);
        Section s = (Section) sections.get(key);
        sortedSections.add(s);
      }
```

❑ We now have a Vector containing all Sections that were originally in the Hashtable, but in alphabetically sorted order.

```
    return sortedSections;
  }
```

The Student Class (Retrofitting Attributes)

When we modeled the SRS throughout Part 2 of the book, it didn't occur to us to allow for a Student to have a password, since this is more of a computer-related artifact than it is a real-world attribute of a student. But, as is frequently the case, we find that we must expand the attributes and methods of a class once we begin implementation to accommodate what we often refer to as 'solution space' or 'implementation space' features. Such is the case with the password attribute of Student.

Because the Student class code is so long (over six pages when printed!), and because you've seen much of the Student class code in previous chapters, we're only going to present those chunks of code that are new as of the Chapter 16 version. Again, we encourage you to have a printed copy of the complete class available for comparison purposes.

❑ First, we add the attribute:

```
private String password;
```

❑ Next, we acknowledge the existence of this new attribute by adding initialization code to both versions of the Student constructor. Most of the constructor code is unaltered from its Chapter 15 version; we've repeated it all here, but have highlighted the only changes that were necessary:

```
//----------------
// Constructor(s).
//----------------

public Student(String ssn) {
    // First, construct a "dummy" Student object. Then,
    // attempt to pull this Student's information from the
    // appropriate file (ssn.dat: e.g., 111-11-1111.dat).
    // The file consists of a header record, containing
    // the student's basic info. (ssn, name, etc.), and
    // 0 or more subsequent records representing a list of
    // the sections that he/she is currently registered for.

    this();
```

```java
String line = null;
BufferedReader bIn = null;
boolean outcome = true;
String pathToFile = ssn + ".dat";

try {
  // Open the file.

  bIn = new BufferedReader(new FileReader(pathToFile));

  // The first line in the file contains the header info.

  line = bIn.readLine();
  if (line != null) parseData(line);

  // Any remaining lines contain section references.
  // Note that we must instantiate an empty vector
  // so that the parseData2() method may insert
  // items into the Vector.

  attends = new Vector();

  line = bIn.readLine();
  while (line != null) {
    parseData2(line);
    line = bIn.readLine();
  }

  bIn.close();
}
catch (FileNotFoundException f) {
  // Since we are encoding a "dummy" Student to begin
  // with, the fact that his/her name will be equal
  // to "???" flags an error. We have included
  // a boolean method successfullyInitialized()
  // which allows client code to verify the success
  // or failure of this constructor (see code below).
}
catch (IOException i) {
  // See comments for FileNotFoundException above.
}

// Initialize the password to be the first three digits
// of the student's ssn.

setPassword(getSsn().substring(0, 3)); // added for GUI purposes

// Create a brand new Transcript.
// (Ideally, we'd read in an existing Transcript from
// a file, but we're not bothering to do so in this
// example).
```

```
        setTranscript(new Transcript(this));
    }

    // A second form of constructor, used when a Student's data
    // file cannot be found for some reason.

    public Student() {
        // Reuse the code of the parent's constructor.
        // Question marks indicate that something went wrong!

        super("???", "???");

        setMajor("???");
        setDegree("???");

        // Placeholders for the remaining attributes (this
        // Student is invalid anyway).

        setPassword("???"); // added for GUI purposes
        setTranscript(new Transcript(this));
        attends = new Vector();
    }
```

❑   Then, we added an accessor and a modifier method for this attribute:

```
    //------------------
    // Get/set methods.
    //------------------

    // This next method was added for use with the GUI.

    public void setPassword(String pw) {
        password = pw;
    }

    // This next method was added for use with the GUI.

    public String getPassword() {
        return password;
    }
```

❑   And under the heading:

```
    //-----------------------------
    // Miscellaneous other methods.
    //-----------------------------
```

we add a method that will be used to validate the password that a user types in when logging into the GUI against his/her 'official' password. The argument 'pw' represents the value that a user has typed in (we'll see how this is determined when we visit the event handling code of the PasswordPopup class), and of course 'password' represents the 'authentic' password for this student user.

```
// This next method was added for use with the GUI.

public boolean validatePassword(String pw) {
  if (pw == null) return false;
  if (pw.equals(password)) return true;
  else return false;
}
```

As it turns out, there are a few more information retrieval methods that we're going to need in support of the GUI – methods that we didn't anticipate needing when we modeled the SRS in Part 2 of the book, but which only surfaced when we designed the SRS GUI.

- ❑ We want a method that will enable the MainFrame to retrieve a Vector of all Section objects that the Student is currently enrolled in, so that it may be used to populate the studentCourseList JList:

```
// This next method was added for use with the GUI.

public Vector getSectionsEnrolled() {
  return attends;
}
```

- ❑ We also need a method to use in retrieving the total number of sections that a Student is registered for, so that we may use this value to update the totalCoursesLabel component on the GUI:

```
// This next method was added for use with the GUI.

public int getCourseTotal() {
  return attends.size();
}
```

- ❑ In the Chapter 15 version of the Student class, we provided a method isEnrolledIn() which accepted an argument of type Section and returned a boolean value indicating whether or not the Student in question was enrolled in this exact section:

```
// Determine whether the Student is already enrolled in this
// exact Section.

public boolean isEnrolledIn(Section s) {
  if (attends.contains(s)) return true;
  else return false;
}
```

After development of the GUI was underway, we recognized the need to not only determine whether a Student was enrolled in a specific Section, but furthermore whether or not the student was enrolled in a *different* section of the *same* course. So, we added this next method as a variation on isEnrolledIn():

```
    // Determine whether the Student is already enrolled in another
    // Section of this same Course.

    public boolean isCurrentlyEnrolledInSimilar(Section s1) {
      boolean foundMatch = false;
```

We get a handle on the Course that this Section represents; then, we step through all enrolled sections with an Enumeration, and for each of these, we obtain the Course that it represents; then, we check to see if the two courses represent exactly the same object (recall our discussion of Object identities in Chapter 13).

Please see the in-line comments below for further details.

```
      Course c1 = s1.getRepresentedCourse();
      Enumeration e = getEnrolledSections();
      while (e.hasMoreElements()) {
        Section s2 = (Section) e.nextElement();
        Course c2 = s2.getRepresentedCourse();
        if (c1 == c2) {
          // There is indeed a Section in the attends() Vector
          // representing the same Course. Check to see if the
          // Student is currently enrolled (in other words whether
          // or not he has yet received a grade). If there is no
          // grade, he/she is currently enrolled; if there is a
          // grade, then he/she completed the course some time in
          // the past.
          if (s2.getGrade(this) == null) {
            // No grade was assigned! This meant that the Student
            // is currently enrolled in a Section of this same Course.
            foundMatch = true;
            break;
          }
        }
      }

      return foundMatch;
    }
```

Other than these few changes, the Student class is unaltered from its Chapter 15 version.

The Section Class (Making Up for Past Mistakes)

The Section class for this chapter differs from the version that we presented in Chapter 15 by only *one line of code*.

❑ In the Chapter 15 version of Section, the enroll() method started out as follows:

```
    public int enroll(Student s) {
      // First, make sure that this Student is not already
      // enrolled for this Section, and that he/she has
      // never taken and passed the course before.
```

```
Transcript transcript = s.getTranscript();

if (s.isEnrolledIn(this) ||
    transcript.verifyCompletion(this.getRepresentedCourse()))
    return PREVIOUSLY_ENROLLED;

// etc.
```

That is, we used the `isEnrolledIn()` method of Student to determine whether or not the Student about to be enrolled in this particular Section was already enrolled in this Section; if so, then we returned a status of PREVIOUSLY_ENROLLED from the enroll() method. (Recall that PREVIOUSLY_ENROLLED is declared as a `public static final int` variable in the Section class.)

However, we missed one minor detail: if a Student attempted to enroll in two *different* sections of the *same* course in the same semester – for example, in 'CMP101 – 1' and 'CMP101 – 2' – then the enroll() method would not detect this situation, and the Student would be allowed to enroll in both sections. This is an undesirable situation.

❑ Fortunately, as we discussed just a few moments ago, we introduced a new method for the Student class in support of the SRS GUI called isCurrentlyEnrolledInSimilar(). We subsequently realized that the Section class's enroll() method could be improved upon by taking advantage of this new method of the Student class, and so we did! We only had to change one line of code in the enroll() method to make this happen:

```
public int enroll(Student s) {
    // First, make sure that this Student is not already
    // enrolled for this Section, and that he/she has
    // never taken and passed the course before.

    Transcript transcript = s.getTranscript();

    if (s.isCurrentlyEnrolledInSimilar(this) ||
        transcript.verifyCompletion(this.getRepresentedCourse()))
        return PREVIOUSLY_ENROLLED;

    // etc.
```

In the course of developing a system, it's natural to uncover functional 'flaws'; adding a GUI to an application often brings to light limitations of the model that we hadn't previously detected, because it enables us to test the application from a new perspective. The important thing to note was that, in this particular instance, we were able to effect a 'repair' to the Section class's enroll() method fairly painlessly, thanks to the natural modularity of classes and their methods.

The SRS 'Driver' Class – Significantly Streamlined

Now that we have a GUI to use in interacting with the SRS, many of the extra steps that we went through in the Chapter 15 version of the SRS driver class are now unnecessary.

To illustrate both what we've removed from the old version of SRS.java as well as what we've added to accommodate the GUI, we've repeated the old version of the SRS.java file below first, and are using gray text to illustrate what we've been able to eliminate:

```
// SRS.java - the old Chapter 15 version
import java.util.*;

public class SRS {
    // We can effectively create "global" data by declaring
    // public static attributes in the main class.

    // Entry points/"roots" for getting at objects.

    public static Faculty faculty = new Faculty();

    public static CourseCatalog courseCatalog = new CourseCatalog();

    public static ScheduleOfClasses scheduleOfClasses =
                                new ScheduleOfClasses("SP2001");

    // We don't create a collection for Student objects, because
    // we're only going to worry about one Student at a time -- namely,
    // whichever Student is logged on.

    public static void main(String[] args) {
        // Initialize the key objects by reading data from files.
        // Setting the second argument to true causes the
        // initializeObjects() method to use the parseData()
        // method instead of parseData2().

        faculty.initializeObjects("Faculty.dat", true);
        courseCatalog.initializeObjects("CourseCatalog.dat", true);
        scheduleOfClasses.initializeObjects("SoC_SP2001.dat", true);

        // We'll handle the students differently:  that is,
        // rather than loading them all in at application outset,
        // we'll pull in the data that we need just for one
        // Student when that Student logs on -- see the Student
        // class constructor for the details.
```

We no longer need to create Student objects to simulate log-ons, since we now have a GUI for this purpose:

```
        // Let's temporarily create Students this way as a test,
        // to simulate Students logging on.  Note that only the
        // first Student has "preregistered" for courses based
        // on the content of his/her ssn.dat file (see Student.java
        // for details).

        Student s1 = new Student("111-11-1111");
        Student s2 = new Student("222-22-2222");
        Student s3 = new Student("333-33-3333");

        // Establish some prerequisites (c1 => c2 => c3 => c4).
        // Setting the second argument to false causes the
        // initializeObjects() method to use the parseData2()
        // method instead of parseData().
```

```
courseCatalog.initializeObjects("Prerequisites.dat", false);

// Recruit a professor to teach each of the sections.
// Setting the second argument to false causes the
// initializeObjects() method to use the parseData2()
// method instead of parseData().

faculty.initializeObjects("TeachingAssignments.dat", false);
```

Neither do we need to simulate a Student enrolling in a section, since we can perform that function via the GUI now, too:

```
// Let's have one Student try enrolling in something, so
// that we can simulate his/her logging off and persisting
// the enrollment data in the ssn.dat file (see Student.java
// for details).

Section sec = scheduleOfClasses.findSection("ART101 - 1");
sec.enroll(s2);
s2.persist();  // Check contents of 222-22-2222.dat!
```

And, since we can now verify the outcome of our interactions with the SRS simply by viewing the state of the GUI, we no longer need to use System.out.println() calls to display the internal state of objects (although we may wish to retain this code, and simply comment it out, in our SRS program, to help us with debugging the application at a later date).

```
// Let's see if everything got initialized properly
// by calling various display methods!

System.out.println("====================");
System.out.println("Course Catalog:");
System.out.println("====================");
System.out.println("");
courseCatalog.display();

System.out.println("====================");
System.out.println("Schedule of Classes:");
System.out.println("====================");
System.out.println("");
scheduleOfClasses.display();

System.out.println("=======================");
System.out.println("Professor Information:");
System.out.println("=======================");
System.out.println("");
faculty.display();

System.out.println("====================");
System.out.println("Student Information:");
System.out.println("====================");
System.out.println("");
s1.display();
System.out.println("");
s2.display();
System.out.println("");
s3.display();
```

The only *new* logic that we had to add to the SRS class was the code needed to create and display an instance of the main GUI window:

```
    // Create and display an instance of the main GUI window.

    new MainFrame();
  }
}
```

The resultant streamlined class is as follows:

```
// SRS.java - new Chapter 16 version!
// A main driver for the GUI version of the SRS.

import java.util.*;

public class SRS {
  // We can effectively create "global" data by declaring
  // PUBLIC STATIC attributes in the main class.

  // Entry points/"roots" for getting at objects.

  public static Faculty faculty = new Faculty();

  public static CourseCatalog courseCatalog = new CourseCatalog();

  public static ScheduleOfClasses scheduleOfClasses =
    new ScheduleOfClasses("SP2001");

  // We don't create a collection for Student objects, because
  // we're only going to handle one Student at a time -- namely,
  // whichever Student is logged on per instance of the application

  public static void main(String[] args) {
    // Initialize the key objects by reading data from files.

    faculty.initializeObjects("Faculty.dat", true);
    courseCatalog.initializeObjects("CourseCatalog.dat", true);
    scheduleOfClasses.initializeObjects("SoC_SP2001.dat", true);

    // We'll handle the students differently:  that is,
    // rather than loading them all in at application outset,
    // we'll pull in the data that we need just for one
    // Student when that Student logs on -- see the Student
    // class constructor for the details.

    // Establish some prerequisites (c1 => c2 => c3 => c4).

    courseCatalog.initializeObjects("Prerequisites.dat", false);

    // Recruit a professor to teach each of the sections.

    faculty.initializeObjects("TeachingAssignments.dat", false);

    // Create and display an instance of the main GUI window.

    new MainFrame();
  }
}
```

The MainFrame Class, Revisited: Adding Behaviors

Earlier in this chapter, we took a look at the first half of the MainFrame class – in particular, the attributes representing the component 'building blocks' of the frame, and the constructor that glued these together. Now, let's pick up where we left off, and take a look at all of the code required to implement the desired behaviors of the SRS GUI.

By way of review, we had stated before that we were going to need to provide listeners for each of the following GUI components, as these are the components that the user will be interacting with:

- ❏ We'll need the GUI to recognize when a user has typed his/her student ID number into the ssnField as a signal that he/she wishes to log on.

- ❏ We'll need to program the logic for what is to happen behind the scenes when each of the four buttons at the bottom of the GUI -- addButton, dropButton, saveScheduleButton, and logoffButton – is clicked.

- ❏ We'll need to recognize when a user has made a selection in either the studentCourseList or scheduleOfClassesList.

- ❏ We'll also want to provide a WindowListener to enable us to close down the application as a whole 'gracefully' if the user clicks the window close button at the upper right hand corner of the window.

The following code is the 'bottom half' of the MainFrame.java file; because this file is so long (10+ pages!), we won't clutter the chapter by repeating the first half of this class from earlier in the chapter, but encourage you to download and print out the entire file from the Wrox website. We'll provide editorial comments on those segments of code that are most unusual or complex, but please do take the time to read through all of the in-line documentation, as well.

As mentioned in the comments for this program, different types of components require different types of listeners:

- ❏ Text fields respond to an ActionListener whenever the Enter key is pressed.

- ❏ Buttons respond to an ActionListener whenever the button is clicked.

- ❏ JLists respond to a ListSelectionListener whenever an item is selected.

So, we'll declare a reference variable for each of these three listener types.

```
// ------------------
// Add all behaviors.
// ------------------
```

```
ActionListener aListener;
ListSelectionListener lListener;
WindowAdapter wListener;
```

Then, we'll proceed to instantiate the appropriate listeners one by one, using the technique that we learned earlier in this chapter for creating anonymous inner classes.

ssnField

```
// ssnField
```

The `ssnField` is the field that the user types his/her student ID into, such that the SRS system can recognize that a student wishes to log on. So, we need to listen for the `ActionEvents` that are generated when a user presses the Enter key after typing in this field, and an `ActionListener` is designed to do just that.

```
aListener = new ActionListener() {
  public void actionPerformed(ActionEvent e) {
```

We've created a private 'housekeeping' method, `clearFields()`, which steps through the three components on the GUI that represent student-specific information – `nameField`, `totalCoursesLabel`, and `studentCourseList` – clearing them of any information that is still being displayed for a previously logged on student. You'll see the code for this method, along with several other 'housekeeping' methods, toward the end of this discussion.

```
// First, clear the fields reflecting the
// previous student's information.
clearFields();
```

Then, we use the `getText()` method to pull whatever `String` the user has typed into the field, and attempt to instantiate a new `Student` object representing the 'real' student user (an example of a boundary class, as we discussed in Chapter 11):

```
// We'll try to construct a Student based on
// the ssn we read, and if a file containing
// Student's information cannot be found,
// we have a problem.
String id = ssnField.getText();
Student theStudent = new Student(id);
```

We use the `successfullyInitialized()` method that we added to the `Student` class in Chapter 15; recall that this method was defined to return a `boolean` value: `true` if the `Student` contructor was able to open the associated student's data file (for example, `111-11-1111.dat` for a `Student` with a student ID of `111-11-1111`), and `false` otherwise.

If the result of this method call was `false`, we reset the `currentUser` attribute of the `MainFrame` class to `null`, to signify that no user is logged on; this has the added effect of causing reference variable `currentUser` to drop any handle that it might still have been holding on a previously logged in `Student` object.

```
if (!theStudent.successfullyInitialized()) {
  // Drat! The ID was invalid.
  currentUser = null;
```

Then, we formulate a warning message dialog to that effect using the `JOptionPane` class, a technique that we discussed earlier in this chapter.

```
// Let the user know that login failed,
// unless the ID typed was blank,
// signalling a successful log-off.
JOptionPane.showMessageDialog(null,
        "Invalid student ID; please try again.",
        "Invalid Student ID",
        JOptionPane.WARNING_MESSAGE);
}
```

If, on the other hand, the `successfullyInitialized()` method returned a value of `true`, then we know that the `Student` class's constructor successfully read in the contents of the Student's data file, populating all of the `Student` object's attributes, and that his/her password attribute has been initialized, as well. So, it's time to ask the user to provide a password, for us to check against this Student's correct password. (It is conceivable that someone might be trying to impersonate a particular student by typing in his/her ID number, which would indeed retrieve that student's data from a file; but, if this student is an impostor who doesn't know the correct password, we want to find out before *displaying* the student's 'private' information.)

```
else {
    // Hooray!  We found one!  Now, we need
    // to request and validate the password.
    PasswordPopup pp = new PasswordPopup(MainFrame.this);
```

The preceding line of code is responsible for instantiating and displaying a `PasswordPopup` dialog, which is a special class that we defined as a subclass of `JDialog`. (We'll see the code for `PasswordPopup` in its entirety after we finish stepping through the `MainFrame` class.)

The `PasswordPopup` dialog happens to be a modal dialog, which means that as long as the `PasswordPopup` dialog is displayed on the screen, the user will be unable to interact with the rest of the SRS GUI. More importantly, though, as long as the dialog is displayed on the screen, the JVM will be awaiting events from that dialog, and the code for the `MainFrame` method that we're in the middle of executing is also suspended.

By the time we reach the next line of code, we know that the password dialog was dismissed by the user, so we can use a method that we've written for the `PasswordPopup` class called `getPassword()` that allows us to 'fetch' whatever the user has typed into the dialog; we'll see the code for that method when we study `PasswordPopup` a bit later in the chapter.

After we fetch the value of whatever password the user typed in, we can dispose of the dialog, because we no longer need to 'talk' with it to request any of its services:

```
String pw = pp.getPassword();
pp.dispose();
```

We attempt to validate the password, and if the attempt succeeds, we retain a handle on the `Student` object whose data we've just loaded in, and whose password we've just validated, in attribute `currentUser`. We then use another 'housekeeping' method, `setFields()`, to populate the various components on the GUI with this student's information so that he/she can see it. (We'll see that method code in a moment.) We also use `JOptionPane` once again to notify the user that the login succeeded.

```
             if (theStudent.validatePassword(pw)) {
               currentUser = theStudent;
               setFields(theStudent);

               // Let the user know that the
               // login succeeded.
               JOptionPane.showMessageDialog(null,
               "Log in succeeded for " +
               theStudent.getName() + ".",
               "Log In Succeeded",
               JOptionPane.INFORMATION_MESSAGE);
             }
```

And, of course, if the logon failed, we notify the user of this, as well.

```
             else {
               // Password validation failed;
               // notify the user of this.
               JOptionPane.showMessageDialog(null,
               "Invalid password; please " +
               "try again.",
               "Invalid Password",
               JOptionPane.WARNING_MESSAGE);
             }
           }
```

We force the GUI to refresh itself, to make sure that the new data appears. (It should do so automatically, but this is extra 'insurance' to make *sure* that it does.)

```
             MainFrame.this.repaint();
```

And, since the state of the application has changed – a new user is now logged on – we use a third 'housekeeping' method to enable/disable the buttons at the bottom of the screen, as appropriate. (We'll see the code for resetButtons() toward the end of our discussion of the MainFrame class.)

```
             // Check states of the various buttons.
             resetButtons();
           }
         };
         ssnField.addActionListener(aListener);
```

addButton

```
             // addButton
```

For the Add button, we first must pull the user-selected line item from the scheduleOfClassesList via the getSelectedValue() method. This method returns a generic Object, so we must cast it back into a Section object; we maintain a handle on that Section object via the 'selected' reference variable.

```
        aListener = new ActionListener() {
          public void actionPerformed(ActionEvent e) {
          // Determine which section is selected
          // (note that we must cast it, as it
          // is returned as an Object reference).
          Section selected = (Section)
              scheduleOfClassesList.getSelectedValue();
```

Now, we have numerous validations to do! We send two messages:

❏   `currentUser.isCurrentlyEnrolledInSimilar()` , to determine whether this
    Student is (a) already enrolled in this class, (b) already enrolled in another section of this
    same class, (c) has ever attended this course. If the outcome of this message is true, meaning
    that this would indeed be a duplicate course, we notify the user of this via a `JOptionDialog`,
    and our processing of this event is concluded.

❏   `selected.enroll(currentUser)`, which is an attempt to actually enroll the Student in
    the selected Section.

```
          // Check to see if this COURSE is already
          // one that the student registered for,
          // even if the SECTION is different.
          // If so, warn them of this.
          if (currentUser.isCurrentlyEnrolledInSimilar(selected)) {
```

Note the technique of displaying two lines of message text on the message dialog:

```
          // Create a String array of TWO lines
          // of messsage text, so that the popup
          // window won't be too wide.
          String[] message = { "You are already enrolled in " +
                          "(or have already successfully completed) "
                          + "a section of this course."," " };
          // Then, we can just hand the String
          // array in to the showMessageDialog()
          // call.
          JOptionPane.showMessageDialog(null, message, "Request Denied",
            JOptionPane.WARNING_MESSAGE);
          } else {
          // Attempt to enroll the student, noting
          // the status code that is returned.
          int success = selected.enroll(currentUser);
```

We study the outcome of the enrollment request; note the use of public static final variables
`Section.SECTION_FULL`, `Section.PREREQ_NOT_SATISFIED`, and
`Section.PREVIOUSLY_ENROLLED` to return a status value from the `enroll()` method. In each case, we
formulate the appropriate dialog message with `JDialogPane`, and our processing of this event is finished.

```
        // Report the status to the user.
        if (success == Section.SECTION_FULL) {
          JOptionPane.showMessageDialog(null,
                "Sorry - that section is full.",
                "Request Denied",
                JOptionPane.WARNING_MESSAGE);
        }
        else if (success == Section.PREREQ_NOT_SATISFIED) {
          JOptionPane.showMessageDialog(null,
                "You haven't satisfied all " +
                "of the prerequisites for " +
                "this course.",
                "Request Denied",
                JOptionPane.WARNING_MESSAGE);
        }
        else if (success ==
          Section.PREVIOUSLY_ENROLLED) {
            String[] message = { "You are already enrolled in " +
                  "(or have already",
                  "successfully completed) a " +
                  "section of this course.",
                  " " };

          JOptionPane.showMessageDialog(null, message,
                "Request Denied",
             JOptionPane.WARNING_MESSAGE);
        }
```

If we make it to this point in the code, we've indeed succeeded in getting this student enrolled in the selected class!

```
        else { // success!
          // Display a confirmation message.
          JOptionPane.showMessageDialog(null,
            "Seat confirmed in " +
            selected.getRepresentedCourse().getCourseNo() + ".",
            "Request Successful",
            JOptionPane.INFORMATION_MESSAGE);
```

We must reflect the newly added section to the student's course list on the GUI; it's easy enough to just repopulate the entire list with all of the sections for which this student is enrolled presently. We also update the field representing the total enrolled course count.

```
        // Update the list of sections
        // that this student is registered for.
        studentCourseList.setListData(currentUser.getSectionsEnrolled());

        // Update the field representing
        // student's course total.
        int total = currentUser.getCourseTotal();
        totalCoursesLabel.setText("" + total);
```

And, as a housekeeping measure, we clear out the user's 'clicked' entry in the scheduleOfClassesList, so that it is ready for another selection to be made:

```
            // Clear the selection in the
            // schedule of classes list.
            scheduleOfClassesList.clearSelection();
        }
    }
```

Note another use of the resetButtons() 'housekeeping' method.

```
        // Check states of the various buttons.
        resetButtons();
    }
};
addButton.addActionListener(aListener);
```

dropButton

```
            // dropButton
```

The code for responding to a press of the 'Drop' button is quite similar to that for the 'Add' button, albeit a bit less elaborate; here, all we need to do is:

❑ Determine which item the user selected in his/her studentCourseList

❑ Drop the course

❑ Display a confirmation message

❑ Refresh the user-related information displayed on the screen

We present the code without further discussion; please refer to in-line comments in the code.

```
        aListener = new ActionListener() {
          public void actionPerformed(ActionEvent e) {
            // Determine which section is selected
            // (note that we must cast it, as it
            // is returned as an Object reference).
            Section selected = (Section) studentCourseList.getSelectedValue();

            // Drop the course.
            selected.drop(currentUser);

            // Display a confirmation message.
            JOptionPane.showMessageDialog(null,
              "Course " + selected.
              getRepresentedCourse().
              getCourseNo() + " dropped.",
              "Request Successful",
              JOptionPane.INFORMATION_MESSAGE);
```

```
            // Update the list of sections that
            // this student is registered for.
            studentCourseList.setListData(
               currentUser.
               getSectionsEnrolled());

            // Update the field representing
            // student's course total.
            int total = currentUser.getCourseTotal();
            totalCoursesLabel.setText("" + total);

            // Check states of the various buttons.
            resetButtons();
         }
      };
      dropButton.addActionListener(aListener);
```

saveScheduleButton

```
            // saveScheduleButton
```

This is a means of invoking the Student class's persist() method on the currentUser, a method that we studied in depth in Chapter 15. In a nutshell, this method saves all information about the student, including all sections in which he/she is enrolled, to a file by the name of *ssn*.dat, for example, 111-11-1111.dat.

```
      aListener = new ActionListener() {
         public void actionPerformed(ActionEvent e) {
            boolean success = currentUser.persist();
            if (success) {
               // Let the user know that his/her
               // schedule was successfully saved.
               JOptionPane.showMessageDialog(null,
               "Schedule saved.",
               "Schedule Saved",
               JOptionPane.INFORMATION_MESSAGE);
            }
            else {
               // Let the user know that there
               // was a problem.
               JOptionPane.showMessageDialog(null,
               "Problem saving your " +
               "schedule; please contact " +
               "the SRS Support Staff for " +
               "assistance.",
               "Problem Saving Schedule",
               JOptionPane.WARNING_MESSAGE);
            }
         }
      };
      saveScheduleButton.addActionListener(aListener);
```

logoffButton

```
// logoffButton
```

When a user logs off, we clear out various GUI components:

```
aListener = new ActionListener() {
  public void actionPerformed(ActionEvent e) {
    clearFields();
    ssnField.setText("");
    currentUser = null;
    // Clear the selection in the
    // schedule of classes list.
    scheduleOfClassesList.clearSelection();

    // Check states of the various buttons.
    resetButtons();
  }
};
logoffButton.addActionListener(aListener);
```

studentCourseList and scheduleOfClassesList

Both the studentCourseList and scheduleOfClassesList components are JLists, and so they both generate ListSelectionEvents whenever an item in either list is clicked. We will implement a ListSelectionListener for these components, rather than an ActionListener; this requires us to program a valueChanged() method rather than an actionPerformed() event, but the concept is the same.

Note that we are using these two listeners to make sure that there is never an item selected in both lists simultaneously:

```
// studentCourseList
lListener = new ListSelectionListener() {
  public void valueChanged(ListSelectionEvent e) {
    // When an item is selected in this list,
    // we clear the selection in the other list.
    if (!(studentCourseList.isSelectionEmpty()))
      scheduleOfClassesList.clearSelection();

    // Check states of the various buttons.
    resetButtons();
  }
};
studentCourseList.addListSelectionListener(lListener);

// scheduleOfClassesList

lListener = new ListSelectionListener() {
  public void valueChanged(ListSelectionEvent e) {
```

```
        // When an item is selected in this list,
        // we clear the selection in the other list.
        if (!(scheduleOfClassesList.isSelectionEmpty()))
          studentCourseList.clearSelection();

        // Check states of the various buttons.
        resetButtons();
      }
    };
    scheduleOfClassesList.addListSelectionListener(lListener);
```

We also add a listener to the frame to enable us to close the window via the Close (X) button.

```
    wListener = new WindowAdapter() {
      public void windowClosing(WindowEvent e) {
        System.exit(0);
      }
    };
    this.addWindowListener(wListener);

    this.setVisible(true);
  }
```

Housekeeping Methods

As mentioned throughout this discussion, we've outfitted the MainFrame class with a few 'housekeeping' methods; note that these are all declared to be private, meaning that they are only used within MainFrame. Note, in particular, our approach to the resetButtons() method (please read in-line comments below).

```
    // Because there are so many different situations in which one or
    // more buttons need to be (de)activated, and because the logic is
    // so complex, we centralize it here and then just call this method
    // whenever we need to check the state of one or more of the buttons.
    // It is a tradeoff of code elegance for execution efficiency:
    // we are doing a bit more work each time (because we don't need to
    // reset all four buttons every time), but since the execution time
    // is minimal, this seems like a reasonable tradeoff.

    private void resetButtons() {

      // There are four conditions which collectively govern the
      // state of each button:

      // 1: Whether a user is logged on or not.
      boolean isLoggedOn;
      if (currentUser != null) isLoggedOn = true;
      else isLoggedOn = false;

      // 2: Whether the user is registered for at least one course.
```

```
    boolean atLeastOne;
    if (currentUser != null && currentUser.getCourseTotal() > 0)
      atLeastOne = true;
    else atLeastOne = false;


    // 3: Whether a registered course has been selected.
    boolean courseSelected;
    if (studentCourseList.isSelectionEmpty())
      courseSelected = false;
    else courseSelected = true;


    // 4: Whether an item is selected in the Schedule of Classes.
    boolean catalogSelected;
    if (scheduleOfClassesList.isSelectionEmpty())
      catalogSelected = false;
    else catalogSelected = true;


    // Now, verify the conditions on a button-by-button basis.

    // Drop button:
    if (isLoggedOn && atLeastOne && courseSelected)
      dropButton.setEnabled(true);
    else dropButton.setEnabled(false);


    // Add button:
    if (isLoggedOn && catalogSelected)
      addButton.setEnabled(true);
    else addButton.setEnabled(false);


    // Save My Schedule button:
    if (isLoggedOn) {
      saveScheduleButton.setEnabled(true);

      // Because of the way that we created the latter two
      // buttons, we have to do a bit of extra work to make them
      // appear to be turned on or off.
      l1.setEnabled(true);
      l2.setEnabled(true);
    } else {
      saveScheduleButton.setEnabled(false);
      l1.setEnabled(false);
      l2.setEnabled(false);
    }


    // Log Off button:
    if (isLoggedOn) logoffButton.setEnabled(true);
    else logoffButton.setEnabled(false);
  }


  // Called whenever a user is logged off.
  private void clearFields() {
    nameField.setText("");
    totalCoursesLabel.setText("");
```

```
        studentCourseList.setListData(new Vector());
    }

    // Set the various fields, lists, etc. to reflect the information
    // associated with a particular student. (Used when logging in.)
    private void setFields(Student theStudent) {
        nameField.setText(theStudent.getName());
        int total = theStudent.getCourseTotal();
        totalCoursesLabel.setText("" + total);

        // If the student is registered for any courses, list these, too.
        if (total > 0) {
            // Because we already have a vector containing the
            // sections that the student is registered for,
            // and because these objects have defined a toString()
            // method, we can merely hand the vector to the JList.
            studentCourseList.setListData(theStudent.
                getSectionsEnrolled());
        }
    }
}
```

The PasswordPopup Class (Techniques for Sharing Information Across Windows/Classes)

We've already seen one technique for sharing data throughout the various classes of an application, through the use of public static attributes of the main class/window (or, for that matter, any window), as we did with the various collections declared by the SRS driver program in Chapter 14.

Another approach to application-wide data sharing is to allow a class/window 'A' to collect data from the user, and to then have that class 'A' provide **state retrieval methods** for other classes/windows 'B', 'C', etc. to use in requesting access to the data that 'A' has collected. The PasswordPopup class is such a class: the PasswordPopup collects the user's password as typed, and then makes it available to client code (the MainFrame class, in our application) through the public getPassword() method.

```
// PasswordPopup.java

// A GUI class.

import java.awt.*;
import java.awt.event.*;
import java.util.*;
import javax.swing.*;
```

```
public class PasswordPopup extends JDialog {
```

We create a password attribute, so that this class may save the information gathered from the user until such time as it is asked to divulge it via a call to the getPassword() method.

```
    private String password;
```

```
    // Attributes representing the GUI components.
```

```
private Container contentPane;
private JLabel passwordLabel;
private JPasswordField passwordField;

// Constructor.
public PasswordPopup(Frame parent) {
  // Invoke the generic JDialog constructor first.

  super(parent, "Enter Password", true);

  contentPane = this.getContentPane();
  contentPane.setLayout(new GridLayout(1, 2));

  passwordLabel = new JLabel("Password:  ", JLabel.RIGHT);
  passwordLabel.setForeground(Color.black);
```

We create an `ActionListener` to listen to the `passwordField` component:

```
passwordField = new JPasswordField();
ActionListener aListener = new ActionListener() {
  public void actionPerformed(ActionEvent e) {
```

When we retrieve the password, we use the `trim()` method of the string class to strip off any leading or trailing blank spaces (recall our discussion of the use of a `char[]` array to retrieve passwords when we discussed `JPasswordField` earlier in this chapter).

```
    // Retrieve the password.
    char[] pw = passwordField.getPassword();
    password = new String(pw).trim();
```

We hide the window, but do not dispose of it; it will wait, invisibly, until client code asks it to divulge the password; then, as we saw in the `MainFrame` class's code, it is the client code that calls the `dispose()` method on this popup.

```
    // Hide, but don't dispose of, this window ...
    // we need to give the client code a chance to
    // retrieve the user's typed response via
    // the getPassword() method first.
    PasswordPopup.this.setVisible(false);
  }
};
passwordField.addActionListener(aListener);

contentPane.add(passwordLabel);
contentPane.add(passwordField);

this.setSize(200, 60);

// Center it on the screen.
Dimension screenSize = Toolkit.getDefaultToolkit().getScreenSize();
Dimension popupSize = this.getSize();
int width = popupSize.width;
int height = popupSize.height;
this.setLocation((screenSize.width - width)/2,
  (screenSize.height - height)/2);
```

```
      this.setVisible(true);
  }
```

Here's the method to be used to retrieve whatever the user typed:

```
    public String getPassword() {
       return password;
    }
```

We saw an example of the use of a 'spare' main() method as a test scaffold in Chapter 15. Here is another such example:

```
  // Test scaffold.
  public static void main(String[] args) {
    PasswordPopup pp = new PasswordPopup(new JFrame());
    System.out.println("Password typed:  " + pp.getPassword());
    pp.dispose();
    System.exit(0);
  }
```

With the addition of a main() method to class PasswordPopup, we can now run it from the command line as:

java PasswordPopup

rather than having to run the main driver:

java SRS

This is useful if we want to see how our popup looks early on in its development.

Note that there is no harm in leaving this main() method in the PasswordPopup class even after our testing is finished – in fact, it is a handy thing to keep around in case we change the look of the GUI later, and want to retest it.

Summary

We've covered a tremendous amount of ground in this chapter!

❑ We discussed the two primary Java APIs – AWT and Swing.

❑ We've learned specifically about the following building blocks of GUIs:

  ❑ Swing top-level containers: JFrame, JPanel, JDialog

  ❑ Other Swing components: JLabel, JButton, JList, JTextField, JPasswordField

  ❑ AWT layout managers: BorderLayout, GridLayout, FlowLayout

  ❑ AWT/Swing listeners: ActionListener (AWT), WindowListener (AWT), ListSelectionListener (Swing)

  ❑ Other: JOptionPane (Swing)

❑ We talked about planning the 'look' of a GUI, and creative uses of GridLayout to help us in assembling components into 'layers'.

❑ We learned about the Java event handling model; in particular, about creating and registering listeners.

❑ We've discussed the philosophy and advantages of model-view separation.

❑ We talked about the development of a concept of operations, or 'storyboard', as a means for getting sponsor/client/user buy-in before any code has been written, to ensure that the proposed look and flow of a GUI meets the use case requirements for the system.

❑ We've discussed data sharing techniques: public static attributes, state retrieval methods.

And, we saw the piece de resistance – adding a GUI front end to the SRS application! We've now come through the full lifecycle of the SRS application, beginning with an expression of requirements via use cases in Chapter 9, to an object model in Chapters 10 and 11, to a command line driven program in Chapter 14; a program with file persistence in Chapter 15; and a GUI-driven application in Chapter 16.

Exercises

1. Improve the `Calculator4` example found in this chapter so that it performs proper exception handling; right now, if the user clicks the + or − buttons without typing in two proper numbers, a `NumberFormatException` run-time exception arises. (Hint: you'll need to wrap the code that manipulates the values retrieved from the text fields on the GUI in a `try` – `catch` block.)

2. For all of the `catch` blocks located in the various SRS classes, use JOptionPane to display an appropriate error message to the user.

3. Advanced Project: Modify the SRS application to provide the user with the capability for setting his/her own password. This will involve:

❑ Adding a **Set Password** button on the `MainFrame`.

❑ Changing the structure of the `Student.dat` file to accommodate a password, which will in turn require changing the following methods of the Student class:

    ❑ `parseData()`

    ❑ `persist()`

    ❑ and the `Student` constructor

❑ Popping up a dialog to request that the user enter the old and new password (consider reuse of the `PasswordPopup` class).

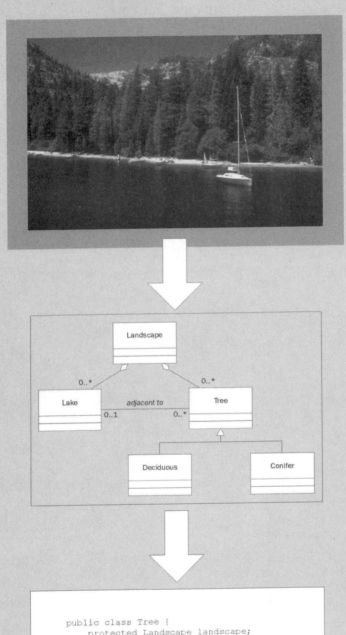

```
public class Tree {
    protected Landscape landscape;
    protected Lake nextTo;

    public void setNextTo(Lake l) {
        nextTo = l;
    }
    public Lake getNextTo() {
        return nextTo;
    }

    public abstract Color getLeafColor();
}
```

Next Steps

Congratulations! You've made it through quite a learning curve, from object concepts, to object modeling, to Java programming. What you do next will depend on what your intentions were for learning this material in the first place:

- ❑ If you are a software developer primarily interested in building Java applications, you'll want to get some hands-on Java programming experience if you haven't already done so. A good first step is to tackle some of the exercises at the end of each chapter in Part 3 of the book; if you have already done so, then you may be ready to try your hand at a full-lifecycle object oriented development project. See Jacquie's 'Tried and True' Method for Learning Java Properly below for a game plan on how to proceed, and Recommended Reading for other books that might be appropriate next steps in your continued professional development.

- ❑ If you are a systems analyst primarily interested in object modeling, be certain to attempt the exercises at the ends of the chapters in Part 2 of the book if you haven't already done so. Then, seek out an opportunity to engage in an object modeling project within your organization, ideally with a senior object modeler to guide and mentor you.

- ❑ If you are a manager whose goal was to become better versed in these technologies, this may be an appropriate time to conduct a technology review of ongoing projects in your company to see how the techniques touched upon in this book are being carried out within your organization.

- ❑ If you are an instructor, review Appendix A for suggestions on how to use this material as the basis of a beginning object methods/Java curriculum.

Whatever your focus, be sure to visit my website, http://objectstart.com, for additional suggestions as well as links to related web sites that you may find of interest.

Jacquie's 'Tried and True' Method for Learning Java Properly

1. Understand OO analysis and design – hopefully, this book has gone a long way toward helping you to accomplish this, and our recommended reading suggestions later in this chapter will help you to deepen this understanding.

2. Obtain a good beginning book on Java – again, this book has hopefully given you a good jump start with the language, and you can follow that up by obtaining a copy of *Ivor Horton's Beginning Java 2*.

3. Download and install a free copy of the latest release of the Java 2 Platform, Standard Edition (J2SE) Software Developer's Kit from Sun's website as described in Appendix C.

4. Compile and run a simple 'Hello, World' program from the command line to ensure that all Java SDK components are installed and working properly.

5. Choose a **simple** first problem to automate: one that (a) you are very familiar with the requirements for – perhaps an application that you have already built in some other language, or an application based upon some hobby – and (b) which only requires a handful of domain classes when modeled.

6. Produce a class diagram for your application based on the object modeling techniques that we learned in Part 2 of the book.

7. Write the code for your 'core' model classes, and get the application to work as a command-line driven application first as we did for the Student Registration System (SRS) in Chapter 14. (This is your **model**, without a graphical **view**.)

8. Learn more about the Java Abstract Windowing Toolkit and Swing components for constructing GUIs, and buy a good reference book(s) about this subject.

9. Add a GUI front-end onto the code you produced in step 7, as we did for the SRS in Chapter 16. My personal bias is that you do so by writing the GUI code from scratch, without using a 'drag and drop' GUI building tool, as I believe that you learn GUI concepts more thoroughly by doing so.

10. Learn about the Java Database Connectivity (JDBC) API, and buy a good reference book about this subject.

11. Acquire the appropriate JDBC driver for your particular DBMS, if necessary. Or, check my website for links regarding free, single-user DBMS's in the public domain that are ideal for educational use.

12. Connect your application to a database 'back-end' so as to persist your objects. You may wish to experiment with an object DBMS (ODBMS) vs. a relational DBMS; visit http://objectstart.com for some suggestions in this regard.

13. (Optional) If you are inclined to use an integrated development environment (IDE), invest in a commercially available Java IDE such as Kawa or Symantec Café, or investigate Sun's Forte IDE, which is available as a free download from Sun's website. Make sure to **avoid** any IDE that introduces platform-**dependent** extensions to the Java language – focus on producing 100% pure Java code for ultimate portability whenever possible. (My personal bias is to avoid drag and drop GUI builders; the time you save in creating the GUI may be ultimately lost when you try to work around the code that was automatically generated.)

14. From this point forward, your options are open-ended! For example, you may wish to become familiar with Java 2 Enterprise Edition, which provides support for enterprise-level server-side applications; you may wish to study up on the Java 2D and 3D graphics APIs; or your interests may lie with the Java 2 Micro Edition (J2ME), a highly optimized Java runtime environment targeting consumer products such as cellular phones and pagers. Whichever direction you choose to take, you can rest assured that there will be plenty of new Java-related innovations in the months and years to come.

Recommended Reading

Many fine books have been written and published on the subject of OO software development by a variety of publishers, and it would be virtually impossible to do justice to them all here. Consider this list to represent some of my personal recommendations (visit my website, objectstart.com, for more recommendations), but please do peruse the titles available from your favorite technical bookseller, as new titles are being released literally every day.

Booch, Rumbaugh, Jacobson, **The Unified Modeling Language User Guide**, Addison Wesley, 1998. *A definitive reference on UML, written by its creators; definitely worth adding to your library if you are serious about object modeling.*

Rumbaugh, Jacobson, Booch, **The Unified Modeling Language Reference Manual**, Addison Wesley, 1999. *A second definitive reference by the same gentlemen; see my comments above.*

Jacobson, Booch, Rumbaugh, **Unified Software Development Process**, Addison Wesley, 1999. *And a third!*

Quatrani, Terry, **Visual Modeling with Rational Rose and UML**, Addison Wesley, 1998. *A practical, step by step guide for how to use Rational Rose, one of the industry's leading object modeling CASE tools, to prepare UML models.*

Eriksson, Hans and Magnus Penker, **UML Toolkit**, John Wiley & Sons, Inc., 1998. *Comes with a CD-ROM containing a demo copy of Rational Rose 4.0, numerous UML models, and Java code.*

Taylor, David A., **Object Technology: A Manager's Guide**, Addison Wesley, 1998. *A classic, high-level review of the direction in which the OO industry as a whole is headed.*

Gamma, Helm, Hohnson, Vlissides, **Design Patterns: Elements of Reusable Object-Oriented Software**, Addison Wesley, 1994. *An in-depth look at identifying and reusing common design patterns.*

Meyer, Bertrand, **Object-oriented Software Construction**, Prentice Hall, 1988.
An academic treatment of object-orientedness in a programming language, based on Eiffel.

Kernighan, Brian W. and Dennis M. Ritchie, **The C Programming Language**, Prentice Hall, 1988
A solid, basic treatment of C, for those of you who are interested in the most basic of Java's 'roots'!

The entire 'Core Java' and 'Graphic Java' series of books published jointly by Sun Microsystems and Prentice Hall.

Your Comments, Please!

In the interest of making this book as useful as possible to our readers, I'd love to hear from you if you have suggestions for how the book could be improved! Please visit my website at http://objectstart.com for more information on how to get in touch with me.

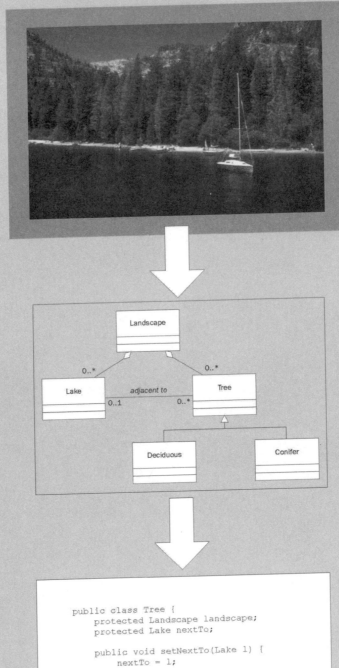

```
public class Tree {
    protected Landscape landscape;
    protected Lake nextTo;

    public void setNextTo(Lake l) {
        nextTo = l;
    }
    public Lake getNextTo() {
        return nextTo;
    }

    public abstract Color getLeafColor();
}
```

Part 4

Appendices

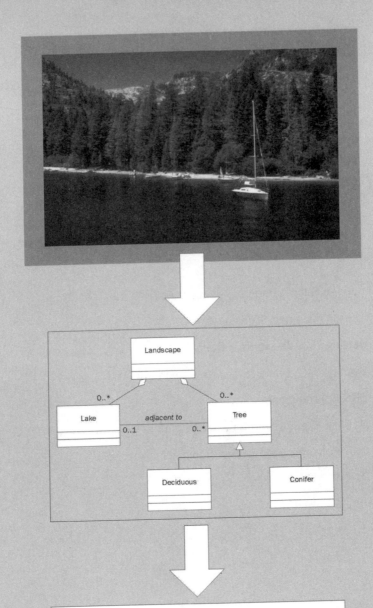

```
public class Tree {
    protected Landscape landscape;
    protected Lake nextTo;

    public void setNextTo(Lake l) {
        nextTo = l;
    }
    public Lake getNextTo() {
        return nextTo;
    }

    public abstract Color getLeafColor();
}
```

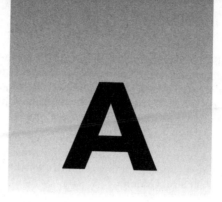

Suggestions for Using This Book as a Textbook

The material in this book is based on two semester-long courses that I developed and teach, on object methods and their application in Java programming. This material can be covered in a variety of ways:

❑ **As the basis for a single semester OO methodology course.**

I focus on the subject matter content in Parts 1 and 2, making sure to give students ample 'hands on' experience with object modeling through both in-class group exercises as well as through homework assignments. Time permitting at the end of the semester, I cover the material in Chapter 14, for I have found that exposing students to the way an object model translates into the syntax of an OO language such as Java really helps to cement object concepts, even for those students who are not aspiring to be professional programmers.

For this type of course, I don't typically assign programming assignments – I leave this to a follow-on Java course – but I do examine students on the object aspects of the Java language by giving them code to analyze on paper as a homework assignment or final exam question.

❑ **As the basis for a single semester Java programming course.**

I devote the first two lectures, respectively, to teaching the main points of Part 1 and reviewing UML notation as covered in Chapter 10, and then devote the rest of the semester to the Java material in Chapter 1 and all of the chapters in Part 3.

❑ **Ideally, the entire book should be used from cover to cover in two consecutive semesters.**

I am extremely passionate about the notion that people learning Java (or, for that matter, any other OO language) should learn about objects **first**. I sometimes have students who come to my Objects Methods course having already taken a Java course elsewhere. Such students still get a lot out of the OO material, but invariably wind up saying 'I wish I had taken your Object Methods course first, so that I could have appreciated more of what my professor was trying to teach us about Java'.

Because students will have already purchased my book for the first (OO) course, it can be used as the core 'pacing' text for the second (Java) course. One big advantage of using my book is that it uses a consistent case study as the basis for object concepts, object modeling, and Java programming. Students can actually see how an object model evolves from a requirements specification, and how that same object model translates into a working Java application, something that few other books present.

Students should be encouraged to buy an optional Java reference book of their own choosing, to be used as a supplemental programming reference for the second course; Ivor Horton's *Beginning Java 2* is one such suggestion.

As a learning/teaching tool, Java is an ideal language for many of the reasons cited in Chapter 1. From my perspective as an instructor:

- One of Java's *biggest* advantages is that it is platform independent and consistent across most commonly used platforms. If you encourage students to use Sun's Java Software Development Kit (SDK) as their sole development environment, you will dramatically lessen the 'hassle factor' as compared with teaching a language like C++ to a group of students who are using a multitude of different programming environments/tools on their home/work computers.

- Java is, in my opinion, a simpler language to grasp than C++, at least as far as the core language is concerned; C++ pointers have historically sent many a student running for a 'course drop' slip! The biggest challenge with learning Java is the phenomenal number of APIs and classes therein; but, I believe that I have successfully distilled these down to just those that a beginning student needs to know: namely, the Java topics covered in Part 3 of my book.

- It is free: all students really need is Sun's Java Software Development Kit (SDK), downloadable for free as detailed in Appendix C, and a text editor.

    If you prefer to expose students to the use of an Integrated Development Environment (IDE), some free Java IDEs that you might wish to consider are:

    Forte for Java Community Edition (http://www.sun.com/forte/ffj/ce/download.html)

    VisualAge for Java Entry Edition (http://www-4.ibm.com/software/ad/vajava/download.htm)

    Please check my website http://objectstart.com for suggestions of simple, low cost (or, in some cases free) Java IDEs that you might wish to consider, along with suggestions for free or low cost object modeling tools.

Other teaching suggestions:

- In addition to the Student Registration System case study that is used as the backbone of the book, I recommend using a second case study as the basis for homework assignments and/or in-class group exercises. Either have students devise their own (see suggested exercise no. 3 at the end of Chapter 2), or use either the Conference Room Reservation System or Airline Ticketing System case study provided in Appendix B.

- Each time a new technique is introduced in lectures, a classroom exercise and/or a homework assignment should be assigned to the students so that they may apply that technique.

❏   Spend the beginning of each class for which a homework assignment is due discussing students' and instructor's solutions to the assignment. (I often have students submit their homework solutions to me in advance of the class meeting via FAX, email, or web posting so that I may prepare overhead transparencies of these.)

❏   For purposes of object modeling, students should be encouraged to work in small teams for both the classroom exercises and the homework assignments. A great deal of the learning that takes place from object modeling comes with 'hammering out' differences of opinion among a group. It's useful to give the same set of requirements to multiple teams, and group projects give students a real taste of the teamwork required in the business world.

❏   It's also enlightening to give the same set of requirements to multiple teams, and to then have the teams review each other's proposed solutions, pointing out what works and what doesn't.

Keep an eye on my website http://www.objectstart.com for additional suggestions on how to use this material effectively in an academic setting. And, if you come up with a particularly effective approach or idea, I'd love to hear about it, so that it may be shared with others through my website.

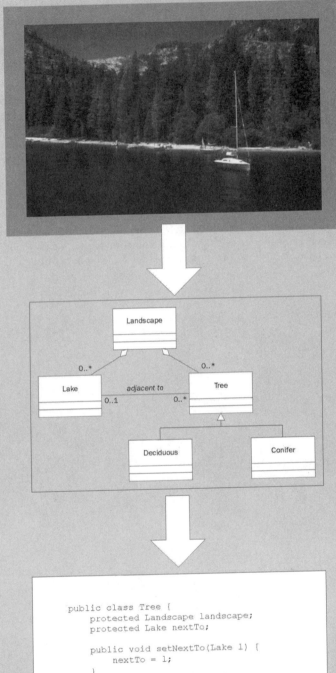

Alternative Case Studies

This appendix is meant to be a companion appendix to Appendix A, as well as a supplement to many of the end-of-chapter exercises found throughout the book.

Case Study #1: Conference Room Reservation System

Background

You have been asked to develop an automated Conference Room Reservation System (CRRS) for your company. This system is motivated by the fact that, at present, the process used to reserve conference rooms throughout your office complex is hit and miss, as follows.

❑   A total of a dozen conference rooms are scattered across the four different buildings that comprise your facility. These rooms differ in terms of their seating capacity as well as other amenities (discussed below).

❑   At present, each of these is overseen by a different administrative staff member, known as a Conference Room Coordinator.

❑   Room reservations are being recorded manually by the various Conference Room Coordinators as follows:

    ❑   The name of the person reserving the room, as well as their telephone number, is jotted by hand in an appointment book; the start and stop time of the meeting is also noted.

    ❑   At present, no supplemental information regarding the number of attendees or planned audio-visual (A/V) equipment usage is being noted for a given meeting.

❑   The following problems have been noted regarding the present manual system:

    ❑   If someone planning a meeting involving only four people schedules a room with the capacity for 20, the excess capacity in that room will be wasted. Meanwhile, someone truly needing a room for 20 people will be left short.

❑ Whenever the Coordinator is away from their desk, information about room availability is unavailable, unless the inquirer wishes to walk to the Coordinator's office and inspect the appointment book directly. However, due to the size of the office complex, this is not practical, so inquirers typically leave a voicemail message or send an email to the Coordinator, who gets back to them at a later point in time.

❑ People are lax about canceling reservations when a room is no longer needed, so rooms often sit vacant that could otherwise be put to good use.

❑ Pertinent information about the rooms (for example, their seating capacity; whether or not they have a white board; whether or not they have built-in AV facilities; whether or not they are 'wired' into the company's LAN) is not presently published anywhere.

❑ A separate, central organization called the A/V Equipment Group provides loan of A/V equipment to supplement any equipment that may be permanently installed in a given conference room. Equipment that is available for temporary use through this group includes: conventional overhead projectors, televisions, VCRs, overhead projectors used for direct connections with PCs, electronic whiteboards, laptop PCs, software installed on those PCs (e.g. PowerPoint), tape recorders, and slide projectors. Personnel from this group deliver equipment directly to the locale where it is needed, and pick it up after the meeting is concluded.

You have been asked by management to design a system for providing on-line, automated conference room and equipment scheduling.

Goals for the System

The goals of this project are to provide the ability for any employee to directly connect into the system to perform the following tasks:

❑ If the user is interested in scheduling a room for a meeting, they will be required to complete an on-line questionnaire regarding the parameters of the meeting, to include:

    ❑ The scheduler's name, title, department, and telephone number

    ❑ The number of attendees anticipated

    ❑ A date range, indicating the earliest and latest acceptable date for the meeting

    ❑ The length of time that the room will be required, in half hour increments

    ❑ An earliest acceptable start time and latest acceptable stop time

    ❑ A list of all A/V equipment required

❑ As soon as this questionnaire is completed, the system will present the user with a list of all available suitable room alternatives. The user will be able to select from these options to reserve a room, or change their criteria and repeat the search.

❑ After a room has been selected, the system will then determine what loan equipment will be needed to supplement the installed equipment in that room, and will automatically arrange for its delivery. (For purposes of this case study, we won't worry about running out of equipment – we'll assume an infinite supply of everything – although in real life this would also have to be a consideration.)

❑ If no rooms meeting the user's requirements are available, the user will be presented with a list of suitable rooms with the number of people wait listed for each. The user will be able to place their name on a waiting list for one or more of the rooms.

  ❑ When such a request is posted, the system is to send a courtesy email to the person holding that room's reservation, asking them to rethink their need for the room.

  ❑ Should the room on the waiting list become available, it will automatically be temporarily reserved for the first person on the waiting list. An email message is to be sent automatically to the requestor, giving them 72 hours to confirm their selection before the room is either (a) reassigned (again, temporarily) to the next person on the waiting list or (b) goes 'up for grabs' if the waiting list has been exhausted.

❑ A user should be permitted to query the system as to who has a particular room reserved, the number of persons attending, and the purpose of the meeting, as long as the person holding the room reservation is not a member of the Executive Committee. (Only another Executive Committee member may see the details of a fellow Executive Committee member's meetings; to someone else, only the simple message 'Room unavailable' will be displayed.)

❑ The user must be able to cancel a room reservation at any time.

Case Study #2: Blue Skies Airline Reservation System

Background

Blue Skies Airline, a fairly new airline, offers services between any two of the following cities: Denver, Washington D.C., Los Angeles, New York City, Atlanta, and Cleveland.

When a customer calls Blue Skies to make a flight reservation, the reservation agent first asks them for:

❑ The desired travel dates

❑ The departure and destination cities

❑ The seat grade desired (first class, business class, or economy)

The reservation agent then informs the customer of all available flights that meet their criteria; for each flight, the flight number, departure date and time, arrival date and time, and round-trip price are communicated to the customer. If the customer finds any of the available flights acceptable, they may either pay for the ticket via credit card, or may request that the seat be held for 24 hours. (A specific seat assignment – row and seat number – is not issued until the seat is paid for.)

A limited number of seats on each flight are earmarked as frequent flyer seats. A customer who is a frequent flyer member may reserve and 'pay for' one of these seats by giving the agent their frequent flyer membership number; the agent then verifies that the appropriate balance is available in their account before the seat can be confirmed, at which point those miles are deducted from the account.

The customer has two ticketing options: they may request that a conventional 'paper' ticket be issued and mailed to their home address, or an electronic ticket (E-ticket) may instead be assigned, in which case the customer is simply informed of the E-ticket serial number by telephone. (With an E-ticket, the customer simply reports to the airport at the time of their departure, and presents suitable ID to a ticket agent at the gate; no paperwork is exchanged.) In either case, the reservation agent records the serial number of the (conventional or E) ticket issued to this customer.

The number of seats available for a given flight in each of the seat grade categories is dependent on the type of aircraft assigned to a given flight.

Other Simplifying Assumptions

❑ Assume that all flights are round-trip between two cities (no three-legged itineraries are permitted).

❑ Disregard the complication that airlines sometimes have to switch aircraft at the last minute due to mechanical difficulties, thus disrupting the seating assignments.

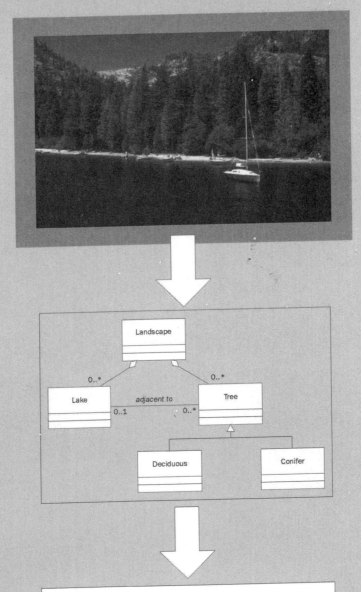

```
public class Tree {
    protected Landscape landscape;
    protected Lake nextTo;

    public void setNextTo(Lake l) {
        nextTo = l;
    }
    public Lake getNextTo() {
        return nextTo;
    }

    public abstract Color getLeafColor();
}
```

Setting Up a Basic Object Modeling/Java Environment

In this Appendix, I explain the 'bare bones' requirements for downloading a trial version of an OO modeling tool and the Java Software Developer's Kit so that you may experiment with these technologies while reading my book.

I also provide a number of 'tips' that I've gathered up over the years as to how to get Java to 'behave' under various operating system scenarios. Note that these tips are not all inclusive; they are simply provided as a professional courtesy, in the hope that you may find something useful among them. Please visit my website, http://objectstart.com, for an evolving version of these 'tips'.

Object Modeling Tools

Visit my website for suggestions on object modeling tools that you might wish to download and evaluate, as these change on a regular basis. Vendor offerings change regularly; links to these offerings change regularly; and the details for downloading and installing various tools are highly vendor dependent.

The Java Software Developer's Kit

The Java Software Developer's Kit (SDK) is available as a free download from Sun Microsystem's website. Among other things, the SDK comes with:

- ❑ A command-line driven compiler (javac).

- ❑ A copy of the Java Virtual Machine (JVM), the engine that runs compiled Java byte code, appropriate for your platform (for example, Windows, Unix, Linux).

- ❑ A command-line driven Java Archive ('jar') utility; see Appendix D for more information on the relevance of jar files.

and much more. In addition, as a separate (but very worthwhile!) download, Sun has made on-line documentation available in HTML format, so that it is viewable from your Web browser.

> *Note: since URLs and links are continuously changing, the directions for finding the proper location within Sun's domain may change after this book is published; check for updates to these instructions on Apress's website (www.apress.com).*

At the time of publication of this book, there were at least two reliable ways to download the Java SDK from Sun Microsystems websites, the first being the preferred means of doing so:

❑ Go to http://java.sun.com, then click on the **Products & APIs** link.

❑ Go to http://www.sun.com/download – and click the FREE Products link.

Either way, follow the posted instructions for downloading and installing the latest release of the Java 2 SDK, **Standard Edition** for your desired platform (Windows, Solaris, or Linux). Make sure to download the Standard Edition, not the Enterprise Edition, or the Micro Edition. Download the Java 2 SDK documentation, as well.

> **From this point on, consider this material to be 'helpful hints', provided merely as a professional courtesy! We don't profess to have ALL of the answers for ALL permutations and combinations of platform scenarios...**

'Odds and Ends' Tips for Getting Java Working

After you get the SDK downloaded and installed per the instructions on Sun's web page, there are a few additional things you'll need to do to get Java up and running.

If you are working under Windows 95 or 98

❑ Open a DOS window by selecting the Windows **Start => Programs => MS-DOS Prompt** menu option.

❑ Type the following DOS commands:

```
C:
cd \
dir autoexec.bat
```

❑ If there is already a file by the name of `autoexec.bat` in the 'root' directory (\) on C:, make a copy of it for safekeeping:

```
copy autoexec.bat autoexec.sav
```

❏ Next, edit or create the file, as appropriate:

edit autoexec.bat

and look for a line which starts with 'SET PATH'; for example:

SET PATH=C:\ThinkPad;C:\vim\win

Note that the above is merely an example of what the path is set to on my computer – yours will almost certainly be different!

❏ If there is such a line, add a semicolon (;) to the end of whatever is already in the PATH statement, and then append the full path to the directory in which you installed the SDK binary executables (the 'bin' subdirectory under the Java SDK home directory). For example, if you downloaded the latest release of Java to C:\jdk1.3, then you'd add the following to the end of the PATH statement:

SET PATH=*existing contents of your PATH statement*;C:\jdk1.3\bin;

(make sure to tack the '\bin;' onto the end).

❏ Conversely, if you found no 'SET PATH' statement in the autoexec.bat file, or if you are creating the autoexec.bat file from scratch, insert a 'SET PATH' statement as follows:

SET PATH=%PATH%;*path to the Java SDK 'bin' subdirectory*

for example:

SET PATH=%PATH%;C:\jdk1.3\bin;

❏ Next, look for a line that starts with 'SET CLASSPATH'. If there is such a line, make sure that a lone period (.) is reflected as one of the entries. For example, the following statement reflects a single period as the first entry:

SET CLASSPATH=.;*other_stuff*;

whereas the next statement shows it as being embedded in the middle:

SET CLASSPATH=*stuff*;.;*other_stuff*

If the statement does *not* reflect a lone period as *one* of the entries, add a period followed by a semicolon right after the equals (=) sign:

SET CLASSPATH=.;*other_stuff*

❏ If there is no 'SET CLASSPATH' statement in the `autoexec.bat` file, insert one as follows:

SET CLASSPATH=.

(note that there is a single period (.) at the end of the line, right after the equals sign (=)).

By way of background, the purpose of the SET CLASSPATH *statement is to tell the Java Virtual Machine where to find executable Java* `.class` *files which are not part of the 'core' Java language – that is,* `.class` *files that you have written and compiled yourself.*

❏ Exit the editor to save your changes to `autoexec.bat`, then exit the DOS window by typing:

exit

at the DOS prompt.

❏ You must restart your computer via the Windows **Start => Shutdown => Restart** menu so that your changes to the `autoexec.bat` file take effect.

❏ See further instructions under 'For Either Platform:' below.

If You Are Working Under Another Version of Windows (For Example, NT, 2000, ME)

See the instructions above for Windows 95/98 for a general sense of what needs to be done; then, obtain assistance from someone with expertise in your particular operating system in 'translating' those instructions to their equivalent version for your platform. (And, time permitting, pass along any helpful tips you might have via my website, http://objectstart.com, so that I might share these with other folks.)

If You Are Working Under Unix (Solaris, Linux)

You need to declare or amend two environment variables – PATH and CLASSPATH. The notes below reflect how I've done so under Solaris.

❏ In my `.cshrc` file, I declared the following:

setenv JAVA_HOME *'path to where I installed the Java SDK'*

For example:

setenv JAVA_HOME '/apps/java/jdk/Solaris_JDK_1.2.1_02'

❑ In my .login file, I declared the following:

setenv PATH ${JAVA_HOME}/bin:${PATH}
setenv CLASSPATH '.'

❑ See further instructions under 'For Either Platform:' below.

For Either Platform:

❑ Create a working directory in which you plan to store your various Java experiments, and then download the example code for this book into that directory (see Appendix D for download instructions).

Do not put anything in the Java SDK home directory (for example, C:\jdk1.3 in the Windows examples above) or any of its subdirectories unless specifically instructed to do so!

❑ Your Java environment should now, hopefully, be up and running. To give it a test drive, type, compile, and run the following trivially simple program:

```
public class Success {
  public static void main(String[] args) {
    System.out.println("Hooray!");
  }
}
```

You must first enter the above program text *exactly* as shown into a file named Success.java (note the precise use of upper case and lower case in naming the file). You can use a variety of methods to enter a Java program into a file. Here are four alternatives:

❑ Use the Windows Notepad editor.
❑ Use any other Windows-based text editor that you prefer.
❑ Use your favorite DOS or Unix text editor (e.g. vi).
❑ Use an interactive development environment (IDE) of your choice – see my web site, http://objectstart.com, for suggestions.

❑ Next, we'll attempt to compile and run this program from the command line. Make sure to 'cd' to the directory in which the program resides, if you aren't already there, and then type the following at the operating system prompt to compile the program:

javac Success.java

If the program compiles without errors, an executable Success.class byte code file will be created in the same directory where the Success.java file resides.

❑ Assuming there were no compilation errors, type the following at the operating system prompt to run the program:

java Success

(We don't type the '.class' part of the executable file name; again, note the precise use of upper/lower case – Java is case sensitive!) If all goes well, the following should appear as output (Windows/DOS version shown):

C:\>javac Success.java

C:\>java Success

Hooray!

C:\>

Troubleshooting Your Installation

All of the following examples show problems that might occur under Windows/DOS; comparable problems (but with different error messages, of course!), with similar resolutions, can arise under Solaris or Linux.

❑ If you get the following error message when attempting to compile:

C:\MyDir> javac Success.java

Bad command or file name

this means that the Java compiler could not be found; i.e. you either have improperly installed the Java SDK download, or that your PATH statement is incorrect.

❑ If you get the following error message when attempting to compile:

C:\MyDir> javac Success.java

error: Can't read: Success.java

this means that the computer cannot find your source code. Make sure that (a) you are in the correct directory where the program source code file resides, and (b) that you are spelling the name of the file correctly, including proper use of upper/lower case.

❑ If you get the following type of compilation error:

C:\MyDir> javac Success.java

Success.java:1: Public class success must be defined in a file called

'success.java'

public class success {

                 ^

check to make sure that the prefix on the external file name – e.g. `Success.java` – exactly matches the name of the file in the `public class classname {` line, including the use of upper-lower case.

❑ If you get any other compilation errors, for example,

C:\MyDir> javac Success.java

Success.java:3: String not terminated at end of line.

    System.out.println("Hooray!);
                   ^

check to make sure that you've typed in the program exactly as shown above. (In this particular example, we're missing the quote mark after "Hooray!".)

❑ If you get the following error message when attempting to run a successfully compiled program:

C:\MyDir> java Success

Exception in thread 'main' Java.lang.NoClassDefFoundError: Success

this could mean one of several different things: either (a) you are spelling the name of the program incorrectly (again, pay attention to upper/lower case); (b) the program did not compile correctly, thus failing to produce a `Success.class` file; (c) your CLASSPATH has not been properly established; see instructions above.

❑ It is important that you not type the '.class' suffix, as you'll get an error if you do:

C:\MyDir> java Success.class
Exception in thread "main" java.lang.NoClassDefFoundError: Simple/class

Using the On-Line Java Documentation with Windows

Note: these instructions were written for Java version 1.2.2; later versions of Java may vary!

If you downloaded the optional Java documentation from Sun's website, it is most likely located in directory *Java home directory\docs*, for example, `C:\jdk1.2.2\docs`. The documentation is usable from your web browser by using the browser's **File => Open File ...** menu option, then opening the file named *Java home directory*\docs\api\index.html. This brings up the initial Java documentation window as shown after:

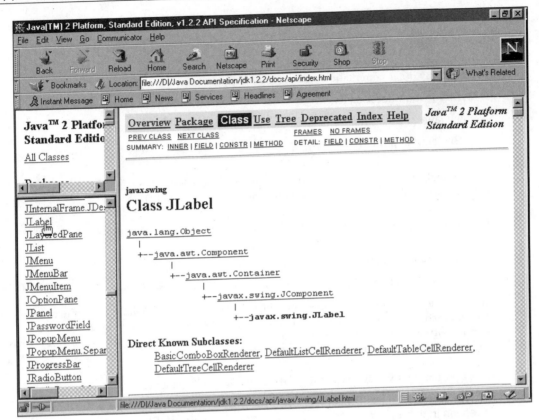

Spend time getting familiar with the on-line Java documentation – it is tremendously useful!

Special Tips for Using DOS Under Microsoft Windows

Rule No. 1: All DOS Environments Aren't Created Equal!

The various different versions of Windows – Windows 95, Windows 98, Windows NT, Windows 2000, and Windows ME – each implement DOS a bit differently. Therefore, rules regarding how 'true' DOS behaves won't necessarily apply on your particular implementation of Windows/DOS. You'll have to experiment a bit with your particular 'flavor' of DOS to find out what does or doesn't work well.

Here are some of my experiences with using Windows 98:

Capturing Program Output to a File

Under 'true' DOS, there are easy ways of capturing program output and compilation error messages to files via the file redirection symbol '>'; this is known as redirecting standard output. For example, the command:

```
C:\>java Success > somefile
```

stores what would normally appear as output to the screen (the 'Hooray!' message from an earlier example) in a text file instead. In addition, to capture compilation error messages to a file, the command:

```
C:\>javac Success.java  2> stderr.log    (When using NT/2000)
                        >& errors.log    (When using UNIX)
```

should, in theory, do the trick, taking advantage of a technique known as standard error redirection. Alas, standard error redirection doesn't appear to be available under Windows 98.

The use of '>' for program output redirection seems to work fairly consistently across all versions of Windows/DOS, but standard error redirection does not.

Long Filenames and Use of the Wildcard Character

Another inconsistency among DOS implementations has to do with the way that wildcard characters (*) and long filenames are handled. On my Windows 98 PC, for example, if I type the command:

```
C:\> mkdir MyJavaDirectory
```

to create a new directory, and then type:

```
C:\>dir My*
```

the wildcard character works fine, and I see the following output:

```
    Volume in drive C has no label
    Volume Serial Number is 3437-14EF
    Directory of C:\

    MYIMAG~1        <DIR>         01-20-00  7:05p My Images
    MYDOCU~1        <DIR>         08-13-98  1:34p My Documents
    MYZIPF~1        <DIR>         11-18-98  5:19p My ZIP Files
    MYDOWN~1        <DIR>         06-27-99 10:02a My Download Files
    MYJAVA~1        <DIR>         09-17-00  9:09a MyJavaDirectory
             0 file(s)                 0 bytes
             6 dir(s)         96,403,456 bytes free
```

Note that the new directory that I created is reflected as both 'MYJAVA~1' and 'MyJavaDirectory'. If, however, I try to use a wildcard character to move into that directory:

```
C:\>cd MyJ*
```

I get the error message:

```
Invalid directory
```

If I try to use the long version of the filename to move into that directory:

```
C:\>cd MyJavaDirectory
```

I get the error message:

Too many parameters – MyJavaDirectory

It is possible to surround the directory name in double quotes:

C:\>cd "MyJavaDirectory"

This will then allow me to move into the directory, or I can type:

C:\>cd MyJava~1

which also works.

Resizing the DOS Window

If you wish to make the DOS window larger, so that more lines of text can appear at once, right click on the DOS window header bar and select **Properties** on the pop-up menu that appears; then explore the settings available for your particular 'flavor' of DOS under the Memory and Screen 'tabs' of the window that subsequently appears. (Again, what this window allows you to do is Windows-version dependent.)

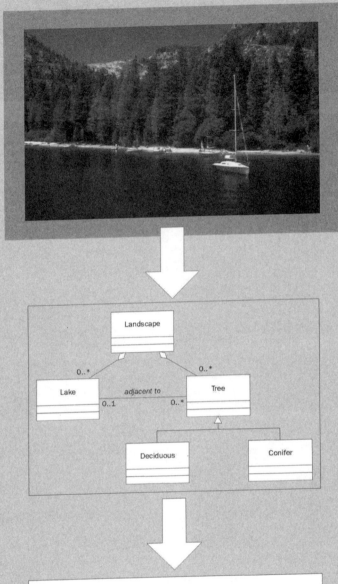

```
public class Tree {
    protected Landscape landscape;
    protected Lake nextTo;

    public void setNextTo(Lake l) {
        nextTo = l;
    }
    public Lake getNextTo() {
        return nextTo;
    }

    public abstract Color getLeafColor();
}
```

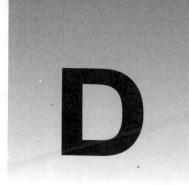

SRS Source Code

Downloading the Example Code

All of the source code and supporting data files for the key example programs in Chapters 14, 15, and 16 is available for download from the Apress website, http://www.apress.com as a single file named 4176.zip. When downloaded and unzipped, this will create the following directory structure beneath your *home* directory (make sure to that you want to use directory names from the ZIP file, so that this directory structure is preserved):

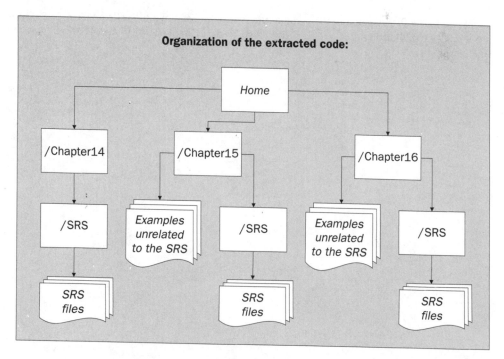

Organization of the extracted code:

❏ For chapters 15 and 16, small example programs unrelated to the SRS – for example, `FrameTest.java` from Chapter 16 – will be located in the Chapter15 and Chapter16 subdirectories, respectively.

❏ For all three chapters, the SRS specific files will be located one subdirectory further down.

To compile the SRS code for a particular chapter, change your default working directory to the appropriate `.../SRS` subdirectory, and type:

```
javac *.java
```

Note that the examples were written and tested using Java version 1.2.2; it is recommended that you upgrade your version of the Java SDK if you aren't already using that version or later.

Then, to run the SRS example for that chapter, type:

```
java SRS
```

To compile and run individual example files such as `FrameTest.java`, change your default working directory to the appropriate 'Chapter' subdirectory (`.../Chapter15` or `.../Chapter16`), and type:

```
javac program.java
java program
```

For example:

```
javac FrameTest.java
java FrameTest
```

You will also find a PDF version of the code on the Apress website in a file called `4176_SRS_Code.pdf`. This is a read-only full listing of all the SRS code discussed in Chapters 14, 15 and 16 which can be printed or viewed online.

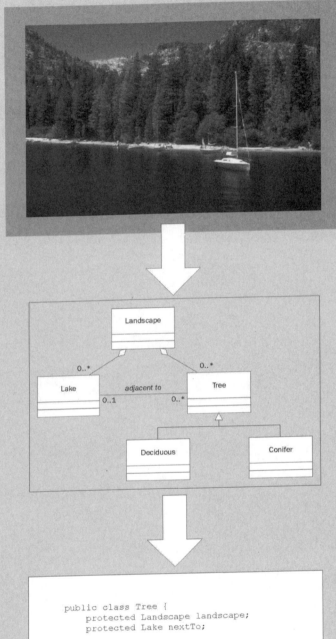

```
public class Tree {
    protected Landscape landscape;
    protected Lake nextTo;

    public void setNextTo(Lake l) {
        nextTo = l;
    }
    public Lake getNextTo() {
        return nextTo;
    }

    public abstract Color getLeafColor();
}
```

Note to Experienced C++ Programmers

This appendix is intended for folks who are C++ 'power programmers'; we assume a great deal of C++ proficiency in this section, and so as a result we don't explain a lot of the background necessary to understand this material. So, if you are not a C++ 'expert', please skip this appendix!

Although there are many similarities between the C++ and Java languages – Java was in part patterned after C++ – some of the most complex, error-prone features of C++ were eliminated in creating Java to make it a 'safer' language, one of the most significant being:

No More Pointers!

Pointers vs. References

Those of you who have programmed in C or C++ know how easy it is to manipulate memory addresses directly via **pointers**, which can quickly get a programmer into trouble! It is an all too common experience to get a **segmentation violation**: that is, an accidental (or intentional!) attempt to access 'forbidden' memory, which causes the program to crash.

Instead of using pointers, Java uses **references**. Java references work the same way that C++ pointers do when it comes to instantiating objects dynamically: that is, you declare a reference/pointer variable first, and then use the 'new' operator to dynamically create the object at run time. Then, you later use the reference/pointer to access the object that it references, a technique known as **de-referencing**.

One big difference between pointers and references is that we can do arithmetic on pointers in C++, but not on references in Java. That is, in C++, we can treat a pointer as a 'raw' numeric memory address, and can add/subtract arbitrary numeric values to the address before de-referencing it, thus accessing some alternative location in memory. This is not permitted with references in Java.

Dynamic vs. Static Object Creation

With C++, we can create objects in one of two ways:

- ❏ At compile time, known as **static instantiation**;
- ❏ At run time, known as **dynamic instantiation**.

Here is a comparison of Java versus C++ syntax with respect to dynamically instantiated objects (assume the existence of a class named `Student` in both cases):

Approach to Object Creation	Java Syntax for Doing So	C++ Syntax for Doing So

Dynamic Instantiation (i.e., at run time)	`// Declare a reference`
	`variable.`
	`Student s;`
		`// Declare a pointer.`
		`Student* s;`

	`// Instantiate a Student`
	`// object.`
	`s = new Student();`
		`// Instantiate a Student object`
		`// in one of two ways: either:`
		`s = new Student();`
		
		`// or (shorthand form):`
		`s = new Student;`

	`// Invoke a method on the`
	`// object via dot notation.`
	
	`s.setName("Fred");`
		`// Invoke a method on the`
		`// object in one of two ways:`
		`// either`
		`// via dot notation ...`
		`(*s).setName("Fred");`
		
		`// ... or via "arrow" notation.`
		`s->setName("Fred");`

Note that the Java syntax is a lot cleaner, in that we don't use asterisks (*), or arrows (->) when declaring or de-referencing pointers.

In Java, however, there is no concept of static/compile time object instantiation, as there is with C++... *all* Java objects are created *dynamically* via the 'new' operator. Note that the syntax for creating and manipulating objects *statically* in C++ resembles the syntax for *dynamic* object creation and manipulation in Java:

Approach to Object Creation	Java Syntax for Doing So	C++ Syntax for Doing So

Static Instantiation (i.e., at compile time)	* Not available *	`// Declare a reference variable.`
		`Student s;`
		
		`// No need to instantiate!`
		
		`// Invoke a method via dot`
		`// notation.`
		`s.setName("Fred");`

Exception Handling

The elimination of true pointers from Java virtually eradicates the potential for getting a segmentation violation, which was one of the main causes of run-time exceptions, or 'crashes'. Java also has an extensive system of **exception handling**, which we discuss in Chapter 13. When something illegal happens, Java throws an exception, which your program can catch and gracefully recover from without crashing.

Exception handling was also introduced in C++, but is optional in C++, *mandatory* in Java: if you use a language construct in a Java program that is capable of throwing an exception, but do not explicitly intercept ('catch') it, you will receive a compilation error.

'Breaking' the OO 'Rules' with C++

We talk at great length in Part 1 of the book about the advantages of encapsulation, information hiding, inheritance, and polymorphism in OO languages. Although C++ does indeed take advantage of these benefits, it provides a few 'back doors' that allow you to break the spirit of these features. Here are a few examples:

❑ **Friend functions**: These functions reside outside the bounds of any class. They are given permission to access private attributes of one or more classes, thus breaking the spirit of encapsulation.

❑ **Virtual functions**: In C++, we have to designate a method as `virtual` in order to get overriding to take place; this means that the developer of a C++ class must anticipate the future need to override a particular method. With Java, the reverse is true: all methods are automatically 'overridable' unless they are flagged with the keyword `final`, which *prohibits* overriding.

This goes hand in glove with polymorphism. In Java, the ability for objects to perform the correct version of a method is automatic. With C++, if we fail to designate a method in a base class as virtual, then we may think we are overriding the method – we may indeed write method code in a subclass to 'mask' the parent's version – but at run time, the subclassed objects will only 'see', and hence be able to run, the parent's version of the method.

Platform Portability

Another disadvantage of C++ with respect to Java is its relative lack of platform portability; this manifests itself in several ways:

❑ The executable code that you produce by compiling a C++ program is specific to a certain underlying operating system architecture, and hence is platform dependent, whereas Java executable code is inherently platform independent, as we discuss at length in Chapter 1. (In defense of C++, a native executable is lightning fast, but there also happen to be native compilers available for Java. These compromise Java's portability, of course, for the sake of speed.)

❑ Even C++ source code is not necessarily portable; if you stray from the absolute core of ANSI standard C++, you may find yourself with source code that must be rewritten in order to compile it for a different platform. This is particularly true of C++ applications that avail themselves of platform specific operating system or windowing calls. As we discuss in Chapter 1, Java provides platform-independent means of doing all of these things, such that both source code as well as executable code is truly platform independent.

Abstract Methods and Abstract Classes

C++ and Java differ in the specific manner in which methods, and therefore classes, are flagged as being abstract. In Java, we flag the signature of a method with the keyword 'abstract', and if we have one or more abstract methods in a class, the compiler then forces us to also add the 'abstract' keyword to the class definition as a whole:

```
public abstract class Course {
  // details omitted ...
  public abstract void establishCourseSchedule();
}
```

whereas in C++, we designate a (virtual) method to be abstract by 'zeroing out' the method body:

```
virtual void establishCourseSchedule() = 0;
```

which is a bit more obscure. (Such a method, by the way, is called a **pure virtual function** in C++.)

Also, in Java, we are permitted to label a class abstract in order to prevent instantiation of the class even if it contains no abstract methods, whereas we are not permitted to do so in C++.

Other Simplifications

❑ There are no more 'memory leaks' with Java - **garbage collection** takes care of this automatically, as we discuss in Chapter 13.

It is possible to get the occasional 'out of memory' error with the JVM itself, however, if we consume memory allocated to the JVM faster than the garbage collector can recycle it, and/or we fail to release object handles that are no longer in service.

❑ There is no support in Java for multiple inheritance, which as we discuss in Chapter 5 was deemed problematic in C++ – Java introduces the notion of interfaces as a work-around, as we discuss in Chapters 7 and 13.

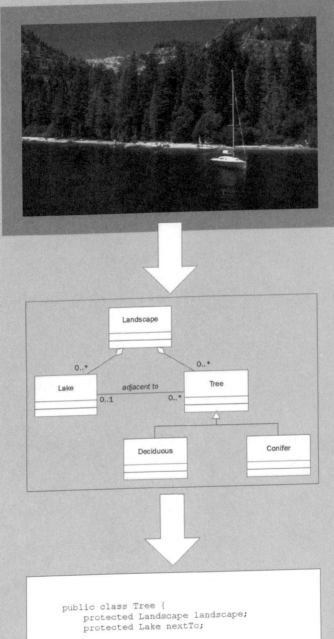

```
public class Tree {
    protected Landscape landscape;
    protected Lake nextTo;

    public void setNextTo(Lake l) {
        nextTo = l;
    }
    public Lake getNextTo() {
        return nextTo;
    }

    public abstract Color getLeafColor();
}
```

How Polymorphism Works 'Behind the Scenes' (Static vs. Dynamic Binding)

> Warning: this material is fairly technically deep! The good news, however, is that it is not necessary to understand how polymorphism works 'behind the scenes' in order to make use of it in the applications that you develop, any more than it is necessary to understand how an automobile engine works in order to drive a car. So, if you are curious about the 'mechanics' of polymorphism, read on; otherwise, feel free to skip this material. As long as you feel comfortable with our discussion of polymorphism in Chapter 7, you're good to go!

In Chapter 3, we discuss the fact that with Java, simply declaring a variable to be of type `Student` doesn't actually make a student object 'materialize'; we have to explicitly instantiate an object through the use of the `new` operator and a constructor method call:

```
Student y;
y = new Student();
```

The fact that a method must be called to create an object implies that the allocation of sufficient memory to house a `Student` object takes place when the program runs, that is, at run time, not at compile time. This is known as **dynamic instantiation**. (When this program is compiled, only enough memory is set aside to hold a reference, which in Java is 64 bits long regardless of the type of object that a reference variable will eventually be referencing!)

The concept of dynamic instantiation is closely tied with another concept called **dynamic** or **run-time binding**, which is at the very heart of what makes polymorphism and *overriding* (which was discussed in Chapter 5) 'tick'. In contrast to dynamic binding, we have **static** or **compile time binding**, which comes into play with *overloading* (which was also discussed in Chapter 5). We'd like to explain these two concepts to round out your understanding of how polymorphism works 'behind the scenes'.

Static Binding

Let's look at static binding first. When a program is compiled, the job of a compiler is to make sure that every line of code that you have written makes sense, meaning that, among other things:

- All of the variables mentioned in the code – simple data types as well as objects – have been properly declared.

```
int x;
int y;

x = y + z;   // Problem!  z was not declared, and so the compiler will
             // complain!
```

- All of the functions (methods) that you are calling have also been properly declared. That is to say, each method call is compared against all of the method signatures you've declared to make sure that the call properly agrees with exactly one such signature. (As we saw when we talked about overloading in Chapter 5, it is impossible to overload the same method *name* with different argument signatures, so we are guaranteed that there will be one and only one match.)

```
int x;
int y;
Student s;

int z = s.print(x, y);   // Compiler will look for a method belonging
                         // to class Student whose name is 'print' and
                         // whose argument signature calls for two int(egers).
```

When the compiler finds such a match, bingo! – it knows what method code body needs to be executed when that method actually gets called at run time, and 'locks in' that code at compile time, as illustrated conceptually in the figure below.

If for some reason the compiler does not find such a match, then it complains that the method call is invalid:

```
int x;
Student s;

// There is no method "foobar" for the Student class!
s.foobar(x);
```

The compiler would produce the following error on the last line of code above:

Method foobar(int) not found in class Student.

Imagine that you are going to be taking a road trip from Washington, D.C. to Cleveland, Ohio. Compile time binding is analogous to having a specific driving route planned in advance – route 95N to route 70N to route 83E, etc. – with no flexibility for changing this route when you actually set forth on your trip (i.e. at 'run time').

Dynamic Binding

Let's contrast what we've just learned about static binding with dynamic or run-time binding: a language feature that defers the decision of which method code body will be exercised for a particular method call until the time at which the program actually runs.

- ❑ In the diagram that follows, we show the main application as declaring a reference p of type Person. The program logic (reflected via an 'if' statement) shows that based upon some condition at *run time* (for example, some input provided by the user, perhaps), we will create either a Student object or a Professor object, which p will hold onto.

- ❑ At *compile time*, since we don't know what the future runtime conditions will be, we cannot guess as to whether we'll need to invoke the Student class's version of print() or the Professor class's version, so we have to defer this decision.

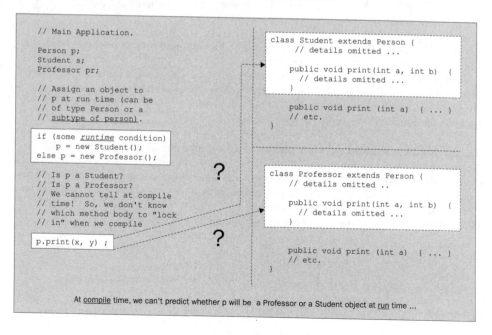

❑ At *run time* – that is, at the very moment when the `print()` method is called in our application – p will be holding onto a *specific* object, the run time environment will be able to determine its type/class, and the proper version of the `print()` method will automatically be selected, thanks to polymorphism!

```
// Main Application.

Person p;
Student s;
Professor pr;

// Assign an object to
// p at run time (can be
// of type Person or
// subtype of person).

if (some runtime condition)
    p = new Student();
else p = new Professor();

// Is p a Student?
// Is p a Professor?
// We cannot tell at compile
// time! So, we don't know
// which method body to "lock
// in" when we compile

p.print(x, y) ;
```

```
class Student extends Person {
    // details omitted ...

    public void print(int a, int b) {
        // details omitted ...
    }

    public void print(int a) { ... }
    // etc.

}


class Professor extends Person {
    // details omitted ..

    public void print(int a, int b) {
        // details omitted ...
    }

    public void print(int a) { ... }
    // etc.

}
```

... but by the time this program is run, we will know what type of object p is referring to, and can choose the right method!

Going back to our road trip analogy, this would be like taking a road trip where you know you plan on going from Washington, D.C. to Cleveland, Ohio, AND you know that there is at least one way (if not many!) to get there, because you checked a map; but, you are going to defer the decision about which route to take until you are actually behind the steering wheel of the car and departing for your trip, to allow for 'run time' road conditions such as ice, snow, road construction, and the like. (You don't wish to 'lock in' your route at the planning stage of your trip.)

Dynamic binding enables polymorphism. If a programming language were not able to hold off on choosing a particular method to execute until the precise moment that it is needed – that is, if a language only supports static, or compile time, binding – then the compiler's only option in the preceding example would be to play it safe by choosing a version of print that it knows would work for either a `Student` or a `Professor` – namely, the version of `print()` defined by their common superclass, `Person` – and no overriding or polymorphism would be possible.

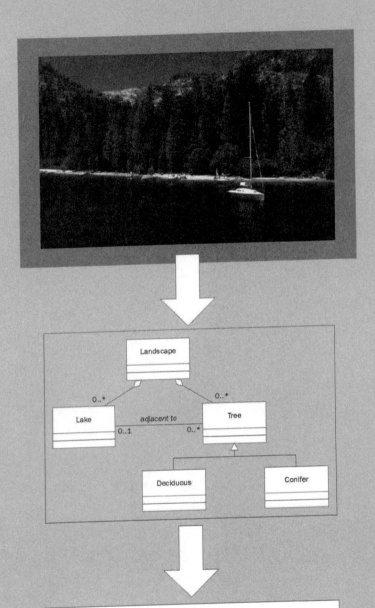

```
public class Tree {
    protected Landscape landscape;
    protected Lake nextTo;

    public void setNextTo(Lake l) {
        nextTo = l;
    }
    public Lake getNextTo() {
        return nextTo;
    }

    public abstract Color getLeafColor();
}
```

Index

A Guide to the Index

The index is arranged hierarchically, in alphabetical order, with symbols preceding the letter A. Most second-level entries and many third-level entries also occur as first-level entries. This is to ensure that users will find the information they require however they choose to search for it.